The Essential AMERICA

The Essential

W • W • NORTON & COMPANY
NEW YORK • LONDON

AMERICA

VOLUME 1

George B. Tindall

David E. Shi

Thomas Lee Pearcy

Editor: Steve Forman
Associate Managing Editor—College Books: Jane Carter
Director of Manufacturing—College: Roy Tedoff
Manuscript Editor: Kate Lovelady
Project Editor: Nan Sinauer
Book Designer: Rubina Yeh
Photograph Editor: Kate Nash
Editorial Assistant: Lory Frenkel
Cartographer: Cartographics

The text of this book is composed in Melior, with the display set in Eurostile.
Composition by The PRD Group.
Manufacturing by R. R. Donnelley & Sons Company.

The Library of Congress has cataloged the one-volume edition as follows:

Tindall, George Brown.
    The essential America / George B. Tindall, David E. Shi [and] Thomas Lee Pearcy.
        p.   cm.
    Includes bibliographical references and index.
    ISBN 0-393-97699-8 (pbk.)
    1. United States—History.   I. Shi, David E.   II. Pearcy, Thomas L., 1960–   III. Title.

    E178.T56   2000
                                                        00-053698

ISBN 0-393-97623-8 (pbk.)

W. W. Norton & Company, Inc., 500 Fifth Avenue, New York, N.Y. 10110
www.wwnorton.com
W. W. Norton & Company Ltd., 10 Coptic Street, London WC1A 1PU

2 3 4 5 6 7 8 9 0

For Bruce and Blair
For Jason and Jessica
For Shauna

CONTENTS

ESSENTIAL THEMES
CRITICAL QUESTIONS

How did the political bases of
independence evolve over the colonial
period?

How did the colonists build thriving
economies from their subsistence
beginnings?

How did the distinctive social groups
in early America interact?

How did the European settlers
respond to their encounters with
the peoples and places of America?

What was America's position in the
Atlantic world during the colonial
period?

ESSENTIAL THEMES

CRITICAL QUESTIONS

 How did the cross-currents of nationalism and sectionalism gain force in this period?

 How did the Federalists and Republicans address the issues of economic development in the new nation?

How did issues of race and class enter into debates over the shape of the new nation?

How did Americans develop a more independent culture in the early national period?

How did the new nation seek to enhance its international status?

ESSENTIAL THEMES
CRITICAL QUESTIONS

 How did westward expansion affect the politics of nationalism and sectionalism?

How did the Industrial Revolution affect regional economic distinctions?

Was the early 19th century a period of growing equality or inequality in American society?

How did the twin themes of Enlightenment reason and revivalist faith find expression in this period?

What were the international implications of America's westward expansion in this period?

ESSENTIAL THEMES
CRITICAL QUESTIONS

 Why were the nation's political leaders unable to solve the problems that led to the Civil War?

Did the northern economy give Union forces a decisive advantage in the war?

What were the social effects of the Civil War in the North and the South?

Had the North and South come to embrace irreconcilable values at the time of the Civil War?

What were the most important international implications of the Civil War?

MAPS

Most observers agree that we are living through a digital revolution. There is less agreement, however, about the impact this revolution will have on our habits of reading and learning. Some confidently predict that printed books will be outmoded in the twenty-first century, completely replaced by digital technologies. At the other end of the spectrum, there are those who express alarm at our willingness to embrace new digital technologies at the expense of the book. Such critics warn that we are sacrificing the opportunity for thinking deeply in our rush to gain access to information.

To a surprising degree, the warring champions of the pixel and the page share the assumption that these technologies represent fundamentally opposed forces that cannot coexist in our high-tech future. We beg to differ. The printed book and the new multimedia technologies can complement each other very well.

This assumption undergirds the publication before you: The printed *Essential America* and the electronic *Essential America* were conceived together and developed in tandem. Printed book and E-book, each makes the most of its distinctive medium to convey the basics of American history to beginning students and arouse in them the desire to know more.

The aim of *The Essential America* is to furnish students with the fundamental elements of American history. To do so, we have compressed the brief version of *America* by at least one-third, omitting some supporting detail, examples, and quotations while maintaining the book's broad coverage, accuracy, and, we hope, appeal. As you can see, the look of *The Essential America* represents a major departure. With its four-color design, large trim size, and clear double-column page, this version of *America* allows us to enrich the essentials with many color illustrations, a new full-color map program, and some new pedagogical features.

The new educational tools aim to help students grasp the essentials while never losing sight of the larger themes running through the book. The seven parts of the book open with multipage spreads that identify and outline five basic themes: political, economic, social, cultural, and global. Each theme is stated by way of a general question that applies to that part of the book. We hope these thematic questions suggest to students the larger developments at work over longer periods of time. The questions can guide students' reading or serve as essay topics. Each theme is also outlined at the start of each part so that students can readily follow its development through the relevant chapters. Finally, each theme is highlighted by an icon that appears "lit" (in color) at the top of each page that addresses that theme. Students can use these icons to follow a thematic thread through the book or to keep themselves oriented thematically as they read chapters. Our aim is to give students thematic guidance throughout the text.

In the electronic *Essential America*, we hope to have realized some of the potential that the new digital technologies hold for teaching and learning. The E-book delivers the full text, maps, and illustrations of the printed text enhanced with multimedia materials for review and enrichment. It employs a technology that achieves a smooth integration of text and multimedia elements. It has an attractive on-screen design, readable type, and intuitive navigation devices. The E-book also furnishes students with a suite of study tools, from highlighters and sticky notes to custom searches and a personal notebook for assembling multimedia materials. For a preview of the electronic *Essential America*, visit the Web site at www.wwnorton.com/eamerica.

To offer a more complete integration of pixel and page, we have also created *The Essential America* On-line Tutor, which students can access at no charge, whether they are using the printed or the electronic *Essential America*. The On-line Tutor features review and research materials developed specifically for *The Essential America*. Its on-line quizzes test the students' grasp of the text; the on-line topic for each chapter encourages further research, since documents, still images, audio, and video materials are accessible through the site.

Just as the pencil has survived the typewriter, we are confident that printed books will survive in our digital world. Through this distinctive attempt to harness the considerable powers of both print and digital technologies, we hope we are advancing the efforts of all to teach and learn American history ever more effectively.

This new version of *America* features an outstanding ancillary package that supplements the text. *For the Record: A Documentary History of America*, by David E. Shi and Holly A. Mayer (Duquesne University), is a rich resource with over 300 primary-source readings from diaries, journals, newspaper articles, speeches, government documents, and novels. It also has four special chapters on interpreting illustrations and photographs as historical documents. The Study Guide, by Charles Eagles (University of Mississippi), is another valuable resource. It contains chapter outlines, learning objectives, timelines, vocabulary exercises, short-answer questions, and essay questions, as well as source readings for each chapter. Norton Presentation Maker is a CD-ROM slide and text resource that includes all the images from the text as well as four-color maps, 1,000 additional images from Library of Congress archives, and 30 audio clips from significant historical speeches. Finally, the Instructor's Manual and Test Bank, by Jonathan Lee (San Antonio College), includes a test bank of short-answer and essay questions as well as detailed chapter outlines, lecture suggestions, and bibliographies that include the addresses of useful Web sites.

This version of *America* benefited from the insights and suggestions of many people. The following scholars have provided close readings at various stages: Lucy Barber (University of California at Davis), Michael Barnhart (State University of New York at Stony Brook), Saul Cornell (Ohio State University), Charles Eagles (University of Mississippi), Timothy Gilfoyle (Loyola University), Tera Hunter (Carnegie-Mellon University), Walter Johnson (New York University), Peter Kolchin (University of Delaware), Christopher Morris (University of Texas at Arlington), Arwen Mohun (University of Delaware), David Parker (Kennesaw State University), Thomas Sugrue (University of Pennsylvania), and Marilyn Westerkamp (University of California at Santa Cruz). Once again, we thank our friends at W. W. Norton & Company, especially Steve Forman, Jon Durbin, Steve Hoge, Kate Lovelady, Kate Nash, Lory Frenkel, Matthew Arnold, Rubina Yeh, and Nan Sinauer for their care and attention along the way.

—George B. Tindall
—David E. Shi
—Thomas L. Pearcy

A New World

Long before Christopher Columbus accidentally discovered the New World in his effort to find a passage to Asia, the tribal peoples he mislabeled "Indians" had occupied and shaped the lands of the Western Hemisphere. By the end of the fifteenth century, when Columbus began his voyage west, there were millions of Native Americans living in the "New World." Over the centuries, they had developed stable, diverse, and often highly sophisticated societies, some rooted in agriculture, others in trade or imperial conquest.

The Native American cultures were, of course, profoundly affected by the arrival of peoples from Europe and Africa. The Indians were exploited, enslaved, displaced, and exterminated. Yet this conventional tale of conquest oversimplifies the complex process by which Indians, Europeans, and Africans interacted. The Indians were more than passive victims; they were also trading partners and rivals of the transatlantic newcomers. They became enemies and allies, neighbors and advisors, converts and spouses. As such they fully participated in the creation of the new society known as America.

The Europeans who risked their lives to settle in the New World were themselves quite diverse. Young and old, men and women, they came from Spain, Portugal, France, Great Britain, the Netherlands, Italy, and the various German states. A variety of motives inspired them to undertake the transatlantic voyage. Some were adventurers and fortune seekers, eager to find gold and spices. Others were fervent Christians determined to create kingdoms of God in the New World. Still others were convicts, debtors, indentured servants, or political or religious exiles. Many were simply seeking higher wages and greater economic opportunity. A settler in Pennsylvania noted that "poor people (both men and women) of all kinds can here get three times the wages for their labour than they can in England or Wales."

Yet such enticements were not sufficient to attract enough workers to keep up with the rapidly expanding colonial economies. The Europeans began to force Indians to work for them, but there were never enough of them to meet the unceasing demand. Moreover, Indian slaves often escaped or were so rebellious that several colonies banned their use. The Massachusetts legislature did so because Indians were of such "a malicious, surly and revengeful spirit; rude and insolent in their behavior, and very ungovernable."

Beginning early in the seventeenth century, more and more colonists turned to the African slave trade for their labor needs. This development would transform American society in unexpected ways. Few Europeans during the colonial era saw the contradiction between the New World's promise of individual freedom and the expanding institution of race slavery. Nor did they reckon with the problems associated with introducing into the new society a race of peoples they considered alien and unassimilable.

The intermingling of peoples, cultures, and plants and animals from the three continents of Africa, Europe, and North America gave colonial American society its distinctive vitality and variety. In turn, the diversity of the environment and climate led to the creation of quite different economies and patterns of living in the various regions of North America. As the original settlements grew into prosperous and populous colonies, the transplanted Europeans had to fashion social institutions and political systems to manage growth and control tensions.

At the same time, imperial rivalries among the Spanish, French, English, and Dutch produced numerous intrigues and costly wars. The monarchs of Europe had a difficult time trying to manage and exploit this fluid and often volatile colonial society. Many of the colonists brought with them to the New World a feisty independence that resisted government interference in their affairs. A British official in North Carolina reported that the colonists who settled in the Piedmont region were "without any Law or Order. Impudence is so very high, as to be past bearing." As long as the reins of imperial control were loosely applied, the two parties maintained an uneasy partnership. But as the British authorities tightened their control during the mid–eighteenth century, they met resistance, which escalated into revolt, and culminated in revolution.

ESSENTIAL THEMES

CRITICAL QUESTIONS

How did the political bases of independence evolve over the colonial period?

How did the colonists build thriving economies from their subsistence beginnings?

How did the distinctive social groups in early America interact?

How did the European settlers respond to their encounters with the peoples and places of America?

What was America's position in the Atlantic world during the colonial period?

An emerging social and political order
Slavery in the South
New England trade
Diversity in the middle colonies
The cities

Royal Proclamation of 1763
George Grenville, first lord of the Treasury
Sugar Act (1764)
Currency Act of 1764
Stamp Act (1765)
Quartering Act (1765)
Charles Townshend, chancellor of the Exchequer
Townshend Acts (1767)
Revenue Act of 1767
Board of Customs Commissioners established in Boston (1767)
Lord North, chancellor of the Exchequer
Tea Act of 1773
Boston Port Act, seeking remuneration for Boston Tea Party (1774)
A new Quartering Act (1774)
Massachusetts Governing Act (1774)
Conciliatory Resolution (1775)
Colonial responses to British political intransigence
Virginia House of Burgesses responds to Stamp Act (1765)
Declaration of Rights and Grievances of the Colonies (1765)
First Continental Congress assembles in Philadelphia (1774)
Suffolk Resolves declare null and void 1774 Intolerable Acts
Declaration of American Rights adopted
Continental Association of 1774 promotes boycott of all British goods
Revolutionary War begins April 18–19 at Lexington and Concord, Massachusetts (1775)
Continental Congress assumes role of government
Second Continental Congress convenes in Philadelphia in May (1775)
Declaration of Independence issued July 4, 1776

CHAPTER 1

Discovery and Settlement

Native-American empires and the extension of European hegemony in the "New World"

CHAPTER 2

Colonial Ways of Life

Diversity and authority

CHAPTER 3

The Imperial Perspective

Precursors to self-government

CHAPTER 4

From Empire to Independence

The culmination of political tensions between England and America

Zenith of Mayan civilization (300–900 A.D.)
Collapse of Mayan civilization (approximately A.D. 900)
Aztecs found capital city of Tenochitlàn
Conquest of Aztecs by Cortés (1521)
The Spanish empire in America
English exploration and settlements
Jamestown (1607)
Plymouth and the Mayflower Compact (1620)
John Winthrop and Massachusetts Bay Colony (1630)
The Massachusetts Charter
Roger Williams and Rhode Island (1636)
Connecticut (1637)
"Fundamental Orders of Connecticut" (1639)
The Restoration colonies
Other European settlements in the Americas
French Québec (1608)
Spanish St. Augustine, Fla. (1565), and Santa Fe, N.M. (1610)

English administration of the colonies
The Glorious Revolution in America
An emerging colonial system
The habit of self-government
Judiciaries
Governors
Colonial assemblies
House of Burgesses (Virginia)
House of Delegates (Maryland)
House of Representatives (Massachusetts)
War and self-rule

CHAPTER 1

Discovery and Settlement

Economic motives for
exploration and empire •

Regional distinctions in early
English colonies •

The Virginia Company
John Rolfe and Virginia tobacco
Competition for land triggered by
  tobacco
The Southern colonies
Trading furs with the Carolina Native
  Americans
Tobacco and the emergence of an export
  economy in the South
Slave labor in the emerging economy
New England
Lumber as an economic staple in the
  North
The sea and shipbuilding in the
  northern economy
Trade in the middle colonies
Fur trading on the western frontier
  The Iroquois League
**Economic success of the English
  colonies**
Women as a workforce

**Southern crops and access to British
  markets**
Plantation economics and the increasing
  demand for slaves
**Northern lumber and abundant fishing
  grounds fueled trade**
**Northern lack of staples: comparatively
  sparse agriculture and pastoral
  resources**
The "Triangular Trade" network
Agriculture and trade in the middle
  colonies
Urban economies

CHAPTER 2

Colonial Ways of Life

• Integration into the North Atlantic
  trade Network

CHAPTER 3

The Imperial Perspective

Challenges to British mercantilism •

CHAPTER 4

From Empire to Independence

• Economic tensions between
  crown, colonists

**Dutch shipping competes with British
  merchants**
**French trading posts dot waterways
  and reach the heartland**
The Great Lakes, Des Moines, Terre
  Haute
**British efforts to protect their colonial
  markets**
The Navigation Acts (1651, 1660, 1663,
  1673)

**British efforts to raise revenues in the
  colonies**
**Colonists issue paper money (early
  1760s)**
**Townshend Acts heighten colonial
  resistance (1767)**
**Colonists impose embargo on British
  manufacturers (1765)**
Tea Act (1773)
**Colonists boycott all British goods
  (1774)**

How did the distinctive social groups in early America interact?

CHAPTER 1

Discovery and Settlement

New World social structures •

Indian society
Hierarchies in Spanish America
Social structure in the Chesapeake
Religion and gender in New England
Anne Hutchinson's trial (1637) and
    banishment (1638)
Indian-white relations in the colonies

The origins of slavery
Ethnic diversity of African slaves
Adapting to slavery
Social relations in New England
Cohesive forces
Diversity and social strains
The Salem witch trials (1692)
Social relations in the middle colonies
Class
Ethnic mix
Cities
The social order
The urban web
Education and society
Founding of first colleges
**The Great Awakening as a social
    movement**
Revivalism and clerical authority

CHAPTER 2

Colonial Ways of Life

• Demography, gender, and race

CHAPTER 3

The Imperial Perspective

Heightened tensions in the colonies •

The Glorious Revolution in America
Social effects
Claims of white settlers on Indian lands
King Philip's War (1675–1676)
Bacon's Rebellion (1676)
Social effects of the colonial wars

CHAPTER 4

From Empire to Independence

• Surging American nationalism
Resistance on the frontier •

Sons of Liberty and popular discontent
Social strains on the frontier
The mob as a political force
**Committees of Correspondence
    (1772–1773)**
Boston Tea Party (1773)

**Ethan Allen and the Green Mountain
    Boys (late 1770s)**
The Paxton Boys of Pennsylvania
**The Regulators of North Carolina and
    the Battle of Alamance (1771)**
**Daniel Boone and settlers create the
    Wilderness Road (1774)**

British folkways
Conflicting views regarding the land:
    communal resource vs.
    privately-owned commodity
African roots and black culture
Kinship ties
Agricultural techniques
Religion
Lifestyles
Southern plantations
    Tidewater gentry
    Religion
New England townships
    Dwellings and daily life
    Enterprise
    Religion
The American Enlightenment
The Great Awakening

British wars with the Native Americans
British wars with France

Newspapers incite colonists against
    Grenville's measures (1765)
Colonists boycott British goods (1765)
John Dickinson's *Letters of a*
    ***Pennsylvania Farmer* criticizes**
    Townshend Acts (1767)
Thomas Paine's *Common Sense* (1776)

CHAPTER 1
Discovery and Settlement
The "New World"

CHAPTER 2
Colonial Ways of Life
The genesis of "American" culture

CHAPTER 3
The Imperial Perspective
Cultures at War

CHAPTER 4
From Empire to Independence
American nationalism and the
Revolutionary War

Pre-Columbian Indian civilizations
Maya, Inca, Aztec—the "classic"
    civilizations
Smaller North American indigenous
    nations
Earliest European contacts with Native
    Americans
Encounter at Hispaniola
Enslavement and transport to Europe
The great biological exchange and the
    ecological consequences of
    contact
Europeans adopt New World plants,
    clothing, words
Devastating effects of European diseases
Spanish America
Conquests by Hernando Cortés,
    Francisco Pizarro
Christianity in the New World: the
    spiritual conquest
Patterns of life in Spanish America:
    European culture
French explorations
Québec
Beyond discovery and exploration: a
    permanent English presence
The Chesapeake
    Relations with Indians in Virginia
        and Maryland
New England
    The Pilgrims
    William Bradford
Puritan culture
    The first Thanksgiving (1621)
    John Winthrop's "city upon a hill"
Relations with Native Americans
    The Powhatan Confederation
    John Smith and Pocahontas
    Pequot War of 1637 (Massachusetts)
    Yamasee War (1715–1717)
Dutch New York
Quaker culture in Pennsylvania

CHAPTER 1

Discovery and Settlement

European exploration and settlement •

Cromwell governs England as Lord
    Protector (1653–1658) •

Restoration in England (1660) •

> Columbus's first voyage to the New
>   World (1492)
> **Portugese arrive in Brazil (1500)**
> **Ponce de Léon explores Florida coast
>   (1513)**
> **Spaniards conquer Aztec capital
>   (1519–1521)**
> **Jacques Cartier explores the St.
>   Lawrence River (1542)**
> **Sir Walter Raleigh sails for North
>   America (1548)**

> **Waves of British colonists**
> Puritans to Massachusetts, 1629–1641
> Wealthier persons from southern
>   England to Virginia
> Quakers from England's north midlands
>   to West Jersey, Pennsylvania, and
>   Delaware
> Celtic-Britons and Scotch-Irish to the
>   Appalachian Mountains,
>   1717–1775
> **Indentured servants**

CHAPTER 2

Colonial Ways of Life

• Continuing migrations

CHAPTER 3

The Imperial Perspective

Developments in Europe affect
the British colonies in America •

British supremacy in North America •

> **English Civil War and Restoration**
> **LaSalle traverses Mississippi River to
>   the Gulf of Mexico (1682)**
> **The Glorious Revolution (1688–1689)**
> **King William's War (1689–1697)**
> **The War of the Spanish Succession
>   (1702–1713)**
> **Spanish America in decline**
> **The French and Indian War
>   (1754–1763)**
> **Peace of Paris (1763)**

CHAPTER 4

From Empire to Independence

• Legacy of Seven Years War

> **The Revolutionary controversy and
>   Britain's global interest**

CHAPTER

1

Discovery and Settlement

This chapter focuses on

- The reasons for the founding of the different colonies.

- The ways in which Europeans and Native Americans adapted to each other's presence.

- The factors making for England's success in colonizing North America.

THE *ESSENTIAL AMERICA* ON-LINE TUTOR

www.wwnorton.com/eamerica/ch1

- **Topic: The great biological exchange**
  www.wwnorton.com/eamerica/ch1/topic.htm

  The European "discovery" of America brought different worlds into contact. Explore the great biological exchange and its significance through woodcuts and other images, contemporary accounts by Native Americans and European settlers, maps, and historical analyses. What were the consequences of this exchange?

- **Chapter review: On-line quiz and chapter summary**
  www.wwnorton.com/eamerica/ch1/review.htm

- **Chapter resources: Multimedia index**
  www.wwnorton.com/eamerica/ch1/media.htm

The Western Hemisphere was originally an uninhabited frontier. But like all frontiers, it served as a powerful magnet for dreamers and adventurers. Until recent years, archeologists and anthropologists believed that the first people to settle in the Western Hemisphere were northeastern Asians. Some 11,500 years ago, according to the traditional interpretation, Asian immigrants entered the New World from Siberia to what is now Alaska. New archaeological discoveries, however, have raised questions about the conventional view of America's human origins. Skeletal remains found in Brazil, Nebraska, Washington, and Minnesota resemble South Asians or Europeans—not northeastern Asians. And such evidence also suggests that people were in the Western Hemisphere more than 12,000 years ago.

Pre-Columbian Indian Civilizations

Whatever their place of origin and time of arrival, the first Americans spread across North and South America, establishing new communities and cultures. In the high altitudes of Mexico and Peru, the Mayas, Aztecs, Incas, and others built great empires supported by large-scale agriculture and a far-flung commerce.

The Mayas, Aztecs, and Incas

By about 2000–1500 B.C., the nomadic Indian tradition began to give way in what is today Central America to more permanent farming settlements. The more settled life in turn fostered more complex cultures through the cultivation of religion, crafts, art, science, civic administration—and organized warfare. A stratified social structure also developed. From about A.D. 300–900, this Middle American region reached its cultural peak, with great religious centers,

This page from the Codex Mendoza, a European-style picture book painted by a native artist for the first Viceroy of New Spain, depicts Aztec officers at the time of conquest. Note the tall emblems worn on the officers' backs, which identified rank to troops being led into battle.

gigantic pyramids and temples, and ceremonial courts, all supported by the surrounding villages.

The Mayas, living in present-day Yucatán, Guatemala, Belize, and western Honduras and El Salvador, were a warlike people who ruled a loosely controlled empire. They built dozens of pyramids, devised a complex writing system based on hieroglyphs, and developed enough mathematics and astronomy to devise a calendar more accurate than the one used by Columbus.

Then, about A.D. 900, for reasons unknown, Mayan culture abruptly collapsed, and the religious centers were abandoned. The Mayas were succeeded by the Toltecs, who conquered most of the region in the tenth century. But around A.D. 1200, the Toltecs too mysteriously withdrew.

The equally warlike Aztecs, who arrived from the northwest, founded the city of Tenochtitlán (now Mexico City) in 1325 and gradually extended their control over central Mexico. When the Spaniards invaded in 1519, the Aztec Empire under Montezuma II ruled over 5 million people. Their economy depended on agriculture, and their religious practices included human sacrifices to the sun god. Farther south, Incas by the fifteenth century controlled an

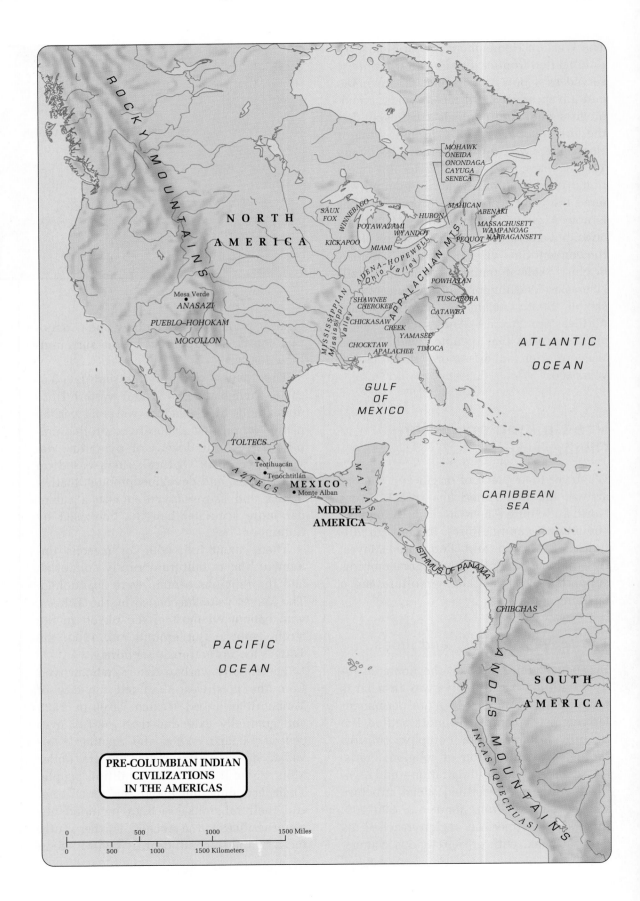

ROCKY MOUNTAINS

NORTH
AMERICA

SAUX
FOX
WINNEBAGO
POTAWATAMI
KICKAPOO
MIAMI
HURON
WYANDOT

MOHAWK
ONEIDA
ONONDAGA
CAYUGA
SENECA

MAHICAN
ABENAKI
MASSACHUSETT
WAMPANOAG
PEQUOT NARRAGANSETT

ADENA–HOPEWELL
Ohio Valley

APPALACHIAN MTS.

POWHATAN

Mesa Verde
ANASAZI

PUEBLO–HOHOKAM

MOGOLLON

MISSISSIPPIAN
Mississippi Valley

SHAWNEE
CHEROKEE
CHICKASAW
CREEK
CHOCKTAW
APALACHEE

TUSCARORA
CATAWBA
YAMASEE
TIMOCA

ATLANTIC
OCEAN

GULF
OF
MEXICO

TOLTECS
Teotihuacán
Tenóchtitlán
AZTECS
MEXICO
Monte Alban
MIDDLE
AMERICA

MAYAS

CARIBBEAN
SEA

ISTHMUS OF PANAMA

CHIBCHAS

PACIFIC
OCEAN

SOUTH
AMERICA

ANDES MOUNTAINS
INCAS (QUECHUAS)

**PRE-COLUMBIAN INDIAN
CIVILIZATIONS
IN THE AMERICAS**

0   500   1000   1500 Miles
0   500   1000   1500 Kilometers

empire that stretched a thousand miles along the Andes Mountains from Ecuador to Chile, connected by an elaborate system of roads and organized under an autocratic government that dominated community life.

Indian Cultures of North America

The North American tribes tended to be smaller, more scattered, and less settled than the Mayas or Aztecs. Most of them migrated with the seasons in search of food—fish, deer, rabbits, maize (corn), nuts, berries—and temperate locales. They built few permanent structures and tended to own land communally.

Indian societies of the sixteenth century were ill-equipped to resist the dynamic European cultures invading their world. The Indians of Mexico, for example, had copper and bronze but no iron. They had domesticated dogs, turkeys, and llamas, but horses were unknown until the Spaniards arrived. When fighting erupted, arrows and tomahawks were seldom a match for guns. And the new diseases contracted from European invaders proved to be catastrophic for the Native American peoples.

Yet the Indians resisted European invaders for centuries. They displayed an amazing capacity for adapting to changing circumstances, incorporating European technology and weaponry, forging new alliances, changing their own community structures, and converting whites to their way of life. Many Spanish, English, and French settlers voluntarily joined Indian society or chose to stay after being captured.

First Contacts

The European discovery of the New World coincided with the extension of European power and culture around the world. Such expansion derived from the revival of learning and the rise of an inquiring spirit; the

explosive growth of trade, towns, and modern corporations; the decline of feudalism and the rise of nations; the religious zeal generated by the Protestant Reformation and the Catholic Counter-Reformation; and on the darker side, some old sins—greed, conquest, racism, and slavery.

By the fifteenth century, these forces had combined to focus European eyes on new lands to conquer or settle and on new peoples to convert, civilize, or exploit. Europeans were especially attracted by the lure of Asia, a near-mythical land of spices, silks, jewels, and millions of "heathens" to be Christianized.

The Voyages of Columbus

The Orient's storied wealth caught the expansive vision of Christopher Columbus, a gold-loving adventurer. Born in 1451, the son of an Italian weaver, Columbus hatched a scheme to reach Asia by sailing west. He turned to Spain for backing, and after years of disappointment and disgrace, he finally won the support of Ferdinand and Isabella, the Spanish monarchs.

On August 2, 1492, Columbus set off across the Atlantic with a squadron of three small ships and eighty-seven men. Early on October 12, 1492, a lookout called out, "*Tierra! Tierra!* [Land! Land!]" It was an island in the Bahamas that Columbus named San Salvador (Blessed Savior). Assuming that he was near the Indies, he called the islanders "Indios," Indians. He described them as naked people, "very well made, of very handsome bodies and very good faces." The Indians paddled out in dugout logs, which they called *canoa,* and offered gifts of parrots and javelins to the strangers.

At the moment, however, Columbus was more interested in gold than gifts. He continued to explore the Bahamian Cays down to Cuba, a place name that suggested Cipangua (Japan), and then eastward to the island he named Española (or Hispaniola), where he first found significant amounts of gold jewelry.

On the night before Christmas in 1492, the *Santa María* ran aground off Hispaniola, and Columbus, still believing he had reached Asia, decided to return home. He left about forty men behind and seized a dozen natives to present as gifts to Spain's royal couple. After Columbus reached Spain, the news of his discovery spread rapidly throughout Europe, and Ferdinand and Isabella instructed him to prepare for a second voyage.

Columbus made three more voyages to the New World. In each instance, he grew more greedy for gold and more brutal in his treatment of the people he called Indians. His savagery eventually led to his arrest and return to Spain in chains. To the end, Columbus insisted that he had discovered parts of Asia.

Ironically, the New World was named not for its discoverer but for another Italian, Amerigo Vespucci. Vespucci was a Florentine merchant and navigator who helped outfit Columbus for the transatlantic crossing. Later, Vespucci himself made several voyages to the New World. In 1507 a young geographer named Martin Waldseemuller published a book in which he mistakenly credited Vespucci with having reached South America before Columbus. For that reason, Waldseemuller suggested that the new continent be named "America" in his honor.

Actually, Vespucci's first voyage began in 1499, and there is no firm evidence that he, any more than Columbus, ever believed he had discovered anything other than a part of East Asia. Waldseemuller's idea stuck, however, and the name for the New World took hold.

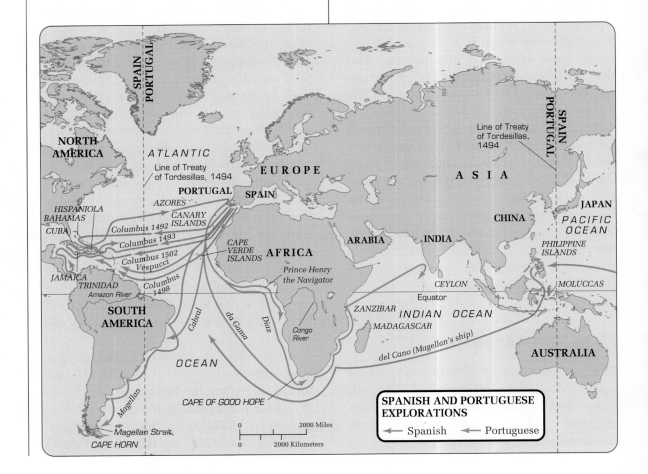

SPANISH AND PORTUGUESE EXPLORATIONS

← Spanish ← Portuguese

The Great Biological Exchange

European contact with the New World produced more than a diffusion of human cultures. If anything, the plants and animals of the two worlds were more different than the people and their ways of life. Europeans, for instance, had never seen creatures such as the iguana, flying squirrel, catfish, rattlesnake, or anything quite like several other species native to America: bison, cougars, armadillos, opossums, sloths, anacondas, electric eels, vampire bats, toucans, condors, or hummingbirds. Nor did the Native Americans know of horses, cattle, pigs, sheep, goats, and (maybe) chickens, which soon arrived from Europe in abundance.

The transfer of plant life worked a revolution in the diets of both hemispheres. Before 1492 three main staples of the modern diet were unknown in the Old World: maize (corn), potatoes (sweet and white), and many kinds of beans (snap, kidney, lima, and others). Other New World food plants were peanuts, squash, peppers, tomatoes, pumpkins, pineapples, papayas, avocados, cacao (the source of chocolate), and chicle (for chewing gum). Europeans in turn introduced rice, wheat, barley, oats, wine grapes, melons, coffee, olives, bananas, "Kentucky" bluegrass, daisies, and dandelions.

The beauty of the ecological exchange between old and new worlds was that the food plants were more complementary than competitive. They grew in different soils and climates, or in different seasons. Indian corn, it turned out, could flourish almost anywhere, and it spread quickly throughout the world. Before the end of the 1500s, American maize and sweet potatoes were staple crops in China. The green revolution exported from the Americas thus helped nourish a worldwide population explosion probably greater than any since the invention of agriculture.

Europeans also adopted many Native American devices, such as snowshoes, hammocks, kayaks, dogsleds, toboggans, and parkas. The rubber ball and the game of lacrosse had Indian origins. Indian words entered the European vocabulary: succotash, tobacco, moose, skunk, opossum, woodchuck, chipmunk, tomahawk, hickory, pecan, raccoon, and hundreds of others. There were still other New World contributions: tobacco and a number of other drugs, including coca (for cocaine and novocaine), curare (a muscle relaxant), and cinchona bark (for quinine).

Unfortunately, the Europeans in exchange presented the Indians with illnesses they could not handle. Even minor diseases such as measles killed Indians who had never encountered them and had built no immunity to them. Major infections such as smallpox and typhus killed all the more speedily. The first contacts with some of Columbus's sailors devastated whole Indian communities. The epidemics spread rapidly into the interior, and some tribes lost 90 to 95 percent of their population within the first century of European colonization. In central Mexico alone, some 8 million people, perhaps a third of the entire population, died of disease within a decade after the Spaniards arrived.

Exploration and Conquest of the New World

Excited by Columbus's discoveries, professional explorers, mostly Italians, probed the shorelines of America during the early sixteenth century in the vain search for a passage to China. In the process they greatly increased European knowledge of the New World. Yet during the sixteenth century the New World remained a Spanish preserve, except for Brazil, which was a Portuguese colony. After establishing colonies on Hispaniola and at Santo Domingo, which became the capital of the West Indies, the Spaniards proceeded eastward to Puerto Rico (1508) and westward to Cuba (1511–

1514). Their motives were explicit. Said one soldier: "We came here to serve God and the king, and also to get rich."

A Clash of Cultures

The great adventure of mainland conquest began in 1519, when Spaniard Hernando Cortés and 600 men landed on the site of Vera Cruz, Mexico, which he founded. Cortés then set about a daring conquest of the Aztec Empire. The 200-mile march from Vera Cruz through difficult mountain passes to the magnificent Aztec capital of Tenochtitlán, and the subjugation of the Aztecs, were two of the most remarkable—and tragic—feats in human history.

After a year of fighting, in 1521 Cortés and his officers replaced the former Aztec overlords as rulers over the Indian empire. In doing so, they set the style for other conquistadors (Spanish soldiers) to follow. Within twenty years, conquistadors had established an empire for Spain that was far larger than Rome's had ever been. Between 1522 and 1528, various lieutenants of Cortés conquered the remnants of Indian culture in Yucatán and Guatemala. Then in 1531 Francisco Pizarro led a band of soldiers down the Pacific coast from Panama toward Peru, where they subdued the Inca Empire. From Peru, conquistadors extended Spanish authority through Chile, and to the north, in present-day Colombia.

Spanish America

The Spanish conquistadors transferred to Amer-

Unarmed Aztecs are killed by Cortés's men during a religious festival in the month of Toxcatl.

ica a system known as the *encomienda*, whereby favored officers became privileged landowners (*encomenderos*) who controlled Indian villages. The *encomenderos* protected the villages and supported missionary priests. In turn, they required tribute from the villagers in the form of goods and labor. Spanish America therefore developed from the start a society of extremes: affluent European conquistadors and native peoples who were held in poverty.

Yet by the mid-1500s Indians were nearly extinct in the West Indies, killed more by European diseases than by Spanish exploitation. To take their place, the colonizers as early as 1503 began to import slaves from Africa. They eventually would transport over 9 million people across the Atlantic in bondage. In all of Spain's New World empire, the Indian population dropped from about 50 million at the outset to 4 million in the seventeenth century, and slowly rose again to 7.5 million. Whites, who totaled no more than 100,000 in the mid–sixteenth century, numbered over 3 million by the end of the colonial period.

For most of the colonial period, much of what is now the United States belonged to Spain, and Spanish culture has left a lasting imprint upon American ways of life. Spain's colonial presence lasted more than three centuries, much longer than either England's or France's, and its possessions were much more far-reaching. New Spain was centered in Mexico, but its frontiers extended from the Florida Keys to Alaska and included areas not currently thought of as formerly Spanish, such as the Deep South (Memphis was founded as San Fernando, Vicksburg as Nogales) and the lower Midwest. Hispanic influences in art, architecture, literature, music, law, and cuisine survive today.

Although Spain's influence was strongest from Mexico southward, the "Spanish borderlands" of the southern United States from Florida to California preserve many reminders of the Spanish presence. The earliest known exploration of Florida was made in 1513 by Juan Ponce de León, then governor of Puerto Rico. He sought the mythic fountain of youth but instead found alligators, swamps, and abundant wildlife. Meanwhile, other Spanish explorers skirted the Gulf coast from Florida to Vera Cruz, scouted the Atlantic coast from Cuba to Newfoundland, established a town at St. Augustine, Florida, and a mission at Santa Fe, New Mexico.

Spain established provinces in North America not so much as commercial enterprises but as defensive buffers protecting its more lucrative trading empire in Mexico and South America. The Spaniards were concerned about French traders infiltrating from Louisiana, English settlers crossing into Florida, and Russian seal hunters wandering down the California coast. Yet the Spanish settlements in what is today the United States never flourished. The Spaniards failed to realize that a prosperous and

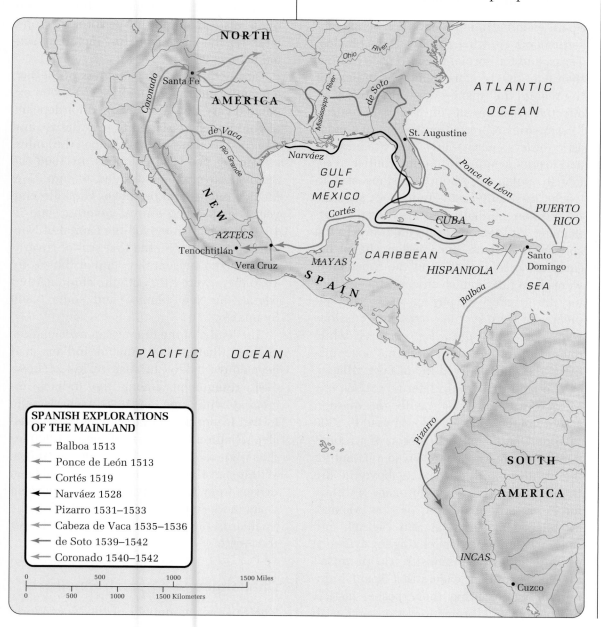

SPANISH EXPLORATIONS OF THE MAINLAND

← Balboa 1513
← Ponce de León 1513
← Cortés 1519
← Narváez 1528
← Pizarro 1531–1533
← Cabeza de Vaca 1535–1536
← de Soto 1539–1542
← Coronado 1540–1542

enduring colonial empire depended on self-sustaining economic development. England and France surpassed Spain in the development of an American presence because Spain failed to embrace what the other imperial powers decided early on: that developing a thriving Indian trade in goods was more important than the conversion of "heathens" and the vain search for gold and silver.

The Spanish Southwest

Spain eventually founded other permanent settlements in what is now New Mexico, Texas, and California. Eager to pacify rather than fight the far more numerous Indians of the region, the Spanish used religion as an effective instrument of colonial control. Missionaries representing the various monastic orders, particularly the Franciscans and Jesuits, ventured into the frontier to establish isolated Catholic missions and to teach Christianity to the Indians. A successful mission gradually became a secular settlement: its lands were divided among the converted Indians, the mission chapel became a parish church, and the inhabitants were given full Spanish citizenship—including the privilege of paying taxes. The soldiers who were sent to protect the missions were housed in *presidios,* or forts, while their families and the merchants accompanying the soldiers lived in adjacent villages.

The land that would later be called New Mexico was the first center of mission activity in the American Southwest. In 1598 Juan de Oñate, the wealthy son of a prominent family in Mexico, received a patent for the territory north of Mexico above the Rio Grande. With an expeditionary military force, he took possession of New Mexico, established a capital at San Gabriel, and sent out search parties looking for evidence of gold and silver deposits. He promised the Pueblo Indian leaders that Spanish dominion would bring them peace, justice, prosperity, and protection. Conversion to Catholicism offered even greater benefits:

"an eternal life of great bliss" instead of "cruel and everlasting torment."

Some Indians welcomed the missionaries as "powerful witches" capable of easing their burdens. Others tried to use the Spanish as allies against rival Indian tribes. Still others saw no alternative but to submit. The Spanish priests smashed, burned, or confiscated the objects deemed sacred by the Indians and suppressed spiritual rituals and ceremonial dances. The Indians living in Spanish New Mexico were required to pay tribute to their *encomenderos.* Indians were often also required to perform personal tasks for the *encomenderos,* including sexual favors.

During the first three-quarters of the seventeenth century, Spanish New Mexico expanded very slowly. The hoped-for deposits of gold and silver failed to materialize, and a limited food supply also helped dull interest among potential colonists. In 1608 the Spanish government decided to turn New Mexico into a royal province. The following year it dispatched a royal governor, and in 1610 the Spanish moved the capital of New Mexico to Santa Fe, the first seat of government in the present-day United States. By 1630 there were fifty Catholic churches and friaries in New Mexico and some 3,000 Spaniards.

The leader of the Franciscan missionaries claimed that 86,000 Pueblo Indians had been converted to Christianity. In fact, however, resentment among the Indians increased with time. In 1680 a charismatic Indian leader named Popé organized a massive rebellion that involved some 17,000 Indians spread across hundreds of miles. Within a few weeks, the Spaniards had been driven from New Mexico. It took fourteen years and four military assaults for the Spaniards to reestablish their control over the territory.

Challenges to Spanish Empire

The Spanish monopoly of the New World colonies remained intact throughout the sixteenth century, but not without challenge from national rivals lusting for New World booty. The French were the first to pose a serious threat. In 1524 the French king sent an Italian named Giovanni da Verrazano in search of a passage to Asia. Sighting land (probably at Cape Fear, North Carolina), Verrazano ranged along the coast as far north as Maine, but it was not until a decade later that the French made their first colonization effort. On three voyages, Jacques Cartier explored the Gulf of St. Lawrence and ventured up the St. Lawrence River as far as present-day Montréal. Near Québec he established a short-lived colony in 1542.

Thereafter, however, French interest in Canada waned, as the French were preoccupied with the religious civil wars wracking their country. Not until the early seventeenth century, when the bold explorer Samuel de Champlain established new settlements in Acadia (Nova Scotia) and at Québec, did French colonization in America begin in earnest. Enterprising French traders negotiated with Indians for their fur pelts, and French Jesuit missionaries cultivated their souls. Unlike many Spanish missionaries, the French Jesuits were not determined to strip their converts of all vestiges of Indian culture. Instead they displayed considerable respect for Native American values.

Acquiring furs and converts took the French southward as well. In 1673 Louis Jolliet and Père Jacques Marquette, a Jesuit priest, took the first expedition down the Mississippi River, but fearing an encounter with the Spaniards, they turned back before reaching the Gulf of Mexico. Nine years later, Robert Cavalier, sieur de La Salle, ventured all the way to the Gulf of Mexico. There, near the river's delta, the French in the early eighteenth century would establish a settlement called New Orleans. The French thereby came to control not only Canada but also the major inland waterway in North America. It was a deceptive control, however, because the French monar-

chy never emphasized permanent settlement. Instead it viewed the region almost solely as a source for trade, and French America remained only sparsely populated.

From the mid-1500s, greater threats to Spanish power in the New World arose from the growing strength of the Dutch and English. The prosperous provinces of the Netherlands, which had passed by inheritance to the Spanish king, and which had become largely Protestant, rebelled against Spanish rule in 1567. A protracted, bloody struggle for independence was interrupted by a twelve-year truce, but Spain did not accept the independence of the Dutch republic until 1648.

Almost from the beginning of the revolt, Dutch privateers plundered Spanish ships. While Queen Elizabeth of England steered a tortuous course to avoid open war with Catholic Spain, she encouraged both Dutch and English sea captains to attack the Spanish. Sporadic British piracy against the Spanish continued until 1587, when Queen Elizabeth had her Catholic cousin, Mary, Queen of Scots, beheaded for her involvement in an unsuccessful coup. In revenge, Spain's Philip II decided to crush Protestant England and began to gather his ill-fated Armada. The ambitious enterprise quickly became a case of incompetence and mismanagement accompanied by bad luck. The heavy Spanish galleons fell victim to the smaller, faster English vessels commanded by Sir Francis Drake and others. Defeat of the Armada convinced the English that the Spanish navy was no longer invincible and cleared the way for English colonization of the Americas.

Early English Explorations

English colonization in North America began in 1584 when Sir Walter Raleigh, eager "to seek new worlds for gold, for praise, for glory," sent an expedition to explore prospects for founding a colony in America. Sailing by way of the West Indies, they came to the Outer Banks of North Carolina

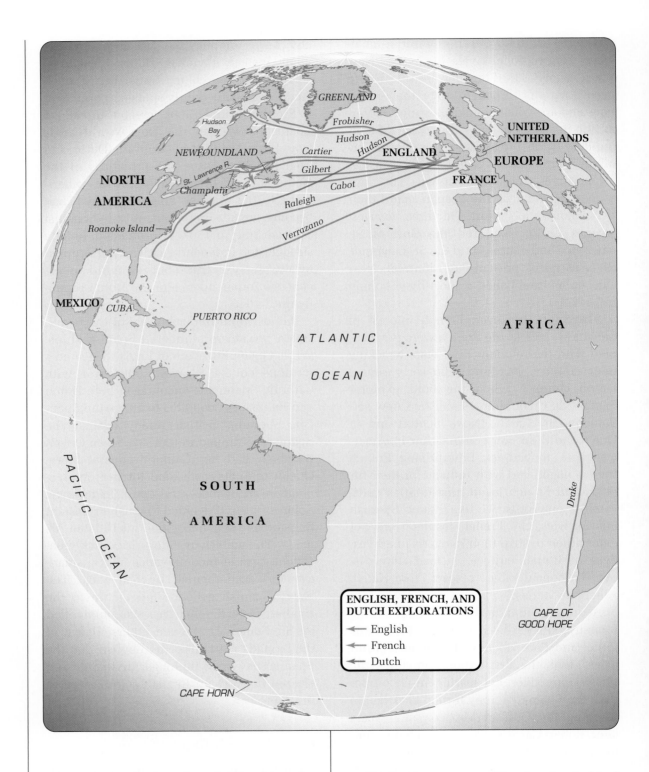

ENGLISH, FRENCH, AND
DUTCH EXPLORATIONS

← English
← French
← Dutch

and discovered Roanoke Island, where the soil seemed fruitful and the natives friendly. Three years later, 117 settlers arrived, including women and children, under the leadership of Governor John White. After a month in Roanoke, White returned to England to get supplies, leaving behind the other colonists, including his daughter, Eleanor, her husband, and her baby, Virginia Dare, the first English child born in the New World. White, however, was long delayed because of the war with Spain.

When he finally returned in 1590, he found the village of "Ralegh" abandoned and pillaged, possibly by hostile Indians or by Spaniards. No trace of the "lost colonists" was ever found. When Queen Elizabeth died in 1603, there were no English settlers in North America.

Settling the Chesapeake

With the death of Queen Elizabeth, the Tudor line ended and the throne fell to her cousin James VI of Scotland, the son of the ill-fated Mary, Queen of Scots. The first of the Stuarts, he ruled England as James I. The Stuart dynasty spanned most of the seventeenth century, a turbulent time of religious and political tensions, civil war, and foreign intrigues. During these eventful years in English history, all but one of the thirteen North American colonies and several more in the Caribbean were founded. They were quite diverse in geography, motives, and composition.

In 1606, having made peace with Spain, thereby freeing up resources and men for colonization, James I chartered the Virginia Company with two divisions, the First Colony of London and the Second Colony of Plymouth. The stockholders expected a potential return from gold and products such as wine, citrus fruits, olive oil, pitch, tar, potash, and other forest products needed for naval use. Many also still hoped to discover a passage to India. Few if any investors foresaw what the first English colony would become: a bountiful source of tobacco.

From the outset, the pattern of English colonization diverged significantly from the Spanish emphasis on conquest and conversion. The English settled along the Atlantic seaboard, where the native populations were relatively weak. There was no Aztec or Inca Empire to conquer and rule. The colonists thus had to establish their own communities within a largely wilderness setting and among a more diverse array of Indian tribes.

Virginia

The London group of the Virginia Company planted the first permanent colony in Virginia, named after Elizabeth I, the "Virgin Queen." On May 6, 1607, three ships loaded with about 100 men reached Chesapeake Bay after four storm-tossed months at sea. They chose a river with a northwest bend—in hope of a passage to Asia—and settled about 40 miles inland to hide from marauding Spaniards.

The river they called the James, and the colony Jamestown. After building a fort, thatched huts, a storehouse, and a church, the colonists began planting, but most were either townsmen unfamiliar with farming or "gentlemen" adventurers who scorned manual labor. They had come to find gold, not to establish a farm settlement. Supplies from England were undependable, and only firm leadership and their trade with the Indians, who taught the colonists to grow maize, enabled them to survive.

The Indians of the region were loosely organized. Wahunsonacock, called Powhatan by the English after the name of his tribe, was the chief of some thirty Algonquian-speaking tribes in eastern Virginia. The Indians making up the so-called Powhatan Confederacy were largely an agricultural people who lived along rivers in fortified towns and resided in framed houses sheathed with bark. Despite occasional clashes with the colonists, the Indians of Virginia initially adopted a stance of nervous assistance and watchful waiting. Powhatan apparently hoped to develop a lucrative trade and military alliance with the newcomers; he realized too late that the English intended to expropriate his lands and subjugate his people.

The colonists, as it happened, had more than a match for Powhatan in Captain John Smith, a soldier of fortune with rare powers of leadership and self-promotion. The Virginia Company appointed Smith a member of the resident council to manage the new colony in America. With the colonists on the verge of starvation, he imposed strict discipline and forced all to labor, declaring that "he that will not work shall not eat." Smith also bargained with the Indians and mapped the Chesapeake region. Through his efforts, Jamestown survived the first two winters, but in 1609 Smith suffered a gunpowder burn and sailed back to England. The colony lapsed into anarchy and suffered the "starving time" of the winter of 1609–1610, during which most of the colonists, weakened by hunger, fell prey to disease. A relief party found only about sixty settlers still alive in 1610. All poultry and livestock (including horses) had been eaten, and one man reportedly had dined on his wife.

For the next seven years, the colony limped along until it gradually found a reason for being: tobacco. In 1612 John Rolfe had begun to experiment with the harsh-tasting Virginia tobacco, and by 1616 a smoother-tasting variety had become an export staple. Meanwhile Rolfe had made another contribution to stability by marrying Pocahontas, the daughter of Powhatan. Their marriage helped to ease deteriorating relations between the Indians and English settlers, who continued to try to take the Indians' crops, either through extortion or plundering. Distinguished Virginians still boast of their descent from the Indian "princess," who died of smallpox in London in 1620.

In 1618 officials in London initiated a series of reforms intended to shore up their struggling American colony. They first inaugurated a new "headright" policy. Anyone who bought a share in the company, or who could transport himself to Virginia, could have fifty acres, and fifty more for any servants he might send or bring. The following year the company promised that the settlers should have the "rights of Englishmen," including a representative assembly. On July 30, 1619, the first General Assembly of Virginia met in the Jamestown church. It was an eventful year in two other respects.

During 1619, a ship arrived with ninety "young maidens," to be sold to likely husbands of their own choice for the cost of transportation (about 125 pounds of tobacco). And a Dutch vessel dropped off "20 Negars," the first blacks in English America.

Yet despite its successes, Jamestown again fell upon evil days. The profitable tobacco trade intensified the settlers' lust for Indian lands because they had already been cleared and were ready to be planted. In 1622 the Indians tried to repel the land-grabbing English. They killed some 350 colonists, including John Rolfe.

The English thereafter sought to wipe out the Indian presence along their frontier. In 1623 Captain William Tucker and a band of soldiers met with Indian leaders to negotiate a settlement. After signing a treaty, Tucker invited the Indians to drink a toast to celebrate their truce. Unwittingly, the Indians drank the proffered wine, only to realize too late that it had been poisoned. Two hundred Indians died from the doctored brew. The soldiers then burned Indian villages and plundered their corn, killed another fifty and "brought home part of their heads." This process of "continual incursions" into Indian territory spanned the decade.

Yet the English foothold in Virginia remained tenuous. Some 14,000 people had migrated to the colony since 1607, but the population in 1624 stood at a precarious 1,132. The king appointed a commission to investigate the running of the struggling colony by the Virginia Company, and on the commission's recommendation a court dissolved the company. In 1624 Virginia became a royal colony.

Maryland

In 1634, ten years after Virginia became a royal colony, a neighboring settlement named Maryland appeared on the northern shores of Chesapeake Bay. It was the first so-called proprietary colony, granted not to a joint-stock company but to an individual, Lord Baltimore. Sir George Calvert, the first Lord Baltimore, had announced in 1625 his conversion to Catholicism and sought the colony as a refuge for English Catholics, who were subjected to discrimination at home.

His son, Cecilius Calvert, the second Lord Baltimore, actually founded the colony in 1634 at St. Mary's near the mouth of the Potomac River. Calvert brought along Catholic gentlemen as landholders, but a majority of the servants were Protestants. The charter gave Calvert power to make laws with the consent of the freemen (all property holders). The first legislative assembly met in 1635 and later divided into two houses, with the governor and council sitting separately. The charter also empowered the proprietor to grant huge manorial estates, and Maryland had some sixty before 1676. But the Lords Baltimore soon found that to draw large numbers of settlers they had to offer small farms. The colony was meant to rely on mixed farming, but its fortunes, like those of Virginia, soon came to depend on tobacco.

Settling New England

Plymouth

Meanwhile, far to the north of the Chesapeake, quite different colonies were taking shape. The Pilgrims who established Plymouth Colony were bent not on finding gold or making a fortune but on building a Christian commonwealth. They belonged to the most uncompromising sect of Puritans, the Separatists, who had severed all ties with the Church of England. Persecuted by James I and Anglican officials, they fled to Holland in 1607. The Calvinistic Dutch, who shared their belief in predestination and a rigid moral code, granted them asylum and toleration, but restricted them mainly to unskilled laboring jobs. After ten

years in Holland, the Pilgrims had wearied of such discrimination, and they decided to found a colony in the New World.

In 1620, 101 men, women, and children, led by William Bradford, crammed into the *Mayflower* for the transatlantic voyage. Only half of the voyagers were Pilgrim "Saints"—people recognized as having been elected by God for salvation; the rest were non-Pilgrim "Strangers"—ordinary settlers, hired hands, and indentured servants. The leaders undertook the voyage, as Bradford asserted, "for the glorie of God, and advancements of the Christian faith and honour of our king & countrie."

A stormy voyage led them to Cape Cod, far north of Virginia. They called their settlement Plymouth. Forty-one of the Pilgrims entered into a formal agreement to abide by laws made by leaders of their own choosing—the Mayflower Compact of November 21, 1620. Later used as a model by other New England settlers, the compact helped establish the distinctive American tradition of consensual government.

The Pilgrims built and occupied their dwellings amid the winter snows, and nearly half of them died of exposure and disease. In the spring of 1621, the colonists met a Wampanoag Indian named Squanto, who showed them how to grow maize. By autumn the Pilgrims had a bumper crop of corn, a flourishing fur trade, and a supply of lumber for shipment. To celebrate, they held a harvest feast with the Wampanoags, an annual ritual that later would be dubbed Thanksgiving.

Massachusetts Bay

Plymouth Colony's population never rose above 7,000, and after ten years it was overshadowed by its larger neighbor, the Massachusetts Bay Colony. It, too, was intended to be a holy commonwealth made up of religious folk bound together in the harmonious worship of God. Like the Pilgrims, the Puritans who colonized Massachusetts Bay

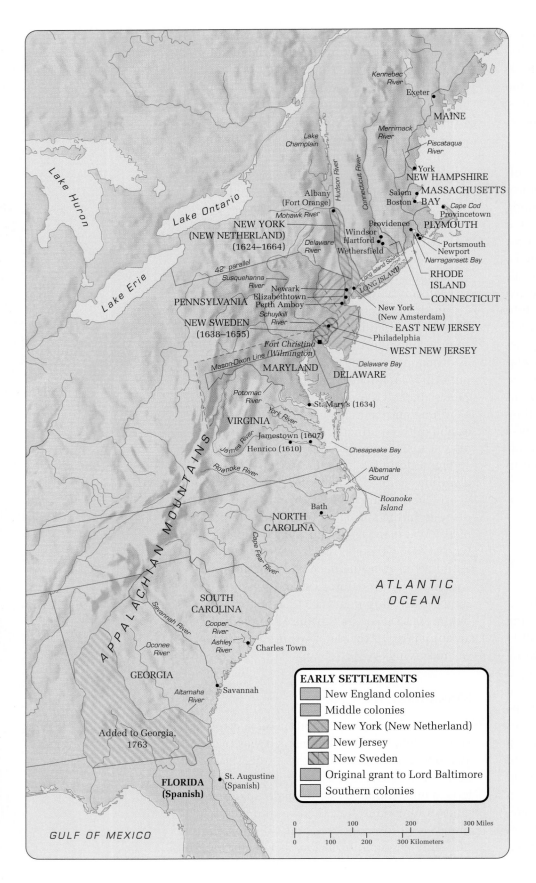

EARLY SETTLEMENTS

New England colonies

Middle colonies

New York (New Netherland)

New Jersey

New Sweden

Original grant to Lord Baltimore

Southern colonies

| 0 | | 100 | | 200 | | 300 Miles |
| 0 | 100 | 200 | | 300 Kilometers | | |

were primarily Congregationalists who wanted self-governing churches whose members would be limited to "visible saints," those who could demonstrate their receipt of the gift of God's grace. Unlike the Plymouth Separatists, however, the Puritans who settled Massachusetts hoped that the Church of England could be reformed. Thus they were called Non-Separating Congregationalists, or Nonconformists.

In 1629 a group of Puritans and merchants convinced King Charles I to grant their newly formed Massachusetts Bay Company an area north of Plymouth Colony for settlement. Leaders of the company at first looked upon it mainly as a business venture, but a majority faction led by John Winthrop, a respected lawyer, resolved to use the colony as a refuge for persecuted Puritans.

In 1630 the *Arbella,* with Governor John Winthrop and the charter aboard, embarked with six other ships for Massachusetts. In a speech entitled "A Model of Christian Charity," delivered on board, Winthrop told his fellow Puritans "we must consider that we shall be a city upon a hill"—an exemplary beacon showing all people what a truly godly community could be. By the end of 1630, seventeen more ships bearing an additional 1,000 colonists joined Winthrop's band of colonists. As settlers—Puritan and non-Puritan—poured into the region, Boston became the chief city and capital. The next several years witnessed the Great Migration, in which 80,000 people left their homeland, including some 40,000 to 50,000 English settlers who went to the New World, fleeing persecution and economic depression at home.

Winthrop was a courageous leader who shrewdly took advantage of a fateful omission in the charter for the

Massachusetts Bay Company: the usual proviso that the company maintain its home office in England. Winthrop's group took its charter with them, thereby transferring the entire government of the colony to Massachusetts Bay, where they hoped to ensure Puritan control.

The transfer of the Massachusetts charter, whereby an English trading company evolved into a provincial government, was a unique venture in colonization. Under this royal charter, power rested with the General Court, which elected the governor and his assistants and which consisted of shareholders, called freemen (those who had the "freedom of the company").

At first the freemen had no power except to choose legislators known as assistants, who in turn elected the governor and deputy governor. The procedure violated provisions of the charter, but Winthrop kept the document hidden, and few knew of its exact provisions. Controversy simmered until 1634, when each town sent two delegates to Boston to confer on matters coming before the General Court. There they demanded to see the charter, which Winthrop reluctantly produced, and they read that the power to pass laws and levy taxes rested in the General Court. Winthrop argued that the body of freemen had grown too large, but when it met, the General Court responded by turning itself into a representative body with two or three deputies to represent each town. They also chose a new governor, and Winthrop did not resume the office until three years later. A final stage in the evolution of the government, a two-house legislature, came in 1644, with the deputies and assistants sitting apart and all decisions requiring a majority in each house.

Thus over a period of fourteen years, the Massachusetts Bay Company, a trading corporation, evolved into the governing body of a commonwealth. Membership in a Puritan church replaced the purchase of stock as a means of becoming a freeman, which was to say a voter. The General Court, like Parliament, became a representative body of two houses, with the House of Assistants corresponding roughly to the House of Lords, and the House of Deputies to the House of Commons.

Rhode Island

More by accident than design, Massachusetts became the staging area for the rest of New England, as new colonies grew out of religious quarrels within the fold. Puritanism created a volatile mixture: on the one hand, the search for God's will could lead to a rigid orthodoxy; on the other hand, it could lead troubled consciences to diverse, radical, or even bizarre convictions.

Young Roger Williams, who arrived in 1631, was among the first to cause problems, precisely because he was the purest of Puritans, a Separatist troubled by the failure of the Massachusetts Nonconformists to repudiate the Church of England entirely. Williams's belief that a true church must have no relations with the English government, the Anglican establishment, or with the unregenerate led him to the conclusion that no true church was possible, unless perhaps consisting of himself and his wife— and he may have had doubts about her.

The purity of the church that Williams espoused required complete separation of church and state and freedom from coercion in matters of faith. "Forced worship," he declared, "stinks in God's nostrils." Such views were too advanced even for the radical church of Salem, which finally removed him. In 1635 a provoked General Court banished him to England. Aided by Narragansett Indian friends, however, Williams and a few followers fled into the wilderness, and they eventually were taken in by the Narragansetts. In the spring of 1636 Williams bought some land from the Indians and established the town of Providence at the head of Narragansett Bay, the first permanent settlement in Rhode Island, and the first in America to legislate freedom of religion.

Governor John Winthrop, who envisioned the Massachusetts Bay Colony as "a city upon a hill."

Anne Hutchinson quarreled with the Puritan leaders for different reasons. Strong-willed and articulate, she worked as a healer and midwife and hosted meetings in her Boston home to discuss sermons. Soon, however, those discussions turned into forums for Hutchinson to provide her own commentaries on religious matters. She claimed to have had direct revelations from the Holy Spirit that convinced her that only two or three Puritan ministers actually preached the appropriate "covenant of grace." The others, she charged, were deluded and were promoting a "covenant of works" that led people to believe that good conduct would ensure their salvation.

Hutchinson's beliefs were provocative for several reasons. Puritan theology affirmed the Calvinist doctrine that people could be saved only by God's grace rather than through their own willful actions. But Puritanism in practice also insisted that ministers were necessary to interpret God's will for the people so as to "prepare" them for the possibility of their being selected for salvation. In challenging the very legitimacy of the ministerial community as well as the hard-earned assurances of salvation enjoyed by current church members, Hutchinson was undermining the stability of an already fragile social system and theological order. What made the situation worse in such a male-dominated society, of course, was that a *woman* had the audacity to make such charges and assertions.

A pregnant Hutchinson was hauled before the General Court in 1637, and for two days she verbally sparred on equal terms with the presiding magistrates and testifying ministers. As the intense trial continued, Hutchinson was eventually lured into convicting herself by claiming direct divine inspiration. Banished in 1638 as "a woman not fit for our society," she settled with her family and a few followers on an island near what is now Portsmouth, Rhode Island. The arduous journey had taken a toll, however. Hutchinson grew sick and her baby was stillborn. Hutchinson's spirits never recovered. After her husband's death in 1643, she moved to Long Island, then under Dutch jurisdiction, and the following year she and five of her children were massacred during an Indian attack.

Thus the colony of Rhode Island, the smallest in America, grew up in Narragansett Bay as a refuge for dissenters who believed that the state had no right to coerce religious belief. In 1640 they formed a confederation and in 1643 secured their first charter. Roger Williams lived until 1683, an active and beloved citizen of the commonwealth he founded in a society that, during his lifetime at least, lived up to his principles of religious freedom and a government based on the consent of the people.

Connecticut, New Hampshire, and Maine

Connecticut had a more orthodox beginning than did Rhode Island. It was founded by groups of Massachusetts Puritans seeking better lands and access to the fur trade farther west. In 1636 three entire church congregations trekked westward by the "Great Road," and moved to the Connecticut River towns of Wethersfield, Windsor, and Hartford.

Led by Thomas Hooker, they organized the self-governing colony of Connecticut in 1637 as a response to the danger of attack from the Pequot Indians, who lived east of the river. In 1639 the Connecticut General Court adopted the "Fundamental Orders of Connecticut," a series of laws providing for a government like that of Massachusetts. Voting in the Connecticut colony, however, was not limited to church members.

To the north of Massachusetts, most of what is now New Hampshire and Maine was granted in 1622 by the Council for New England to Sir Ferdinando Gorges and Captain John Mason and their associates. In 1629 Mason and Gorges divided their territory at the Piscataqua River, Mason taking the southern part, which he named New Hampshire, and Gorges taking the northern part, which became the province of Maine. In the 1630s, Puritan immigrants began filtering in, and in 1638 the Reverend John Wheelwright, one of Anne Hutchinson's group, founded Exeter. Maine consisted of a few scattered and small settlements, mostly fishing stations.

Indians in New England

The settlers who poured into New England found not a "virgin land" of uninhabited wilderness but a developed region populated by over 100,000 Indians. The Native Americans coped with the newcomers and changing circumstances in different ways. Some resisted, others sought accommodation, and still others grew dependent on European culture. In some areas, Indians survived and even flourished in concert with European settlers over long periods of time. In other areas, land-hungry Europeans quickly displaced or decimated the native populations. The interactions of the two cultures involved misunderstandings, the mutual need for trade and adaptation, and sporadic outbreaks of epidemics and warfare.

In general, the English colonists adopted a different strategy for dealing with the Native Americans than that of the French and the Dutch. Merchants from France and the Netherlands were preoccupied with exploiting the fur trade. To do so, they established permanent trading outposts among the Indians. This nurtured amicable relations with the far more numerous Indians in the region. In contrast, the English colonists were more interested in fish and farms. They were quite willing to manipulate and exploit Indians rather than deal with them on an equal footing. Their goal was subordination rather than reciprocity.

In Maine the Abenakis were mainly hunters and gatherers dependent upon the natural offerings of the land and waters. The men did the hunting and fishing, women the gathering and cooking. Women were also responsible for setting up and breaking camp and raising the children. The Algonquian tribes of southern New England—the Massachusetts, Nausets, Narragansetts, Pequots, and Wampanoags—were more horticultural. While the men still hunted, fished, or traded surplus grain, women planted crops.

Although often portrayed as a monolithic group, the various Indian tribes of New England often fought among themselves, usually over disputed land. Had they been able to forge a solid alliance, they would have been better able to resist the encroachments of white settlers. As it was, they not only were fragmented but also vulnerable to the infectious diseases carried on board the ships transporting European settlers to the New World. Epidemics of smallpox devastated the coastal Indian population. Between 1610 and 1675, the Abenakis declined from 12,000 to 3,000, and the southern New England tribes from 65,000 to 10,000.

Those Indians who survived the epidemics and refused to yield their lands were often dislodged by force. In 1636 white settlers in Massachusetts accused a Pequot of murdering a colonist. Joined by Connecticut colonists, they retaliated by setting fire to a Pequot village. As the Indians fled their burning huts, the Puritans shot and killed them—men, women, and children. In less than an hour, all but seven escapees were dead.

Sassacus, the Pequot chief, then organized the survivors and attacked the whites. During the Pequot War of 1637, the colonists and their Narragansett allies massacred hundreds of Pequots. Most of the survivors were sold into slavery in Bermuda. Under the terms of the Treaty of Hartford (1638), the Pequot nation was dissolved.

After the Pequot War, the prosperous fur trade contributed to peaceful relations between whites and the remaining Indians, but the relentless growth of the colony and the decline of the animal population began to reduce the eastern tribes to relative poverty. The colonial government repeatedly encroached upon the Indian settlements, forcing them to acknowledge English laws and customs. Colonial leaders argued that the Indians should be deprived of their land because they were not using it as efficiently as the English would.

The era of fairly peaceful coexistence that began with the Treaty of Hartford came to an end during the last quarter of the seventeenth century. In 1675 Philip (Metacom), chief of the Wampanoags, forged an alliance among the remaining tribes of southern New England—the Narragansetts, Mohegans, and Wampanoags. Provoked by the hanging of three Indians for murder, Metacom's forces attacked English settlements. What came to be known as King Philip's War lasted through 1676. In the end, Metacom and over 3,000 Indians were killed. With them died organized resistance to white expansion.

Renewed Settlement

Before 1640, English settlers in New England and around Chesapeake Bay had established two great beachheads on the Atlantic coast, separated by the Dutch colony of New Netherland. After 1640, however, the power struggle back in England between king and Parliament, which erupted into civil war in 1642 between those who backed Parliament and those who supported the king, distracted attention from colonization. As a result, British migration dwindled to a trickle for more than twenty years. During the time of the English Civil War and Oliver Cromwell's Puritan dictatorship, the struggling colonies were left pretty much alone.

The Restoration of King Charles II in England in 1660 involved scarcely any changes in colonial governments, since little had occurred there under Cromwell. Renewed emigration rapidly expanded the populations of Virginia and Maryland. Fears of reprisals against Puritan New England by the reestablishment of the Anglican Church as the official church of England proved unfounded, at least for the time being. Massachusetts gained reconfirmation of its charter in 1662, and Connecticut and Rhode Island received the first royal charters in 1662 and 1663. All three retained their status as self-governing corporations.

The Restoration of the king also rekindled enthusiasm for colonial expansion. Within twelve years, the English had conquered New Netherland, had settled Carolina, and had nearly filled out the shape of the colonies. In the middle region formerly claimed by the Dutch, four new colonies sprang into being: New York, New Jersey, Pennsylvania, and Delaware. Without exception, the new colonies were proprietary, awarded by the king to "proprietors," men who had remained loyal during the civil war.

Settling the Carolinas

Carolina from the start comprised two widely separated areas of settlement. The northernmost part, long called Albemarle, remained a remote scattering of settlers along the shores of Albemarle Sound, isolated from Virginia by the Dismal Swamp and lacking easy access for oceangoing vessels. Albemarle had no governor until 1664, no assembly until 1665, and not even a town until a group of French Huguenots (Protestants) founded the village of Bath in 1704.

The eight Lords Proprietors to whom the king gave Carolina neglected Albemarle from the outset and focused on more promising sites to the south. Eager to find settlers who had already been seasoned in the colonies, they looked first to Barbados. The rise of large-scale sugar production in Barbados had persuaded small planters to try their luck elsewhere. Sir Anthony Ashley-Cooper finally spurred the enterprise by convincing his fellow proprietors to take on more of the financial burden of settlement. In 1669 three ships left London with about 100 settlers recruited in England; they sailed first to Barbados to pick up more settlers and then north to Bermuda. The expedition finally landed in America at a place several miles up the Ashley River. There Charles Town (later known as Charleston) remained from 1670 to 1680, when it was moved downstream to Oyster Point.

The government rested on one of the most curious documents of colonial history, the "Fundamental Constitutions of Carolina," drawn up by Lord Ashley-Cooper with the help of his secretary, the philosopher John Locke. Its cumbersome form of government and its provisions for an almost feudal social system and an elaborate nobility had little effect in the colony except to encourage a practice of large land grants, but from the beginning smaller "headrights" were given to immigrants who paid their own way. The provision that had greatest effect was a grant of religious toleration, designed to encourage immigration, which gave South Carolina a distinctive degree of indulgence (extending even to Jews and heathens) and ethnic pluralism.

Ambitious English planters from Barbados dominated the colony and soon organized a major trade in Indian slaves, whom the Westo Indians obligingly drove to the coast for shipment to the Caribbean. The first major export other than furs and slaves was cattle, and a true staple crop was not developed until the introduction of rice in the 1690s.

South Carolina became a separate royal colony in 1719. North Carolina remained under the proprietors' rule for ten more years, when they surrendered their governing rights to the crown.

The Southern Indians

The major Indian tribes in Florida, the Carolinas, Georgia, and what is today Alabama and Mississippi—the Apalachee, Timucua, Catawba, Cherokee, Chickasaw, Choctaw, Creek, and Tuscarora—combined farming with hunting and fishing to produce a thriving culture. They clustered in matrilineal clans (in which authority and property descended through the maternal line). The women raised beans, potatoes, and especially corn. The men hunted, traded, and made war.

Beginning in the late seventeenth century, the Creeks developed a flourishing trade with the British settlers, exchanging deerskins for manufactured goods—hoes, copper kettles, knives, beads, blankets, and clothing. During this same time, English merchants—mostly illiterate adventurers—began traveling southward from Virginia into the Piedmont region of Carolina, where they did business with the Catawbas. By 1690 traders from Charleston, South Carolina, made their way up the Savannah River to arrange deals with the Cherokees, Creeks, and Chickasaws. Between 1699 and 1715, Carolina exported an average of 54,000 deerskins per year. The voracious demand for the soft skins almost exterminated the deer population.

Trading with the English exposed the Indians to contagious diseases and also entwined them in a dependent relationship that would prove disastrous to their traditional way of life. Eager to receive more manufactured goods, weapons, and ammunition, the Indians were easily manipulated by English entrepreneurs and government officials. The English traders began providing the Indians with firearms and rum as incentives to capture rival tribesmen to be sold as slaves.

The continuing Indian trade led to repeated troubles. In 1715, Creeks, Choctaws, and members of smaller tribes organized a massive revolt against English control. This so-called Yamasee War began when Indians killed several English traders. The English colonists won out by playing the Indians against one another, convincing the Cherokees to join their side. When the Creek leaders visited the Cherokees in an effort to gain

(*Left*) Carolina Indians fishing, by John White, one of the earliest English settlers in America. Two methods of fishing are depicted here—nets and spears for daylight, and by firelight for night. (*Right*) Secotan dance, watercolor by John White.

their support, the Cherokees killed them, an incident that engendered hatred between the two tribes for years thereafter. The Yamasee War ended in 1717, when the Creeks signed a peace treaty, but infighting among the Indians continued.

New Netherland Becomes New York

Meanwhile, to the west of New England, the English resolved to pluck out that old thorn in their side—New Netherland. The Dutch colony was older than New England and had been planted when the two Protestant powers of England and the Netherlands enjoyed friendly relations in opposition to Catholic Spain. The Dutch East India Company (organized in 1602) had hired an English captain, Henry Hudson, to seek the elusive passage to China. In 1609 Hudson had discovered Delaware Bay and had explored the river named for him to a point probably beyond Albany, where he and a group of Mohawks made merry with brandy. From that contact stemmed a lasting trade between the Dutch and Iroquois nations. In 1614 the Dutch established fur-trading posts on Manhattan Island and upriver at Fort Or-

ange (later Albany). Ten years later, a newly organized West India Company began permanent settlements. In 1626 Governor Peter Minuit purchased Manhattan from the Indians, and the new village of New Amsterdam became the capital of New Netherland.

Like the French, the Dutch were interested mainly in the fur trade and less in agricultural settlements. In 1629, however, the Dutch West India Company (organized in 1621) provided that any stockholder might obtain a large estate (a patroonship) if he peopled it with fifty adults within four years. The patroon supplied cattle, tools, and buildings. His tenants, in turn, paid him rent, used his gristmill (a mill for grinding grain), gave him first option to buy their surplus crops, and submitted to a court he established. It amounted to transplanting the feudal manor into the New World. Volunteers for serfdom were hard to find, however, when there was land to be had elsewhere, and most settlers took advantage of the company's provision that one could have as farms all the lands one could improve.

The colony's government was under the almost absolute control of a governor sent out by the Dutch West India Company. The governors were mostly stubborn autocrats, either corrupt or inept, especially at Indian relations. They depended on a small professional garrison for defense, and the inhabitants (including a number of English settlers on Long Island) showed almost total indifference in 1664 when Governor Peter Stuyvesant called them to arms against a threatening British fleet. Almost defenseless, old soldier Stuyvesant blustered about on his wooden leg, but he finally surrendered to the English without firing a shot.

The plan of conquest had been hatched by Charles II's brother, James, the duke of York, later King James II. When James and his advisers counseled that New Netherland could easily be conquered, Charles II granted the region to his brother. The English transformed New Amsterdam into New York and Fort Orange into Albany, and they held the country thereafter, except for a brief Dutch reoccupation in 1673–1674. Nonetheless, the Dutch left a permanent imprint on the land and the language. While the Dutch vernacular faded away, places like Wall Street (the original wall provided protection against Indians) and Broadway (Breede Wegh) remained, along with family names like Rensselaer, Roosevelt, and Van Buren. The Dutch presence lingered in the Dutch Reformed church; in words like *boss, cookie, crib, snoop, stoop, and spook;* and in the legendary Santa Claus and Rip Van Winkle.

The Iroquois League

One of the most significant effects of European settlement in North America during the seventeenth century was the intensification of warfare between Indian peoples. The same combination of forces that weakened the Indian population of New England and the Carolinas befell the tribes around New York City and the lower Hudson Valley. Dissension among the Indians and susceptibility to infectious disease left them vulnerable to exploitation by whites and by other Indians.

In the interior of New York, however, a different situation arose. There the Iroquois (an Algonquian term signifying "snake" or "terrifying man") nation would eventually forge an alliance so strong that the outnumbered Dutch and, later, English traders were forced to work with the federation of five tribes that spoke related languages—the Mohawk, Oneida, Onondaga, Cayuga, and Seneca (a sixth tribe, the Tuscaroras, joined them from Carolina in 1712).

By the early 1600s, some fifty sachems (chiefs) governed the 12,000 members of the Iroquois League. The well-organized Iroquois tribes lived in rectangular "long houses" sheathed in bark. Although a patriarchal society, the Iroquois granted considerable powers to women, who controlled the nominations for the tribal councils and could remove ineffective leaders.

When the Iroquois began to deplete the local game supply during the 1640s, they used firearms furnished by their Dutch trading partners to seize the Canadian hunting grounds of the neighboring Hurons and Eries. During the so-called Beaver Wars, the Iroquois defeated the western tribes and thereafter hunted the region's beavers to extinction. Other Indian nations such as the Fox, Sauk, and Kickapoo fled in terror at the approach of the Iroquois.

During the second half of the seventeenth century, the relentless search for furs and captives led Iroquois war parties to range far and wide across eastern North America. They gained control over a huge area from the St. Lawrence River to Tennessee and from Maine to Michigan. These wars helped reorient the political relationships in the eastern half of the continent, especially in the area from the Ohio Valley northward across the Great Lakes basin. Besieged by the Iroquois League, the western tribes forged defensive alliances with the French.

In the 1690s the French and their Indian allies gained the advantage over the Iroquois. They destroyed their crops and villages, infected them with smallpox, and re-

A Quaker meeting. The presence of women is evidence of Quaker views on the equality of the sexes.

duced the male population by more than a third. Facing extermination, the Iroquois made peace with the French in 1701. They had tired of serving the English as a "Pack of Hounds" to harass the French. During the first half of the eighteenth century, the Iroquois maintained a shrewd neutrality between the two rival European powers that enabled them to play off the British against the French, all the while creating a thriving fur trade for themselves.

New Jersey

Shortly after the conquest of New York, still in 1664, the duke of York granted his lands between the Hudson and the Delaware Rivers to Sir George Carteret and Lord John Berkeley and named the territory for Carteret's native island of Jersey. In East New Jersey, peopled at first by perhaps 200 Dutch who had crossed the Hudson, new settlements gradually arose: disaffected Puritans from New Haven founded Newark, and a group of Scots founded Perth Amboy. In the west, which faced the Delaware, a scattering of Swedes, Finns, and Dutch remained, soon to be overwhelmed by swarms

of English Quakers. In 1702 East and West Jersey were united as a royal colony.

Pennsylvania and Delaware

The Quaker sect, as the Society of Friends was called in ridicule (because they told their followers to "tremble at the word of the Lord"), became the most influential of many radical groups that sprang from the turbulence of the English Civil War. Founded by George Fox about 1647, the Quakers carried further than any other group the doctrine of individual spiritual inspiration and interpretation—the "inner light," they called it. They discarded all formal sacraments and formal ministry, refused deference to persons of rank, used the familiar "thee" and "thou" in addressing everyone, declined to take oaths because that was contrary to Scripture, and embraced simple living and pacifism. Quakers experienced intense persecution—often in their zeal they seemed to invite it—but never inflicted it on others. Their toleration extended to complete religious freedom for all and the equality of the sexes, including the full participation of women in religious affairs.

In 1673 George Fox returned to England from a visit to America with the vision of a Quaker commonwealth in the New World and enticed others with his idea. The entrance of Quakers into New Jersey encouraged other Friends to migrate, especially to the Delaware River side. Soon, across the river arose the Quaker Commonwealth, the colony of Pennsylvania.

William Penn, the colony's founder, was born in 1644 and raised as a proper gentleman, but in 1667 he converted to Quakerism. In 1681 King Charles II awarded Penn a huge tract of land in America, and Penn named it, at the king's insistence, for his father: Pennsylvania (literally Penn's Woods). Penn vigorously recruited settlers to his new colony, and religious dissenters from England and the Continent—Quakers,

Mennonites, Amish, Moravians, Baptists—flocked to the region. Indian relations were good from the beginning because of the Quakers' friendliness and Penn's careful policy of purchasing land titles from the Indians.

Pennsylvania's government resembled that of other proprietary colonies, except that the councilors as well as the assembly were elected by the freemen (taxpayers and property owners) and the governor had no veto—although Penn as proprietor did. Penn hoped to show that a government could run in accordance with Quaker principles, that it could maintain peace and order without oaths or wars, that religion could flourish without an established church and with absolute freedom of conscience.

In 1682 the duke of York also granted Penn the area of Delaware, another part of the Dutch territory. At first Delaware became part of Pennsylvania, but after 1701 the settlers were granted the right to choose their own assembly. From then until the American Revolution, Delaware had a separate assembly but the same governor as Pennsylvania.

Georgia

Georgia was the last of the British continental colonies to be established, half a century after Pennsylvania. In 1732 George II gave the land between the Savannah and Altamaha Rivers to the twenty-one trustees of Georgia. In two respects Georgia was unique among the colonies: it was set up both as a philanthropic experiment and a military buffer against Spanish Florida. General James E. Oglethorpe, who accompanied the first colonists as resident trustee, represented both concerns: as a soldier who organized the colony's defenses, and as a philanthropist who championed prison reform and sought a colonial refuge for the poor and religiously persecuted.

In 1733 Oglethorpe and a band of 120 colonists founded Savannah near the mouth of the Savannah River. Soon thereafter they were joined by Protestant refugees from central Europe, who made the colony for a time more German than English. The addition of Scottish Highlanders, Portuguese Jews, Welsh, and others gave the early colony a cosmopolitan character much like that of Charleston, South Carolina.

As a buffer against Spanish Florida the colony succeeded, but as a philanthropic experiment it failed. Efforts to develop silk and wine production floundered. Landholdings were limited to 500 acres, rum was prohibited, and the importation of slaves forbidden, partly to leave room for servants brought on charity, partly to ensure security. But the utopian rules soon collapsed. The regulations against rum and slavery were widely disregarded and finally abandoned. By 1759 all restrictions on landholding were removed.

In 1753 the trustees' charter expired and the province reverted to the crown. As a royal colony, Georgia acquired for the first time an effective government. The province developed slowly over the next decade but grew rapidly in population and wealth after 1763. Instead of wine and silk, Georgians exported rice, indigo, lumber, naval stores, beef, and pork, and they carried on a lively trade with the West Indies. The colony finally had become a commercial success.

Thriving Colonies

After a late start and with little design, the English outstripped both the French and the Spanish in the New World. The lack of plan marked the genius of English colonization, for it gave free rein to a variety of human impulses. The centralized control imposed by the monarchs of Spain and France got their colonies off the mark more quickly but eventually brought their downfall because it hobbled innovation and responsiveness to new circumstances. The British preferred private investment with a minimum of royal control. In the English colonies, poor immigrants had a much greater chance of getting at least a small parcel of land, and a degree of self-government made the English colonies more responsive to new challenges—if sometimes stalled by controversy.

Moreover, the compact model of English settlement contrasted sharply with the pattern of Spain's far-flung conquests or France's far-reaching trade routes to the interior by way of the St. Lawrence and Mississippi Rivers. Geography reinforced Eng-

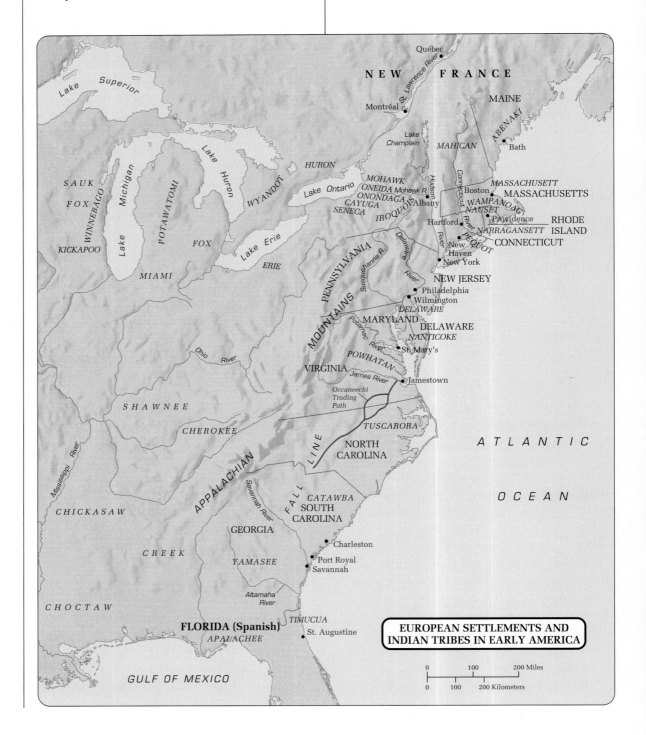

EUROPEAN SETTLEMENTS AND INDIAN TRIBES IN EARLY AMERICA

land's bent for concentrated occupation and settlement of its colonies. The rivers and bays indenting the coasts served as veins of communication along which colonies first sprang up, but no great river offered a highway to the far interior. About a hundred miles back in Georgia and the Carolinas, and nearer the coast to the north, the "fall line" of the rivers presented rocky rapids that marked the head of navigation and the end of the coastal plain. About a hundred miles beyond that, and farther back in Pennsylvania, stretched the rolling expanse of the Piedmont, literally the foothills. The final backdrop of English America was the Appalachian Mountain range running from New England to Georgia. For 150 years, the western outreach of settlement stopped at the slopes of the mountains. To the east lay the wide expanse of ocean, which served as a highway for the transit of European culture to America, but also as a barrier beyond which Old World values and folkways took to new paths in a new environment.

CHAPTER

2

Colonial Ways of Life

This chapter focuses on

- The social and economic differences among the southern, middle, and New England colonies.

- How various groups of people of different genders, races, and classes fit into colonial society.

- The impact of the Enlightenment and the Great Awakening on the American colonies.

28

THE *ESSENTIAL AMERICA* ON-LINE TUTOR

www.wwnorton.com/eamerica/ch2

- **Topic: The trans-Atlantic slave trade**
  www.wwnorton.com/eamerica/ch2/topic.htm

  The trans-Atlantic slave trade brought millions of Africans to the Americas. Examine the trans-Atlantic slave trade and its implications using slave narratives, historical analyses, maps, and art. How did slavery affect its victims?

- **Chapter review: On-line quiz and chapter summary**
  www.wwnorton.com/eamerica/ch2/review.htm

- **Chapter resources: Multimedia index**
  www.wwnorton.com/eamerica/ch2/media.htm

Those who colonized America during the seventeenth and eighteenth centuries were part of a massive social migration occurring throughout Europe and Africa. People were migrating from farms to villages, from villages to cities, and from homelands to colonies. They moved for different reasons. Most were responding to powerful social and economic forces: rapid population growth, the rise of commercial agriculture, and the early stages of the industrial revolution. Others sought political security or religious freedom. Moreover, Africans were moved to new lands against their will.

The Shape of Early America

Most of the migrants to America were young (over half were under twenty-five), and most were male. Almost half were indentured servants or slaves, and during the eighteenth century, England transported some 50,000 convicts to the North American colonies. About a third of the settlers journeyed with their families, but most arrived alone. A very few were wealthy, but many more were impoverished. Most immigrants were of the "middling sort," neither very rich nor very poor.

British Folkways

The vast majority of early settlers came from Great Britain. Four mass migrations from distinct regions of Britain occurred during the seventeenth and eighteenth centuries. The first involved some 20,000 Puritans who settled in Massachusetts between 1629 and 1641; most of these settlers hailed from the East Anglian counties east of London. A generation later, a smaller group of wealthy royalist cavaliers and their indentured servants migrated from southern England to Virginia. These English aristocrats, mostly Anglicans, were already accustomed to severe social inequalities and so had few

qualms about the introduction of African slavery.

The third migratory wave brought some 23,000 Quakers from the north midlands of England to the Delaware Valley colonies of West Jersey, Pennsylvania, and Delaware. They imported with them a social system stressing spiritual equality, suspicion of class distinctions and powerful elites, and commitment to plain living and high thinking. The fourth and largest surge of colonization occurred between 1717 and 1775. It included hundreds of thousands of Celtic Britons and Scotch-Irish from northern Ireland, the Scottish Lowlands, and the northern counties of England; these were mostly coarse, feisty, clannish folk who settled in the rugged backcountry along the Appalachian Mountains.

Although most British settlers spoke a common language and shared the Protestant faith, they were in fact diverse people who carried with them—and retained—sharply different cultural attitudes and customs from their home regions. They spoke distinct dialects, ate different foods, built their houses in contrasting architectural styles, engaged in disparate games and forms of recreation, and organized their societies differently.

Seaboard Ecology

The ecology of America was shaped both by Native Americans and by European settlers. For thousands of years, Indian hunting practices produced what one scholar has called the "greatest known loss of wild species" in American history. In addition, the Indians burned woods and undergrowth to provide cropland, to ease travel through hardwood forests, and to nourish the grasses, berries, and other forage for the animals they hunted. This "slash and burn" agriculture halted the normal forest succession and, especially in the Southeast, created large stands of longleaf pines, still the most common source of timber in the region.

Whereas the Native Americans tended to be migratory, considering land and animals as communal resources to be shared and consumed only as necessary, many European colonizers viewed natural resources as privately owned commodities. Settlers quickly set about evicting Indians, clearing, fencing, improving, and selling land, growing cash crops, and trapping game for commercial use.

In time, a more dense population of humans and their domestic animals created a landscape of fields, meadows, fences, barns, and houses. Such innovations radically altered the ecology of the New World environment. Cleared and grazed land is warmer and drier, more subject to flooding and erosion. Foraging cattle, sheep, horses, and pigs gradually changed the distribution of trees, shrubs, and grasses. Indians, far from being passive observers, contributed to the process of environmental change by trading furs for metal or glass trinkets. This decimated the populations of large mammals that had earlier been central to Indian culture—and to the ecological balance. By 1750 such unintended consequences had transformed the physical environment from what it had been in 1600. New England, for example, by then had become a commercial success but an agricultural wasteland.

Birthrates and Death Rates

America's plentiful land beckoned immigrants and induced them to replenish the earth with large families. Where labor was scarce, children could lend a hand, and once grown, they could find new land for themselves if need be. Colonists tended, as a result, to marry and start new families at an earlier age than their European counterparts.

The initial scarcity of women in the colonies had significant social effects. Whereas in England the average age of women at marriage was twenty-five to twenty-six, in America it dropped to twenty or twenty-

one. Men also married younger in the colonies than in the Old World. The birthrate rose accordingly, since those who married earlier had time for about two additional pregnancies during the childbearing years. Later a gradual reversion to a more even sex ratio brought the average age at marriage back toward the European norm. Even so, given the better economic prospects in the colonies, a greater proportion of American women married, and the birthrate remained much higher than in Europe.

Equally important in explaining rapid population growth in the New World was its much lower death rate, at least in the New England colonies (in the South, death rates remained higher due to malaria, dysentary, and other diseases). After the difficult first years of settlement, infants generally had a better chance to reach maturity, and adults had a better chance to reach old age than their counterparts in England and Europe. This greater longevity resulted less from a more temperate climate than from the character of the settlements themselves. Since the land was more bountiful, famine seldom occurred after a settlement's first year. Though the winters were more severe than in England, firewood was plentiful. Being younger on the whole—the average

"A little commonwealth." This eighteenth-century American family shows the "stairstep" pattern of childbearing, in which children were born at approximately two-year intervals.

age in the colonies in 1790 was sixteen!—Americans were less susceptible to disease than were Europeans in the Old World. More widely scattered, they were also less exposed to disease. This began to change, of course, as cities grew and trade and travel increased. By the mid–eighteenth century, the colonies were beginning to experience levels of contagion much like those in Europe.

Women in the Colonies

Colonists brought to America deeply rooted convictions concerning the inferiority of women. God and nature, it was widely assumed, had stained women with original sin and made these "weaker vessels" smaller in stature, feebler in mind, and prone to both excited emotions and psychological dependency. Women were expected to be meek and model housewives. Their role in life was clear: to obey and serve their husbands, nurture their children, and maintain their households. Both social custom and legal codes ensured that women remained deferential and powerless. They could not vote, preach, hold office, attend public schools or colleges, bring lawsuits, make contracts, or own property except under extraordinary conditions.

In the eighteenth century, "women's work" typically involved activities in the house, garden, and yard. Farm women usually rose at four in the morning and prepared breakfast by five-thirty. They then fed and watered the livestock, awakened the children, churned butter, tended the garden, prepared lunch, played with the children, worked the garden again, cooked dinner, milked the cows, readied the children for bed, and cleaned the kitchen before retiring about nine.

Despite the conventional mission of women to serve in the domestic sphere, the scarcity of labor in the colonies opened new social opportunities. Quite a few women, either by necessity or choice, assumed gainful occupations outside the home. In the towns, women commonly served as tavern hostesses and shopkeepers, but some women also worked as doctors, printers, upholsterers, painters, silversmiths, and shipwrights. These women often, but not always, were widows who carried on their husbands' trades. Some women in the South managed plantations.

The acute shortage of women in the early years of colonial settlement made them more highly valued than in Europe, and the Puritan emphasis on well-ordered family life led to laws protecting wives from physical abuse and allowing for divorces. In addition, colonial laws gave wives greater control over property that they contributed to a marriage or that was left after a husband's death. But the traditional notion of female subordination and domesticity remained firmly entrenched in the New World.

Society and Economy in the Southern Colonies

Crops and Land

The southern colonies had one unique economic advantage—the climate, which enabled them to grow exotic staples (market crops) prized by the mother country. Tobacco smoking had become the rage among Europeans during the seventeenth century, and Virginia planters took full advantage of the situation. As one of them stressed, "all our riches for the present do consist in tobacco." Tobacco, however, was only one of many cash crops in the southern colonies. After 1690 rice became the staple in South Carolina. The southern woods also provided harvests of lumber and naval stores (tar, pitch, and turpentine).

In 1614 each of the Virginia Company's colonists received three acres, and this marked the beginning of a "headright" policy that provided every settler in the colony with a plot of land. In 1618 the Virginia Company increased land grants, giving 100 acres each to those already in the colonies, and 50 acres each to new settlers or to anyone paying the passage of immigrants (for example, indentured servants) to Virginia. Lord Baltimore adopted the same practice in Maryland, and successive proprietors in the other southern and middle colonies offered variations on the plan.

Indentured Servants and Slaves

The plantation economy depended upon manual labor, and voluntary indentured servitude accounted for probably half the white settlers in all the colonies outside New England. The name derived from the indenture, or contract, by which a person would agree to work for a fixed number of years in return for transportation to the New World.

Although many migrants saw the opportunity to go to the New World as a chance to better themselves, not all went voluntarily. One servant recalled how he and others were "stolen in Ireland" by English soldiers. On occasion, orphans were bound off to the New World, and from time to time the mother country sent convicts into colonial servitude. Once the indenture had run its course, usually after four to seven years, the servant claimed the "freedom dues" set by law—some money, tools, clothing, food—and often took up land-owning.

Slavery, long a dying institution in Europe, evolved in the Chesapeake Bay colonies after 1619, when a Dutch vessel dropped off twenty Africans in Jamestown. Some of the first were treated as indentured servants, with a limited term. Those who worked out their term of indenture gained freedom and a fifty-acre parcel of land. They themselves sometimes acquired slaves and white indentured servants. But gradually, with rationalizations based on color difference or heathenism, the practice of perpetual black slavery became the custom and the law of the land.

An idyllic view of a Tidewater plantation. Note the easy access to ocean-going vessels.

As colonists developed staple crops for commercial markets, the demand for slaves grew, and as readily available lands diminished, Virginians were less eager to bring in indentured servants who would lay claim to land at the end of their service. Though British North America brought less than 5 percent of the total slave imports to the Western Hemisphere during the more than three centuries of that traffic—400,000 out of some 9,500,000—it offered slaves better chances for survival, if few for human fulfillment. The natural increase of black immigrants in America approximated that of whites, and by the end of the colonial period, over 20 percent of the American population was black. In South Carolina blacks were in the majority.

African Roots and Black Culture

Slaves are so often lumped together as a social group that their great ethnic diversity is overlooked. They came from lands as remote from each other as the Congo and Senegal, the west coast of Africa, and the area around the hump in between, and they

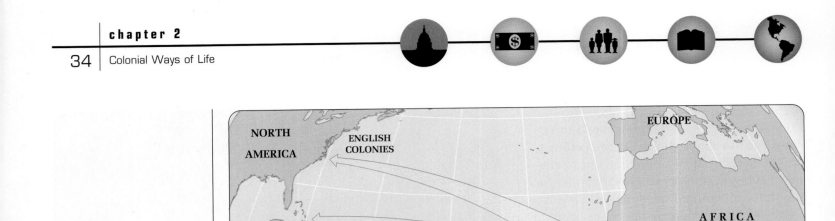

NORTH
AMERICA
ENGLISH
COLONIES

EUROPE

AFRICA

Principal area of slave supply

SENEGAL
GAMBIA
GUINEA
SIERRA LEONE
IVORY COAST
GOLD COAST
TOGO
DAHOMEY
NIGERIA
CAMEROON

GABON

CONGO

ANGOLA

From East Africa

WEST INDIES

GUIANA
NEW GRANADA
(SPAIN)

SOUTH
AMERICA

BRAZIL
(PORTUGAL)

ATLANTIC
OCEAN

PACIFIC OCEAN

THE AFRICAN SLAVE TRADE,
1500–1800

spoke Mandingo, Ibo, Kongo, and countless other languages. For all of their differences, however, the many peoples of Africa did share similar kinship and political systems. African societies were often matrilineal; property and political status descended through the mother rather than the father. Priests and the nobility lorded over the masses of farmers and craftspeople. Below the masses were the slaves, typically war captives, criminals, or debtors.

Most of the slaves who arrived in English North America during the seventeenth century did not come directly from Africa. Instead, they had first been taken from Africa to the sugar-producing colonies in Brazil and the Caribbean. Many had Spanish or Portuguese surnames, spoke a European language, and had been exposed to Christianity. Once in America, they often worked alongside white indentured servants. A surprising number of the early slaves were able to earn money on the side and buy their freedom. Thus, seventeenth-century slaves had a more fluid and independent existence than their successors.

During the eighteenth century, with the rapid development of a plantation economy in the Chesapeake region and the low country of South Carolina, the demand for slaves grew so quickly that a much higher proportion came directly from the African interior—Angola, Biafra, and Senegambia. Planters wanted field hands, so most of these newer slaves were young males who had had no exposure to European culture or languages, a factor that discouraged relations between the races in America. As plantation slave culture evolved during the eighteenth century, discipline was more harshly enforced.

Some of the slaves rebelled against their masters, resisting work orders, sabotaging crops and tools, or running away to the frontier. In a few cases, slaves organized rebellions that were ruthlessly suppressed. After capturing slaves who participated in the Stono uprising in South Carolina in 1739, enraged planters "Cutt off their heads and set them up at every Mile Post."

Outnumbered and unarmed, most slaves resigned themselves to the overwhelming authority of their owners. Yet in the process of being forced into lives of bondage, blacks from diverse homelands forged a new identity as African Americans, while at the same time leaving entwined in the fabric of American culture many strands of African heritage.

On one level, slaves used songs, stories, and sermons to distract them from their toil; on another level, these modes of expression conveyed coded protests against masters or overseers. Slave religion, a unique blend of African and Christian beliefs, was frequently practiced in secret. Its fundamental theme was deliverance: God, they believed, would eventually free them from slavery and open up the gates to the promised land. The planters, however, sought to strip slave religion of its liberationist hopes. They insisted that being "born again" had no effect upon their workers' status as slaves. In 1667 the Virginia legislature declared that "the conferring of baptism does not alter the condition of the person as to his bondage or freedom."

The Gentry

By the early eighteenth century, Virginia and South Carolina were being led by a so-cial elite known as the Tidewater gentry. The new aristocracy tried to replicate the life of the English country gentleman, indulging in the pleasures of hunting, fishing, riding, and gambling on horse races, cards, and dice. In their zest for the good life, the planters purchased the latest London luxury goods, buying on credit extended for future years' crops. Indebtedness to London merchants remained a chronic southern problem lasting far beyond the colonial period.

Religion

Although Americans during the seventeenth century took religion more seriously than at any time since, the proportion of church members to residents in the southern colonies was less than one in fifteen. The tone of religious belief and practice in the Chesapeake colonies was quite different from that in Puritan New England or Quaker Pennsylvania. Anglicanism predominated in the region, and it proved especially popular among the large landholders. As in England, colonial Anglicans were more conservative, rational, and formal in their forms of worship than their Puritan, Quaker, or

The survival of African culture among American slaves is evident in this late-eighteenth-century painting of a South Carolina plantation. The musical instruments, pottery, and clothing are of African origin, probably Yoruba.

Baptist counterparts. Anglicans tended to stress collective rituals over personal religious experience. Through most of the seventeenth century, the Church of England was "established" (tax supported) only in Virginia and Maryland, but by the early eighteenth century it had become the established church throughout the South.

In the colonial environment, the Anglican church evolved into something quite unlike the state church of England. The scattered population and the absence of bishops in America made centralized control difficult. In practice therefore, if not in theory, the Anglican churches became as independent of any hierarchy as the Puritan congregations of New England. Standards were often lax, and the Anglican clergy around the Chesapeake became notorious for its "sporting parsons," addicted to fox-hunting, gambling, drunkenness, and worse. Their congregations showed little toleration for being chastised from the pulpit. One minister lamented that the powerful planters removed any preacher who "had the courage and resolution to preach against any Vices taken into favor by the leading Men of his Parish."

Society and Economy in New England

Townships

By contrast to the seaboard planters who transformed the English manor into the southern plantation, the Puritans transformed the English village into the New England town, although there were many varieties. Land policy in New England had a stronger social and religious purpose than elsewhere. The headright system of the Chesapeake never took root in New England. There were cases of large individual land grants, but the standard practice was one of township grants to organized groups of settlers, often gathered already into a congregation.

Dwellings and Daily Life

The first colonists in New England arrived to find what one called a "hideous and desolate wilderness, full of wild beasts & wild men." Forced first to live in caves, tents, or "English wigwams," they soon built simple, small frame houses clad with hand-split clapboards. The roofs were steeply pitched to reduce the buildup of snow and were covered with thatched grasses or reeds.

By the end of the seventeenth century, most New England homes were plain but sturdy dwellings centered on a fireplace. Some had glass windows brought from England. The interior walls were often plastered and whitewashed, but the exterior boards were rarely painted. The interiors were dark, illuminated only by candles or oil lamps, both of which were expensive; most people usually went to sleep soon after sunset.

Family life revolved around the main room on the ground floor, called the "hall." Here meals would be cooked within a large fireplace. Pots would be suspended on an iron rod over the fire, and food would be served at a table made of rough-hewn planks called "the board." The father was sometimes referred to as the "chair man" because he sat in the only chair. The rest of the family usually stood to eat or sat on stools or benches.

Below the main floor of a New England house was a cellar for storing food and other supplies for the long winters. Above the hall was a loft where older children might sleep on bedrolls.

Enterprise

New England farmers and their families led hard lives. Simply clearing the glacier-scoured soil of rocks might require sixty days of strenuous labor per acre. The growing season was short, and the harsh climate precluded any profitable cash crops such as tobacco. With virgin forests ready for conversion into masts, lumber, and ships, and

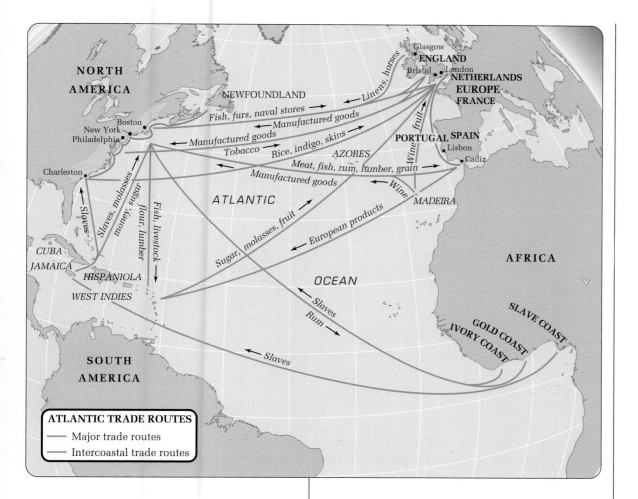

ATLANTIC TRADE ROUTES
— Major trade routes
— Intercoastal trade routes

Trade

abundant fishing grounds that stretched northward to Newfoundland, New Englanders turned to the sea for their livelihood, and the region became America's most important maritime center. Whales, too, abounded in New England waters and supplied oil for lighting and lubrication.

New England's fisheries, unlike its farms, provided profitable exports to Europe, while lesser grades of fish went to the West Indies as food for slaves. Fisheries encouraged the development of shipbuilding, and experience at seafaring spurred commerce. This in turn led to wider contacts in the Atlantic world and a degree of materialism and cosmopolitanism that clashed with the Puritan credo of plain living and high thinking.

By the end of the seventeenth century, America had become part of a great North Atlantic commercial network, trading not only with the British Isles and the British West Indies, but also—and often illegally—with Spain, France, Portugal, Holland, and their colonies. Since they lacked the means to produce goods themselves, the colonists had to import manufactured items from Britain and Europe. Their central economic problem was to find the means of paying for these imports.

The mechanism of trade in New England and the middle colonies differed from that in the South in two respects: the northern colonies were at a disadvantage in their lack of staples to exchange for English goods, but the abundance of their own shipping and mercantile enterprise worked in their favor. After 1660, in order to protect English agriculture and fisheries, the English government raised prohibitive duties (taxes) against certain major imports from the northern colonies—fish, flour, wheat, and meat—while leaving the door open to timber, furs, and whale oil. As a consequence, in the early eighteenth century New York and New England bought more from England than they sold there, incurring an unfavorable trade balance.

The northern colonies met the problem in two ways: they used their own ships and merchants, thus avoiding the charges to British merchants for trade and transport; and they found other markets for the staples excluded from England, thus acquiring goods or gold to pay for imports from the mother country. American lumber and fish went to southern Europe for money or in exchange for wine; lumber, rum, and provisions went to Newfoundland; and all of these and more went to the West Indies, which became the most important outlet of all. American merchants could sell fish, flour, corn, pork, beef, and horses to West Indian planters who specialized in sugarcane. In return they got money, sugar, molasses, rum, indigo, and other products, much of which went eventually to England. This gave rise to the famous "triangular trade" (more a descriptive convenience than a rigid pattern) in which New Englanders shipped rum to the west coast of Africa and bartered for slaves, took the slaves to the West Indies, and returned home with various commodities, including molasses, from which they manufactured rum. In another version, they shipped provisions to the West Indies, carried sugar and molasses to England, and returned with manufactured goods from Europe.

The unfavorable balance of trade left the colonies with a chronic shortage of hard money, which drifted away to pay for imports. Various expedients met the currency shortage. Most of the colonies at one time or another issued bills of credit, on promise of payment in hard currency later (hence the dollar "bill"), and most set up land banks that issued paper money for loans to farmers on the security of their lands, which were mortgaged to the banks. Colonial farmers, recognizing that an inflation of paper money led to an inflation of crop prices, asked for more and more paper. Thus began in colonial politics what was to become a recurrent problem in later times, the issue of currency inflation. Wherever the issue arose, debtors commonly favored growth in the money supply, which would make it easier for them to settle accounts, whereas creditors favored a limited money supply, which would increase the value of their capital.

Religion

The Puritans for many years had a bad press. The picture of the dour Puritan, hostile to all pleasures, rings false. Puritans, especially those of the upper class, wore colorful clothing, enjoyed secular music, and drank rum, though a person found incapacitated by reason of strong drink was subject to arrest, and repeat "drunkards" were forced to wear the letter "D" in public.

Moderation in all things except piety was the Puritan guideline. This was true for sexual activity as well. Contrary to prevailing images of the Puritans as prudes, they readily recognized natural human desires. One minister emphasized that "the Use of the Marriage Bed" is "founded in man's Nature." Churches occasionally expelled members for failing to satisfy their partner's sexual needs. Sexual activity outside the bounds of marriage was strictly forbidden, but, like most prohibitions, the rule seemed to provoke transgression. New England court records bulge with cases of adultery and fornication. In part the abundance of sexual offenses reflected the disproportionate number of men in the colonies. Many were unable to find a wife and were therefore tempted to satisfy their sexual desires outside of marriage.

The Puritans who settled Massachusetts, unlike the Separatists of Plymouth, proposed only to form a purified version of the Anglican church. They believed that they could remain loyal to the Church of England, the unity of church and state, and the principle of compulsory uniformity. But their remoteness from England led them very quickly to a congregational form of church government identical to that of the Pilgrim Separatists.

In the Puritan theology, God had voluntarily entered into a covenant, or contract, with people through which his creatures could secure salvation. By analogy, therefore, an assembly of true Christians could enter into a church covenant, a voluntary union for the common worship of God. From this it was a fairly short step to the idea of a voluntary union for purposes of government.

The covenant theory contained certain kernels of democracy in both church and state. Democracy, however, was no part of Puritan political thought, which like so much else in Puritan belief began with original sin. Innate human depravity made governments necessary. The Puritan was dedicated to seeking not the will of the people but the will of God. The ultimate source of authority resided in the Bible, but the Bible had to be interpreted by those trained to the purpose.

While Puritan New England has often been called a theocracy, the church in theory was entirely separated from the state—except that town residents were taxed for its support. And if not all inhabitants were church members, they were to be present for church services. Life in the small rural townships was intimate and essentially cooperative. Studies of Andover, Dedham, and Plymouth, Massachusetts, among other towns, suggest that, at least in the seventeenth century, family ties grew stronger and village life more cohesive than in the homeland.

Diversity and Social Strains

Such harmony, however, was frequently short-lived. Increasing diversity and powerful disruptive forces combined to erode the consensual society envisioned by the founding settlers. Despite long-enduring myths, New England towns were not always pious, harmonious, static, and self-sufficient rural utopias populated by praying Puritans. Many communities were founded as centers of fishing, trade, and commerce rather than farming, religion, and morality, and the animating concerns of residents in such towns tended to be more entrepreneurial than spiritual.

Sectarian disputes and religious indifference often developed. The emphasis on a direct accountability to God, which lay at the base of all Protestant theology, led believers to challenge authority in the name of private conscience. Massachusetts repressed such heresy in the 1630s, but it resurfaced during the 1650s among Quakers and Baptists, and in 1659–1660 the colony hanged four Quakers who persisted in returning after they were expelled. The hangings caused such revulsion—and an investigation by the crown—that they were not repeated, although heretics continued to face harassment and persecution.

More damaging to the Puritan utopia was the increasing pluralism and worldliness of New England, which placed growing strains on church discipline. More and more children of the "visible saints" found themselves unable to testify that they had received the gift of God's grace. In 1662 an assembly of ministers at Boston accepted the "Half-Way Covenant," whereby baptized children of church members could be admitted to a "half-way" membership. Their own children could be baptized, but

such "half-way" members could neither vote nor take communion. A further blow to Puritan convention and control came with the Massachusetts royal charter of 1691, which required toleration of dissenters and based the right to vote on property rather than on church membership.

New England Witchcraft

The strains accompanying Massachusetts's transition from Puritan utopia to royal colony reached a bizarre climax in the witchcraft hysteria at Salem Village (now the town of Danvers) in 1692. Belief in witchcraft pervaded European and New England society in the seventeenth century. Prior to the dramatic episode in Salem, almost 300 New Englanders (mostly lower-class, middle-aged, marginal women—spinsters or widows) had been accused as witches, and more than thirty had been hanged.

Still, the Salem outbreak exceeded all precedents in its scope and intensity. The episode began when a few teenage girls became entranced listeners to voodoo stories told by Tituba, a West Indian slave. The girls began acting strangely—shouting, barking, groveling, and twitching for no apparent reason. The town doctor concluded that they had been bewitched, and the girls pointed to Tituba and two older white women as the culprits. Town dwellers panicked as word spread that the devil was in their midst. At a hearing before the magistrates, the "afflicted" girls rolled on the floor in convulsive fits as the three women were questioned by the magistrates. The crazed girls accused dozens of residents, including several of the most respected members of the community. Within a few months, the Salem jail overflowed with townspeople—men, women, and children—accused of practicing witchcraft. Before the hysteria ran its course ten months later, nineteen people (including some men) had been hanged, one man—stubborn Giles Corey, who refused to plead either guilty or not guilty—pressed to death by heavy stones, and more than 100 others jailed.

When the afflicted girls accused Samuel Willard, the distinguished pastor of Boston's First Church and president of Harvard College, the stunned magistrates had seen enough. Shortly thereafter, the governor intervened when his own wife was accused of serving the devil. He disbanded the special court and ordered the remaining suspects released. A year after it had begun, the fratricidal event was finally over. Nearly everybody responsible for the Salem executions later recanted, and nothing quite like it happened in the colonies again.

What explains the witchcraft hysteria at Salem? Some have argued that it may have represented nothing more than a contagious exercise in adolescent imagination intended to enliven the dreary routine of everyday life. Yet it was adults who pressed the formal charges against the accused and provided most of the testimony. This has led some scholars to speculate that long-festering local feuds and property disputes may have triggered the prosecutions.

More recently, historians have focused on the fact that almost all of the accused witches were women who had in some way defied the traditional roles assigned to females. Some had engaged in business transactions outside the home, others did not attend church; some were curmudgeons. Most of them were middle-aged or older, beyond child-bearing age, and without sons or brothers. They thus stood to inherit property and live as independent women. The notion of autonomous spinsters flew in the face of prevailing social conventions.

Society and Economy in the Middle Colonies

An Economic Mix

Both geographically and culturally the middle colonies stood between New England

and the South, blending their own influences with elements derived from the older regions on either side. In so doing, they more completely reflected the diversity of colonial life and more fully foreshadowed the pluralism of the later American nation than the regions on either side. Their crops were those of New England but more bountiful, owing to better land and a longer growing season, and they developed surpluses of foodstuffs for export to the plantations of the South and the West Indies: wheat, barley, and livestock. Three great rivers—the Hudson, Delaware, and Susquehanna—and their tributaries gave the middle colonies easy access to their backcountry and to the fur trade of the interior, where New York and Pennsylvania long enjoyed friendly relations with the Indians. As a consequence, the region's commerce rivaled that of New England, and Philadelphia in time supplanted Boston as the largest city in the colonies.

Land policies followed the headright system of the South. In New York the early royal governors carried forward, in practice if not in name, the Dutch device of the patroonship, granting to influential favorites vast estates on Long Island and up the Hudson and Mohawk Valleys. These estates most nearly approached the Old World manor. They were self-contained domains farmed by tenants who paid fees to use the landlords' mills, warehouses, smokehouses, and wharves. But with free land elsewhere, New York's population languished, and the new waves of immigrants sought the promised land of Pennsylvania.

An Ethnic Mix

In the makeup of their population, the middle colonies stood apart from both the mostly English Puritan settlements and the biracial plantation colonies to the south. In New York and New Jersey, for instance, Dutch culture and language lingered for some time, along with the Dutch Reformed Church. Up and down the Delaware River, the few Swedes and Finns, the first settlers, were overwhelmed by the influx of English and Welsh Quakers, followed in turn by the Germans and Scotch-Irish.

The Germans came mainly from the Rhineland. William Penn's brochures on the bounties of Pennsylvania had circulated in German translation, and his promise of religious freedom brought an excited response from persecuted sects, especially the Mennonites, whose beliefs resembled those of the Quakers. They were but the vanguard of a swelling migration in the eighteenth century that included Lutherans, Reformed Calvinists, Moravians, Dunkers, and others, a large proportion of whom paid their way as indentured servants or "redemptioners," as they were commonly called. West of Philadelphia these thrifty farmers and artisans created a belt of settlement in which the "Pennsylvania Dutch" (a corruption of "Deutsch," meaning German) predominated.

The Scotch-Irish began to arrive later and moved still farther out in the backcountry. "Scotch-Irish" is an enduring misnomer for Ulster Scots, Presbyterians transplanted from Scotland to confiscated lands in northern Ireland to give that country a more Protestant tone. The Ulster Scots suffered economic disaster and Anglican persecution. They fled mainly to Pennsylvania and the fertile valleys stretching southwestward into Virginia and Carolina. Unlike the more communal and pastoral Germans, they tended to settle in the backcountry—wilderness areas, usually the western portions of the colonies, where they cleared the land, built isolated log cabins, and lived by hunting and scratch farming. The Scotch-Irish were virulently anti-English and suspicious of all governments. From such rugged, hardheaded, and hardfisted people would come many powerful leaders, such as John Calhoun, Andrew Jackson, Sam Houston, and Woodrow Wilson.

The Germans and Scotch-Irish became the most numerous of the non-English

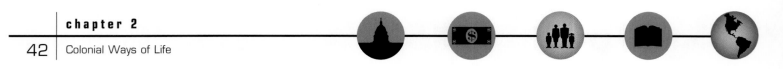

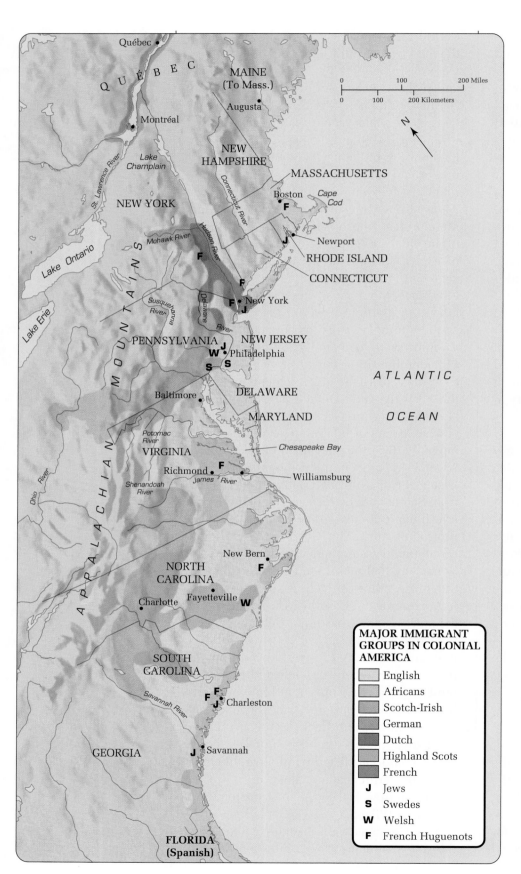

MAJOR IMMIGRANT GROUPS IN COLONIAL AMERICA

- English
- Africans
- Scotch-Irish
- German
- Dutch
- Highland Scots
- French
- **J** Jews
- **S** Swedes
- **W** Welsh
- **F** French Huguenots

groups in the colonies, but others also enriched the diversity of population in New York and the Quaker colonies: French Huguenots, Irish, Welsh, Swiss, Jews, and others. By 1790 barely half the populace could trace their origins to England.

Colonial Cities

Since commerce was their chief reason for being, colonial cities hugged the coastline or, like Philadelphia, sprang up on rivers where oceangoing vessels could reach them. Never having more than 10 percent of the colonial population, they exerted a disproportionate influence in commerce, politics, and culture. By the end of the colonial period, Philadelphia had some 30,000 people and was the largest city in the colonies, second only to London in the British Empire; New York, with about 25,000, ranked second; Boston numbered 16,000; Charleston, 12,000; and Newport, 11,000.

The Social and Political Order

Merchants formed the upper crust of urban society, and below them resided a middle class of craftspeople, retailers, innkeepers, and artisans who met a variety of needs. Almost two-thirds of adult male workers were artisans, people who made their living at handicrafts. At the bottom of the pecking order were sailors and unskilled workers. Such class stratification in the cities became more pronounced during the eighteenth century and after.

Problems created by urban growth are nothing new. Colonial cities had traffic that required not only paved streets and lighting but regulations to protect children and animals in the streets from reckless riders. Other regulations restrained citizens from tossing their garbage into the streets. Devastating fires led to building codes, restrictions on burning rubbish, and the organization of fire companies. Crime and violence made necessary more police protection. And in cities the poor became more visible than in the countryside. Colonists brought with them the English principle of public responsibility for the needy. The number of Boston's poor receiving public assistance rose from 500 in 1700 to 4,000 in 1736; New York's rose from 250 in 1698 to 5,000 in the 1770s. Most of the aid went to "outdoor" relief in the form of money, food, clothing, and fuel, but almshouses also appeared in colonial cities.

The Urban Web

Transit within and between early American cities was difficult. The first roads were likely to be Indian trails, which themselves often followed the tracks of bison through the forests. The trails widened with travel, then were made roads by order of provincial and local authorities. Land travel at first was by horse or by foot. The first stagecoach line for the public opened in 1732. From the main ports, good roads might reach thirty or forty miles inland, but all were dirt roads subject to washouts and mudholes. There was not a single hard-surfaced road during the entire colonial period, aside from city streets.

Roadside taverns were an important adjunct of colonial travel, since movement by night was too risky. By the end of the seventeenth century, there were more taverns in America than any other business. Like private clubs today, colonial taverns and inns were places to drink, relax, read the newspaper, play cards or billiards, gossip about people or politics, learn news from travelers, or conduct business. Local ordinances regulated and licensed the taverns, setting their prices and usually prohibiting them from serving liquor to blacks, Indians, servants, or apprentices.

Postal service through the seventeenth century was almost nonexistent—people entrusted letters to travelers or sea captains. Under a parliamentary law of 1710, the postmaster of London named a deputy in charge of the colonies and a postal system eventually extended the length of the Atlantic seaboard. Benjamin Franklin, who served as deputy postmaster from 1753 to 1774, speeded up the service with shorter routes and night-traveling post riders, and he increased the volume by inaugurating lower rates.

More reliable deliveries gave rise to newspapers in the eighteenth century. Before 1745, twenty-two newspapers had been started, seven in New England, ten in the middle colonies, and five in the South. An important landmark in the progress of freedom of the press was John Peter Zenger's trial for seditious libel for publishing criticisms of New York's governor in his newspaper, the *New York Weekly Journal*. Zenger was imprisoned for ten months and brought to trial in 1735. The established rule in English common law held that one might be punished for criticism that fostered "an ill opinion of the government." The jury's function was only to determine whether the defendant had published the opinion. Zenger's lawyer startled the court with his claim that the editor had published the truth—which the judge ruled an unacceptable defense. The jury, however, agreed with the assertion and held the editor not guilty. The libel law remained standing as before, but editors thereafter were emboldened to criticize officials more freely.

The Enlightenment

In the world of ideas a new fashion dazzled minds: the Enlightenment. During the seventeenth century, Europe experienced a scientific revolution in which the prevailing notion of an earth-centered universe was overthrown by the new sun-centered system of Polish astronomer Nicolaus Copernicus. The revolution climaxed in 1687 when England's Sir Isaac Newton set forth his theory of gravitation. Newton disclosed a mechanistic universe moving in accordance with natural laws that could be grasped by human reason and explained by mathematics.

By analogy from Newton's view of the world as a machine, one could reason that natural laws governed all things—the orbits of the planets and also the orbits of human relations: politics, economics, and society. People reasoned, for instance, that the natural law of supply and demand governed economics and that natural rights to life, liberty, and property determined the limits and functions of government.

The way to improve both society and human nature was by the application and improvement of Reason—which was the highest Virtue (Enlightenment thinkers often capitalized both words).

The American Enlightenment

However interpreted, such ideas profoundly affected the climate of thought in the eighteenth century. As a Connecticut minister recognized in 1788, "The present age is an enlightened one." Anybody who pretended to a degree of learning revealed a curiosity about natural philosophy, and some carried it to considerable depth.

Benjamin Franklin epitomized the Enlightenment more than any other single person. Born in Boston in 1706, Franklin left home at the age of seventeen and relocated to Philadelphia. There he owned a print shop, where he edited and published the *Pennsylvania Gazette* and *Poor Richard's Almanac*. Before he retired from business at the age of forty-two, Franklin, among other achievements, had founded a library, set up a fire company, helped start the academy that became the University of Pennsylvania,

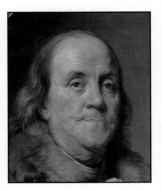

Benjamin Franklin. By the time he retired from business at the age of forty-two, Franklin had, among other things, owned a print shop, edited and published a newspaper, established a fire company, and invented the lightning rod and Franklin stove.

and organized a debating club that grew into the American Philosophical Society.

After his early retirement, Franklin devoted himself to public affairs and the sciences. His speculations and inventions extended widely to the fields of medicine, meteorology, geology, astronomy, physics, and music.

Education in the Colonies

The Age of Enlightenment prized education. And in the American colonies people promoted schooling for a variety of reasons. The Puritan emphasis on Scripture reading, which all Protestants shared to some degree, implied an obligation to ensure literacy. In 1647 Massachusetts Bay required every town of fifty or more families to set up a grammar school (a Latin school that could prepare a student for college). Although the act was widely evaded, it set an example that the rest of New England emulated.

In Pennsylvania, the Quakers financed a number of private schools teaching practical as well as academic subjects. In the southern colonies, efforts to establish schools were hampered by the more scattered populations, and in parts of the backcountry by indifference and neglect. Some of the wealthiest planters and merchants of the Tidewater sent their children to England or hired tutors, who in some cases would also serve the children of neighbors. In some places, wealthy patrons or the people collectively managed to raise some kind of support for secondary academies.

The Great Awakening

The new currents of learning and the Enlightenment prompted many people to drift away from orthodox religion. Many of the best educated were attracted to deism (which denied that God interfered with the laws and working of the universe) and to skepticism (which questioned accepted assumptions and religious beliefs). Meanwhile, out along the fringes of settlement there grew up a great backwater of the unchurched, people who had no minister to preach or administer sacraments or perform marriages. By the 1730s, the sense of falling away from religious orthodoxy prompted a widespread revival of faith, the Great Awakening, a wave of evangelism that within a few years swept the colonies from one end to the other.

Edwards and Whitefield

In 1734–1735 a remarkable spiritual revival occurred in the congregation of Jonathan Edwards, a Congregationalist minister in Northampton, in western Massachusetts. One of America's most brilliant philosophers and theologians, Edwards took charge of the Congregational church in Northampton in 1726 and found the congregation's spirituality at low ebb. He was convinced that Christians had become too preoccupied with making and spending money and that religion had become too intellectual and in the process had lost its emotional force. His vivid descriptions of the torments of hell and the delights of heaven helped rekindle spiritual fervor among his congregants.

The true catalyst of the Great Awakening, however, was a twenty-seven-year-old English minister, George Whitefield, whose reputation as a spellbinding evangelist preceded him to the colonies. Congregations were lifeless, he claimed, "because dead men preach to them." To restore the fires of religious fervor to American congregations, Whitefield reawakened the notion of individual salvation. In the autumn of 1739 he made a triumphal procession from Georgia to New England, drawing great crowds and releasing "Gales of Heavenly Wind" that dispersed sparks throughout the colonies.

Young and magnetic, possessed of a golden voice and a squinting left eye, Whitefield enthralled audiences with his unparalleled eloquence. The English re-

vivalist stressed the need for individuals to experience a sudden and emotional moment of conversion and salvation—and the dangers of an unconverted ministry that had not experienced such rebirth. By the end of his sermon, one listener reported, the entire congregation was "in utmost Confusion, some crying out, some laughing, and Bliss still roaring to them to come to Christ, as they answered, *I will, I will, I'm coming, I'm coming.*"

Piety and Reason

Whatever their motive or method, the revivalists succeeded in awakening the piety of many Americans. Between 1740 and 1742, some 25,000 to 50,000 New Englanders, out of a total population of 300,000, joined churches. The Great Awakening spawned a proliferation of new religious groups and sects that helped undermine the notion of state-supported churches. Everywhere the revivals brought splits, especially in the more Calvinistic churches. Traditional clergymen found their position undermined as church members chose sides and either dismissed their ministers or deserted them. Many of the revivalists, or "New Lights," went over to the Baptists, and others flocked to Presbyterian or, later, Methodist groups, which in turn divided and subdivided into new sects.

By the middle of the eighteenth century, New England Puritanism had finally fragmented. The precarious balance in which the founders had held the elements of piety and reason was shattered, and Baptists, Presbyterians, Anglicans, and other denominations began establishing footholds in formerly Congregationalist Puritan communities. Yet the revival frenzy scored its most lasting victories along the chaotic frontiers of the middle and southern colonies. In contrast, in the more sedate churches of Boston, rational religion ultimately got the upper hand in a reaction against the excesses of revival emotion. The rationality of the Enlightenment crept more and more into the sermons of Boston ministers, and they embarked on the road to Unitarianism and Universalism.

In reaction to taunts that the "born-again" revivalist ministers lacked learning, the Great Awakening gave rise to denominational colleges. The three colleges already in existence had originated earlier from religious motives: Harvard, founded in 1636, because the Puritans dreaded "to leave an illiterate ministry to the church when our present ministers shall lie in the dust"; the College of William and Mary, in 1693, to strengthen the Anglican ministry; and Yale College, in 1701, to serve the Puritans of Connecticut, who felt that Harvard was drifting from the strictest orthodoxy. Over the next hundred and fifty years, scores of other denominational colleges and academies were founded across the country.

The Great Awakening, like the Enlightenment, set in motion powerful currents that still flow in American life. It implanted permanently in American culture evangelical principles and the appeal of revivalism. The movement weakened the status of the established clergy and encouraged believers to exercise their own judgment, and it thereby weakened habits of deference generally. The proliferation of denominations heightened the need for toleration of dissent. In some respects, the Great Awakening, characterized by piety and emotion, and the Enlightenment, dominated by reason and rationality, led by different roads to similar ends. Both emphasized the power and right of individual choice and popular resistance to established authority, and both aroused millennial hopes that America would become the promised land in which people might approach the perfection of piety or reason, if not of both. Such hopes had both social and political, as well as religious, implications. As the eighteenth century advanced, fewer and fewer people were willing to defer to the ruling social and political elite, and many such rebellious, if pious, folk would be transformed into revolutionaries.

CHAPTER

3

The Imperial Perspective

This chapter focuses on

- England's changing policies in the political and economic administration of the colonies.

- How colonial governments were structured.

- The relations between English colonists and their neighbors in North America: the French and the Indians.

47

THE *ESSENTIAL AMERICA* ON-LINE TUTOR

www.wwnorton.com/eamerica/ch3

- **Topic: The French and Indian War**
  www.wwnorton.com/eamerica/ch2/topic.htm

  The French and Indian War ended French domination of northern North America while altering relations between the British crown and its thirteen colonies. Study the French and Indian War using a variety of historical analyses, maps, primary documents, and period cartoons. What was at issue in the French and Indian War, and how did it affect the colonists?

- **Chapter review: On-line quiz and chapter summary**
  www.wwnorton.com/eamerica/ch3/review.htm

- **Chapter Resources: Multimedia index**
  www.wwnorton.com/eamerica/ch3/media.htm

For the better part of the seventeenth century, England remained too distracted by the struggle between Parliament and the Stuart kings to perfect either a systematic colonial policy or effective agencies of imperial control. After the Restoration of the Stuart dynasty in 1660, the British government slowly developed a new plan of colonial administration. By the end of the century, however, it still lacked coherence and efficiency, leaving Americans accustomed to rather loose colonial reins.

English Administration of the Colonies

Throughout the colonial period, the British king was the source of legal authority in America, and land titles derived ultimately from royal grants. After the Restoration, the king tried to reassert his control over the colonies, but administration by the mother country continued to be inefficient, lax, and often inconsistent. For instance, the British government granted home rule to the settlements along the Atlantic coast and then sought to keep them from exercising it. It regarded English colonists as citizens, but it refused to grant them the privileges of citizenship. It insisted that the settlers contribute to the expense of maintaining the colonies, but it refused to allow them a voice in the shaping of administrative policies. Such inconsistencies bred festering tensions. By the mid–eighteenth century, when the British tried to impose on their American colonies the kind of controls that were reaping huge profits in India, it was too late. British Americans had developed a far more powerful sense of their rights than any other colonial people, and they were determined to assert and defend those rights.

The Mercantile System

Like all the other major European powers of the seventeenth and eighteenth centuries, England adopted the mercantile system, or mercantilism, which assumed that the total of the world's gold and silver remained essentially fixed, with only a nation's share in that wealth subject to change. Thus a nation could gain wealth only at the expense of another country—by seizing its gold and silver and dominating its trade. To get and keep gold and silver, the government had to direct all economic activities, limiting foreign imports and preserving a favorable balance of trade. This required the government to encourage manufacturing, through subsidies and monopolies if need be, to develop and protect its own shipping, and to make use of colonies as sources of raw materials and markets for its finished goods.

During the English Civil War, colonial trade had fallen largely to Dutch shipping. To win back this trade, Oliver Cromwell, in 1651, convinced Parliament to adopt a Navigation Act requiring that all goods imported into England or the colonies must arrive on English ships, and that the majority of each crew must be English.

The Navigation Act of 1660 added a new twist to Cromwell's act of 1651. Ships' crews now had to be three-quarters English, and certain articles not produced by the mother country were to be shipped from the colonies only to England or other English colonies. The list of "enumerated goods" included tobacco, cotton, indigo dye, and sugar. Later, rice, naval stores, masts, copper, and furs were added. Not only did England (and its colonies) become the sole outlet for these colonial exports, but three years later the Navigation Act of 1663 sought to make England the funnel through which all colonial imports had to be routed. The act was sometimes called the Staple Act because it made England the staple market (or trade center) for goods sent to the colonies. Virtually all ships carrying goods from Europe to America had to dock in England, be offloaded, and pay a duty before proceeding. A third major act rounded out the trade system. The Navigation Act of 1673 (some-

This view of eighteenth-century Boston shows the importance of shipping and its regulation in the colonies, especially in Massachusetts Bay.

times called the Plantation Duty Act) required that every ship loading enumerated articles in the colonies had to pay a duty or tax on the item.

Enforcing the Navigation Acts

The Navigation Acts supplied a convenient rationale for a colonial system to serve the economic needs of the mother country. Their enforcement in far-flung colonies, however, was another matter. In 1675 King Charles II designated certain of his advisers as Lords of Trade, a name reflecting the overall importance of economic factors. The Lords of Trade were to make the colonies abide by the mercantile system and to make them more profitable to the crown. To these ends, they named colonial governors, wrote or reviewed the governors' instructions, and handled all reports and correspondence dealing with colonial affairs.

Between 1673 and 1679, British collectors of customs duties arrived in all the colonies, and with them appeared the first seeds of colonial resentment. New England's expanding commercial interests counseled prudence and accommodation, but the Puritan leaders harbored a persistent distrust of Stuart intentions. Consequently, the Massachusetts Bay Colony not only ignored royal wishes; it tolerated violations of the Navigation Acts. This led the Lords of Trade to begin legal proceedings against the colonial charter, and in 1684, the Lords of Trade won a court decision annulling the Massachusetts charter.

The Dominion of New England

The Massachusetts Bay government was placed in the hands of a special royal commission. Then in 1685 Charles II died and was succeeded by his brother, the duke of York, as James II, the first Catholic sovereign since Queen Mary. James II asserted his prerogatives more forcefully than his brother. The new king readily approved a proposal to create a Dominion of New England and to place under its jurisdiction all colonies south through New Jersey.

The Dominion was to have a government named by royal authority, a governor and council that would rule without any colonial assembly. The royal governor, Sir Edmund Andros, appeared in Boston in 1686 to establish his rule, which he soon extended over Connecticut and RhodeIsland, and in 1688 over New York and East and West Jersey. Andros was honest, efficient, and loyal to the crown, but tactless in circumstances that called for the utmost diplomacy—the uprooting of long-established institutions in the face of popular hostility.

Andros levied taxes without consent of the Massachusetts General Court, and when residents protested against such taxation without representation, he imprisoned or fined a number of them. Andros suppressed town governments, enforced the trade laws, and clamped down on smuggling. Most ominous of all, he and his lieutenants took over one of Boston's Puritan churches for Anglican worship.

But the Dominion of New England was scarcely established before word arrived from Britain of the Glorious Revolution of 1688–1689. James II, like Andros in New England, had aroused resentment in England by his arbitrary measures and, what was more, by openly parading his Catholic faith. In 1688, parliamentary leaders, their patience exhausted, invited James's Protestant daughter Mary and her husband, the Dutch leader William of Orange, to assume the throne as joint monarchs. James II, his support dwindling, fled to France.

The Glorious Revolution in America

When news reached Boston that William and Mary had landed in England, Boston staged its own Glorious Revolution, as bloodless as that in England. Andros and his councilors were arrested, and Massachusetts reverted to its former government, as did the other colonies that had been absorbed into the Dominion. All were permitted to retain their former status except Massachusetts and Plymouth, which, after some delay, were united under a new charter in 1691 as the royal colony of Massachusetts Bay.

The Glorious Revolution had significant long-term effects on American history. The Bill of Rights and Toleration Act, passed in England in 1689, limited the powers of rulers and affirmed freedom of worship for Christians. These acts influenced attitudes and the course of events in the colonies. The overthrow of James II also set a precedent for revolution against the monarch. In defense of that action, the English philosopher John Locke published his *Two Treatises on Government* (1690), which had an enormous impact on political thought in the colonies. Locke's contract theory of government argued that people were endowed with natural rights to life, liberty, and property. When rulers violated these rights, the people had the right—in extreme cases—to overthrow the monarch and change their government.

An Emerging Colonial System

William and Mary oversaw a refinement of the Navigation Acts and the administrative system for regulating the American colonies. The Navigation Act of 1696 required colonial governors to enforce the Navigation Acts, allowed customs officials to use "writs of assistance" (general search warrants that did not have to specify the place to be searched), and ordered that accused violators be tried in admiralty courts, because colonial juries habitually refused to convict their peers. Admiralty cases were decided by judges whom the governors appointed.

Also in 1696, William III created a Board of Trade to take the place of the Lords of Trade. Colonial officials were required to report to the board, which continued to make policy through the remainder of the colonial period. Intended to ensure that the colonies served the mother country's economy, the board oversaw the enforcement of the Navigation Acts and recommended ways to limit manufacturing in the colonies and to encourage their production of raw materials.

From 1696 to 1725 the Board of Trade subjected the colonies to a more efficient royal control. After 1725, however, its energies and activities waned. This was during the reign of the Hanoverian monarchs, George I (1714–1727) and George II (1727–1760), German princes who became English kings by virtue of their descent from James I. At the same time, the cabinet (a kind of executive committee in the Privy Council) emerged as the central agency of administration in England. Robert Walpole, as first minister (1721–1742), deliberately followed a lenient policy toward the colonies, a policy that the philosopher Edmund Burke later called "a wise and salutary neglect."

The Habit of Self-Government

Government within the colonies, like colonial policy, evolved essentially without plan. In broad outline, the governor, council, and assembly in each colony corresponded to the king, lords, and commons of the mother country. However, over the years certain anomalies appeared as colonial governments diverged from trends in England. On the one hand, the governors retained powers and prerogatives that the king had lost in the course of the seventeenth century. On the other hand, the assemblies acquired powers, particularly with respect to appointments, that Parliament had yet to gain.

Powers of the Governors

The crown never vetoed acts of Parliament after 1707, but the colonial governors still held an absolute veto over the assemblies, and the crown could disallow (in effect, veto) colonial legislation on advice of the Board of Trade. With respect to the assembly, the governor still had the power to determine when and where it would meet, to prorogue (adjourn or recess) sessions, and to dissolve the assembly for new elections or to postpone elections indefinitely. In contrast, in the mother country, the crown had

pledged to summon Parliament every three years and call elections at least every seven, and could not prorogue sessions.

With respect to the judiciary, in all but the charter colonies, the governor still held the prerogative of creating courts and of naming and dismissing judges, powers explicitly denied the king in England. Over time, however, the colonial assemblies generally made good their claim that courts should be created only by legislative authority, although the crown repeatedly disallowed acts to grant judges life tenure in order to make them more independent.

As chief executive, the colonial governor could appoint and remove officials, command the militia and naval forces, grant pardons, and, as his commission often put it, "execute everything which doth and of right ought to belong to the governor"—which might cover a multitude of powers. Yet as the eighteenth century unfolded, colonial assemblies nibbled away at the governors' power of appointment; at the same time, the authorities in England increasingly drew the control of colonial patronage into their own hands.

Powers of the Assemblies

Unlike the governor and council, appointed by either king or proprietor, the colonial assembly was elected. Whether called the House of Burgesses (Virginia), or Delegates (Maryland), or Representatives (Massachusetts), or simply "assembly," the lower houses were chosen by popular vote in counties or towns or, in South Carolina, parishes. Religious tests for voting were abandoned during the seventeenth century, and the chief restriction left was a property qualification, based on the notion that only men who held a "stake in society" could vote responsibly. Yet the property qualifications generally set low hurdles in the way of potential voters. A greater proportion of the population could vote in the colonies than anywhere else in the world of the eighteenth century. Women, Indians, and blacks were excluded.

By the early eighteenth century, the assemblies, like Parliament, held two important strands of power. First, they held the power of the purse string in their right to vote on taxes and expenditures. Second, they held the power to initiate legislation and not merely, as in the early history of some colonies, the right to act on proposals from the governor and council. Governors were held on a tight leash by the assembly's control of political salaries.

Throughout the eighteenth century, the assemblies expanded their power and influence, sometimes in conflict with the governors and sometimes in harmony with them. Often in the course of routine business, the assemblies passed laws and set precedents, the collective significance of which neither they nor the imperial authorities fully recognized. Once established, however, these laws and practices became fixed principles, parts of the "constitution" of the colonies. Self-government in the colonies became first a habit, then a "right."

Troubled Neighbors

Relations between the colonists and Indians were at times cooperative and at times viciously hostile. Indian-white relations transformed the human and ecological landscape of colonial North America, stirred up colonial politics, and disrupted or destroyed the fabric of Indian culture. Relations between European settlers and North American Indians were themselves agitated by the fluctuating balance of power in Europe. The French and the English each sought to use Indians to their advantage in fighting one another for control of New World territory.

Displacing the Indians

The English invasion of North America would have been a different story, maybe a shorter and simpler one, had the English encountered greater Indian resistance. Instead, they encountered scattered and mutually hostile tribes whom they subjected to a policy of divide and conquer. Whether tempted by trade goods or the promise of alliances, or intimidated by a show of force, most of the Native Americans let matters drift until the English were too entrenched to be pushed back into the sea.

In the mid-1670s, both New England and Virginia went through a time of troubles: in New England an Indian war, and in Virginia a civil war masquerading as an Indian war. For a long time in New England, the Indian fur trade had contributed to peaceful relations, but the growth of settlement and the decline of the animal population were reducing the eastern tribes to relative poverty. Colonial governments encroached on the Indians repeatedly, forcing Indians to acknowledge English laws and customs, including Puritan codes of behavior, and to permit English arbitration of disputes. On occasion, colonial justice imposed fines, whippings, and worse. At the same time, Puritan missionaries reached out to the tribes. By 1675 several thousand converts had settled in special "praying Indian" towns.

The spark that set New England ablaze was struck by the murder of Sassamon, a "praying Indian" who had attended Harvard, later strayed from the faith while serving King Philip of the Wampanoag tribe, and then returned to the Christian fold. When Plymouth tried and executed three Wampanoags for the murder of Sassamon, King Philip's tribesmen attacked.

Thus began "King Philip's War," which the land-hungry leaders of Connecticut and Massachusetts quickly enlarged by assaulting the peaceful Narragansetts at their chief refuge in Rhode Island—a massacre the Rhode Island authorities were helpless to prevent. During 1675, Indian attacks ravaged the interior of Massachusetts and Plymouth, and sporadic fighting continued through 1676. Finally, depleted supplies and the casualty toll wore down Indian resistance. Philip's wife and son were captured and sold into slavery, and Philip himself was tracked down and killed. Sporadic fighting continued until 1678 in New Hampshire and Maine. Indians who survived the slaughter had to submit to colonial authority and accept confinement to ever-dwindling plots of land.

Bacon's Rebellion

The news from New England heightened tensions among settlers in the interior of Virginia and contributed to the tangled events thereafter known as Bacon's Rebellion. Depressed tobacco prices, rising taxes, and crowds of freed servants lusting for Indian lands provided the fuel for the rebellion. The discontent turned to violence in 1675 when a petty squabble between a frontier planter and local Indians on the Potomac River led to a series of killings. Soon a force of Virginia and Maryland militiamen laid siege to the Susquehannocks and murdered in cold blood five chieftains who came out for a parley. The enraged Indian survivors took their revenge on frontier settlements. Scattered attacks continued on down to the James River, where Nathaniel Bacon's overseer was killed.

In 1676 Bacon defied Governor William Berkeley's authority by assuming command of a group of frontier vigilantes. The twenty-nine-year-old Bacon had a talent for trouble and an enthusiasm for punitive expeditions against peaceful Indians. After threatening to kill the governor and the assembly if they tried to intervene, Bacon began preparing for a total war against all Indians. To prevent any governmental interference, he ordered the governor arrested, thus pitting his followers (who were largely servants, small farmers, and even slaves) against the wealthy planters and political leaders of Virginia. Berkeley's forces resisted—but only feebly—and Bacon's men burned Jamestown in 1676. But Bacon could not sa-

vor the victory long; he fell ill and died of swamp fever a month later.

Governor Berkeley quickly regained control and subdued the leaderless rebels. A royal commission made treaties of pacification with the remaining Indians, but the fighting had opened new lands to the colonists and confirmed the power of an inner group of established landholders who sat on the Virginia council.

Spanish America in Decline

At the start of the eighteenth century, the Spanish ruled over a huge colonial empire spanning North America. Yet their settlements in the borderlands north of Mexico were a colossal failure when compared to the colonies of the other European powers.

The Spanish failed to create thriving North American colonies for several reasons. Perhaps the most obvious was that the region lacked the gold and silver as well as the large native populations that attracted Spain to Mexico and Peru. In addition, the Spanish were distracted by their need to control the perennial unrest in Mexico among the natives and *mestizos* (people of mixed Indian and European ancestry). Moreover, those Spaniards who led the colonization effort in the borderlands were so preoccupied with military and religious exploitation that they never developed viable settlements with self-sustaining economies. Instead they concentrated on building missions and forts and looking—in vain—for gold. Whereas the French and the English built their Indian policies around trading relationships (including firearms), Spain emphasized conversion to Catholicism and stubbornly adhered to an outdated mercantilism that forbade manufacturing within the colonies and strictly limited trade with the natives.

New France and Louisiana

Permanent French settlement in the New World began soon after the Jamestown landing, far away at Port Royal, Acadia (later Nova Scotia). In 1608, the French explorer Samuel de Champlain founded a settlement at Québec, and from there pushed his explorations into the Great Lakes as far as Lake Huron, and southward to the lake that still bears his name. There, in 1609, he joined a band of Huron and Ottawa allies in a fateful encounter, fired his gun into the ranks of their Iroquois foes, and thereby kindled a hatred that pursued New France to the end. Thenceforth the Iroquois stood as a buffer against any French designs to invade New York and Pennsylvania.

From the Great Lakes, French explorers moved southward. In 1673 Louis Joliet and Père Jacques Marquette ventured into Lake Michigan and then journeyed down the Mississippi. In 1682, the daring explorer La Salle went down the Mississippi River all the way to the Gulf of Mexico and named the area Louisiana after King Louis XIV. Actual settlement of the Louisiana region occurred later, when the French built several fortified towns, the most important of which was New Orleans, founded in 1718.

The French thus enjoyed access to the great water routes that led to the heartland of the continent. In the Illinois region, scattered settlers began farming the fertile soil, and courageous priests established missions at places such as Terre Haute ("high land") and Des Moines ("some monks"). In the dense woods around the Great Lakes, rugged French Canadians became adept trappers and traders. Unlike their English counterparts, many of these hardy *coureurs de bois* (runners of the woods) shed their Old World culture and adopted Indian ways of dress and living. Some of them married Indian women.

Yet French involvement in North America never approached that of the British. In part this was because the French-held areas were less inviting than the English seaboard settlements. Few French settlers were willing to challenge the interior's rugged terrain, fierce winters, and hostile Indians. In addition, the French government impeded colonization by refusing to allow French Protestants (Huguenots) to migrate. New France was to remain Roman Catholic. It also remained largely a wilderness, home to a mobile population of traders, trappers, missionaries—and, mainly, Indians. In 1750, when the English colonists numbered about 1.5 million, the French population was no more than 80,000.

In some ways, however, the French had the edge on the British. Their relatively small numbers forced the French to develop cooperative relationships with the Indians. Unlike the English settlers, the French established trading outposts (to trade European goods for fur) rather than farms, mostly along the St. Lawrence River, on lands not claimed by Indians. Thus they did not have to confront initial hostility. In addition, the French served as effective mediators between rival Great Lakes tribes. This diplomatic role gave them much more local authority and influence than their English counterparts, who disdained such mediation. The heavily outnumbered and disproportionately male French settlers sought to integrate themselves with Indian culture rather than to displace it. They also encouraged the Indians to embrace Catholicism and hate the English. This fraternal bond between the French and the Indians proved to be a source of strength in the wars with the English. French governors could mobilize for action without any worry about quarreling assemblies or ethnic and religious diversity. New France was thus able to survive until 1760, despite the lopsided disparity in numbers between the colonies of the two powers.

An Iroquois warrior in an eighteenth-century French engraving.

Benjamin Franklin's symbol of the need to unite the colonies against the French in 1754 would become popular again twenty years later, when the colonies faced a different threat.

The Colonial Wars

For most of the seventeenth century, the French and British Empires developed in relative isolation from each other; for most of that century, the homelands remained at peace. After the Restoration, the British and French monarchs cooperated. The Glorious Revolution of 1688, however, abruptly reversed English diplomacy. William III, the new British king from the Dutch Republic, had fought a running conflict against French ambitions in the Netherlands. His ascent to the throne brought England into a Grand Alliance against the French in the War of the League of Augsburg, known in the colonies simply as King William's War (1689–1697). This was the first of four great European and intercolonial wars over the next sixty-four years.

The other three major European wars were: the War of the Spanish Succession (known in the colonies as Queen Anne's War, 1702–1713), the War of the Austrian Succession (known in the colonies as King George's War, 1744–1748), and the Seven Years' War (known in the colonies as the French and Indian War, which lasted nine years in America, 1754–1763). In all except the last, the battles in America were but a sideshow to greater battles in Europe. The alliances shifted from one fight to the next, but Britain and France were pitted against each other every time.

So for much of the century, after the great Indian conflicts of 1676, the colonies were embroiled in wars and rumors of wars. The effect on much of the population was devastating. It is estimated that 900 Boston men (about 2.5 percent of the eligible males) died in the fighting. One result of such carnage was that Boston's population stagnated through the eighteenth century while the population of Philadelphia and New York continued to grow, and Boston had to struggle to support a large population of widows and orphans. Eventually, the economic impact of the four wars left increasing numbers of poor people in New England, and many of them would participate in the popular unrest leading to the Revolutionary movement. Moreover, frequent conflict with France led the English government to incur an enormous debt, establish a huge navy and standing army, and excite a fervent nationalism. These changes would ultimately lead to a reshaping of the relationship between the mother country and its American colonies.

The French and Indian War

Of the four major wars involving the European powers and their New World colonies, the climactic conflict between Britain and France in North America was the French and Indian War. It began in 1754 after enterprising Virginians crossed the Appalachians into the upper Ohio Valley in order to trade with Indians and survey 200,000 acres granted them by King George. This infuriated the French, who saw such activity as a threat to their holdings, and they set about building a string of forts in the disputed area.

When news of the forts reached Williamsburg, the governor sent an emissary to warn off the French. An ambitious young officer in the Virginia militia, Major George Washington, volunteered for the mission. With a few companions, he made his way to Fort LeBoeuf and returned with a polite but firm French refusal to give way. The Virginia governor then sent a small force to erect a fort at the strategic fork where the Allegheny and Monongahela Rivers meet to form the great Ohio. No sooner was it started than a larger French force appeared, ousted the Virginians, and proceeded to build Fort Duquesne on the same strategic site.

Meanwhile, George Washington had been organizing a force of volunteers, and in the spring of 1754 he set out with an advance guard and a few Indian allies. Their clash with a French detachment marked the first bloodshed of a long—and finally decisive—war that reached far beyond America. Washington fell back with his prisoners and hastily constructed a stockade, Fort Necessity, which soon fell under siege by a larger French force. On July 4, 1754, Washington surrendered and was permitted to withdraw with his survivors.

In London the government decided to force a showdown with the French in America, but things went badly at first. In 1755 the British fleet failed to halt the landing of French reinforcements in Canada, but it scored one success in Nova Scotia with the capture of a fort. The British buttressed their hold on the area by expelling most of its French population. Some 5,000 to 7,000 Acadians scattered through the colonies from Maine to Georgia refused to take an oath of allegiance to the British crown. Impoverished and homeless, many of them desperately found their way to French Louisiana, where they became the "Cajuns" (a corruption of "Acadians") whose descendants still preserve elements of the French language along the remote bayous and in many urban centers.

A World War

For two years, war raged along the American Canadian frontier without becoming the cause of war in Europe. In 1756, however, the colonial war merged with what became the Seven Years' War in Europe. There

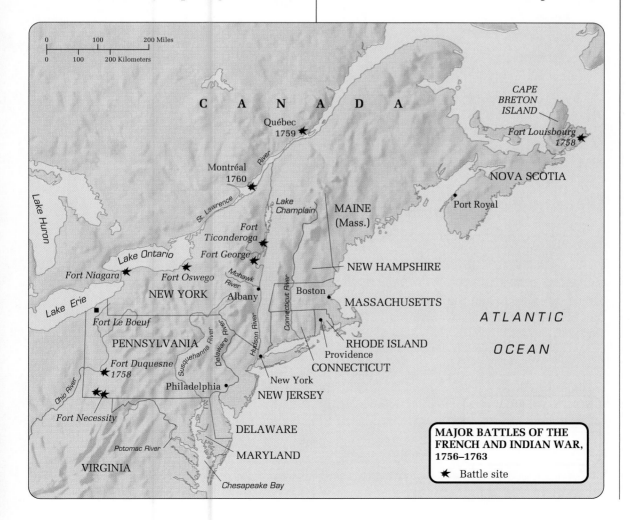

MAJOR BATTLES OF THE FRENCH AND INDIAN WAR, 1756–1763

★ Battle site

Austria allied with its old enemy, France, to oppose Prussia and its new ally, Britain. British sea power soon began to cut off French reinforcements and supplies to the New World—and the trading goods with which they bought Indian allies. In 1758 the British captured several key French forts. The following year, the decisive battle occurred at Québec.

Commanding the British expedition up the St. Lawrence was General James Wolfe.

For two months Wolfe probed the defenses of Québec, seemingly impregnable on its fortified heights. Finally Wolfe's troops found a path up the cliffs behind Québec. During the night of September 12–13, they scrambled up the sheer walls and emerged on the Plains of Abraham, athwart the main roads to the city. There, in a battle more like conventional European warfare than a frontier skirmish, the British forces allowed the French to advance within close range and

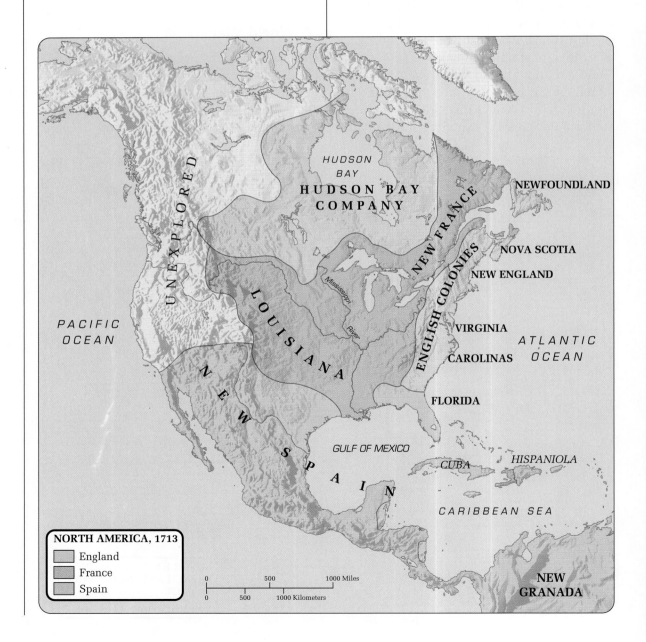

HUDSON BAY

HUDSON BAY COMPANY

NEWFOUNDLAND

NEW FRANCE

NOVA SCOTIA

NEW ENGLAND

ENGLISH COLONIES

UNEXPLORED

PACIFIC OCEAN

LOUISIANA

Mississippi River

VIRGINIA

CAROLINAS

ATLANTIC OCEAN

NEW SPAIN

FLORIDA

GULF OF MEXICO

CUBA

HISPANIOLA

CARIBBEAN SEA

NORTH AMERICA, 1713

England
France
Spain

0   500   1000 Miles
0   500   1000 Kilometers

NEW GRANADA

then fired two devastating volleys that ended French power in North America for all time.

The war dragged on until 1763, but the rest was a process of mopping up. In the South, where little significant action had occurred, the Cherokee nation flared into belated hostility, but a force of British regulars and provincials broke Cherokee resistance in 1761. In the North, just as peace was signed, an Ottawa chief, Pontiac, attempted to unify all the Indians of the frontier and launched a series of attacks that were not finally suppressed until the end of 1764, after the backwoods had been ablaze for ten years.

The Peace of Paris

The war culminated in the Peace of Paris of 1763. It ended French power in North America. Britain took all of France's possessions east of the Mississippi River (except

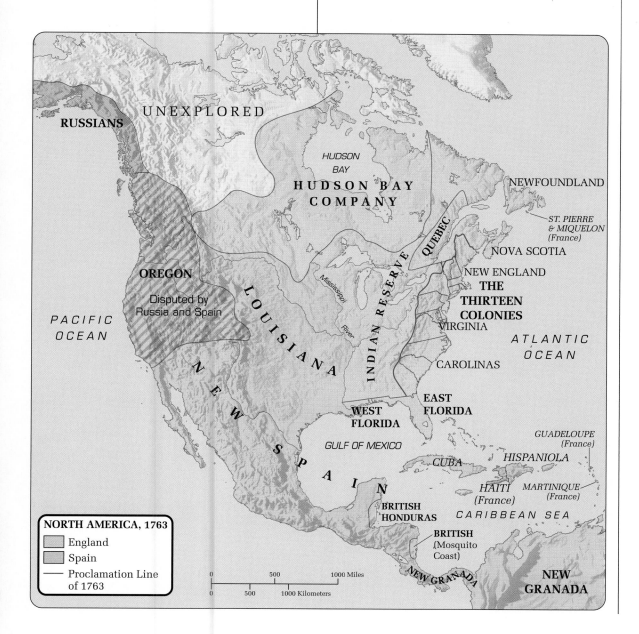

NORTH AMERICA, 1763
- England
- Spain
- Proclamation Line of 1763

New Orleans), several islands in the West Indies, and all of Spanish Florida. In compensation for the loss of Florida, Spain received Louisiana (New Orleans and all French land west of the Mississippi River) from France. Spain would hold title to Louisiana for nearly four decades, but it would never succeed in erasing the region's French roots. The French-born settlers always outnumbered the Spanish.

The loss of Louisiana left France with no territory on the continent of North America. British power reigned supreme over North America east of the Mississippi. But a fatal irony would pursue the British victory. In gaining Canada, the British government put in motion a train of events that would end twenty years later with the loss of all the rest of British North America. France, humiliated in 1763, thirsted for revenge.

From Empire
to Independence

This chapter focuses on

- The changes in British colonial policy after 1763.

- How the Whig ideology shaped the colonial response to changes in British policy.

- The role of Revolutionary leaders, including Samuel Adams, John Dickinson, Thomas Paine, and Thomas Jefferson.

Seldom if ever since the days of Queen Elizabeth had England thrilled with such pride as in the closing years of the Great War for Empire. The victories of 1759 had delivered Canada and India to British control. In 1760 the young, vigorous George III ascended to the throne. Three years later, the Peace of Paris confirmed the possession of a great new British empire. The end of the French imperial domain in North America unleashed development of the sprawling region between the Appalachian Mountains and the Mississippi River and from the Gulf of Mexico to Hudson Bay.

The American colonists shared in the euphoria of victory, but the moment of celebration served to mask festering resentments and new problems. Underneath the pride in the growing British Empire was a maturing sense of American nationalism. For over a generation, the colonists had essentially been allowed to govern themselves and were beginning to think and speak of themselves more as Americans than as English or British.

The Heritage of War

In the aftermath of victory, the British ministry faced new problems. How should it manage the defense and governance of the new possessions it had acquired from France and Spain? What should be done with the western American lands? How were the British to pay an unprecedented debt built up during the war and bear the new burdens of greater colonial administration and more far-flung defense? And—the thorniest problem of all, as it turned out—what role should the colonies play in all this? The problems were of a magnitude and complexity to challenge men of the greatest statesmanship and vision, but those qualities were rare among the ministers of George III. The king himself, while a conscientious and deeply religious man, was obstinate

and unimaginative, and overly dependent on his advisers and ministers.

In the British politics of the day, Whigs predominated. "Whig" had been the name given to those who had opposed James II, led the Glorious Revolution of 1688, and secured the Protestant Hanoverian succession in 1714. The Whigs were the champions of individual liberty and parliamentary supremacy, but with the passage of time Whiggism had drifted into complacency, and leadership settled upon an aristocratic elite of the Whig gentry. Throughout the 1760s, the king turned first to one and then to another prime minister, and the government grew more and more unstable just as the new problems of empire required forceful solutions. Colonial policy remained marginal to the chief concerns of British politics. The result was first inconsistency and vacillation, followed by stubborn inflexibility.

Western Lands

No sooner was peace arranged in 1763 than events rapidly thrust the problem of America's new western lands upon the British government. The Indians of the Ohio region, unable to believe that their French friends were helpless and fearing the incursion of English settlers, grew restless and receptive to the warnings of Pontiac, chief of the Ottawa. In 1763, the western tribes joined Pontiac's attempt to reopen frontier warfare, and within a few months wiped out every British post in the Ohio region except Fort Detroit and Fort Pitt.

To secure peace on the frontier, the ministers in London postponed further settlement of the western lands. The immediate need was to stop Pontiac's warriors and pacify the Indians. The king signed the Royal Proclamation of 1763, which drew an imaginary line along the crest of the Appalachians beyond which settlers were forbidden to go. It also established the new British colonies of Quebec and East and West Florida.

But Pontiac did not agree to peace until 1766, and Britain's Proclamation Line did not remain intact for long. During the turbulent decade that followed, hardy pioneers pushed over the Appalachian ridges. By 1770 the town of Pittsburgh had twenty log houses. Four years later, Daniel Boone and a party of settlers cut the Wilderness Road through the Cumberland Gap in southwestern Virginia to the Kentucky River.

Grenville's Colonial Policy

As the Proclamation of 1763 was being drafted, a new ministry in London began to grapple with the problems of imperial finances. The new chief minister, George Grenville, first lord of the Treasury, was much like the king: industrious, honest, meticulous, and unaware of the complexities of colonial relations. Grenville assumed the need for British redcoats to defend the frontier, although the colonies had been left mostly to their own devices before 1754. He also wanted to keep a large army in America to avoid a rapid demobilization that would force many influential officers to retire and thereby provoke political criticism at home. But on top of an already staggering debt, he faced sharply rising costs for American defense.

Customs and Currency

Because there was a heavy tax burden at home and a much lighter one in the colonies, Grenville reasoned that the Americans must share the cost of their own defense. He also learned that the American customs service was amazingly inefficient. Evasion and corruption were rampant. Grenville thus issued stern orders to colonial officials and dipatched the navy to patrol the coasts for smugglers. Parliament agreed to set up a new maritime or vice-admiralty court in Halifax with jurisdiction over all the colonies. Decisions would be made by judges appointed by the crown rather than by juries of colonists sympathetic to smugglers. The old habits of salutary neglect in the enforcement of the Navigation Acts were coming to an end, causing no little annoyance to American shippers.

The old Molasses Act of 1733 had set a sixpence-per-gallon duty on molasses in order to prevent trade with the French sugar islands. New England merchants evaded this duty, smuggling in French molasses to make rum. Recognizing that the duty, if enforced, would ruin the business of the rum distillers, Grenville put through the Sugar Act (1764), which cut the duty in half. This, he believed, would reduce the temptation to smuggle or to bribe customs officers. In addition, the Sugar Act levied new duties on imports into the colonies of foreign textiles, wines, coffee, indigo, and sugar. The act, Grenville estimated, would bring in enough revenue to help defray "the necessary expenses of defending, protecting, and securing" the colonies. For the first time, Parliament had adopted customs duties designed to raise revenues in the colonies rather than just to regulate trade.

Another measure in Grenville's new colonial program that had an important impact on the colonies was the Currency Act of 1764. The colonies faced a chronic shortage of hard money, which kept going out to pay debts in England. To meet the shortage, they issued their own paper money. British creditors, however, feared receiving payment in such a depreciated currency. To alleviate their fears, Parliament in 1751 had forbidden the New England colonies to make their currency legal tender. Now Grenville extended the prohibition to all the colonies. The value of existing paper money soon plummeted, since nobody was obligated to accept it in payment of debts, even within the colonies. The deflationary impact of the Currency Act, combined with new duties and stricter enforcement, delivered a severe shock to a colonial economy already suffering a postwar slump.

The Stamp Act

Grenville's new design entailed two more key provisions. Because the Sugar Act would defray only part of the cost of maintaining the 10,000 British troops to be stationed along the western frontier, he proposed another measure to raise money in America, a stamp tax. Enacted on February 13, 1765, the Stamp Act created revenue stamps that were to be attached to printed matter and legal documents of all kinds: newspapers, pamphlets, almanacs, bonds, leases, deeds, licenses, insurance policies, ship clearances, college diplomas, even dice and playing cards. The requirement would go into effect on November 1, 1765.

In March 1765 Grenville put through the final measure of his new program, the Quartering Act. It required the colonies to supply British troops with provisions and to provide them barracks or submit to their use of inns and vacant buildings. It applied to all colonies, but affected mainly New York, headquarters of the British forces.

The Ideological Response

The cumulative effect of Grenville's measures raised colonial suspicions to a fever pitch. Unwittingly, the king's chief minister had stirred up a storm of protest and set in motion a profound reassessment of America's relation to England. Grenville had loosed upon the colonies the very engines of tyranny from which Parliament had rescued England in the seventeenth century. A standing army encouraged despots, and now several thousand British soldiers remained in the colonies. Among fundamental English rights were trial by jury and the presumption of innocence, but the new vice-admiralty courts excluded juries and put the burden of proof on the defendant.

Most important, the English had the right to be taxed only by their elected representatives. Parliament claimed that privilege in England, and the colonial assemblies had long exercised it in America. Now, with the Stamp Act, Parliament was usurping the assemblies' power of the purse strings.

Protest in the Colonies

The Stamp Act became the chief target of colonial protest. It affected the most articulate elements in the community: merchants, planters, lawyers, printer-editors—all strategically placed to influence public opinion. In a flood of colonial pamphlets, speeches, and resolutions, debate on the Stamp Tax turned mainly on the point expressed in a slogan familiar to all Americans: "no taxation without representation."

Through the spring and summer of 1765, popular resentment against Grenville boiled over into mass meetings, parades, bonfires, and other demonstrations. To be sure, only a minority engaged in such public protests. They included farmers, laborers, dock workers, and seamen. But lawyers, editors, and merchants took the lead or lent support. Calling themselves Sons of Liberty, they met underneath "Liberty Trees"—in Boston a great elm, in Charleston a live oak.

The widespread protests encouraged colonial unity, as Americans discovered that they had more in common with each other than with London. In May 1765, the Virginia House of Burgesses struck the first blow against the Stamp Act in the Virginia Resolves, a series of resolutions inspired by young Patrick Henry. Virginians, the burgesses declared, were entitled to all English rights, and the English could be taxed only by their own representatives. Virginians, moreover, had always been governed by laws passed with their own consent. Newspapers spread the resolutions throughout the colonies, along with even more radical statements that were kept out of the final version, and other assemblies hastened to

Two examples of British stamps.

copy Virginia's example. In June 1765, the Massachusetts House of Representatives invited the various assemblies to send delegates to confer in New York on appeals for relief from the king and Parliament.

Nine colonial assemblies responded, and on October 7 the Stamp Act Congress of twenty-seven delegates convened and issued expressions of colonial sentiment: a Declaration of the Rights and Grievances of the Colonies, a petition to the king for relief, and a petition to Parliament for repeal of the Stamp Act. The delegates argued that Parliament might have powers to legislate for the regulation of colonial trade, but it had no right to levy taxes, which were a gift granted by the people through their representatives.

By November 1, its effective date, the Stamp Act was a dead letter. Business went on without the stamps. Newspapers appeared with the skull and crossbones where the stamp belonged. Colonial rebels were beginning to sense their power. After passage of the Sugar Act, a movement had begun to boycott British goods. Now colonists adopted nonimportation agreements to exert pressure on British merchants. Americans knew they had become a major market for British products. By shutting off imports they could exercise real leverage.

Repeal of the Stamp Act

Colonial resistance had scarcely begun before Grenville's ministry was turned out of office, dismissed not because of the turmoil in America but because of tensions with the king over the distribution of lucrative government offices. In July 1765 the king installed a new minister, the marquis of Rockingham, leader of the "Rockingham Whigs," who sympathized with the colonists' views. Rockingham resolved to end the quarrel with America by repealing the Stamp Act. When Parliament assembled early in 1766, Parliamentary leader William Pitt demanded that the Stamp Act be re-

pealed "absolutely, totally, and immediately," but he urged that Britain's authority over the colonies "be asserted in as strong terms as possible," except on the point of taxation. In March 1766 Parliament passed the repeal, but at the same time it passed the Declaratory Act, which asserted the full power of Parliament to make laws binding the colonies "in all cases whatsoever." It was a cunning evasion that made no concession with regard to taxes but made no mention of them either. Amid the rejoicing and relief on both sides of the Atlantic there were no omens that the quarrel would be reopened within a year.

Fanning the Flames

Meanwhile, the king continued to have his ministers play musical chairs. Rockingham fell because he lost the confidence of the king, and his own administration suffered a paralyzing fragmentation. The king invited William Pitt to form a ministry that included the major factions of Parliament. Soon thereafter, however, Pitt slipped over the fine line between genius and madness, and he resigned in 1768. For a time in 1767 the guiding force in the ministry was Charles Townshend, chancellor of the Exchequer, whose "abilities were superior to those of all men," according to Horace Walpole, "and his judgment below that of any man." Townshend took advantage of Pitt's absence to reopen the question of colonial taxation and seized upon the notion that "external" taxes on exports and imports were tolerable to the colonies—not that he believed it for a moment.

The Townshend Acts

In May and June 1767 Townshend put his plan through the House of Commons, and in September he died, leaving a bitter legacy: the Townshend Acts. Their first objective was to bring the New York assembly to its senses. That body had defied the Quartering Act and refused to provide beds or supplies for the king's troops. Parliament, at Townshend's behest, suspended all acts of the New York assembly until it yielded. New York finally caved in, inadvertently confirming the British suspicion that too much indulgence had encouraged colonial bad manners. Townshend followed up with the Revenue Act of 1767, which levied duties ("external taxes") on colonial imports of glass, lead, paints, paper, and tea. Next, he set up a Board of Customs Commissioners at Boston, the colonial headquarters of smuggling. Finally, he reorganized the vice-admiralty courts, providing four in the continental colonies—at Halifax, Boston, Philadelphia, and Charleston.

The Townshend duties did increase government revenues, but the intangible costs were greater. The duties taxed goods exported from England, indirectly hurting British manufacturers, and they had to be collected in colonial ports, increasing collection costs. More important, the new taxes accelerated colonial resistance. The Revenue Act of 1767 posed a more severe threat to colonial assemblies than Grenville's taxes, for Townshend proposed to apply the revenues to pay the salaries of governors and other officers and thereby release them from financial dependence on the assemblies.

Dickinson's *Letters*

The Townshend Acts provoked the colonists to boycott British goods and to develop their own manufactures. Once again the colonial press spewed out expressions of protest, most notably the essays of John Dickinson, a Philadelphia lawyer. Late in 1767 his twelve *Letters of a Pennsylvania Farmer* (as he chose to style himself) began to appear in the *Pennsylvania Chronicle*, from which they were copied in other papers and in pamphlet form. He argued that Parliament might regulate commerce and collect duties incidental to that purpose, but it had no right to levy taxes for revenue, whether they were internal or external taxes. Dickinson used moderate language throughout. The colonists, he declared, should "speak at the same time the language of affliction and veneration" toward the mother country.

Samuel Adams and the Sons of Liberty

But the affliction grew and the veneration waned. British ministers could neither conciliate moderates like Dickinson nor cope with firebrands like Boston's Samuel Adams, who was now emerging as the supreme genius of revolutionary agitation. Adams insisted that Parliament had no right to legislate for the colonies, that Massachusetts must return to the spirit of its Puritan founders and defend itself from a new conspiracy against its liberties. Adams whipped up the Sons of Liberty, writing incendiary newspaper articles and letters and organizing protests in the Boston pubs, town meetings, and the provincial assembly. The royal governor called him "the most dangerous man in Massachusetts." Early in 1768 Adams and Boston lawyer James Otis formulated another Massachusetts circular letter, which the assembly dispatched to the other colonies. The letter restated the illegality of parliamentary taxation, warned that the new duties would be used to pay colonial officials, and invited the other colonies to join in a boycott of British goods.

The Boston Massacre

In Boston roving gangs enforced the boycott of goods from England, intimidating Tory merchants and their customers. This led the governor to appeal for military support, and two British regiments sailed from Halifax. The presence of soldiers in Boston had always been a source of provocation, but now tensions boiled over. On March 5, 1770, in the square before the customs house, a mob

Paul Revere's partisan engraving of the Boston Massacre.

of toughs began heaving taunts, snowballs, and oyster shells at the British sentry, whose call for help brought reinforcements. Then somebody rang the town firebell, drawing a larger crowd to the scene. At its head, or so the story goes, was Crispus Attucks, a runaway mulatto slave. The riotous crowd began striking at the British troops with sticks and knocked one soldier down. He rose to his feet and fired into the crowd. Others fired too, and when the smoke cleared, five people lay dead or dying and eight more were wounded.

The cause of colonial resistance now had its first martyrs, and the first to die was Crispus Attucks. Governor Thomas Hutchinson moved the soldiers out of town to avoid another incident. The troops involved in the shooting were indicted for murder but were defended by John Adams, who portrayed them as the victims of circumstance, provoked, he said, by a "motley rabble of saucy boys, negroes and mulattoes, Irish teagues and outlandish Jack tars." All were acquitted except two, who were convicted of manslaughter and branded on their thumbs.

The Boston Massacre sent shock waves through the colonies. The incident, remembered one Bostonian, "created a resentment which emboldened the timid" and "determined the wavering." But late in April 1770 news arrived that Parliament had repealed all the Townshend duties save one. The cabinet, by a vote of five to four, had advised keeping the tea tax as a token of parliamentary authority. Colonial diehards insisted that pressure should be kept on British merchants until Parliament gave in altogether, but the nonimportation movement soon faded. Parliament, after all, had given up the substance of the taxes, with one exception, and much of the colonists' tea was smuggled in from Holland anyway.

For two years thereafter, discontent simmered down, and suspicions began to fade on both sides of the ocean. The Stamp Act was gone, as were all the Townshend duties, except that on tea. Yet most of the hated innovations remained in effect: the Sugar Act, the Currency Act, the Quartering Act, the vice-admiralty courts, the Board of Customs Commissioners. The redcoats had left Boston, but they remained nearby, and the British navy still patrolled the coast. Each remained a source of irritation and the cause of occasional incidents. Colonial patriots were primed to resist new tyrannies.

Discontent on the Frontier

Many colonists showed no interest in the disputes over British regulatory policies raging along the seaboard. Parts of the backcountry had stirred with quarrels that had nothing to do with the Stamp and Townshend Acts. Rival land claims to the east of Lake Champlain pitted New York against New Hampshire, and the Green Mountain Boys led by Ethan Allen against both. Eventually the residents of the area would simply create their own state of Vermont in 1777, although it was not recognized as a member of the Union until 1791.

In Pennsylvania a group of frontier ruffians took the law into their own hands. Outraged at the lack of frontier protection provided by the Quaker-influenced assembly during Pontiac's rebellion, a group called the "Paxton Boys" took revenge by massacring peaceful Conestoga Indians in Lancaster County, then threatened the so-called Moravian Indians, a group of Moravian converts near Bethlehem. When the Moravian Indians took refuge in Philadelphia, some 1,500 Paxton Boys marched on the capital, where Benjamin Franklin talked them into returning home by promising that more protection would be forthcoming.

Farther south, South Carolina frontier folk voiced similar complaints about the lack of settled government and the need for protection against horse thieves, cattle rustlers, and Indians. They organized societies called "Regulators" to administer vigilante justice in the region and refused to pay taxes until they gained effective government. In 1769 the assembly finally set up six new circuit courts in the region and revised the taxes, but it still did not respond to the backcountry's demand for representation in the legislature.

In North Carolina the protest was less over the lack of government than over the abuses and extortion inflicted by government appointees from the eastern part of the colony. Farmers felt especially oppressed at the government's refusal either to issue paper money or to accept produce in payment of taxes, and in 1766 they organized to resist. Efforts of these Regulators to stop seizures of property and other court proceedings led to more disorders and a new law that made the rioters guilty of treason. In the spring of 1771 the royal governor and 1,200 militiamen defeated some 2,000 ill-organized Regulators in the Battle of Alamance. The pitched battle illustrated the growing tensions between backcountry settlers and the wealthy planters in the eastern part of the colony, tensions that would erupt again during and after the Revolution.

These internal disputes and revolts within the colonies illustrate the fractious diversity of opinion and outlook evident among Americans on the eve of the Revolution. Colonists were of many minds about many things, including British rule. The disputatious frontier in colonial America also helped convince British authorities that the colonies were inherently unstable and that they required even firmer oversight, even to the extent of using military force to ensure civil stability.

A Worsening Crisis

Two events in June 1772 shattered the period of calm in the quarrels with the mother country. Near Providence, Rhode Island, a British schooner, the *Gaspee,* patrolling for smugglers, accidentally ran aground. Under cover of darkness a crowd from the town boarded the ship, removed the crew, and set fire to the vessel. Four days after the burning, Massachusetts' governor, Thomas Hutchinson, told the provincial assembly that his salary thenceforth would come out of the customs revenues. Superior Court judges would be paid from the same source and would thereby no longer be dependent on the assembly for their income. The assembly feared that this portended "a despotic administration of government."

To keep the pot simmering, in November 1772 Sam Adams convinced the Boston Town Meeting to form a Committee of Correspondence, which issued a statement of rights and grievances and invited other towns to do the same. Committees of Correspondence sprang up in Massachusetts and other colonies. In March 1773 the Virginia assembly proposed the formation of such committees on an intercolonial basis, and a network of the committees spread across the colonies, mobilizing public opinion and fanning colonial resentments.

The Boston Tea Party

Lord North, who had replaced Townshend as chancellor of the Exchequer, soon brought colonial resentment from a simmer to a boil. In May 1773 he contrived a scheme to bail out the foundering East India Company. The company had in its British warehouses some 17 million pounds of unsold tea. Under the Tea Act of 1773, the government would refund the British duty of twelvepence per pound on all tea shipped to the colonies and collect only the existing threepence duty payable at the colonial port. By this arrangement, colonists could get tea more cheaply than the English could, for less even than the black market Dutch tea. North, however, miscalculated in assuming that price alone would govern colonial reaction. And he erred even worse by permitting the East India Company to serve retailers directly through its own agents or consignees, bypassing the colonial wholesalers who had handled it before. Once that kind of monopoly was established, colonial merchants began to wonder, how soon would the precedent apply to other commodities?

The Committees of Correspondence, backed by colonial merchants, alerted people to the new danger. The government, they reported, was trying to purchase their loyalty and passivity with cheap tea. Before the end of the year, large shipments of tea went out to major colonial ports. In Boston, Governor Hutchinson and Sam Adams engaged in a test of will. The tea ships' captains, alarmed by the radical opposition, proposed to turn back, but Hutchinson refused permission until the tea was landed and the duty paid. On December 16, 1773, a group of colonial Patriots disguised themselves as Mohawk Indians, boarded the three ships, and threw the 342 chests of tea overboard—cheered on by a crowd along the shore.

British authorities were now convinced that the very existence of the empire was at stake. "The colonists must either submit or triumph," George III wrote to Lord North, and North hastened to make the king's judgment a self-fulfilling prophecy.

The Coercive Acts

In April 1774 Parliament enacted harsh measures designed by North to discipline Boston. The Boston Port Act closed the port from June 1, 1774, until the lost tea was paid for. A new Quartering Act directed local authorities to provide lodging for British soldiers, in private homes if necessary. The Massachusetts Government Act made the colony's council and law-enforcement officers all appointive, rather than elected; sheriffs would select jurors; no town meeting could be held without the governor's consent, except for the annual election of town officers.

Designed to isolate Boston and make an example of the colony, the actions instead cemented colonial unity and emboldened resistance. If these "Intolerable Acts," as the colonists labeled the Coercive Acts, were not resisted, they would eventually be applied to the other colonies.

Colonists throughout America rallied to the cause of besieged Boston, taking up collections and sending provisions. When the Virginia assembly met in May 1774, a young member of the Committee of Correspon-

Americans Throwing the Cargoes of the Tea Ships into the River, at Boston (1773).

dence, Thomas Jefferson, proposed to set aside June 1, the effective date of the Boston Port Act, as a day of fasting and prayer in Virginia. The irate colonial governor thereupon dissolved the assembly, whose members retired to a nearby tavern and drew up a resolution for a "Continental Congress" to make representations on behalf of all the colonies. Similar calls were coming from Providence, New York, Philadelphia, and elsewhere, and in June the Massachusetts assembly suggested a September meeting in Philadelphia. Shortly before George Washington left to represent Virginia at the meeting, he wrote to a friend that "the crisis is arrived when we must assert our rights, or submit to every imposition, that can be heaped upon us, till custom and use shall make us as tame and abject slaves, as the blacks we rule over with such arbitrary sway."

The Continental Congress

On September 5, 1774, the First Continental Congress assembled in Philadelphia. The fifty-five delegates represented twelve continental colonies, all but Georgia, Quebec, Nova Scotia, and the Floridas. The Congress endorsed the radical Suffolk Resolves, resolutions that declared the Intolerable Acts null and void, urged Massachusetts to arm for defense, and called for economic sanctions against British commerce. The Congress also adopted a Declaration of American Rights, which denied Parliament's authority with respect to internal colonial affairs. In addition, the Congress sent the king a petition for relief and issued addresses to the people of Great Britain and the colonies.

Finally, the Congress adopted the Continental Association of 1774, which recommended that every county, town, and city form committees to enforce a boycott on all British goods. These committees would become the organizational and communications network for the Revolutionary move-

ment, connecting every locality to the leadership. The Continental Association also included provisions for the nonimportation of British goods and the nonexportation of American goods to Britain.

British critics of the American actions reminded the colonists that Parliament had absolute sovereignty. Power could not be shared. Parliament could not relinquish its claim to authority in part without abandoning it altogether. So Parliament declared Massachusetts in rebellion, forbade the New England colonies to trade with any nation outside the empire, and excluded New Englanders from the North Atlantic fisheries. Lord North's Conciliatory Resolution, adopted February 27, 1775, was as far as they would go. Under its terms, Parliament would levy taxes only to regulate trade and would grant to each colony the duties collected within its boundaries, provided the colonies would contribute voluntarily to a quota for defense of the empire. It was a formula not for peace but for new quarrels.

Forging Fetters for the Americans. A cartoon attacking British parliamentary measures of 1775–1776.

Shifting Authority

Events were already moving beyond conciliation. All through late 1774 and early 1775, the Patriot defenders of American rights were seizing the initiative. The uncertain and unorganized Loyalists (also called Tories) were put on the defensive. The Continental Congress urged each colony to mobilize its militia. Royal and proprietary officials were losing control as provincial congresses assumed authority and colonial militias organized and gathered arms and gunpowder. Still, British military officers remained smugly confident. Major John Pitcairn wrote home from Boston in March: "I am satisfied that one active campaign, a smart action, and burning two or three of their towns, will set everything to rights."

Lexington and Concord

Pitcairn soon had his chance. On April 14, 1775, General Thomas Gage, the new royal governor of Massachusetts, received orders to suppress the "open rebellion." Gage decided to seize Sam Adams and John Hancock in Lexington and to destroy the militia's supply depot at Concord, about twenty miles away from his Boston headquarters. On the night of April 18, Lieutenant-Colonel Francis Smith and Major Pitcairn gathered 700 men on Boston Common and set out to Concord by way of Lexington. But local Patriots got wind of the plan, and Boston's Committee of Safety sent silversmith Paul Revere and tanner William Dawes by separate routes on their famous ride to spread the alarm. Revere reached Lexington about midnight and alerted Hancock and Adams. Joined by Dawes and Dr. Samuel Prescott, who had been visiting in Lexington, he rode on toward Concord. A British patrol intercepted the trio, but Prescott slipped through with the warning.

At dawn on April 19, the British advance guard found Captain John Parker and about seventy Minute Men lined up on the dewy Lexington village green. Parker apparently intended only a silent protest, but Pitcairn rode onto the green, swung his sword, and brusquely yelled, "Disperse, you damned rebels! You dogs, run!" The Americans already had begun backing away when someone fired a single pistol shot, whereupon the British soldiers loosed a volley into the Minute Men and then charged them with bayonets, leaving eight dead and ten wounded.

The British officers hastily reformed their men and proceeded to Concord. There the Americans had already carried off most of their valuable supplies, but the British destroyed what they could. In the meantime, enraged Patriots were swarming over the countryside, eager to wreak vengeance on the hated British troops. At Concord's North Bridge, the growing American forces inflicted fourteen casualties on a British platoon, and about noon the exhausted redcoats began marching back to Boston.

By then, however, the road back had turned into a gauntlet of death as the embattled colonists from "every Middlesex village and farm" sniped at the redcoats from behind stone walls, trees, barns, and farmhouses, all the way back to Charlestown peninsula. By nightfall the British survivors were safe under the protection of the fleet and army at Boston, having suffered over 250 killed or wounded; the Americans had lost nearly a hundred. A British general reported to London that the rebels, though untrained, had earned his respect: "Whoever looks upon them as an irregular mob will find himself much mistaken."

The Spreading Conflict

The war had started. When the Second Continental Congress convened at Philadelphia on May 10, 1775, British-held Boston was under siege by the Massachusetts militia.

The Retreat. An American cartoon showing the retreat of British forces at Lexington and Concord, April 1775.

On the very day that Congress met, a force of Green Mountain Boys under Ethan Allen of Vermont and Massachusetts volunteers under Benedict Arnold of Connecticut captured strategic Fort Ticonderoga in New York. In a prodigious feat of daring energy, the Americans then managed to transport sixty captured British cannon down rivers and over ridges to support the siege of Boston.

The Continental Congress, with no legal authority and no resources, met amid reports of spreading warfare and had little choice but to assume the role of Revolutionary government. The Congress accepted a request that it "adopt" the motley army gathered around Boston, and on June 15 it named George Washington commander-in-chief. He accepted on the condition that he receive no pay.

On June 17, the very day that Washington was commissioned, the colonial rebels and British troops engaged in their first major fight, the Battle of Bunker Hill. While the Congress deliberated, both American and British forces in and around Boston had increased in strength. Militiamen from Rhode Island, Connecticut, and New Hampshire joined in the siege. British reinforcements included three major-generals—Sir William Howe, Sir Henry Clinton, and John Burgoyne. On the day before the battle, Americans began to fortify the high ground of Charlestown peninsula, overlooking Boston. Breed's Hill was the battle location, nearer to Boston than Bunker Hill, the site first chosen (and the source of the battle's erroneous name).

The rebels were spoiling for a fight. As Joseph Warren, a dapper Boston physician, put it, "The British say we won't fight; by heavens, I hope I shall die up to my knees in blood!" He soon got his wish. With civilians looking on from rooftops and church steeples, Gage ordered a conventional frontal assault in the blistering heat, with 2,200 British troops moving in tight formation through tall grass. The Americans watched from behind hastily built earthworks as the waves of brightly uniformed British troops advanced up the hill. Ordered not to fire until they could "see the whites of their eyes," the militiamen waited until the attackers came within fifteen to twenty paces, then loosed a shattering volley. Through the cloud of oily smoke, the Americans could see fallen bodies "as thick as sheep in a fold." The militiamen cheered as they watched the greatest soldiers in the world retreating in panic.

Within a half hour, however, the British had re-formed and attacked again. Another sheet of flame and lead greeted them, and the vaunted redcoats retreated a second time. Still, the proud British generals were determined not to be humiliated by such ragtag rustics. On the third attempt, when the colonials began to run out of gunpowder and were forced to throw stones, a bayonet charge ousted them. The British took the high ground, but at the cost of 1,054 casualties. Colonial losses were about 400. "A dear bought victory," recorded General Clinton; "another such would have ruined us."

The Battle of Bunker Hill had two profound effects. First, the high number of British casualties made the English generals more cautious in subsequent encounters with the Continental Army. Second, Congress recommended after the battle that all able-bodied men enlist in the militia. This tended to divide the male population into Patriot and Loyalist camps. A middle ground was no longer tenable.

While Boston remained under siege, the Continental Congress sought a possible compromise. On July 5 and 6, 1775, the delegates issued two major documents: an appeal to the king, thereafter known as the Olive Branch Petition, and a Declaration of the Causes and Necessity of Taking Up Arms. The Olive Branch Petition, written by John Dickinson, professed continued loyalty to George III and begged him to restrain further hostilities pending a reconciliation. The Declaration, also largely Dickinson's work, rejected independence but affirmed the colonists' purpose to fight for their rights rather than submit to slavery. Such efforts failed to impress the outraged king. On August 22 he declared the colonists "as open and avowed enemies."

As the fighting spread north into Canada and south into Virginia and the Carolinas, the Continental Congress assumed the functions of government. It appointed commissioners to negotiate peace treaties with Indian tribes, organized a Post Office Department with Benjamin Franklin as postmaster-general, and authorized formation of a navy and a marine corps. A committee began to explore the possibility of gaining foreign military alliances. Still, the delegates continued to hold back from the seeming abyss of formal independence. Yet through late 1775 and early 1776, word came of one British action after another that proclaimed rebellion and war. In December 1775 Parliament declared the colonies closed to all commerce, and the king began hiring German soldiers. Eventually almost 30,000 Germans served, about 17,000 of them from the region of Hesse-Kassel, and "Hessian" became the epithet applied to them all.

When Washington arrived outside of Boston to take charge of the American forces after the Battle of Bunker Hill, the military situation was stalemated, and so it remained through the winter, until early March 1776. At that time, American forces occupied Dorchester Heights to the south of Boston, bringing the city under threat of bombardment with cannon and mortars. General William Howe, who had replaced Gage as British commander, retreated with his forces by water to Halifax, Nova Scotia. The last British troops, along with fearful American Loyalists, embarked from Boston on March 17, 1776. By that time, British power had collapsed nearly everywhere, and the British faced not the suppression of a rebellion but the reconquest of a continent.

Common Sense

In early 1776 Thomas Paine's pamphlet *Common Sense* was published anonymously in Philadelphia, transforming the revolutionary controversy. Born of Quaker parents, Paine had distinguished himself in England chiefly as a drifter, a failure in marriage and business. At age thirty-seven, he sailed for America with the purpose of setting up a school for young ladies. When that did not work out, he moved into the political controversy as a freelance writer and, with *Common Sense*, proved himself the consummate revolutionary rhetorician. Until his pamphlet appeared, the squabble had been mainly with Parliament, but Paine directly attacked allegiance to the monarchy, the last frayed connection to Britain. The common sense of the matter, to Paine, was that King George III and his advisers bore the responsibility for the malevolence toward the colonies. Americans should consult their own interests, abandon George III, and declare their independence: "The blood of the slain, the weeping voice of nature cries, 'TIS TIME TO PART."

Independence

Within three months, more than 100,000 copies of Paine's pamphlet were in circulation, an enormous number for the time. One by one the provincial governments authorized their delegates in the Continental Congress to take the final step. On June 7, 1776, Richard Henry Lee of Virginia moved "that these United Colonies are, and of right ought to be, free and independent states." Sam Adams immediately endorsed the idea, but others balked. South Carolina and Pennsylvania initially opposed severing ties with England. After feverish lobbying by radical Patriots, however, the dissenters changed their minds, and the resolution passed on July 2. The more memorable date, however, became July 4, 1776, when Congress adopted the Declaration of Independence.

Jefferson's Declaration

Although Jefferson is often called the "author" of the Declaration of Independence, he is more accurately termed its draftsman. In June 1776 the Continental Congress appointed a committee of five men—Jefferson, Benjamin Franklin, John Adams, Robert Livingston of New York, and Roger Sherman of Connecticut—to explain the reasons for colonial discontent and to provide a rationale for independence. The group asked Adams and Jefferson to produce a first draft, whereupon Adams deferred to Jefferson because of the thirty-three-year-old Virginian's reputation as an eloquent writer.

During two days in mid-June 1776, Jefferson wrote the first statement of American grievances and principles. Jefferson drew primarily upon two sources: his own draft preamble to the Virginia Constitution written a few weeks earlier, and George Mason's draft of Virginia's Declaration of Rights, which appeared in Philadelphia newspapers in mid-June. It was Mason's text that stimulated many of Jefferson's most famous phrases.

The Continental Congress made eighty-six changes in Jefferson's declaration, including shortening its overall length by one-fourth. Jefferson said his colleagues had "mangled" the document. But overall the legislative editing improved the declaration, making it more concise, accurate, and coherent—and, as a result, more powerful.

The Declaration of Independence constitutes an eloquent restatement of John Locke's contract theory of government—the theory, in Jefferson's words, that governments derive "their just Powers from the consent of the people," who are entitled to "alter or abolish" those that deny their "unalienable rights" to "life, Liberty, and the

The Continental Congress votes for independence, July 2, 1776.

pursuit of Happiness." The appeal was no longer simply to "the rights of Englishmen" but to the broader "laws of Nature and Nature's God." The document set forth "a history of repeated injuries and usurpations, all having in direct object the establishment of an absolute Tyranny over these States." The "Representatives of the United States of America," therefore, declared the thirteen "United Colonies" to be "Free and Independent States."

"We Always Had Governed Ourselves"

So it had come to this, thirteen years after Britain had won domination of North America. Historians have advanced numerous explanations as to what caused the Revolutionary controversy: "unfair" trade regulation, the restrictions on British settlement of western lands, the tax controversy, the debts to British merchants, the lack of representation in Parliament, ideologies of Whiggery and the Enlightenment, the abrupt shift from a mercantile to an "imperial" policy after 1763.

Each of these factors contributed something to collective colonial grievances that rose to a climax in a gigantic failure of British statesmanship. A conflict between British sovereignty and American rights had come to a point of confrontation that adroit statesmanship might have avoided, sidestepped, or outflanked. Irresolution and vacillation in the British ministry finally gave way to the stubborn determination to force an issue long permitted to drift. The colonists saw these developments as the conspiracy of a corrupted oligarchy—and finally, they decided, of a despotic king—to impose an "absolute Tyranny."

Perhaps the last word on how the Revolution came about should belong to an obscure participant, Levi Preston, a Minute Man from Danvers, Massachusetts. Asked sixty-seven years after Lexington and Concord about British oppressions, he responded, as his young interviewer reported later: "'What were they? Oppressions? I didn't feel them.'" When asked about the hated Stamp Act, he claimed that he "'never saw one of those stamps,'" and was "'certain I never paid a penny for one of them.'" Nor had he ever heard of John Locke or his theories. "'We read only the Bible, the Catechism, Watts's Psalms and Hymns, and the Almanack.'" When his exasperated interviewer asked why, then, did he support the Revolution, Preston replied: "'Young man, what we meant in going for those redcoats was this: we always had governed ourselves, and we always meant to. They didn't mean we should.'"

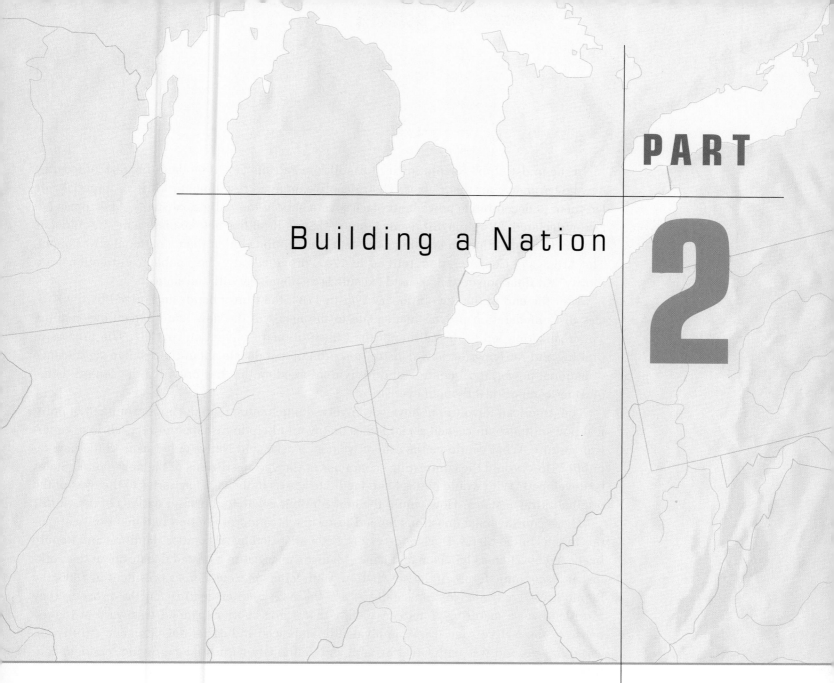

PART 2

Building a Nation

The signing of the Declaration of Independence generated great excitement among the rebellious colonists. Yet it was one thing for Patriot leaders to declare American independence from British authority; it was quite another to win it on the battlefield. Barely a third of the colonists actively supported the revolution, the new nation was politically fragile, and George Washington found himself in command of a poorly supplied, untested army.

Yet the Revolutionary movement would persevere and prevail. The skill and fortitude of Washington and his lieutenants enabled the Americans to exploit their geographic advantages. Equally important was the intervention of the French on behalf of the Revolutionary cause. The Franco-American alliance proved to be decisive. After eight years of sporadic fighting and heavy human and financial losses, the British gave up the fight and their American colonies.

In the midst of the Revolutionary turmoil, the Patriots faced the daunting task of forming new governments for themselves. Their deeply engrained resentment of British imperial rule led them to decentralize power and place sovereignty in the individual states. As Thomas Jefferson declared, "Virginia, Sir, is my country." Such local ties help explain why the colonists focused their attention on creating new state constitutions rather than a national government. The Articles of Confederation, ratified in 1781, provided only the semblance of national authority. All final power to make and execute laws remained with the states.

After the end of the Revolutionary War in 1783, the flimsy bonds authorized by the Articles of Confederation proved inadequate to the needs of the new—and expanding—nation. This realization led to the calling of the Constitutional Convention in 1787. The process of drafting and ratifying the new constitution prompted a debate about the relative significance of national power, local control, and individual freedom that has provided the central theme of American political thought ever since.

The American Revolution, however, involved much more than the apportionment of political power. It also unleashed social forces that would help to reshape the very fabric of American culture. What would be the role of women, blacks, and Native Americans in the new republic? How would the contrasting economies of the various regions of the new United States be developed? Who would control and facilitate access to the vast territories to the west of the original thirteen states? How would the new republic relate to the other nations of the world?

These controversial questions helped foster the creation of the first national political parties in the United States. During the 1790s, Federalists led by Alexander Hamilton and Republicans led by Thomas Jefferson and James Madison engaged in a heated debate about the political and economic future of the new nation. With Jefferson's election as president in 1800, the Republicans controlled national politics for the next quarter century. In the process, they presided over a maturing American society that aggressively expanded westward at the expense of the Native Americans, ambivalently embraced industrial development, fitfully engaged in a second war with Great Britain, and ominously witnessed a growing sectional controversy over slavery.

ESSENTIAL THEMES

CRITICAL QUESTIONS

How did the cross-currents of nationalism and sectionalism gain force in this period?

How did the Federalists and Republicans address the issues of economic development in the new nation?

How did issues of race and class enter into debates over the shape of the new nation?

How did Americans develop a more independent culture in the early national period?

How did the new nation seek to enhance its international status?

CHAPTER 5
The American Revolution
Independence ●

Critical junctures in the Revolutionary War
Trenton and Princeton (1776–1777)
Saratoga (1777)
Valley Forge (1778)
Yorktown (1781)
British peace overtures following Saratoga
Transition to a republic
Articles of Confederation establish weak central government (1781)
New state constitutions (1776–1787)

CHAPTER 6
Shaping a Federal Union
● Western lands, states' rights, and the constitution

Northwest Ordinance regulates population and government of western lands (1787)
The Constitutional Convention (1787)
The Virginia and New Jersey Plans
The Great Compromise
The Federalist: Hamilton, Madison, and Jay (1787–1788)
Confederation Congress yields to constitutional rule (October 1788)

CHAPTER 7
The Federalists: Washington and Adams
Federalist rule ●

Washington elected first president of the United States (March 1789)
John Jay becomes first chief justice of the Supreme Court (1789)
Alexander Hamilton named first secretary of the treasury (1789)
The Bill of Rights protects individual liberties (1791)
Land policy and the frontier policy (1796)
John Adams wins nation's first partisan election (1796)
Congress creates Department of the Navy (1798)
Jefferson wins presidency in 1800

CHAPTER 8
Republicanism: Jefferson and Madison
● An orderly transfer of power in 1800

Thomas Jefferson as president (1800–1804)
Republican simplicity and the "Revolution of 1800"
Marbury v. *Madison* (1803) defines relationship between court, executive branch
The Louisiana Purchase (1803)
Divisions in the Republican party
John Randolph and the *Tertium Quid* (1806)
The Burr Conspiracy
Jefferson and the politics of war

CHAPTER 9
Nationalism and Sectionalism
Nationalism and sectionalism ●

Judicial nationalism: Chief Justice John Marshall
Dartmouth College v. *Woodward* (1819)
McCulloch v. *Maryland* (1819)
Gibbons v. *Ogden* (1824)
Expansion and sectional tension: the Missouri Compromise (1820)
John Quincy Adams becomes president (1824)
The 1828 election

CHAPTER 5

The American Revolution

• Economic dimensions of the revolutionary war

Destruction and confiscation of property
Inflation and war profiteering

CHAPTER 6

Shaping a Federal Union

Confederation finance •

Acute economic contraction between 1770 and 1790
Robert Morris establishes Bank of North America (1781)
Currency crisis, mounting debt
Tariffs and foreign trade
Shays's Rebellion (1787) and the debt problem
Economic interests and the Constitution

Hamilton promulgates a strong central government that favors capitalist development
Establishment of a national bank, national mint (1790–1791)
Protective tarrifs to raise revenue and assist nascent American industry (1790s)
Treasury begins retiring Revolutionary War debt, attracting foreign investment (1790s)
Jefferson and Madison favor a decentralized, agricultural republic

CHAPTER 7

The Federalists: Washington and Adams

• Conflicting economic ideologies of Federalists and Republicans

CHAPTER 8

Republicanism: Jefferson and Madison

Republican finance •

Republicans repeal whiskey tax (1802) and other Federalist excises
Government finances depend on tariff revenues and sale of western lands
Economic effects of war in Europe
Lewis and Clark and the fur trade (1804–1806)
Economic causes of the War of 1812

CHAPTER 9

Nationalism and Sectionalism

• Economic effects of the War of 1812

President Madison promotes economic balance and a "national" economy
Tariff of 1816 protects American manufacturing
Canals and new roads improve transportation
Second Bank of the United States established (1816)
Early industrialization
The Panic of 1819
Tariff of 1824 and sectional interests
The Marshall Court and the economy (1819)

CHAPTER 5
The American Revolution
Revolution and society •

CHAPTER 6
Shaping a Federal Union
The ongoing struggle for equality

CHAPTER 7
The Federalists: Washington and Adams
The new nation •

CHAPTER 8
Republicanism: Jefferson and Madison
• Jeffersonian America

CHAPTER 9
Nationalism and Sectionalism
Race and the national agenda •

The Confederation
Northwest Ordinance prohibits slavery, guarantees religious freedom in Northwest (1787)
Social unrest under the Confederation
The Constitution (1787)
Race: the Three-Fifths Compromise and racial inequality
Gender: women continue to lack basic constitutional rights
Indian nations forced to yield their lands to American expansion (1780s)
Congress funds public schools on the western frontier (1785)

Social effects of the Revolution
Social realignment and the erosion of social deference
The status of women
The paradox of slavery
Religious pluralism
Virginia's Declaration of Rights (1776) and Statute of Religious Freedom (1786)
Emergence of national church bodies
Indian-white relations
Revolution weakens tribes along frontier, clearing way for later settlement
The home front during the war
Tories vs. Loyalists
Demands for social equality by working classes

The first census (1790)
In 1790, 750,000 African Americans and 150,000 Native Americans living in the United States
Unrest on the frontier
The Whiskey Rebellion (1794)
Cherokees, Chickasaws, Choctaws, Creeks, and Seminoles reject American authority (1790s)
Federalist-Antifederalist debate between centralized capitalism and decentralized agrarianism
Alien and Sedition Acts and the politics of nationality (1798)

Worsening white-Indian relations during the War of 1812
Tecumseh (Shawnee), William Henry Harrison, and the Battle of Tippecanoe (1811)
Tecumseh's death at the Battle of the Thames (1813)
Creeks cede two-thirds of their lands to the United States (1814)
Jefferson outlaws foreign slave trade effective January 1, 1808
Nearly 300,000 slaves smuggled into southern states 1808–1861

Jackson pursues Seminoles into Florida; Jackson takes Seminole lands for the United States (1817–1818)
The Missouri Compromise (1819)
Rapid territorial expansion

CHAPTER 5

The American Revolution

The ideology of republicanism ●——

> Emergence of an American culture
> America's "mission" and the sense of
>   common nationality
> American painting
> Education
> State-supported public education
> Chartering of state universities

CHAPTER 6

> *The Federalist* and the foundations of
>   American political thought
> Thomas Pritchard Rossiter and Charles
>   Willson Peale

Shaping a Federal Union

——● Literature and art in the
confederation

CHAPTER 7

The Federalists: Washington

and Adams

Life and values in early America ●——

> **Thomas Jefferson's enlightened world**
> Monticello, the Virginia Capitol, and
>   the University of Virginia
> **Life on the American frontier**
> Daniel Boone and the Wilderness Road
>   (1770)
> Corn-based foods and "likker"
> **Westward migration**

CHAPTER 8

> The Louisiana Purchase
> Exploring the trans-Mississippi
>   wilderness: Lewis and Clark
>   (1804–1806)
> The War of 1812—the "Second War of
>   Independence"

Republicanism: Jefferson and

Madison

——● American identity in the first
years of nationhood

CHAPTER 9

Nationalism and Sectionalism

Culture and the expansion of
territorial boundaries ●——

> Slavery and the "cotton culture"
>   expand into Missouri and
>   Arkansas
> French and Spanish culture in Florida
>   and the Southwest

CHAPTER 5

The American Revolution

A world war: England fights the
four powers ●

American diplomacy
France enters the war on the side of the
    Americans (1778)
Spain joins France against England
    (1779)
England declares war on Holland
    (1780)
Peace of Paris (1783)

British forts along the Canadian border
American trade
The United States and Spain negotiate
    boundaries, navigation of
    Mississippi (1780s)
Spanish governor of Louisiana incites
    Creeks, Choctaws, Chicasaws,
    and other tribes against the
    United States (1780s)

CHAPTER 6

Shaping a Federal Union

● American diplomacy following
the war

CHAPTER 7

The Federalists: Washington
and Adams

Events in Europe affecting the
United States ●

The French Revolution and the Terror
    (1789–1794)
Britain, Spain, and Holland go to war
    with France (1793)
President Washington declares U.S.
    neutrality in British-French
    hostilities (1793)
Free American navigation of the
    Mississippi River
Jay's Treaty aims to soothe U.S.–British
    relations (1794)
Pinckney's Treaty (1795)
The XYZ Affair and war with France
    (1797–1800)
Congress renounces 1778 alliance with
    France
Napoleon's dictatorship sets stage for
    Louisiana Purchase

Jefferson's abhorrence of "entangling
    alliances"
The Louisiana Purchase (1803)
Spaniards remain in Florida
The "paper blockade" (1806)
Napoleon's Continental System
    (1806–1807)
Jefferson's Embargo Act and "peaceable
    coercion" (1807)
The Non-Intercourse Act (1809)
Macon's Bill Number 2 (1810)
The War of 1812
Trade issues
Land issues
Anti-British sentiment
British burn Washington, D.C. (1814)
Treaty of Ghent ends war (1814)

CHAPTER 8

Republicanism: Jefferson
and Madison

● Ongoing relations with Europe

CHAPTER 9

Nationalism and Sectionalism

New nationalism and improving
relations with Britain ●

Andrew Jackson attacks Spanish
    strongholds in Florida
    (1817–1818)
Spain cedes Florida with
    Transcontinental Treaty (1819)
Russia cedes Pacific Northwest (1824)
The Monroe Doctrine (1823)
Origins
Significance

The American Revolution

This chapter focuses on

- American and British military strategies and the Revolutionary War's major turning points.

- The effect of the war on the home front.

- The American Revolution considered as a "social revolution" in matters of social equality, slavery, the rights of women, and religious freedom.

- The beginnings of a distinctive American culture.

77

THE *ESSENTIAL AMERICA* ON-LINE TUTOR

www.wwnorton.com/eamerica/ch5

- **Topic: The paintings of Charles Willson Peale**
www.wwnorton.com/eamerica/ch5/topic.htm

The paintings of Charles Willson Peale helped shape the American memory of the Revolution and its advocates. Explore Peale's work and its significance using paintings, historical analyses, and personal correspondence. What does Peale's work contribute to our understanding of the Revolution?

- **Chapter review: On-line quiz and chapter summary**
www.wwnorton.com/eamerica/ch5/review.htm

- **Chapter resources: Multimedia index**
www.wwnorton.com/eamerica/ch5/media.htm

The Americans lost most of the battles in the Revolutionary War, but they eventually forced the British to sue for peace and grant the colonists their independence. The surprising result was due to the tenacity of the Patriots, the importance of the French alliance, and the peculiar difficulties facing the British as they tried to conduct a demanding military campaign thousands of miles from home.

Like all major military events, the Revolution had unexpected consequences. It not only secured American independence, generated a new sense of nationalism, and created a unique system of self-governance; it also began a process of societal definition and change that has yet to run its course. The turmoil of the Revolution upset traditional class and social relationships and helped transform the lives of people who have long been relegated to the periphery of historical concern—blacks, women, and Indians. In important ways, then, the Revolution was much more than simply a war for independence. It was an engine for political experimentation and social change.

1776: Washington's Narrow Escape

On July 2, 1776, the day that Congress voted independence, British redcoats landed on Staten Island, off the coast of New York City. They were the vanguard of a gigantic effort to reconquer America and the first elements of an enormous force that gathered around New York Harbor over the next month. By mid-August, General William Howe, with the support of a fleet under his older brother, had some 32,000 men at his disposal, including 9,000 German Hessians—the biggest single force ever mustered by the British in the eighteenth century. To counter the British, Washington transferred most of his men from Boston, but he could muster only about 19,000 Continental soldiers and militiamen. Such a

force could not defend New York, but Congress wanted it held. This forced Washington to expose his men to entrapments from which they escaped more by luck and Howe's caution than by the American commander's skill. Washington was still learning the art of generalship, and the New York campaign taught him some costly lessons.

Fighting in New York and New Jersey

By invading and occupying New York, the British sought to sever New England from the rest of the rebellious colonies. In late August 1776, Howe inflicted heavy losses and forced Washington to evacuate Long Island and withdraw to Manhattan. Had Howe moved quickly, he could have trapped Washington's army in lower Manhattan. But the main American force of 6,000 men withdrew northward to mainland New York, crossed the Hudson River, and then retreated slowly across New Jersey and the Delaware River into Pennsylvania.

In the retreating army marched a volunteer from England, Thomas Paine. Having opened an eventful year with his inspiring pamphlet *Common Sense*, he now composed *The American Crisis*, in which he exhorted Americans to fight on with the immortal line "These are the times that try men's souls." The eloquent pamphlet, ordered read in the Revolutionary army camps, helped restore shaken morale.

General Howe, comfortably based in New York (which the British held throughout the war), settled down with his army to wait out the winter. But Washington was not yet

George Washington at Princeton, detail of a painting by Charles Willson Peale.

ready to hibernate; instead he seized the initiative. On Christmas night 1776, he slipped across the icy Delaware River with 2,400 men. Near dawn at Trenton, New Jersey, the Americans surprised a garrison of 1,500 Hessians. The daring raid was a total rout from which only 500 royal soldiers escaped death or capture. Washington's men suffered only six casualties. At nearby Princeton, on January 3, the Americans repelled three regiments of redcoats before taking refuge in winter quarters at Morristown, in the hills of northern New Jersey. The campaigns of 1776 had ended, after repeated American defeats, with two minor but uplifting victories. Howe had missed his great chance to bring the rebellion to a speedy end.

American Society at War

Divided Loyalties

The Revolution seemed to have been a fight between the Americans and the British, but the War for Independence was also a civil war that divided families and communities. After the outbreak of war, opinion concerning the Revolution divided in three ways: Patriots or Whigs (as the revolutionaries called themselves), Tories (as Patriots called the Loyalists, recalling the die-hard royalists in England), and an indifferent middle group swayed by the better organized and more energetic radicals.

American Tories were concentrated mainly in the seaport cities, but they came from all walks of life. Almost all governors, judges, and other royal officials were loyal to Britain; most Anglican ministers also preferred the mother country; colonial merchants might be tugged one way or the other, depending on how much they had benefited or suffered from mercantilist regulation; the great planters were swayed one way by dependence on British bounties, another by their debts to British merchants. In the backcountry of New York and the Carolinas, many humble folk rallied to the crown. Whereas planter aristocrats tended to be Whig, as in North Carolina, backcountry farmers (many of them recently Regulators) leaned toward the Tories. When Patriots took control of an area, Loyalists in the region faced a difficult choice: either accompany the British and leave behind their property or stay and face the wrath of the Patriots.

Militia and Army

Since the end of the French and Indian War, the colonies had required all adult males between the ages of fifteen and sixty to enroll in their local militia company, to attend monthly drills, and to turn out on short notice for emergencies. The Patriot militia kept springing to life whenever the redcoats appeared nearby, and all adult white males, with few exceptions, were obligated under state law to serve when called.

In the backcountry, the militia engaged in a brutal warfare that defied prevailing rules of combat. Dressed in hunting shirts and armed with muskets with long, grooved barrels, they preferred to ambush their opponents or engage them in hand-to-hand

"One of those ubiquitous American frontiersmen-turned-soldier," second from right. Sketches of the American militia by a French soldier at Yorktown.

combat rather than fight in traditional formations. They also tended to kill unnecessarily and to torture prisoners. To repel an attack, the militia somehow materialized; the danger past, it evaporated, for there were chores to do at home. They "come in, you cannot tell how," George Washington said in exasperation, "go, you cannot tell when, and act you cannot tell where, consume your provisions, exhaust your stores, and leave you at last at a critical moment."

The Continental Army was on the whole better trained and motivated than the militias. While many American troops were attracted by bounties of land or cash, and some deserted, most harbored a genuine patriotic fervor and a thirst for adventure that enabled them to survive the horrors of combat and camp life. Unlike the full-time professional soldiers in the British army, Washington's army, which fluctuated in size from 5,000 to 20,000, was populated mostly by citizen-soldiers, poor native-born Americans or immigrants who had been indentured servants or convicts.

Behind the Lines

Civilians saw their lives profoundly altered by the Revolutionary War. British forces occupied the major cities (Boston, New York, Philadelphia, Savannah, Charleston). They also confiscated crops and livestock.

Some civilians took selfish advantage of the war. The inflationary spiral generated by a scarcity of consumer goods and the supplies needed for the military effort created new opportunities for quick profits and graft. Throughout the war years, George Washington complained that "speculation, peculation, and an insatiable thirst for riches seems to have got the better of every other of Men."

The poor suffered most amid the war's disruptions and skyrocketing prices. A bushel of wheat that sold for less than a dollar in 1777 brought $80 two years later. Many consumers appealed to authorities to institute price controls so they could afford basic necessities. Others took more direct action. In Boston a throng of women paraded a merchant accused of hoarding through the streets while "a large concourse of men stood amazed." No longer willing to defer quietly to gouging merchants and retailers, the working classes grabbed the opportunity afforded by the Revolution to claim new economic and political rights.

To Revolutionary leaders such as John Adams, the "democratical" demands for political and social equality put forward by the laboring classes were as odious as British regulatory measures. The specter of unlearned mechanics and laborers exercising political power horrified him. The American people, he and others insisted, must accept social inequality as a fact of human existence and defer to the leadership of their betters.

1777: Setbacks for the British

Indecision, overconfidence, and poor communications plagued British military planning for the campaigns of 1777. The profoundly confident General "Gentleman Johnny" Burgoyne sought to bisect the colonies. His men would advance southward from Canada to the Hudson River while another force moved eastward down the Mohawk Valley. Howe had proposed a similar plan, combined with an attack on New England. Had he stuck to it, he might have cut the colonies in two and delivered them a disheartening blow. But he changed his mind and decided to move against the Patriot capital, Philadelphia, expecting that the Pennsylvania Tories would then rally to the crown and secure the colony.

Washington, sensing Howe's purpose, withdrew most of his men from New Jersey to meet the new threat. At Brandywine Creek, south of Philadelphia, Howe pushed Washington's forces back on September 11,

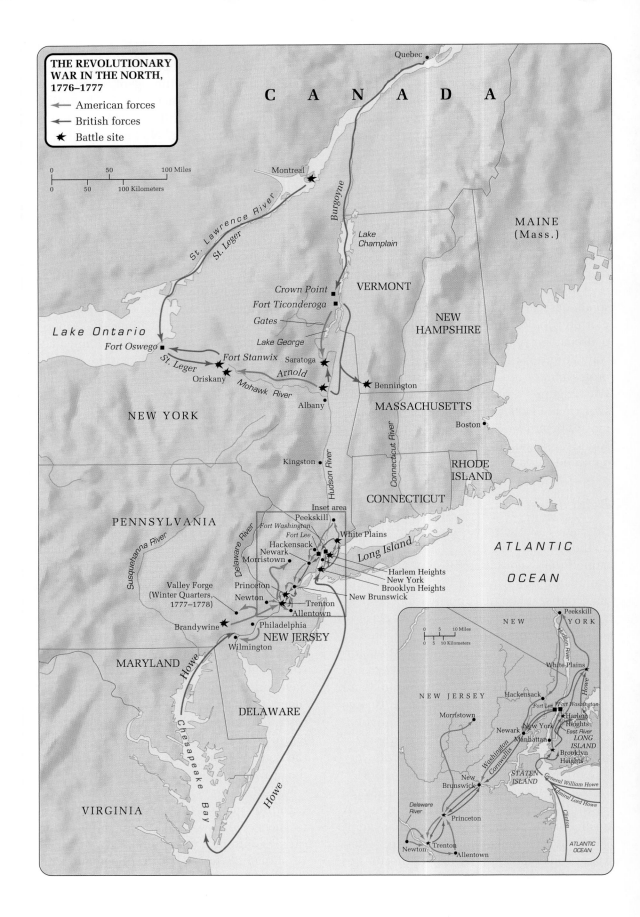

THE REVOLUTIONARY
WAR IN THE NORTH,
1776–1777

⟵ American forces
⟵ British forces
★ Battle site

0   50   100 Miles
0   50   100 Kilometers

Quebec

C A N A D A

Montreal

St. Lawrence River

St. Leger

St. Leger

Burgoyne

Lake Champlain

MAINE
(Mass.)

Lake Ontario

Fort Oswego

St. Leger

Fort Stanwix

Oriskany

Mohawk River

Arnold

NEW YORK

Crown Point

Fort Ticonderoga

Gates

Lake George

Saratoga

Bennington

Albany

VERMONT

NEW
HAMPSHIRE

MASSACHUSETTS

Boston

Kingston

Hudson River

Connecticut River

RHODE
ISLAND

CONNECTICUT

Long Island

ATLANTIC

OCEAN

PENNSYLVANIA

Susquehanna River

Delaware River

Inset area

Peekskill

Fort Washington

Fort Lee

White Plains

Hackensack

Newark

Morristown

Harlem Heights

New York

Brooklyn Heights

New Brunswick

Valley Forge
(Winter Quarters,
1777–1778)

Princeton

Newton

Trenton

Allentown

Brandywine

Philadelphia

NEW JERSEY

Wilmington

MARYLAND

Howe

DELAWARE

Chesapeake Bay

VIRGINIA

Howe

Peekskill

NEW

YORK

0   5   10 Miles
0   5   10 Kilometers

Hudson River

White Plains

Howe

NEW JERSEY

Hackensack

Morristown

Fort Lee

Fort Washington

Harlem Heights

East River

LONG
ISLAND

Newark

New York

Manhattan

Brooklyn
Heights

Washington

Cornwallis

STATEN
ISLAND

General William Howe

Admiral Lord Howe

New
Brunswick

Delaware
River

Princeton

Newton

Trenton

Allentown

Clinton

ATLANTIC
OCEAN

and fifteen days later British troops occupied Philadelphia. Washington retired into winter quarters at Valley Forge while Howe and his men remained for the winter in the relative comfort of Philadelphia, twenty miles away. Howe's plan had succeeded, up to a point. He had taken Philadelphia, but the Tories there proved fewer than he expected. Meanwhile, Burgoyne was stumbling into disaster in the north.

Saratoga

Burgoyne moved southward toward Lake Champlain in 1777 with about 7,000 men, his mistress, and a baggage train that included some thirty carts filled with his personal trappings and a large supply of champagne. A powerful force on paper, the expedition was in fact much too cumbersome to be effective in the dense forests and rugged terrain of upstate New York. Burgoyne sent part of his army down the St. Lawrence River with Lieutenant-Colonel Barry St. Leger and a force of Iroquois allies. This combined group headed east toward Albany. When they met the more mobile Americans, the British suffered two serious reversals.

At Oriskany, New York, on August 6, 1777, a band of militia thwarted an ambush by Tories and Indians and gained time for General Benedict Arnold to bring a thousand Continentals to the relief of Fort Stanwix, which had been under siege by St. Leger. The Indians, convinced they faced a force greater than they actually did, deserted, and the Mohawk Valley was secured for the Patriot forces. To the east, at Bennington, Vermont, on August 16, New England militia repulsed a British foraging party. American reinforcements continued to gather, and after two sharp clashes, Burgoyne pulled back to Saratoga, where American forces under General Horatio Gates surrounded him. On October 17, 1777, Burgoyne, resplendent in his scarlet, gold, and white uniform, surrendered to the plain, blue-coated Gates. Most of Burgoyne's soldiers were imprisoned in Virginia, but "Gentleman Johnny" himself was permitted to go home, where he received an icy reception. The victory at Saratoga proved critically important to the American cause.

Alliance with France

On December 2, 1777, news of the American triumph at Saratoga reached London; two days later it reached Paris, where it was celebrated almost as if it were a French victory. Its impact on the French made the Battle of Saratoga a decisive turning point of the war. In 1776 the French had taken their first step toward aiding the colonists by sending fourteen ships with military supplies to America; most of the Continental Army's gunpowder in the first years of the war came from this source. Besides arms, artillery, and ammunition, the French had also secretly sent clothing, shoes, and other supplies to help the Americans. After Saratoga, the French saw their chance to strike a sharper blow at their hated enemy and entered into serious negotiations with the Americans.

On February 6, 1778, France and America signed two treaties: a Treaty of Amity and Commerce, in which France recognized the United States and offered trade concessions, including important privileges to American shipping, and a Treaty of Alliance. Under the latter, both agreed, first, that if France entered the war, both countries would fight until American independence was won; second, that neither would conclude a "truce or peace" without the consent of the other; and third, that each guaranteed the other's possessions in America "from the present time and forever against all other powers." France further bound itself to seek neither Canada nor other British possessions on the mainland of North America.

By June 1778, British vessels had fired on French ships, and the two nations were at war. In 1779, after extracting promises from the French to help it regain territories taken by the British in the previous war, including Gibraltar, Spain entered the war as an ally of France, but not of the United States. The following year, Britain declared war on the Dutch, who persisted in a profitable trade with the French and Americans. Thus, the American Revolution sparked another world war, and the fighting now spread to the Mediterranean, Africa, India, the West Indies, and the high seas.

1778: Both Sides Regroup

Revolutionary Army at Valley Forge

For Washington's army, bivouacked at Valley Forge, near Philadelphia, the winter of 1777–1778 was a season of suffering far worse than the previous winter at Morristown. The American force, encamped in crowded, lice-infested log huts, endured cold, hunger, and disease. Many died and others deserted or resigned their commissions. Much of the suffering and lack of rations was because the local farmers refused to sell their cattle, bread, and meat to Washington's army for paper money, preferring to send their produce to Philadelphia for British gold and silver.

Desperate for relief, Washington ordered foraging expeditions. His troops confiscated horses, cattle, and livestock in exchange for "receipts" to be honored by the Continental Congress. By March, the once-gaunt troops at Valley Forge saw their strength restored. Their improved health enabled Washington to begin a training program designed to bring unity and order to his motley forces. By the end of March, the ragtag soldiers were beginning to resemble a professional army. Moreover, as winter drew to an end, the army's morale gained strength from congressional promises of extra pay and bonuses after the war.

British Peace Overtures and Withdrawal

After the defeat at Saratoga, Lord North, the British prime minister, knew that winning the war was unlikely, but the king refused to let him either resign or make peace. On March 16, 1778, the House of Commons adopted a program that in effect granted all the American demands prior to independence. Parliament repealed the Townshend tea duty, the Massachusetts Government Act, and the Prohibitory Act, which had closed the colonies to commerce. It then dispatched a peace commission to negotiate an end to the war, but its members did not reach Philadelphia until after Congress had ratified the French treaties. The Congress refused to begin any negotiations until independence was recognized or British forces withdrawn, neither of which the commissioners could promise.

Unbeknownst to the British commissioners, the crown had already authorized the evacuation of British troops from Philadelphia, a withdrawal that further weakened what little bargaining power the commissioners had. After Saratoga, General Howe resigned his command and Sir Henry Clinton replaced him. Clinton pulled his troops out of Philadelphia and sent them to New York by sea and land. His orders were to abandon New York, if necessary, but to keep Newport, Rhode Island, taking a defensive stance except in the South, where the British government believed Tory sentiment in the backcountry needed only a visible British presence for its release. The pro-British sentiment turned out once again, as in other theaters of war, to be weaker than it seemed.

As General Clinton's forces withdrew eastward toward New York, Washington pursued them across New Jersey. On June 28, 1778, he engaged the British in an indecisive battle at Monmouth Court House. Clinton's forces then slipped away into New York while Washington took up a position at White Plains, north of the city. From that time on, the northern theater, scene of the major campaigns and battles in the first years of the war, settled into a long stalemate, interrupted by minor and mostly inconclusive engagements.

Actions on the Frontier

The one major American success of 1778 occurred far from the New Jersey battlefields. Out to the west, at Forts Niagara and Detroit, the British under Colonel William Hamilton had incited frontier Tories and Indians to raid western settlements and had offered to pay for American scalps. To end such attacks, young George Rogers Clark took 175 frontiersmen and a flotilla of flatboats down the Ohio River in early 1778. They marched through the woods and on the evening of July 4 surprised the British at Kaskaskia. At the end of the year, Clark marched his men (almost half French volunteers) through icy rivers and flooded prairies and captured an astonished British garrison at Vincennes.

Meanwhile, Tories and Iroquois Indians in western Pennsylvania continued to terrorize frontier settlements through the summer of 1778. Led by the charismatic Mohawk Joseph Brant, the Iroquois killed hundreds of militiamen along the Pennsylvania frontier. In response, Washington dispatched 4,000 men under General John Sullivan to the area. At Newton (now Elmira) the American force defeated the only serious opposition on August 29, 1779. The American troops burned about forty Seneca and Cayuga villages together with their orchards and food stores. The destruction broke the power of the Iroquois federation for all time.

In the Kentucky territory, Daniel Boone and his small band of settlers risked constant attack from the Shawnees and their British and Tory allies. During the Revolution, they survived frequent ambushes, at least seven skirmishes, and three pitched battles. Despite such ferocious fighting and dangerous circumstances, the white settlers refused to leave Kentucky.

By thus weakening the major Indian tribes along the frontier, the American Revolution, among its other results, cleared the way for rapid settlement of the trans-Appalachian West after the war ended.

The War in the South

At the end of 1778, the focus of British military action shifted suddenly to the South. The whole region from Virginia southward had been free from major action since 1776. Now the British would test King George's belief that a sleeping Tory power in the South needed only the presence of a few redcoats to awaken it. The war in the Carolinas eventually involved not only opposing British and American armies, but also guerrilla-style civil conflicts between local Loyalists and local Patriots.

The Carolinas

In November 1778, British forces took Savannah, Georgia. The British then headed for Charleston, South Carolina, plundering plantation houses along the way. Outside Charleston, the British encamped and awaited additional naval and land forces from New York and New Jersey. After their arrival with General Clinton and General Charles Cornwallis in February 1780, the British launched a massive assault against the Patriot defenders, and on May 12 American general Benjamin Lincoln surrendered the city and its 5,500 defenders. This was the single greatest American loss of the war.

At this point, against Washington's advice, Congress turned to Horatio Gates, the victor of Saratoga, and sent him south to take command of the Revolutionary troops there. Meanwhile, General Clinton sailed back to New York, leaving General Corn-

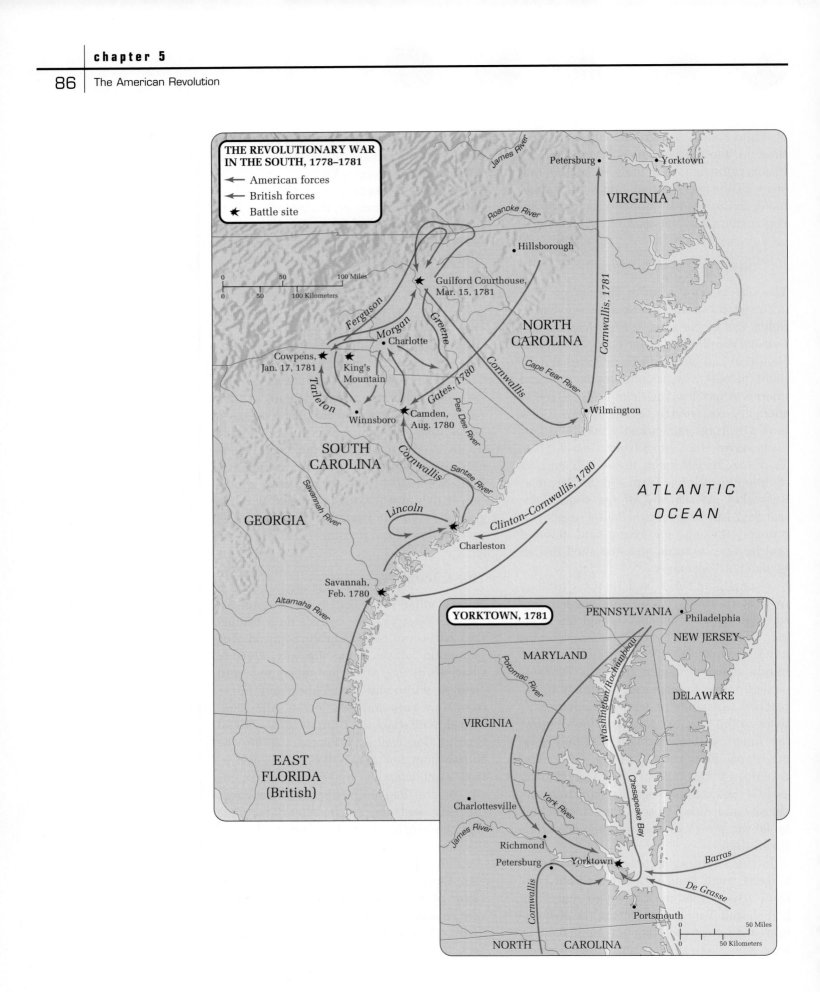

THE REVOLUTIONARY WAR IN THE SOUTH, 1778–1781

→ American forces
→ British forces
★ Battle site

James River

Roanoke River

VIRGINIA

Petersburg •   • Yorktown

• Hillsborough

Guilford Courthouse, Mar. 15, 1781

0   50   100 Miles
0   50   100 Kilometers

Ferguson

NORTH CAROLINA

Morgan
• Charlotte

Greene

Cowpens, Jan. 17, 1781 ★   ★ King's Mountain

Cornwallis, 1781

Tarleton

Gates, 1780

Cornwallis

Cape Fear River

Camden, Aug. 1780

Pee Dee River

Winnsboro

• Wilmington

SOUTH CAROLINA

Cornwallis

Santee River

Savannah River

GEORGIA

Lincoln

ATLANTIC OCEAN

Clinton–Cornwallis, 1780

Charleston

Savannah, Feb. 1780 ★

Altamaha River

EAST FLORIDA (British)

YORKTOWN, 1781

PENNSYLVANIA   • Philadelphia

MARYLAND

NEW JERSEY

Potomac River

Washington/Rochambeau

DELAWARE

VIRGINIA

Chesapeake Bay

• Charlottesville

York River

James River

• Richmond

Petersburg •   Yorktown ★

Barras

Cornwallis

De Grasse

• Portsmouth

0   50 Miles
0   50 Kilometers

NORTH   CAROLINA

wallis in charge of the British troops in the South. Cornwallis's troops clashed with Gates's forces outside Camden in August 1780, and the American army was routed by the British. The Patriots retreated all the way to Hillsborough, North Carolina, 160 miles away.

Cornwallis had South Carolina just about under British control, but his cavalry leaders, Banastre Tarleton and Patrick Ferguson, who mobilized Tory militiamen, overreached themselves in their effort to subdue the Whigs. "Tarleton's Quarter" became bywords for savagery, because "Bloody Tarleton" ordered rebels killed after they surrendered. Ferguson sealed his own doom when he threatened to march over the mountains and hang the revolutionary leaders there. Instead the feisty "overmountain men" went after Ferguson. Allied with other backcountry Whigs, they caught him and his Tories on Kings Mountain along the border between North and South Carolina. There, on October 7, 1780, they routed his force. Kings Mountain was the turning point of the war in the South. By proving that the British were not invincible, it emboldened small farmers to join guerrilla bands under partisan leaders like Francis Marion, "the Swamp Fox," and Thomas Sumter, "the Gamecock."

While the "overmountain men" were closing in on Ferguson, Congress had chosen a new commander for the southern theater, General Nathanael Greene, the "fighting Quaker" of Rhode Island. Greene shrewdly lured Cornwallis and his troops into chasing the Americans across the Carolinas, thus taxing British energies and supplies. Splitting his army, Greene sent out about 700 men under General Daniel Morgan toward Cornwallis's headquarters in Winnsboro in western Carolina. With his force of militia and Continental soldiers, Morgan faced off with Tarleton's 1,000 men at Cowpens, a cow-grazing area in northern South Carolina, on January 17, 1781. The Americans routed the British. Morgan and

his men then linked up with Greene's main force, and the combined army offered battle near Guilford Courthouse on March 15, 1781. After inflicting heavy losses, Greene prudently withdrew. Cornwallis was left in possession of the field, but at a cost of nearly 100 men killed and more than 400 wounded. In London, when the word arrived, a parliamentary leader moaned, "Another such victory and we are undone."

Cornwallis marched off toward the coast at Wilmington to lick his wounds and take on new supplies. Greene then resolved to go back into South Carolina in the hope of drawing Cornwallis after him or forcing the British to give up the state. There he joined forces with the guerrillas already on the scene, and in a series of brilliant actions he kept losing battles while winning the war: "We fight, get beat, rise, and fight again," he said. By September 1781, he had narrowed British control in the Deep South to Charleston and Savannah, although for more than a year longer Whigs and Tories slashed at each other "with savage fury" in the backcountry, where there was "nothing but murder and devastation in every quarter," Greene said.

Meanwhile, Cornwallis had headed north away from Greene, reasoning that Virginia must be eliminated as a source of reinforcement before the Carolinas could be subdued. In 1781 Cornwallis met up with Benedict Arnold, now a *British* general. From July until September 1780, he had been American commander at West Point. Overweening in ambition, lacking in moral scruples, and a reckless spender, he had nursed a grudge over an official reprimand for his extravagances as commander of reoccupied Philadelphia. Arnold plotted to sell out the West Point garrison to the British. The American seizure of the British go-between, Major John André, ended Arnold's plot. Forewarned that his plan had been discovered, Arnold joined the British in New York, and the Americans hanged André as a spy.

Yorktown

Cornwallis arrived at Yorktown, Virginia, with an army of 7,200, far more than the small American force they faced. There appeared to be little reason to worry about a siege, since Washington's main land force seemed preoccupied with attacking New York and the British navy controlled American waters.

To be sure, there was a small American navy, but it was no match for the British fleet. Most celebrated were the exploits of Captain John Paul Jones, who sailed east across the Atlantic in 1778 and on September 23, 1779, won a desperate battle off England's coast with a British frigate, which he captured and occupied before his own ship sank. This was the occasion for his stirring and oft-repeated response to a British demand for surrender: "I have not yet begun to fight."

Such heroics, however, were little more than nuisances to the British. But at a critical point, thanks to the French navy, the British lost control of the Chesapeake waters off Virginia. Indeed, it is impossible to imagine an American victory in the Revolution without the assistance of the French. As long as the British navy maintained supremacy at sea, the Americans could not hope to force a settlement to their advantage. For three years, Washington had waited to get some military benefit from the French alliance. In July 1780 the French had finally landed a force of about 6,000 at Newport, but the French army under the comte de Rochambeau sat there for a year, blockaded by the British fleet.

Then, in 1781, the elements for combined action suddenly fell into place. As Cornwallis moved into Virginia in May, Washington persuaded Rochambeau to join forces for an attack on New York. The two armies linked up in July, but before they could strike at New York, word came from the West Indies that Admiral De Grasse was bound for Chesapeake Bay with his entire French fleet and some 3,000 soldiers. Washington and his troops secretly slipped out of New York and met up with the French in Philadelphia. The combined American-French forces immediately set out toward Yorktown. Meanwhile, the French fleet finally evaded the British barricade at Newport and sailed south toward Chesapeake Bay.

On August 30, De Grasse's fleet reached Yorktown, where his troops joined the American force already watching Cornwallis. On September 6, De Grasse forced the British to give up the effort to relieve Cornwallis, whose fate was quickly sealed. De Grasse then sent ships up the Chesapeake to ferry to Williamsburg Washington's 16,000 American and French forces, double the size of Cornwallis's army.

The siege began on September 28. On October 14, two major outposts guarding the left of the British line fell to French and American attackers, the latter led by Washington's aide Alexander Hamilton. A British counterattack failed to retake them. Later that night, a squall forced Cornwallis to abandon a desperate plan to escape with his troops across the York River. On October 17, 1781, four years to the day after Saratoga, a red-coated drummer boy

Surrender of Lord Cornwallis. John Trumbull completed his painting of the pivotal British surrender at Yorktown in 1794.

climbed atop the British parapet and began beating the call for a truce. Cornwallis sued for peace, and on October 19 the British force marched out, their flags furled, to the tune of "The World Turned Upside Down." Cornwallis himself claimed to be too "ill" to appear.

Negotiations

Whatever lingering hopes of victory the British may have harbored vanished at Yorktown. "Oh God, it is all over," Lord North groaned at news of the surrender. On February 27, 1782, the House of Commons voted against continuing the war, and on March 5 it authorized the crown to make peace. On March 20, Lord North resigned. The new ministry included old friends of the Americans headed by the duke of Rockingham, who had brought about repeal of the Stamp Act. The new colonial minister, Lord Shelburne, became chief minister after Rockingham's death in September and directed the Paris negotiations with American commissioners appointed by the Continental Congress.

The American peace commissioners in Paris were John Adams; John Jay, minister to Spain; Benjamin Franklin; Henry Laurens from South Carolina; and Franklin's nephew, William Temple Franklin. Their difficult task was immediately complicated by commitments France had made to Spain. The United States and Spain were both allied with France, but not with each other. America was bound by its alliance to fight on until the French made peace, and the French had pledged to help the Spanish recover Gibraltar from England. Unable to deliver Gibraltar, or so the tough-minded Jay reasoned, the French might try to bargain off American land west of the Appalachians in its place. Fearful that the French were angling for a separate peace with the British, Jay persuaded Franklin to play the same game. Ignoring their instruc-

tions to consult fully with the French, they agreed to further talks with the British. On November 30, 1782, the talks produced a preliminary treaty with Great Britain. If it violated the spirit of the alliance, it did not violate the strict letter of the treaty with France, for the French minister was notified the day before it was signed, and final agreement still depended on a Franco-British settlement.

The Peace of Paris

Early in 1783, France and Spain gave up on acquiring Gibraltar and reached an armistice with Britain. The Peace of Paris was finally signed on September 3, 1783. In accord with the bargain already struck, Great Britain recognized the independence of the United States and agreed to a Mississippi River boundary to the west. Both the northern and southern borders left ambiguities that would require further definition. Florida, as it turned out, passed back to Spain. The British further granted Americans the "liberty" of fishing off Newfoundland and in the Gulf of St. Lawrence, and the right to dry their catches on the unsettled coasts of Canada. On the matter of pre–Revolutionary War debts, the best the British could get was a promise that British merchants should "meet with no legal impediment" in seeking to collect them. And on the tender point of Loyalists whose property had been confiscated, the negotiators agreed that Congress would "earnestly recommend" to the states the restoration of confiscated property. Each of the last two points was little more than a face-saving gesture for the British.

The Political Revolution

Republican Ideology

The Revolutionary War served as the catalyst for a prolonged debate about what new

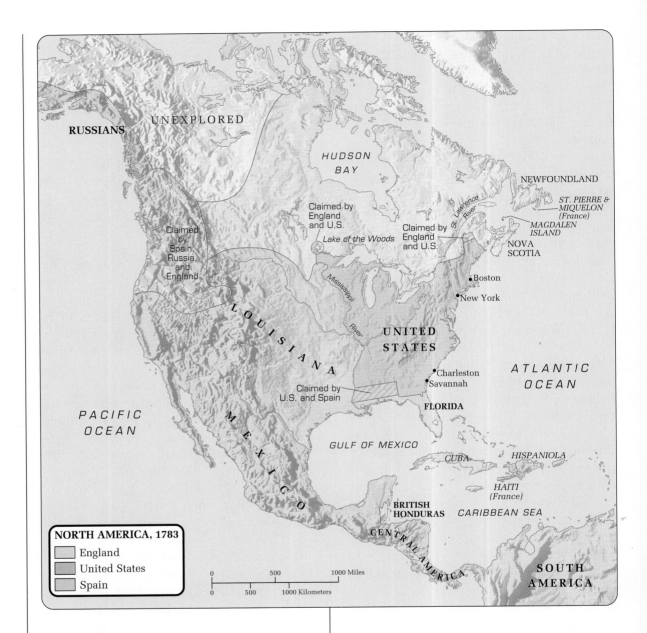

NORTH AMERICA, 1783

England
United States
Spain

UNEXPLORED

RUSSIANS

HUDSON BAY

NEWFOUNDLAND

ST. PIERRE & MIQUELON (France)

MAGDALEN ISLAND

Claimed by England and U.S.

Claimed by England and U.S.

Lake of the Woods

St. Lawrence River

NOVA SCOTIA

Claimed by Spain, Russia, and England

Mississippi

River

•Boston

•New York

UNITED STATES

ATLANTIC OCEAN

•Charleston
•Savannah

Claimed by U.S. and Spain

FLORIDA

PACIFIC OCEAN

M E X I C O

L O U I S I A N A

GULF OF MEXICO

CUBA

HISPANIOLA

HAITI (France)

BRITISH HONDURAS

CARIBBEAN SEA

CENTRAL AMERICA

SOUTH AMERICA

0   500   1000 Miles
0   500   1000 Kilometers

forms of government would best serve an independent republic. Americans knew that they must develop new political assumptions and institutions. They had no monarchy or aristocracy. Yet how could sovereignty reside in the common people? How could Americans ensure the survival of a republican form of government, long assumed to be the most fragile? The war thus provoked a spate of state constitution-making that remains unique in history.

Such ideas as the contract theory of government, the sovereignty of the people, the separation of powers, and natural rights found their way quickly, almost automatically, into the new frames of government that were devised while the fight went on—amid other urgent business.

The very idea of republican government—a balanced polity animated by civic virtue—was a far more radical departure in that day than it would seem to later generations. The new American republic, people assumed, would endure only as long as the majority of the people were virtuous and willingly placed the good of society above the self-interest of individuals. Herein lay the hope and the fragility of the American experiment in popular government: even as leaders enthusiastically fashioned new state constitutions, they feared that their experiments in republicanism would fail because of a lack of civic virtue.

New State Constitutions

Most political experimentation between 1776 and 1787 occurred at the state level. Innovations devised in the state constitutional conventions created the core principle of the American political system: representative government defined in written constitutions in which the people are sovereign and delegate limited authority to the government. In addition, the states initiated bills of rights to protect individuals and fashioned procedures for constitutional conventions that have also remained an essential part of the American political system.

At the onset of the fighting, every colony experienced the departure of governors and other British officials. Loyalists were usually expelled from the assemblies, which then assumed power as provincial "congresses" or "conventions." But they were acting as revolutionary bodies without any legal basis for the exercise of authority. In two of the states this presented little difficulty. Connecticut and Rhode Island, which had been virtually little republics as corporate colonies, simply purged their charters of any reference to colonial ties. Massachusetts followed their example until 1780.

In the other states, the prevailing notions of social contract and popular sovereignty led to written constitutions that specified the framework and powers of government. Constitution-making began even before independence. In May 1776, Congress advised the colonies to set up new governments "under the authority of the people."

The first state constitutions varied mainly in detail. They formed governments much like the colonial administrations, with elected governors and senates instead of appointed governors and councils. Generally they embodied, sometimes explicitly, a separation of powers as a safeguard against abuses. Most of them also included a bill of rights that protected the time-honored rights of petition, freedom of speech, trial by jury, freedom from self-incrimination, and the like. Most state constitutions tended to limit the powers of governors and increase the powers of the legislatures, which had led the people in their quarrels with the colonial governors. Pennsylvania went so far as to eliminate the governor and upper house of the legislature altogether. It had a twelve-man executive council and operated until 1790 with a unicameral legislature limited only by a house of "censors," who reviewed its work every five years.

The Articles of Confederation

The central government, like the state governments, grew out of an extralegal revolutionary body. The Continental Congress exercised governmental powers without any constitutional sanction before 1781. Plans for a permanent frame of government were started very early, however, when on July 12, 1776, a committee headed by John Dickinson produced a draft constitution, the "Articles of Confederation and Perpetual Union." For more than a year Congress debated the articles in between more urgent matters and finally adopted them in November 1777, subject to ratification by all the states.

The central government created by the Articles of Confederation was intentionally weak. The Congress was not a legislature, nor a sovereign entity unto itself, but a collective substitute for the monarch. In

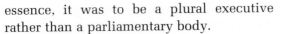

essence, it was to be a plural executive rather than a parliamentary body.

For all the weaknesses of the central government proposed by the Articles of Confederation, it represented the most appropriate structure for the new nation. After all, the Revolution on the battlefields had yet to be won, and the statesmen did not have the luxury of engaging in prolonged and perhaps divisive debates over the distribution of power that proposals for other systems would have provoked. There would be time later for modifications.

The Social Revolution

Americans formed a consensus on the general frame of government—the forms grew naturally out of the experience and the ideas of the colonial period. On other issues raised by the Revolution, however, there was sharp disagreement. What did the Revolution mean to those workers, servants, farmers, and freed slaves who participated in the Stamp Act demonstrations, supported the boycotts, idolized Tom Paine, and fought with Washington and Greene?

Many laboring folk hoped that the Revolution would remove, not reinforce, the traditional political and social advantages exercised by colonial elites. The more conservative Patriots would have been content to replace royal officials with the rich, the well-born, and the able, and let it go at that. But more radical elements, in the apt phrase of one historian, raised the question not only of home rule, but of who shall rule at home.

Equality and Its Limits

This spirit of equality weakened old habits of deference. Participation in the army or militia stirred to action people who had taken little interest in politics. The large number of new political opportunities afforded by the creation of new state governments thus led more ordinary citizens into participation than ever before. The social base of the new legislatures was much broader than that of the old assemblies.

Men fighting for their liberty found it difficult to justify denying other white men the rights of suffrage and representation. The property qualifications for voting, which already admitted an overwhelming majority of white males, were lowered still further in some states. In Pennsylvania, Delaware, North Carolina, Georgia, and Vermont, any male taxpayer could vote, although office-holders had to meet higher property requirements. In the state legislatures, older representatives, some of whom had been Loyalists, were often replaced by newcomers with less property and little education. Some states concentrated much power in a legislature chosen by a wide suffrage, but not even Pennsylvania, which adopted the most radical state constitution, went quite so far as universal male suffrage. Others, like New York and Maryland, took a more conservative stance and instituted stiff property requirements for voting.

The Paradox of Slavery

The Revolutionary generation of leaders was the first to confront the issue of slavery and to consider abolishing it. The principles of liberty and equality so crucial to the rebellion had clear implications for America's enslaved blacks. Jefferson's draft of the Declaration of Independence had indicted the king for having violated the "most sacred rights of life and liberty of a distant people" by encouraging the slave trade in the colonies, but he deleted the clause to satisfy leaders from South Carolina and Georgia.

Black soldiers or sailors were present at most of the major battles, from Lexington to Yorktown; most were on the Loyalist side. Slaves who served in the cause of independence got their freedom and in some cases land bounties. But the British army, which freed probably tens of thousands of slaves during the war, was a greater instrument of emancipation than the American forces. Most of the newly freed blacks found their way to Canada or to British colonies in the Caribbean.

In the northern states, which had fewer slaves than the southern, the doctrines of liberty led swiftly to emancipation for all either during the fighting or shortly afterward. South of Pennsylvania the potential consequences of emancipation were so staggering—South Carolina had a black majority—that whites refused to extend the principle of liberty to their slaves. Although some southern slaveholders like Washington, Jefferson, Patrick Henry, and others were troubled, most could not bring themselves to free their own slaves.

Slaves, especially in the upper South, also earned freedom through their own actions during the Revolutionary era, frequently by running away. They often gravitated to the growing number of African-American communities in the North. Because of emancipation laws in the northern states, and with the formation of free black neighborhoods in the North and in several southern cities, runaways found refuge and the opportunities for new lives. It is estimated that 55,000 slaves fled to freedom during the Revolution.

The Status of Women

The logic of liberty applied to the status of women as much as to that of slaves. Women had remained essentially confined to the domestic sphere during the eighteenth century. They could not vote or preach or hold office. Few had access to formal education. Although in some colonies women could own property and execute contracts, in other colonies they could not legally own even their own clothes, and they had no legal rights over their children. Divorces were extremely difficult to obtain.

The Revolutionary ferment offered women new opportunities and new roles. They plowed fields and melted down pots and pans to make shot. Women also assisted the armies in various ways, such as handling supplies and serving as spies or couriers. Wives sometimes followed their husbands to camp, where they nursed the wounded and sick, cooked and washed for the able, and frequently buried the dead. On occasion, women took their places in the firing line.

Yet the legal status of women did not benefit dramatically from the equalitarian doctrine fostered by the Revolution. Most women retained the narrow domestic outlook that had long been imposed on them. A few free-spirited reformers, however, argued that only educated and independent mothers could raise children fit for republican citizenship. Some demanded equal treatment. In an essay entitled "On the Equality of the Sexes," written in 1779 and published in 1790, Judith Sargent Murray of Gloucester, Massachusetts, stressed the importance of mutuality in marriage: "Mutual esteem, mutual friendship, mutual confidence, begirt about by mutual forbearance." Murray and others insisted that women were perfectly capable of excelling outside the domestic sphere.

Freedom of Religion

The Revolution also set in motion a transition from the toleration of religious dissent to a complete freedom of religion in the separation of church and state. The Anglican church, established as the official religion in five colonies and parts of two others, was especially vulnerable because of its association with the crown and because dissenters outnumbered Anglicans in most states except Virginia. All but Virginia removed tax support for the church before the fighting was over. In 1776, the Virginia Declaration of Rights (a bill of rights) guar-

The Congregational church developed a national body in the early nineteenth century; Lemuel Haynes, depicted here, was its first black preacher.

anteed the free exercise of religion, and in 1786 the Virginia Statute of Religious Freedom (written by Thomas Jefferson) declared that "no man shall be compelled to frequent or support any religious worship, place or ministry whatsoever," and "that all men shall be free to profess and by argument to maintain, their opinions in matters of religion." These statutes and the Revolutionary ideology that spawned them helped shape the course that religion would take in the new United States: pluralistic and voluntary rather than monolithic and state supported.

In churches as well as in government, the Revolution set off a period of constitution-making, as some of the first national church bodies emerged. In 1784 the Methodists, who at first were an offshoot of the Anglicans, organized a general conference at Baltimore. The Anglican church, rechristened Episcopal, gathered in a series of meetings which by 1789 had united the various dioceses in a federal union; in 1789 the Presbyterians also held their first general assembly in Philadelphia. The following year, 1790, the Catholic church had its first bishop in the United States when John Carroll was

named bishop of Baltimore. Other churches would follow in the process of organizing on a national basis.

Emergence of an American Culture

The Revolution generated among some Americans a sense of common nationality. As early as the Stamp Act Congress of 1765, Christopher Gadsden, leader of the Charleston radicals, had said: "There ought to be no New England man, no New Yorker, known on the Continent; but all of us Americans." In the first Continental Congress Patrick Henry asserted that such a sense of national identity had come to pass: "The distinctions between Virginians, Pennsylvanians, New Yorkers, and New Englanders are no more. I am not a Virginian but an American." Henry claimed too much. Before long he and others would reassert state loyalties, but for now an American spirit was in the air.

Art in the New Nation

The Revolution provided the first generation of native artists with inspirational subjects. It also filled them with high expectations that individual freedom would release creative energies and vitalize both commerce and the arts.

Ironically, the best American painters of the time spent all or most of the Revolution in England, studying with Benjamin West of Pennsylvania and John Singleton Copley of Massachusetts, both of whom had set up shop in London before the outbreak of hostilities. Even John Trumbull, who had served in the siege of Boston and the Saratoga campaign, somehow managed a visit to London during the war. Later he highlighted patriotic themes in numerous canvases celebrating scenes from the Revolution. Similarly, Charles Willson Peale, who fought at Trenton and Princeton and survived the winter at Valley Forge, produced a virtual portrait gallery of Revolutionary War figures. Over twenty-three years he painted George Washington seven times from life and produced in all sixty portraits of the general.

Education

The most lasting cultural effect of postwar nationalism may well have been its mark on education. The colonies had founded a total of nine colleges, but after the Revolution eight more sprang up in the 1780s and six more in the 1790s. Several of the state constitutions provided for state universities. Georgia's was the first chartered, in 1785, but the University of North Carolina (chartered in 1789) was the first to open, in 1795.

Even more important, the Revolution provided the initial impetus for state-supported public school systems. Many of the founders believed that the survival of the new nation depended upon instilling in the public an appreciation for the fragility of republican government and its utter dependence on private and civic virtue. They viewed public schools as the best agencies for such moral and civic development. Yet schemes for most public schools came to naught.

Wealthy critics opposed spending tax money on schools that would mingle their sons "in a vulgar and suspicious communion" with the masses.

Mission

In a special sense, American nationalism embodied an idea of divine mission. Many people, at least since the time of the Pilgrims, had thought America to be singled out by God for a special identity, a special mission. This sense of mission was neither limited to New England nor rooted solely in Calvinism. From the democratic rhetoric of Jefferson, to the pragmatism of Washington, to heady toasts bellowed in South Carolina taverns, patriots everywhere articulated a special American leadership role in human history. The mission was now a call to lead the way toward liberty and equality. Meanwhile, however, Americans had to address more immediate problems created by their new nationhood. Benjamin Rush, the Philadelphia patriot, doctor, and scientist, issued a prophetic statement in 1787: "The American war is over: but this is far from being the case with the American Revolution. On the contrary, but the first act of the great drama is closed."

Shaping a Federal Union

This chapter focuses on

- The achievements and weaknesses of the Confederation government.

- The issues involved in writing the Constitution.

- The debate over ratifying the Constitution.

THE *ESSENTIAL AMERICA* ON-LINE TUTOR

www.wwnorton.com/eamerica/ch6

- **Topic: The Constitutional Convention**
  www.wwnorton.com/eamerica/ch6/topic.htm

  The Constitutional Convention of 1787 was a remarkable moment of political creation, notable for its achievements and its shortcomings. Explore the convention through paintings, primary source materials, historical analyses, personal correspondence, and biographical sketches. How did such a diverse group successfully arrive at conclusions that have endured for more than two centuries?

- **Chapter review: On-line quiz and chapter summary**
  www.wwnorton.com/eamerica/ch6/review.htm

- **Chapter resources: Multimedia index**
  www.wwnorton.com/eamerica/ch6/media.htm

In an address to fellow graduates at the Harvard commencement in 1787, young John Quincy Adams lamented "this critical period" when the country was struggling to establish itself as a new nation. Historians thereafter used his phrase to designate the years when the United States operated under the Articles of Confederation, 1781 to 1787. Fear of government power dominated the period, and such concerns ensured that the new Confederation would not threaten state sovereignty. Yet while there were weaknesses of the Confederation, there were also major achievements during the so-called critical period. Moreover, lessons learned under the Confederation would prompt the formulation of a new Constitution intended to balance central and local authority.

The Confederation

The Congress of the Confederation had little authority. It could only request money from the states; it could make treaties with foreign countries but could not enforce them; it could borrow money but lacked the means to ensure repayment. The Congress was virtually helpless to cope with the postwar problems of diplomacy and economic depression, problems that would have challenged the resources of a much stronger government. It was not easy to find men of stature to serve in such a body, and often hard to gather a quorum of those who did. Yet, in spite of its handicaps, the Confederation Congress somehow managed to keep afloat and to lay important foundations for the future. It concluded the Peace of Paris in 1783, created the first executive departments, and formulated principles of land distribution and territorial government that guided expansion all the way to the Pacific coast.

The Articles of Confederation

When the Articles of Confederation took effect in 1781, they did little more than make legal the status quo. Congress had a multitude of responsibilities but little authority to carry them out. It had full power over foreign affairs and questions of war and peace; it could decide disputes between the states; it had authority over coinage, postal service, and Indian affairs, and responsibility for the government of the western territories. But it had no courts and no power to enforce its resolutions and ordinances upon either states or individuals. The Confederation had neither an executive nor a judicial branch; there was no administrative head of government (only the president of the Congress, chosen annually) and no federal courts. It also had no power to levy taxes but had to rely on requisitions, which state legislatures could ignore at their will.

The states, after their colonial battles with Parliament, were in no mood for a strong central government. The Congress in fact had less power than the colonists had once accepted in Parliament, since it could not regulate interstate and foreign commerce. For certain important acts, moreover, a "special majority" was required. Nine states had to approve measures dealing with war, privateering, treaties, coinage, finances, or the army and navy. Unanimous approval by the states was needed to levy tariffs (often called "duties") on imports. Amendments to the Articles of Confederation also required unanimous ratification by the states.

Throughout most of the War for Independence, the Congress had remained distrustful of executive power. It had assigned administrative duties to its committees and thereby imposed a painful burden on conscientious members. At one time or another John Adams, for instance, had served on some eighty committees. In 1781, however, anticipating ratification of the Articles of Confederation, Congress began to set up three departments: Foreign Affairs, Finance, and War. Each was to have a single head responsible to Congress. Given time and stability, Congress and the department heads might have evolved into something like the parliamentary cabinet system. As it turned out, these agencies were the forerunners of the government departments to be established under the Constitution.

Finance

Since there was neither president nor prime minister, but only the presiding officer of Congress and its secretary, the closest thing to an executive head of the Confederation was Robert Morris, who was superintendent of finance in the final years of the war. Morris wanted to make both himself and the Confederation more powerful. He envisioned a coherent program of taxation and debt management to make the government financially stable.

As the foundation of his plan, Morris secured in 1781 a congressional charter for the Bank of North America, which would hold government deposits, lend money to the government, and issue bank notes that would provide a stable currency for the country at large. But his program depended ultimately on a secure source of revenue for the Confederation government, and it proved impossible to win the unanimous approval of the states for the necessary amendments to the Articles of Confederation. Local interests and the fear of a central authority hobbled action. As a consequence, the Confederation never put its finances in order. The Continental currency quickly proved worthless, and each year Congress ran a deficit on its operating expenses.

Land Policy

The one source from which Congress might hope to draw an independent income was the sale of western lands, but throughout the Confederation period that income remained more a fleeting promise than an accomplished fact. The Confederation nevertheless dealt more effectively with the western lands than with anything else. There Congress had direct authority, at least on paper. Thinly populated by Indians, French settlers, and a growing number of American squatters, the region north of the Ohio River had long been the site of overlapping claims by colonies and speculators. By 1786 all states had abandoned their claims in the area except for a 120-mile strip along Lake Erie, which Connecticut held until 1800 as its "Western Reserve."

As early as 1779, Congress had decided not to treat the western lands as colonies but as equal states. Between 1784 and 1787, policies for western development emerged in three major ordinances of the Confederation Congress. These documents, which rank among its greatest achievements, set precedents that the United States would follow in its future expansion. Thomas Jefferson wanted to grant self-government to western territories at an early stage, when settlers would meet and choose their own officials. Under Jefferson's Ordinance of 1784, when a territory's population equaled that of the smallest existing state, it would achieve full statehood.

In the Land Ordinance of 1785, the delegates outlined a plan of surveys and sales that eventually stamped a rectangular pattern on much of the nation's surface. Wherever Indian titles had been extinguished, the Northwest was to be surveyed into townships six miles square along east-west and north-south lines. Each township in turn was to be divided into thirty-six lots (or sections), each one mile square (or 640 acres). The 640-acre sections were to be auctioned for no less than $1 per acre, or $640 total. Such terms favored land speculators, of course, since few common folk had that much money or were able to work that much land. In later years, new land laws would make smaller lots available at lower prices. In each township, Congress reserved the income from the sixteenth section for the support of schools—a significant departure at a time when public schools were rare.

Robert Morris, the most influential figure in the Confederation government, in a portrait by Charles Willson Peale.

Spurred by the plans for land sales and settlement, Congress drafted a more specific form of territorial government to replace Jefferson's Ordinance of 1784. The new plan backed off from the commitment to early self-government. Because of the trouble that might be expected from squatters who were clamoring for free land, the Northwest Ordinance of 1787 required a period of colonial tutelage. At first the territory fell subject to a governor, a secretary, and three judges, all chosen by Congress. When any territory in the Northwest region had 5,000 free male adults, it could choose an assembly, and Congress would name a governing council from names proposed by the assembly. The governor would have a veto and so would Congress.

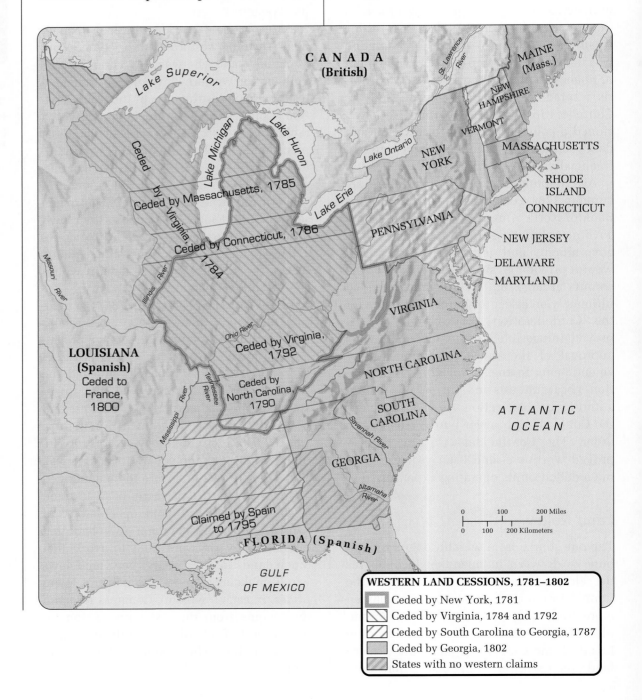

WESTERN LAND CESSIONS, 1781–1802

- ☐ Ceded by New York, 1781
- ☒ Ceded by Virginia, 1784 and 1792
- ▨ Ceded by South Carolina to Georgia, 1787
- ▦ Ceded by Georgia, 1802
- ▨ States with no western claims

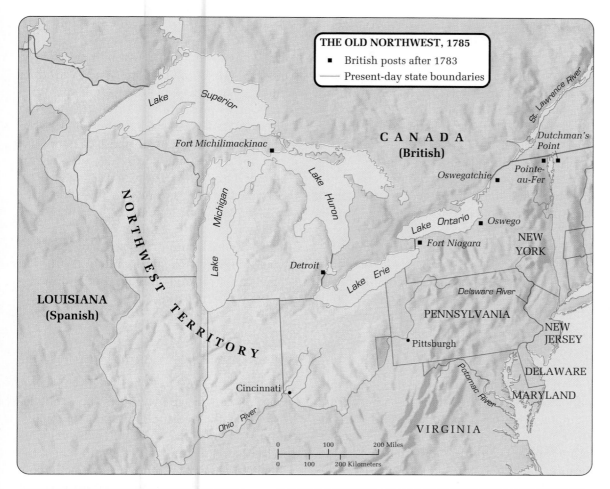

THE OLD NORTHWEST, 1785

- ■ British posts after 1783
- —— Present-day state boundaries

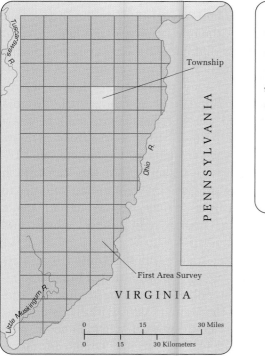

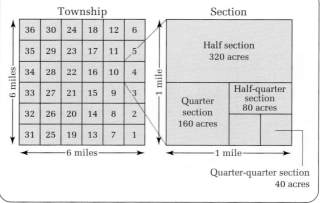

The resemblance of these territorial governments to the old royal colonies is clear, but there were two significant differences. For one, the Ordinance anticipated statehood when any territory's population reached 60,000. At that point, a convention could be called to draft a state constitution and to apply to Congress for statehood. For another, it included a bill of rights that guaranteed religious freedom, proportional representation, trial by jury, habeas corpus, and the application of common law. Finally, the Northwest Ordinance excluded slavery permanently from the Northwest. This proved a fateful decision. As the progress of emancipation in the existing states gradually freed all slaves above the Mason-Dixon line, the Ohio River boundary of the Old Northwest extended the line between freedom and slavery all the way to the Mississippi.

The lands south of the Ohio River followed a different process of development. Title to the western lands remained with Georgia, North Carolina, and Virginia for the time being, but settlement proceeded at a far more rapid pace during and after the Revolution, despite the Indians' fierce resentment. Substantial population centers grew up in Kentucky and Tennessee.

During the mid-1780s, the Iroquois were forced to cede land in western New York and Pennsylvania, and the Cherokees forced to give up all claims in South Carolina, much of western North Carolina, and large portions of present-day Kentucky and Tennessee. At the same time, the major Ohio tribes lost their claim to most of Ohio, except for a segment bordering the western part of Lake Erie. The Creeks, pressed by Georgia to cede portions of their lands in 1784–1785, went to war in the summer of 1786 with covert aid from Spanish Florida. When Spanish support lapsed, however, the Creek chief struck a bargain in 1791 that gave the Creeks favorable trade arrangements with the United States but did not restore the lost lands.

Trade and the Economy

In its economic life, as in planning westward expansion, the young nation dealt vigorously with the difficult wartime problems. Congress had little to do with achievements in the economy, but neither could it bear the blame for an acute economic contraction between 1770 and 1790, the result primarily of the war and separation from the British Empire. Although farmers enmeshed in local markets maintained their livelihood during the Revolutionary era, commercial agriculture dependent upon trade with foreign markets suffered a severe downturn. Virginia suffered a loss of slave labor, much of it carried off by the British. Chesapeake planters also lost their lucrative foreign markets. Tobacco was especially hard hit. The British decision to close its West Indian colonies to American trade devastated what had been a thriving commerce in timber, wheat, and other foodstuffs.

British trade with the United States resumed after 1783. American ships were allowed to deliver American products and return to the United States with British goods, but they could not carry British goods anywhere else. The pent-up demand for famil-

Merchants' Counting House. Americans involved in overseas trade, such as the merchants depicted here, were sharply affected by the dislocations of war.

iar goods created a vigorous market in America for imports, fueled by British credits and the hard money that had come into the new nation from foreign aid, the expenditures of foreign armies, and wartime trade and privateering. The result was a quick cycle of postwar boom and bust, a buying spree followed by a money shortage and economic troubles that lasted several years.

In colonial days the chronic trade deficit with Britain had been offset by the influx of coins from trade with the West Indies. Now American ships found themselves legally excluded from the British West Indies. But the islands still demanded wheat, fish, lumber, and other products from the mainland, and American shippers had not lost their talent for smuggling. By 1787, Americans were also trading with the Dutch, Swedes, Prussians, Moroccans, and Chinese, and American seaports were flourishing more than ever. By 1790, American commerce and exports had far outrun the trade of the colonies. American merchants had more ships than before the war. Farm exports were twice what they had been. Although most of the exports were the products of American forests, fields, and fisheries, during and after the war more workers had turned to small-scale manufacturing—shoes, textiles, soap—mainly for domestic markets.

Diplomacy

The achievements of the flourishing young nation are more visible in hindsight than they were at the time. Until 1787, the shortcomings and failures of the Confederation government remained far more apparent—and the advocates of a stronger central government were extremely vocal on the subject. In diplomacy, there remained the nagging problems of relations with Great Britain and Spain, both of which kept military posts on American soil and conspired with Indians and white settlers in the West. The British, despite the peace treaty of 1783, held on to a string of forts along the Canadian border. From these they kept a hand in the fur trade and a degree of influence with the Indian tribes.

Another major irritant was the confiscation of Loyalist property. The peace treaty had obligated Congress to stop confiscations, to guarantee immunity to Loyalists for twelve months during which they could return and wind up their affairs, and to recommend that the states return confiscated property. Persecutions, even lynchings, of Loyalists still occurred until after the end of the war. Some Loyalists returned unmolested, however, and once again took up their lives in their former homes. By the end of 1787, moreover, all the states had rescinded laws discriminating against former Tories.

With Spain, the chief issues were the southern boundary and the right to navigate the Mississippi. According to the preliminary treaty with Britain, the United States claimed as its traditional boundary a line running eastward from the mouth of the Yazoo River. The American treaty with Britain had also specified the right to navigate the Mississippi River to its mouth, but the river was entirely within Spanish Louisiana in its lower reaches. The right to navigation assumed importance because of the growing settlements in Kentucky and Tennessee, but in 1784 Louisiana's Spanish governor closed the river to American commerce. He also began to intrigue with the Creeks, Choctaws, Chickasaws, and other Indians of the Southwest against the American settlers and with the settlers themselves against the United States. The issue of American access to the lower Mississippi remained unsettled for nearly another decade.

The Confederation's Problems

Of greatest concern to most Americans were protection for infant American industries and the currency shortage. Mechanics (skilled workers who made, used, or repaired tools and machines) and artisans (skilled workers who made products) were developing exports ranging from crude iron nails to the fine silver bowls of Paul Revere. They were frustrated by British policies excluding them from British markets, and in retaliation they sought from the states tariffs (taxes on imports) on foreign goods that competed with theirs. The country would be on its way to economic independence, they argued, if only the money that flowed into the country were invested in domestic manufactures instead of being paid out for foreign goods. Nearly all the states gave some preference to American goods, but the lack of consistency in their laws put them at cross purposes, and so urban mechanics along with merchants were drawn into the movement demanding a stronger central government in the interest of uniform regulation of trade.

The shortage of cash and other economic difficulties generated demands for paper currency as legal tender, for postponement of tax and debt payments, and for laws to "stay" the foreclosure of mortgages. Farmers who had profited during the war found themselves squeezed by depressed crop prices and mounting debts while merchants

sorted out and opened up new trade routes. Creditors demanded hard money, but it was in short supply—and paper money was both scarce and virtually worthless after the depreciation of the Continental currency. The result was an outcry among debtor groups for relief, and around 1785 the demand for new paper money became the most divisive issue in state politics. In 1785–1786 seven states (Pennsylvania, New York, New Jersey, South Carolina, Rhode Island, Georgia, and North Carolina) issued paper money. In spite of the cries of calamity at the time, the money served positively as a means of credit to hard-pressed farmers through state loans on farm mortgages. It was also used to fund state debts and to pay off the claims of veterans.

Shays's Rebellion

Many Americans—especially bankers and merchants—hated such inflationary policies. Developments in Massachusetts provided the final proof (some said) that the country was poised on the brink of anarchy: Shays's Rebellion. After 1780, Massachusetts had remained in the grip of a rigidly conservative regime. Ever higher poll and land taxes were levied to pay off a large war debt, held mainly by wealthy creditors in Boston. The taxes fell most heavily upon beleaguered farmers and the working poor in general.

When the legislature adjourned in 1786 without providing either paper money or any other relief from taxes and debts, three western counties erupted into spontaneous revolt. Armed bands closed the courts and prevented foreclosures, and a ragtag "army" of some 1,200 disgruntled farmers led by Captain Daniel Shays, a destitute farmer and "brave and good" war veteran, advanced upon the federal arsenal at Springfield in 1787. Shays and his followers sought a more flexible monetary policy, laws allowing them to use corn and wheat as money, and the right to postpone paying taxes until the depression lifted.

Led by Daniel Shays, a band of disgruntled farmers attacked the federal arsenal at Springfield, Massachusetts, in January 1787, but were repulsed by the militia.

A small militia force scattered Shays's men with a single volley that left four dead. The rebels nevertheless had a victory of sorts. The new state legislature included members sympathetic to the agricultural crisis. They omitted direct taxes the following year, lowered court fees, and exempted clothing, household goods, and tools from the debt process. But a more important consequence was the impetus the rebellion gave to conservatism and nationalism.

Rumors, at times deliberately inflated, greatly exaggerated the extent of Shays's rebellion. The uprising seemed to provide an ominous example of possible greater turmoil, and panic set in among the republic's elite. New York's Gouverneur Morris was typically blunt: "The mob begin to think and reason. Poor reptiles! They bask in the sun and ere noon they will bite, depend upon it. The gentry begin to fear this."

Calls for a Stronger Government

Shays's Rebellion convinced many political leaders that the Articles of Confederation were incapable of providing an effective basis for the new republican government. Self-interest frequently led bankers, merchants, and mechanics to promote a stronger central government. At the same time, many public-spirited men saw it as the only alternative to anarchy. Gradually people were losing the ingrained fear of central authority as they saw evidence that tyranny might come from other quarters, including the common people themselves.

By the mid-1780s, in fact, several prominent political spokesmen had become convinced that the new state governments were being run by uneducated entrepreneurs pursuing selfish economic and petty political interests. Men of humble origins and parochial points of view were allegedly displacing the "wise and virtuous" from seats of power. Such inexperienced and frequently uncouth lawmakers were passing an avalanche of legislation merely to serve particular interest groups and constituents rather than the general welfare. They were printing excessive amounts of paper money and passing "stay" laws (laws that granted stays, or postponements of debt payments) preventing judicial action against debtors.

Such developments led many of the Revolutionary leaders to revise their assessment of American character. "We have, probably," concluded George Washington in 1786, "had too good an opinion of human nature in forming our confederation." The following year James Madison reported to Jefferson that America was displaying "symptoms . . . truly alarming, which have tainted the faith of most orthodox republicans." People were stretching the meaning of liberty far beyond what he and others had envisioned. He found a "spirit of *locality*" rampant in the state legislatures that was destroying the "aggregate interests of the community." Even worse, he saw people taking the law and other people's property into their own hands. Such developments led Madison and others to revise their assumptions about the degree of republican virtue in the American people. At any given time, they decided, only a distinct minority could be relied upon to set aside their private interests in favor of the common good. Madison and these so-called Federalists concluded that the new republic must now depend for its success on the constant virtue of the few rather than the public-spiritedness of the many. For these reasons and others, nationalists demanded revisions to the Articles of Confederation.

Adopting the Constitution

After stalling for several months, Congress, in 1787, passed a resolution endorsing a convention "for the sole and express purpose of revising the Articles of Confederation." By then five states had already named

James Madison was only thirty-six when he assumed a major role in the drafting of the Constitution. This miniature is by Charles Willson Peale (c. 1783).

delegates; before the meeting, six more states had acted. Rhode Island kept aloof throughout, leading critics to label it "Rogue Island."

The Constitutional Convention

Twenty-nine delegates began work in Philadelphia on May 25. Altogether seventy-three men were elected by the state legislatures, fifty-five attended at one time or another, and after four months, thirty-nine signed the Constitution they had drafted.

The document's durability and flexibility testify to the remarkable quality of the men who made it. The delegates were surprisingly young—forty-two was the average age. Only two were small farmers. Most were planters, merchants, lawyers, judges, bankers—many of them widely read in history, law, and political philosophy, yet at the same time practical men of experience, tested in the fires of the Revolution. Twenty-one had fought in the conflict, seven had been state governors, most of them had served in the Continental Congress, and eight had signed the Declaration of Independence.

The delegates spent four sweltering months fighting flies, the humidity, and each other. They worked with a sense of urgency, five to six hours a day, six days a week, hammering out the compromises embedded in the Constitution. On certain fundamentals they generally agreed: that government derived its just powers from the consent of the people, but that society must be protected from the tyranny of the majority; that the people at large must have a voice in their government, but that checks and balances must be provided to keep any one group from dominating; that a stronger central authority was essential, but that all power was subject to abuse. Even the best of people were naturally selfish, they believed, and therefore government could not be founded upon a trust in goodwill and virtue. Yet by carefully checking power

with countervailing power, the Founding Fathers hoped to devise institutions that could somehow constrain individual sinfulness and channel individual self-interest on behalf of the public good.

The Virginia and New Jersey Plans

James Madison was the key figure at the convention. He arrived in Philadelphia with trunks of books and a head full of ideas, and he set about drafting the proposals that came to be called the "Virginia Plan," presented on May 29. This plan called for separate legislative, executive, and judicial branches, and a truly national government whose laws would be binding upon individual citizens as well as upon states. Congress would be divided into two houses, a lower house to be chosen by popular vote and an upper house to be chosen by the lower house from nominees of the state legislatures. Congress could disallow state laws under the plan and would itself define the extent of its and the states' authority.

On June 15 William Paterson submitted the "New Jersey Plan," which kept the existing equal representation of states in a unicameral Congress but gave the Congress power to levy taxes, regulate commerce, and name a plural executive (with no veto) and a Supreme Court. The different plans presented the convention with two major issues: whether to amend the Articles of Confederation or draft an entirely new document, and whether to apportion congressional representation by population or by states.

On the first point, the Convention voted to work toward a national government as envisioned by the Virginians. Experience had persuaded the delegates that an effective central government, as distinguished from a confederation, needed the power to levy taxes, to regulate commerce, to raise an army and navy, and to make laws binding upon individual citizens. The lessons of the

1780s suggested to them, moreover, that in the interest of order and uniformity the states must be denied certain powers: to issue money, to void contracts, to make treaties or wage war, and to levy tariffs.

But other issues provoked furious disagreements. The first clash in the Convention involved the issue of representation, and it was solved by the "Great Compromise," sometimes called the "Connecticut Compromise," offered by Roger Sherman. In the House of Representatives, apportionment would be by population, which pleased the more populous states; in the Senate, there would be equal representation of each state (although votes would be by individuals and not by states), which protected state power.

An equally contentious struggle ensued between northern and southern delegates over slavery, an omen of future sectional controversies. Few if any of the framers even considered the possibility of abolishing slavery in those states—mostly southern—where it was still legal. The interest of southern delegates, with slaves so numerous in their states, dictated that slaves be counted as part of the population in determining the number of representatives. Northerners were willing to have slaves counted in deciding each state's share of direct taxes but not for purposes of representation. The delegates, with little dissent, agreed in a compromise to count three-fifths of the slaves as a basis for apportioning both representatives and direct taxes.

A more sensitive issue involved an effort to prevent the new central government from stopping the transatlantic slave trade. Eventually a compromise emerged whereby the delegates established a time limit after which the slave trade would be prohibited. Congress could not prohibit the traffic until 1808, but it could levy a tax of $10 a head on all slaves imported. In drafting both provisions, a sense of delicacy—and hypocrisy—dictated the use of euphemisms. The Constitution thus spoke of "free persons" and "all other persons," of persons "held to Service of Labor." The odious word "slavery" did not appear in the Constitution until the Thirteenth Amendment (1865) abolished the "peculiar institution" by name.

If the delegates found the slavery issue distracting, they considered irrelevant any discussion of the legal or political role of women under the new Constitution. There was never any formal discussion of women's rights at the Convention. The new nationalism still defined politics and government as outside the realm of female endeavor.

The Separation of Powers

Some delegates displayed a thumping disdain for any democratizing of the political system. Alexander Hamilton called the people "a great beast," and Elbridge Gerry asserted that most of the nation's problems "flow from an excess of democracy." These elitist views were incorporated into the Constitution's mixed legislative system, which allowed direct popular choice of just one chamber of the Congress. The lower house was designed to be closest to the voters, who elected it every two years. The House of Representatives would be, according to Virginia's George Mason, "the grand repository of the democratic principle of the Government." Its members should "sympathize with their constituents, should think as they think, and feel as they feel; and for these purposes should even be residents among them." The upper house, or Senate, was elected by state legislatures rather than directly by the voters. Staggered six-year terms prevented the choice of a majority in any given year, and thereby further isolated senators from the passing fancies of public passion.

The decision that a single person be made the chief executive caused the delegates "considerable pause," according to Madison. George Mason protested that this would create a "fetus of monarchy." Indeed, although subject to election every four years, the

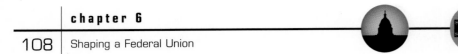

Signing the Constitution, September 17, 1787. Thomas Pritchard Rossiter's painting shows George Washington presiding over what Thomas Jefferson called "an assembly of demigods."

chief executive would wield powers that would exceed those of the British king. This was the sharpest departure from the recent experience in state government, in which the office of governor had commonly been diluted because of the memory of struggles with the colonial executives. The president could veto acts of Congress, subject to being overridden by a two-thirds vote in each house, was commander-in-chief of the armed forces, and was responsible for the execution of the laws. The chief executive could make treaties with the advice and consent of two-thirds of the Senate and appoint diplomats, judges, and other officers with the consent of a Senate majority.

But the president's powers were limited in certain key areas. The chief executive could neither declare war nor make peace; those powers were reserved for Congress. Unlike the British king, moreover, the president could be removed. The House could impeach (indict) the chief executive—and other civil officers—on charges of treason, bribery, or "other high crimes and misde-

meanors"; the president could then be removed by the Senate with a two-thirds vote to convict.

The third branch of government, the judiciary, caused surprisingly little debate. Both the Virginia and New Jersey Plans had called for a Supreme Court, which the Constitution established, providing specifically for a chief justice of the United States and leaving up to Congress the number of other justices. Article VI declared the federal constitution, federal laws, and treaties to be the "supreme law of the land," state laws or constitutions to the contrary notwithstanding.

While the Constitution extended vast new powers to the national government, the delegates' mistrust of unchecked power is apparent in repeated examples of countervailing forces: the separation of the three branches of government, the president's veto, the congressional power of impeachment and removal, the Senate's power over treaties and appointments, the courts' implied right of judicial review. In addition,

Adopting the Constitution | 109

the new form of government specifically forbade Congress to pass ex post facto laws (laws adopted after the fact to make past deeds criminal). It also reserved to the states large areas of sovereignty—a reservation soon made explicit by the Tenth Amendment. By dividing sovereignty between the people and the government, the framers of the Constitution provided a distinctive contribution to political theory. That is, by vesting ultimate authority in the people, they divided sovereignty *within* the government. This constituted a dramatic break with the colonial tradition. The British had always insisted that the sovereignty of the king-in-Parliament was indivisible.

The Fight for Ratification

The final article of the Constitution provided that it would become effective upon ratification by nine states (not quite the three-fourths majority required for amendment). The Congress submitted the Convention's work to the states on September 28, 1787. In the ensuing political debate, advocates of the new Constitution, who might properly have been called Nationalists because they preferred a strong central government, assumed the more reassuring name of Federalists. Opponents, who favored a more decentralized federal system, became Antifederalists.

The Federalists were not only better prepared but better organized, and on the whole they represented the more articulate elements in the community. The Federalists were usually clustered in or near cities and tended to be more cosmopolitan, urbane, and well educated. Antifederalists tended to be small farmers and frontiersmen who saw little to gain from the promotion of interstate commerce and much to lose from prohibitions on paper money and "stay" laws. Many of them also feared that an expansive land policy was likely to favor speculators.

Historians have long debated what motivated the advocates of the new Constitution. Some, like Charles A. Beard, have argued that the Philadelphia Convention was made up of men who held large amounts of depreciated government securities and otherwise stood to gain from the power and stability of the new central government. But most of the delegates had no compelling economic interests at stake. Many prominent nationalists had no western lands or bonds. Some opponents of the Constitution, on the contrary, held large blocks of bonds and securities. Economic interests certainly figured in the process of constitution-making, but they functioned in a complex interplay of state, sectional, group, and individual interests that turned largely on how well people had fared under the Confederation.

The Federalist

Among the supreme legacies of the debate over the Constitution was a collection of essays called *The Federalist,* originally published in New York newspapers between 1787 and 1788. Initiated by Alexander Hamilton, the eighty-five articles published under the name "Publius" included about thirty by James Madison, nearly fifty by Hamilton, and five by John Jay. Written in support of ratification, the essays defended the principle of a supreme national authority but at the same time sought to reassure doubters that there was little reason to fear tyranny by the new government.

In perhaps the most famous single essay, Number Ten, Madison argued that the country's very size and diversity would make it impossible for any single faction to form a majority that could dominate the government. This contradicted prevailing notions of republican government. Republics, the conventional wisdom of the times insisted, could work only in small, homogeneous countries like Switzerland and the Netherlands. In larger countries, republican government would descend into anarchy and tyranny through the influence of factions. Quite the contrary, Madison argued. A republic with a balanced federal government could survive in a large and diverse country better than in a smaller country. "Extend the sphere," he wrote, "and you take in a greater variety of parties and interests; you make it less probable that a majority of the whole will have a common motive to invade the rights of other citizens."

The Federalists insisted that the new union would contribute to prosperity, in part to link their movement with the economic recovery already under way. The Antifederalists, however, highlighted the dangers of power. They noted the absence in the proposed Constitution of a bill of rights protecting individuals and states, and they found the ratification process highly irregular, which it was—indeed, illegal under the Articles of Confederation. The two groups disagreed, however, more over means than ends. Both sides for the most part agreed that a stronger national authority was needed, and that it required an independent income to function properly. Both were convinced that the people must erect safeguards against tyranny, even the tyranny of the majority. Once the new government had become an accomplished fact, few diehards were left who wanted to undo the work of the Philadelphia Convention.

The Decision of the States

Ratification of the new federal Constitution gained momentum throughout 1787, and New Hampshire was the ninth to ratify, on June 21, 1788. The Confederation Congress then began to draft plans for an orderly transfer of power. On September 13, 1788, it selected New York City as the seat of the new government and fixed the date for elections. On October 10, 1788, the Confederation Congress transacted its last business and passed into history. "Our constitution is in actual operation," the elderly Ben Franklin wrote to a friend; "everything appears to promise that it will last; but in this world nothing is certain but death and taxes." George Washington was even more uncertain about the future under the new plan of government. He had told a fellow delegate as the convention adjourned: "I do not expect the Constitution to last for more than twenty years."

"A More Perfect Union"

The Constitution has lasted much longer, of course, and in the process it has provided a model of republican government whose features have been repeatedly borrowed by other nations through the years. Yet what makes the American Constitution so distinctive is not its specific provisions but its remarkable harmony with the particular "genius of the people" it governs. The Constitution has been neither a static abstraction nor a "machine that would go of itself," as the poet James Russell Lowell would later assert. Instead it has provided a flexible system of government that presidents, legislators, judges, and the people have modified to accord with a fallible human nature and changing social, economic, and political circumstances. In this sense, the Founding Fathers not only created "a more perfect Union" in 1787; they engineered a form of government whose resilience has enabled later generations to continue to perfect their republican experiment. But the framers of the Constitution failed in one significant respect. In skirting the issue of slavery so as to cement the new union, they unknowingly allowed tensions over what southerners came to call their "peculiar institution" to reach the point at which there would be no political solution—only civil war.

The Federalists:
Washington and Adams

This chapter focuses on

- The early operation of the new government.

- Alexander Hamilton's Federalist program.

- The beginnings of the first party system (Federalists and Republicans).

- The elements of Federalist foreign policy.

111

THE *ESSENTIAL AMERICA* ON-LINE TUTOR

www.wwnorton.com/eamerica/ch7

- **Topic: Pierre L'Enfant and the federal city**
  www.wwnorton.com/eamerica/ch7/topic.htm

  In 1791 French architect Pierre L'Enfant drew up plans for the nation's new capitol—plans that included fifteen major public squares connected by broad, tree-lined avenues. Explore L'Enfant's design of Washington, D.C., using his drawings, historical analyses, personal correspondence, and maps. How did L'Enfant's design differ from the more traditional gridiron pattern used elsewhere in the young nation?

- **Chapter review: On-line quiz and chapter summary**
  www.wwnorton.com/eamerica/ch7/review.htm

- **Chapter resources: Multimedia index**
  www.wwnorton.com/eamerica/ch7/media.htm

The adoption of the new Constitution set in motion the creation of a new central government to deal more effectively with the problems of the vast new nation. The election of the first president, the writing of a bill of rights, and numerous domestic and foreign crises faced the fledgling nation.

A New Nation

The framers of the Constitution sought to create a new federal government capable of administering a rapidly expanding territory and population. In 1789 the United States and the western territories covered an area from the Atlantic Ocean to the Mississippi River and included almost 4 million people. The United States was predominantly a rural society. Eighty percent of households were involved in agricultural production. Only a few cities had more than 5,000 people. The first national census, taken in 1790, reported that there were 750,000 African Americans, almost one-fifth of the population. Most of them lived in the five southernmost states. Less than 10 percent of blacks lived outside the South. Most African Americans, of course, were slaves, but there were many free blacks as a result of the Revolutionary turmoil. In fact, the proportion of free blacks to slaves was never higher than in 1790.

The 1790 census did not include the many Indians still living east of the Mississippi River. Most Americans still viewed the Native Americans as those peoples whom the Declaration of Independence dismissed as "merciless Indian savages." It is estimated that there were over eighty tribes numbering perhaps as many as 150,000 persons in 1790. In the South, the five most powerful tribes—the Cherokees, Chickasaws, Choctaws, Creeks, and Seminoles—numbered between 50,000 and 100,000. They steadfastly refused to recognize American authority and used Spanish-supplied weapons to thwart white settlement.

Only about 125,000 whites and blacks lived west of the Appalachian Mountains in 1790. But that was soon to change. The great theme of nineteenth-century American history would be the ceaseless stream of migrants flowing westward from the Atlantic seaboard. By foot, horse, boat, and wagon, pioneers and adventurers headed west. Rapid population growth, cheap land, and new economic opportunities fueled western development. Although immigrants contributed significantly to the rising numbers, the extraordinary growth rate resulted primarily from natural increase. The average white woman gave birth to eight children, and the white population doubled approximately once every twenty-two years. This made for a very young population on average. In 1790 almost half of all white Americans were under sixteen.

A New Government

The men who drafted the Constitution knew that many questions were left unanswered, and they feared that putting the new form of government into practice would pose unexpected challenges. The new Congress of the United States opened with a whimper rather than a bang. On March 4, 1789, the appointed date of its first session in bustling New York City, only eight senators and thirteen representatives took their seats. A month passed before both chambers gathered a quorum. Only then could the temporary presiding officer of the Senate count the ballots and certify the foregone conclusion that George Washington, with sixty-nine votes, was the unanimous choice of the electoral college for president. John Adams, with thirty-four votes, the second-highest number, became vice-president.

Washington was a reluctant president. He greeted the news with "a heart filled with distress," yet he felt compelled to serve because he had been "summoned by my country." A self-made man with little formal education, Washington had a remarkable capacity for moderation and mediation that helped keep the infant republic from disintegrating.

Governmental Structure

Washington inherited but the shadow of a federal government: a foreign office with John Jay at its head and two clerks; a Treasury Board with little or no treasury; a 300-pound secretary of war, Henry Knox, with a lightweight army of 672 officers and men, and no navy at all; a heavy federal debt and almost no federal revenue.

During the summer of 1789, Congress created executive departments corresponding in each case to those already formed under the Confederation. To head the Department of State, Washington named Thomas Jefferson, recently back from his mission to France. Leadership of the Department of the Treasury went to Washington's wartime aide Alexander Hamilton, who had since become a prominent lawyer in New York. Tall, graceful Edmund Randolph, former governor of Virginia and owner of a plantation worked by 200 slaves, assumed the new position of attorney-general.

In 1789 Washington named New Yorker John Jay as the first chief justice of the Supreme Court, and he served until 1795. Born in New York City in 1745, Jay graduated from King's College (now Columbia University). His distinction as a lawyer led New York to send him as its representative to the First and Second Continental Congresses. After serving as president of the Continental Congress in 1779, Jay became the American minister in Spain. While in Europe, he helped John Adams and Benjamin Franklin negotiate the Treaty of Paris in 1783. After the Revolution, Jay served as secretary of foreign affairs. He then joined Madison and Hamilton as co-author of *The Federalist* and became one of the most effective champions of the Constitution.

The Bill of Rights

In the new House of Representatives, James Madison made a bill of rights one of the first items of business. The lack of protection for individual rights had been one of the Antifederalists' major objections to the Constitution. During the ratification debate, Madison and other Federalists had argued that the Constitution needed no enumeration of specific "rights" because, as Madison said, "everything not granted is reserved." Madison and other Federalists also worried that specifying such rights might imply the existence of a parallel set of powers never meant to be delegated to the central government.

But public anxiety about individual rights persisted, so in May 1789 Madison reluctantly drew the first eight amendments from the Virginia Declaration of Rights, which George Mason had written in 1776. These provided safeguards for certain fundamental individual rights: freedom of religion, press, speech, and assembly; the right to keep and bear firearms; the right to refuse to house soldiers in private homes; protection from unreasonable searches and seizures; the right to refuse to testify against oneself; the right to a speedy public trial before an impartial jury and to have legal counsel present; and protection against cruel and unusual punishment. The states voted separately on each proposed amendment, and the Bill of Rights became effective December 15, 1791.

Hamilton's Vision of America

Revenue was the new federal government's most critical need, and Congress quickly enacted a tariff on imports intended to raise revenue and protect America's new manufacturers from foreign competition. Yet tariffs resulted in higher prices on imported goods bought by Americans, most of whom were tied to the farm economy. This raised a basic and perennial question: should these rural consumers be forced to subsidize the nation's infant manufacturing sector?

The import tariff launched the effort to get the country on a sound financial basis. In finance, with all its broad implications for policy in general, it was thirty-four-year-old Alexander Hamilton who seized the initiative. The first secretary of the treasury was the protégé of the president. Born out of wedlock on a Caribbean island, Hamilton found his way at seventeen to New York, attended King's College, and entered the Revolutionary army, where he became a favorite of George Washington. After the Revolution, he studied law, established a legal practice in New York, and served as collector of revenues and member of the Confederation Congress. An early convert to nationalism, he played a crucial part in promoting the Constitutional Convention and defending its work in *The Federalist*.

The new government needed all of Hamilton's ambition and brilliance. In a series of classic reports submitted to Congress in 1790 and 1791, he outlined his program for government finances and the economic development of the United States.

Establishing the Public Credit

The First Report on the Public Credit made two key recommendations: first, funding of the federal debt at face value, which meant that those citizens holding government securities could exchange them for new interest-bearing bonds of the same face value; and second, the federal government's assumption of state debts from the Revolution to the amount of $21 million. The funding scheme was controversial because many farmers and soldiers in need of immediate money had sold their securities for a fraction of their value to speculators. Spokesmen for these Americans argued that they should be reimbursed for their losses; otherwise, the speculators would gain a windfall. Hamilton

sternly resisted. The speculators, he argued, had "paid what the commodity was worth in the market, and took the risks."

Payment of the national debt, Hamilton felt, would be not only a point of national honor and sound finance, ensuring the country's credit for the future; it would also be an occasion to assert a federal taxing power and thus instill respect for the authority of the national government. It was on this point, however, that Madison, who had been Hamilton's close ally in the movement for a stronger government, broke with him. Madison did not question that the debt should be paid, but he was troubled that speculators and "stock-jobbers" would become the chief beneficiaries. Also disturbing to the Virginian was that northerners held most of the debt. Madison's opposition touched off a vigorous debate that deadlocked the whole question of debt funding and assumption through much of 1790.

The stalemate finally ended when Hamilton, Jefferson, and Madison reached an understanding. In return for northern votes in favor of locating the permanent national capital on the Potomac River on the Virginia border, Madison pledged to seek enough southern votes to pass the debt assumption bill, with the further arrangement that those states with smaller debts would get in effect outright grants from the federal government to equalize the difference. These arrangements secured enough votes to carry Hamilton's funding and assumption plans. The national capital would be moved from New York to Philadelphia for ten years, after which it would be located in a new federal city on the Potomac River, the site to be chosen by the president. In August 1790 Congress finally passed the legislation for Hamilton's plan.

A National Bank

Through this vast program of funding and assumption, Hamilton had called up from nowhere, as if by magic, a great sum of cap-

Alexander Hamilton, secretary of the treasury from 1789 to 1795.

ital for the new federal government. Having established the public credit, Hamilton moved on to a related measure essential to his vision of national greatness. He called for a national bank, which by issuance of bank notes (paper money) might provide a uniform currency as well as a source of capital for the developing economy. Government bonds held by the bank would back up the currency. The national bank, chartered by Congress, would remain under governmental surveillance, but private investors would supply four-fifths of the $10 million capital and name twenty of the twenty-five directors; the government would purchase the other fifth of the capital and name five directors. Government bonds would be received in payment for three-fourths of the stock in the bank, and the other fourth would be payable in gold and silver.

Once again Madison rose to lead the opposition, arguing that he could find no basis in the Constitution for such a bank. That was enough to raise in President Washington's mind serious doubts as to the constitutionality of the measure, which Congress passed over Madison's objections. Before signing the bill into law, therefore, the president sought the advice of his cabinet and found an equal division of opinion. This resulted in the first great debate on constitutional interpretation. Should there be a strict or a broad construction of the document? Were the powers of Congress only those explicitly stated in the Constitution or were others implied? The argument turned chiefly on Article I, Section 8, which authorized Congress to "make all laws which shall be necessary and proper for carrying into execution the foregoing Powers."

Such language left room for disagreement and led to a confrontation between Jefferson and Hamilton. Jefferson pointed to the Tenth Amendment, which reserved to the states and the people powers not delegated to Congress. A bank might be a convenient aid to Congress in collecting taxes and regu-

lating the currency, but it was not, as Article I, Section 8, specified, *necessary*. Hamilton insisted that the power to charter corporations was included in the sovereignty of any government, whether or not expressly stated. The president accepted Hamilton's argument and signed the bill. By doing so, in Jefferson's words, he opened up "a boundless field of power," which in coming years would lead to a further broadening of implied powers with the approval of the Supreme Court.

Encouraging Manufactures

Hamilton's imagination and his ambitions for the new country were not yet exhausted. At the end of 1790, he submitted a Second Report on Public Credit, which included a proposal for an excise tax on alcoholic beverages to aid in raising revenue to cover the nation's debts. Six weeks later, the secretary proposed a national mint, which was established in 1792. And finally, on December 5, 1791, as the culmination of his basic reports, in his Report on Manufactures he proposed an extensive program of government aid to the development of manufacturing enterprises.

In the Report on Manufactures, Hamilton argued for the active encouragement of manufacturing to provide productive uses for the new capital he had created by his funding, assumption, and banking schemes. To secure his ends, Hamilton advocated protective tariffs, "which in some cases might be put so high as to keep out foreign products altogether; restraints on the export of raw materials; bounties and premiums to encourage certain industries; inducements to inventions and discoveries; and finally, the encouragement of internal improvements in transportation, the development of roads, canals, and navigable streams."

Some of Hamilton's tariff proposals were enacted in 1792. Otherwise the program was filed away—but not forgotten. It provided an arsenal of arguments for the manufacturing sector in years to come. Hamilton denied that his scheme favored the northern states. If, as seemed likely, the northern and middle states should become the chief sites for manufacturing, he claimed, they would create robust markets for agricultural products, some of which the southern states were peculiarly qualified to produce. The nation as a whole would benefit, he argued, as commerce between North and South increased, supplanting the trade across the Atlantic.

Hamilton's Achievement

Largely because of the skillful Hamilton, the Treasury Department began retiring the Revolutionary War debt, enhanced the value of a "Continental" dollar, secured the government's credit, and attracted foreign investment capital. Prosperity, so elusive in the 1780s, began to flourish once again during the 1790s, although President Washington cautioned against attributing "to the Government what is due only to the goodness of Providence."

Hamilton professed a truly nationalist outlook, and he focused his energies on the rising power of commercial capitalism. Tying the government closely to the rich and the well-born, Hamilton believed, promoted the government's financial stability and guarded the public order against the potential turbulence that had always haunted him.

But many Americans then and since have interpreted such views as elitist and self-serving. To be sure, Hamilton never understood the people of the small villages and farms, the people of the frontier. They were foreign to his world, despite his own humble beginnings. And they, along with the planters of the South, would be at best only indirect beneficiaries of his programs. There were, in short, vast numbers of people who saw little gain from the Hamiltonian program and thus were drawn into opposition.

Indeed, Jefferson claimed that he and Hamilton were "pitted against each other every day in the cabinet like two fighting-cocks."

The Republican Alternative

The split over the Hamiltonian program planted the seeds of the first national political parties. Hamilton emerged as the embodiment of the party known as the Federalists; Madison and Jefferson assumed the leadership of those who took the name Republicans and thereby implied that the Federalists really aimed at a monarchy. Yet parties were slow in developing, or at least in being acknowledged as legitimate. All the political philosophers of the age deplored the spirit of party, or faction.

Neither side in the disagreement over national policy deliberately set out to create parties. But there were important differences of both philosophy and self-interest that simply would not dissolve, and the strongly partisan newspapers of the day ensured that such differences were repeatedly accented for the reading public.

The crux of the debate centered on the relative power of the federal government and the states. At the outset, Madison assumed leadership of Hamilton's opponents in the Congress, and he argued that Hamilton was trampling upon states' rights in forging a consolidated central government. After the compromise on the funding of state debts, Jefferson joined Madison in ever more resolute opposition to Hamilton's policies. They opposed his move to place an excise tax on whiskey, which would especially burden the trans-Appalachian farmers, whose grain was the source of the whiskey; and they opposed his proposal for a national bank and his Report on Manufactures. As these differences developed, the personal hostility between Jefferson and

Thomas Jefferson.

Hamilton festered, much to the distress of President Washington. In the process, Jefferson, the secretary of state, emerged as the leader of the opposition to Hamilton's policies within the administration, while Madison continued to direct the opposition in Congress.

Jefferson's Agrarian View

Thomas Jefferson, twelve years Hamilton's senior, was in most respects his opposite. Displaying little of Hamilton's ordered intensity, Jefferson instead conveyed an aristocratic carelessness and a breadth of cultivated interests that ranged perhaps more widely in science, the arts, and the humanities than those of any contemporary, even Franklin. Jefferson read or spoke seven languages. He was an architect of some distinction (Monticello, the Virginia Capitol, and the University of Virginia are monuments to his talent), a man who understood mathematics and engineering, an inventor, an agronomist.

Philosophically, Hamilton and Jefferson had contrasting visions of the character of the Union, and their opposite views defined certain fundamental issues of American life that still echo two centuries later. Hamilton foresaw a diversified capitalistic economy, agriculture balanced by commerce and industry, and was thus the better prophet. Jefferson feared the growth of crowded cities divided into a capitalistic aristocracy on the one hand and a deprived working class on the other. Hamilton feared anarchy and loved order; Jefferson feared tyranny and loved liberty.

Whereas Hamilton wanted a strong central government run by a wealthy elite promoting capitalistic enterprise, Jefferson desired a decentralized agrarian republic. Jefferson's ideal republic was to remain one in which small farmers predominated: "Those who labor in the earth," he wrote, "are the chosen people of God." Jefferson feared that the unlimited expansion of commerce and industry would produce a class of propertyless wage laborers who were dependent on others for their livelihood and therefore subject to political manipulation and economic exploitation.

Crises Foreign and Domestic

As the disputes between Jefferson and Hamilton intensified, Washington proved ever more adept at holding things together with his unmatched prestige. In 1792 he won unanimous reelection. No sooner had his second term begun than problems of foreign relations leapt to center stage, brought there by the consequences of the French Revolution, which had begun during the first months of Washington's presidency. Americans supported the popular revolt against the French monarchy, up to a point. By the spring of 1792, though, the experiment in liberty, equality, and fraternity had turned into a monster that plunged France into war with Austria and Prussia and began devouring its own children along with its enemies in the Terror of 1793–1794.

After the execution of King Louis XVI in 1793, Great Britain joined with the monarchies of Spain and Holland in a war against the French Republic. For the next twenty-two years, Britain and France were at war, with only a brief respite, until the final defeat of the French forces under Napoleon in 1815.

Americans wanted no part of the war. They were determined to maintain their lucrative trade with both sides of the European conflict. Of course, the combatants resented and resisted America's profitable neutrality. For their part, Hamilton and Jefferson found in the neutrality policy one issue on which they could agree. Where they differed was in how best to implement the policy. On April 22, 1793, President Washington issued a neutrality proclamation that simply declared the United States "friendly and impartial toward the belligerent powers."

Citizen Genêt

At the same time, Washington accepted Jefferson's argument that the United States should recognize the new revolutionary French government (becoming the first country to do so) and receive its new ambassador, Edmond Charles Genêt. Early in 1793, Genêt landed at Charleston, South Carolina, and made his way northward to Philadelphia. Along the way, he brazenly engaged in un-neutral activities. He outfitted privateers for use against the British royal navy and intrigued with frontiersmen and land speculators to attack Spanish Florida and Louisiana in retaliation for Spain's opposition to the French Revolution.

Genêt quickly became an embarrassment even to his Republican friends. "His conduct has been that of a madman," Madison charged. The cabinet finally agreed unanimously that he had to go, and Washington demanded his recall. Genêt's foolishness and the growing excesses of the French radicals were fast cooling American support for their revolution. The French made it hard even for Republicans to retain sympathy for the French Revolution, but Jefferson and others swallowed hard and made excuses. Nor did the British make it easy for Federalists to rally to their side. Near the end of 1793, they announced Orders in Council, which allowed them to seize the cargoes of American ships with provisions for or produce from French islands in the Caribbean. Despite the offenses by both sides, the French and British causes polarized American opinion and the two parties.

Jay's Treaty

Early in 1794, Republican leaders in Congress were gaining support for commercial retaliation to bring the British to their senses, when the British gave President Washington a timely opening for a settlement. They repealed the Orders under which American ships were being seized, and on April 16, 1794, Washington named Chief Justice John Jay as a special envoy to Great Britain. Jay left with instructions to settle all major issues: to get the British soldiers out of their posts along the northwestern frontier and to win reparations for the losses of American shippers, compensation for slaves carried away in 1783, and a commercial treaty that would legalize American commerce with the British West Indies.

The pro-British Jay, however, had little leverage with which to wring concessions from the British, and after seven months of negotiations he won only two pledges: the British promised to evacuate the northwestern military posts by 1796 and to pay damages for the seizures of American ships and cargoes in 1793–1794. In exchange for these concessions, Jay agreed to the British definition of neutral rights. He accepted the principles that naval stores, food, and military supplies headed to enemy ports on neutral ships were contraband, and that trade with enemy colonies prohibited in peacetime could not be opened in wartime (the "Rule of 1756"). Britain also gained most-favored-nation treatment in American commerce and a promise that French privateers would not be outfitted in American ports. Finally, Jay conceded that the British need not compensate Americans for the slaves who had escaped during the Revolutionary War, and he promised that the long-standing American debts to British merchants would be paid by the American government. Perhaps most important, he failed to gain unrestricted access for American shippers to the British West Indies.

Public outrage greeted the terms of Jay's Treaty. Even Federalist shippers, ready for settlement on almost any terms, criticized Jay's failure to open fully the British West Indies to American commerce. But much of the outcry came from disappointed Republican partisans who sought an escalation of conflict with hated England. Jay remarked that he could travel across the country by the light of his burning effigies. Yet the Senate debated the treaty in secret, and in the end moderation prevailed. Without a single vote to spare, Jay's Treaty won the necessary two-thirds majority on June 24, 1795.

The Frontier Stirs

Other events also had an important bearing on Jay's Treaty, adding force to the importance of its settlement of the Canadian frontier. While Jay was haggling in London, frontier conflict with Indians escalated, with American troops suffering two defeats. At last, Washington named General Wayne, known as "Mad Anthony," to head an expedition into the Northwest Territory. In the fall of 1793, Wayne marched into Indian country with some 2,600 men.

On August 4, 1794, Indians representing eight tribes, and reinforced by some Canadian militia, attacked Wayne's force at the Battle of Fallen Timbers. The Americans repulsed them with heavy Indian losses, after which American detachments destroyed their fields and villages. Dispersed and decimated, the Indians finally agreed to the Treaty of Greenville, signed in 1795. In the treaty, at the cost of a $10,000 annuity, the United States bought from twelve tribes the rights to the southeastern quarter of the Northwest Territory (now Ohio and Indiana) and enclaves at the sites of Vincennes, Detroit, and Chicago.

The Whiskey Rebellion

Wayne's forces were still mopping up after the Battle of Fallen Timbers when the administration decided on another show of strength in the backcountry against the so-called Whiskey Rebellion. Hamilton's excise tax on liquor, levied in 1791, had angered frontier farmers because it taxed their staple crop. Their grain was more easily transported to market in concentrated liquid form than in bulk. A pack horse, for example, could carry two bushels of unprocessed rye, but it could carry two barrels of whiskey representing twenty-four bushels of rye. Frontiersmen considered the tax another part of Hamilton's scheme to pick the pockets of the poor to enrich privileged speculators. All through the backcountry, from Georgia to Pennsylvania and beyond, the liquor tax provoked resistance and evasion.

In the summer of 1794, the rumblings of discontent broke into open rebellion in Pennsylvania's four western counties, where vigilantes, mostly of Scottish or Irish descent, terrorized federal revenue agents. On August 7, 1794, President Washington issued a proclamation ordering the rebels to disperse and go home, and calling out militiamen from Virginia, Maryland, Pennsylvania, and New Jersey. Getting no response from the "Whiskey Boys," he issued a proclamation for suppression of the rebellion.

Under the command of Virginia's governor, General Henry (Light-Horse Harry) Lee, 13,000 men, a force larger than any Washington had ever commanded in the Revolution, marched out from Harrisburg across the Alleghenies, itching to smite the insurgents. But the rebels vaporized like corn mash when heated. By dint of great effort and much marching, the troops finally rounded up twenty barefoot, ragged prisoners, whom they paraded down Market Street in Philadelphia and clapped into prison.

The government had made its point in defense of the rule of law and federal authority. The use of force, however, led many who sympathized with the frontiersmen to become Republicans, who scored heavily in the next Pennsylvania elections.

Pinckney's Treaty

While these stirring events were transpiring in Pennsylvania, Spain was suffering setbacks to its schemes to consolidate control over Florida and the Louisiana territory. Spain had refused to recognize the legitimacy of America's southern boundary established by the Treaty of Paris in 1783, and its agents thereafter sought to thwart American expansion southward. Spanish intrigues among the Indians were keeping up the same turmoil the British had fomented along the Ohio.

But for reasons growing out of the shifting balance of power in Europe, Spain decided in the mid-1790s to end its designs on America. This change of heart resulted in Pinckney's Treaty (1795), by which the U.S. minister, Thomas Pinckney, won acceptance of an American boundary at the thirty-first parallel; free navigation of the Mississippi River; the right to deposit goods at New Orleans without having to pay customs duties for a period of three years (with promise of renewal); a commission to settle American claims against Spain; and a promise on each side to refrain from inciting Indian attacks on the other.

Land Settlement

Now that Jay and Pinckney had settled matters with Britain and Spain, and General Wayne in the Northwest had ended organized Indian resistance, settlers flocked to the West. New lands, ceded by the Indians in the Treaty of Greenville, revealed Congress once again divided on land policy. There were two basic viewpoints on the matter: one that the public domain should serve mainly as a source of revenue; the other that it was more important to accommodate settlers with low prices, even free land, and get the country settled. Policy would evolve from the first toward the second viewpoint, but for the time being the government's need for revenue took priority.

Land Policy

Opinions on land policy, like other issues, separated Federalists from Republicans. Federalists involved in speculation might prefer lower land prices, but the more influential Federalists like Hamilton and Jay preferred to build the population of the eastern states first, lest the East lose political influence and a labor force important to the future growth of manufactures. Men of their persuasion favored high land prices to enrich the Treasury, and the sale of relatively large parcels of land to speculators rather than small tracts to actual settlers. Jefferson and Madison were reluctantly prepared to go along with such a land policy for the sake of reducing the national debt, but Jefferson yearned for a plan by which the lands could be more readily settled.

The Federalist land policy prevailed in the Land Act of 1796, which retained the 640-acre minimum size mandated by the Northwest Ordinance of 1787 while doubling the price per acre to $2 and requiring that the full amount be paid within a year. This was well beyond the means of most settlers and even many speculators. As a result, by 1800, government land offices had sold fewer than 50,000 acres. Continuing demands for cheaper land led to the Land Act of 1800, which reduced the minimum sale to 320 acres and spread the payments over four years. Thus with a down payment of $160 one could get a farm. The Land Act of 1804 further reduced the minimum parcel to 160 acres, which became the traditional homestead, and the price per acre went down to $1.64.

The Wilderness Trail

The lure of western lands led thousands of settlers to follow Daniel Boone into the territory known as Kentucky or "Kaintuck"— from the Cherokee name Ken-ta-ke ("great meadow"). In the late eighteenth century, Kentucky was a farmer's fantasy and a hunter's paradise, with its fertile soils and abundant forests teeming with buffalo, deer, and wild turkeys.

In 1773 Boone led the first group of settlers through the Appalachian Mountains at

Daniel Boone Escorting Settlers through the Cumberland Gap by George Caleb Bingham.

Transfer of Power

By 1796 President Washington had decided that two terms in office were enough. Tired of the political quarrels and the venom of the partisan press, he was ready to retire to Mount Vernon. He left behind a formidable record of achievement: the organization of a national government with demonstrated power, establishment of the national credit, the settlement of territory previously held by Britain and Spain, stabilization of the northwestern frontier, and the admission of three new states: Vermont (1791), Kentucky (1792), and Tennessee (1796).

Cumberland Gap in southwestern Virginia. Two years later, Boone and thirty woodsmen used axes to create what became known as the Wilderness Road, a passage that more than 300,000 settlers would use over the next twenty-five years.

A steady stream of settlers, mostly Scotch-Irish folk from Pennsylvania, Virginia, and North Carolina, poured into Kentucky during the last quarter of the eighteenth century. The backcountry settlers came on foot or on horseback, often leading a mule or cow that carried their few tools and possessions. On a good day they might cover fifteen miles.

On their new farms, corn was the preferred crop because it kept well and had so many uses. Ears were roasted and eaten on the cob, and kernels were ground into meal for making mush, hominy grits, hoecake, and "johnnycake" (a dry biscuit suitable for travelers that was originally called journeycake). Pigs and cows provided pork and milk, butter and cheese. Many of the frontier families also built crude stills to manufacture a potent whiskey known as "corn likker."

Washington's Farewell

Washington's farewell address focused on domestic policy and particularly on the need for unity among Americans in backing their new government. He decried the "baneful effects" of sectionalism and partisanship, while acknowledging that parties were "useful checks upon the administration of the government, and serve to keep alive the spirit of liberty."

In foreign relations, Washington asserted, America should show "good faith and justice toward all nations" and avoid either "an habitual hatred or an habitual fondness" for other countries. The United States should also "steer clear of permanent alliances with any portion of the foreign world." Later spokesmen for such an isolationist policy would distort Washington's position by claiming that he had opposed any "entangling alliances." On the contrary, Washington was not preaching isolationism; he was instead warning against any further permanent arrangements like the one with France, still technically in effect. Washington recognized that "we may safely trust to temporary alliances for extraordinary emergencies." Washington's warning against permanent foreign entanglements thereafter served as a fundamental principle in American foreign policy until the early twentieth century.

The Election of 1796

With Washington out of the race, the United States in 1796 held its first partisan election for president. The logical choice of the Federalists would have been Washington's protégé Hamilton, the chief architect of their programs. But Hamilton's policies had left scars and made enemies. Nor did he suffer fools gladly, a common affliction of Federalist leaders, including the man on whom the choice fell. In Philadelphia a caucus of Federalist congressmen chose John Adams as heir apparent, with Thomas Pinckney of South Carolina, fresh from his triumph in Spain, as nominee for vice-president. As expected, the Republicans drafted Jefferson and added geographical balance to the ticket with Aaron Burr of New York.

The rising strength of the Republicans, largely due to the smoldering resentment toward Jay's Treaty, very nearly swept Jefferson into office, and perhaps would have but for the public appeals of the French ambassador for Jefferson's election—an action that backfired. The Federalists won a majority among the electors, but Alexander Hamilton hatched an impulsive scheme that very nearly threw the election away after all. Thomas Pinckney, Hamilton thought, would be easier to influence than the strong-minded Adams. He therefore sought to have South Carolina Federalists withhold a few votes from Adams and bring Pinckney in first. The Carolinians cooperated, but New Englanders got wind of the scheme and dropped Pinckney. The upshot of Hamilton's intrigue was to cut Pinckney out of both offices and elect Jefferson as vice-president with sixty-eight votes, second to Adams's seventy-one.

The Adams Years

Adams had behind him a distinguished career as a Massachusetts lawyer; as a leader in the Revolutionary movement and the Continental Congress; as a diplomat in France, Holland, and Britain; and as vice-president. His political philosophy fell somewhere between Jefferson's and Hamilton's. He shared neither the one's faith in the common people nor the other's fondness for an aristocracy of "paper wealth." He favored the classic republican balance of aristocratic, democratic, and monarchical elements in government. A man of powerful intellect, forthright convictions, and uncontrollable vanity, Adams was haunted by the feeling that he was never properly appreciated—and he may have been right. On the overriding issue of his administration, war and peace, he kept his head when others about him were losing theirs—probably at the cost of his reelection.

War with France

Adams inherited from Washington his divided cabinet—there was as yet no precedent for changing personnel at the start of each new administration. Adams also inherited a menacing quarrel with France, a byproduct of Jay's Treaty. When Jay accepted the British position that food supplies and naval stores—as well as war matériel—bound for enemy ports were contraband subject to seizure, the French reasoned that American cargoes in the British trade were subject to the same interpretation. The French loosed their corsairs with even more devastating effect than the British had in 1793–1794. By the time of Adams's inauguration in 1797, the French had plundered some 300 American ships and had broken diplomatic relations with the United States.

John Adams.

Adams immediately acted to restore relations in the face of an outcry for war from the "High Federalists." Hamilton, however, agreed with Adams on this point and approved his last-ditch effort for a settlement. In 1797 Charles C. Pinckney (brother of Thomas) sailed for Paris with John Marshall (a Virginia Federalist) and Elbridge Gerry (a Massachusetts Republican) for further negotiations. After long, nagging delays, the three commissioners were accosted by three French counterparts (whom Adams labeled X, Y, and Z in his report to Congress). The three French diplomats delicately let it be known that negotiations could begin only if there were a loan to France of $12 million, a bribe of $250,000 to the five directors then heading the government, and suitable apologies for remarks recently made in Adams's message to Congress.

Such bribes were common eighteenth-century diplomatic practice—Washington himself had bribed a Creek chieftain, as well as ransomed American sailors from Algerian pirates at a cost of $100,000 each—but Talleyrand's price was high merely for a promise to negotiate. The answer, according to the commissioners' report, was "no, no, not a sixpence." When the XYZ Affair was reported in Congress and the public press, this was translated into the more stirring slogan "Millions for defense but not one cent for tribute." Expressions of hostility toward France rose in a crescendo—even the most partisan Republicans were hard put to make any more excuses—and many of them joined a chorus for war. An undeclared naval war in fact raged from 1798 to 1800, but Adams resisted a formal declaration of war. Congress, however, authorized the capture of armed French ships, suspended commerce with France, and renounced the alliance of 1778, which was already defunct.

Adams used the French crisis to strengthen American defenses. An American navy had ceased to exist at the end of the Revolution, but after Algerian pirates began to prey on American merchant vessels in the Mediterranean, Congress, in 1794, authorized the arming of six ships. Three of these—the *Constitution*, the *United States*, and the *Constellation*—were eventually completed in 1797. In 1798 Congress created a Department of the Navy, and by the end of 1799 the number of naval ships had increased to thirty-three. By then American ships had captured eight French vessels and provided secure passage for American commerce.

By the fall of 1798, even before the naval war was fully under way, the French began to make peace overtures. Adams named three peace commissioners, who arrived in Paris to find themselves confronting a new government under First Consul Napoleon Bonaparte. They sought two objectives: $20 million to pay for the American ships seized by the French, and the formal cancellation of the 1778 Treaty of Alliance. By the Convention of 1800, ratified in 1801, the French agreed only to terminate the alliance and the quasi-war.

The War at Home

The real purpose of the French crisis all along, the more ardent Republicans suspected, was to create an excuse to put down

A cartoon indicating the anti-French feeling generated by the XYZ Affair. The three American ministers at left reject the "Paris Monster's" demand for money.

domestic political opposition. The Alien and Sedition Acts of 1798 lent credence to their suspicions. These four measures, passed amid the wave of patriotic war fever, limited freedom of speech and the press and the liberty of aliens. Three of the four acts reflected native hostility to foreigners, especially the French and Irish, a large number of whom had become active Republicans and were suspected of revolutionary intent.

The Naturalization Act changed the residence requirement for citizenship from five to fourteen years. The Alien Act empowered the president to deport "dangerous" aliens at his discretion. The Alien Enemy Act authorized the president in time of declared war to expel or imprison enemy aliens at will. Finally, the Sedition Act defined as a high misdemeanor any conspiracy against legal measures of the government, including interference with federal officers and insurrection or riot. What is more, the law forbade writing, publishing, or speaking anything of "a false, scandalous and malicious" nature against the government or any of its officers.

The purpose of such laws was transparently partisan, designed to punish Republicans. Of the ten convictions under the act, all were directed at Republicans. To offset the Alien and Sedition Acts, Jefferson and Madison promoted what came to be known as the Kentucky and Virginia Resolutions. These passed the legislatures of the two states in late 1798. The resolutions, much alike in their arguments, denounced the Alien and Sedition Acts as unconstitutional and advanced the state-compact theory. Since the Constitution arose as a compact among the states, the resolutions argued, it followed logically that the states retained the right to say when Congress had exceeded its powers. The states could "interpose" their judgment on acts of Congress and "nullify" them if necessary.

These doctrines of interposition and nullification, revised and edited by later theorists, were destined to be used for causes unforeseen by the authors of the Kentucky and Virginia Resolutions. At the time, it seems, both Jefferson and Madison intended the resolutions to serve chiefly as propaganda, the opening guns in the political campaign of 1800. Neither Kentucky nor Virginia took steps to nullify or interpose its authority against enforcement of the Alien and Sedition Acts. Instead, both called upon the other states to help them win a repeal in Congress.

Republican Victory

As the presidential election of 1800 approached, many grievances were mounting against Federalist policies: taxation to support an unneeded army, the Alien and Sedition Acts, the hostilities aroused by Hamilton's programs, the suppression of the Whiskey Rebellion, and Jay's Treaty. When Adams decided for peace in 1800, he probably doomed his one chance for reelection. Only a wave of patriotic war fever with a united party behind him could have gained him victory at the polls. His decision gained him much goodwill among the people at large, but it left the Hamiltonians unreconciled and his party divided.

In 1800 the Federalists summoned enough unity to name Adams and Charles C. Pinckney as their candidates. But the Hamiltonians continued to snipe at the president and his policies, and soon after his renomination Adams removed two of them from his cabinet. Hamilton struck back with a pamphlet questioning Adams's fitness to be president, citing his "disgusting egotism." Intended for private distribution among Federalist leaders, the pamphlet reached the hands of Aaron Burr, who put it in general circulation.

Jefferson and Burr, as the Republican candidates, once again represented the alliance of Virginia and New York. Jefferson, perhaps even more than Adams, became the target of abuse. Unscrupulous opponents labeled him an atheist and a supporter of the excesses of the French Revolution. Jefferson refused to answer the attacks and directed the campaign by mail from his home at Monticello. He was portrayed as the farmers' friend, the champion of states' rights, frugal government, liberty, and peace.

Adams proved more popular than his party, whose candidates generally fared worse than the president, but the Republicans edged him out by seventy-three electoral votes to sixty-five. Still, the result was not final, for Jefferson and Burr had tied with seventy-three votes each, and the choice of the president was thrown into the House of Representatives, where Federalist diehards tried vainly to give the election to Burr. This was too much for Hamilton, who opposed Jefferson but held a much lower opinion of Burr. Eventually the deadlock was broken when a confidant of Jefferson assured a Federalist congressman from Delaware that Jefferson would refrain from wholesale removals of Federalists and would uphold the new fiscal system. The

representative resolved to vote for Jefferson, and several other Federalists agreed simply to cast blank ballots, permitting Jefferson to win without any of them actually having to vote for him.

Before the Federalists relinquished power to the Jeffersonian Republicans on March 4, 1801, Congress passed the Judiciary Act of 1801. Intended to ensure Federalist control of the judicial system, this act provided that the next vacancy on the Supreme Court should not be filled, created sixteen Circuit Courts with a new judge for each, and increased the number of attorneys, clerks, and marshals. Before he left office, Adams named John Marshall to the vacant office of Chief Justice and appointed Federalists to all the new positions, including forty-two justices of the peace for the new District of Columbia. The Federalists, defeated and destined never to regain national power, had in the words of Jefferson "retired into the judiciary as a stronghold."

CHAPTER 8

Republicanism:
Jefferson and Madison

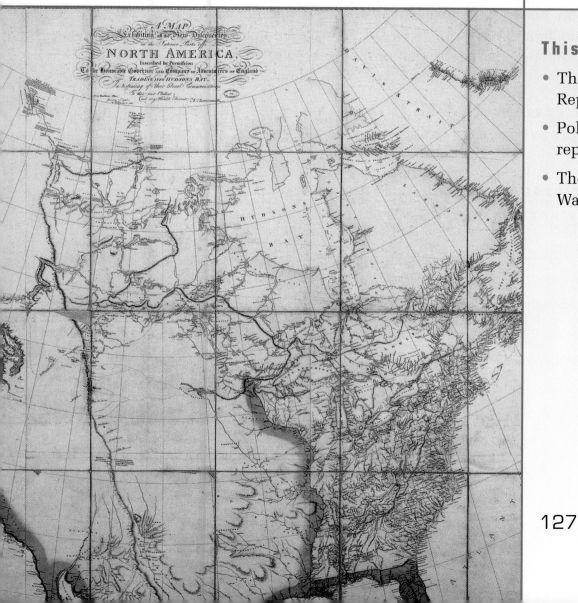

This chapter focuses on

- The domestic policies of the Republicans in power.

- Political divisions in the early republic.

- The causes and effects of the War of 1812.

127

THE *ESSENTIAL AMERICA* ON-LINE TUTOR

www.wwnorton.com/eamerica/ch8

- **Topic: The Lewis and Clark expedition**
  www.wwnorton.com/eamerica/ch8/topic.htm

  In 1804 the "Corp of Discovery" led by Merriwether Lewis and William Clark set out on a scientific and commercial exploration of the vast trans-Mississippi West. Employing images, maps, journal entries, and historical analyses, consider the significance of the Lewis and Clark expedition. How did their experiences and findings affect the popular perception of the American West?

- **Chapter review: On-line quiz and chapter summary**
  www.wwnorton.com/eamerica/ch8/review.htm

- **Chapter resources: Multimedia index**
  www.wwnorton.com/eamerica/ch8/media.htm

On March 4, 1801, the soft-spoken, brilliant, and charming Thomas Jefferson became the first president to be inaugurated in the new federal city, Washington, District of Columbia. Tall and thin, with ill-fitting clothes, chiseled features, red hair, and a ruddy complexion, the new president walked two blocks to the unfinished Capitol, entered the Senate chamber, took the oath from the recently appointed Chief Justice John Marshall, and returned to his boardinghouse for dinner.

Jefferson in Office

The deliberate display of republican simplicity at Jefferson's inauguration set the style of his administration. He took pains to avoid the monarchical trappings of his Federalist predecessors. Jefferson, a widower, discarded the coach and six in which Washington and Adams had traveled to state occasions and rode about the city on horseback. He also continued to attire himself in plain clothes. But Jefferson had by no means ceased to be the Virginia gentleman, nor had he abandoned elegant manners or the good life. The cuisine of his French chef and the wines for his frequent dinners strained his budget to the point that he had to borrow money.

Jefferson liked to think of his election as the "Revolution of 1800." He placed in policy-making positions men of his own party, and he was the first president to pursue the role of party leader, cultivating congressional support at his dinner parties and otherwise. In the cabinet the leading figures were Secretary of State James Madison, a longtime neighbor and political ally, and Swiss-born Secretary of the Treasury Albert Gallatin, a Pennsylvania Republican. In an effort to cultivate Federalist New England, Jefferson chose men from that region for the positions of attorney-general, secretary of war, and postmaster-general.

In lesser offices, however, Jefferson resisted the wholesale removal of Federalists, preferring to wait until vacancies appeared. But pressure from Republicans often forced him to yield and remove Federalists, trying as best he could to assign some other than partisan causes for the removals. In one area, however, he managed to remove the offices rather than the appointees. In 1802 Congress repealed the Judiciary Act of 1801, and so abolished the circuit judgeships and other offices to which Adams had made his "midnight appointments." A new judiciary act restored to six the number of Supreme Court justices and set up six circuit courts, each headed by a justice.

Marbury v. Madison

Adams's "midnight appointments" as he left office sparked the important case of *Marbury* v. *Madison* (1803), the first in which the Supreme Court asserted its right to declare an act of Congress unconstitutional. The case involved the appointment of William Marbury as justice of the peace in the District of Columbia. Marbury's official letter of appointment, or commission, signed by President Adams two days before he left office, remained undelivered when Madison became secretary of state, and Jefferson directed him to withhold it. Marbury then sued for a court order (a writ of mandamus) directing Madison to deliver his commission.

John Marshall, Jefferson's distant Virginia cousin with staunch Federalist views, wrote the Court's opinion. He held that Marbury deserved his commission, but he then denied that the Court had jurisdiction in the case. Marshall and the court ruled that Section 13 of the Judiciary Act of 1789, which gave the Court original jurisdiction in mandamus proceedings, was unconstitutional because the Constitution specified that the Court should have original jurisdiction only in cases involving ambassadors or states.

A painting of the president's house during Jefferson's term in office. Jefferson called it "big enough for two emperors, one pope, and the grand lama in the bargain."

The Court, therefore, could issue no order in the case. With one bold stroke, Marshall thus had chastised the Jeffersonians while avoiding an awkward confrontation with an administration that might have defied his order. At the same time, he established the precedent that the Court could declare a federal law invalid on the grounds that it violated provisions of the Constitution.

Domestic Reforms

Jefferson's first term was a succession of triumphs in both domestic and foreign affairs. He did not set out to discard Hamilton's economic program. Under Treasury Secretary Gallatin's tutoring, he learned to accept the national bank as an essential convenience. It was too late, of course, to undo Hamilton's funding and debt assumption operations, but none too soon, in the opinion of both Jefferson and Gallatin, to begin retiring the resultant federal debt. In 1802 Jefferson won the repeal of the whiskey tax, much to the relief of backwoods distillers, drinkers, and grain farmers.

Without the revenue from excise taxes, frugality was all the more necessary to a government dependent for income on tariffs and the sale of western lands. Happily for the federal Treasury, both flourished. The European war brought a continually in-creasing traffic to American shipping and revenues to the Treasury. At the same time, settlers flocked to the western lands, which were coming more and more within their reach. The admission of Ohio in 1803 increased the number of states to seventeen.

By the "wise and frugal government" promised in the inaugural, Jefferson and Gallatin reasoned, the United States could live within its income, like a prudent farmer. The basic formula was simple: cut back expenses on the military. A standing army threatened a free society anyway. It therefore should be kept to a minimum, with defense left to the militia. The navy, which the Federalists had already reduced after the quasi-war with France, ought to be reduced further. Coastal defense, Jefferson argued, should rely on fortifications and a "mosquito fleet" of small gunboats.

In 1807 Jefferson crowned his reforms by signing an act that outlawed the foreign slave trade as of January 1, 1808, the earliest date possible under the Constitution. South Carolina was the only state that still permitted the trade, but for years to come an illegal traffic in African slaves would continue. Perhaps 300,000 slaves were smuggled into southern states between 1808 and 1861.

The Barbary Pirates

Issues of foreign relations intruded on Jefferson early in his term, when events in the Mediterranean gave him second thoughts about the need for a navy. On the Barbary Coast of North Africa, the rulers of Morocco, Algiers, Tunis, and Tripoli (now part of Libya) had for years practiced piracy and extortion. After the Revolution, American shipping in the Mediterranean became fair game, no longer protected by British payments of tribute. The new American government paid protection money too, first to Morocco in 1786, then to the others in the 1790s. In 1801, however, the pasha of Tripoli upped his demands and declared war on the United States. Jefferson thereupon sent warships to blockade Tripoli.

A wearisome war dragged on until 1805, punctuated in 1804 by the notable exploit of Lieutenant Stephen Decatur, who slipped into Tripoli Harbor by night and set fire to the frigate *Philadelphia*, which had been captured (along with its crew) after it ran aground. In 1805 the pasha settled for $60,000 ransom and released the *Philadelphia*'s crew (mostly British subjects), whom he had held hostage for more than a year. It was still tribute, but less than the $300,000 the pasha had demanded, and much less than the cost of the war.

The Louisiana Purchase

Meanwhile, events elsewhere had conspired to produce the greatest single achievement of the Jefferson administration. The Louisiana Purchase of 1803 more than doubled the territory of the United States by acquiring the entire Mississippi Valley west of the river itself. Soon after taking power in France in 1799, Napoleon Bonaparte forced the Spanish to return the territory to France and expressed his intention of creating a North American empire. When word of the deal reached Washington in 1801, Jefferson hastened Robert R. Livingston, the new minister to France, on his way to Paris. Napoleon in control of the Mississippi outlet could only mean serious trouble.

Livingston and the French engaged in a series of frustrating negotiations that dragged out into 1803. In April Napoleon's minister, Talleyrand, suddenly asked if the United States would like to buy the whole of Louisiana. Livingston snapped up the offer. Napoleon had apparently decided simply to cut his losses in the New World, turn a quick profit, please the Americans, and go back to reshaping the map of Europe.

By the treaty of cession, dated April 30, 1803, the United States paid about $15 million for the huge territory. In defining the boundaries of Louisiana, the treaty's vague language could be stretched to provide a tenuous claim on Texas and a much stronger claim on West Florida, from Baton Rouge on the Mississippi River past Mobile to the Perdido River on the east. When Livingston asked about the boundaries, Talleyrand responded: "I can give you no direction. You have made a noble bargain for yourselves, and I suppose you will make the most of it."

The turn of events had indeed presented Jefferson with a noble bargain, a great new "empire of liberty," but also with a constitutional dilemma. Nowhere did the Constitution mention the purchase of territory. Jefferson at first thought to resolve the matter by amendment, but his advisers argued against delay lest Napoleon change his mind. The power to purchase territory, they reasoned, resided in the power to make treaties. Jefferson relented, trusting, he said, "that the good sense of our country will correct the evil of loose construction when it shall produce ill effects." New England Federalists boggled at the prospect of new western states that would probably strengthen the Jeffersonian party, and in a reversal that foreshadowed many future reversals on constitutional issues, Federalists found themselves arguing strict construction of the Constitution while Republicans brushed aside such scruples.

The Senate ratified the treaty by an overwhelming vote of 26 to 6, and on December 20, 1803, American representatives took formal possession of Louisiana. The Spanish kept West Florida, but within a decade it would be ripe for the plucking. American settlers in 1810 staged a rebellion in Baton Rouge and proclaimed the Republic of West Florida, which was quickly annexed and occupied by the United States as far eastward as the Pearl River. In 1812 the state of Louisiana absorbed the region. The following year, with Spain itself a battlefield for French and British forces, American troops

took over the rest of West Florida, now the Gulf coast of Mississippi and Alabama.

Exploring The Continent

An amateur scientist long before he was president, Jefferson asked Congress in 1803 for money to send an expedition to explore the far Northwest, beyond the Mississippi River, in what was still foreign territory. Jefferson was keenly interested in mapping the trans-Mississippi wilderness and collecting scientific information, as well as promoting trade with the Indians of the interior. Congress approved the project, and Jefferson assigned as commanders twenty-nine-year-old Meriwether Lewis, the president's private secretary, and another Vir-

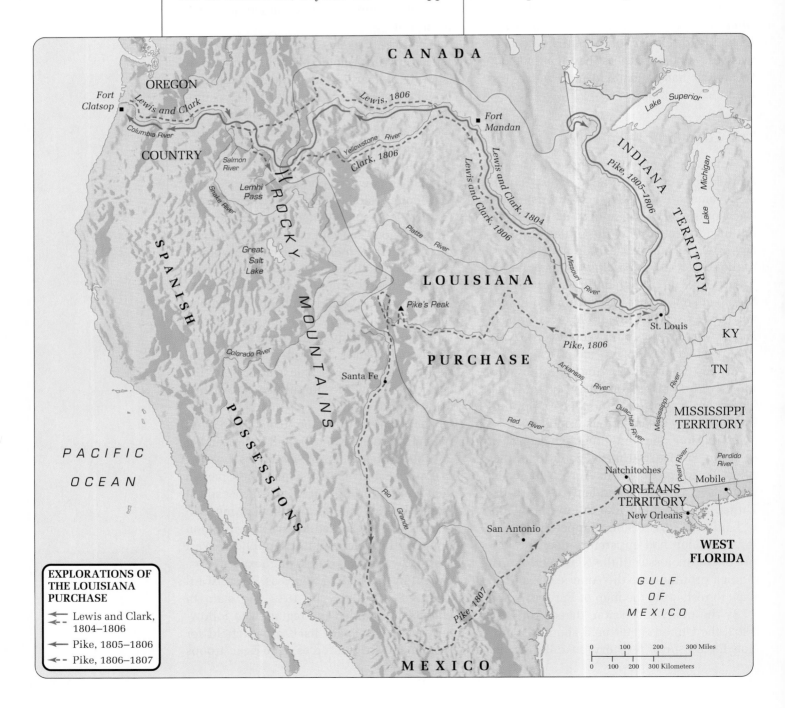

EXPLORATIONS OF THE LOUISIANA PURCHASE

- ← Lewis and Clark, 1804–1806
- ← Pike, 1805–1806
- ←- Pike, 1806–1807

Documented in an illustration from William Clark's diary, the eulachon, or candlefish, was one of many new species encountered on the expedition.

ginian, William Clark, the much younger brother of the Revolutionary hero George Rogers Clark.

In 1804 the "Corps of Discovery," numbering nearly fifty, set out from St. Louis to ascend the Missouri River. Six months later, near the Mandan Sioux villages in what is now North Dakota, they built a fort for the winter. In the spring they added to the main party a French guide and his remarkable Shoshone wife, Sacajawea ("Canoe Launcher"), who proved an enormous help as interpreter among the Indians of the region, and they set out once again upstream. At the head of the Missouri River, they took the north fork, thenceforth the Jefferson River, crossed the Continental Divide, braved attacks by grizzly bears, and in dugout canoes descended the Snake and Columbia Rivers to the Pacific. The following spring, they split into two parties, with Lewis heading back east by almost the same route, and Clark going by way of the Yellowstone River. They reunited at the juncture of the Missouri and Yellowstone Rivers, returning together to St. Louis in 1806, having been gone nearly two and a half years. Their reports of friendly Indians and abundant pelts attracted many traders and trappers to the region.

The Jeffersonians in Power

Jefferson's policies, including the Louisiana Purchase, brought him almost solid support in the South and West. Even New Englanders were moving to his side. By 1809 even John Quincy Adams, the son of the second president, would become a Republican. Diehard Federalists read the handwriting on the wall. The acquisition of a vast new empire in the West would reduce New England to insignificance in political affairs, and along with it the Federalist cause. Under the leadership of Senator Timothy Pickering, a group of bitter Massachusetts Federalists

called the Essex Junto considered seceding from the Union, an idea that would simmer in New England for another decade.

Randolph and the Tertium Quid

The presidential campaign of 1804 began when a Republican congressional caucus renominated Jefferson. Opposed by the Federalist Charles C. Pinckney, Jefferson won 162 of 176 electoral votes.

Freed from a strong opposition—Federalists made up only a quarter of the new Congress—the Republican majority began to lose its cohesion. John Randolph, a Jeffersonian mainstay in the first term, became the most conspicuous of the dissidents. Randolph became the crusty spokesman for a shifting group of "Old Republicans," whose adherence to party principles had rendered them more Jeffersonian than Jefferson himself. Their philosopher was John Taylor, a Virginia planter-pamphleteer whose theories reflected the continuing fear that the national government was growing in power and scope at the expense of individual liberty and states' rights.

Randolph broke with Jefferson in 1806, when the president sought an appropriation of $2 million for a thinly disguised bribe to win French influence in persuading Spain to give up the Floridas. "I found I might co-operate or be an honest man—I have therefore opposed and will oppose them," Randolph pledged. Thereafter he resisted Jefferson's initiatives almost out of reflex. Randolph and his colleagues were sometimes called "Quids," or the Tertium Quid (the "third something"), and their dissents gave rise to talk of a third party, neither Republican nor Federalist. But Quids never coalesced into a party.

The Burr Conspiracy

If feisty John Randolph was sincerely committed to principle, opportunistic Aaron Burr was sincerely committed to himself.

Sheer brilliance and shrewdness carried the New Yorker to the vice-presidency, and he might have become heir apparent to Jefferson, but for his taste for intrigue. He ended his political career once and for all when he killed Alexander Hamilton in a duel. Indicted in New York and New Jersey for murder and heavily in debt, Burr fled first to Spanish-held Florida. Once the furor subsided, he boldly returned to Washington to preside over the Senate. As long as he stayed out of New York and New Jersey, he was safe.

But Burr focused his attention less on the Senate than on a cockeyed scheme to carve out a personal empire for himself in the West. The so-called Burr Conspiracy originated when Burr met with General James Wilkinson, an old friend with a tainted Revolutionary War record who was a spy for the Spanish and had a penchant for easy money, a taste for rum, and an eye for intrigue. Just what he and Burr were up to probably will never be known. The most likely explanation is that they sought to organize a secession of Louisiana and set up an independent republic. Wilkinson developed cold feet, however, and sent a letter to Jefferson warning of "a deep, dark, wicked and wide-spread conspiracy." Traveling south to recruit adventurers, Burr was apprehended in disguise and taken to Richmond, Virginia, for trial.

Charged with treason, Burr was brought for trial before Chief Justice John Marshall. Events then revealed both Marshall and Jefferson at their partisan worst. Jefferson, determined to get a conviction at any cost, published relevant affidavits in advance and promised pardons to conspirators who helped to convict Burr. The Federalist Marshall in turn was so indiscreet as to attend a dinner given by the defense counsel at which Burr himself was present.

The case established two major constitutional precedents. First, on the grounds of executive privilege, Jefferson ignored a subpoena requiring him to appear in court with certain papers. He believed that the independence of the executive branch would be compromised if the president were subject to a court writ. The second major precedent was the rigid definition of treason. On this issue, John Marshall adopted the strictest of constructions. Treason under the Constitution, he concluded, consisted of "levying war against the United States or adhering to their enemies" and required "two witnesses to the same overt act" for conviction. Since the prosecution failed to produce two such witnesses, the jury found him not guilty. To avoid further legal entanglements, Burr left the country for France. He returned in 1812 to practice law in New York and died at age eighty.

War in Europe

Burr was more an annoyance than a threat to Jefferson. The more intractable problems of his second term involved the renewal of the European war in 1803, which helped resolve the problem of Louisiana but put more strains on Jefferson's desire to avoid "entangling alliances" and the quarrels of Europe. In 1805 Napoleon's defeat of Russian and Austrian forces gave him control of western Europe. The same year, the British defeat of the French and Spanish fleets in the Battle of Trafalgar secured Britain's control of the seas. Napoleon was dominant on land, the British dominant on the water, neither able to strike a decisive blow at the other, and neither restrained by an appreciation of neutral rights or international law.

Harassment by Britain and France

For two years after the renewal of hostilities in Europe, American shippers took over trade with the French and Spanish West Indies. But in the case of the *Essex* (1805), a British court ruled that the practice of shipping French and Spanish goods through

Preparation for War to Defend Commerce. In 1806 and 1807 American shipping was caught in the crossfire of war between Britain and France.

first, he declared his own paper blockade of the British Isles; in the second, he ruled that neutral ships that complied with British regulations were subject to seizure when they reached continental ports. The situation presented American shippers with a dilemma. If they complied with the demands of one side, they were subject to seizure by the other.

The risks were daunting, but the prospects for profits were so great that shippers ran the risk. Seamen faced a more dangerous risk: a renewal of the practice of impressment. The use of press gangs to kidnap men in British (and colonial) ports was a long-standing method of recruitment for the British navy. The seizure of British subjects from American vessels became a new source of recruits, justified on the principle that British subjects remained British subjects for life: "Once an Englishman, always an Englishman."

In the summer of 1807, a British frigate, the *Leopard*, accosted an American naval vessel, the *Chesapeake*, just outside territorial waters off Norfolk. After the *Chesapeake*'s captain refused to allow his ship to be searched, the *Leopard* opened fire, killing three and wounding eighteen. The *Chesapeake*, caught unready for battle, was forced to surrender. A British search party seized four men, one of whom was later hanged for desertion from the British navy. Soon after the *Chesapeake* limped back into Norfolk, a Washington newspaper editorialized: "We have never, on any occasion, witnessed such a thirst for revenge. . . ." Public wrath was so aroused that Jefferson could have had war on the spot. But like Adams before him, he resisted the war fever and suffered politically as a result. One Federalist called Jefferson a "dish of skim milk curdling at the head of our nation."

American ports while on their way elsewhere did not neutralize enemy goods. Such a practice violated the British rule of 1756, under which trade closed in time of peace remained closed in time of war. Goods shipped in violation of the rule, the British held, could be seized at any point under the doctrine of continuous voyage. After 1807, British interference with American shipping increased, not just to keep supplies from Napoleon's continent but also to hobble competition with British merchant ships.

In 1806, the British ministry set up a paper blockade of Europe. Vessels headed for continental ports had to get licenses and accept British inspection or be liable to seizure. It was a "paper blockade" because even the powerful British navy was not large enough to monitor every European port. Napoleon retaliated with his "Continental System," proclaimed in the Berlin Decree of 1806 and the Milan Decree of 1807. In the

The Embargo

Jefferson resolved to channel public indignation into an effort at "peaceable coercion." In December 1807, in response to his request, Congress passed the Embargo Act, which stopped all export of American goods and prohibited American ships from leaving for foreign ports. It also effectively ended imports, since it was unprofitable for foreign ships to return from America empty. The constitutional basis of the embargo was the power to regulate commerce, which in this case Republicans interpreted broadly as the power to prohibit commerce.

Jefferson's embargo, however, failed from the beginning, for the public was unwilling to make the necessary sacrifices. Trade remained profitable despite the risks, and violating the embargo was almost laughably easy. Neither France nor Great Britain was significantly hurt by Jefferson's policy.

But Jefferson's presidency was seriously injured. The embargo revived the languishing Federalist party in New England, which renewed the charge that Jefferson was in league with the French. Jefferson finally accepted failure and on March 1, 1809, he repealed the embargo shortly before he relinquished the "splendid misery" of the presidency. In the election of 1808, the presidency passed to another Virginian, Secretary of State James Madison.

The Drift to War

Madison was entangled in foreign affairs from the beginning of his presidency. Still insisting on neutral rights and freedom of the seas, he pursued Jefferson's policy of "peaceful coercion" by different but equally ineffective means. In place of the embargo, Congress had substituted the Non-Intercourse Act, which reopened trade with all countries except France and Great Britain and authorized the president to reopen trade with whichever warring nation gave up its restrictions. Nonintercourse proved as ineffective as the embargo. In the vain search for an alternative, in 1810, Congress reversed its ground and adopted a measure introduced by Nathaniel Macon of North Carolina. Macon's Bill Number 2 reopened trade with the warring powers but provided that, if either dropped its restrictions, nonintercourse would be restored with the other.

Napoleon's foreign minister, the duc de Cadore, informed the American minister in Paris that he had withdrawn the Berlin and Milan Decrees, but the carefully worded Cadore letter had strings attached: revocation of the decrees depended on the British revoking their paper blockade. The strings were plain to see, but either Madison misunderstood or, more likely, went along in hope of putting pressure on the British. In response to the Cadore letter, he restored nonintercourse with the British. London refused to give in, but Madison clung to his policy despite Napoleon's continued seizure of American ships.

The seemingly hopeless effort did finally work. With more time, patience, or a transatlantic cable, Madison's policy would have been vindicated without resort to war. On June 16, 1812, the British foreign minister, facing economic crisis, revoked its blockade. Britain preferred not to risk war with the United States on top of its war with Napoleon. But it was too late. On June 1 Madison had asked for war, and on June 18, 1812, the Congress concurred, unaware of the British repeal.

The War of 1812

Causes

The main cause of the war—the demand for neutral rights—seems clear enough. Neutral rights dominated Madison's war message and provided the salient reason for mounting public hostility toward the British. Yet the geographical distribution of the congressional vote for war raised a troubling question. Most votes for war came from the farm regions that stretched from Pennsylvania southward and westward. The maritime

Tecumseh, the Shawnee leader who tried to unite the tribes in defense of their lands. He was killed in 1813 at the Battle of the Thames.

states of New York and New England, the region that bore the brunt of British attacks on American trade, voted against the declaration of war. One explanation for this seeming anomaly is simple enough. The farming regions suffered damage to their markets for grain, cotton, and tobacco, while New England shippers made profits in spite of British restrictions.

Other plausible explanations for the sectional vote, however, include frontier Indian attacks that were blamed on the British, western land hunger, and the desire for territory in British Canada and Spanish Florida. The constant pressure to open new lands repeatedly forced or persuaded Indians to sign treaties they did not always understand, causing stronger resentment among tribes that were losing more and more of their lands. It was an old story, dating from the Jamestown settlement, but one that took a new turn with the rise of a powerful Shawnee leader, Tecumseh.

Tecumseh recognized the consequences of Indian disunity and set out to form a confederation of tribes to defend hunting grounds. He insisted that no land cession was valid without the consent of all tribes, since they held the land in common. By 1811 Tecumseh had matured his plans and headed south from the Indiana Territory to win the Creeks, Cherokees, Choctaws, and Chickasaws to his cause.

General William Henry Harrison, governor of the Indian Territory, learned of Tecumseh's plans, met with him twice, and pronounced him "one of those uncommon geniuses who spring up occasionally to produce revolutions and overturn the established order of things." In the fall of 1811,

Harrison decided that Tecumseh must be stopped. He gathered a thousand troops near Tecumseh's capital on the Tippecanoe River. The Indians took the bait and attacked Harrison's encampment. The Shawnees lost the Battle of Tippecanoe, although about a quarter of Harrison's men died or were wounded in the battle. Harrison then burned the Shawnee town and destroyed all its supplies. Tecumseh's dreams of an Indian confederacy went up in smoke, and he fled to British protection in Canada.

The Battle of Tippecanoe reinforced suspicions that the British were inciting the Indians. To eliminate the Indian menace, frontier settlers reasoned, they needed to remove its foreign support. Conquest of Canada, they decided, would end British influence among the Indians and open a new empire for land-hungry Americans. East Florida, still under the Spanish flag, also posed a threat, since Spain was either too weak or unwilling to prevent sporadic Indian attacks across the frontier. Moreover, the British were suspected of smuggling through Florida and intriguing with the Indians on the southwest border.

Such concerns helped generate a war fever within the frontier states. In the Congress that assembled in 1811, a number of young members from southern and western districts began to clamor for war in defense of "national honor." Among them were Henry Clay of Kentucky, who became Speaker of the House; Richard M. Johnson, also of Kentucky; and John C. Calhoun of South Carolina. John Randolph of Roanoke christened these "new boys" the "War Hawks." After they entered the House, Randolph said, "We have heard but one word—like the whip-poor-will, but one eternal monotonous tone—Canada! Canada! Canada!"

Preparations

As it turned out, the War Hawks would get neither Canada nor Florida. For in 1812 James Madison had led into war a country that was ill prepared both financially and militarily. The year before, despite urgent pleas from Treasury Secretary Gallatin, Congress had let the twenty-year charter of the Bank of the United States expire. A combination of strict-constructionist Republicans and Anglophobes, who feared the large British interest in the Bank, caused its demise. Meanwhile, trade had collapsed and tariff revenues had declined. Loans were needed for about two-thirds of the war costs, but northeastern opponents of the war were reluctant to lend money.

The military situation was almost as bad. War had been likely for nearly a decade, but Republican budgetary constraints had prevented preparations. When the war began, the army numbered only 6,700 men, illtrained, poorly equipped, and led by aging officers. The navy, on the other hand, was in comparatively good shape, with able officers and trained men whose seamanship had been tested in the fighting against France and Tripoli. Its ships were well outfitted and seaworthy—all sixteen of them. In the first year of the war, the navy produced the only American victories in isolated duels with British vessels, but their effect was mainly an occasional lift to morale. Within a year, the British had blockaded the coast, except for New England, where they hoped to cultivate antiwar feeling, and most of the little American fleet was bottled up in port.

The War in the North

The only place where the United States could effectively strike at the British was Canada. The administration opted for a three-pronged drive against Canada: along the Lake Champlain route toward Montreal, with General Henry Dearborn in command; along the Niagara River, with forces under General Stephen Van Rensselaer; and into Upper Canada (north of Lake Erie and Lake Ontario) from Detroit, with General William Hull and some 2,000 men. In Detroit, the sickly and senile Hull procrastinated, while his position worsened and the news arrived that an American fort isolated at the head of Lake Huron had surrendered. The British commander cleverly played upon Hull's worst fears. Gathering what redcoats he could to parade in view of Detroit's defenders, he announced that thousands of Indian allies were at the rear and that once fighting began he would be unable to control them. Fearing massacre, Hull, without consulting his officers and without a shot being fired, surrendered his entire force.

Along the Niagara front, General Van Rensselaer was more aggressive. An advance party of 600 Americans crossed the Niagara River and worked its way up the bluffs on the Canadian side to occupy Queenstown Heights. The stage was set for a major victory, but the New York militia refused to reinforce Van Rensselaer's men, claiming that their military service did not obligate them to leave the country. They complacently remained on the New York side and watched their outnumbered countrymen fall to a superior force across the river.

On the third front, the old invasion route via Lake Champlain, the incompetent General Dearborn led his army north from Plattsburgh toward Montreal. He marched them up to the border, where the local militia once again stood on its alleged constitutional rights and refused to cross, and then marched them back to Plattsburgh.

Madison's navy secretary now pushed vigorously for American control of inland waters. At Presque Isle (Erie), Pennsylvania, twenty-eight-year-old Commodore Oliver H. Perry, already a fourteen-year veteran who had seen action against Tripoli, was busy building ships from green timbers. By the end of the summer, Perry set out in search of the British, whom he found at Lake Erie's Put-in-Bay on September 10, 1813.

Two British warships used their superior weapons to pummel the *Lawrence*, Perry's flagship, at long distance. After four hours of intense shelling, none of the *Lawrence*'s guns was left working and most of the crew were dead or wounded. The British ex-

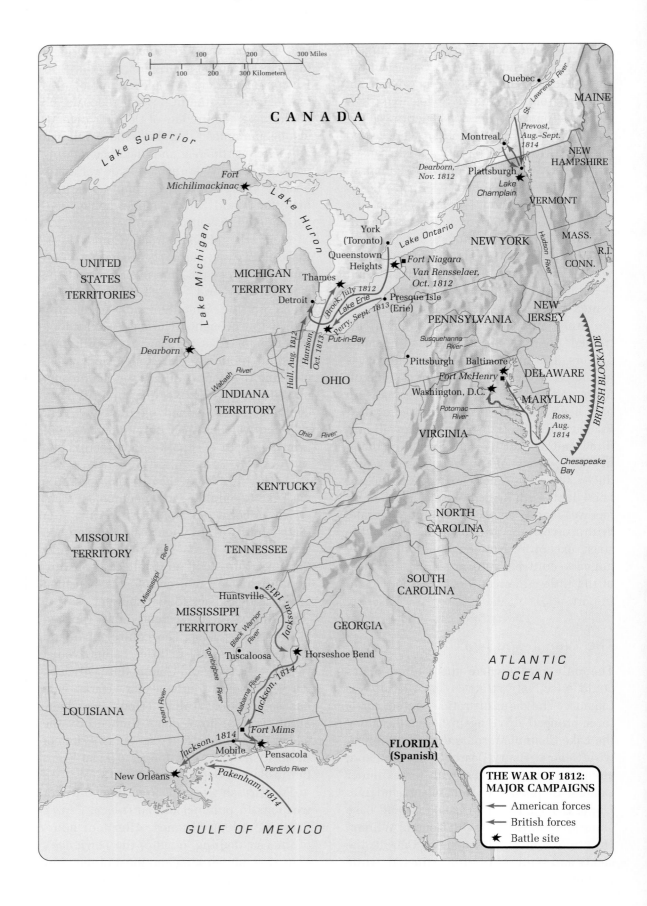

THE WAR OF 1812:
MAJOR CAMPAIGNS
⟵ American forces
⟵ British forces
★ Battle site

pected the Americans to turn tail, but Perry refused to quit. He himself rowed to another vessel, carried the battle to the enemy, and finally accepted surrender of the entire British squadron. Hatless, begrimed, and bloodied, Perry sent General William Henry Harrison the long-awaited message: "We have met the enemy and they are ours."

More good news followed. At the Battle of the Thames (October 5), in Canadian territory east of Detroit, General William Henry Harrison eliminated British power in Upper Canada and released the Northwest from any further threat. In the course of the battle, Tecumseh was killed, and his persistent dream of Indian unity died with him.

The War in the South

In the Southwest, too, the war flared up in 1813. On August 30 the Creeks attacked Fort Mims, on the Alabama River above Mobile, killing almost half the people in the fort. The news found Andrew Jackson home in bed in Nashville, recovering from a street brawl with Thomas Hart Benton, later a senator from Missouri. As major-general of the Tennessee militia, a recovered Jackson summoned about 2,000 volunteers and set out on a campaign that crushed Creek resistance. The decisive battle occurred on March 27, 1814, at the Horseshoe Bend of the Tallapoosa River, in the heart of the upper Creek country. In the Treaty of Fort Jackson, the Indians ceded two-thirds of their lands to the United States, including part of Georgia and most of Alabama.

British Strategy

Four days after the Battle of Horseshoe Bend, Napoleon's empire collapsed. Now free to deal with America, the British developed a threefold plan of operations for 1814. They would launch a two-pronged invasion of America via Niagara and Lake Champlain to increase the clamor for peace in the Northeast; extend the naval blockade to New England, subjecting coastal towns to raids; and seize New Orleans to cut the Mississippi River, lifeline of the West.

The main British effort focused on the invasion via Lake Champlain. A land assault might have taken Plattsburgh and forced American troops out of their protected positions nearby. But England's army, led by General George Prevost, bogged down while its navy engaged an American naval squadron, led by Commodore Thomas Macdonough, in a deadly battle on Lake Champlain. The battle ended in September 1814 with the entire British flotilla either destroyed or captured.

Fighting in the Chesapeake

Meanwhile, American forces suffered the most humiliating experience of the war, the capture and burning of Washington, D.C. With attention focused on the Canadian front, the Chesapeake Bay offered the British a number of inviting targets, including Baltimore, then the fourth-largest city in America. On the evening of August 24, 1814, the British marched unopposed into Washington. They burned the White House, the Capitol, and most other government buildings.

The attack on Baltimore was a different story. Some 13,000 American soldiers, chiefly militia, fortified the heights behind the city. About 1,000 men held Fort McHenry, on an island in the harbor. When the British finally came into sight of the city, they halted in the face of American defenses. All through the following night the British fleet bombarded Fort McHenry to no avail, and the invaders abandoned the attack on the city. Francis Scott Key, a Washington lawyer, watched the siege from a vessel in the harbor. The sight of the flag still in place at dawn inspired him to draft the verses of "The Star-Spangled Banner." Later revised and set to the tune of an English drinking song, it eventually became the national anthem.

Andrew Jackson's defeat of the British at the Battle of New Orleans, January 1815.

The Battle of New Orleans

The British failure at Baltimore followed by three days their failure on Lake Champlain, and their offensive against New Orleans had yet to run its course. Along the Gulf coast, General Andrew Jackson had been busy shoring up the defenses of Mobile and New Orleans. In late 1814, without authorization, he invaded Spanish Florida and took Pensacola, ending British intrigues there. Back in Louisiana by the end of November, he began to erect defenses on the approaches to New Orleans. But the British fleet, with some 8,000 troops under General Sir Edward Pakenham, cautiously took up positions on a level plain near the Mississippi just south of New Orleans.

Pakenham's painfully careful approach—he waited until all his artillery was available—gave Jackson time to build earthworks bolstered by cotton bales. It was an almost invulnerable position, but Pakenham, contemptuous of Jackson's motley array of frontier militiamen, Creole aristo-crats, free blacks, and pirates, ordered a frontal assault at dawn on January 8, 1815. His redcoats emerged out of the morning fog and ran into a murderous hail of enemy fire. Before the British withdrew, about 2,000 had been killed or wounded, including Pakenham himself.

The Battle of New Orleans occurred after a peace treaty had already been signed. But this is not to say that it was an anticlimax or that it had no effect on the outcome of the war. The treaty was yet to be ratified and the British might have exploited to advantage the possession of New Orleans had they won it. The battle assured ratification of the treaty as it stood, and both governments acted quickly.

The Treaty of Ghent and the Hartford Convention

Peace efforts had begun in 1812, even before hostilities commenced, but negotiations bogged down after the fighting started. The British were stalling, awaiting news of smashing victories to strengthen their hand. Word of the American victory on Lake Champlain weakened the British resolve. Their will to fight was further eroded by a continuing power struggle in Europe, by the eagerness of British merchants to renew trade with America, and by the war weariness of a tax-burdened public. The British finally decided that the war was not worth the cost. Envoys from both sides eventually agreed to end the fighting, return prisoners, restore previous boundaries, and to settle nothing else. The Treaty of Ghent was signed on Christmas Eve, 1814.

While the diplomats converged on a peace settlement, an entirely different kind of meeting took place in Hartford, Connecticut. The Hartford Convention represented the climax of New England's disaffection with "Mr. Madison's War." New England had managed to keep aloof from the war and extract a profit from illegal trading and privateering. After the fall of Napoleon, however, the British extended their blockade to New England, occupied part of Maine, and conducted several raids along the coast. Even Boston seemed threatened. Instead of rallying to the American flag, however, Federalists in the Massachusetts legislature voted to convene a meeting of New England states to plan independent action.

On December 15, the Hartford Convention assembled with delegates chosen by the legislatures of Massachusetts, Rhode Island, and Connecticut, two delegates from Vermont and one from New Hampshire: twenty-two in all. They proposed seven constitutional amendments designed to limit Republican influence, including the requirement of a two-thirds vote to declare war or admit new states, a prohibition on embargoes lasting more than sixty days, a one-term limit for the presidency, and a ban on successive presidents from the same state.

Their call for a later convention in Boston carried the unmistakable threat of secession if the demands were ignored. Yet the threat quickly evaporated. When messengers from Hartford reached Washington, they found the battered capital celebrating the good news from Ghent and New Orleans. The consequence was a fatal blow to the Federalist party, which never recovered from the stigma of disloyalty and narrow provincialism stamped on it by the Hartford Convention.

The War's Aftermath

For all the ineptitude with which the War of 1812 was fought, it generated intense patriotic feeling. Despite the standoff with which it ended at Ghent, the American public felt victorious, thanks to Andrew Jackson and his men at New Orleans as well as to the heroic exploits of American frigates in their duels with British ships. Remembered too were the vivid words of the dying Captain James Lawrence on the *Chesapeake*: "Don't give up the ship." Under Republican leadership, the nation had survived a "Second War of Independence" against the greatest military power on earth and emerged with new symbols of nationhood and a new gallery of heroes.

The war revealed America's need for a more efficient system of internal transportation—roads, bridges, canals. Even more important, the conflict launched the United States toward economic independence, as the interruption of trade encouraged the birth of American manufactures. This was a profound development, for the emergence of an American factory system would generate far-reaching social effects as well as economic growth. After forty years of independence, it dawned on the world that the new republic might not simply survive but might flourish.

As if to underline the point, Congress authorized a quick, decisive blow at the Barbary pirates. During the War of 1812, they had renewed plundering American ships. On March 3, 1815, little more than two weeks after the Senate ratified the Treaty of Ghent, Congress authorized a naval expedition against the Mediterranean pirates. On May 10, Captain Stephen Decatur sailed from New York with ten vessels. He first seized two Algerian ships and then sailed boldly into the harbor of Algiers. On June

We Owe Allegiance to No Crown. The War of 1812 generated a new feeling of nationalism.

30, 1815, the pirates' leaders agreed to cease molesting American ships and to return all American prisoners. Decatur then forced similar concessions from Tunis and Tripoli. Piracy against American vessels was over.

One of the strangest results of the War of 1812 was a reversal of roles by the Republicans and Federalists. Out of the wartime experience the Republicans had learned some lessons in nationalism. The necessities of war had "Federalized" Madison, or "re-Federalized" the father of the Constitution. Perhaps, he reasoned, a peacetime army and navy would not be so bad after all. He also had come to see the value of a national bank and of higher tariffs to protect infant American industries from foreign competition. But while Madison was embracing such nationalistic measures, the Federalists were borrowing the Jeffersonian theory of states' rights and strict construction. It was yet another reversal of roles in constitutional interpretation. It would not be the last.

CHAPTER

9

Nationalism and Sectionalism

This chapter focuses on

- The elements of the "Era of Good Feelings."

- How economic policies, diplomacy, and judicial decisions reflected the nationalism of these years.

- The various issues that promoted sectionalism.

- The fate of the Republican party after the collapse of the Federalists.

145

THE *ESSENTIAL AMERICA* ON-LINE TUTOR

www.wwnorton.com/eamerica/ch9

- **Topic: The Monroe Doctrine**
  www.wwnorton.com/eamerica/ch9/topic.htm

  The Monroe Doctrine (1823) became one of the keynotes of American foreign policy. Relying on government documents, maps, historical analyses, and personal correspondence, explore the significance of the Monroe Doctrine. What was the purpose of Monroe's declaration, and how did the international community receive it?

- **Chapter review: On-line quiz and chapter summary**
  www.wwnorton.com/eamerica/ch9/review.htm

- **Chapter resources: Multimedia index**
  www.wwnorton.com/eamerica/ch9/media.htm

Amid the jubilation after the War of 1812 Americans began to transform their young republic into a sprawling nation. Hundreds of thousands of people began to stream westward at the same time that what had been a largely local economy was maturing into a national market. The dispersion of plantation slavery and the cotton culture from the Atlantic coast into the Old Southwest—Georgia, Alabama, Mississippi, Louisiana, and Texas—disrupted family ties and changed social life. In the North and West, meanwhile, a dynamic middle class began to emerge and grow within towns and cities. Such dramatic changes prompted strident political debates over economic policies, transportation improvements, and the extension of slavery into the new territories. In the process, the nation began to divide into three powerful regional blocs—North, South, and West—whose shifting coalitions shaped the political landscape until the Civil War.

Economic Nationalism

After the War of 1812, the idea spread that the country needed a more balanced and "national" economy of farming, commerce, and manufacturing, as well as a more muscular military. President Madison, in his first annual message to Congress after the war, recommended several steps toward these ends: better fortifications, a standing federal army and a strong navy, a new national bank, effective protection of the new infant industries, a system of canals and roads for commercial and military use, and to top it off, a great national university, to be located in Washington, D.C. "The Republicans have out-Federalized Federalism," one observer remarked.

The Bank of the United States

The trinity of what came to be called economic nationalism—proposals for a second national bank, protective tariffs, and inter-nal improvements—inspired the greatest controversies of the time. After the national bank's charter expired in 1811, the country had fallen into a financial muddle. State-chartered banks mushroomed with little or no control, and their bank notes (paper money) flooded the channels of commerce with money of uncertain value. Because hard money had been so scarce during the war, many state banks had suspended specie (gold or silver) payments in redemption of their notes, thereby further depressing their value. And this was the money on which Americans depended.

To remedy this situation, in 1816 Congress created a new Bank of the United States (B.U.S.), which would be located in Philadelphia. Modeled after Hamilton's bank, its charter again ran for twenty years, the government owned a fifth of the stock and named five of the twenty-five directors, and it served as the depository for government funds. Its bank notes were accepted in payments to the government. In return for its privileges, the Bank had to keep the government's funds without charge, lend the government $5 million on demand, and pay the government a cash bonus of $1.5 million.

The bitter debate about the Bank set the pattern of regional alignment for most other economic issues. Western senators predicted that the currency-short western towns would be at the mercy of such a centralized eastern bank.

The debate over the national bank featured the great triumvirate of John C. Calhoun of South Carolina, Henry Clay of Kentucky, and Daniel Webster of New Hampshire, later of Massachusetts. Calhoun, as an economic nationalist and leading War Hawk who helped maneuver the United States into war with Great Britain in 1812, introduced the measure and pushed it through, justifying its constitutionality by citing the congressional power to regulate the currency. Clay, who had earlier opposed Hamilton's bank, now asserted that new circumstances had made the Bank indispensable. Webster, however, led the opposition of the New Englanders who did not want Philadelphia to displace Boston as the nation's banking center. Later, after he moved from New Hampshire to Massachusetts, Webster would return to Congress as the champion of a much stronger national power, while events would carry Calhoun in the other direction.

A Protective Tariff

Peace in 1815 brought a sudden renewal of cheap British imports and provoked a movement for the protection of young American industries from foreign competition. The self-interest of the manufacturers, who as yet had little political impact, was reinforced by a patriotic desire for economic independence from Britain.

The Tariff of 1816, the first intended more for the protection of industry against foreign competition than for revenue, easily passed Congress. The South and New England both split their votes, with New England registering a majority of its votes for the tariff and the South directing a majority of its votes against the bill, while the Middle States and Old Northwest cast only five negative votes altogether. Led by Calhoun, the minority of southerners who voted for the tariff had hoped that the South might itself become a manufacturing center. Although in 1810 the southern states had almost as many manufacturers as New England, within a few years New England moved ahead of the South, and Calhoun turned against tariff protection. The tariff then became a sectional issue, with manufacturers and food growers favoring higher tariffs, while export-crop planters and shipping interests favored lower duties.

Internal Improvements

The third major economic issue of the time involved the government-financed road construction and the development of water transportation. The federal government had entered the field of internal improvements under Jefferson. In 1803, when Ohio became a state, Congress decreed that 5 percent of the proceeds from state land sales would go to building a National Road from the Atlantic coast into Ohio and beyond as the territory developed. Construction of the National Road began in 1811.

Originally called the Cumberland Road, it was the first federally financed interstate road network. By 1818, the road ran from Cumberland, Maryland, to Wheeling on the Ohio River; by 1838 the road extended all the way to Vandalia, Illinois. By reducing transportation costs and opening up new markets, the National Road and privately financed turnpikes helped accelerate the commercialization of agriculture.

In 1817 Calhoun put through the House a bill to place in a fund for internal improvements the $1.5 million bonus the Bank of the United States had paid for its charter, as well as all future dividends on the government's bank stock. Opposition centered in New England and the South, regions that expected to gain least from transportation improvements. Support came largely from the West, which urgently needed good roads. Madison, bothered by its constitutionality, vetoed the bill. For another hundred years, internal improvements remained, with few exceptions, the responsibility of states and private enterprise.

Nonetheless, despite disagreements about funding, improved transportation and communications (mass newspapers, express mail service, the telegraph) during the second quarter of the nineteenth century helped create a national market for goods and services. No longer limited to local or regional markets, farmers and manufacturers rapidly expanded production. Banks offered easy access to capital, and enterprising Americans rushed to take advantage of unprecedented entrepreneurial opportunities. Commercial agriculture and the factory system began to displace subsistence farming and household production. Mills and factories sprouted across the countryside. New technologies greatly increased productivity and in the process changed the rhythms of work and the relationships between laborers and employers. These first stirrings of an industrial revolution spawned a sustained economic expansion that would transform American society and politics.

"Good Feelings"

James Monroe

As President James Madison approached the end of a turbulent tenure he, like Jefferson, turned to a fellow Virginian, another secretary of state, as his successor: James Monroe. Monroe never displayed the depth in scholarship or political theory of his Republican predecessors, but what he lacked in intellect he made up in dedication to public service. Monroe served in the Virginia assembly, as governor, in the Confederation Congress and United States Senate, and as U.S. minister to France, England, and Spain. Under Madison he had been secretary of state and twice had doubled as secretary of war. In the 1816 presidential election he overwhelmed his Federalist opponent, Rufus King of New York. Tall, rawboned Monroe, with his powdered wig, cocked hat, and knee breeches, was the last of the Revolutionary generation to serve in the White House.

Firmly grounded in traditional Republican principles of states' rights and a limited role for the national government, Monroe was never able to keep up with the onrush of the "new nationalism," which advocated federal economic policies, such as a central national bank and a tariff on imports. In his veto of the Cumberland Road Bill (1822), he denied the authority of Congress to collect tolls for its repair and maintenance. Rather he urged a constitutional amendment, as

had Jefferson and Madison, to remove all doubt about federal authority in the field of internal improvements.

Whatever his limitations, Monroe surrounded himself with some of the ablest young Republican leaders: John Quincy Adams became secretary of state, William Crawford of Georgia continued as secretary of the treasury, and John C. Calhoun headed the War Department. The new administration took power with America at peace and the economy flourishing. The period became known as the "Era of Good Feelings." Like many a maxim, it conveys just enough truth to be sadly misleading. The collapse of the Federalist party did not mean that the Republicans grew more unified. They continued to suffer from rancorous internal tensions. Moreover, the social order began to show signs of increasing stratification as the nation experienced dramatic economic growth and rapid westward migration. Finally, a resurgence of sectionalism erupted just as the postwar prosperity collapsed in the Panic of 1819.

For a time, however, general harmony in national politics reigned, and even when troubles arose, little of the blame fell on Monroe. In 1820 he was reelected without opposition, as the Federalists were too weak to put up a candidate. Monroe won all the electoral votes except for three abstentions and one vote from New Hampshire for John Quincy Adams.

The Union Manufactories of Maryland in Patapsco Falls, Baltimore County, c. 1815. A textile mill begun during the embargo of 1807; by 1825 the Union Manufactories would employ over 600 people.

Improving Relations with Britain

Adding to the prevailing contentment after the war was a growing rapprochement with England. American shippers resumed trade with Britain in 1815. The Treaty of Ghent had left unsettled a number of minor disputes, but thereafter, two important compacts—the Rush-Bagot Agreement of 1817 and the Convention of 1818—removed several potential causes of irritation. In the first, resulting from an exchange of notes between Acting Secretary of State Richard Rush and British minister Charles Bagot, the threat of naval competition on the Great Lakes vanished with an arrangement to limit forces there. Although the exchange made no reference to the land boundary between the United States and Canada, its spirit gave rise to the tradition of an unfortified border, the longest in the world.

The Convention of 1818 covered three major points. The northern limit of the Louisiana Purchase was settled by extending the national boundary along the Forty-ninth Parallel west from Lake of the Woods to the crest of the Rocky Mountains. West of that point the Oregon country would be open to joint U.S.-British occupation. The right of Americans to fish off Newfoundland and Labrador, granted in 1783, was acknowledged once again.

Extension of Boundaries

A whole sequence of developments came into focus in 1819, one of the more fateful years in American history. Controversial efforts to expand American territory, a sharp financial panic, a tense debate over the extension of slavery, and several landmark Supreme Court cases combined to bring an unsettling end to the "Era of Good Feelings."

The aggressive new nationalism reached a climax with the acquisition of Florida. Spanish sovereignty over Florida was more a technicality than an actuality. The thinly populated province had been a thorn in the side of the United States during the recent war, a center of British intrigue, a military haven for Creek refugees who were beginning to take the name Seminole ("runaway" or "separatist"), and a harbor for runaway slaves and criminals.

Spain, once the dominant power of the Americas, was now a nation in rapid decline, suffering from both internal and colonial revolt, and unable to enforce its obligations under the Pinckney Treaty of 1795 to pacify the frontiers. In 1817 Secretary of War Calhoun authorized a military campaign against the Seminoles in Florida and summoned General Andrew Jackson from Nashville to take command.

Jackson's orders allowed him only to pursue the offenders into Spanish territory, not to attack any Spanish post, but the general was not a man to bother with technicalities. Jackson pushed eastward through Florida, reinforced by Tennessee volunteers and friendly Creeks, taking a Spanish post and skirmishing with the Seminoles. Jackson hanged two of their leaders without a trial. The Florida panhandle was in American hands by the end of May 1818.

News of Jackson's exploits aroused anger in Madrid and concern in Washington. Spain demanded the return of its territory, reparations, and the punishment of Jackson. Monroe's cabinet at first prepared to disavow Jackson's action, especially his direct attack on Spanish posts. Calhoun, as secretary of war, wanted to discipline Jackson for disregarding orders—a stand that later caused bad blood between the two men—but privately confessed a certain pleasure at the outcome. In any case, a man as popular as Jackson was almost invulnerable. And he had one important friend in Washington, Secretary of State John Quincy Adams, who realized that Jackson had strengthened his hand in negotiations already under way with the Spanish minister. American forces withdrew from Florida, but negotiations resumed with the knowledge that the United States could retake Florida at any time.

With Florida's fate a foregone conclusion, Adams cast his eye on a larger purpose, a final definition of the western boundary of the Louisiana Purchase and—his boldest stroke—extension of a boundary to the Pacific coast. In lengthy negotiations, Adams gradually gave ground on claims to Texas, but he stuck to his demand for a transcontinental boundary line. Agreement finally came early in 1819. With the Transcontinental Treaty, Spain ceded all of Florida to the United States in return for American assumption of private claims against Spain up to $5 million. The western boundary of the Louisiana Purchase would run along the Sabine River and then in stair-step fashion up to the Red River, along the Red, and up to the Arkansas River. From the source of the Arkansas it would go north to the Forty-second Parallel and thence west to the Pacific coast. Florida became a territory, and its first governor was briefly Andrew Jackson. In 1845 Florida finally achieved statehood.

Crises and Compromises

The Panic of 1819

Adams's Transcontinental Treaty was a triumph of foreign policy and the climactic event of America's postwar nationalism. Even before it was signed in early 1819, however, two thunderclaps signaled the end of the brief "Era of Good Feelings" and gave warning of stormy weather ahead: the financial Panic of 1819 and the controversy over statehood for Missouri. The panic resulted from a sudden collapse of cotton prices in the English market, as British textile mills turned away from American sources to cheaper East Indian cotton. The price collapse set off a decline in the demand for other American goods and suddenly revealed the fragility of the prosperity that had begun after the War of 1812.

Since 1815, much of the economic boom had been built on a shaky foundation. Businessmen, bankers, farmers, and land specu-

lators had caused a volatile expansion of credit. Even the directors of the Second Bank of the United States engaged in the same reckless extension of loans that state banks had pursued. In 1819, Langdon Cheves, former congressman from South Carolina, assumed control of the Bank and established sounder policies.

Cheves rescued the B.U.S. from near-ruin, but only by putting heavy pressure on the state banks. They in turn put pressure on their debtors, who found it harder to renew old loans or get new ones. The Cheves policies were the result rather than the cause of the Panic, but hard-pressed debtors found it all the more difficult to meet their obligations. Hard times lasted about three years, and in the popular mind the Bank deserved much of the blame. The Panic passed, but resentment of the national bank lingered, and it never fully regained the confidence of the South and the West.

The Missouri Compromise

Just as the Panic was breaking over the country, another cloud appeared on the horizon, the onset of a sectional controversy over slavery. By 1819, the country had an equal number of slave and free states, eleven of each. The line between them was defined by the southern and western boundaries of Pennsylvania and the Ohio River. Although slavery lingered in some places north of the line, it was on the way to extinction there. Beyond the Mississippi River, however, no move had been made to extend the dividing line across the Louisiana Purchase territory, where slavery had existed from the days when France and Spain had colonized the area. At the time, the Missouri Territory embraced all of the Louisiana Purchase except the state of Louisiana (1812) and the Arkansas Territory (1819). In the westward rush of population, the old French town of St. Louis became the funnel through which settlers pushed on beyond the Mississippi. These were largely settlers from the South who brought their slaves with them.

In early 1819, the House of Representatives debated legislation enabling Missouri to draft a state constitution, its population having passed the minimum of 60,000. Representative James Tallmadge, Jr., a New York congressman, introduced a resolution prohibiting the further introduction of slaves into Missouri, which already had some 10,000 slaves, and providing freedom at age twenty-five to those born after the territory's admission as a state. After brief but fiery exchanges, the House passed the Tallmadge amendment on an almost strictly sectional vote, and the Senate rejected it by a similar tally, but with several northerners joining the opposition. With population at the time growing faster in the North, a political balance between the free and slave states could be held only in the Senate. In the House, slave states had 81 votes while free states had 105; a balance was unlikely to be restored in the House.

Maine's application for statehood made it easier to arrive at an agreement. Since colonial times Maine had been the northern province of Massachusetts. The Senate linked its request for separate statehood with Missouri's and voted to admit Maine as a free state and Missouri as a slave state, thus maintaining the balance between free and slave states in the Senate. An Illinois senator further extended the compromise by an amendment to exclude slavery from the rest of the Louisiana Purchase north of 36°30′, Missouri's southern border. Slavery thus would continue in the Arkansas Territory and in Missouri, and be excluded from the remainder of the area. On August 10, 1821, President Monroe proclaimed the admission of Missouri as the twenty-fourth state. For the time, the controversy was settled. "But this momentous question," the aging Thomas Jefferson wrote to a friend, "like a firebell in the night awakened and filled me with terror. I considered it at once as the knell of the Union."

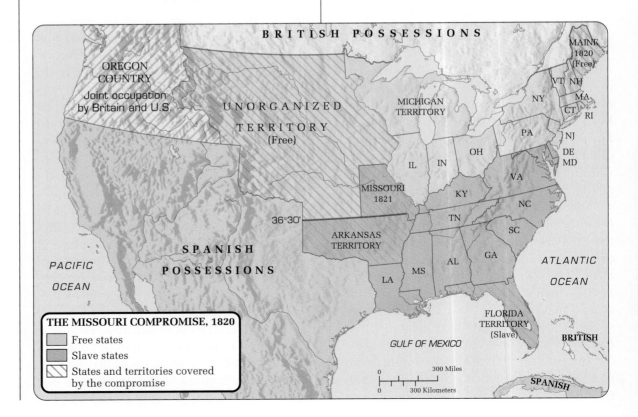

THE MISSOURI COMPROMISE, 1820
Free states
Slave states
States and territories covered by the compromise

Judicial Nationalism

John Marshall

During the early nineteenth century, many of the nation's leading attorneys and judges were nationalists. They believed that an expanding nation needed a central government with enough power and responsibility to override local interests. And they argued that an independent judiciary system should have the authority to settle disputes between the states and the federal government. The leader among these judicial nationalists was John Marshall. A Virginia lawyer who served as secretary of state for John Adams, Marshall established the power of the Supreme Court by his force of mind and determination. During Marshall's early years on the Court (altogether he served thirty-four years), he affirmed the principle of judicial review of legislative acts. In *Marbury* v. *Madison* (1803) and *Fletcher* v. *Peck* (1810), the Marshall Court first struck down a federal law and then a state law as unconstitutional.

Expanding Power of Federal Government

In the fateful year 1819, Marshall and the Court made two decisions of major importance in checking the power of the states and expanding the power of the federal government: *Dartmouth College* v. *Woodward*, and *McCulloch* v. *Maryland*.

The Dartmouth College case involved an attempt by the New Hampshire legislature to alter a charter granted the college by King George III in 1769, under which the governing body of trustees became a self-perpetuating board. In 1816 the state's Republican legislature, irritated by this residue of monarchical rule as well as by the fact that Federalists dominated the board of trustees, placed Dartmouth under the control of a new board named by the governor. The original trustees sued and lost in the state courts, but with Daniel Webster as

their counsel, they gained a hearing before the Supreme Court. The charter, declared Marshall in speaking for the Court, was a valid contract that the legislature had violated, an action expressly forbidden by the Constitution. This decision implied a new and enlarged definition of *contract* that seemed to put private corporations beyond the reach of the states that chartered them. "If business is to prosper," Marshall explained, "men must have the assurance that contracts will be enforced."

Marshall's single most important interpretation of the constitutional system appeared in *McCulloch* v. *Maryland* (1819). In the unanimous decision, the Court upheld the "implied powers" of Congress to charter the Bank of the United States and denied the state of Maryland's attempt to tax the Bank. In a lengthy opinion, Marshall rejected Maryland's argument that the federal government was the creature of sovereign states. Instead, he insisted, it arose directly from the people acting through the conventions that ratified the Constitution ("We, the people of the United States, . . . do ordain and establish . . ."). While sovereignty was divided between the states and the national government, the latter, "though limited in its powers, is supreme within its sphere of action."

Maryland's effort to tax the Bank conflicted with the supreme law of the land. One great principle that "entirely pervades the Constitution," Marshall wrote, was "that the Constitution and the laws made in pursuance thereof are supreme: that they control the Constitution and laws of the respective states, and cannot be controlled by them." The state tax therefore was unconstitutional, for "the power to tax involves the power to destroy"—which was precisely what the legislatures of Maryland and several other states had in mind with respect to the Bank.

Marshall's last great decision, *Gibbons* v. *Ogden* (1824), established national supremacy in regulating interstate commerce,

Chief Justice John Marshall, pillar of judicial nationalism.

and it thereby dealt another blow to proponents of states' rights. In 1808 the New York legislature granted Aaron Ogden the exclusive ferry rights across the Hudson River between New York and New Jersey. A competitor, Thomas Gibbons, protested the state's right to grant such a monopoly. On behalf of a unanimous Court, Marshall ruled that the state's action conflicted with the federal Coasting Act under which Gibbons operated. Congressional power to regulate commerce among the states, the Court said, "like all others vested in Congress, is complete in itself, may be exercised to its utmost extent, and acknowledges no limitations other than are prescribed in the Constitution." In striking down the monopoly created by the state, the nationalist Marshall had opened the way to extensive interstate development of steamboat navigation and, soon afterward, steam railroads. Such judicial nationalism provided an important support for economic expansion.

Nationalist Diplomacy

The Pacific Northwest

In foreign affairs, too, nationalism continued to be an effective force. Within two years after final approval of John Quincy Adams's Transcontinental Treaty, the secretary of state was able to draw another important transcontinental line. In 1819 Spain had abandoned its claim to the Oregon country above the Forty-second Parallel. Russia, however, had claims along the Pacific coast as well, including trading outposts from Alaska as far south as California. In 1823 Secretary of State Adams contested "the right of Russia to any territorial establishment on this continent." The American government, he informed the Russian minister, assumed the principle "that the American continents are no longer subjects for any new European colonial establishments." The upshot of his protest was a treaty signed in 1824 whereby Russia accepted the line of

54°40' as the southern boundary of its claim. The Oregon Territory, to the south of the line, remained subject to joint occupation by the United States and Great Britain under their agreement of 1818.

The Monroe Doctrine

Adams's disapproval of further colonization also had clear implications for Latin America. One consequence of the Napoleonic Wars and French occupation of Spain and Portugal had been a series of wars of liberation in Latin America. Within little more than a decade after the flag of rebellion was first raised in 1811, Spain had lost almost its entire empire in the Americas. All that was left were the islands of Cuba, Puerto Rico, and Santo Domingo.

In 1823 rumors began to circulate that France might try to help Spain regain its American empire. Monroe and Secretary of War Calhoun were alarmed at the possibility. British foreign minister George Canning was also worried about French and Spanish intentions, and he urged Anglo-American protection of Latin America.

Adams recommended to Monroe and the cabinet that the United States adopt its own unilateral policy against the restoration of Spain's colonies. "It would be more candid," Adams said, "as well as more dignified, to avow our principles explicitly to Russia and France, than to come in as a cockboat in the wake of the British man-of-war." Adams knew that to protect Britain's trade with the area, the British navy would stop any action by a European power in Latin America. The British wanted the United States to agree not to acquire any more Spanish territory, including Cuba, Texas, or California, but Adams preferred to avoid such a commitment.

Monroe incorporated the substance of Adams's views in his annual message to Congress in 1823. The Monroe Doctrine, as it was later called, comprised four major points: (1) that "the American continents . . . are henceforth not to be considered as subjects for future colonization by any European powers"; (2) the political system of European powers was different from that of the United States, which would "consider any attempt on their part to extend their system to any portion of this hemisphere as dangerous to our peace and safety"; (3) the United States would not interfere with existing European colonies; and (4) the United States would keep out of the internal affairs of European nations and their wars.

At the time, the statement drew little attention either in the United States or abroad. Over the years, however, the Monroe Doctrine, not even so called until 1852, became one of the cherished principles of American foreign policy.

One-Party Politics

Almost from the start of Monroe's second term the jockeying for the presidential succession in 1824 had begun. Three members of Monroe's cabinet were active candidates: Secretary of War John Calhoun, Secretary of the Treasury William Crawford, and Secretary of State John Quincy Adams. Henry Clay, longtime Speaker of the House, also thirsted after the office. And on the fringes of the Washington scene a new force appeared in the person of Andrew Jackson, the scourge of the British, Spaniards, and Seminoles, who was elected a senator from Tennessee in 1823. All were Republicans, for again no Federalist stood a chance, but they were competing in a new political world, complicated by the crosscurrents of nationalism and sectionalism. With only one party there was in effect no party, for there existed no generally accepted method for choosing a "regular" candidate.

The "Corrupt Bargain"

The outcome of the election of 1824 turned more on personalities and sectional alle-

giance than on issues. Adams, the only northern candidate, carried New England, the former bastion of the Federalist party, and won most of New York's electoral votes. Clay took Kentucky, Ohio, and Missouri, while Crawford carried Virginia, Georgia, and Delaware. Jackson swept the Southeast, plus Illinois and Indiana, and with Calhoun's support the Carolinas, Pennsylvania, Maryland, and New Jersey.

The result was inconclusive in both the electoral vote and the popular vote. In the electoral college, Jackson had 99, Adams 84, Crawford 41, and Clay 37; in the popular vote, the proportion ran about the same. Whatever might have been said about the outcome, it was a defeat for Clay's program: New England and New York opposed him on internal improvements, the South and Southwest on the protective tariff. Sectionalism had defeated the national program, yet the advocate of the American System now assumed the role of president-maker, since the election was thrown into the House of Representatives, where Speaker Clay's influence was decisive. Clay had little trouble in choosing, since he regarded Jackson as unfit for the office. "I cannot believe," he muttered, "that killing 2,500 Englishmen at New Orleans qualifies for the various, difficult and complicated duties of the Chief Magistracy." He eventually threw his support to Adams. The final vote in the House, which was by state, carried Adams to victory with thirteen votes to Jackson's seven and Crawford's four.

It was a costly victory, for it united Adams's foes and crippled his administration before it got under way. There is no evidence that Adams entered into any bargain with Clay to win his support, but the charge was widely believed after Adams made Clay his secretary of state, the office from which three successive presidents had risen. A campaign to elect Jackson next time was launched almost immediately after the 1824 decision. "The people have been cheated," Jackson growled. The Crawford people, in-

Henry Clay.

cluding Martin Van Buren, the "Little Magician" of New York politics, soon moved into the Jackson camp.

John Quincy Adams's Presidency

John Quincy Adams was one of the ablest men, hardest workers, and finest intellects ever to enter the White House, but he lacked the common touch and the politician's gift for maneuver. A stubborn man, he suffered from chronic bouts of depression that provoked in him a grim self-righteousness and self-pity, qualities that did not endear him to fellow politicians.

Adams's first annual message to Congress provided a grandiose blueprint for national development, set forth in such a blunt way that it became a political disaster. In the boldness and magnitude of its conception, the Adams plan outdid those of both Hamilton and Clay. The central government, the president asserted, should promote internal improvements, set up a national university, finance scientific explorations, and create a new Department of the Interior.

Adams's federalist presidential message hastened the emergence of a new party system. The minority who cast their lot with Adams and Clay were turning into National-Republicans; the opposition, the growing party of Jacksonians, were the Democratic-Republicans, who would eventually drop the name Republican and become Democrats.

Adams's headstrong plunge into nationalism and his refusal to play the game of politics condemned his administration to utter frustration. Congress ignored his domestic proposals, and in foreign affairs the triumphs he had scored as secretary of state had no sequels. The climactic effort to discredit Adams came on the tariff issue. The Panic of 1819 had provoked calls for a higher tariff in 1820, but the effort failed by one vote in the Senate. In 1824 the advo-

cates of protection renewed the effort, with greater success. The Tariff of 1824 favored the Middle Atlantic and New England manufacturers with higher duties on woolens, cotton, iron, and other finished goods. Clay's Kentucky won a tariff on hemp, a fiber used for making rope. A tariff on raw wool brought the wool-growing interests to the support of the measure. Additional revenues were provided by duties on sugar, molasses, coffee, and salt.

Three years later, Jackson's supporters sought to advance their candidate through an awkward scheme hatched by John Calhoun. The plan was to propose such outrageously high tariffs on raw materials that the eastern manufacturers would join the commercial interests there, and, with the votes of the agricultural South and Southwest, combine to defeat the measure. In the process, Jackson men in the Northeast could take credit for supporting the tariff, and Jackson men, wherever it fitted their interests, could take credit for opposing it—while Jackson himself remained in the background. Virginia's John Randolph saw through the ruse. The bill, he asserted, "referred to manufactures of no sort of kind, but the manufacture of a President of the United States."

The complicated scheme did help elect Jackson in 1828, but in the process Calhoun became a victim of his own shenanigans. His high tariff bill, to his chagrin, passed, thanks to the growing strength of manufacturing interests in New England and to several crucial amendments that exempted certain raw materials. Daniel Webster, now a senator from Massachusetts, explained that he was ready to deny all he had said before against the tariff because New England had built up her manufactures on the understanding that the protective tariff was a settled policy.

When the bill passed on May 11, 1828, it was Calhoun's turn to explain his newfound opposition to the gospel of protection, and

John Quincy Adams, a president of great intellect but without the common touch.

nothing so well illustrates the flexibility of constitutional principles as the switch in positions by Webster and Calhoun. Back in South Carolina, Calhoun prepared the *South Carolina Exposition and Protest* (1828), which asserted the right of a state to nullify an act of Congress that it found unconstitutional.

Jackson Sweeps In

Thus far the stage was set for the election of 1828, which might more truly be called a political revolution than that of 1800. But if the issues of the day had anything to do with the election, they were hardly visible in the campaign, in which politicians on both sides reached depths of scurrilousness that had not been plumbed since 1800.

Jackson was denounced as a hot-tempered, ignorant barbarian, whose fame rested on his reputation as a killer. In addition, Jackson's enemies dredged up the old story that he had lived in adultery with his wife, Rachel, before they had been legally married. In fact they had been married for two years in the mistaken belief that her divorce from a former husband was final. As soon as the official divorce had come through, Jackson and Rachel had been remarried. But such distinctions escaped his opponents. Anxiety over this humiliation and her probable reception in Washington may have contributed to an illness from which Rachel died before her husband took office, a tragedy for which Jackson could never forgive his enemies. Jackson blamed Clay and Adams for not restraining their supporters from having made such scurrilous charges against his family.

The Jacksonians, however, were not averse to mudslinging. They got in their licks against Adams, condemning him as a man corrupted by foreigners in the courts of Europe. They called him a gambler and a spendthrift for having bought a billiard table and a chess set for the White House, and a puritanical hypocrite for despising the common people and warning Congress to ignore the will of its constituents. Adams had finally reached the presidency, the Jacksonians claimed, by a "corrupt bargain" with Henry Clay.

In the campaign of 1828, Jackson held most of the advantages. As a military hero, he stirred the patriotism of voters. As a son of the West, he was almost unbeatable there. As a planter and slaveholder, he had the trust of southern planters. Debtors and local bankers who hated the national bank turned to Jackson. In addition, his vagueness on the issues protected him from attack by various interest groups. Not least of all, Jackson benefited from a spirit of democracy in which the common folk were no longer satisfied to look to elites for leadership, as they had done in the past.

Since the Revolution, and especially after 1800, more people were voting as states expanded the suffrage from only those with property to taxpaying white males, and even in some states, to universal male suffrage. After 1815 the new states of the West entered the Union with either white manhood suffrage or a low taxpaying requirement, and older states such as Connecticut (1818), Massachusetts (1821), and New York (1821) abolished their property requirements for voting. As more people voted and participated in political activities, the ideal of social equality took on more importance in the political culture.

Jackson embodied this new, more democratic political world. A tall, sinewy frontiersman born in South Carolina, he had scrambled his way up by will and tenacity.

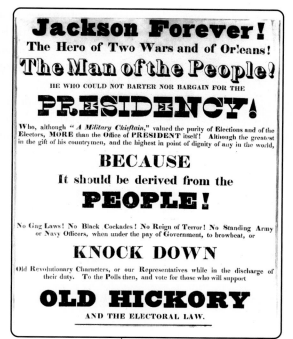

This 1828 handbill identifies Jackson, "The Man of the People," with the democratic impulse of the time.

His toughness inspired his soldiers to nick-name him "Old Hickory." As a fighter, horse trader, land speculator, and frontier lawyer, Jackson symbolized the rugged new western temperament. A fellow law student described him as a "most roaring, rollicking, game-cocking, horse-racing, card-playing, mischievous fellow."

The 1828 returns revealed that Jackson had won by a comfortable margin. The electoral vote was 178 to 83. Adams won all of New England, except for one of Maine's nine electoral votes, and a scattering of votes in New York and Maryland. All the rest belonged to Jackson. A new, convulsive era in American politics was about to begin.

An Expansive Nation

The election of Andrew Jackson signaled a new era in American history. By 1828 the United States was no longer an infant nation hugging the Atlantic coast. The maturing republic now included twenty-four states and almost 13 million people. Many Americans were on the move during the early nineteenth century. They formed a relentless migatory stream that spilled over the Appalachian Mountains, spanned the Mississippi River, and in the 1840s reached the Pacific Ocean. Wagons, canals, flatboats, steamboats, and eventually railroads transported the settlers westward.

The feverish expansion of the United States into new western territories brought Americans into conflict with Native Americans, Mexicans, and the British. Only a few Americans, however, expressed moral reservations about displacing others. Most believed it was the "manifest destiny" of the United States to spread across the entire continent—at whatever cost and at whomever's expense. Americans generally felt that they enjoyed the blessing of Providence in consolidating the entire continent under their control.

While most Americans during the Jacksonian era continued to earn their living from the soil, textile mills and manufacturing plants began to dot the landscape and transform the nature of work and the pace of life. By mid-century the United States was emerging as one of the world's major industrial powers. In addition, the lure of cheap land and plentiful jobs, as well as the promise of political equality and religious freedom, attracted hundreds of thousands of immigrants from Europe. These newcomers, mostly from Germany and Ireland, faced ethnic prejudices, religious persecution, and language barriers that made assimilation into American culture all the more difficult.

All these developments gave to American life in the second quarter of the nineteenth century its dynamic and fluid quality. The United States, said the philosopher-poet Ralph Waldo Emerson, was "a country of beginnings, of projects, of designs, of expectations." A restless optimism characterized the period. People of lowly social status who heretofore had accepted their lot in life now strove to climb the social ladder and enter the political arena. The patrician republicanism espoused by Jefferson and Madison gave way to the frontier democracy promoted by the Jacksonians. Americans were no longer content to be governed by an aristrocracy of talent and wealth. They began to demand—and obtain—government of, by, and for the people.

The fertile economic environment during the antebellum era helped foster the egalitarian idea that individuals (except African Americans, Native Americans, and women) should have an equal opportunity to better themselves and should be granted political rights and privileges. In America, observed a journalist in 1844, "One has as good a chance as another according to his talents, prudence, and personal exertions."

The exuberant individualism embodied in such mythic expressions of economic equality and political democracy also spilled over into the cultural arena during the Jacksonian era. The so-called romantic movement applied democratic ideals to philosophy, religion, literature, and the fine arts. In New England, Ralph Waldo Emerson, Henry David Thoreau, and Margaret Fuller joined other transcendentalists in espousing a radical individualism. Other reformers were motivated more by a sense of spiritual mission that democratic individualism. In striving to enhance personal morality and the general welfare, mostly middle-class reformers sought to create public-supported schools, abolish slavery, promote temperance in the use of alcoholic beverages, and improve the lot of the disabled, insane, and imprisoned. Their efforts helped address some of the problems created by the frenetic pace of economic growth and territorial expansion. But the reformers made little headway against slavery. It would take a brutal civil war to dislodge America's "peculiar institution."

ESSENTIAL THEMES

CRITICAL QUESTIONS

How did westward expansion affect the politics of nationalism and sectionalism?

How did the Industrial Revolution affect regional economic distinctions?

Was the early nineteenth century a period of growing equality or inequality in American society?

How did the twin themes of Enlightenment reason and revivalist faith find expression in this period?

What were the international implications of America's westward expansion in this period?

How did westward expansion affect the politics of nationalism and sectionalism?

CHAPTER 10
The Jacksonian Impulse
Jacksonian politics ●

Expansion of the franchise among white males
Development of political party activity
Voter participation
The Jackson administration
Nullification and sectional tensions
The tariffs of 1828 and 1832
John C. Calhoun's *South Carolina Exposition and Protest* (1828)
The Webster-Hayne debate (1830)
South Carolina's nullification ordinance (1832)
Clay's compromise and the Force Bill (1833)
Indian policy
The Bank of the United States controversy
The new party system
The Whigs

CHAPTER 11
The Dynamics of Growth
● Government and the economy

Internal improvements
The politics of immigration
Labor politics
Commonwealth v. *Hunt* (1842) legalizes trade unions

CHAPTER 12
An American Renaissance: Religion, Romanticism, and Reform
The politics of reform ●

CHAPTER 13
Manifest Destiny
● National politics in the 1840s

The Indian wars: the clash between white interests and Native Americans
The Ft. Laramie Treaty and the beginnings of the reservation system (1851)
The Annexation of Texas (1836)
The Alamo (1836)
Sam Houston
Polk's presidency (1845–1849)
The Mexican War

Education and citizenship
Horace Mann
Female seminaries
American Temperance Union formed (1833)
Prison reform
State-run asylums
Dorthea Dix
The civil rights of women: Seneca Falls (1848)

The development of the market economy
Industrialization and regional specialization
The spread of wage labor
Jackson and the Bank of the United States
Sectionalism and the tariff question: the South Carolina nullification ordinance (1832)
Distribution of the federal surplus to the states
The Panic of 1837

CHAPTER 10

The Jacksonian Impulse

Jackson and the economy

CHAPTER 11

The Dynamics of Growth

The Industrial Revolution in America

The cotton gin (1793)
The cotton economy and slavery
The transportation revolution
Turnpikes
Canals and steamboats
Railroads
Government and the economy
Technology and the growth of industry
The "Lowell System"
The McCormick reaper (1840s)
Goodyear rubber (1844)
Morse's telegraph
Industry and the cities
Immigrant labor
Organized labor

CHAPTER 12

An American Renaissance: Religion, Romanticism, and Reform

American culture in the new industrial landscape

Literature: introduction of cheap penny newspapers
Movements and social and economic change
Reform: in response to factory system
Owens founds New Harmony (1825)

CHAPTER 13

Manifest Destiny

Economic motives for westward migration

Pioneers seek to exploit the natural resources of the new western lands

Politics and the changing social order
Politics and gender
Politics and race
Racism in Northern cities
Antiblack riots in Philadelphia (1834)
Pennsylvania disenfranchises blacks
    (1838); other states follow suit
Antiblack riots occur in many northern
    cities (1830s–1850s)
**Congress approves the Indian Removal
    Act (1830)**
Cherokee Nation v. *Georgia* **(1831)**
Trail of Tears (late 1830s)
**Indian wars devastate Native-American
    populations**
Growth of America's urban population

CHAPTER 10
The Jacksonian Impulse
Jacksonian democracy

CHAPTER 11
The Dynamics of Growth
Inequality in Jacksonian America

**Workers begin organizing: National
    Trades' Union (1834)**
Increasing social stratification
Irish immigration
German immigration
Nativist backlash to immigrant labor
Anti-Catholic violence
Labor organizations grow
The growth of cities and urban poverty

CHAPTER 12
An American Renaissance: Religion, Romanticism, and Reform
Early social reform

CHAPTER 13
Manifest Destiny
The social order on the western frontier

Western Indians
The Spanish West
California
Movements westward

**Spread of public education and
    university training**
Rise of urban middle class
Temperance movement
Women's rights movement
Seneca Falls Convention organized by
    Lucretia Mott and Elizabeth Cady
    Stanton (1848)
Declaration of Sentiments, fashioned
    after the Declaration of
    Independence
Utopian communities

CHAPTER 10

The Jacksonian Impulse

• Political culture

> "Log Cabin and Hard Cider"
> presidential campaign (1839-
> 1840)
> **Jacksonian democracy**
> Cultural expressions of partisanship

CHAPTER 11

The Dynamics of Growth

The Culture of Industry •

> **Lowell and the values of industry**
> **Literary lectures**
> Ralph Waldo Emerson
> Henry Ward Beecher
> **Popular entertainment**
> Blood sports
> Theaters and minstrel shows

CHAPTER 12

An American Renaissance: Religion,
Romanticism, and Reform

• The American Renaissance

> **Romanticism**
> **The flowering of American literature**
> **Newspapers and the popular press**
> **Public education**
> **Unitiarianism and Universalism**
> **The Second Great Awakening**
> Charles Grandison Finney and the
>   Burned-Over District
> Joseph Smith establishes Mormon
>   church (1830)
> Brigham Young leads exodus of
>   Mormons westward
> **Transcendentalism**
> **The women's movement**
> **Utopian communities**
> Shakers
> Brook Farm
> Oneida Community (1840s–1850s)

CHAPTER 13

Manifest Destiny

The Multicultural Southwest •

> **The Indians of the West**
> **The Spanish West**
> **Mountain men of the fur trade**
> The arduous Oregon Trail

What were the international implications of America's westward expansion in this period?

CHAPTER 10
The Jacksonian Impulse
Jacksonian America and events abroad

> The tariff issue and international prices
> Influx of foreign silver triggers
>   inflation, financial situation
>   (mid-1830s)
> The world economy and the Panic of
>   1837

CHAPTER 11
The Dynamics of Growth
America's industrial development
and the world economy

> The cotton South
> Textile manufactures
> Irish labor migrates to America
>   (1840s–1850s)
> German professionals migrate to
>   America (1840s–1850s)

CHAPTER 12
An American Renaissance: Religion, Romanticism, and Reform
America's cultural independence

> Romanticism and American culture
> An indigenous culture

CHAPTER 13
Manifest Destiny
American pioneers encroach on
Indian lands and Mexican territory
as they move westward

Britain and America clash over the
suppression of the slave trade

> Webster-Ashburton Treaty (1842)

> Mexico welcomes American settlers as
>   a means of stabilizing the
>   Mexican–U.S. border (1823)
> Manifest Destiny
> Annexation of Texas from Mexico
>   (1843)
> Santa Anna's costly victory at the
>   Alamo (1836)
> Sam Houston and the independence of
>   Texas (1836)
> Oregon: "Fifty-four forty or fight" and
>   relations with Britain
> Texas gains statehood (1845)
> Polk asks Congress for permission to
>   end joint occupation of Oregon
>   with Britain (1845)
> Annexation of California (1847)
> Treaty of Guadalupe Hidalgo completes
>   continental United States (1848)

The Jacksonian Impulse

This chapter focuses on

- The social and political context of the Jackson/Van Buren administrations.

- Andrew Jackson's attitudes and actions concerning the tariff (and nullification), Indian policy, and the Bank of the United States.

- The rise of a new party system (Democrats and Whigs).

THE *ESSENTIAL AMERICA* ON-LINE TUTOR

www.wwnorton.com/eamerica/ch10

- **Topic: The Trail of Tears**
  www.wwnorton.com/eamerica/ch10/topic.htm

  The "Trail of Tears" was forged by thousands of Cherokees, Choctaws, Chickasaws, Creeks, and Seminoles during their forced removal from tribal lands in the Southeast to reservations west of Arkansas. Utilizing tribal records, maps, historical analyses, and Native art, study the plight of these nations as they made their trek westward to new lands.

- **Chapter review: On-line quiz and chapter summary**
  www.wwnorton.com/eamerica/ch10/review.htm

- **Chapter resources: Multimedia index**
  www.wwnorton.com/eamerica/ch10/media.htm

The election of Andrew Jackson coincided with a distinctive new era in American politics, economic development, and social change. Jackson was the first president not to come from a prominent colonial family. As a self-made soldier-politician-land speculator from the backcountry, he symbolized a transformation in the nation's social structure and political temper.

Profound economic and social forces were reshaping the young United States. In 1828 there were twenty-four states and almost 13 million people, many of them recent arrivals from Germany and Ireland. Surging foreign demand for cotton and other goods helped fuel a transportation revolution and an economic boom. Textile mills and shoe factories sprouted like mushrooms across the New England countryside, their spinning looms fed by cotton grown in the newly cultivated lands of Alabama and Mississippi.

Cities increasingly became the centers of the nation's commerce, industry, finance, and political activity. The urban population grew twice as fast as the rural population during the second quarter of the nineteenth century. A more urban society and a more diversified and speculative economy created more instability as people took greater risks to make money. A more stratified social order also emerged, as some people acquired great wealth while most others worked for wages.

An agrarian economy that earlier had produced crops and goods for household use or for local exchange expanded into a market-oriented economy engaged in national and international commerce. New canals and roads opened up eastern markets to western farmers in the Ohio Valley. The new economic order brought with it regional specialization and increasing division of labor. As more land was put into cultivation and commercial farmers came to rely on banks for credit to buy land and seed, they were subject to greater risks and the volatility of the market. In the midst of periodic financial panics and sharp business depressions, farmers unable to pay their debts lost their farms to "corrupt" banks that they believed had engaged in reckless speculative ventures and had benefited from government favoritism.

For many people, the transition to cash-crop agriculture and capitalist manufacturing was painful and unsettling. A traditional economy of independent artisans and subsistence farmers was giving way to a new system of centralized workshops, mills, and factories based on wage labor. Chartered corporations and commercial banks began to dominate local economies. The onset of the factory system and urban commerce called into question the assumption of Thomas Jefferson and others that a republic could survive only if most of its citizens were independent, self-reliant property owners, neither too rich to dominate other people nor too poor to become dependent and subservient.

A New Political Culture

At the same time that the urban population was increasing and more people were engaging in wage labor, many states, especially those on the frontier, were reducing or eliminating the property requirement for voting. The easing of voting restrictions reflected the feeling that a more democratic ballot would help combat the rising influence of commercial and manufacturing interests. Four times as many people voted in the 1828 presidential election as had voted in the 1824 election.

The mass-based Democratic party that ushered Jackson into the White House reflected the emergence of a new political culture during the 1820s. Up to that time, well-organized national political parties had been virtually nonexistent. The Jacksonian era witnessed the crystallization of formal parties (the Democratic party and the Whig party), which took particular stands on issues and held formal nominating conventions for selecting presidential and vice-presidential candidates.

This era also ushered in a new style of politicking that featured fierce polemics, expensive and well-organized campaigns, tightly controlled local party "machines," and intense partisan loyalties. Politics during the Jacksonian era was a vibrant public phenomenon that involved mass marches, spontaneous chanting, vigorous debates, and high voter turnout. The local party machines used a partisan network of employers and landlords to help party members find jobs and housing; in return, they could expect their members to vote without question for the candidates designated by the machine.

The Democratic party that arose during this time was an unstable coalition of northern industrial workers (many of them Irish and German immigrants) and small farm owners, landless farm laborers, and aspiring entrepreneurs from all sections of the country. Their shared concern was the preservation of a "just" and "virtuous" society in which most people were small property holders jealous of their freedom from mo-

nopolists or corrupt politicians. Democrats therefore opposed tariffs and the national bank, and any other efforts to centralize governmental power. At the same time, frontier folk settling in the new states of the Old Northwest (Ohio, Indiana, Illinois) and the Old Southwest (Alabama, Mississippi, Louisiana) were no longer willing to defer to traditional political and social elites.

Yet to call the Jacksonian era the "age of the common man," as many historians have done, is misleading. While political participation increased during the Jacksonian era, most of the common folk remained *common* folk. The period never produced true economic and social equality. Power and privilege, for the most part, remained in the hands of an "uncommon" elite. Moreover, many Jacksonians in power proved to be as opportunistic and manipulative as the "corrupt" politicians they displaced. And, for all of their egalitarian rhetoric, Jacksonian Democrats never embraced the principle of economic equality. "True republicanism," one commentator declared, "requires that every man . . . shall be free to become as unequal as he can." But in the afterglow of Jackson's election victory, few observers troubled with such distinctions. It was time to celebrate the commoner's ascension to the presidency.

Jackson Takes Office

Inauguration

On Inauguration Day, March 4, 1829, the new president, a sixty-two-year-old widower, said that he favored retirement of the national debt, a proper regard for states' rights, a "just" policy toward Indians, and rotation in federal office holders, which he pronounced "a leading principle in the republican creed"—a principle his enemies would dub the "spoils system."

After his speech, Jackson mounted his horse and rode off to the White House,

George Caleb Bingham's *Verdict of the People* depicts the increasingly democratic politics of the early to middle nineteenth century.

where he hosted a reception for all who chose to come. A huge crowd pushed into the White House, surged through the rooms, leaped onto the furniture—all in an effort to shake the president's hand or at least get a glimpse of him. To Supreme Court Justice Joseph Story, "the reign of 'King Mob' seemed triumphant."

Appointments and Political Rivalries

Jackson believed that government workers who stayed too long in office became corrupted. So he set about replacing Adams's appointees with his own supporters. But his use of the "spoils system" has been exaggerated. During his first year in office, Jackson replaced only about 9 percent of the appointed officials in the federal government, and during his entire term fewer than 20 percent.

Jackson's administration was from the outset a house divided between the partisans of Secretary of State Martin Van Buren of New York and Vice-President John C. Calhoun of South Carolina. Much of the political history of the next few years would turn upon the rivalry between the two, as each man jockeyed for position as Jackson's heir apparent. Van Buren held most of the advantages, foremost among them his skill at timing and tactics. Jackson, new to political administration, leaned heavily on him for advice and for help in soothing the ruffled feathers of rejected office seekers.

But Calhoun could not be taken lightly. He, too, expected to be Jackson's successor. A man of towering intellect, he possessed a demonic sense of duty. Since returning from Washington to his plantation in South Carolina in 1825, Calhoun had nurtured his crops and his ardent love for his native region. Now, as vice-president, he was determined to defend southern interests against the advance of northern industrialism and abolitionism.

The Eaton Affair

In his battle for political power with Calhoun, Van Buren had luck as well as political skill on his side. Fate had quickly handed him a trump card: the succulent scandal of the Peggy Eaton affair. Peggy Eaton was a vivacious Irish widow whose husband supposedly had committed suicide upon learning of her affair with Tennessee senator John Eaton. Her marriage to Eaton, three months before he entered Jackson's cabinet as secretary of war, had scarcely made a virtuous woman of her in the eyes of the proper ladies of Washington. Floride Calhoun, the vice-president's wife, especially objected to Peggy Eaton's lowly origins and unsavory past. She pointedly snubbed her, and other cabinet wives followed suit.

Peggy's plight reminded Jackson of the gossip that had pursued his wife, Rachel, and he pronounced Peggy "chaste as a virgin." But the cabinet members were unable to cure their wives of what Van Buren dubbed "the Eaton Malaria." Van Buren, however, was a widower, and therefore free to lavish on poor Peggy all the attention that Jackson thought was her due. Mrs. Eaton herself finally wilted under the chill and withdrew from society. The outraged Jackson came to link Calhoun with what he called a conspiracy against her and drew even closer to Van Buren.

Internal Improvements

During the chilly winter of 1829–1830, Van Buren delivered some additional blows to Calhoun. It was easy to bring Jackson into opposition to internal improvements and thus to federal programs with which Calhoun had long been identified. In 1830 the Maysville Road Bill, passed by Congress, offered Jackson a happy chance for a dual thrust at both Calhoun and Henry Clay. The bill authorized the government to buy stock in a road from Maysville to Clay's home-

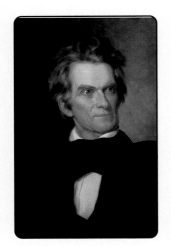

John C. Calhoun (detail).

town of Lexington. The road lay entirely within the state of Kentucky, and though part of a larger scheme to link up with the National Road via Cincinnati, it could be viewed as a purely local undertaking. On that ground, Jackson vetoed the bill, prompting widespread popular acclaim. Yet while Jackson continued to oppose federal aid to local projects, he supported projects such as the National Road, as well as road building in the territories, and rivers and harbors bills, the "pork barrels" of federal funds from which every congressman tried to pluck a morsel for his district. Even so, Jackson's attitude toward the Maysville Road set an important precedent, on the eve of the railroad age, for limiting federal initiative in internal improvements. Railroads would be built altogether by state and private capital at least until 1850.

Nullification

Calhoun's Theory

Calhoun was now in midpassage from his early phase as an economic nationalist to his later phase as a states'-rights sectionalist—and open to thrusts on both flanks. Conditions in his home state had brought on this change. Suffering from agricultural depression, South Carolina lost almost 70,000 people to emigration during the 1820s, and it would lose nearly twice that number in the 1830s. Most South Carolinians blamed the protective tariff, which tended to raise the prices of manufactured goods. Insofar as tariffs discouraged the sale of foreign goods in the United States, they reduced the ability of British and French traders to acquire the American money with which to buy American cotton. This worsened already existing problems of low cotton prices and exhausted lands. The South Carolinians' malaise was compounded by the increasing criticism of slavery. Hardly had the country emerged from the Missouri controversy when the city of Charleston was thrown into panic by the thwarted Denmark Vesey slave insurrection of 1822.

The unexpected passage of the Tariff of 1828, called the Tariff of Abominations by its critics because of its high taxes on imports, left Calhoun no choice but to join the opposition or give up his home base. Calhoun's *South Carolina Exposition and Protest* (1828), written in opposition to that tariff, contained a finespun theory of nullification, whereby a state could impose state authority and in effect repeal a federal law. This theory stopped just short of justifying secession from the Union. The unsigned statement accompanied resolutions of the South Carolina legislature protesting the tariff. Calhoun, however, had not entirely abandoned his earlier nationalism. He wanted to preserve the Union by protecting the minority rights that the agricultural and slaveholding South claimed. The fine balance he struck between states' rights and central authority was actually not far removed from Jackson's own philosophy, but growing tension between the two men would complicate the issue. The flinty Jackson, in addition, was determined to draw the line at any defiance of federal law.

The Webster-Hayne Debate

South Carolina had proclaimed its dislike for the tariff, but it had postponed any action against its enforcement, awaiting with hope the election of 1828 in which Calhoun was the Jacksonian candidate for vice-president. The state anticipated a new tariff policy from the Jackson administration. There the issue stood until 1830, when the great Webster-Hayne debate sharpened the lines between states' rights and the Union. The immediate occasion for the debate, however, was the question of lands owned by the federal government.

Late in 1829 a Connecticut senator, fearing the continued drain of able-bodied folk from New England, sought to restrict land sales in the West. When his resolution came before the Senate in 1830, Missouri's Thomas Hart Benton, who for years had been calling for lower land prices, denounced it as a sectional attack designed to impede the settlement of the West so that the East might maintain its supply of cheap factory labor.

Robert Y. Hayne of South Carolina took Benton's side. Hayne saw in the public-lands issue a chance to strengthen the alliance of South and West reflected in the vote for Jackson. The government, said Hayne, endangered the Union by imposing a hardship upon one section to the benefit of another. The use of public lands as a source of revenue to the central government would create "a fund for corruption—fatal to the sovereignty and independence of the states."

At this point Daniel Webster of Massachusetts, widely recognized as the nation's foremost orator and lawyer, rose to offer a dramatic defense of the East. With the gallery hushed, he began by denying that the East had ever sought to restrict development of the West. He then lured Hayne into defending states' rights and upholding the doctrine of nullification.

Hayne took the bait. Young, handsome, and himself an accomplished speaker, Hayne launched into a defense of Calhoun's *South Carolina Exposition*, arguing that the union was a compact of the states, and therefore the states remained free to judge when the national government had overstepped the bounds of its constitutional authority. The right of state "interposition," whereby a state could interpose its authority over a federal law in order to thwart an unjust federal statute, was as "full and complete as it was before the Constitution was formed."

In rebuttal to the state-compact theory, Webster defined a nationalistic view of the Constitution. From the beginning, he asserted, true sovereignty resided in the people as a whole, for whom both federal and state governments acted as agents in their respective spheres. If a single state could nullify a law of the general government, then the Union would be a "rope of sand," a practical absurdity. A state could neither nullify a federal law nor secede from the Union. The practical outcome of nullification would be a confrontation leading to civil war.

Those sitting in the Senate galleries and much of the country at large thrilled to Webster's eloquence. His closing statement has become justly famous: "Liberty and Union, now and forever, one and inseparable." In the practical world of coalition politics, Webster also had the better of the argument, for the Union and majority rule meant more to westerners, including Jackson, than the abstractions of state sovereignty and nullification. As for the public lands, the disputed resolution was soon defeated anyway.

The Rift with Calhoun

As yet, however, the enigmatic Jackson had not spoken out on the issue. Like Calhoun, he was a slaveholder, albeit a westerner, and he might be expected to sympathize with South Carolina, his native state. Soon all doubt was removed, at least on the point of nullification. On April 13, 1830, the Jefferson Day Dinner, honoring the birthday of the former president, was held in Washington. Jackson and Van Buren agreed that the president should offer a toast that would indicate his opposition to nullification. When his turn came, Jackson rose, raised his glass, pointedly stared at Calhoun, and announced: "Our Union—it must be preserved!" Calhoun tried quickly to retrieve the situation with a toast to "The Union, next to our liberty most dear!" But Jackson had set off a bombshell that exploded the plans of the states'-righters.

Nearly a month afterward, the final nail was driven into the coffin of Calhoun's presidential ambitions. On May 12, 1830, Jackson saw a letter confirming reports that in 1818 Calhoun, as secretary of war, had proposed to discipline Jackson for his reckless behavior during the Florida invasion. This discovery provoked a tense correspondence between President Jackson and Calhoun and ended with a curt note from the president cutting it off. "Understanding you now," Jackson wrote, "no further communication with you on this subject is necessary."

The growing rift prompted Jackson to remove all Calhoun partisans from the cabinet. He then named Van Buren as minister to London, pending Senate approval. In the fall of 1831 Jackson announced his readiness for one more term, with the idea of returning Van Buren from London in time for the New Yorker to succeed him as president in 1836. But in 1832, when the Senate reconvened, Van Buren's enemies opposed his appointment as minister and gave Calhoun, as vice-president, a chance to reject the nomination by a tie-breaking vote. "It will kill him [Van Buren], sir, kill him dead," Calhoun told Senator Thomas Hart Benton. Benton disagreed: "You have broken a minister, and elected a Vice-President." So, it turned out, he had. Calhoun's vote against Van Buren aroused popular sympathy for the New Yorker, who would soon be nominated to succeed Calhoun as vice-president.

His own presidential hopes blasted, Calhoun eagerly became the public leader of the nullificationists. These South Carolinians believed that tariff rates remained too high. By the end of 1831, Jackson was calling for further reductions of tariffs to take the wind out of the nullificationists' sails, and the tariff of 1832 did cut revenues another $5 million, but mainly on unprotected items. Average tariff rates were about 25 percent, but rates on cottons, woolens, and iron remained around 50 percent.

The South Carolina Ordinance

In the South Carolina state elections of 1832, the advocates of nullification took the initiative in organization and agitation. A special legislative session called for the election of a state convention, which overwhelmingly adopted a nullification ordinance repudiating the tariff acts of 1828 and 1832 as unconstitutional and forbidding collection of the duties in the state after February 1, 1833. The legislature also chose Robert Hayne as governor and elected Calhoun to succeed him as senator. Calhoun promptly resigned as vice-president to defend nullification on the Senate floor.

In the crisis, South Carolina found itself standing alone. The Georgia legislature dismissed nullification as "rash and revolutionary." Alabama pronounced it "unsound in theory and dangerous in practice." Mississippi stood "firmly resolved" against nullification. Jackson's response was measured and firm, but not rash—at least not in public. In private he threatened to hang Calhoun and all other traitors—and later expressed regret that he had failed to hang at least Calhoun. In his annual message on December 4, 1832, Jackson announced his firm intention to enforce the tariff, but once again he urged Congress to lower the rates. On December 10 he followed up with his Nullification Proclamation, which characterized nullification as an "impractical absurdity." Jackson appealed to the people of his native state not to follow false leaders: "The laws of the United States must be executed. . . . Those who told you that you might peaceably prevent their execution, deceived you. . . . Their object is disunion. But be not deceived by names. Disunion by armed force is treason."

Clay's Compromise

Jackson sent General Winfield Scott to Charleston Harbor with reinforcements of federal soldiers. The nullifiers mobilized the state militia while their local opponents, called Unionists, organized a volunteer force. In 1833 the president requested from

Congress a "Force Bill" authorizing him to use the army to compel compliance with federal law in South Carolina. At the same time, he endorsed a bill in Congress that would have lowered tariff duties to a maximum of 20 percent within two years.

When the Force Bill was introduced, Calhoun immediately rose in opposition, denying that either he or his state favored disunion. He did not want the South to leave the Union; he wanted the region to regain its political dominance of the Union. Passage of the bill eventually came to depend on the support of Henry Clay, who finally yielded to those urging him to save the day. On February 12, 1833, he introduced a plan to reduce the tariff gradually until 1842, by which time no rate would be more than 20 percent.

On March 1, 1833, the compromise tariff and the Force Bill passed Congress, and the next day Jackson signed both. The South Carolina convention then met and rescinded its nullification ordinance. Both sides were able to claim victory. The president had upheld the supremacy of the Union, and South Carolina had secured a reduction of the tariff. Calhoun, worn out by the controversy, returned to his plantation. "The struggle, so far from being over," he ominously wrote, "is not more than fairly commenced."

Racial Prejudice in the Jacksonian Era

The Jacksonian era is filled with contradictions. Many of the same social factors and economic forces that promoted the democratization of the political process during the 1820s also led Democrats, North and South, to justify white supremacy, slavery, and the subjugation of Indians and women.

What explains such contradictory behavior? By asserting the racial inferiority of Indians and blacks, white wage earners could, in a tortured sense, enhance their own self-esteem and justify their own economic interests. In addition, many northern workers feared for their own jobs if runaway slaves continued to stream northward or if all the slaves in the South were freed.

Attitudes toward Blacks

Roger B. Taney, the man Andrew Jackson appointed as the nation's attorney-general, declared in 1831 that blacks were a "separate and degraded people" and therefore could be discriminated against by local and state governments. Free blacks in most northern states during the Jacksonian era were denied basic civil rights and forced to live and operate under segregated conditions. In 1829 government officials in Cincinnati, Ohio, a haven for runaway slaves, ordered all blacks out of the city within thirty days. A mob of whites decided to hurry them on, and they destroyed most of the black neighborhoods in the city.

Such antiblack riots were common in northern cities. Whites who participated in an 1834 riot against blacks in Philadelphia explained that they were simply defending themselves against the efforts of blacks and abolitionists "to break down the distinctive barrier between the colors [so] that the poor whites may gradually sink into the degraded condition of the Negroes—that, like them, they may be slaves and tools" of economic elites. Four years later, in 1838, the state of Pennsylvania officially disenfranchised blacks. By 1860, almost every state, old and new, had disenfranchised free blacks while easing voting qualifications for white males.

The Democratic coalition that elected Jackson thus depended for its survival on a widely shared "white racism" and the ability to avoid potentially divisive discussions of slavery. In the South, the majority of farmers who supported the slaveholding Jackson and identified with the Democrats did not own slaves, but they still embraced theories of racial superiority.

Indian Policy

The attitude of Jackson and many of his followers toward the Indians was the typically western one—that they were barbaric impediments to white social progress and territorial expansion. By the time of his election in 1828, Jackson was convinced that a "just, humane, liberal policy toward Indians" dictated moving them onto the plains west of the Mississippi River, an area fit mainly for horned toads and rattlesnakes. Congress agreed, and in 1830 it approved the Indian Removal Act.

Although sometimes the tribes rebelled, there was, on the whole, remarkably little resistance. In Illinois and Wisconsin Territory an armed clash known as the Black Hawk War sprang up in 1832, when the Sauk and Fox under Chief Black Hawk sought to reoccupy some lands they had abandoned in the previous year. The Illinois militia mobilized to expel them, chased them into Wisconsin Territory, and massacred women and children as they tried to escape across the Mississippi.

Sioux Encamped on the Upper Missouri, Dressing Buffalo Meat and Robes (1832), by George Catlin. Catlin's romantic paintings of Indian life appeared just as the tribes of the Southeast were rooted up and moved west.

In the South two proud Indian nations, the Seminoles and Cherokees, also put up a stubborn resistance. The Seminoles were in fact a group of different tribes that had gravitated to Florida in the eighteenth century. They fought a protracted guerrilla war in the Everglades from 1835 to 1842, but most of the vigor went out of their resistance after 1837, when their leader, Osceola, was seized by treachery under a flag of truce, imprisoned, and left to die. After 1842 only a few hundred Seminoles remained, hiding out in the swamps. Most of the rest had been banished to the West.

The Trail of Tears

The Cherokees had by the end of the eighteenth century fallen back into the mountains of northern Georgia and western North Carolina, onto land guaranteed to them in 1791 by treaty with the United States. In 1827 the Cherokees, relying on their treaty rights, adopted a constitution in which they said pointedly that they were not subject to any other state or nation. The next year Georgia responded with a law stipulating that after June 1, 1830, the authority of state law would extend over the Cherokees living within the boundaries of the state.

The discovery of gold in 1829 whetted the whites' appetite for Cherokee lands and brought bands of rough prospectors into the country. The Cherokees sought relief in the Supreme Court, but in *Cherokee Nation v. Georgia* (1831) John Marshall ruled that the Court lacked jurisdiction because the Cherokees were a "domestic dependent nation" rather than a foreign state in the meaning of the Constitution. Marshall added, however, that the Cherokees had "an unquestionable right" to their lands until they wished to cede them to the United States.

In 1830 a Georgia law had required whites in the Cherokee territory to get licenses authorizing their residence there, and to take an oath of allegiance to the state of Georgia. Two New England missionaries

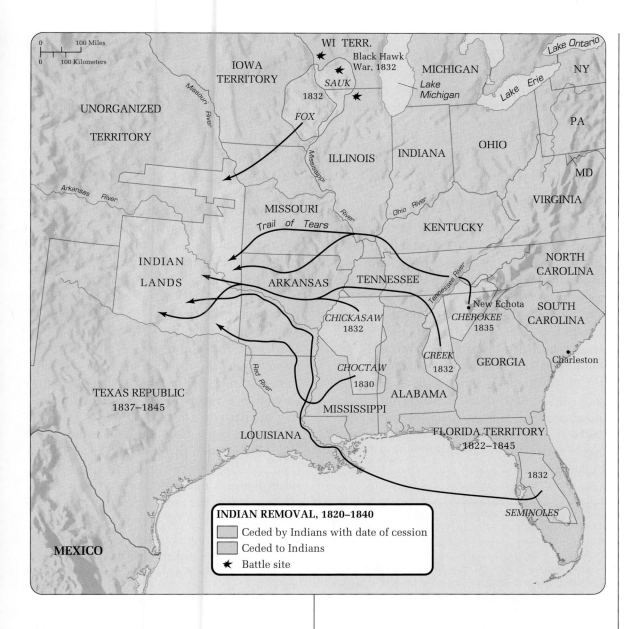

INDIAN REMOVAL, 1820–1840
- Ceded by Indians with date of cession
- Ceded to Indians
- ★ Battle site

among the Indians refused and were sentenced to four years at hard labor. On appeal, their case reached the Supreme Court as *Worcester* v. *Georgia* (1832), and the court held that the Cherokee nation was "a distinct political community" within which Georgia law had no force. The Georgia law was therefore unconstitutional. Now Georgia faced down the Supreme Court with the tacit consent of the president. Jackson is supposed to have said privately: "Marshall has made his decision, now let him enforce it!" In the circumstances, there was nothing

for the Cherokees to do but give in and sign a treaty, which they did in 1835. They gave up their lands in the Southeast in exchange for lands in the Indian Territory west of Arkansas, $5 million from the federal government, and expenses for transportation.

By 1838 some 12,000 Cherokees had departed on the thousand-mile "Trail of Tears" westward, following the Choctaws, Chickasaws, Creeks, and Seminoles. It was a grueling journey marked by the cruelty and neglect of soldiers and private contractors, and scorn and pilferage by whites along the way. Four thousand Cherokees did not survive the trip. A few never left their homeland. They held out in their native mountains and acquired title to lands in North Carolina; thenceforth they were the "Eastern Band" of Cherokees.

The Bank Controversy

The Bank's Opponents

The overriding national issue in the presidential campaign of 1832 was neither Jackson's Indian policy nor South Carolina's obsession with nullification. It was the question of rechartering the Bank of the United States (B.U.S), whose legal mandate would soon lapse. Jackson had absorbed the West's hostility toward the Bank after the Panic of 1819, and he insisted that it was unconstitutional no matter what Marshall had said in *McCulloch* v. *Maryland.* Banks in general had fed a speculative mania, and Jackson, suspicious of all banks, preferred a hard-money policy based solely on gold and silver coins rather than paper bank notes.

Jackson battling the hydra-headed Bank of the United States.

Under the management of Nicholas Biddle, the Second Bank of the United States had prospered during the early 1830s. The Bank had facilitated business expansion and supplied a stable currency by forcing state banks to keep a specie (gold or silver) reserve on hand to back up their paper currency. The Bank also acted as the collecting and disbursing agent for the federal government, which held one-fifth of the Bank's $35 million capital stock. From the start, many were suspicious of this combination of private and public functions. As the government's revenues soared, the Bank became the most powerful lending institution in the country, a central bank, in effect, whose huge size enabled it to determine the amount of available credit for the nation. Moreover, by issuing paper money of its own, the B.U.S. provided a stable and uniform currency for the expanding economy as well as a regulating mechanism controlling the pace of growth.

Arrayed against the Bank were powerful enemies: some of the state and local banks that had been forced to reduce their volume of paper money, debtor groups that had suffered from the reduction, and businessmen and speculators "on the make" who wanted easier credit. States'-rights groups questioned the Bank's constitutionality. Financiers on New York's Wall Street resented the supremacy of the Bank on Philadelphia's Chestnut Street. Many westerners and workingmen, like Andrew Jackson, felt that the Bank was a powerful monopoly controlled by the wealthy few and that this was irreconcilable with a democracy.

The Recharter Effort

Henry Clay, already the presidential candidate of the National-Republicans, proposed to make the Bank the central issue of the 1832 presidential election. Friends of the Bank held a majority in Congress, and Jackson would risk loss of support in the election if he vetoed renewal. But they failed to grasp the depth of popular prejudice against the Bank. They succeeded mainly in handing over to Jackson a charged issue on the eve of the election. "The Bank," Jackson told Martin Van Buren in May 1832, "is trying to kill me. But I will kill it."

Both houses passed the recharter bill by comfortable margins, but without the two-thirds majority needed to override a presidential veto. On July 10, 1832, Jackson vetoed the bill, sending it back to Congress with a ringing denunciation of monopoly and special privilege. An effort to overrule the veto failed in the Senate, where the vote of twenty-two to nineteen for the Bank fell far short of the needed two-thirds majority. The stage was set for a nationwide financial crisis.

Campaign Innovations

The 1832 presidential campaign included a third political party for the first time. The Anti-Masonic party was, like the Bank, the object of strong emotions then sweeping the new democracy. The group had grown out of popular hostility toward the Masonic order, a fraternal organization whose members were suspected of having kidnapped and murdered a New Yorker for revealing the "secrets" of his lodge. Opposition to a secret fraternal order was hardly the foundation on which to build a lasting national political organization, but the Anti-Masonic party had three important "firsts" to its credit: in addition to being the first third party, it was the first party to hold a national nominating convention and the first to announce a platform, all of which it accomplished in 1831 when it nominated William Wirt of Maryland for president.

The major parties followed its example by holding national conventions of their own. In 1831 National-Republican party delegates assembled in Baltimore to nominate Henry Clay for president. Jackson endorsed the idea of a nominating convention for the Democratic party to demonstrate popular support for its candidates. To that purpose, the convention adopted the two-thirds rule for nomination (which prevailed until 1936), and then named Martin Van Buren as Jackson's running mate. The Democrats, unlike the other two parties, adopted no formal platform at their first convention, and they relied substantially on hoopla and the president's personal popularity to carry the election.

The outcome was an overwhelming endorsement of Jackson in the electoral college by 219 votes to 49 for Clay, and a less overwhelming but solid victory in the popular vote, 688,000 to 530,000. William Wirt carried only Vermont. South Carolina, preparing for nullification and unable to stomach either Jackson or Clay, delivered its eleven votes to the governor of Virginia.

Removal of Government Deposits

Jackson viewed the election as a mandate to proceed further against the B.U.S., and he now resolved to remove all government deposits and distribute them to state banks. When Secretary of the Treasury Louis McLane opposed removal of the government deposits and suggested a new and modified version of the Bank, Jackson shook up his cabinet. He kicked McLane upstairs to head the State Department and replaced him with William J. Duane of Philadelphia. Yet Duane saw no merit in removing deposits from the central bank for deposit in countless state banks. So Jackson summarily dismissed Duane and moved Attorney-General Roger Taney to the Treasury, where the new secretary gladly complied with the president's wishes, which corresponded to his own views.

By the end of 1833, there were twenty-three state banks that had the benefit of governmental deposits, "pet banks" as they came to be called. Transferring the government's deposits was a highly questionable action under the law, and the Senate voted to censure Jackson for his actions. Nicholas Biddle refused to surrender. He ordered that

King Andrew the First. This opposition cartoon shows King Andrew Jackson trampling on the Constitution, internal improvements, and the Bank of the United States.

the B.U.S. curtail loans throughout the nation and demand the immediate redemption of state bank notes in specie as fast as possible. He sought to bring the economy to a halt, create a sharp depression, and reveal to the nation the importance of maintaining the Bank. By 1834 the tightness of credit was creating widespread complaints of business distress.

The financial contraction resulting from the bank war quickly gave way, however, to a speculative binge encouraged by the deposit of government funds in the pet state banks. With the restraint of the B.U.S. removed, the state banks unleashed their wildcat tendencies, issuing bank notes without keeping sufficient gold reserves on hand. (The term "wildcat," used in this sense, originated in Michigan, where one of the fly-by-night banks featured a panther, or wildcat, on its worthless notes.) New banks mushroomed, blissfully printing bank notes to lend to speculators. Sales of public lands rose from 4 million acres in 1834 to 15 million in 1835 and to 20 million in 1836. At the same time, the states plunged heavily into debt to finance the building of roads and canals, inspired by the success of New York's Erie Canal in opening up the entire state's economy to the markets of the Eastern Seaboard and Europe. By 1837 total state indebtedness had soared to $170 million, a very large sum for that time.

Fiscal Measures

Still the federal revenues continued to mount as the widespread speculation in public lands continued, and this set off an intense debate over how to deal with the growing federal surplus. Many westerners proposed simply to lower the price of land; southerners preferred to lower the tariff—but such action would now upset the compromise achieved in the Tariff of 1833. Finally, in 1836, the Distribution Act was passed. This was a compromise that allowed the government to distribute most of the surplus as loans to the states in proportion to each state's representation in Congress.

About a month after passage of this Distribution Act, Jackson's treasury secretary issued the Specie Circular of July 11, 1836. With that document, the president belatedly applied his hard-money convictions to the sale of public lands. According to his order, the government after August 15 would accept only gold and silver in payment for lands. Doing so would supposedly "repress frauds," withhold support "from monopoly of the public lands in the hands of speculators and capitalists," and discourage the "ruinous extension" of bank notes and credit.

Both the Distribution Act and the Specie Circular put many state banks in a precarious plight. The distribution reduced their deposits, or at least threw things into disarray by shifting them from bank to bank, and the increased demand for specie put an added strain on the supply of gold and silver. The distribution of the federal surplus to the state governments entailed the removal of large deposits from state banks. In turn, the state banks had to call in many of their loans in order to accumulate enough money to make the transfer of federal funds to the state governments. This disrupted the already chaotic state banking community.

Boom and Bust

But the boom and bust of the 1830s had causes larger even than Andrew Jackson, causes that were beyond his control. The inflation of mid-decade was rooted not solely in a sudden expansion of bank notes, as it seemed at the time, but also in an increase of gold and silver flowing in from England and France, and especially from Mexico, for investment and for the purchase of American cotton and other products.

Contrary to appearances, the specie reserves in American banks actually kept pace with the increase of bank notes, despite reckless behavior by some banks. But by 1836 a tighter economy caused a decline in British investments abroad and in British demand for American cotton, just when the new western lands were creating a rapid increase in cotton supply. Fortunately for Jackson, the Panic of 1837 did not break until he was out of the White House and safely back at his plantation near Nashville. His successor would serve as the scapegoat.

Van Buren and the New Party System

The Whig Coalition

By 1834, Jackson's opponents began to pull together a new coalition of diverse elements united chiefly by their hostility to the president. The imperious demeanor of that champion of democracy had given rise to the name of "King Andrew I." His followers therefore were "Tories," supporters of the king, and his opponents "Whigs," a name that linked them to the patriots of the American Revolution. This diverse coalition clustered around its center, the National-Republican party of John Quincy Adams, Clay, and Webster. Into the combination streamed remnants of the Anti-Masons and Democrats who, for one reason or another, were alienated by Jackson's stands on the Bank, Indian removal, hard money, or internal improvements.

The core Whigs were the supporters of Henry Clay and his "American System" of industrial development, high tariffs, and internal improvements. In the South the Whigs enjoyed the support of the urban banking and commercial interests, as well as their planter associates, owners of most of the slaves in the region. In the West,

farmers who valued internal improvements joined the Whig ranks. Most states'-rights supporters eventually dropped away, and by the early 1840s the Whigs were becoming the party of economic nationalism, even in the South. Unlike the Democrats, who attracted Catholic immigrants from Germany and Ireland, Whig voters tended to be native-born and British-American Protestants—Presbyterians, Baptists, and Congregationalists—who were active in promoting social reforms such as abolitionism and temperance.

The Election of 1836

By the presidential election of 1836, a new two-party system was emerging out of the Jackson and anti-Jackson forces, a system that would remain in fairly even balance for twenty years. In 1835, the Democrats held their second national convention and nominated Jackson's handpicked successor, Vice-President Martin Van Buren. The Whig coalition, united chiefly in its opposition to Jackson, adopted a strategy of multiple candidacies, hoping to throw the election into the House of Representatives.

The result was a free-for-all reminiscent of 1824, except that this time one candidate stood apart from the rest. It was Van Buren against the field. In the popular vote, Van Buren outdistanced the entire Whig field, with 765,000 votes to 740,000 votes for the Whigs.

Martin Van Buren, the eighth president, was the first of Dutch ancestry. Son of a tavernkeeper in Kinderhook, New York, he had been schooled in a local academy, read law, and entered politics. Although he kept up a limited legal practice, he had been primarily a professional politician, so skilled in the arts of organization and manipulation that he was dubbed the "Little Magician." After a brief tenure as governor of New York, Van Buren resigned to join Jackson's cabinet and, because of Jackson's support, became minister to London and then vice-president.

Martin Van Buren, the "Little Magician."

The Panic of 1837

Van Buren inherited Jackson's favor and a good part of his following, but he also inherited a financial panic. An already precarious economy was tipped over into crisis by depression in England, which resulted in a drop in the price of cotton from 17½ cents to 13½ cents a pound, and caused English banks and investors to contract their activities in the New World and to refuse extensions of loans. This was a particularly hard blow, since much of America's economic expansion depended on European—and mainly English—capital. As creditors hastened to foreclose, the inflationary spiral went into reverse. States curtailed ambitious plans for roads and canals and in many cases felt impelled to repudiate their debts. In the crunch, many of the wildcat banks succumbed.

By the fall of 1837, a third of the workforce was jobless. Those still fortunate enough to have jobs saw their wages cut by 30 to 50 percent within two years. At the same time, prices for food and clothing skyrocketed. There was no government aid, only that provided by churches and voluntary societies.

Van Buren's advisers and supporters were inclined to blame speculators and bankers for the hard times. At the same time, they expected the evildoers to get what they deserved in a healthy shakeout that would bring the economy back to stability. Van Buren did not believe that he or the government had any responsibility to rescue hard-pressed farmers or businessmen, or to provide public welfare. But he did feel obliged to keep the government itself in a healthy financial situation. To that end, he called a special session of Congress in 1837, which quickly voted to postpone indefinitely the distribution of the federal surplus because of a probable upcoming deficit, and also approved an issue of Treasury notes to cover immediate expenses.

An Independent Treasury

Van Buren proposed that the government cease risking its deposits in shaky banks and set up an Independent Treasury. Under this plan, the government would keep its funds in its own vaults and do business entirely in hard money. Van Buren's Independent Treasury Act encountered stiff opposition from a combination of Whigs and conservative Democrats who feared deflation, and it took the president several years of maneuvering to get what he wanted. Van Buren gained western support for the plan by backing a more liberal federal land policy. Congress finally passed the Independent Treasury Act on July 4, 1840. Although the Whigs repealed it in 1841, it would be restored in 1846.

The protracted struggle over the Treasury was only one of several issues that kept Washington preoccupied through the Van Buren years. Petitions asking Congress to abolish slavery and the slave trade in the District of Columbia provoked tumultuous debate, especially in the House of Representatives. A dispute over the Maine boundary kept British-American animosity at a simmer. But basic to the spreading malaise of the time was the depressed condition of the economy, which lasted through Van Buren's entire term. Fairly or not, the administration became the target of growing discontent. The president won renomination easily enough, but the general election was another matter.

The "Log Cabin and Hard Cider" Campaign

The Whigs got an early start on their 1840 campaign when they met at Harrisburg, Pennsylvania, on December 4, 1839, to choose a candidate. The delegates turned to William Henry Harrison, victor at the battle of Tippecanoe against the Shawnees in 1811, governor of the Indiana territory, and briefly a congressman and a senator from

Ohio. To rally their states'-rights wing, the Whigs chose for vice-president John Tyler of Virginia, Clay's close friend.

The Whigs had no platform. That would have risked dividing a coalition united chiefly by opposition to the Democrats. But they had a slogan, "Tippecanoe and Tyler too," that went trippingly on the tongue. And they soon had a rousing campaign theme, which a Democratic paper unwittingly supplied them when it declared sardonically "that upon condition of his receiving a pension of $2,000 and a barrel of cider, General Harrison would no doubt consent to withdraw his pretensions, and spend his days in a log cabin on the banks of the Ohio." The Whigs seized upon the cider and log cabin symbols to depict Harrison as a simple man sprung from the people. Actually, he sprang from one of the first families of Virginia, was a college graduate, and lived in a commodious Ohio farmhouse.

The campaign produced the largest turnout of any election up to that time. To the general public, Van Buren had come to symbolize the economic slump as well as aristocratic snobbery. "Van! Van! Is a Used-up Man!" went one of the Whig campaign slogans, and down he went by the thumping margin of 234 electoral votes to 60.

Assessing the Jackson Years

The Jacksonian impulse had permanently altered American politics. Long-standing ambivalence about political parties had been purged in the fires of political conflict, and mass political parties had arrived to stay. They were now widely justified as a positive good. By 1840 both parties were tightly organized down to the precinct level, and the proportion of adult white males who voted in the presidential election nearly tripled, from 27 percent in 1824 to 78

percent in 1840. That much is beyond dispute, but the phenomenon of Jackson, the great symbol for an age, has inspired conflicts of interpretation as spirited as those among his supporters and opponents at the time. Was he the leader of a vast democratic movement that welled up in the West and mobilized a farmer-laborer alliance to sweep the "Monster" bank into the dustbin of history? Or was he essentially a frontier tycoon, an opportunist for whom the ideal of democracy provided effective political rhetoric?

Whatever else Jackson and his supporters had in mind, they followed an ideal of republican virtue, of returning to the Jeffersonian vision of the Old Republic in which government would leave people largely to their own devices. In the Jacksonian view, the alliance of government and business invited special favors and provided an eternal source of corruption. The central bank epitomized such evil. Good governmental policy, at the national level in particular, refrained from granting special privileges and let free competition regulate the economy.

In the bustling world of the nineteenth century, however, the idea of a return to agrarian simplicity represented a futile exercise in nostalgia. Instead, Jackson's laissez-faire policies actually opened the way for a host of aspiring entrepreneurs eager to replace the established economic elite with a new order of free enterprise capitalism. And in fact there was no great conflict in the Jacksonian mentality between the farmer or planter who delved in the soil and the independent speculator and entrepreneur who won his way by other means. Jackson himself was all these things. The ultimate irony would be that Jackson's laissez-faire rationale for republican simplicity eventually became the justification for the growth of unregulated centers of economic power far greater than any ever wielded by the Bank of the United States.

CHAPTER

11

The Dynamics of Growth

This chapter focuses on

- The expansion of agriculture, industry, and transportation.
- Patterns of immigration at mid-century.
- The emergence of labor unions.

THE *ESSENTIAL AMERICA* ON-LINE TUTOR

www.wwnorton.com/eamerica/ch11

- **Topic: Industrialization, urbanization, and immigration**
  www.wwnorton.com/eamerica/ch11/topic.htm

  One of the great waves of immigration to America occurred in the 1840s and 1850s, bringing millions of Northern Europeans to the United States. Explore the significance of this immigration utilizing personal accounts, maps, paintings, contemporary newspaper accounts, and historical analyses. How did this wave of immigration affect the United States?

- **Chapter review: On-line quiz and chapter summary**
  www.wwnorton.com/eamerica/ch11/review.htm

- **Chapter resources: Multimedia index**
  www.wwnorton.com/eamerica/ch11/media.htm

The Jacksonian-era political debate between democratic and elitist elements was rooted in a profound transformation of American social and economic life. Between 1815 and 1850, the United States expanded all the way to the Pacific coast. An industrial revolution in the Northeast began to reshape the contours of the economy and propel an unrelenting process of urbanization. In the West an agricultural empire began to emerge based upon the foundation of corn, wheat, and cattle. In the South cotton became king, and its profits came to depend on an expanding institution of slavery. At the same time, innovations in transportation—horse-drawn wagons, canals, steamboats, and railroads—knit together a national market. These economic developments in turn generated changes in every other area of American life, from politics to the legal system, from the family to social values.

Agriculture and the National Economy

The first stage of industrialization brought with it an expansive commercial and urban outlook that by the end of the century would supplant the agrarian philosophy espoused by Thomas Jefferson and many others. "We are greatly, I was about to say fearfully, growing," John C. Calhoun told his congressional colleagues in 1816, and many other statesmen shared his ambivalent outlook. Would the Republic retain its virtue and cohesion amid the turmoil of commercial development?

Cotton

A major source of economic opportunity in the South after 1815 was provided by the cultivation of cotton, the profitable new staple crop that was spreading from South Carolina and Georgia into the new lands of Mississippi and Alabama. For many years, cotton had remained rare and expensive be-

cause of the need for hand labor to separate the lint from the tenacious green seeds. But that problem was solved in 1793 when Eli Whitney devised a machine for removing the sticky seeds. The cotton gin enabled a person to separate cotton fifty times faster than could be done by hand.

By inventing the cotton gin, Whitney had unwittingly begun a revolution. Cotton production soared during the first half of the nineteenth century, and planters found a new and profitable use for slavery. Planters and their slaves migrated westward into Kentucky, Tennessee, Alabama, Mississippi, Louisiana, and Texas, and the cotton culture became a way of life that tied together the Old Southwest and the coastal Southeast.

After Napoleon's defeat in 1815, European demand for cotton skyrocketed. From 1815 to 1819, American cotton exports averaged 39 percent of the value of all exports, and from the mid-1830s to 1860 they accounted for more than half the total. For the national economy as a whole during the first half of the century, cotton precipitated a phenomenal expansion. The South supplied the North both raw materials and markets for manufactures. Income from the North's role in handling the cotton trade then provided surpluses for capital investment.

Farming the West

The westward flow of planters and their slaves to Alabama and Mississippi during these flush times mirrored another migration through the Ohio Valley and the Great Lakes region, where the Indians had been steadily pushed westward. By 1860, more than half the nation's population resided west of the Appalachian Mountains, and the restless movement had long since spilled across the Mississippi River and touched the shores of the Pacific.

North of the expanding cotton belt in the Gulf states, the fertile woodland soils, riverside bottom lands, and black loam of the prairies drew farmers from the rocky land of

New England and the exhausted soils of the Southeast. The development of effective iron plows greatly eased the grueling job of breaking the soil. In 1819 a New York farmer developed an improved iron plow with parts that could be replaced separately without buying a whole new plow. Demand for plows grew so fast that the manufacturer could not supply the need. Further improvements would follow, including John Deere's steel plow (1837), which was better suited for breaking up the rock-hard soil of the Great Plains.

A new federal land law of 1820 reduced the minimum price per acre and the minimum plot from 160 to 80 acres. The settler could now buy a homestead for as little as $100, and over the years the proliferation of state banks made it possible to continue buying on credit. Even that was not enough for westerners who began a long—and eventually victorious—agitation for further relaxation of the land laws. They favored *preemption*, the right of squatters to purchase land at the minimum price, and *graduation*, the progressive reduction of the price on lands that did not sell.

Congress eventually responded with two new laws. Under the Preemption Act of 1830, squatters could stake out claims ahead of the land surveys and later get 160 acres at the minimum price of $1.25 per acre. In effect, the law recognized a practice enforced more often than not by frontier vigilantes. Under the Graduation Act of 1854, prices of unsold government lands were to go down in stages until the lands could sell for 12½¢ per acre after thirty years.

Transportation and the National Economy

New Roads

Transportation improvements helped spur the development of a national market. In 1795 the Wilderness Road, which followed the trail blazed by Daniel Boone twenty years before, was opened to wagon and stagecoach traffic, thereby easing the route through the Cumberland Gap in Kentucky. In the Deep South there were no such major highways. South Carolinians and Georgians

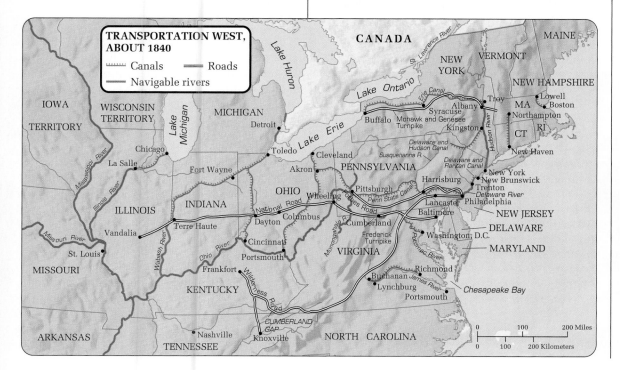

TRANSPORTATION WEST, ABOUT 1840

- Canals
- Roads
- Navigable rivers

pushed westward on whatever trails or rutted roads had appeared.

To the northeast, public demand for paved roads packed with crushed stones gathered momentum after completion of the Philadelphia-Lancaster Turnpike in 1794 (the term derives from a pole or pike at the tollgate, turned to admit the traffic). By 1821 there were some 4,000 miles of turnpikes, mainly connecting eastern cities, but western traffic could move along the Frederick Turnpike to Cumberland and thence along the National Road to Wheeling on the Ohio River in 1818, then to Columbus, Ohio, in the Northwest Territory, and to Vandalia, Illinois, by about mid-century.

Water Transport

Once turnpike travelers had reached the Ohio River, they could float westward in comparative comfort on flatboats. In the early 1820s some 3,000 flatboats went down the Ohio River every year, and for many years thereafter the flatboat remained the chief means for conveying heavy traffic downstream.

By the early 1820s, the turnpike boom was giving way to new developments in water transportation: the river steamboat and

Lockport, New York. Eighty-three locks were required for the Erie Canal to cross the rise in elevation in western New York, including five at Lockport.

the canal barge, which carried bulk commodities far more cheaply than did Conestoga wagons on the National Road. The first commercially successful steamboat appeared when Robert Fulton and Robert R. Livingston sent the *Clermont* up the Hudson River to Albany in 1807.

By 1836, 361 steamboats navigated the far reaches of the Mississippi Valley, up rivers such as the Wabash, the Monongahela, the Cumberland, the Tennessee, the Missouri, and the Arkansas. By bringing cheaper and faster two-way traffic to the Mississippi Valley, the steamboats helped create a continental market and an agricultural empire that became the new breadbasket of America. Along with the new farmers came promoters, speculators, and retailers. Villages at strategic trading points along the streams evolved into centers of commerce and urban life. The port of New Orleans grew in the 1830s and 1840s to lead all others in exports.

But by then the Erie Canal was drawing eastward much of the trade that once went down to the Gulf. In 1817 the New York legislature had endorsed Governor De Witt Clinton's dream of a canal connecting the Hudson River with Lake Erie. Eight years later, in 1825, the canal was open for its entire 350 miles from Albany to Buffalo; branches soon put most of the state within reach of the canal. The completion of the canal reduced travel time from New York City to Buffalo from twenty days to six, and the cost of moving a ton of freight plummeted from $100 to $5.

The speedy success of the New York system inspired a mania for canals that lasted more than a decade and created about 3,000 miles of waterways by 1837. But no canal ever matched the spectacular success of the Erie. It rendered the entire Great Lakes region an economic tributary to New York City and had major economic and political consequences tying together the West and East while further isolating the Deep South. With the addition of new canals spanning Ohio and Indiana from north to south, much of the upper Ohio Valley was also drawn within New York's economic sphere.

Railroads

In 1825, the year the Erie Canal was completed, the world's first commercial steam railway began operations in England, and soon the port cities of Baltimore, Charleston, and Boston were alive with schemes to penetrate the hinterlands by rail. By 1840, American railroads, with a total of 3,328 miles, had outdistanced the canals by just two miles. Over the next twenty years,

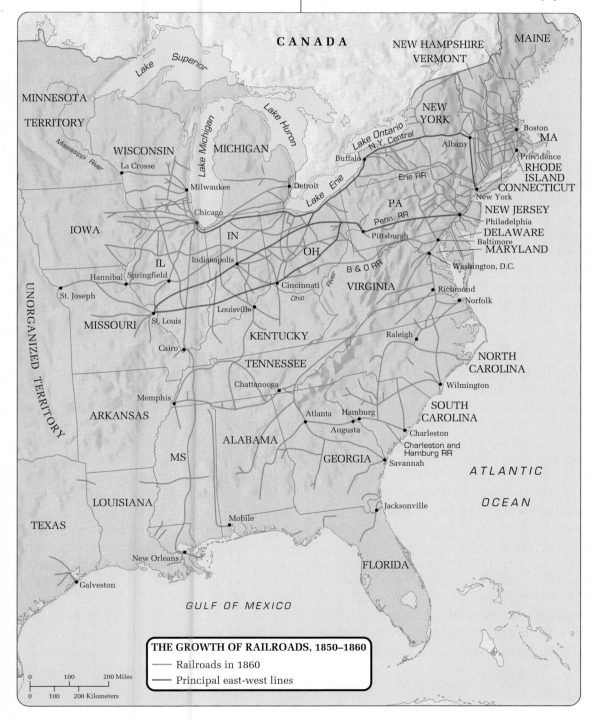

THE GROWTH OF RAILROADS, 1850–1860

—— Railroads in 1860

—— Principal east-west lines

though, railroads grew nearly tenfold to cover 30,626 miles; more than two-thirds of this total was built in the 1850s. But it was not until the eve of the Civil War that railroads surpassed canals in total haulage: in 1859 they carried a little over 2 billion tons compared to 1.6 billion on canals.

Travel on the early railroads tested the courage of passengers. Wood was used for fuel, and the sparks often caused fires along the way or damaged passengers' clothing. Invention of the "spark arrester" and the use of coal for fuel alleviated but did not eliminate the hazard. Different track widths often forced passengers to change trains until a standard gauge became national in 1882. Land travel, whether by stagecoach or train, was a jerky, bumpy, wearying ordeal.

Water travel, where available, offered far more comfort, but railroads gained supremacy over other forms of transport because of their economy, speed, and reliability. Early trains averaged ten miles an hour, doubling the speed of stagecoaches and canal boats. Railroads provided indirect benefits by encouraging frontier settlement and boosting farming. During the antebellum period, the reduced shipping costs provided by the railroads aided the expansion of farming more than manufacturing, since manufacturers in the Northeast, especially in New England, had better access to water transportation. The railroads' demand for iron and equipment of various kinds, however, did provide an enormous market for the industries that made these capital goods. And the ability of railroads to operate year round in all kinds of weather gave them an advantage in carrying finished goods, too.

But the epic railroad boom had negative effects as well. By opening up new possibilities for quick and often shady profits, it helped to corrupt political life, and by opening up access to the trans-Appalachian West, it helped accelerate the decline of Indian culture. In addition, the railroad dramatically quickened the tempo and mobility of life.

Ocean Transport

For oceangoing traffic, the start of service on regular schedules was the most important change of the early 1800s. In the first week of 1818, ships of the New York–based Black Ball Line inaugurated a weekly transatlantic service between New York and Liverpool, England. By 1845 some fifty-two transatlantic lines ran square-riggers on schedule from New York, with three regular sailings per week. Many others ran in the coastwise trade, to Charleston, Savannah, New Orleans, and elsewhere.

The same year, 1845, witnessed a great innovation with the launching of the first clipper ship, the *Rainbow*. Built for speed, the sleek clippers were the nineteenth-century equivalent of the supersonic jetliner. They doubled the speed of the older merchant vessels. Long and lean, with taller masts and more sails, they cut dashing figures during their brief but colorful career, which lasted less than two decades. What provoked the clipper boom was the lure of Chinese tea, a drink long coveted in America but in scarce supply. The tea leaves were a perishable commodity that had to reach market quickly, and the new clippers made this possible. Even more important, the discovery of California gold in 1848 lured thousands of prospectors and entrepreneurs from the Atlantic seaboard. These new settlers generated an urgent demand for goods, and the clippers met the need. In 1854 the *Flying Cloud* took eighty-nine days and eight hours to get from New York to San Francisco, a speed that took steamships several decades to equal. But clippers, while fast, lacked ample cargo space, and after the Civil War they would give way to the larger steamship.

The Role of Government

The massive internal improvements of the antebellum era were the product of both state government and private initiatives, sometimes undertaken jointly and sometimes separately. After the Panic of 1837, however, the states left railroad development mainly to private corporations, the source of most investment capital. Still, several southern and western states built their own lines, and most states granted generous tax concessions to private developers.

The federal government helped, too, despite the constitutional scruples of some against direct involvement in internal improvements. The government bought stock in turnpike and canal companies and, after the success of the Erie Canal, extended land grants to several western states for the support of canal projects. Congress provided for railroad surveys by government engineers, granted tracts of land, and reduced the tariff duties on iron used in railroad construction.

The Growth of Industry

While the South and West developed the agricultural basis for a national economy, the Northeast was laying the foundation for an industrial revolution. Technology in the form of the cotton gin, the grain harvester, and improvements in transportation quickened agricultural development and to some extent decided its direction. But technology altered the economic landscape even more profoundly by giving rise to the textile factory system.

The beginnings of an American textile industry were slow and faltering until Jefferson's embargo in 1807 and the War of 1812 restricted imports and encouraged New England merchant capitalists to switch their resources into manufacturing. New England had one distinct advantage in that its ample rivers were near the coast, where water transportation was readily available. By 1815, New England textile mills numbered in the hundreds. The foundations of textile manufacture were laid, and they spurred the growth of garment trades and a machine-tool industry to build and service the mills.

Technology in America

Meanwhile, American ingenuity was adding other bases for industrial growth. In 1804 Oliver Evans developed a high-pressure steam engine adapted to a variety of uses in ships and factories. Thirty years later, in 1834, Cyrus Hall McCormick of Virginia invented a primitive grain reaper, a development as significant to the agricultural economy of the Old Northwest as the cotton gin was to the South.

With a hand-operated sickle a farmer could harvest half an acre of wheat a day; with a McCormick reaper two people could work twelve acres a day. McCormick's success attracted other manufacturers and inventors, and soon there were mechanical threshers to separate the grains of wheat from the straw. As the volume of agricultural products soared, prices dropped, income rose, and the standard of living for many farm families in the Old Northwest improved.

A spate of inventions in the 1840s generated profound changes in American life. In 1844 Charles Goodyear patented a process for vulcanizing rubber, which made it stronger and more elastic and in the process created the fabric for rainproof coats. In the same year the first intercity telegraph message was transmitted from Baltimore to Washington on the device Samuel F. Morse had invented back in 1832. The telegraph was slow to catch on at first, but seventeen years after that demonstration, with the completion of connections to San Francisco, an entire continent had been wired for instant communication. In 1846 Elias Howe invented the sewing machine, soon improved by Allen B. Wilson and Isaac Merritt Singer.

It is hard to exaggerate the importance of science and technology in changing the ways people lived by mid-century. To cite but a few examples: improved transportation and a spreading market economy combined with innovations in canning and refrigeration to provide people a more healthful and varied diet. Fruit and vegetables, heretofore available only during harvest season, could be shipped during much of the year. Scientific breeding of cattle helped make meat and milk more abundant.

Technological advances also helped improve living conditions: houses were larger, better heated, and better illuminated. Although working-class residences had few creature comforts, the affluent were able to afford indoor plumbing, central heating, gas lighting, bathtubs, iceboxes, and sewing machines. Even the lower classes were able to afford new coal-burning, cast-iron cooking stoves that facilitated more varied meals and improved heating. The first sewer systems began to help rid city streets of human and animal waste, while underground water lines enabled fire companies to use hydrants rather than bucket brigades.

The Lowell System

Before the 1850s, the factory system still had not become widespread. Handicraft and domestic production remained common,

Women workers carding, drawing, and roving cotton cloth in a textile mill, 1834.

and as late as 1860 the United States was still preponderantly rural and agricultural. But modern industrialism made significant inroads, especially in New England. At Lowell, Massachusetts, along the Merrimack River, the Merrimack Manufacturing Company in 1822 developed a new plant similar to one in Waltham, Massachusetts, in which spinning and weaving by power machinery had been brought under one roof for the first time in 1813. The town of Lowell grew dramatically, and it soon provided the model for other mill towns in Massachusetts, New Hampshire, and Maine.

The chief features of the "Lowell System" were a large capital investment, the concentration of all production processes in one plant under unified management, and specialization in a relatively coarse cloth requiring minimum skill by the workers. Lowell's founders insisted that they could design model factory centers that would enhance rather than corrupt the social fabric. The drab, crowded, and wretched life of English mill villages would be avoided by locating American mills in the countryside and then establishing an ambitious program of paternal supervision for the workers. The operatives were mostly young women from New England farm families who were increasingly without gainful employment and faced diminishing prospects for finding husbands. With so many men migrating westward, New England had been left with a surplus of women. Moreover, much of the household production previously carried out by daughters had given way to "store-bought" goods. Many women workers were also drawn to the mills by the chance to escape the routine of farm life and to earn money to help the family or improve their own circumstances.

Initially visitors to Lowell praised the well-designed mills. The laborers appeared "healthy and happy." The women workers lived in dormitories staffed by matronly supervisors, church attendance was mandatory, and temperance regulations and curfews were rigidly enforced. Despite the thirteen-hour days and six-day workweek, one woman operative described Lowell's community life as approaching "almost Arcadian simplicity." But Lowell soon lost its innocence as it experienced mushrooming growth. By 1840, Lowell had thirty-two mills and factories in operation, and the blissful rural town had become a bustling, grimy, bleak industrial city.

Other factory centers began sprouting up across New England, displacing forests and farms and engulfing villages, filling the air with smoke, noise, and stench. Between 1820 and 1840, the number of Americans engaged in manufactures increased eightfold, and the number of city dwellers more than doubled.

During the 1830s, as prices and wages dropped, relations between workers and managers rapidly deteriorated. A new generation of owners and foremen stressed efficiency and profit margins over community values. The machines and their operatives were worked at a faster pace, and workers organized strikes to protest deteriorating conditions. Visitors now noted the growing similarity between Lowell and the dismal factory towns of England immortalized in Charles Dickens's writings.

Industry and Cities

In 1855 a journalist exclaimed that "the great phenomenon of the Age is the growth of cities." Using the census definition of "urban" as places with 8,000 inhabitants or more, the proportion of urban population grew from 3 percent in 1790 to 16 percent in 1860. Because of their strategic locations and their importance as centers of trade and transportation, the Atlantic seaports of New York, Philadelphia, Baltimore, and Boston were the four largest U.S. cities throughout the pre–Civil War period. New York outpaced all its competitors and the nation as a whole in its population growth. By 1860, it was the first American city to boast a population of more than a million, largely because of its superior harbor and its unique access to commerce afforded by the Erie Canal.

Pittsburgh, at the head of the Ohio River, was already a center of iron production by 1800, and Cincinnati, at the mouth of the Little Miami, soon surpassed all other centers of meat packing, with pork a specialty. Louisville, because it stood at the falls of the Ohio River, became an important trade center. On the Great Lakes, the leading cities also benefited from easy access to water transportation: Buffalo, Cleveland, Detroit, Chicago, and Milwaukee. Chicago was especially well located to become a hub of both water and rail transportation on into the trans-Mississippi West. During the 1830s, St. Louis tripled in size, mainly because most of the trans-Mississippi grain and fur trade was funneled down the Missouri River.

The Popular Culture

During the colonial era, working Americans had little time for play or amusement. Their priority was simply survival. Yet over time they fashioned engaging forms of recreation and entertainment. In rural areas people participated in barn raisings and cornhusking parties, shooting matches and foot races, while on the seacoast people sailed and fished. In colonial cities, people attended balls, sleigh rides, picnics, and played "parlor games" at home—billiards, cards, and chess.

By the early nineteenth century, however, a more urban society could indulge in new forms of recreation. As more people moved into cities in the first half of the nineteenth century, they began to create a distinctive urban culture. Laborers and shopkeepers sought new forms of leisure and entertainment as pleasant diversions from their long workdays.

Bare Knuckles. Blood sports emerged as a popular entertainment in the cities for men of all social classes.

Urban Recreation

In working-class neighborhoods at mid-century, young men formed volunteer fire companies and fraternal societies whose primary activities were drinking and gambling. The more affluent and educated people viewed leisure time as an opportunity for self-improvement and attended lectures by prominent figures such as philosopher Ralph Waldo Emerson and minister Henry Ward Beecher. Circuses began touring the country. Foot races, horse races, and boat races began attracting thousands of spectators.

So-called blood sports were also a popular form of amusement. Cockfighting and dogfighting at saloons attracted excited crowds and frenzied betting. Prizefighting (also known as boxing) eventually displaced the animal contests. Imported from Britain, boxing surged into prominence at mid-century, and then, as now, proved popular with all social classes. Contestants fought with bare knuckles, and the results were brutal. A match ended only when a contestant could not continue. One such bout in 1842 lasted 119 rounds and ended when one fighter died in his corner. Such matches prompted clergymen to condemn prizefighting, and several cities outlawed the practice, only to see it reappear as an underground activity.

The Performing Arts

The most popular form of indoor entertainment was theatrical. During the first half of the nineteenth century, the theater played the popular role that movie houses would provide in the first half of the twentieth century. People of all social classes flocked to opera houses and theaters to watch a wide spectrum of performances: Shakespeare's tragedies, "blood and thunder" melodramas, comedies, minstrel shows, operas, magic shows, acrobatic troupes, and local pageants.

The audiences were predominantly young and middle-aged men. "Respectable" women were deterred from attending because of the boisterous atmosphere and the prevailing "cult of domesticity" that kept women in the home. People went to the theater not simply to watch the performances but also to socialize, to see and be seen, to talk business and gossip. Patrons were participants as well as spectators. Audiences cheered the heroes and heroines and hissed the villains. They often joined the actors in reciting famous passages or yelled out the punch lines for familiar jokes. If an actor did not meet expectations, audiences would hurl epithets, nuts, eggs, fruit, shoes, or chairs.

By mid-century, the arbiters of taste dealt with the problem of cultural rowdiness by creating separate theaters for the genteel elite and for laboring folk. As historian Lawrence Levine has remarked, the theaters and opera houses "no longer functioned as an expressive form that embodied all classes within a shared public space." Theaters grew darker, quieter, and more secure; audiences grew more affluent and passive.

Minstrel Shows

The 1830s witnessed the emergence of the first uniquely American form of mass entertainment: the blackface minstrel show featuring white performers made up as blacks.

"Minstrelsy" drew upon African-American subjects and reinforced prevailing racial stereotypes. It featured banjo and fiddle music, "shuffle" dances, and low-brow humor. Between the 1830s and 1870s, the minstrel shows were immensely popular throughout the nation, especially among northern working-class ethnics and southern whites, who were eager to flaunt their presumed superiority to blacks. The shows expanded to include entire troupes of performers who would tour the country, often using riverboats as their means of transportation, giving performances that included jokes, sentimental songs, dances, comedy routines, and skits.

Although antebellum minstrel shows usually portrayed slaves as blissfully contented and caricatured free blacks in the North as superstitious buffoons who preferred slavery to freedom, minstrelsy represented more than an expression of virulent racism and white exploitation of black culture; it also provided a medium for the expression of authentic African-American art forms.

Immigration

Throughout the nineteenth century, land remained plentiful and relatively cheap, while labor was scarce and relatively expensive. A decline in the birthrate coinciding with the onset of industry and urbanization reinforced this condition. The United States in the nineteenth century remained a strong magnet to immigrants, offering them chances to take up farms in the country or jobs in the cities. Glowing reports from early arrivals who made good also reinforced romantic views of American economic opportunity and political and religious freedom.

During the forty years from the outbreak of the Revolution until the end of the War of 1812, immigration had slowed to a trickle. The wars of the French Revolution and Napoleon restricted travel from Europe un-til 1815. Within a few years, however, passenger ships had begun to cross the north Atlantic. The years from 1845 to 1854 saw the greatest proportionate influx of immigrants in American history, 2.4 million, or about 14.5 percent of the total population in 1845.

Most European immigrants entered the United States through the Port of New York. Ships would discharge passengers at wharves, and the newcomers would have to fend for themselves in their alien environment. Thieves, thugs, and con men preyed upon the new arrivals. The infectious diseases that many of the immigrants brought with them also aroused popular concern. In 1855 the problems associated with the immigrants' arrival in America provoked the New York State legislature to lease Castle Garden, at the southern tip of Manhattan, for use as an immigration receiving center. Inside the depot, clerks would record the names, nationalities, and destinations of the new arrivals, physicians would give them a cursory physical exam, and labor bureau representatives would assist them in seeking jobs.

The Irish

In 1860 America's population was 31 million, with more than one of every eight foreign born. The largest groups among the immigrants were 1.6 million Irish, 1.2 million Germans, and 588,000 British (mostly English). The Irish had a long-standing reason for migrating from their country: resentment of British rule, British landlords, British Protestantism, and British taxes. But what caused so many Irish to flee their homeland in the nineteenth century was the onset of a prolonged depression that brought immense social hardship. The most densely populated country in Europe, Ireland was so ravaged by the economic collapse that in rural areas the average age at death declined to nineteen. By the 1830s, the number of Irish migrants to America was growing quickly, and after an epidemic of potato rot in 1845 brought a famine to rural Ireland that killed upward of a million peasants, the flow of Irish immigrants to Canada and the United States rose to a flood.

By 1850, the Irish constituted 43 percent of the foreign-born population in the United States. Unlike the German immigrants, who were predominantly male, the Irish newcomers were more evenly apportioned by sex; in fact a slight majority of them were women, most of them single young adults.

Many Irish men hired on with construction gangs building the canals and railways—about 3,000 set to work on the Erie Canal as early as 1818. Others worked in iron foundries, steel mills, warehouses, and shipyards. Many Irish women found jobs as domestic servants, laundresses, or textile mill workers in New England. In 1845, the Irish constituted only 8 percent of the workforce in the Lowell mills; by 1860, they made up 50 percent.

Landing from an Immigrant Ship. In 1847, nearly 214,000 Irish emigrated to the United States and Canada, 30 percent of whom died on board ship.

Few immigrants during the Jacksonian era found their way into the South, where land was expensive and industries scarce. The widespread use of slaves also left few opportunities in the region for manual laborers. Too poor to move inland, most of the destitute Irish congregated in the eastern cities, in or near their port of entry. By the 1850s, the Irish made up over half the populations of Boston and of New York City, and they were almost as prominent in Philadelphia. They clustered in murky slums and around Catholic churches, both of which became familiar features of the urban scene. Irish newcomers crowded into filthy, poorly ventilated buildings plagued by high rates of crime, infectious disease, prostitution, alcoholism, and infant mortality. The archbishop of New York City at mid-century described the Irish as "the poorest and most wretched population that can be found in the world."

But many enterprising Irish immigrants seized opportunities in their new environment to forge remarkable success stories. Twenty years after arriving in New York, Alexander T. Stewart became the owner of America's largest department store and thereafter accumulated vast real estate holdings in Manhattan. Michael Cudahy, who began work in a Milwaukee meat-packing business at age fourteen, became head of the Cudahy Packing Company and developed the process for the summer curing of meats under refrigeration. Dublin-born Victor Herbert emerged as one of America's most revered composers, and Irish dancers and playwrights came to dominate the American stage. Irishmen were equally successful in the boxing arena.

These accomplishments did little to quell the intense anti-Irish sentiments prevalent in nineteenth-century America. Irish immigrants confronted demeaning stereotypes and violent anti-Catholic prejudices. It was commonly assumed that the Irish were ignorant, filthy, clannish folk incapable of assimilation. "No Irish Need Apply" signs sprouted in every eastern city. But the Irish could be equally contemptuous of other groups, such as free blacks who competed with them for low-status jobs. In 1850 the *New York Tribune* expressed consternation at the fact that the Irish, having themselves escaped from "a galling, degrading bondage" in their homeland, typically voted against any proposal for equal rights for the Negro. For their part, many blacks viewed the Irish with equal disdain.

The Irish, after becoming naturalized citizens, formed powerful blocs of voters and found their way into American politics more quickly than any other immigrant group. Drawn mainly to the party of Andrew Jackson, they set a crucial pattern of identification with the Democrats that other ethnic groups by and large followed.

Although property requirements initially kept most Irish Americans from voting, a New York State law extended the franchise in 1821, and five years later the state removed the property qualification altogether. The following year masses of Irish voters made the difference in the election between Jackson and John Quincy Adams. Although women, blacks, and Indians still could not vote, the Irish newcomers were able to use the franchise to exert a remarkable political influence.

Perhaps the greatest collective achievement of the Irish immigrants was stimulating the growth of the Catholic Church in the United States. Years of persecution had instilled in Irish Catholics a fierce loyalty to the doctrines of the church, leading one Irish American to proclaim that religion "overrides all other sovereigns, and has the supreme authority over all the affairs of the world." Such passionate attachment to Catholicism generated both community cohesion among Irish Americans and fear among American Protestants.

The Germans, Scandinavians, and Chinese

During the eighteenth century, Germans had responded to William Penn's offer of free re-

ligious expression and cheap, fertile land by coming in large numbers to America. As a consequence, when a new wave of German migration formed in the 1830s, there were still large German enclaves in Pennsylvania and Ohio.

The new German migration took on a markedly different cast. It peaked in 1854, just a few years after the crest of Irish arrivals, when 215,000 Germans disembarked at American ports. These immigrants included a large number of learned, cultured professional people—doctors, lawyers, teachers, engineers—some of them refugees from the failed German revolutions of 1830 and 1848. The Germans brought with them a variety of religious preferences. A third of the new arrivals were Catholic, most were Protestants (usually Lutherans), and a significant number were Jewish, free-thinking atheists, or agnostics.

Unlike the Irish, the Germans included many independent farmers, skilled workers, and shopkeepers who arrived with enough money to get themselves established in skilled labor or on the land. They also migrated in families and groups rather than as individuals, and this clannish quality helped them sustain elements of German language and culture in their New World environment.

Among those who prospered in America were Ferdinand Schmacher, who began peddling oatmeal in glass jars in Ohio and eventually formed the Quaker Oats Company; Heinrich Steinweg, a piano maker from Lower Saxony, who in America changed his name to Steinway and became famous for the quality of his pianos; and Levi Strauss, a Jewish tailor who followed the gold rushers to California and began making long-wearing denim work pants that later were dubbed blue jeans or Levi's.

Two other groups that began to arrive in some number during the 1840s and 1850s were but the vanguard of greater numbers to come later. Annual arrivals from Scandinavia, most of them religious dissenters, did not exceed 1,000 until 1843, but by 1860 a total of 72,600 Scandinavians lived in America. The Norwegians and Swedes gravitated usually in family groups to Wisconsin and Minnesota, where the climate and woodlands reminded them of home.

By the 1850s, the sudden development of California after the discovery of gold attracted Chinese, who, like the Irish in the East, did the heavy work of construction. Infinitesimal in numbers until 1854, the Chinese in America numbered 35,500 by 1860. The migrants were mostly married, illiterate men desperate for work. Single women did not travel abroad, and married women usually stayed behind to raise the children. During the mid–nineteenth century, a laborer in southern China might earn five dollars a month; in California, he could work for a railroad or a mine and make six times as much. After three or four years of such work, an immigrant could return to China with his savings and become a "big, very big gentleman."

Nativism

For many native-born Americans, these waves of strangers posed a threat of unknown languages, mysterious customs, and, perhaps worst, feared religions. The flood of Irish and German Catholics aroused Protestant hostility to "popery." A militant Protestantism growing out of the early nineteenth-century revivals heated up the climate of suspicion. There were fears of political radicalism among the Germans and of voting blocs among the Irish, but above all hovered the menace of unfamiliar religious practices. Catholic authoritarianism was widely perceived as a threat to hard-won American liberties, religious and political.

By the 1830s, nativism was conspicuously on the rise. In 1834 a series of anti-Catholic sermons by the leading New England minister of the era, revivalist and later abolitionist Lyman Beecher, aroused feelings to the extent that a mob attacked and burned a convent in Charlestown, Massa-

chusetts. In 1844 armed clashes between Protestants and Catholics in Philadelphia ended with about twenty killed and one hundred injured. Sporadically, the nativist spirit took organized form in groups that proved their patriotism by hating foreigners and Catholics.

In 1854 delegates from thirteen states gathered to form the American political party, which had the trappings of a secret fraternal order. Members pledged never to vote for any foreign-born or Catholic candidate. When asked about the organization, they were to say "I know nothing," and in popular parlance the American party thus became the Know-Nothing party. In state and local campaigns during 1854, the Know-Nothings carried one election after another. They swept the Massachusetts legislature, winning all but two seats in the lower house. That fall they elected more than forty congressmen. For a while the Know-Nothings threatened to control New England, New York, and Maryland and showed strength elsewhere, but the movement subsided when slavery became the focal issue of the 1850s.

The Know-Nothings demanded the exclusion of immigrants and Catholics from public office and the extension of the period for naturalization from five to twenty-one years, but the party never gathered the political strength to effect such legislation. Nor did Congress act during the period to restrict immigration in any way.

Immigrant Labor

By meeting the need for cheap, unskilled labor, immigrants made a twofold contribution to economic growth: they moved into jobs vacated or bypassed by those who went into the factories, and they themselves made up a pool of labor from which in time factory workers were drawn.

In New England the large numbers of Irish workers, accustomed to hard treatment and willing to work for what natives considered low wages, spelled the end of the "Lowell girls." By 1860, immigrants made up more than half the labor force in New England mills. Even so, their pay was generally higher than that of the women and children who worked to supplement family incomes. The flood of immigration never rose fast enough to stop the long-term rise in wages. Factory labor thus continued to draw people from the countryside. Work in the cities offered higher real wages than work on the farm. Labor costs encouraged factory owners to seek ever more efficient machines in order to increase production without hiring more workers. In addition, the owners' desire to control the upward pressure on wage rates accelerated the emphasis on mass production.

By stressing high production and low prices, owners made it easier for workers to buy the items they made. Artisans who emphasized quality and craftsmanship found it hard to meet such competitive conditions. Many artisans in fact found that their skills were going out of style. Some took work as craftsmen in factories, while others went into small-scale manufacturing or shopkeeping, and some bought homesteads to practice their crafts in the West.

Organized Labor

As early as the colonial period, craftsmen had formed fraternal and mutual-benefit societies, much like the medieval guilds, through which they regulated a system for training apprentices. These organizations continued to flourish well into the national period. After the Revolution, however, organizations of journeymen carpenters, masons, shipfitters, tailors, printers, and cordwainers (as shoemakers were called) became concerned with wages, hours, and working conditions and began to back up their demands with devices such as the strike and the closed shop (in which only union members could work). These organi-

zations were local, often largely social in purpose, and frequently lasted only for the duration of the dispute with the employer. During the 1820s and 1830s, few workers belonged to unions. Increasingly, however, a growing fear that they were losing status led artisans of the major cities into intense activity in labor politics and unions.

Early Unions

Early efforts to form labor unions faced serious legal obstacles. Unions were prosecuted as unlawful conspiracies. In 1806, for instance, Philadelphia shoemakers were found guilty of a "combination to raise their wages." The decision broke the union. Such precedents were used for many years to hamstring labor organizations until the Massachusetts Supreme Court made a landmark ruling in the case of *Commonwealth* v. *Hunt* (1842). The court ruled that forming a trade union was not in itself illegal, nor was a demand that employers hire only members of the union.

Until the 1820s, labor organizations took the form of local trade unions, confined to one city and one craft. During the ten years from 1827 to 1837, organization on a larger scale began to take hold. In 1834 the National Trades' Union was set up to federate the city societies. At the same time, national craft unions were established by the shoemakers, printers, combmakers, carpenters, and hand-loom weavers, but all the national groups and most of the local ones vanished in the economic collapse of 1837.

Labor Politics

With the widespread removal of property qualifications for voting, labor politics flourished briefly in the 1830s. Working Men's parties appeared in New York, Boston, Philadelphia, and about fifteen states. These labor parties faded quickly for a variety of reasons: the inexperience of labor politicians that left the parties prey to manipulation by political professionals; the fact that some of their issues were also espoused by the major parties; and their vulnerability to attack on grounds of radicalism. In addition, they often splintered into warring factions, which limited their effectiveness.

Once the labor parties had faded, many of their supporters found their way into a radical wing of the Jacksonian Democrats, which became the Equal Rights party. In 1835 party members acquired the name "Locofocos" when their opponents from New York City's regular Democratic organization, Tammany Hall, turned off the gas lights at one of their meetings, and the Equal Rights supporters produced candles, lighting them with the new friction matches known as Locofocos. The Locofocos soon faded as a separate group but endured as a radical faction within the Democratic party.

Though the labor parties elected few candidates, they did draw notice to their demands, many of which attracted the support of middle-class reformers. Above all they called for free government-funded education and the abolition of imprisonment for debt, causes that won widespread popular support. The labor parties and unions also actively promoted the ten-hour workday. In 1836 President Andrew Jackson established the ten-hour workday at the Philadelphia Navy Yard in response to a strike, and in 1840 President Martin Van Buren extended the limit to all government offices and projects. In private jobs the ten-hour workday became increasingly common, although by no means universal, before 1860.

The Revival of Unions

After the Panic of 1837, the nascent labor movement went into decline, but it began to revive with improved business conditions in the early 1840s. Still, the unions of the time remained local, weak, and given to sporadic activity. Often they came and went with a single strike. The greatest labor dispute before the Civil War came on February 22, 1860, when shoemakers at Lynn and Natick, Massachusetts, walked out for higher wages. Before the strike ended, it had spread throughout New England, involving perhaps twenty-five towns and 20,000 workers. It stood out also because it was a strike the workers won. Most of the employers agreed to wage increases, and some also agreed to recognize the union as a bargaining agent.

This reflected the growing tendency of workers to view their unions as permanent. Workers sought union recognition and regular collective bargaining agreements. They also shared a rising sense of solidarity. In 1852 the National Typographical Union revived the effort to organize skilled crafts on a national scale. Others followed, and by 1860 about twenty such organizations had appeared, although none was strong enough as yet to do much more than hold national conventions and pass resolutions.

Jacksonian Inequality

During the years before the Civil War, the United States had begun to develop a distinctive working class, and the gap between rich and poor visibly widened. In 1828 the top 1 percent of New York's families (owning $34,000 or more) held 40 percent of the wealth, and the top 4 percent held 76 percent. Similar circumstances prevailed in Philadelphia, Boston, and other cities.

A supreme irony of the times was that the so-called age of the common man, the age of Jacksonian Democracy, seems actually to have been an age of increasing social stratification. Years before, in the late eighteenth century, slavery aside, American society probably approached equality more closely than any other population of its size anywhere else in the world. During the last half of the 1700s, social mobility was higher than either before or since. By the time popular egalitarianism caught up with reality,

reality was moving back toward greater inequality.

Why this happened is difficult to say, except that the boundless wealth of the untapped frontier narrowed as the land was occupied and claims on various opportunities were staked out. Such developments took place in New England towns even before the end of the seventeenth century. But despite growing social distinctions, it seems likely that the majority of the white population of America, at least, was better off than the general run of European peoples. New frontiers, both geographical and technological, raised the level of material well-being for all.

An American Renaissance: Religion, Romanticism, and Reform

This chapter focuses on

- The rise of new religious movements.

- The development of a distinctive American literary culture.

- The variety of social reform movements.

THE *ESSENTIAL AMERICA* ON-LINE TUTOR

www.wwnorton.com/eamerica/ch12

- **Topic: The Seneca Falls Convention**
www.wwnorton.com/eamerica/ch12/topic.htm

  The Seneca Falls Convention of 1848 helped launch the Women's Rights movement in the United States and began the long struggle for women's suffrage. Using photographs, newspaper articles, personal accounts, speech texts, and historical analyses, examine the convention and its significance for the women's movement. How did the convention affect the women's movement?

- **Chapter review: On-line quiz and chapter summary**
www.wwnorton.com/eamerica/ch12/review.htm

- **Chapter resources: Media index**
www.wwnorton.com/eamerica/ch12/media.htm

The American novelist Nathaniel Hawthorne once lamented "the difficulty of writing a romance about a country where there is no shadow, no antiquity, no mystery, no picturesque and gloomy wrong." Unlike nations of the Old World, rooted in shadow and mystery, entwined in historic cultures and traditions, the United States was an infant nation swaddled in the commonsense ideas of the Enlightenment. Those ideas, most vividly set forth in Jefferson's Declaration of Independence, had in turn a universal application that would influence religion, literature, and various social reform movements.

Rational Religion

American thought and culture in the early nineteenth century remained rooted in Puritan piety and Enlightenment rationalism. The United States, it was widely believed, had a mission to stand as an example to the world, for the religious fervor quickened in the Great Awakening had reinforced the idea of providential national destiny. In turn, the sense of high calling infused the national character with an element of perfectionism—and an element of impatience when reality fell short of expectations. The combination of religious belief and social idealism brought major reforms and advances in human rights. It also brought disappointments that could fester into cynicism and alienation.

Deism

The currents of the Enlightenment and the Great Awakening, now mingling, now parting, flowed on into the nineteenth century and in different ways eroded the remnants of Calvinist orthodoxy. As time passed, the image of a just but stern God promising predestined hellfire and damnation gave way to a more optimistic religious outlook. Enlightenment rationalism increas-

ingly stressed inherent human goodness rather than depravity, and it encouraged a belief in social progress and the promise of individual perfectibility.

Many leaders of the Revolutionary War era, such as Thomas Jefferson and Benjamin Franklin, became deists, even while nominally attached to churches. Deism, which arose in eighteenth-century Europe, carried the logic of Sir Isaac Newton's image of the world as a smoothly operating machine to its logical conclusion. The God of the deist had planned the universe, built it, set it in motion, and then left it to its own devices. By the use of reason, people might grasp the natural laws governing the universe. Orthodox Christians could hardly distinguish such a doctrine from atheism, but Enlightenment rationalism soon began to make deep inroads into American Protestantism.

Unitarianism and Universalism

By the end of the eighteenth century, many New Englanders were embracing Unitarianism, a belief emphasizing the oneness and benevolence of God, the inherent goodness of humankind, and the primacy of the individual's reason and conscience over established religious creeds and Scriptural literalism. Humans were not inherently depraved, Unitarianism stressed; people were capable of doing tremendous good and all were eligible for salvation. Boston's revered Unitarian minister William Ellery Channing emerged as the chief spokesman for the liberal religious position. "I am surer that my rational nature is from God," he said, "than that any book is an expression of his will."

A parallel movement, called Universalism, attracted people of more humble means. Universalists stressed the salvation of all men and women, not just the predestined elect of the Calvinist doctrine. God, they taught, was too merciful to condemn anyone to eternal punishment; eventually all souls would come into harmony with God. "Thus, the Unitarians and Universalists were in fundamental agreement," wrote one historian of religion, "the Universalists holding that God was too good to damn man; the Unitarians insisting that man was too good to be damned."

The Second Great Awakening

Around 1800, fears that secularism was taking root sparked a revival of religious orthodoxy that grew into the Second Great Awakening. The new wave of evangelical fervor fed upon the spreading notion of social equality. Methodists and Baptists, neither of whom featured an educated clergy, sought to democratize religious practices and congregational structures. Such "populist" tendencies were reinforced by the growing popularity of the concept of "free will." Salvation was available to everyone.

Frontier Revivals

In its frontier phase, the Second Great Awakening, like the first, generated great excitement and strange manifestations. It gave birth, moreover, to a new ritual, the camp meeting, in which the fires of faith were repeatedly rekindled. Missionaries found ready audiences among lonely frontier folk hungry for spiritual meaning and a sense of community. In the backwoods and in small rural hamlets, the traveling revival was as welcome an event as the traveling circus.

The Baptists embraced a simplicity of doctrine and organization that appealed especially to the common people of the frontier. Their theology was grounded in the authority of the Bible and the recognition of a person's innate depravity. But they replaced the Calvinist notion of predestination with the concept of universal redemption and highlighted the ritual of adult baptism. They also stressed the equality of all men and women before God, regardless of wealth, social standing, or educational training.

Methodist Camp Meeting, 1837. Religious revivals at times so infused people with religious fervor that they went into trances or jerked and twitched.

The Methodists, who shared with the Baptists an emphasis on salvation by free will, established the most effective recruiting method of all: the circuit rider who sought out people in the most remote areas with the message of salvation as a gift free for the taking. The system began with Francis Asbury, a tireless British-born revivalist who scoured the trans-Appalachian frontier for lost souls, preaching some 25,000 sermons while defying hostile Indians and suffering through harsh winters. Asbury's mobile evangelism perfectly suited the frontier environment and the new democratic age. By the 1840s the Methodists had grown into the largest Protestant denomination in the country.

The revivals spread quickly through the West and into more settled regions back East. Camp meetings were held typically in late summer or fall, when farm work slackened. People converged from far and wide, camping in wagons, tents, or crude shacks. Blacks, whether slave or free, were allowed to set up their own adjacent camp revivals, often separated from the white camp by a plank partition. On the final meeting day of the week, the wall would be taken down, enabling both groups to join in a song festival and a "marching ceremony." The largest camp meetings tended to be ecumenical affairs, with Baptist, Methodist, and Presbyterian ministers working as a team.

The crowds often numbered in the thousands, and the unrestrained atmosphere made for chaos. If a particular hymn or sermon excited someone, they would cry, shout, dance, or repeat the phrase. Infusions of the spirit provoked some participants into cataleptic trances; others contracted the "jerks," laughed the "holy laugh," babbled in unknown tongues, or got down on all fours and barked like dogs to "tree the Devil."

But dwelling on the bizarre aspects of the camp meetings distorts a social institution that offered a meaningful outlet to isolated rural folk. Camp meetings also brought a more settled community life through the churches they spawned, and they helped spread a more democratic faith among the frontier people.

Finney and the "Burned-Over District"

Regions swept by such revival fevers have been compared to forests devastated by fire. In 1830–1831 alone, the number of churches in New England grew by one-third. Lyman Beecher called the Great Awakening of 1831 "the greatest work of God, and the greatest revival of religion, that the world has ever seen." Western New York from Lake Ontario to the Adirondacks and including Rochester experienced such intense levels of evangelical activity that it was labeled the "Burned-Over District."

The most successful evangelist in the region was a lawyer named Charles Grandison Finney, whose own religious awakening occurred one evening in 1821, when a "mighty baptism of the Holy Ghost overwhelmed him." The next day he announced a new profession as a revivalist. In 1823 Finney was ordained, and during the next decade he became the greatest single exemplar of evangelical Protestantism, and the inventor of professional revivalism.

Finney wrestled with an age-old question that had plagued Protestantism: what

role can the individual play in earning salvation? Orthodox Calvinists had long argued that people could neither earn nor choose salvation on their own accord. Grace was a gift of God, a predetermined decision incapable of human understanding or control. In contrast, Finney insisted that people could control their own salvation. Finney transformed revivals into collective conversion experiences in which spectacular public events displaced private communion and the unregenerate were brought into intense contact with praying Christians.

Untrained in theology, Finney read the Bible and worked out his own theology of free will. His gospel also combined faith and good works; one led to the other. "All sin consists in selfishness," he declared, "and all holiness or virtue, in disinterested benevolence." Regeneration therefore produced "a change from selfishness to benevolence, from having a supreme regard to one's own interest to an absorbing and controlling choice of the happiness and glory of God's Kingdom."

In 1835 Finney became a professor of theology at the new Oberlin College, founded by pious New Englanders in Ohio's Western Reserve. Later he served as its president. From the start, Oberlin radiated a spirit of social reform predicated on faith; it was the first college in America to admit women and blacks, and it was a hotbed of antislavery activity. Finney himself, however, held that people must be reformed from within, and he cautioned against relying primarily on political action for moral ends.

The Mormons

In addition to providing the scene of revivals, the Burned-Over District gave rise to several new religious departures, of which the most important was the Church of Jesus Christ of Latter-day Saints, or the Mormons. The founder of the Mormon church, Joseph Smith, Jr., grew up in the village of Palmyra, New York. In 1820 young Smith (then fourteen) had a vision of "two Personages, whose brightness and glory defy all description." They identified themselves as the Savior and God the Father and cautioned him that all existing religious beliefs were false. About three years later, Smith claimed, an angel named Moroni led him to a hill near his father's farm in upstate New York, where he found the Book of Mormon, a lost section of the Bible. It told the story of ancient Hebrews who had inhabited the New World and to whom Jesus had made an appearance.

On the basis of this revelation, Smith began forming his own church in 1830, and after a few years he was gathering converts by the thousands. Mostly poor New England farmers, these religious seekers found in Mormonism the promise of a pure kingdom of Christ in America and an alternative to the social turmoil and the degrading materialism of the era. Mormons rejected the notion of original sin staining the human race. They instead professed an optimistic creed stressing human goodness and the virtues of common folk.

In their search for a refuge from persecution, the Mormons moved from New York to Ohio, then to several places in Missouri, and finally in 1839 to Nauvoo, Illinois, where they settled for some five years. Nauvoo became a bustling city, and Joseph Smith, "the Prophet," became the community's leading entrepreneur. At Nauvoo he codified the theocratic church organization and instituted the practice of "plural marriage." In 1844 a crisis arose when dissidents accused Smith of justifying polygamy. The upshot was a schism in the church, a gathering movement among non-Mormons in the neighboring counties to attack Nauvoo, and the arrest of Smith and his brother Hyrum. On June 27, 1844, an anti-Mormon mob stormed the feebly defended Nauvoo jail and shot both Joseph and Hyrum Smith.

In Brigham Young, the remarkable successor to Joseph Smith, the Mormons found a leader who was strong-minded, intelligent, and decisive. He was also prolific, eventually marrying sixteen women and fathering fifty-seven children. After the murder of Smith, Young patched up an unsure peace with the neighbors by promising to leave Illinois. Before the year was out, Young had chosen a new destination near the Great Salt Lake in Utah, guarded by mountains to the east and north, deserts to the west and south, yet itself fed by mountain streams of melted snow.

Brigham Young trusted God, but he made careful preparations. As a result, the epic Mormon trek was better organized and less arduous than most of the overland migrations of the time. By the fall of 1846, all 15,000 of the migrants had reached winter quarters on the Missouri River, where they paused until the first bands set out the next spring for the Promised Land. The first arrivals at Salt Lake in July 1847 found only "a broad and barren plain hemmed in by mountains . . . the paradise of the lizard, the cricket and the rattlesnake." But by the end of 1848, the Mormons had developed an efficient irrigation system and over the next decade, by cooperative labor, they brought about a spectacular greening of the desert. They organized at first their own State of Deseret (meaning "land of the honey bee," according to Young), but their independence was short-lived. Congress incorporated the Utah Territory, including the Mormons' Salt Lake settlement, into the United States in 1849. Nevertheless, with Brigham Young named the territorial governor, the new arrangement afforded the Mormons almost the same control. By 1869, some 80,000 Mormons had settled in Utah. Today there are 9 million Mormons, and it is the fastest growing religion in the world.

Romanticism in America

The revival of emotional piety and the founding of new religions during the early 1800s represented a widespread tendency in the Western world to accentuate the stirrings of the spirit over the dry logic of reason. Another great victory of heart over head was the romantic movement in thought, literature, and the arts. By the 1780s, a revolt was brewing in Europe against the well-ordered world of Enlightenment thinkers. Were there not, many wondered, more things in this world than reason and logic could box up and explain: moods, impressions, feelings; mysterious, unknown, and half-seen things?

Transcendentalism

The most intense expression of such romantic ideas in America was the transcendentalist movement of New England, which drew its name from its emphasis on transcending (or rising above) the limits of reason. American transcendentalism was largely inspired by European thinkers such as Immanuel Kant and Samuel Taylor Coleridge, but it was rooted in New England Puritanism, to which it owed a pervasive moral idealism. It also had a close affinity with the Quaker doctrine of the inner light. The inner light, a gift from God's grace, was transformed by transcendentalists into an emphasis on intuition, a faculty of the mind.

In 1836 an informal discussion group named the Transcendental Club began to meet in Boston and Concord. It drew at different times clergymen such as Theodore Parker and George Ripley; philosophical writers such as Henry David Thoreau, Bronson Alcott, and Orestes Brownson; and learned women like Margaret Fuller and Elizabeth and Sophia Peabody. Fuller edited the group's quarterly review, *The Dial* (1840–1844), before the duty fell to Ralph Waldo Emerson, soon to become the acknowledged high priest of transcendentalism.

Emerson and Thoreau

More than any other person, Emerson spread the transcendentalist gospel. Sprung from a line of New England ministers, he set out to be a Unitarian parson, then quit the "cold and cheerless" denomination before he was thirty because of growing doubts about its vitality. After travel to Europe, where he met England's great literary romantics, Emerson settled in Concord to take up the life of an essayist, poet, and popular speaker on the lecture circuit, preaching the good news of optimism, self-reliance, and the individual's unlimited potential. He was determined to *transcend* the limitations of inherited conventions and of rationalism in order to penetrate the inner recesses of the self. As he once suggested, transcendentalism meant belief in a realm "a little beyond" the rational world.

Emerson's young friend and Concord neighbor, Henry David Thoreau, practiced the introspective self-reliance that Emerson preached. Thoreau displayed an uncompromising integrity, outdoor vigor, and tart individuality that Emerson found captivating. Short and sinewy, Thoreau was an acknowledged master of the woodland arts and a probing thinker.

He was also a thoroughgoing individualist. "If a man does not keep pace with his companion," Thoreau wrote, "perhaps it is

Heart of the Andes (1859), by Frederick E. Church. Church, a prominent Hudson River School painter, captured the spirit of the transcendentalist movement in the arts, which emphasized the inspiring beauty of nature.

because he hears a different drummer." After graduating from Harvard, Thoreau settled down in Concord to eke out a living as a part-time surveyor and pencil-maker. But he yearned to be a writer and a philosophical naturalist, and he made almost daily escapes to the woods and fields to drink in the beauties of nature and reflect upon the mysteries of life. The scramble for wealth among his neighbors disgusted rather than tempted him. "The mass of men," he wrote, "lead lives of quiet desperation."

Determined himself to practice "plain living and high thinking," Thoreau embarked on an experiment in self-reliant simplicity. On July 4, 1845, he took to the woods to live in a cabin he had built on Emerson's land beside Walden Pond. He wanted to free himself from the complexities and hypocrisies of modern life and devote his time to reflection and writing. "I went to the woods because I wished to live deliberately," he wrote in *Walden, or Life in the Woods* (1854), ". . . and not, when I came to die, discover that I had not lived."

While Thoreau was at Walden Pond, the Mexican War erupted. He saw the conflict as a corrupt attempt to advance the cause of slavery. So he refused to pay his state poll tax as a gesture of opposition, for which he was put in jail (for only one night; an aunt paid the tax). Out of the incident grew the classic essay "Civil Disobedience" (1849), which would later influence the passive-resistance movements of Mahatma Gandhi in India and Martin Luther King, Jr., in the American South. "If the law is of such a nature that it requires you to be an agent of unjustice to another," Thoreau wrote, "then, I say, break the law. Let your life be a counter friction to stop the machine."

The influence of Thoreau's ideas more than a century after his death shows the impact a contemplative individual can have on the larger world of action. Thoreau and the transcendentalists shied away from orga-nized reform or political activities. They prized their individual freedom and distrusted all institutions—even those promoting causes they deemed worthy. As principled individualists, they primarily supplied the force of an animating idea: people must follow their consciences. In doing so, they inspired reform movements and were the quickening force for a generation of writers who produced the first classic age of American literature.

The Flowering of American Literature

Ever since gaining independence, the United States had suffered from a cultural inferiority complex. The Old World continued to set the standards in philosophy, literature, and the fine arts. As a British critic sneered in 1819, the "Americans have no national literature." That may have been true, but during the Jacksonian era and after, American culture began to flower.

Dickinson

The poet Emily Dickinson lived as a recluse in Amherst, Massachusetts. Only two of her almost 1,800 poems had been published (anonymously) before her death in 1886, and the full corpus of her work remained unknown for years thereafter. Yet she possessed an imaginative power and inventive genius superior to her more famous male peers. Born in Amherst in 1830, she received a first-rate education and then attended the new Mount Holyoke Female Seminary. Neither she nor her sister married, and they both lived out their lives in their parents' home.

Dickinson's intense isolation led her to write about elemental themes: life, death, fear, loneliness, nature, and, above all, God, a "Force illegible," a "distant, stately lover."

Ralph Waldo Emerson, author of *Nature,* America's "intellectual Declaration of Independence."

Henry David Thoreau, author of the American classics *Walden* and "Civil Disobedience."

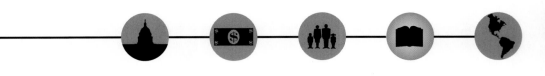

Hawthorne

Nathaniel Hawthorne, the best of the New England group of fiction writers, never shared the sunny optimism of his transcendentalist neighbors or their perfectionist belief in reform. He was haunted by the knowledge of evil bequeathed to him by his Puritan forebears—one of whom had been a judge at the Salem witchcraft trials. After graduating from Bowdoin College in Maine, he worked in obscurity in Salem, gradually began to sell a few stories, and finally earned some degree of fame with his collection of *Twice-Told Tales* (1837). In these, as in most of his later work, he presented powerful moral allegories. His central themes explored evil and its consequences: pride and selfishness, secret guilt, selfish egotism, the impossibility of rooting sin out of the human soul. His greatest novel, *The Scarlet Letter* (1850), explicitly pondered such burdens, focusing on the guilt felt by a woman and a minister who had committed adultery.

Poe

Edgar Allan Poe, born in Boston and reared in Virginia, was a literary genius, and many Europeans considered him the most important American writer of the time. As a poet, he strove to craft verses that would display the classic virtues of restraint, discipline, and unity. "The Raven" is a masterful example of his preoccupation with form as well as his interest in probing the dark recesses of the human soul. The tormented, hard-drinking, quarrelsome Poe was also a master of Gothic horror in the short story and the inventor of the detective story. He judged prose by its ability to provoke emotional tension, and since he considered fear to be the most powerful emotion, he focused his efforts on making the grotesque and supernatural seem disturbingly real to his readers. Anyone who has read the "Tell-Tale Heart" or "The Pit and the Pendulum" can testify to his success.

Melville

Although today considered one of America's greatest novelists, Herman Melville during his later years saw his literary reputation evaporate. Born in New York in 1819, at age twenty he shipped out as a seaman. He wound up in the South Seas and jumped ship with a companion. After a month spent with a friendly tribe in the valley of the Typees, he signed onto an Australian whaler, jumped ship again in Tahiti, was jailed for mutiny, and obtained his release by signing on as a harpooner. After landing in Hawaii, he finally returned to Boston as a seaman aboard a navy frigate. An embroidered account of his exotic adventures, in *Typee* (1846), became an instant popular success, which he repeated in *Omoo* (1847), based on his stay in Tahiti.

Melville then produced a masterpiece in *Moby-Dick* (1851), a novel rich in action as well as symbolism. Unhappily, neither the larger reading public nor many of the critics at the time appreciated the novel, and after the Civil War, Melville's career wound down into futility.

Whitman

The most provocative American writer during the antebellum period was Walt Whitman, a remarkably vibrant personality who disdained inherited social conventions and artistic traditions. There was something elemental in Whitman's character, something bountiful and generous and compelling—even his faults and inconsistencies were ample. Born on a Long Island farm, he moved with his family to Brooklyn, and from the age of twelve worked mainly as a handyman and journalist, frequently taking the ferry across the river to booming, bustling Manhattan. The city fascinated him, and he gorged himself on the urban spectacle—shipyards, crowds, factories, shop windows.

From such material, Whitman drew his editorial opinions and poetic inspiration, but he remained relatively obscure until the first edition of *Leaves of Grass* (1855) caught the eye and aroused the ire of readers. Emerson found it "the most extraordinary piece of wit and wisdom that America has yet contributed," but more conventional critics shuddered at Whitman's explicit homosexual references and groused at his indifference to rhyme and meter as well as his buoyant egotism. The jaunty Whitman, however, refused to conform to genteel notions of art, and he spent most of his career working on his gargantuan collection of poems, *Leaves of Grass*, enlarging and reshaping it in successive editions. He identified the growth of the book with the growth of the country, which he celebrated in all its variety.

The Popular Press

The flowering of American literature came at a time of massive expansion of newspaper circulation. In 1847 Richard Hoe of New York invented the Hoe Rotary Press, which printed 20,000 sheets an hour. It expedited production of cheap "penny" newspapers as well as magazines and books. The availability of newspapers costing only a penny each transformed daily reading into a form of popular entertainment. Circulation soared in every city. As readership grew, the content of newspapers expanded beyond political news and commentary to include social gossip, sports, and sensational crime and accident reports. The *New York Sun*, the first successful penny daily, and others like it often ignored the important news of the day in favor of scandals and sensations, true or false.

Education

Literacy in Jacksonian America was surprisingly widespread, given the condition of public education. In 1840, according to census data, some 78 percent of the total population and 91 percent of the white population could read and write. Since the colonial period, in fact, Americans had enjoyed the highest literacy rate in the Western world.

Early Public Schools

By the 1830s, the demand for state-supported public schools was rising fast. Reformers argued that popular government depended upon a literate and informed electorate. Workers also wanted free schools to give their children an equal chance at economic and social success. Education, it was also argued, would be a means of social reform by improving manners and lessening crime and poverty.

Horace Mann of Massachusetts stood out in the early drive for statewide school systems. He shepherded through the legislature in 1837 a bill that created a state board of education, which he then served as secretary. Mann went on to sponsor many reforms in Massachusetts, including the first state-supported training for teachers, a state association of teachers, and a minimum school year of six months.

While the North made great strides in public education by 1850, the educational pattern in the South continued to reflect the region's aristocratic pretensions and rural isolation: the South had a higher percentage of college students than any other region, but a lower percentage of public school students. And the South had some 500,000 white illiterates, more than half the total number in the country.

Higher Education

The post-Revolutionary proliferation of colleges continued after 1800 with the spread of small church schools and state universities. Of the seventy-eight colleges and universities in 1840, thirty-five had been

War News from Mexico (1848), by Richard Caton Woodville. The immediacy of telegraphic news combined with the invention of the Hoe Rotary Press increased the circulation and popularity of newspapers.

founded after 1830, almost all as church-supported schools. Federal policy abetted the spread of universities into the West. When Congress granted statehood to Ohio in 1803, it set aside two townships for the support of a state university and kept up that policy in other new states.

American colleges and universities during the nineteenth century were tiny when compared to today's institutions of higher learning. Most enrolled a hundred students or less, and the largest rarely had more than 600. Virtually all of these students were men. Elementary education for girls was generally accepted, but training beyond that level was not. Progress began with the academies, some of which taught boys and girls alike. Good "female seminaries" like those founded by Emma Willard at Troy, New York (1824), and Mary Lyon at Mount Holyoke, Massachusetts (1836), prepared the way for women's colleges.

The work in female seminaries usually differed from the courses in men's schools, giving more attention to the social amenities and such "embellishments" as music and art. Vassar, opened at Poughkeepsie, New York, in 1865, is usually credited with being the first women's college to give priority to

conventional academic subjects and standards. In general, the West gave the greatest impetus to coeducation, with state universities in the lead. But once admitted, women students remained in a subordinate status. At Oberlin College in Ohio, for instance, women were expected to clean male students' rooms and were not allowed to speak in class or recite at graduation exercises. Coeducation did not mean equality.

Some Movements for Reform

The urge to eradicate evil from nineteenth-century America had its roots in the American sense of mission, which in turn drew upon rising faith in the perfectibility of humankind. The revival fever of the Second Great Awakening helped generate a widespread belief that people could eradicate many of the evils afflicting society. Transcendentalism, the spirit of which infected even those unfamiliar with its philosophical roots, offered a romantic faith in the individual and the belief that human intuition led to right thinking.

Such a perfectionist bent found outlet in diverse reform movements and activities during the Jacksonian era. Few areas of life escaped the concerns of the reformers: dueling, crime and punishment, the hours and conditions of work, poverty, vice, care of the handicapped, pacifism, temperance, women's rights, the abolition of slavery.

While a perfectionist impulse helped excite the reform movements of the Jacksonian era, social and economic changes helped supply the reformers themselves, most of whom were women. The rise of an urban middle class offered affluent women greater time to devote to social concerns. Material prosperity enabled them to hire maids and cooks, which in turn freed them from household chores. Many of them joined various charitable organizations, most of which were led by men. Some reformers proposed

The George Barrell Emerson School, Boston, c. 1850. Although higher education for women initially met with some resistance, female seminaries like this one were started in the 1820s and 1830s and taught women mathematics, physics, and history, as well as music, art, and the social amenities.

legislative remedies for social ills; others stressed personal conversion or private philanthropy. Whatever the method or approach, social reformers mobilized in great numbers during the second quarter of the nineteenth century.

Temperance

The crusade against alcohol abuse was perhaps the most widespread of all the reform movements. The temperance movement rested on a number of arguments. First and foremost was the religious demand that "soldiers of the cross" lead blameless lives. Others stressed the social and economic costs of drunk workers. The dynamic new economy, with factories and railroads moving on strict schedules, made tippling by the labor force a far greater problem than it had been in a simple agrarian economy. Humanitarians emphasized the relations between drinking and poverty. Much of the movement's propaganda focused on the sufferings of innocent mothers and children.

In 1826 a group of Boston ministers organized the American Society for the Promotion of Temperance. The society pursued its objectives through lecturers, press campaigns, an essay contest, and the formation of local and state societies. A favorite device was to ask those who took the pledge to put by their signatures a T for Total Abstinence. With that a new word entered the language: "teetotaler."

In 1833 the society called a national convention in Philadelphia, where the American Temperance Union was formed. The convention, however, revealed internal tensions: Was the goal moderation or total abstinence, and if the latter, abstinence merely from liquor or also from wine, cider, and beer? Should the movement work by persuasion or by legislation? Like nearly every reform movement of the day, temperance had a wing of perfectionists who rejected all compromises, and in 1836, they called for abstinence from all alcoholic beverages—

which caused moderates to abstain from the reform movement instead. Still, between 1830 and 1860, the temperance agitation drastically reduced Americans' per-capita consumption of alcohol.

Prisons and Asylums

The Jacksonian-age belief that people are innately good and capable of improvement brought major changes in the treatment of prisoners, the handicapped, and dependent children. In the colonial period, prisons were usually places for brief confinement before punishment, which was either death or some kind of pain or humiliation: whipping, mutilation, confinement in stocks, branding, and the like. A new attitude began to emerge after the Revolution, and gradually the idea of the penitentiary developed. It would be a place where the guilty experienced penitence and underwent rehabilitation, not just punishment.

An early model of the new system, widely copied, was the Auburn Penitentiary, commissioned by New York in 1816. The prisoners at Auburn had separate cells and gathered for meals and group labor. Discipline was severe. The men were marched out in lockstep and never put face to face or allowed to talk. But prisoners were at least reasonably secure from abuse by other prisoners. The system, its advocates argued, had a beneficial effect on the prisoners and saved money, since the workshops supplied prison needs and produced goods for sale at a profit. By 1840, there were twelve prisons of the Auburn type in the United States.

The reform impulse also found an outlet in the care of the insane. The Pennsylvania Hospital (1752), one of the first in the country, had a provision in its charter that it should care for "lunaticks," but before 1800 few hospitals provided care for the mentally ill. There were in fact few hospitals of any kind. The insane were usually confined at home with hired keepers or in jails and almshouses. After 1815, however, public asylums that housed the disturbed separately from criminals began to appear.

The most important figure in arousing the public conscience to the plight of these unfortunates was Dorothea Lynde Dix. A Boston schoolteacher, she was called upon to instruct a Sunday-school class at the East Cambridge House of Correction in 1841. She found there a roomful of insane persons completely neglected, fed slop, and left without heat on a cold March day. In a report to the state legislature in 1843, Dix told of persons confined "in *cages, closets, cellars, stalls, pens! Chained, naked, beaten with rods, and lashed into obedience!*" She won the support of leading reformers as well as a large state appropriation for improving the treatment of the insane. From Massachusetts, she carried her campaign throughout the country and abroad. By 1860, she had convinced twenty states to adopt similar programs to improve the conditions in prisons and asylums.

Women's Rights

The official status of women during the antebellum period remained much as it had been in the colonial era. Legally, a woman was unable to vote, and, after marriage, she was denied legal control of her property and even of her children. A wife could not make a will, sign a contract, or bring suit in court without her husband's permission. Her legal status was thus like that of a minor, a slave, or a free black. Gradually, however, more and more women began to complain about their status.

In 1848 two prominent moral reformers and advocates of women's rights, Lucretia Mott, a Philadelphia Quaker, and Elizabeth Cady Stanton, a graduate of Troy Seminary who refused to be merely "a household drudge," decided to call a convention to discuss "the social, civil, and religious condition and rights of women." The hastily organized Seneca Falls Convention, the first of its kind, issued on July 19, 1848, the Declaration of Sentiments, mainly the work of Stanton, who also was the wife of a prominent abolitionist and mother of seven. In a clever paraphrase of Jefferson's Declaration of Independence, the document proclaimed the self-evident truth that "all men and women are created equal," and the attendant resolutions said that all laws placing women "in a position inferior to that of men, are contrary to the great precept of nature, and therefore of no force or authority." Such language was too strong for most of the thousand delegates, and only about a third of them signed the document. Yet the Seneca Falls gathering represented an important first step in the evolving campaign for women's rights.

From 1850 until the Civil War, the women's rights leaders held annual conventions and carried on a program of organizing, lecturing, and petitioning. Susan B. Anthony, an ardent Quaker already active in temperance and antislavery groups, joined the crusade in the 1850s. Unlike Stanton and Mott, Anthony was unmarried and therefore able to devote most of her attention to the women's crusade. As one observer put it, Stanton "forged the thunderbolts and Miss Anthony hurled them."

The primary objective of the women's movement was the right to vote. While women did not win voting rights until the twentieth century, there were some legal gains before the Civil War. The state of Mississippi, seldom regarded as a hotbed of reform, was the first to grant married women control over their property in 1839; by the 1860s eleven more states had such laws.

Elizabeth Cady Stanton (left) and Susan B. Anthony (right).

Still, the only jobs open to educated women in any numbers were nursing and teaching. Yet if women could be teachers, Susan Anthony asked, why not lawyers or doctors or ministers or intellectuals? Why not indeed, replied a small band of hardy women who carved out professional careers. Harriet Hunt of Boston was a teacher who, after nursing her sister through a serious illness, set up shop in 1835 as a self-taught physician and persisted in medical practice although twice rejected by Harvard Medical School. Voted into Geneva Medical College in western New York as a joke, Elizabeth Blackwell of Ohio had the last laugh when she finished at the head of her class in 1849. She founded the New York Infirmary for Women and Children and later had a long career as a professor of gynecology in the London School of Medicine for Women.

An intellectual prodigy among women of the time—the derisory term was "bluestocking"—was Margaret Fuller, who edited *The Dial* for two years and became literary editor and critic for Horace Greeley's *New York Tribune*. From 1839 to 1844, she conducted "conversations" with the cultivated ladies of Boston. From this classroom-salon emerged her pathbreaking book, *Woman in the Nineteenth Century* (1845), a plea for the removal of all intellectual and economic disadvantages. Minds and souls were neither masculine nor feminine, she argued. Genius had no sex.

Utopian Communities

The pervasive climate of reform during the Jacksonian era and after also provoked a quest for utopia. Over a hundred utopian communities sprang up between 1800 and 1900. Among the most durable were the Shakers, officially the United Society of Believers in Christ's Second Appearing, founded by Ann Lee Stanley (Mother Ann), who reached New York State with eight followers in 1774. Believing religious fervor a

sign of inspiration from the Holy Ghost, they had strange fits in which they saw visions and prophesied. These manifestations later evolved into a ritual dance—hence the name Shakers. Mother Ann claimed that she was the female incarnation of God, as Jesus had been the male. She preached celibacy to prepare Shakers for the perfection that was promised them after death.

Mother Ann died in 1784, but the movement found new leaders, and by 1830, about twenty groups were flourishing. In Shaker communities all property was held in common, and strict celibacy was practiced. Men and women not only slept separately but also worked and ate separately. Governance of the colonies was concentrated in the hands of select elders chosen by the ministry. The superbly managed Shaker farms were among the leading sources of garden seed and medicinal herbs, and many of their manufactures, including clothing, household items, and especially furniture, were prized for their simple beauty.

John Humphrey Noyes, founder of the Oneida Community, was the son of a Vermont congressman. After discovering true religion at one of Charles G. Finney's revivals, he entered the ministry but was forced out when he concluded that with true conversion came perfection and a complete release from sin. In 1836 he gathered a group of a dozen or so "Perfectionists"

The Shakers were one of the most durable utopian communities; their services were characterized by a ritual dance of religious fervor around his home in Putney, Vermont. Ten years later Noyes announced a new doctrine of "complex marriage," which meant that every man in the community was married to every woman and vice versa. To outsiders such theology smacked of "free love," and Noyes was arrested. He fled to New York and in 1848 established the Oneida Community, which numbered more than 200 by 1851.

The communal group shared alike in the food, clothing, and shelter produced by their hard work. They eked out a living with farming and logging until the mid-1850s, when the inventor of a new steel trap joined the community. Oneida traps were soon known as the best money could buy. The community then branched out into sewing silk, canning fruits, and making silver tableware. Oneida also carefully regulated its social life. Women enjoyed the same rights as men, and children were raised by the community as a whole, placed in a common nursery, supplied with toys and affection, and allowed to sleep until they awoke themselves.

For well over a generation the passionate community prospered. In 1879, however, it faced a crisis when Noyes fled to Canada to avoid prosecution for adultery. The members then abandoned complex marriage, and in 1881 they decided to convert into a joint-stock company, the Oneida Community, Ltd., which remains today a thriving flatware company.

In contrast to these religious communities, Robert Owen's New Harmony was based on a secular principle. A British capitalist who worried about the social effects of the factory system, Owen bought the town of Harmony, Indiana, and promptly christened it New Harmony. In 1825 about 900 colonists gathered in New Harmony and established a cooperative community. Separate residences were to be built for the married, unmarried, and children. A complete

school system, including nursery and university, was to be built along with a library, lecture halls, laboratories, and gymnasium. There were frequent lectures and social gatherings with music and dancing.

But New Harmony soon fell into discord. Leaders complained of "grumbling, carping, and murmuring" members, and others who had the "disease of laziness." In 1827 Owen returned from a visit to England to find New Harmony insolvent. The following year he dissolved the project and sold or leased the lands on good terms, in many cases to the settlers.

Brook Farm was the most celebrated of all the utopian communities, because it had the support of Ralph Waldo Emerson and countless other well-known literary figures of New England. George Ripley, a Unitarian minister and transcendentalist, conceived of Brook Farm as a kind of early-day "think tank," combining high thinking and plain living. The residents would work together in the mornings so that they could spend the afternoons engaged in intellectual and cultural activities.

Brook Farm and most of the utopian communities were short-lived. While such experiments had little effect on the larger society, they did express the deeply ingrained desire for perfectionism inherent in the American character, a desire that would continue to spawn noble, if frequently naive, experiments thereafter.

Among all the targets of reformers' idealism, however, one great evil would finally take precedence over the others—human bondage. The paradox of American slavery coupled with American freedom, of "the world's fairest hope linked with man's foulest crime," in Herman Melville's words, would inspire the climactic crusade of the age, abolitionism, one that would ultimately move to the center of the political stage and sweep the nation into an epic—and tragic—struggle.

CHAPTER

13

Manifest Destiny

This chapter focuses on

- National politics in the 1840s.

- The factors leading to westward migrations and the conditions faced by western settlers.

- The causes, course, and consequences of the Mexican War.

209

THE *ESSENTIAL AMERICA* ON-LINE TUTOR

www.wwnorton.com/eamerica/ch13

- **Topic: The Oregon Trail**
  www.wwnorton.com/eamerica/ch13/topic.htm

  In the decades following the Lewis and Clark expedition, hundreds of thousands of Americans migrated westward over the Oregon (Overland) Trail. Utilizing maps, sketches, photographs, and historical analyses, investigate the significance of the pioneer experience. What drove these pioneers to brave the wild American West?

- **Chapter review: On-line quiz and chapter summary**
  www.wwnorton.com/eamerica/ch13/review.htm

- **Chapter resources: Multimedia index**
  www.wwnorton.com/eamerica/ch13/media.htm

During the 1840s, the westering impulse, the quest for a better chance and more living room, continued to excite the American imagination. People frustrated by the growing congestion and rising cost of living along the Atlantic seaboard saw in the West a bountiful source of personal freedom, economic opportunity, social democracy—and adventure.

Economic depressions in 1837 and 1841 intensified the appeal of starting anew out West. Texas, Oregon, and Utah were the favored destinations until the discovery of gold in California in 1848 sparked a stampede that threatened to depopulate New England of its young men.

Most of these settlers and adventurers sought to exploit the many economic opportunities afforded by the new lands. Trappers and farmers, miners and merchants, hunters, ranchers, teachers, servants, and prostitutes, among others, headed west seeking their fortunes. Others sought religious freedom or new converts to Christianity. Whatever the reason, they formed an unceasing migratory stream flowing across the Great Plains and the Rocky Mountains. The Indian and Mexican inhabitants of the region soon found themselves swept aside by successive waves of American settlers.

The Tyler Years

When William Henry Harrison took office in 1841, elected like Jackson mainly on the strength of his military record and his lack of a public stand on major issues, the Whig leaders expected him to be a tool in the hands of Daniel Webster and Henry Clay. Webster became secretary of state, and while Clay preferred to stay in the Senate, his friends filled the cabinet. Harrison served the shortest term of any president—after the longest inaugural address. At the inauguration, held on a rainy winter day, he caught cold. The pleadings of office seekers in the following month filled his days and

sapped his strength. On April 4, 1841, exactly one month after the inauguration, Harrison died of pneumonia at age sixty-eight.

John Tyler, the first vice-president to succeed on the death of a president, served practically all of Harrison's term. At age fifty-one, the Virginia slaveholder was the youngest president to date. He already had a long career behind him as legislator, governor, congressman, and senator, and his positions on all the important issues had been forcefully stated and were widely known. Although a Whig, he favored a strict construction of the Constitution and was a stubborn defender of states' rights. When someone asked if he were a "nationalist," Tyler retorted that he had "no such word in my political vocabulary." He ardently opposed Clay's American System of protective tariffs, a national bank, and internal improvements at national expense. He had broken with the Democratic party over Andrew Jackson's denial of a state's right to nullify a federal law and Jackson's imperious use of executive authority. Thus Tyler, the states'-rights Whig, had been chosen to "balance" the ticket by the party leaders in 1840; no one expected that he would actually wield power.

Domestic Affairs

When Congress met in special session in 1841, Henry Clay introduced a series of resolutions designed to supply the platform that the Whig party had evaded in the previous election. The chief points were repeal of the Independent Treasury, establishment of a Third Bank of the United States, distribution to the states of proceeds from federal land sales, and a higher tariff. "Tyler dares not resist me. I will drive him before me," Clay predicted.

Tyler, it turned out, was not easily driven. Although he agreed to the repeal of the Independent Treasury and signed a higher tariff bill in 1842, Tyler vetoed Clay's bill for a new national bank. This provoked his entire cabinet, with the exception of Webster, to resign. Tyler replaced the defectors with anti-Jackson Democrats like himself who had become Whigs. The stubborn Tyler became a president without a party. Irate congressional Whigs expelled him, and Democrats viewed him as an untrustworthy "renegade." Clay's leadership of the Whig party was now established beyond question.

Foreign Affairs

In foreign relations, meanwhile, developments of immense significance were taking place. A major issue between Britain and the United States involved the suppression of the African slave trade, which both countries had outlawed in 1808. In 1841 the British prime minister asserted the right to patrol off the coast of Africa and search vessels flying the American flag to see if they carried slaves. But the American government remembered the impressments and seizures during the Napoleonic Wars and refused to accept such intrusions.

Anglo-American relations were further strained by disputes over boundary lines. The vagueness of the treaty of 1783 ending the American Revolution had led to chronic border disputes between Maine and Canada. In 1842 the British sent Lord Ashburton to Washington to discuss the matter. The negotiations settled the Maine boundary as well as other border disputes by accepting the existing line between the Connecticut and St. Lawrence Rivers, and by compromising on the line between Lake Superior and Lake of the Woods. The Webster-Ashburton Treaty (1842) also provided for joint patrols off Africa to suppress the slave trade.

The Western Frontier

In the 1840s, what stirred the blood of the American people was the mounting evidence that more and more pioneers were hurdling the barriers of the "Great American Desert" and the Rocky Mountains, reaching out toward the Pacific coast. In 1845 an eastern magazine editor labeled this bumptious spirit of expansion. "Our manifest destiny," he wrote, "is to overspread the continent allotted by Providence for the free development of our yearly multiplying millions." At its best, this much-trumpeted notion of "Manifest Destiny" offered a moral justification for American expansion, a prescription for what an enlarged United States could and should be. At its worst, it was a cluster of flimsy rationalizations for naked greed and imperial ambition. Whatever the case, hundreds of thousands of people began streaming into the Far West during the 1840s and after.

As they crossed the Mississippi River and made their way westward, American pioneers entered not only a new environment but a new culture as well. The Great Plains and the Far West were already occupied by Indians and Mexicans, peoples who had lived in the region for centuries and had established their own distinctive customs and ways of life. Now they were joined by Americans of diverse ethnic origin and religious persuasion. It made for a volatile mix.

Western Indians

Over 325,000 Indians inhabited the Southwest, the Great Plains, California, and the Pacific Northwest in 1840. These Native Americans were divided into more than 200 different tribes, each with its own language, religion, economic base, kinship practices, and system of governance. Some were primarily farmers; others were nomadic hunters who preyed upon game animals as well as other Indians.

Some twenty-three tribes resided in the Great Plains, a vast grassland stretching from the Mississippi River west to the Rocky Mountains and from Canada to Mexico. Plains Indians such as the Arapaho, Blackfoot, Cheyenne, Kiowa, and Sioux were horse-borne nomads; they moved across the grasslands with the buffalo herds, carrying their teepees with them.

Several quite different Indian tribes lived to the south and west of the Plains Indians. In the arid region including what is today Arizona, New Mexico, and southern Utah were the peaceful Pueblo tribes—Acoma, Hopi, Laguna, Taos, Zia, Zuni. They were sophisticated farmers who lived in adobe villages along rivers that they used to irrigate their crops of corn, beans, and squash. The word *pueblo* comes from the Spanish term for "village." Their rivals were the Apache and Navajo, warlike hunters who roamed the countryside in small bands and preyed upon the Pueblos. They, in turn, were periodically harassed by their powerful enemies, the Comanches.

To the north, in the Great Basin between the Rocky Mountains and the Sierra Nevada range, tribes such as the Paiutes and Gosiutes struggled to survive in the harsh, arid region of what is today Nevada, Utah, and eastern California. They traveled in family groups and subsisted on berries, pine nuts, insects, and rodents. West of the mountains, along the California coast, the Indians lived in small villages. They gathered wild plants and acorns and fished in the rivers and bays. More than 100,000 Indians lived in coastal California in the 1840s.

The Indian tribes living along the northwest Pacific coast—the Nisqually, Spokane, Yakima, Chinook, Klamath, and Nez Percé (pierced noses)—enjoyed the most abundant natural resources and the most temperate climate. The ocean and rivers provided whales, seals, salmon, and crabs. The lush forests just east of the coast harbored game, berries, and nuts. And the majestic stands of fir, redwood, and cedar offered wood for cooking and shelter.

All of the Indian tribes eventually felt the unrelenting pressure of white expansion. Because Indian life on the Plains depended on the buffalo, the influx of white settlers posed a direct threat to their cultural sur-

Buffalo Lancing in the Snow Drifts, c. 1860s. This painting by George Catlin shows the Sioux hunting buffalo.

vival. Tribal chiefs appealed to Washington for help, but the federal government turned a deaf ear. It continued to build a string of frontier forts to protect the advancing settlers, and it sought to use treaties to gain control of new lands. When officials of the Indian Bureau could not coerce, cajole, or confuse Indian leaders into selling title to their tribal lands, fighting ensued. And after the discovery of gold in California in 1848, the tidal wave of white expansion flowed all the way to the West Coast.

The Spanish West and Mexican Revolution

As American settlers moved westward, they also encountered Spanish-speaking peoples. Many whites were as contemptuous of Hispanics as they were of Indians. Most Americans in the Southwest viewed Mexicans as ignorant, indolent, and conniving. The vast majority of the Spanish-speaking people in what is today called the American Southwest resided in New Mexico. Most of these people were *mestizos* (of mixed Indian and Spanish blood), and they were usually ranch hands or small farmers and herders.

The Spanish had been less successful in colonizing Arizona and Texas than they had been in New Mexico and Florida. The Yuma and Apache Indians in Arizona and the Comanches and Apaches in Texas thwarted efforts to establish Catholic missions. In eastern Texas during the first half of the eighteenth century, French traders from Louisiana undermined the authority and influence of the Spanish missions. The French supplied the Indians with guns, ammunition, and promises of protection. Several of the Texas missions were abandoned and reestablished near San Antonio in 1731. By 1750 the Pawnees, Wichitas, Comanches, and Apaches were using Spanish horses and French rifles to raid Spanish settlements in Texas. By 1790, the Hispanic population in Texas numbered only 2,510 while in New Mexico it exceeded 20,000.

In 1807 French forces occupied Spain and imprisoned the king. This created both consternation and confusion throughout Spain's colonial possessions, including Mexico. Miguel Hidalgo y Costilla, a *creole* (European born in the New World) Mexican priest, organized a revolt of Indians and *mestizos* against Spanish rule in Mexico. The poorly organized uprising failed miserably. In 1811 Spanish troops captured Hidalgo and executed him. Other Mexicans, however, continued to yearn for independence. In 1820, Mexican *creoles* again tried to liberate themselves from Spanish authority. By then, the Spanish forces in Mexico had lost much of their cohesion and dedication. Facing a growing revolt, the last Spanish officials withdrew from Mexico in 1821, and it became an independent nation.

Mexican independence unleashed tremors throughout the Southwest. In New Mexico and Arizona, American fur traders streamed into the region and developed a lucrative commerce in beaver pelts. Soon thereafter, wagon trains carrying American settlers began to make their way from Missouri westward along the Santa Fe Trail. In California, American entrepreneurs flooded into the now-Mexican province and soon became a powerful force for change; by 1848 Americans made up half of the non-Indian population. In Texas, American adventurers decided to promote their own independence from a newly independent—and chaotic—Mexican government. Suddenly, it seemed, the Southwest was a new frontier ripe for American exploitation and settlement.

The Rockies and Oregon Country

In the Northwest, the western frontier consisted of the Nebraska, Washington, and Oregon Territories. Fur traders were especially drawn to the Missouri River with its many tributaries. The heyday of the mountain fur trade began in 1822 when a Missouri businessman sent his first trading party to the upper Missouri River. But by 1840, the great days of the western fur trade were already over. The streams no longer teemed with beavers.

Beyond the mountains, the Oregon country stretched from the Forty-second Parallel north to 54° 40'. Between these parallels, Spain and Russia had given up their claims, leaving Great Britain and the United States as the only claimants. Under the Convention of 1818, the two countries had agreed to

American Settlement of Oregon City (1846), by James Warre. Oregon's fertile soil and temperate climate drew 5,000 settlers by 1845.

"joint occupation." Until the 1830s, however, joint occupation had been a legal technicality, because few Americans were in the area.

Word of Oregon's fertile soil, temperate climate, and magnificent forests gradually spread, largely through the efforts of Methodist missionaries recently settled there. This enticed adventurous Americans, and by the late 1830s, a trickle of emigrants began flowing along the Oregon (Overland) Trail. Soon "Oregon Fever" spread like a contagion. By 1845 there were about 5,000 settlers in the Willamette Valley of Oregon.

California

California also attracted new settlers and entrepreneurs. For all of its rich natural resources, California remained thinly populated by Indians and mission friars well into the nineteenth century. It was a simple, almost feudal, agrarian society, without schools, industry, or defenses. In 1821, when Mexico wrested its independence from Spain, Californians took comfort in the fact that Mexico City was so far away that it would exercise little effective control over its farthest state. During the next two decades, Californians, including many recent American arrivals, staged ten revolts against the governors dispatched to lord over them.

Yet Mexican rule did produce a dramatic change in California history. In 1824, Mexico passed a colonization act that granted hundreds of huge "rancho" estates to Mexican settlers. With free labor extracted from Indians, who were treated like slaves, these *rancheros* lived a life of self-indulgent luxury and ease, gambling, horse-racing, bull-baiting, and dancing. They soon cast covetous eyes on the vast estates controlled by the Franciscan missions, and in 1833–1834 they convinced the Mexican government to confiscate the California missions, exile the Franciscan friars, release the Indians from church control, and make the mission lands

available to new settlement. Within a few years, some 700 huge new rancho grants of 4,500 to 50,000 acres were issued along the coast from San Diego to San Francisco. Organized like feudal estates, these California ranches resembled southern cotton plantations, but the death rate for Indian workers was twice as high as that of slaves in the Deep South.

California's rich natural resources could not long remain a secret, and by the late 1820s, American ships began to enter the "hide and tallow" trade. The *rancheros* produced cowhide and beef tallow in large quantity, and both products enjoyed a brisk demand, cowhides mainly for shoes and the tallow chiefly for candles.

Moving West

Most of the western pioneers during the second quarter of the nineteenth century were American-born whites from the upper South and Midwest. A few free blacks joined in the migration. Between 1841 and 1867, some 350,000 men, women, and children made the arduous trek to California or Oregon, while hundreds of thousands of others settled along the way in Colorado, Texas, Arkansas, and other areas.

The Santa Fe Trail

After gaining its independence in 1821, the new government of Mexico was much more interested in trade with Americans than Spain had been. In Spanish-controlled Santa Fe, in fact, all commerce with the United States had been banned. After 1821, however, trade flourished. Hundreds of entrepreneurs made the thousand-mile trek from St. Louis to Santa Fe, forging a route that became known as the Santa Fe Trail.

The Santa Fe traders pioneered more than a new trail. They showed that heavy wagons could cross the plains and the mountains, and they developed the tech-

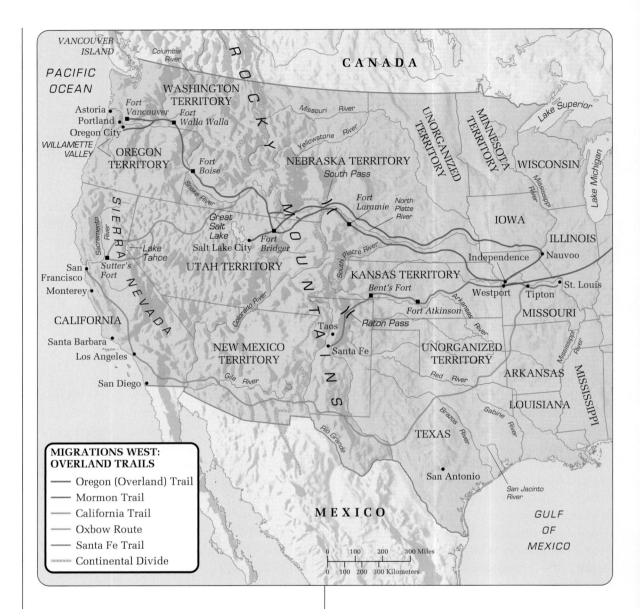

MIGRATIONS WEST:
OVERLAND TRAILS

—— Oregon (Overland) Trail
—— Mormon Trail
—— California Trail
—— Oxbow Route
—— Santa Fe Trail
······ Continental Divide

nique of organized caravans for common protection. Such techniques would also be used by those heading west to California and Oregon.

The Overland Trail

As on the Santa Fe Trail, people bound for Oregon and California traveled in wagon caravans. But on the Overland Trail (also known as the Oregon Trail), most of the people were settlers rather than traders. They usually traveled in family groups and came from all over the United States. The wagon trains followed the trail west from Independence, Missouri, along the North Platte River into what is now Wyoming, through South Pass down to Fort Bridger, then down the Snake River to the Columbia River, and along the Columbia to their goal in the fertile Willamette Valley. They usually left Missouri in late spring, completing the 2,000-mile trek in six months. Traveling in ox-drawn, canvas-covered wagons nicknamed "prairie schooners," they traversed rugged mountains at the rate of about fifteen miles per day. By 1845, about 5,000 people were making the arduous journey annually. The discovery of gold in California in 1848 brought some 30,000 pioneers along the Oregon Trail in 1849. By 1850, the peak year of travel along the trail, the number had risen to 55,000.

The journey west was incredibly difficult. Few who embarked on their western quest were adequately prepared for the ordeals they were to face. Cholera claimed many lives. On average there was one grave every eighty yards along the trail between the Missouri River and the Willamette Valley. Some 20,000 pioneers died in all.

The trail's never-ending routine of necessary chores and grinding physical labor took its toll on once-buoyant spirits. This was especially true for women, whose labors went on day and night. One woman settler complained that, unlike the men, who smoked and talked together after supper while the women cleaned, prepared the next day's food, and tended children, "*we have no time for sociability.*"

Hard labor understandably provoked tensions within families and powerful yearnings for home. Many a tired pioneer could identify with the following comment in a girl's journal: "Poor Ma said only this morning, 'Oh, I wish we had never started.' She looks so sorrowful and dejected." Some turned back, but most continued on. And once in Oregon or California they set about establishing stable communities. Noted one settler:

> Friday, October 27—Arrived at Oregon City at the falls of the Willamette.
> Saturday, October 28—Went to work.

The Indians and the Wagon Trains

Contrary to popular myth, the Indians rarely attacked wagon trains. Less than 4 percent of the fatalities associated with the Overland Trail experience resulted from Indian

The Old Scout's Tale (1853), by William Tylee Ranney. Few settlers traveling in wagon trains were prepared for the hardships of life on the trail.

raids. More often, the Indians either allowed the settlers to pass through their tribal lands unmolested or demanded payment. Many wagon trains never encountered a single Indian, and others received generous aid from Indians who served as guides, advisers, or traders. The Indians, one woman pioneer noted, "proved better than represented." To be sure, as the number of pioneers increased dramatically during the 1850s, tensions between overlanders and Indians increased, but never to the degree portrayed in Western novels and films.

In 1851 U.S. officials invited the Indian tribes from the northern Plains to a conference held in a grassy valley along the North Platte River, near Ft. Laramie in what is now southeastern Wyoming. Almost 10,000 Indians—men, women, and children—attended the treaty council.

After nearly three weeks of heated discussions and after bestowing on the chiefs a mountain of gifts, federal negotiators and tribal leaders agreed to what became known as the Ft. Laramie Treaty. The American government promised to provide an annual cash payment to the Indians as compensation for the damages caused by wagon trains traversing their hunting grounds. In exchange, the Indians agreed to stop harassing white caravans, to allow federal forts to be built, and to confine themselves to a specified area "of limited extent and well-defined boundaries." Specifically, the Indians were restricted to lands north and south of a corridor through which passed the Overland Trail.

As the first comprehensive treaty with the Plains Indians, this agreement foreshadowed the "reservation" concept of Indian management. Several tribes, however, refused to accept the treaty provisions. The most powerful tribe, the Lakota Sioux, reluctantly signed the agreement but thereafter failed to abide by its restrictions.

The Pathfinder: John Frémont

Despite the hardships and dangers of the overland crossing, the Far West remained an irresistible attraction. The premier press agent for California, and the Far West generally, was John Charles Frémont, "the Pathfinder." Born in Savannah, Georgia, and raised in the South, Frémont became the consummate explorer and romantic adventurer.

Frémont was commissioned a second lieutenant in the United States Topographical Corps in 1838. In 1842 he mapped the Oregon Trail beyond South Pass—and met Christopher "Kit" Carson, one of the most knowledgeable of the mountain men. Carson became Frémont's frequent associate and the most famous frontiersman after Daniel Boone. In 1843–1844 Frémont, typically clad in deerskin shirt, blue army trousers, and moccasins, moved on to Oregon, then made a heroic sweep down the eastern slopes of the Sierras, headed southward through the central valley of California, bypassed the mountains in the south, and returned via the Great Salt Lake. His reports on both expeditions, published together in 1845, gained a wide circulation and helped excite the interest of easterners.

Meanwhile, rumors flourished that the British and French were scheming to grab California, though neither government had such intentions. Political conditions in Mexico left the remote territory in near anarchy much of the time, as governors came and went in rapid succession. Amid the chaos, a substantial number of Californians reasoned that they would be better off if they cut ties to Mexico altogether. Some favored an independent state, perhaps under French or British protection. A larger group admired the balance of central and local authority in the United States and felt their interests might best be served by American annexation. By the time the Americans were ready to light the spark of rebellion in California, there was little will in Mexico to resist.

Annexing Texas

American Settlements

America's lust for land was most clearly at work in the most accessible of all the Mexican borderlands, Texas. More Americans resided there than in all the other coveted regions combined. During the 1820s, Texas was rapidly turning into an American province, for Mexico in 1823 began welcoming American settlers into the region as a means of stabilizing the border.

Foremost among the promoters of Anglo-American settlement in Texas was Stephen F. Austin, a Missouri resident who gained from Mexico a huge land grant originally given to his father by Spanish authorities. By 1824 more than 2,000 hardy souls had settled on Austin's lands. Most of the newcomers were southern farmers drawn to rich new cotton lands selling for only a few cents an acre. By 1830 the coastal region of eastern Texas had approximately 20,000 white settlers and 1,000 black slaves brought in to work the cotton. The newcomers quickly outnumbered the 5,000 Mexicans in the area, and they showed little interest in Catholicism or other aspects of Mexican culture.

The Mexican government grew alarmed at the flood of strangers threatening to engulf the province, and it forbade further immigration. But illegal American immigrants crossed the long border just as illegal Mexican immigrants would later cross over in the other direction. By 1835 the American population had mushroomed to around 30,000, about ten times the number of Mexicans in Texas. Friction mounted in 1832 and 1833 as Americans organized conventions to demand greater representation and power from the Mexican government. Instead of granting the request, General Santa Anna, who had seized power in Mexico, dissolved the national congress late in 1834, abolished the federal system, and became dictator. Texans rose in rebellion, summoned a convention, and pledged to fight for the old Mexican constitution. On March 2, 1836, as Santa Anna approached with an army of conquest, the Texans declared their independence.

Independence from Mexico

The Mexican army delivered its first blow at San Antonio, where it assaulted a small garrison of Texans and American volunteers holed up in an abandoned mission, the Alamo. Among the most celebrated of the volunteers was Davy Crockett, the Tennessee frontiersman who had fought Indians under Andrew Jackson and then served as a congressman.

On February 23, 1836, Santa Anna demanded that the Alamo's defenders surrender, only to be answered with a cannon shot. The 5,000 Mexicans then launched a series of frontal assaults. For twelve days they were repulsed, with fearful losses. Then, on March 6, Santa Anna's men attacked from every side. As the defenders ran low on ammunition, the Mexicans broke through the battered north wall.

Davy Crockett and the other frontiersmen used their muskets as clubs, but they were slain. Santa Anna ordered the wounded Americans put to death and their bodies burned with the rest. The only survivors were sixteen women, children, and servants.

Fall of the Alamo. The Americans' twelve-day stand at the Alamo came to an end on March 6, 1836.

It was a complete victory, but a costly one. The defenders of the Alamo gave their lives at the cost of 1,544 Mexicans, and their heroic stand inspired the rest of Texas to fanatical resistance. While Santa Anna dictated a "glorious" victory declaration, his aide wrote in his diary: "One more such 'glorious victory' and we are finished."

The commander-in-chief of the gathering Texas forces was Sam Houston, a flamboyant Tennessee frontiersman who had joined the army in 1813, fighting alongside Andrew Jackson in the Creek wars. He later served two terms in Congress and in 1827 was elected governor of Tennessee. Two years later, Houston married Eliza Allen, a young woman only half his age. For unexplained reasons, however, the marriage was dissolved almost immediately. The scandal shook the state—and Houston. Rumors of infidelity (unfounded) and alcoholism (legitimate) swirled around him, and in 1829 he resigned as governor and moved to the Indian Territory (now Oklahoma), where he lived for six years with the Cherokees. He took a Cherokee wife and adopted Cherokee citizenship. He also drank so heavily that he became widely known among the Cherokees as the "big drunk." In 1835 Houston moved to Texas and soon thereafter he was named commanding general of the revolutionary army.

Sam Houston.

After the Mexican victory at the Alamo, Houston beat a strategic retreat eastward, gathering reinforcements as he went, including volunteers from the United States. Just west of the San Jacinto River, he finally paused near the site of the city that later bore his name, and on April 21, 1836, he surprised a Mexican encampment there. The 800 Texans and American volunteers charged, yelling "Remember the Alamo," and overwhelmed the Mexican force within fifteen minutes. They killed 630 while losing only 9, and they took Santa Anna prisoner. The Mexican dictator bought his freedom by signing a treaty recognizing Texan independence. The Mexican Congress repudiated the treaty, but the war was at an end.

The Move for Annexation

Residents of the Lone Star Republic then drafted a constitution, made Sam Houston their first president, and voted almost unanimously for annexation to the United States as soon as the opportunity arose. Houston's old friend Andrew Jackson was still the American president, but even Old Hickory could be discreet when delicacy demanded it. The addition of a new slave state threatened to cause a serious sectional quarrel that might endanger Van Buren's election. Worse than that, it raised the specter of war with Mexico. Consequently, Jackson and his successor, Van Buren, shied away from the issue of annexation.

Rebuffed in Washington, Texans turned their thoughts to creating a separate country. Under President Mirabeau Bonaparte Lamar, elected in 1838, they began to talk of expanding to the Pacific as a new nation that would rival the United States. France and Britain extended official recognition to the new nation of Texas and began to develop trade relations. Texas supplied them with an independent source of cotton, new markets, and promised also to become an obstacle to American expansion. The British, who had abolished slavery in their empire in 1833, hoped Texans might embrace abolition in exchange for British protection against any Mexican effort to reassert its sovereignty over Texas.

Many Texans, however, had never abandoned their hopes of annexation to the United States. Reports of growing British influence created anxieties in the United States government and among southern slaveholders, who became the chief advocates of annexation. The United States began secret negotiations with Texas in 1843, and in April John C. Calhoun, the new secretary of state, completed a treaty that went to the Senate for ratification.

Calhoun chose this moment also to send the British minister a letter instructing him on the blessings of slavery and stating that annexation of Texas was needed to foil the British abolitionists. Publication of the note fostered the claim that annexation was planned less in the national interest than to promote the expansion of slavery. It was so worded, one editor wrote Jackson, as to "drive off every northern man from the support of the measure." Sectional division, plus fear of a war with Mexico, contributed to the Senate's overwhelming rejection of the treaty. Solid Whig opposition contributed more than anything else to its defeat.

Polk's Presidency

The Election of 1844

Prudent leaders in both political parties had hoped to keep the divisive issue of Texas out of the 1844 campaign. Clay and Van Buren, the leading candidates, both wrote letters opposing annexation because it would risk civil war. Whig party leaders showed no qualms about Clay's stance. The convention nominated him unanimously, and the Whig platform omitted any reference to Texas.

The Democratic convention was a different story. Van Buren's southern supporters, including Jackson, abandoned him because of his opposition to Texas annexation. With the convention deadlocked, expansionist forces nominated James K. Polk of Tennessee. The party platform took an unequivocal stand favoring territorial expansion. To win support in the North and West as well as the South, it called for "the reoccupation of Oregon and the re-annexation of Texas."

The combination of southern and western expansionism constituted a winning strategy that was so popular that Clay began to hedge his statement on Texas. While he still believed the integrity of the Union to be the chief consideration, he had "no personal objection to the annexation of Texas" if it could be achieved "without dishonor, without war, with the common consent of the Union, and upon just and fair terms." His explanation seemed clear enough, but prudence was no match for spread-eagle oratory and the emotional pull of Manifest Destiny. Clay's stand turned more votes to the Liberty party, an antislavery party begun by a group of abolitionists in 1840. In the western counties of New York, the Liberty party drew enough votes away from the Whigs to give the state to Polk. Had he carried New York, Clay would have won the election by seven electoral votes. Polk won a narrow plurality of 38,000 popular votes nationwide but a clear majority of the electoral college, 170 to 105. At forty-nine Polk was the youngest president up to that time.

Polk and His Program

Born near Charlotte, North Carolina, James K. Polk moved to Tennessee as a young man. After studying mathematics and classics at the University of North Carolina, he became a successful lawyer and planter, entered politics early, served fourteen years in Congress (four as Speaker of the House) and two as governor of Tennessee. Young Hickory, as his partisans liked to call him, had none of Jackson's charisma, but he shared Jackson's strong prejudices and his stubborn determination. Single-mindedly committed to the tasks at hand, Polk was a poor diplomat but a formidable leader.

In domestic affairs, Polk adhered to the principles of Jackson, but he and the new Jacksonians subtly reflected the growing influence of the slaveholding South within the party. Abolitionism, Polk warned, could bring the dissolution of the Union, but his proslavery stance further fragmented public opinion. Antislavery northerners had already begun to drift away from the prosouthern Democratic party.

Polk's major objectives were reduction of the tariff, reestablishment of the Independent Treasury, settlement of the Oregon question, and the acquisition of California. He got them all. The Walker Tariff of 1846, in keeping with Democratic tradition, lowered duties, and in the same year, Polk persuaded Congress to restore the Independent Treasury, which the Whigs had eliminated. Twice Polk vetoed internal improvement bills, leading critics to charge that he was determined to further the regional goals of the South at the expense of the national interest.

Polk's chief concern remained geographic expansion. He privately vowed to acquire California and New Mexico as well, preferably by purchase. The acquisition of Texas was already under way before Polk took office. President Tyler, taking Polk's election as a mandate to act, had asked Congress to accomplish annexation by joint resolution, which required only a simple majority in each house and avoided the two-thirds Senate vote needed to ratify a treaty. Congress had read the election returns too, and after a bitter debate over slavery, the resolution passed by votes of 27 to 25 in the Senate and 120 to 98 in the House. Tyler signed the resolution on March 1, 1845, offering to admit Texas to statehood. Texas voters ratified the action in October, and the new state formally entered the Union on December 29, 1845.

Oregon

Meanwhile, the Oregon issue heated up as expansionists insisted that Polk abandon previous offers to settle on the Forty-ninth Parallel and stand by the platform pledge to take all of Oregon from Great Britain. Some expansionists were prepared to risk war. "Fifty-four forty or fight," they insisted. "All of Oregon or none." In his inaugural address, Polk claimed that the American title to Oregon was "clear and unquestionable," but privately he favored a prudent compromise. The British, however, refused his offer to extend the boundary along the Forty-ninth Parallel. Polk then withdrew the offer and renewed his claim to all of Oregon. In the annual message to Congress at the end of 1845, he asked for permission to give Britain a year's notice that joint occupation would be ended. After a long and bitter debate, Congress adopted the resolution.

Fortunately for Polk, the British government had no enthusiasm for war over that remote wilderness at the cost of profitable trade relations with the United States. In June 1846, the British government submitted a draft treaty to extend the border along the Forty-ninth Parallel and through the main channel south of Vancouver Island. On June 18, the Senate ratified the treaty.

The Mexican War

The Outbreak of War

On March 6, 1845, two days after Polk took office, the Mexican ambassador broke off relations and left for home to protest the annexation of Texas. Polk ordered American troops under General Zachary Taylor to take up positions along the Rio Grande River in the new state of Texas. Polk wanted to goad the Mexicans into a conflict in order to secure Texas and obtain California and New Mexico. As Ulysses S. Grant, then a young officer serving under Taylor, later admitted,

"We were sent to provoke a fight, but it was essential that Mexico commence it."

Polk resolved that he could achieve his purposes only by force, and he won the cabinet's approval of a war message to Congress. That very evening, May 9, the news arrived that Mexicans had attacked American soldiers north of the Rio Grande. Eleven Americans were killed, five wounded, and the remainder taken prisoner. Polk's provocative scheme had worked.

In his war message, Polk seized the high ground, declaring that the use of force was a response to aggression, a recognition that war had been forced upon the United States. "The cup of forbearance had been exhausted" before the incident; now, he said, Mexico "has invaded our territory, and shed American blood upon the American soil." The House and Senate quickly passed the war resolution, and Polk signed the declaration of war on May 13, 1846.

Opposition to the War

In the Mississippi Valley, where expansion fever ran high, the war was immensely popular. Likewise in New York, novelist Herman Melville reported that "people here are all in a state of delirium." Whig opinion, however, ranged from lukewarm to hostile. John Quincy Adams, who voted against participation, called it "a most unrighteous war." An obscure one-term congressman from Illinois named Abraham Lincoln, upon taking his seat in 1847, began introducing "spot resolutions," calling on President Polk to name the spot where American blood had been shed on American soil, implying that the troops may in fact have been in Mexico when fired upon. Once again, as in 1812, New England was a hotbed of opposition, largely in the belief that this war was the work of southern slaveholders. Some New Englanders were ready to separate from the slave states, and the Massachusetts legislature pronounced the conflict a war of conquest.

Preparing for Battle

Both the United States and Mexico approached the war ill prepared. The American military was especially small and inexperienced. At the outset of war, the regular army numbered barely over 7,000, in contrast to the Mexican force of 32,000. Many of the Mexicans, however, were pressed into service or recruited from prisons and thus made less than enthusiastic fighters. Before the war ended, the American force grew to 104,000, of whom about 31,000 were regular army troops and marines. The rest were six- and twelve-month volunteers.

Among the volunteers were sons of Henry Clay and Daniel Webster, but most came from coarser backgrounds. Volunteer militia companies, often filled with frontier toughs, made up as raunchy a crew as ever graced the American military—lacking uniforms, standard equipment, and discipline. Repeatedly, despite the best efforts of the commanding generals, these undisciplined forces engaged in plunder, rape, and murder. Nevertheless, these rough-and-tumble Americans consistently defeated larger Mexican forces, which had their own problems with training, discipline, and munitions.

The United States entered the war without even a tentative plan of action, and politics complicated devising one. What Polk wanted, Thomas Hart Benton wrote later, was "a small war, just large enough to require a treaty of peace, and not large enough to make military reputations, dangerous for the presidency." Winfield Scott, general-in-chief of the army, was both a Whig and politically ambitious. Polk nevertheless named him to take charge of the Rio Grande front, but when Scott quarreled with Polk's secretary of war, the exasperated president withdrew the appointment.

There now seemed a better choice. General Zachary Taylor's men had scored two victories over Mexican forces north of the Rio Grande, and on May 18, 1846, they crossed the Rio Grande and occupied Matamoros, which a demoralized and bloodied Mexican army had abandoned. These quick victories brought Taylor instant popularity, and the president responded willingly to the demand that he be made overall commander for the conquest of Mexico. "Old Rough and Ready" Taylor had achieved Polk's main objective, the conquest of Mexico's northern provinces. Taylor became an immediate folk hero to his troops and to Americans back home, so much so that Polk began to see him as a political threat.

Annexation of California

Polk had long coveted the valuable Mexican territory along the Pacific coast and had first tried buying it, but to no avail. He then sought to engineer a Texas-style revolt against Mexican rule among the thousand or so American settlers in California. To that purpose, near the end of 1845, John C. Frémont brought out a band of sixty frontiersmen, including Kit Carson, ostensibly on another exploration of California and Oregon. In 1846 Frémont and his men moved into the Sacramento Valley. Americans in the area fell upon Sonoma on June 14, proclaimed the independent "Republic of California," and hoisted the hastily designed Bear Flag, a California grizzly bear and star painted on white cloth—a version of which became the state flag.

By the end of June, Frémont had endorsed the Bear Flag Republic and set out for Monterey. Before he arrived, the commander of the Pacific Fleet, having heard of the outbreak of hostilities, sent men ashore to raise the American flag and proclaim California a part of the United States. The Republic of California had lasted less than a month, and most Californians of whatever origin welcomed a change that promised order instead of the confusion of the unruly Bear Flaggers. Sporadic clashes with Mexicans continued until 1847, when they finally capitulated. Meanwhile, Colonel

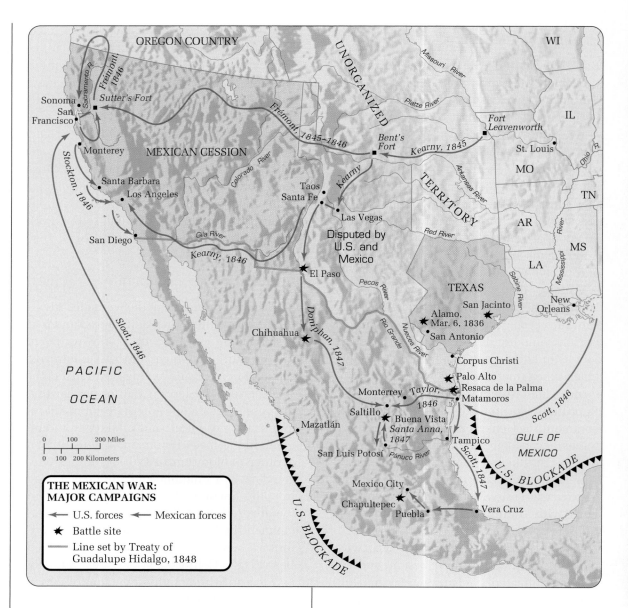

THE MEXICAN WAR:
MAJOR CAMPAIGNS

→ U.S. forces ← Mexican forces

★ Battle site

— Line set by Treaty of
Guadalupe Hidalgo, 1848

Stephen Kearny and 300 soldiers, having earlier captured Santa Fe, ousted the Mexican forces from southern California and occupied Los Angeles.

Taylor's Battles

Both California and New Mexico had been taken from the Mexicans before General Zachary Taylor fought his first major battle in northern Mexico. Having waited for more men and munitions, Taylor finally headed southward in September 1846 toward the heart of Mexico. His first goal was the fortified city of Monterrey, which he took after a five-day siege.

Having never seen the Mexican desert, Polk wrongly assumed that Taylor's men could live off the country and need not depend on resupply. Polk therefore misunderstood the general's reluctance to strike out across several hundred miles of barren land north of Mexico City. On another point the president was simply duped. The old dictator Santa Anna, forced out in 1844, got word to Polk from his exile in Cuba that in return for the right considerations he could bring about a settlement of the war. Polk in turn assured the Mexican leader that Washington would pay well for any territory taken through such a settlement. In 1846, after another overturn in the Mexican government, American forces allowed Santa Anna to return to his homeland. Soon he was again in command of the Mexican army and then was named president once more. But instead of carrying out his pledge to Polk to negotiate an end to the war, Santa Anna prepared to fight Taylor's army. Polk's secret deal had put the ablest Mexican general back in command of the enemy army.

In October 1846, Polk and his cabinet ordered American troops to move against Mexico City from the south by way of Vera Cruz, which left Taylor's forces idle. Polk would have preferred a Democratic general to lead the new offensive, but for want of a better choice, he named Winfield Scott to the field command. Taylor, miffed at his reduction to a minor role and harboring a "violent disregard" for Scott's abilities, disobeyed orders and took the offensive himself.

Near the hacienda of Buena Vista, Santa Anna's large but ill-trained army met Taylor's untested volunteers. The Mexican general invited the vastly outnumbered Americans to surrender. "Tell him to go to hell," Taylor replied. In the hard-fought Battle of Buena Vista (February 22–23, 1847), Taylor saw his son-in-law, Colonel Jefferson Davis, the future president of the Confederacy, lead a regiment that broke up a Mexican cavalry charge. Neither side could claim victory on the strength of the outcome, but Taylor was convinced that only his lack of trained regular troops prevented him from striking a decisive blow.

Scott's Triumph

Meanwhile, the long-planned southern assault on the enemy capital had begun on March 9, 1847, when Scott's army landed

Battle of Buena Vista (1847), by Carl Nebel. The last major action on the northern front, neither side could claim victory in this battle.

on the beaches south of Vera Cruz. It was the first major amphibious operation by American military forces, and it was carried out without loss. The Mexican commander at Vera Cruz surrendered on March 27 after a week-long siege. Scott and some 14,000 soldiers then retraced the 260-mile route to Mexico City taken by Cortés more than 300 years earlier.

Scott directed a brilliant flanking operation around the lakes and marshes guarding the eastern approaches to Mexico City, then another around the Mexican defenses at San Antonio. On September 13, 1847, American forces entered Mexico City.

The Treaty of Guadalupe Hidalgo

After the fall of the capital, Santa Anna resigned and a month later fled the country. By the treaty of Guadalupe Hidalgo, signed on February 2, 1848, Mexico gave up all claims to Texas above the Rio Grande and ceded California and New Mexico to the United States. In return the United States agreed to pay Mexico $15 million and assume the claims of American citizens against Mexico up to a total of $3¼ million.

The seventeen-month-long war had cost the United States 1,721 killed, 4,102 wounded, and far more—11,155—dead of disease, mostly dysentery and chronic diarrhea. It remains the deadliest war in American military history in terms of the percentage of combatants killed. Out of every 1,000 American soldiers in Mexico, some 110 died. The next highest death rate would be in the Civil War, with 65 out of every 1,000 participants.

The military and naval expenditures had been $98 million. For this price, and payments made under the treaty, the United States acquired more than 500,000 square miles of territory (more than a million counting Texas), including the great Pacific harbors of San Diego, Monterey, and San Francisco. Except for a small addition by the Gadsden Purchase in 1853, these annexations rounded out the continental United States.

The War's Legacies

Several important "firsts" are associated with the Mexican War: the first successful American offensive war, the first major amphibious operation, and the nation's first war covered by correspondents. It was also the first significant combat experience for a group of junior officers who would later serve as leading generals during the Civil War: Ulysses S. Grant, Robert E. Lee, Thomas "Stonewall" Jackson, George B. McClellan, George Pickett, George Meade, and others.

Initially, the victory in Mexico provoked a surge of national pride. American triumphs "must elevate the *true* self-respect of the American people," Walt Whitman exclaimed. Others were not so sure. Ralph Waldo Emerson rejected war "as a means of achieving America's destiny," but he then accepted such annexations of new territory by force with the explanation that "most of the great results of history are brought about by discreditable means."

As the years passed, the Mexican War was increasingly seen as a war of selfish conquest. But for a brief season, the glory of victory did add luster to the names of Zachary Taylor and Winfield Scott. Despite Polk's best efforts, he had manufactured the next, and last, two Whig candidates for president. One of them, Taylor, would replace him in the White House, with the storm of sectional conflict already on the horizon.

A House Divided
and Rebuilt

O f all the regions of the United States during the first half of the nineteenth century, the South was the most distinctive. Southern society remained fundamentally rural and agricultural long after the rest of the nation embraced the urban industrial revolution. Likewise, the southern elite's tenacious effort to preserve and expand the institution of slavery muted social reform impulses in the South and ignited a prolonged political controversy that would end in civil war.

The relentless settlement of the western territories set in motion a feverish competition between North and South for political influence in the burgeoning West. Would the new states in the West be "slave" or "free"? The issue of allowing slavery into the new territories involved more than humanitarian concern for the plight of enslaved blacks. By the 1840s, North and South had developed quite different economic interests. The North wanted high tariffs on imported products to "protect" its infant industries from foreign competition. Southerners, on the other hand, favored free trade because they wanted to import British goods in exchange for the cotton they provided British textile mills.

A series of ingenious political compromises glossed over the fundamental differences between the sections during the first half of the nineteenth century. But abolitionists refused to give up their crusade against slavery. Moreover, a new generation of national political leaders emerged in the 1850s, men from both North and South who were less willing to seek political compromises. The continuing debate over allowing slavery into the new western territories kept sectional tensions at a fever pitch. By the time Abraham Lincoln was elected in 1860, many Americans had decided that the nation could not survive half-slave and half-free; something had to give.

In a desperate effort to preserve the institution of slavery, eleven southern states seceded from the Union and created a separate Confederate nation. This, in turn, prompted northerners such as Lincoln to support a civil war to preserve the Union. No one realized in 1861 how prolonged and costly the war between the states would become. Over 630,000 soldiers and sailors died of wounds or disease. The colossal carnage caused even the most seasoned observers to blanch in disbelief. As President Lincoln confessed in his second inaugural address, no one expected the war to become so "fundamental and astonishing."

Nor did people envision how sweeping the war's effects would be on the future of the nation. The northern victory in 1865 restored the Union and in the process helped to accelerate America's transformation into a modern nation-state. National power and a national consciousness began to displace the sectional emphases of the antebellum era. A Republican-led Congress pushed through legislation to foster industrial and commercial development and western expansion. In the process, the United States began to leave behind the Jeffersonian dream of a decentralized agrarian republic.

The Civil War also ended slavery. Yet the actual status of the 4 million freed blacks remained precarious. How would they fare in a society built upon slavery? In 1865 the daughter of a Georgia planter expressed her concern about such issues when she wrote in her diary that "there are sad changes in store for both races. I wonder the Yankees do not shudder to behold their work" ahead in trying to "reconstruct" the defeated South.

The former slaves found themselves legally free, but most were without property, homes, education, or training. Although the Fourteenth Amendment (1867) set forth guarantees for the civil rights of African Americans and the Fifteen Amendment (1870) provided that black males could vote, local white authorities found shrewd—and often violent—ways to circumvent these new laws.

The restoration of the former Confederate states to the Union did not come easily. Much bitterness and resistance remained among the vanquished. Although Confederate leaders were initially disenfranchised, they continued to exercise considerable authority in political and economic matters. Indeed, in 1877, when the last federal troops were removed from the occupied South, former Confederates declared themselves "redeemed" from the stain of occupation. By the end of the nineteenth century, most states of the former Confederacy had devised a complex system of legal discrimination based on race that re-created many aspects of slavery.

ESSENTIAL THEMES

CRITICAL QUESTIONS

Why were the nation's political leaders unable to solve the problems that led to the Civil War?

Did the northern economy give Union forces a decisive advantage in the war?

What were the social effects of the Civil War in the North and the South?

Had the North and South come to embrace irreconcilable values at the time of the Civil War?

What were the most important international implications of the Civil War?

Why were the nation's political leaders unable to solve the problems that led to the Civil War?

Politics in the white South
Honor and politics
The southern frontier
Antislavery in Congress
The abolitionist movement
Abolitionists petition Congress to end
    slavery
Black abolitionists: Frederick Douglass
    and Sojourner Truth

CHAPTER 14

The Old South:
An American Tragedy
The politics of the slave South

CHAPTER 15

The Crisis of Union
Politicizing slavery: the failure
    of compromise

The Wilmot Proviso (1846)
Popular sovereignty
The Free Soilers
Compromise of 1850
The Fugitive Slave Act
Emergence of Republican party (1854)
Kansas-Nebraska Act (1854)
"Bleeding" Kansas
"Bully" Brooks
Dred Scott v. *Sandford* (1857)
Lincoln-Douglas debates (1858)
John Brown's raid
Abraham Lincoln elected president
    (1860)

CHAPTER 16

The War of the Union
The Civil War

Secession (1860–1861)
The outbreak of war
The war's early course
Government during the war
Union politics and civil liberties
Confederate politics
Actions in the Western Theater
McClellan's peninsular campaign
Lincoln issues Emancipation
    Proclamation (January 1, 1863)
The faltering Confederacy
The Confederacy's defeat
General Lee surrenders, April 9, 1865

CHAPTER 17

Reconstruction: North and South
The battle over Reconstruction

The Radical Republican plan
The Freedmen's Bureau
Andrew Johnson's Reconstruction plan
Johnson's impeachment and trial
    (1868)
A second revolution: The Thirteenth,
    Fourteenth, and Fifteenth
    Amendments
Reconstructing the South
Blacks in southern politics (late 1860s)
Carpetbaggers and scalawags
White terror as a political tool
Conservative resurgence in the South
Ulysses S. Grant elected president
    (1868)
Scandals and reform
Compromise of 1877

CHAPTER 14

The Old South:

An American Tragedy

• The economy of the Old South

King Cotton
Agricultural diversity
Industry and trade
Slave labor
The economic argument over slavery

CHAPTER 15

The Crisis of Union

The economic dimension
of sectionalism •

The expansion of slavery
The free labor interest
The gold rush (1849)
Reduced European demand for
    American grain
The panic of 1857
1860 Republican platform: free
    homesteads and a
    transcontinental railroad

CHAPTER 16

The War of the Union

• Economic resources North and South

The organization of resources
Union finances during the war
Confederate finances during the war

CHAPTER 17

Reconstruction: North and South

Economic development in the North •

Northern route for transcontinental
    railroad
The Morrill Tariff
Morrill Land Grant Act (1862)
Homestead Act (1862)
Devastation in the South
Loss of infrastructure
Damage to agriculture
Loss of slave labor
Government debt in the Grant years
The currency question

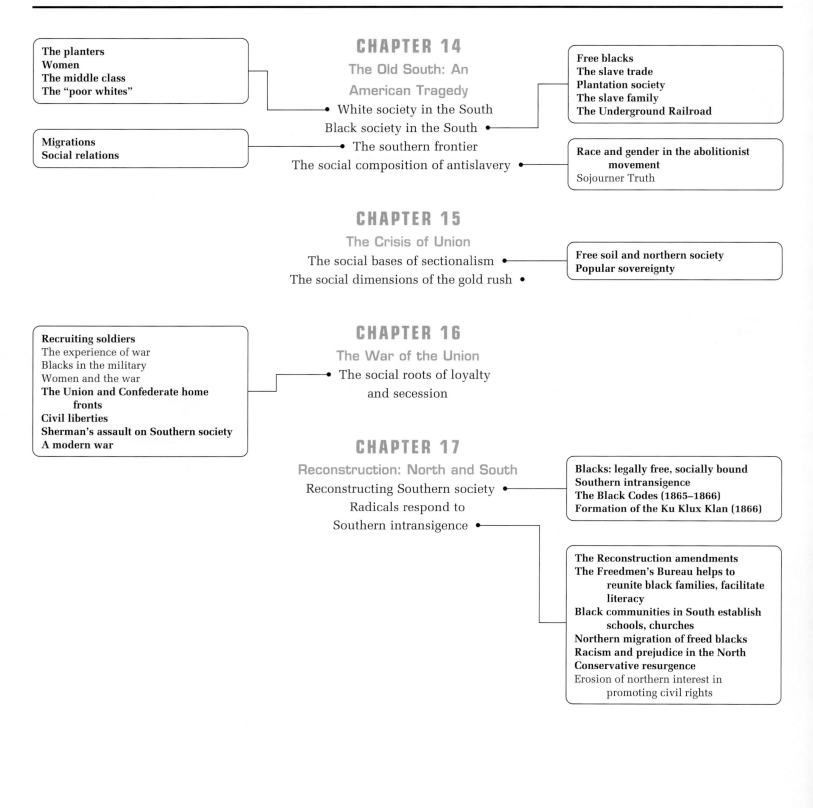

CHAPTER 14

The Old South: An
American Tragedy

White society in the South
Black society in the South
The southern frontier
The social composition of antislavery

The planters
Women
The middle class
The "poor whites"

Migrations
Social relations

Free blacks
The slave trade
Plantation society
The slave family
The Underground Railroad

Race and gender in the abolitionist
movement
Sojourner Truth

CHAPTER 15

The Crisis of Union
The social bases of sectionalism
The social dimensions of the gold rush

Free soil and northern society
Popular sovereignty

CHAPTER 16

The War of the Union
The social roots of loyalty
and secession

Recruiting soldiers
The experience of war
Blacks in the military
Women and the war
The Union and Confederate home
fronts
Civil liberties
Sherman's assault on Southern society
A modern war

CHAPTER 17

Reconstruction: North and South
Reconstructing Southern society
Radicals respond to
Southern intransigence

Blacks: legally free, socially bound
Southern intransigence
The Black Codes (1865–1866)
Formation of the Ku Klux Klan (1866)

The Reconstruction amendments
The Freedmen's Bureau helps to
reunite black families, facilitate
literacy
Black communities in South establish
schools, churches
Northern migration of freed blacks
Racism and prejudice in the North
Conservative resurgence
Erosion of northern interest in
promoting civil rights

CHAPTER 14

The Old South: An American Tragedy

- The Old South

The slave community
Language, folklore, and religion among slaves
"Free persons of color"
***Narrative of the Life of Frederick Douglass* (1845)**
The plantation culture
The culture of the Southern frontier

CHAPTER 15

The Crisis of Union

- A culture of extremes

Sectionalism and compromise
Sectionalism and violence
The impact of *Uncle Tom's Cabin*
The impact of John Brown's raid
California's mining camps: a multicultural moment

CHAPTER 16

The War of the Union

- A culture divides

The justifications for secession
A clash of cultures
The impact of emancipation

CHAPTER 17

Reconstruction: North and South

- Recovering a Nation

The impact of war
The impact of defeat on the South
Anarchy and guerilla war on southern frontier (late 1860s)

What were the most important international implications of the Civil War?

CHAPTER 14

The Old South:

An American Tragedy

• The Southern economy and
foreign trade

The slave trade
American Colonization Society
Approximately 15,000 blacks
       migrate to West Africa (Liberia)
       to escape American slavery
Antislavery as an international
       movement
Waning of British textile industry
       (1860)

CHAPTER 15

The Crisis of Union

American expansionism and the
sectional crisis •

Cuba and the expansion of slavery
Diplomacy in the Pacific
Commodore Matthew Perry visits
       Tokyo (1853)
Harris Convention opens five Japanese
       ports to American trade (1858)
The international dimension of the gold
       rush

CHAPTER 16

The War of the Union

• European trade interests and alliances
in the Civil War

The Emancipation Proclamation and
       alliances abroad
Civil War diplomacy: foreign funding
       and supply

CHAPTER 17

Reconstruction: North and South

A new nation: the aftermath of the
Civil War •

Centralizing political power
Developing the national economy
Harnessing the nation's resources

The Old South:
An American Tragedy

This chapter focuses on

- Industry and agriculture in the Old South.

- Southern society, black and white.

- The antislavery movement and southern reactions to it.

227

THE *ESSENTIAL AMERICA* ON-LINE TUTOR

www.wwnorton.com/eamerica/ch14

- **Topic: The Underground Railroad**
  www.wwnorton.com/eamerica/ch14/topic.htm

  Thousands of black Americans escaped enslavement in the South by following the Underground Railroad to freedom. Explore the Underground Railroad using maps, photographs, drawings, and historical analyses. Who were the principle organizers of the railroad, and how did they insure the safety of those seeking freedom?

- **Chapter review: On-line quiz and chapter summary**
  www.wwnorton.com/eamerica/ch14/review.htm

- **Chapter resources: Multimedia index**
  www.wwnorton.com/eamerica/ch14/media.htm

The South is a region wrapped in enduring myths and stereotypes. The South portrayed in Hollywood films such as *Gone With the Wind* was a stable agrarian society led by paternalistic white planters who lived in white-columned mansions and represented a "natural" aristocracy of virtue and talent within their communities. They were supposedly kind to their slaves and devoted to the rural values of independence and chivalric honor celebrated by Thomas Jefferson.

By contrast, the darker myth about the Old South emerged from abolitionist pamphlets and Harriet Beecher Stowe's best-selling novel *Uncle Tom's Cabin*. These exposés of southern culture portrayed the planters as arrogant autocrats who raped slave women, brutalized slave workers, and lorded over their communities with haughty disdain for the rights and needs of others.

Such contrasting myths died hard, in large part because they are each rooted in reality. Nonetheless, efforts to get at what really set the Old South apart from the rest of the nation generally turn on two lines of thought: the impact of environment (geography and climate) and the effects of human decisions and actions. The South's warm, humid weather fostered the growing of commercial crops, and thus led to the plantation system and slavery. These developments in turn brought sectional conflict and civil war.

Distinctive Features of the Old South

While geography was a key determinant of southern life, explanations that involve human action are more persuasive. In the 1830s, many observers located the origins of southern distinctiveness in the institution of racial slavery. The resolve of whites to maintain such a system muted class conflict. Yet the biracial character of the population influenced other aspects of life. In shaping patterns of speech and folklore, of music and literature, black southerners im-measurably influenced and enriched the region's culture.

The South differed from other sections of the country in that it drew few European immigrants after the Revolution. One reason was that the main shipping lines went to northern ports; another, that immigrants balked at the prospect of competing with slave labor. After the Missouri Controversy of 1819–1821, the South became more and more a self-consciously minority region, its population growth lagging behind that of other sections, its "peculiar institution" of slavery more and more an isolated and odious anachronism.

The South also differed in its hyper-masculine culture. Southern men displayed a penchant for fighting, for guns, and for the military. The preponderance of farming also remained a distinctive southern characteristic, whether pictured as the Jeffersonian yeoman living by the sweat of his brow or the lordly planter dispatching his slave gangs. But in the end, what made the South so distinctive was the widespread assumption that it *was* distinctive.

Agricultural Diversity

The focus on King Cotton and other cash crops such as rice and sugar cane has obscured the degree to which the South fed itself from its own fields. Corn grew everywhere, but it went less into the market than into local consumption, as feed and fodder, as hoecake and grits. On many farms and plantations, the rhythms of the growing season permitted the labor force to alternate attention between the commercial staples and the food crops. Livestock added to the diversity of the farm economy.

Yet the picture was hardly one of unbroken prosperity. The South's staple crops (cotton, sugarcane, tobacco) quickly exhausted the soil, and open-row crops such as tobacco, cotton, and corn left the bare ground in between subject to erosion. By 1860, much of eastern Virginia had aban-

Planting sweet potatoes on the Hopkinson plantation, Edisto Island, South Carolina, April 1862.

of the world. The concentration on land and slaves, as well as the paucity of cities and immigrants, deprived the South of dynamic bases of economic and social innovation. The slaveholding South hitched its wagon to the European demand for cotton. The only perceived threat to "King Cotton" was the growing antislavery sentiment in the North. The unperceived threat was an imminent slackening of the world cotton market. The heyday of expansion in British textiles ended by 1860, but by then the Deep South was locked into cotton production for generations to come.

The Planters

During the first half of the nineteenth century, wealth in the South was increasingly concentrated in the hands of the planter elite. Although great plantations were relatively few in number, they set the tone of economic and social life in the South. What distinguished the plantation from the farm, in addition to its size, was the use of a large slave labor force, managed by overseers. A clear-cut distinction between management and labor set the planter apart from the small slaveholder, who often worked side by side with slaves at the same tasks.

If, to be called a planter, one had to own twenty slaves, only 1 out of every 30 whites in the South in 1860 was a planter. Fewer than 11,000 planters, however, owned fifty or more slaves, and the owners of over one hundred slaves numbered 2,292. The census listed only 11 planters with five hundred slaves and just 1 with as many as one thousand slaves. Yet this privileged elite tended to think of its class interest as synonymous with the interest of the entire South.

The planter group, less than 4 percent of the adult white males in the South, owned more than half the slaves and produced most of the cotton and tobacco and all of the sugar and rice. In a white population numbering just over 8 million in 1860, the total number of slaveholders was only 383,637. But assuming that each family numbered

doned tobacco and in some places had turned to growing wheat for the northern market. The older farming lands had trouble competing with the newer soils farther west, but soon western lands too began to lose their nutrients. So the Southeast and then the Old Southwest faced a growing sense of economic crisis as the nineteenth century advanced.

By 1840, many thoughtful southerners reasoned that by staking everything on agriculture the region had wasted opportunities in manufacturing and trade. After the War of 1812, as cotton growing swept everything before it, the South became increasingly dependent on northern manufacturing and commerce. Cotton and tobacco were exported mainly in northern vessels. Southerners also relied on connections in the North for imported goods. The South became, economically if not formally, a kind of colonial dependency of the North.

White Society in the South

If an understanding of the Old South must begin with a knowledge of potent social myths, it must end with a sense of tragedy. White southerners had won short-term economic gains at the cost of both lagging social development and moral isolation in the eyes five people, the whites with some proprietary interest in slavery came to 1.9 million, or roughly one-fourth of the South's white population. While the preponderance of southern whites belonged to the small-farmer class, the presumptions of the planters were seldom challenged. In part, such deference reflected the desire of many small farmers to become planters themselves. Over time, however, land and slave prices soared, thereby narrowing prospects for upward social mobility. Between 1830 and 1860, the Cotton Belt witnessed a growing concentration of wealth in the hands of a slaveholding elite.

White women reinforced the plantation slave system. The plantation "mistress" supervised the domestic household in the same way her husband took care of the business: overseeing food, linens, housecleaning, the care of the sick, and a hundred other details. While plantation wives also enjoyed entertaining and being entertained, they owed their genteel circumstances to the domestic services provided by slaves.

White women living within a slave-owning culture confronted a double standard in terms of moral and sexual behavior. While they were expected to be models of Christian piety and sexual discretion, their husbands, brothers, and sons enjoyed greater latitude. Many white planters and their sons viewed slave women not only as sources of labor but also as sources of sexual satisfaction.

The Middle Class

Overseers on the largest plantations generally came from the middle class of small farmers or skilled workers (artisans), or were younger sons of planters. Most wanted to become slaveholders themselves, and sometimes they rose to that status, but others were constantly on the move in search of better positions. Occasionally there were black overseers, but the highest management position to which a slave could aspire was usually that of "driver" or leader,

placed in charge of a small group of slaves.

The most numerous white southerners were the yeoman farm families, who lived in modest two-room cabins. They raised a few hogs and chickens, grew some corn and cotton, and traded with neighbors more than with stores. Women and children worked in the fields during harvest time, but most of their days were spent attending to domestic chores. Many of these "middling" farmers owned a handful of slaves, but most owned none.

Small farmers in the South were typically mobile folk, willing to pull up stakes and move west or southwest in pursuit of better land. They tended to be fiercely independent, easily provoked, and suspicious of government authority, and they overwhelmingly identified with the party of Andrew Jackson and the spiritual fervor of evangelical Protestantism. Even though only a minority of the middle-class farmers owned slaves, most of them supported the slave system. They feared that the slaves, if freed, would compete with them for land, and they also enjoyed the "superior" status that racially based slavery afforded them. Such sentiments pervaded the border states as well as the Deep South. Kentucky, for example, held a popular referendum on the issue of slavery in 1849, and the voters, most of whom owned no slaves, resoundingly endorsed the slave system.

Honor and Violence in the Old South

From colonial times, most southern white males prided themselves on adhering to a moral code centered on a prickly sense of honor. The dominant ethical code for the southern white elite included a combative sensitivity to slights, loyalty to family, locality, state, and region, deference to elders and social "betters," and an almost theatrical hospitality. It manifested itself in a fierce defense of female purity and a propensity to magnify personal insults into capital offenses.

Southern white women were the object of masculine chivalry and the subjects of male rule. The mythic southern "lady" was placed on a pedestal celebrating domestic devotion. While men cultivated and defended their *honor*, women paraded and protected their *virtue*. The southern lady presided over the morals and manners of the household—while submitting to patriarchal authority. She subordinated her own individuality in order to serve her husband and children. A southern lady, according to the prevailing standard, was to remain sexually pure, spiritually pious, and domestically submissive—all while she managed the household.

Southern men were preoccupied with an often reckless manliness. As a northern traveler observed, "the central trait of the 'chivalrous southerner' is an intense respect for virility." The duel constituted the ultimate public expression of personal honor and manly courage. Although not confined to the South, dueling was much more common there than in the rest of the young nation, a fact that gave rise to the observation that southerners will be polite until they are angry enough to kill you.

Many of the most prominent southern leaders engaged in duels—congressmen, senators, governors, editors, and planters. The roster of participants included Andrew Jackson, Henry Clay, Sam Houston, and Jefferson Davis. A dueling society, southerners assumed in the early nineteenth century, was a more polite—and honorable—society.

So many duels and deaths occurred in the South that "anti-dueling societies" emerged to lobby against the social ritual. Most states outlawed the practice, but to little avail. As a grand jury in Savannah, Georgia, noted in 1819, "the frequent violations of the law to prevent dueling have made the practice fashionable and almost meritorious among its chivalrous advocates." Judges were reluctant to punish their fellow "gentlemen" for upholding their honor. It was not until after the Civil War that dueling

fell into widespread disgrace and began a rapid decline. Humorist Mark Twain deserves the last word: "I thoroughly disapprove of duels. If a man should challenge me, I would take him kindly and forgivingly by the hand and lead him to a quiet place and kill him."

Black Society in the South

Slavery was one of the fastest growing elements of American life during the first half of the nineteenth century. In 1790 there had been less than 700,000 slaves in the United States. By 1830 there were more than 2 million, and by 1860 there were almost 4 million. Although they all suffered the injustices of white racism, African Americans had diverse experiences in the United States, depending upon their geographic location and the nature of their working and living conditions.

"Free Persons of Color"

Not all blacks were slaves. In the Old South, "free persons of color" occupied an uncertain status, balanced somewhere between slavery and freedom, subject to legal restrictions not imposed on whites. Over the years, some slaves were able to purchase their freedom, while some gained freedom as a reward for service in American wars. Others were simply freed by concerned masters.

By 1830, there were 319,000 free blacks in the United States, about 150,000 of whom lived in the South. The free persons of color included a large number of mulattoes, people of mixed white and black ancestry, some of whom built substantial fortunes and even became slaveholders. In Louisiana a mulatto bought an estate with ninety-one slaves for $250,000.

But black slaveholders were a tiny minority. The 1830 census revealed that only

3,775 free blacks owned 12,760 slaves. Although most of these black slave owners were in the South, some also lived in Rhode Island, Connecticut, Illinois, New Jersey, New York, and the border states. Some blacks owned slaves for humanitarian purposes. One minister, for instance, bought slaves and then enabled them to purchase their freedom from him on easy terms. Most often, black slaveholders were free blacks who bought their own family members with the express purpose of later freeing them. But some blacks engaged in slavery for purely selfish rather than humanitarian reasons. Like their white counterparts, they participated in slave auctions and advertised for the return of runaways.

Free blacks were often skilled artisans (blacksmiths, carpenters, cobblers), farmers, or common laborers. The increase in their numbers slowed as legislatures put more and more restrictions on the right to free slaves, but by 1860 there were 262,000 free blacks in the slave states, a little over half the national total of 488,000. They were most numerous in the upper South and tended to congregate in urban areas.

Free blacks were victims of widespread discrimination. All southern states required them to carry identification passes. Whites often fraudulently claimed that a free black was in fact one of their runaway slaves, and if the African American did not have an official certificate of freedom, he could be enslaved. In many other ways, free blacks were not truly "free." Most southern states prohibited them from voting. Blacks were not allowed to testify in court against whites, and they could not hold church services without the presence of a white minister.

The Trade in Slaves

When the African slave trade was outlawed in 1808, it only added to the value of those slaves already present. The rise in slave value often brought better treatment. "Massa was purty good," one ex-slave recalled later.

"He treated us jus' 'bout like you would a good mule." Some owners hired wage laborers, often Irish immigrants, for ditching and other dangerous work rather than risk the lives of the more valuable slaves.

The end of the foreign slave trade gave rise to a flourishing domestic trade, with slaves being moved mainly from the used-up lands of the Southeast into the booming new country of the Old Southwest. Many slaves moved south and west with their owners, but there also developed an organized business with brokers, slave pens, and auctioneers. The worst aspect of the slave trade was its breakup of families.

Plantation Slavery

More than half of all slaves in 1860 worked on plantations, and most of those were field-hands. The preferred jobs were those of household servants and skilled workers, including blacksmiths, carpenters, and coopers. Fieldhands worked long hours from dawn to dusk and were usually housed in one- or two-room wooden shacks with dirt floors, some without windows. Based on detailed records from eleven plantations in the lower South, scholars have calculated that more than half of all slave babies died in the first year of life, a mortality rate more than twice that of white infants.

The difference between a good owner and a bad one, according to one ex-slave, was the difference between one who did not "whip too much" and one who "whipped till he bloodied you and blistered you." A slave's ultimate recourse was rebellion or flight, but most recognized the futility of such measures, with whites wielding the

African Americans return from laboring in the South Carolina cotton fields.

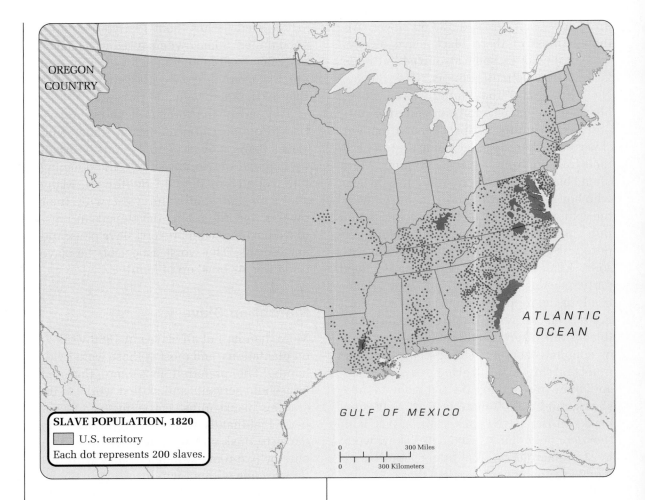

SLAVE POPULATION, 1820

U.S. territory

Each dot represents 200 slaves.

OREGON
COUNTRY

ATLANTIC
OCEAN

GULF OF MEXICO

0   300 Miles

0   300 Kilometers

power and weapons. In the nineteenth century only three slave insurrections drew much notice, and two of those were betrayed before they got under way.

Only the Nat Turner insurrection of 1831 in rural Virginia got beyond the planning stage. Turner, a black overseer, was also a religious exhorter who professed a divine mission in leading the rebellion. The revolt began when a small group killed Turner's master's family and set off down the road repeating the process at other farmhouses, where other slaves joined in. Before it ended, at least fifty-five whites had been killed. Eventually trials resulted in seventeen hangings and seven deportations. The Virginia militia, for its part, killed large numbers of slaves indiscriminately in the process of putting down the rebels.

Forging the Slave Community

The slave experience could be as varied as people are. Slaves were victims, but to stop with so obvious a perception would be to miss an important story of endurance and achievement. If ever there was a melting pot in American history, the most effective may have been that in which Africans from a variety of ethnic, linguistic, and tribal origins fused into a new community and a new culture as African Americans.

Among the most important manifestations of slave culture was its religion, a mixture of African and Christian elements. Most Africans brought with them a concept of a Creator, or Supreme God, whom they could recognize in Jehovah, and lesser gods whom they might identify with Christ, the Holy

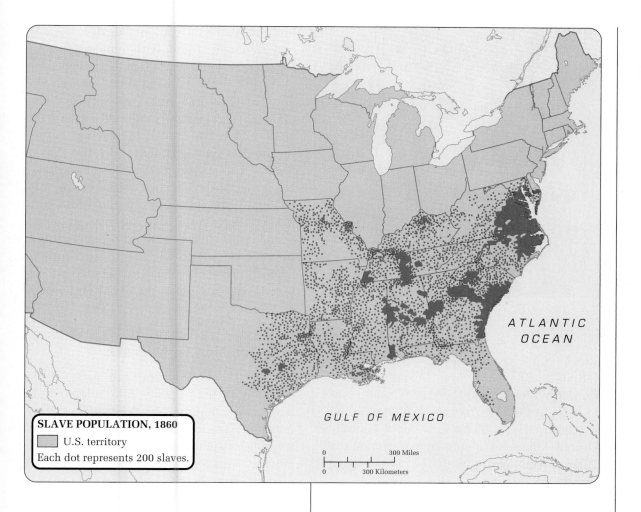

SLAVE POPULATION, 1860

☐ U.S. territory

Each dot represents 200 slaves.

ATLANTIC OCEAN

GULF OF MEXICO

0 — 300 Miles
0 — 300 Kilometers

Ghost, and the saints, thereby reconciling their earlier beliefs with the new Christian religion. Alongside the church, they also retained African beliefs in spirits, magic spells and herbs, and conjuring (the practice of healing and warding off evil spirits). Belief in magic is a common human response to conditions of danger or helplessness.

Slaves, however, found greater comfort in the church. There they could find both balm for the soul and release for their emotions, and they brought with them from Africa a demonstrative spirituality. Some owners openly encouraged religious meetings among their slaves, but those who were denied the open use of "praise houses" held "bush meetings" in secret. The preachers and exhorters who sprang up in the slave world commonly won the acceptance of the owners, if only because efforts to get rid of them proved futile. The peculiar cadences of their exhortations, chants, and spirituals have produced music of great rhythmic complexity, forms of dance and body language, and folk tales.

The Slave Family

Slave marriages had no legal status, but slave owners generally accepted marriage as a stabilizing influence on the plantation. Most slave children were socialized into their culture through the nuclear family, which afforded some degree of independence from white influence. Slaves were not always allowed to realize this norm. In some cases, the matter of family arrangements was ignored or left entirely up to the

Lynchburg Negro Dance, 1853. Slaves successfully maintained some aspects of their African culture, incorporating it into their religion, music, and dance.

slaves on the assumption that black females were simply promiscuous—a convenient rationalization for white sexual exploitation, to which the presence of so many mulattoes attested. The census of 1860 reported 412,000 persons of mixed ancestry in the United States, or about 10 percent of the African-American population, probably a drastic undercount.

The Culture of the Southern Frontier

Despite enduring myths to the contrary, there was substantial social and cultural diversity within the South during the three decades before the Civil War. The antebellum southern frontier, for example, was a quite different region from the more settled areas in the states along the Atlantic seaboard. Of all the many frontiers that have combined to produce a distinctive American culture, the Old Southwest is perhaps the least well known. It included the states and territories west of Georgia—Alabama, Mississippi, Louisiana, Texas, and Arkansas—as well as the frontier areas in Tennessee, Kentucky, and Florida.

Largely unsettled until the 1820s, this region bridged the South and the West, ex-

hibiting characteristics of both areas. Raw and dynamic, filled with dangers, uncertainties, and opportunities, it served as a powerful magnet, luring thousands of settlers from Virginia and the Carolinas when the seaboard economy faltered during the 1820s and 1830s. By the 1830s, most cotton production was occurring in the lower South. The migrating southerners carved out farms, built churches, raised towns, and eventually brought culture and order to a raw frontier. As they took up new lives and occupations, these southern pioneers transplanted many practices and institutions from the coastal states. But they also fashioned a distinctly new set of cultural values and social customs.

The Decision to Migrate

By the Jacksonian era, the agricultural economy of the upper South suffered from depressed commodity prices and soil exhaustion. The dwindling economic opportunities available in the Carolinas and Virginia as well as restrictive kinship ties led many to migrate to the Southwest.

Like their northern counterparts, restless sons of the southern planter and professional elite wanted to make it on their own, to be "self-made men," economically self-reliant and socially independent. To them, speculative profit-seeking was more enticing than family stability. A North Carolinian expected to "rise and soar like an eagle" in the Southwest because he would be freed from the strictures of his family circle, which he perceived as holding him back.

Women were underrepresented among migrants to the Old Southwest. Most dreaded the thought of taking up life on a disease-ridden, violent, and primitive frontier. The new region did not offer them independence or adventure. They would remain part of a patriarchal culture in either area. And their never-ending routine of domestic tasks would only increase in the frontier environment. In general, women regretted more than men the loss of kinship ties that migration would entail. To them a stable family life was more important than the prospect of material gain.

Slaves had many of the same reservations about moving west. Almost a million captive African Americans joined in the migration to the Southwest during the antebellum era, most of them making the journey in the 1830s. Like white women, they feared the harsh working conditions and torpid heat and humidity of the Southwest. They also were despondent at the breaking of their family ties.

Journey and Settlement

Most of the migrants to the Southwest headed for the fertile lands of Alabama, Mississippi, and central Tennessee. The typical trek was about 500 miles long. Along rough roads and trails, the pioneers averaged about fifteen miles per day, occasionally staying overnight in taverns, more often camping in the open amid panthers, bears, and wolves. At times the route was clogged with people. Slaves traveled on foot, tied or chained together. Many drowned while fording rivers.

Once in the Southwest, the pioneers bought land that had been appropriated from the Indians. Parcels of 640 acres sold for as little as two dollars an acre. Land in Alabama's black belt (named for the color of the soil) brought higher prices. As cotton prices soared in the 1830s, aspiring planters bought as much land and as many slaves as possible. As a result, the average size of farms and plantations in the Southwest was larger than that in the Carolinas and Virginia.

But the Old Southwest was much more unhealthy than the Carolina Piedmont. The hot climate, contaminated water, and poor sanitation combined to unleash an epidemic of diseases on the new settlers and their slaves. Malaria was especially common. Life in tents and rude log cabins made many newcomers yearn for the material comforts they had left behind. Many decided to return home or move farther west.

Antislavery Movements

Early Opposition to Slavery

Scattered criticism of slavery developed in the North and the South in the decades after the Revolution, but the emancipation movement accelerated with the formation of the American Colonization Society in 1817. The society proposed to resettle freed slaves in Africa. Its supporters included prominent figures such as James Madison, James Monroe, Henry Clay, John Marshall, and Daniel Webster. Some backed it as an antislavery group, while others saw it as a way to bolster slavery by getting rid of potentially troublesome free blacks. Many in the free black community denounced it from the start. A group of free blacks in Philadelphia, for example, stressed in 1817 that they had "no wish to separate from our present homes for any purpose whatever." America, they insisted, was now their native land.

Nevertheless, in 1821 agents of the society acquired from local chieftains in West Africa a parcel of land that became the nucleus of a new country. In 1822 the first freed slaves arrived there, and twenty-five years later the society relinquished control to the independent republic of Liberia. But given its uncertain purpose, the coloniza-

Several generations of a family raised in slavery. Plantation of J. J. Smith, Beaufort, South Carolina, 1862.

tion movement received only meager support from either antislavery or proslavery elements. By 1860, only about 15,000 blacks had migrated to Africa, approximately 12,000 with the help of the Colonization Society. The number was infinitesimal compared to the number of slave births in the United States.

From Gradualism to Abolitionism

Meanwhile, in the early 1830s the antislavery movement took a new departure. In 1831 William Lloyd Garrison began publication in Boston of a new antislavery newspaper, *The Liberator.* In 1832 Garrison and his followers set up the New England Anti-Slavery Society. A year later two wealthy New York merchants, Arthur and Lewis Tappan, founded a similar group in their state. They then helped start a national organization called the American Anti-Slavery Society, with Garrison and others. They hoped to build on the publicity gained by the British antislavery movement, which in 1833 had induced Parliament to end slavery, with compensation to slaveholders, throughout the British Empire. The American Anti-Slavery Society called for immediate emancipation and argued that blacks should "share an equality with the whites, of civil and religious privileges." The group issued a barrage of propaganda for its cause, including periodicals, tracts, agents, lecturers, organizers, and fund-raisers.

The Movement Splits

As the antislavery movement spread, debates over tactics intensified. The Garrisonians, mainly New Englanders, were radicals who felt that American society had been corrupted from top to bottom. Garrison embraced every important reform movement of the day: antislavery, temperance, pacifism, and women's rights. Deeply affected by the perfectionism of the times, he refused to compromise principle for expediency, to sacrifice one reform for another. Abolition was not enough. He opposed colonization of freed slaves and stood for equal rights. He broke with the organized church, which to his mind was in league with slavery. The federal government was all the more so. The Constitution, he said, was "a covenant with death and an agreement with hell." Garrison therefore refused to vote. He was, however, prepared to collaborate with those who did or with those who disagreed with him on other matters.

Other reformers saw American society as fundamentally sound and concentrated their attention on purging it of slavery. Most of these abolitionists were evangelical Christians, and they promoted pragmatic political organization as the best instrument of reform. Garrison struck them as an impractical fanatic.

A showdown came in 1840 on the issue of women's rights. Women had joined the abolition movement from the start, but quietly and largely in groups without men. The activities of the Grimké sisters brought the issue of women's rights to center stage. Sarah and Angelina Grimké, daughters of a prominent slave-owning family in South Carolina, had broken with their parents and moved north to embrace Quakerism, antislavery, and feminism. They set out speaking to women in New England and slowly widened their audiences to include both men and women.

Such unseemly behavior inspired male leaders to chastise the Grimké sisters and other women activists for engaging in "unfeminine" activity. Angelina Grimké stoutly rejected such conventional arguments. "It is a woman's right," she insisted, "to have a voice in all laws and regulations by which she is to be governed, whether in church or in state."

This debate over the role of women in the antislavery movement crackled and simmered until it finally exploded in 1840. At the American Anti-Slavery Society's annual meeting, the Garrisonians insisted on the right of women to participate equally in the

William Lloyd Garrison.

organization, and they carried their point. They did not commit the group to women's rights in any other way, however. Contrary opinion ranged from outright antifeminism to simple fear of scattering shots over too many reforms. The New Yorkers broke away to form the American and Foreign Anti-Slavery Society.

Black Antislavery Activity

White male antislavery activists also balked at granting full recognition to black abolitionists of either sex. Often blindly patronizing, white leaders expected free blacks to take a back seat in the movement. Blacks became exasperated at whites' tendency to value purity over results, to strike a moral posture at the expense of action. Despite the invitation to form separate black groups, black leaders were active in the white societies from the beginning. Three attended the organizational meeting of the American Anti-Slavery Society in 1833, and some became outstanding agents for the movement, notably the former slaves who could speak from firsthand experience.

Among the black abolitionists, one of the most effective was Sojourner Truth. Born in New York State in 1797, the daughter of slaves owned by a Dutch-American family, she was given the name Isabella. She renamed herself in 1843 after experiencing a mystical conversation with God, who told her "to travel up and down the land" preaching the sins of slavery. She did just that, crisscrossing the country during the 1840s and 1850s, exhorting audiences to support abolitionism and women's rights. Having been a slave until she fled to freedom in 1827, Sojourner Truth was able to speak with added conviction and knowledge about the evils of the "peculiar institution" and the inequality of women. As she reportedly told a gathering of the Ohio Women's Rights Convention in 1851, "I have plowed, and planted, and gathered into barns, and no

man could head me—and ar'n't I a woman? I have borne thirteen children, and seen 'em mos' all sold off into slavery, and when I cried out with a mother's grief, none but Jesus heard—and ar'n't I a woman?" Through such compelling testimony, Sojourner Truth demonstrated the powerful intersection of abolitionism and women's rights agitation, and in the process she tapped the distinctive energies that women brought to reformist causes.

An equally gifted black abolitionist was Frederick Douglass of Maryland. Blessed with an imposing frame and a simple eloquence, he became the best-known black man in America. "I appear before the immense assembly this evening as a thief and a robber," he told a Massachusetts group in 1842. "I stole this head, these limbs, this body from my master, and ran off with them." Fearful of capture after publishing his *Narrative of the Life of Frederick Douglass* (1845), he left for an extended lecture tour of the British Isles and returned two years later with enough money to purchase his freedom. He then started an abolitionist newspaper for blacks, the *North Star*, in Rochester, New York.

Douglass's *Narrative* was the best known among several thousand such accounts. Escapees often made it out on their own—Douglass borrowed a pass from a free black seaman—but many were aided by the Underground Railroad, which grew in legend into a vast system to conceal runaways and spirit them to freedom, often over the Canadian border. Actually, there seems to have been more spontaneity than system about the matter, and blacks contributed more than was credited in the legend.

Reactions to Antislavery

In the 1830s abolitionism took a political turn, focusing at first on Congress. One shrewd strategy was to deluge Congress with petitions calling for the abolition of slavery in the nation's capital, the District of Columbia. Most such petitions were pre-

Sojourner Truth (*top*) and Frederick Douglass (*bottom*) were both leading abolitionists.

sented by former president John Quincy Adams, elected to the House from Massachusetts in 1830. In 1836, however, the House adopted a rule to lay abolition petitions automatically on the table, in effect ignoring them. Adams, "Old Man Eloquent," stubbornly fought this "gag rule" as a violation of the First Amendment and hounded its supporters until the gag rule was finally repealed in 1844.

Meanwhile, in 1840, the year of the schism in the antislavery movement, a small group of abolitionists called a convention in Albany, New York, and launched the Liberty party, with James G. Birney, one-time slaveholder from Alabama and Kentucky, as its candidate for president. In the 1840 election, Birney polled only 7,000 votes, but in 1844 his total rose to 60,000, and from that time forth an antislavery party contested every national election until Abraham Lincoln won the presidency in 1860.

The Defense of Slavery

Birney was but one among a number of southerners propelled north during the 1830s by the South's growing hostility to emancipationist ideas. Antislavery in the upper South had its last stand in 1831–1832, when the Virginia legislature debated a plan of gradual emancipation and colonization, then rejected it by a vote of 73 to 58. Thereafter, southern partisans worked out an elaborate intellectual defense of slavery, presenting it as a positive good.

The evangelical Christian churches, which had widely condemned slavery at one time, gradually turned proslavery, at least in the South. Ministers of all denominations joined in the argument. Had not Saint Paul advised servants to obey their masters and told a fugitive servant to return to his master? And had not Jesus remained silent on the subject, at least so far as the Gospels reported his words? In 1843–1844 disputes over slavery split two great denominations along sectional lines and led to the formation of the proslavery Southern Baptist Convention and Methodist Episcopal Church, South. Presbyterians, the only other major denomination to split, did not divide until the Civil War.

A more fundamental feature of the proslavery argument stressed the intrinsic inferiority of blacks. Other arguments took a more "practical" view of slavery. Not only was slavery profitable, ran one line of argument, it was a matter of social necessity. Jefferson, for instance, in his *Notes on Virginia* (1785), had argued that emancipated slaves and whites could not live together without risk of race war growing out of the recollection of past injustices. What is more, it seemed clear that blacks could not be expected to work if freed. They were too shiftless and improvident, it was believed.

In his books *Sociology for the South; or, The Failure of a Free Society* (1854) and *Cannibals All! or, Slaves Without Masters* (1857), George Fitzhugh of Virginia argued that slavery provided security for the black workers in sickness and old age, whereas workers in the North were exploited for profit and then cast aside. People were not born equal, he insisted. Fitzhugh argued for an organic, hierarchical society, much like the family, in which each had a place with both rights and obligations.

Within one generation, such ideas had triumphed in the white South over the post-Revolutionary apology for slavery as an evil bequeathed by the forefathers. Opponents of the orthodox faith in slavery as a positive good were either silenced or exiled. Freedom of thought in the Old South had become a victim of the nation's growing obsession with slavery.

CHAPTER

15

The Crisis of Union

This chapter focuses on

- The politicization of slavery.

- How the Compromise of 1850 and the Kansas-Nebraska Act reflected sectional tensions.

- The rise of a new party system: Republicans and Democrats.

- The specific events that led to the secession of the southern states.

THE *ESSENTIAL AMERICA* ON-LINE TUTOR

www.wwnorton.com/eamerica/ch15

- **Topic: John Brown's raid on the federal arsenal at Harper's Ferry**
  www.wwnorton.com/eamerica/ch15/topic.htm

  In October of 1859 John Brown shocked many Americans when he led a raid on the Federal arsenal at Harper's Ferry, Virginia. Examine Brown's raid on Harper's Ferry using photographs, newspaper accounts, comments by Brown's contemporaries, and historical analyses. What significance did Brown's actions have for black Americans, and how did the white population view his raid?

- **Chapter review: On-line quiz and chapter summary**
  www.wwnorton.com/eamerica/ch15/review.htm

- **Chapter resources: Multimedia index**
  www.wwnorton.com/eamerica/ch15/media.htm

Wars have a way of corrupting ideals and breeding new wars, often in unforeseen ways. For example, America's victory over Mexico and acquisition of territory gave rise to quarrels over the newly acquired lands. These quarrels set in motion a series of political disputes that would culminate in a crisis of union.

Slavery in the Territories

The Wilmot Proviso

The Mexican War was less than three months old when the seeds of a new conflict began to sprout. On August 8, 1846, a freshman Democrat from Pennsylvania, David Wilmot, stood up in the House of Representatives to discuss President Polk's request for $2 million to expedite negotiations with Mexico. Wilmot favored territorial expansion, even the annexation of Texas as a slave state. But he proposed that in lands acquired from Mexico, "neither slavery nor involuntary servitude shall ever exist in any part of said territory."

Within ten minutes an otherwise obscure congressman had immortalized his name. The Wilmot Proviso politicized slavery once and for all. Since the Missouri Controversy of 1819–1821, the issue of slavery in new territories had been lurking in the wings, kept there most of the time by politicians who feared its disruptive force. But for the two decades following Wilmot's proposal the question would never be far from center stage.

The House adopted the Wilmot Proviso, but the Senate balked. When Congress reconvened in December 1846, Polk prevailed on Wilmot to withhold his amendment, but by then others were ready to take up the cause. When a New York congressman revived the proviso, he signaled a revolt by the Van Burenites in concert with the antislavery forces of the North. Once again the House approved the amendment; again the

Senate refused. The House finally gave up, but in one form or another Wilmot's idea kept being revived. Abraham Lincoln recalled that during one term as congressman, 1847–1849, he voted for it "as good as forty times."

South Carolina Senator John C. Calhoun meanwhile devised a thesis to counter the proviso, and he set it before the Senate in four resolutions on February 19, 1847. The Calhoun Resolutions, which never came to a vote, argued that since the territories were the common possession of the states, Congress had no right to prevent citizens from taking slaves into them. To do so would violate the Fifth Amendment, which forbade Congress to deprive any person of life, liberty, or property without due process of law, and slaves were property. By this clever stroke of logic, Calhoun took the basic guarantee of liberty, the Bill of Rights, and turned it into a basic guarantee of slavery. The irony was not lost on his critics, but the point became established southern dogma— echoed by his colleagues and formally endorsed by the Virginia legislature.

Senator Thomas Hart Benton of Missouri, himself a slaveholder but also a Jacksonian nationalist, found in Calhoun's resolutions a set of abstractions "leading to no result." Wilmot and Calhoun between them, he said, had fashioned a pair of shears. Neither blade alone would cut very well, but joined together they could sever the ties of union.

Popular Sovereignty

Many others, like Benton, refused to be polarized, seeking to bypass the brewing conflict. President Polk was among the first to suggest extending the Missouri Compromise dividing free and slave territory at latitude 36°30' all the way to the Pacific. Senator Lewis Cass of Michigan, an ardent Whig expansionist, suggested that the citizens of a territory "regulate their own internal concerns" like the citizens of a state. Such an approach would combine the merits of expediency and democracy. It would take the issue out of the national arena and put it in the hands of those directly affected.

Popular sovereignty, or squatter sovereignty, as the idea was also called, had much to commend it. Without directly challenging the slaveholders' access to the new lands, it promised to open them quickly to non-slaveholding farmers who would almost surely dominate the territories. With this tacit understanding, the idea of letting the territories decide for themselves the slavery issue prospered in Cass's Old Northwest, where Stephen A. Douglas of Illinois and other prominent Democrats soon endorsed it.

When the Mexican War ended in 1848, the question of bondage in the new territories was no longer hypothetical—unless one reasoned, as many did, that their arid climate excluded plantation crops and therefore excluded slavery. For Calhoun that was beside the point, since the right to carry slaves into the territories was inviolate. In fact, there is little reason in retrospect to credit the argument that slavery had reached its natural limits of expansion. Slavery had been adapted to occupations other than plantation agriculture. On irrigated lands, cotton later became a staple crop of the Southwest.

Nobody doubted that Oregon would become free soil, but it too was drawn into the growing controversy. Oregon's territorial status, pending since 1846, was delayed because its provisional government had excluded slavery. To concede that provision would imply an authority drawn from the powers of Congress, since a territory was created by Congress. After much wrangling, Oregon was allowed to organize without slavery. Polk signed the bill on the principle that Oregon was north of 36°30′.

Polk had promised to serve only one term, and having reached his major goals, he refused to run again in 1848. At the Democratic convention, Lewis Cass, the author of squatter sovereignty, won nomination, but the platform simply denied the power of Congress to interfere with slavery in the states and criticized all efforts to bring the question before Congress. The Whigs devised an even more artful shift. Once again, as in 1840, they passed over Henry Clay, their party leader, for a general, Zachary Taylor, whose popularity had grown since the Battle of Buena Vista. A legal resident of Louisiana and owner of more than a hundred slaves, he was an apolitical figure who had never voted in a national election. Once again, as in 1840, the party adopted no platform at all.

The Free-Soil Coalition

But the antislavery impulse was not easily squelched. Wilmot had raised a standard to which a broad coalition could rally. People who shied away from the abolitionism of William Lloyd Garrison could readily endorse the exclusion of slavery from all the new territories. By doing so, moreover, they could strike a blow for liberty whether or not they cared about slavery itself, or about the slaves. Many simply wanted free soil for white farmers, and to keep the unwelcome blacks far away in the South, where they belonged. Free soil in the new territories, therefore, rather than abolition in the South itself, became the rallying point—and also the name of a new party.

Three major groups entered the free-soil coalition: rebellious northern Democrats, antislavery Whigs, and members of the antislavery Liberty party. Disaffection among the Democrats centered in New York, where the Van Burenites seized on the free-soil issue as a moral imperative. Free-soil principles among the Whigs centered in Massachusetts, where a group of "Conscience" Whigs battled the "Cotton" Whigs. Conscience Whigs rejected the slaveholding nominee of their party, Zachary Taylor.

In 1848 these groups—Van Buren Democrats, Conscience Whigs, and Liberty party followers—organized the Free Soil party in a convention at Buffalo. Its presidential nomination went to Martin Van Buren. The Free Soil party platform pledged to abolish slavery, and it entered the campaign with the catchy slogan of "free soil, free speech, free labor, and free men."

Its impact on the election was mixed. The Free Soilers split the Democratic vote enough to throw New York to Zachary Taylor, and the Whig vote enough to give Ohio to Lewis Cass, but Van Buren's total of 291,000 votes was far below the popular totals of 1,361,000 for Taylor and 1,222,000 for Cass. Taylor won with 163 to 127 electoral votes, and both major parties retained a national following.

The California Gold Rush

Meanwhile, a new dimension had been introduced into the question of the territories. On January 24, 1848, gold was discovered in the California territory, and the rush was on. During 1849 more than 80,000 persons reached California, with 55,000 going overland and the rest by sea.

Unlike the land-hungry pioneers who traversed the overland trails, the miners were mostly unmarried young men representing a wide spectrum of ethnic and cultural backgrounds. Few miners were interested in permanent settlement. They wanted to strike it rich quickly and return home. The mining camps in California valleys, canyons, and along creek beds thus sprang up like mushrooms and disappeared almost as rapidly.

The mining shantytowns were disorderly and often lawless communities where leisure time revolved around saloons and gambling halls. One newcomer reported that "in the short space of twenty-four days, we have had murders, fearful accidents, bloody deaths, a mob, whippings, a hanging, an attempt at suicide, and a fatal duel." Within six months of arriving in California in 1849, one in every five of the gold seekers was dead. The gold fields and mining towns were so dangerous that insurance companies refused to provide coverage. Everyone carried weapons—usually pistols or bowie knives. Suicides were common, and disease was rampant. Cholera and scurvy plagued every camp.

Women were as rare in the mining camps as liquor was abundant. In 1850 less than 8 percent of California's total population was female, and even fewer women risked life in the camps. Those who did could demand quite a premium for their work as cooks, laundresses, entertainers, and prostitutes.

In the camps, the white miners often looked with disdain upon the Hispanics and Chinese who were most often employed as wage laborers to help in the panning process, separating gold from sand and gravel. But the miners focused their contempt on the Indians. In the mining culture it was not a crime to kill Indians or work them to death. American miners tried several times to outlaw foreigners in the mining country but had to settle for a tax on foreign miners that was applied to Mexicans in express violation of the treaty ending the Mexican War.

California Statehood

As civic leaders emerged within the burgeoning California population, they grew increasingly frustrated by the inability of military authorities to maintain law and order. In this context the new president, Zachary Taylor, thought he saw an ideal opportunity to use California statehood as a lever to end the stalemate in Congress caused by the slavery issue.

Born in Virginia and raised in Kentucky, Zachary Taylor had acquired a home in Louisiana and a

Gold Miners, c. 1850. Daguerreotype of miners panning for gold at their claim.

plantation in Mississippi. Southern Whigs had rallied to his support, expecting him to uphold the cause of slavery. Instead they had found a southern man with Union principles. Slavery should be upheld where it existed, Taylor felt, but he had little patience with abstract theories about slavery in territories where it probably could not exist. Why not make the California and New Mexico territories, acquired from Mexico, into states immediately, Taylor reasoned, and bypass the whole issue?

But the Californians, in need of organized government, were already ahead of him. By December 1849, without consulting Congress, California organized a "free-state government," which meant slavery was not permitted. New Mexico responded more slowly, but by 1850 Americans there had adopted another free-state constitution. In Taylor's annual message on December 4, 1849, he endorsed immediate statehood for California and enjoined Congress to avoid injecting slavery into the issue.

The Compromise of 1850

The spotlight fell on the Senate, where the Compromise of 1850, one of the great dramas of American politics, was enacted by a stellar cast: the great triumvirate of Henry Clay, John Calhoun, and Daniel Webster, with support from William H. Seward, Stephen A. Douglas, Jefferson Davis, and Thomas Hart Benton. Seventy-three-year-old Clay once again took the role of the "Great Compromiser," which he had played in the Missouri and nullification controversies.

The Great Debate

In January 1850 Clay presented a package of eight resolutions designed to solve all the disputed issues. He proposed to (1) admit California as a free state, (2) organize the remainder of the Southwest without restric-

tion as to slavery, (3) deny Texas its extreme claim to a Rio Grande boundary up to its source, (4) compensate Texas for this by assuming the Texas debt, (5) uphold slavery in the District of Columbia, but (6) abolish the slave trade across its boundaries, (7) adopt a more effective fugitive slave act, and (8) deny congressional authority to interfere with the interstate slave trade. His proposals, in substance, became the Compromise of 1850, but only after a prolonged debate, the most celebrated in the annals of Congress—and the final great debate for Calhoun, Clay, and Webster.

On February 5–6 Clay summoned all his eloquence in defending the settlement. In the interest of "peace, concord and harmony" he called for an end to "passion, passion—party, party—and intemperance." Otherwise, continued sectional bickering would lead to a "furious, bloody, implacable, exterminating" civil war. To avoid such a catastrophe, he stressed, California should be admitted on the terms that its own people had approved. The debate continued sporadically through February, with Sam Houston rising to support Clay's compromise, Jefferson Davis defending the slavery cause on every point, and none endorsing President Taylor's straightforward plan.

Taylor believed that slavery in the South could best be protected if southerners avoided injecting the issue into the dispute over new territories. Unlike Calhoun, he did not believe the new western territories were suitable for slave-based agriculture. Because in his mind the issue of bringing slaves into the territories was moot, he continued to urge the Congress to admit California and New Mexico without reference to slavery. But few others embraced such a simple solution.

Then on March 4, Calhoun, desperately ill with tuberculosis, from which he would die in a few weeks, dramatically left his sickbed to sit in the Senate chamber. A colleague read his defiant remarks. "I have, Senators, believed from the first that the agitation of the subject of slavery would, if not prevented by some timely and effective measure, end in disunion," wrote Calhoun. Neither Clay's compromise nor Taylor's efforts, he declared, would serve the Union. The South needed simply an acceptance of its rights: equality of treatment in the territories, the return of fugitive slaves, and some guarantee of "an equilibrium between the sections."

Three days later Calhoun returned to hear Daniel Webster. The supreme orator in an age of superb oratory, he chose as his central theme the preservation of the Union: "I wish to speak today, not as a Massachusetts man, not as a Northern man, but as an American . . . I speak today for the preservation of the Union." The extent of slavery was already determined, he insisted, by the Northwest Ordinance, by the Missouri Compromise, and in the new lands by the law of nature. Both sections, to be sure, had legitimate grievances: on the one hand, the excesses of "infernal fanatics and abolitionists" in the North; and on the other hand, southern efforts to expand slavery. But instead of threatening secession, he declared, let people "enjoy the fresh air of liberty and union."

The March 7 speech was a classic gesture of conciliation, and Webster had knowingly brought down a storm upon his head. New England abolitionists labeled him a traitor for not aggressively supporting the free-soil cause and for endorsing the new fugitive slave law. On March 11 William H. Seward, freshman Whig senator from New York, gave the antislavery reply to Webster. Compromise with slavery, he argued, was "radically wrong and essentially vicious." There was "a higher law than the Constitution" that demanded the abolition of slavery.

In mid-April a select Committee of Thirteen bundled Clay's suggestions into one comprehensive bill. Taylor continued to oppose Clay's compromise, and their feud threatened to split the Whig party wide open. Another crisis loomed when word

came that a convention in New Mexico was applying for statehood, with Taylor's support, and with boundaries that conflicted with the Texas claim to the east bank of the Rio Grande.

Toward a Compromise

On July 4, 1850, friends of the Union staged a grand rally at the base of the unfinished Washington Monument. President Taylor attended the ceremonies in the hot sun. Back at the White House he quenched his thirst with iced water and milk, ate some cherries or cucumbers, and contracted cholera morbus (gastroenteritis). Five days later he was dead. The outcome of the sectional quarrel, had he lived, probably would have been different, whether for better or worse one cannot know.

Taylor's sudden death, however, strengthened the chances of compromise. The soldier in the White House was followed by a politician, Millard Fillmore. The son of a poor farmer in upper New York, Fillmore had made his own way as a lawyer and then as a candidate in the rough-and-tumble world of New York politics. Experience had taught him caution, which some saw as indecision, but he had made up his mind to support Clay's compromise and had so informed Taylor. It was a strange switch. Taylor, the Louisiana slaveholder, who had nevertheless stoutly opposed the expansion of slavery, was ready to make war on his native region if it pressed the issue; Fillmore, whom southerners thought was antislavery, was ready to make peace.

At this point, young Senator Stephen A. Douglas of Illinois, a rising star of the Democratic party, rescued Clay's faltering compromise. His strategy was in fact the same one that Clay had used to pass the Missouri Compromise thirty years before. Reasoning that nearly everybody objected to one or another provision of Clay's proposal, Douglas broke it up into six (later five) separate measures. Few members were pre-

Daniel Webster in an 1835 portrait by Francis Alexander.

pared to vote for all of them, but from different elements Douglas hoped to mobilize a majority for each.

It worked. In September 1850, Fillmore signed the last of the five measures into law. The Union had muddled through, and the settlement went down in history as the Compromise of 1850. For the time, it defused an explosive situation and settled each of the major points at issue.

First, California entered the Union as a free state, ending forever the old balance of free and slave states. Second, the Texas and New Mexico Act made New Mexico a territory and set the Texas boundary at its present location. In return for giving up its claims east of the Rio Grande, Texas was paid $10 million. Third, the Utah Act set up another territory. The territorial act in each case omitted reference to slavery except to give the territorial legislature authority over "all rightful subjects of legislation" with provision for appeal to federal courts. For the sake of agreement, the deliberate ambi-

guity of the statement was its merit. Northern congressmen could assume that territorial legislatures might act to exclude slavery on the unstated principle of popular sovereignty. Southern congressmen assumed that they could not do so.

Fourth, a new Fugitive Slave Act put the matter of retrieving runaways wholly under federal jurisdiction and stacked the cards in favor of slave-catchers. Fifth, as a gesture to antislavery forces, the slave trade, but not slavery itself, was abolished in the District of Columbia.

Millard Fillmore pronounced the five measures making up the Compromise of 1850 "a final settlement." Still, doubts lingered that either North or South could be reconciled to the measures permanently. In the South, the disputes of 1846–1850 had transformed the abstract doctrine of secession into a movement animated by such "fire-eaters" as Robert Barnwell Rhett of South Carolina, William L. Yancey of Alabama, and Edmund Ruffin of Virginia. In

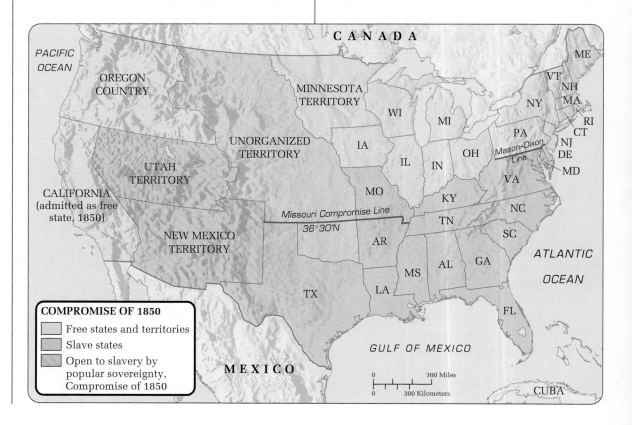

COMPROMISE OF 1850
- Free states and territories
- Slave states
- Open to slavery by popular sovereignty, Compromise of 1850

their view slavery must expand into the territories or it would wither and die—and southern culture would die along with it. They refused to view the matter as settled, and they would do all in their power to see it returned to the center stage of political debate.

The Fugitive Slave Act

Northern abolitionists were equally determined to keep slavery's evils in the forefront of public concerns. Southern intransigence in demanding the Fugitive Slave Act had presented abolitionists an emotional new focus for agitation. The law offered a strong temptation to kidnap free blacks by denying alleged fugitives a jury trial and by providing a fee of $10 for each fugitive delivered to federal authorities. In addition, federal marshals could require citizens to help in its enforcement; violators could be imprisoned for up to six months and fined $1,000. Within a month of the law's enactment, claims were filed in New York, Philadelphia, Harrisburg, Detroit, and other cities. Trouble followed. In Detroit the authorities used military force to stop the rescue of an alleged fugitive by an outraged mob.

There were relatively few such incidents, however. In the first six years of the Fugitive Slave Act, only three runaways were forcibly rescued from the slave-catchers. On the other hand, probably fewer than 200 were returned to bondage during the same years. More than that were rescued by stealth, often through the Underground Railroad. Still, the Fugitive Slave Act had the tremendous effect of widening and deepening the antislavery impulse in the North.

Uncle Tom's Cabin

Antislavery forces found their most persuasive appeal not in opposition to the Fugitive Slave Act but in the fictional drama of Harriet Beecher Stowe's *Uncle Tom's Cabin*

(1852). The novel was filled with unlikely saints and sinners, stereotypes and melodramatic escapades, and was a smashing commercial success. Slavery, seen through Stowe's eyes, subjected its victims either to callous brutality or, at the hands of indulgent masters, to the indignity of extravagant ineptitude and bankruptcy. Stowe poignantly portrayed the evils of the interstate slave trade, especially the breaking up of slave families, and she highlighted the horrors of the Fugitive Slave Act. It took time for the novel to work its effect on public opinion, however. The country was enjoying a surge of prosperity, and the course of the presidential campaign in 1852 reflected a common desire to lay sectional quarrels to rest.

135,000 SETS, 270,000 VOLUMES SOLD.

UNCLE TOM'S CABIN

FOR SALE HERE.

AN EDITION FOR THE MILLION, COMPLETE IN 1 Vol., PRICE 37 1-2 CENTS.
" " IN GERMAN, IN 1 Vol., PRICE 50 CENTS.
" " IN 2 Vols., CLOTH, 6 PLATES, PRICE $1.50.
SUPERB ILLUSTRATED EDITION, IN 1 Vol., WITH 153 ENGRAVINGS,
PRICES FROM $2.50 TO $5.00.

The Greatest Book of the Age.

"The Greatest Book of the Age." *Uncle Tom's Cabin,* as this advertisement indicates, was a tremendous commercial success.

The Election of 1852

As their nominee for president, the Democrats turned to Franklin Pierce of New Hampshire, a personable veteran of the Mexican War with little political experience. The platform pledged the Democrats to "abide by and adhere to a faithful execution of the acts known as the Compromise measures. . . ." Pierce rallied both the southern rights' men and the Van Burenite Democrats. The Free Soilers, as a consequence, mustered only half as many votes as they had totaled in 1848.

The Whigs repudiated the lackluster Fillmore, who had faithfully supported the Compromise, and tried to exploit martial glory by choosing Winfield Scott, the hero of Mexico City, a native of Virginia backed mainly by northern Whigs. The convention dutifully endorsed the Compromise of 1850, but with some opposition from the North. Scott, an able field commander but politically inept, had gained a reputation for antislavery and nativism, alienating German and Irish ethnic voters. In the end, Scott carried only four states. The popular vote was closer: 1.6 million to 1.4 million.

Pierce, a former congressman, senator, and brigadier in Mexico, was, like Polk, touted as another "Young Hickory." But the youngest president turned out to be made of more pliable stuff, unable to dominate the warring factions of his party. By the end of his first year in office, the leaders of his own party had decided he was a failure. By trying to be all things to all people, Pierce looked more and more like a "Northern man with Southern principles."

Foreign Adventures

Cuba

Foreign diversions now distracted attention from domestic quarrels. Cuba, one of Spain's earliest possessions in the New World, had long been an object of American desire, especially to southerners determined to expand slavery into new areas. In 1854 the Pierce administration instructed Pierre Soulé, the American minister in Madrid, to offer $130 million for Cuba, which Spain spurned. Soulé then joined the American ministers to France and Britain in drafting the Ostend Manifesto. It declared that if Spain, "actuated by stubborn pride and a false sense of honor refused to sell," then the United States must ask itself, "does Cuba, in the possession of Spain, seriously endanger our internal peace and existence of our cherished Union?" If so, "we shall be justified in wresting it from Spain." Publication of the supposedly confidential dispatch left the administration no choice but to disavow what northern opinion widely regarded as a "slaveholders' plot" to acquire Cuba.

Diplomatic Gains in the Pacific

In the Pacific, American diplomacy scored some important achievements. In 1844 China signed an agreement with the United States that opened four ports, including Shanghai, to American trade. A later treaty opened eleven more ports and granted Americans the right to travel and trade throughout China. China quickly became a special concern of American Protestant missionaries as well. About fifty were already there by 1855, and for nearly a century, China remained far and away the most active mission field for American evangelism.

Japan meanwhile had remained for two centuries closed to American trade. Moreover, American whalers wrecked on the shores of Japan had been forbidden to leave the country. Mainly in their interest President Fillmore entrusted a special Japanese expedition to Commodore Matthew Perry, who arrived in Tokyo in 1853. Perry attempted to impress—and intimidate—the Japanese with American military and technological superiority. Negotiations followed, and Japan eventually agreed to an American consulate, promised good treatment to castaways, and permitted visits in certain ports for supplies and repairs. Broad commercial relations began after the first envoy, Townsend Harris, negotiated the Harris Convention of 1858, which opened five Japanese ports to American trade. Japan continued to ban emigration to the United States but found the law increasingly difficult to enforce, and by the 1880s the Japanese government abandoned its efforts to prevent Japanese from seeking work abroad.

The Kansas-Nebraska Crisis

American commercial interests in Asia were in part responsible for the growing interest in constructing a transcontinental railroad line linking the eastern seaboard with the

Pacific coast. Other powerful motives were at work as well. Railroad developers and land speculators also promoted this transportation link, as did slaveholders who were eager to expand the area open to slavery. During the 1850s, the idea of building a transcontinental railroad, though a great national goal, spawned sectional rivalries in still another quarter and reopened the slavery issue.

Douglas's Proposal

In 1852 and 1853 Congress debated several likely routes for the rail line. For various reasons, including terrain, climate, and sectional interest, Secretary of War Jefferson Davis favored a southern route and encouraged what became known as the Gadsden Purchase, a barren stretch of land in present New Mexico and Arizona. In 1853, at a cost of $10 million, the United States acquired the area from Mexico as a likely route for a Pacific railroad.

But midwestern spokesmen had other ideas concerning the path of the transcontinental railroad. Since 1845, Illinois senator Stephen A. Douglas and others had offered bills for a new territory in the lands west of Missouri and Iowa, bearing the Indian name Nebraska. In 1854, Douglas put forward yet another Nebraska bill, which included the entire unorganized portion of the Louisiana Purchase to the Canadian border. At this point, fateful connections began to transform his proposal from a railroad bill to a proslavery bill. Douglas needed the support of southerners, and to win that support he needed to make some concession on slavery in the new territories. This he did by writing the principle of "popular sovereignty" into the bill, allowing territories to decide the issue themselves.

It was a clever dodge, since the Missouri Compromise would still exclude slaves until the territorial government had made a decision, preventing slaveholders from getting established before a popular vote decided

the issue. Southerners quickly spotted the problem for them, however, and Douglas as quickly made two more concessions. He supported an amendment for repeal of the Missouri Compromise insofar as it excluded slavery north of 36° 30', and he then agreed to organize two territories: Kansas, west of Missouri; and Nebraska, west of Iowa and Minnesota.

Douglas's motives remain unclear. Railroads were surely foremost in his mind, but he also hoped that popular sovereignty would defuse the slavery issue and open the Great Plains. But he had blundered, thus damaging his presidential chances and setting the country on the road to civil war. He had failed to appreciate the depth of antislavery feelings. Douglas himself preferred that the territories become free. Their climate and geography excluded plantation agriculture, he reasoned, and he could not comprehend how people could get so wrought up over abstract rights. Yet he had in fact opened the possibility that slavery might gain a foothold in Kansas.

Douglas's move to repeal the Missouri Compromise was less than a week old before six antislavery congressmen published a protest called the "Appeal of the Independent Democrats." Their moral indignation quickly spread among those who opposed Douglas. Across the North, editorials, sermons, speeches, and petitions denounced Douglas's bill as a conspiracy to extend slavery. But Douglas had the votes and, once committed, he forced the issue with tireless energy. President Pierce impulsively added his support, and the bill passed in May 1854 by 37 to 14 in the Senate and 113 to 100 in the House.

Very well, many in the North reasoned, if the Missouri Compromise was not a sacred pledge, then neither was the Fugitive Slave Act. On June 2, 1854, Boston witnessed the most dramatic demonstration against the act. After several attempts had failed to rescue a fugitive named Anthony Burns from being returned south, soldiers dispatched

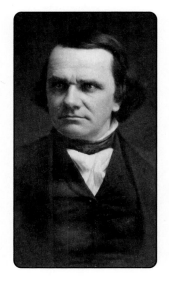

Stephen A. Douglas.

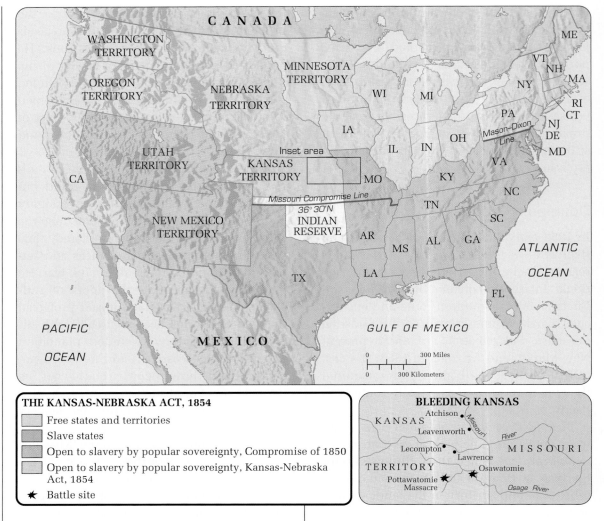

THE KANSAS-NEBRASKA ACT, 1854

☐ Free states and territories

☐ Slave states

☐ Open to slavery by popular sovereignty, Compromise of 1850

☐ Open to slavery by popular sovereignty, Kansas-Nebraska Act, 1854

★ Battle site

BLEEDING KANSAS

by President Pierce marched him to a waiting ship through streets lined with people shouting "Kidnappers!" Burns was the last fugitive slave to be returned from Boston and was himself soon freed through purchase by Boston's black community. New Englanders blamed Pierce for this sorry episode.

The Emergence of the Republican Party

In 1854 what John C. Calhoun had called the cords holding the Union together were fraying. The national church organizations of Baptists and Methodists, for instance, had split over slavery by 1845. The national political parties, which had created mutual interests transcending sectional issues, were beginning to unravel under the strain. The Democrats managed to postpone disruption for yet a while, but their congressional delegation lost heavily in the North, enhancing the influence of the southern wing.

The strain of the Kansas-Nebraska Act, however, soon destroyed the Whig party. Southern Whigs now tended to abstain from voting, while Northern Whigs moved toward two new parties. One was the new American (Know-Nothing) party, which had raised the banner of native Americanism and the hope of serving the patriotic cause of Union. Even more Northern Whigs joined with independent Democrats and Free Soilers in spontaneous antislavery coalitions with an array of confusing names, including "anti-Nebraska," "Fusion," and "People's party." These coalitions finally converged in 1854 on the name "Republican," evoking the memory of Thomas Jefferson.

"Bleeding" Kansas

After passage of the Kansas-Nebraska Act, attention swung to the plains of Kansas, where opposing elements gathered to stage what would turn out to be a dress rehearsal for civil war. All agreed that Nebraska would be free, but Kansas soon exposed the potential for mischief in Douglas's concept of popular sovereignty. The people of Kansas were "perfectly free to form and regulate their domestic institutions in their own way, subject only to the Constitution." That in itself invited conflicting interpretations, but the law failed to specify the time of decision about slavery, adding to each side's sense of urgency about getting control of the territory.

The settlement of Kansas therefore differed from the usual pioneering efforts. Groups sprang up North and South to hurry right-minded settlers westward. In fact, however, few New Englanders migrated to Kansas. Most of the settlers were from Missouri and surrounding states. Although few of them owned slaves, they were not sympathetic to militant abolitionism. Racism was prevalent even among non-slaveholding whites. Many of the Kansas settlers wanted to keep all blacks, slave or free, out of the territory. By 1860, there were only 627 African Americans in the territory.

When Kansas's first territorial governor arrived in 1854, he ordered a census and scheduled an election for a territorial legislature in 1855. On election day, several thousand "Border Ruffians" crossed over from Missouri, illegally cast proslavery votes, and pledged to kill every "God-damned abolitionist in the Territory." The governor denounced the vote as a fraud, but he did nothing to alter the results, for fear of being killed himself. The new legislature expelled the few antislavery members, adopted a drastic slave code, and made it a capital offense to aid a fugitive slave.

Free-state advocates rejected this "bogus" government and quickly formed their own. In 1855 a constitutional convention, the product of an election of dubious legality, met in Topeka, drafted a state constitution excluding both slavery and free blacks from Kansas, and applied for admission to the Union. By 1856 a free-state "governor" and "legislature" were functioning in Topeka. Thus the territory had two illegal governments competing for recognition and control, and both sides began to arm. On May 21, 1856, 700 proslavery thugs entered the free-state town of Lawrence and smashed newspaper presses, set fire to the free-state governor's home, stole property, and destroyed the Free State Hotel.

The "sack of Lawrence" left just one casualty, but the incident aroused a fanatical Kansas Free Soiler named John Brown, who had a history of mental instability. On May 24, two days after the sack of Lawrence, Brown, the father of twenty children, set out

Kansas Free State Battery. The establishment of two illegal governments in Kansas led to fighting in 1856.

with four of his sons and three other men toward Pottawatomie Creek, site of a proslavery settlement, where they dragged five men from their houses and hacked them to death in front of their screaming wives and children, ostensibly as revenge for the deaths of free-state men.

The Pottawatomie Massacre (May 24–25, 1856) set off a guerrilla war in the territory that lasted through the fall. On August 30, Missouri ruffians raided the free-state settlement at Osawatomie. They looted the houses, burned them to the ground, and shot John Brown's son Frederick through the heart. The elder Brown, who barely escaped, swore to his surviving sons and followers that he would "die fighting for this cause." Altogether, by the end of 1856, Kansas lost about 200 killed and $2 million in property destroyed during the territorial civil war.

Violence in the Senate

Violence in Kansas spilled over into Congress itself. On May 20, 1856, Senator Charles Sumner of Massachusetts delivered an inflammatory speech in which he described the proslavery forces' treatment of Kansas as "the rape of a virgin territory." Sumner then called Senator Andrew P. Butler of South Carolina a liar and implied that he kept a slave mistress.

Sumner's rudeness might well have backfired had it not been for Butler's nephew Preston S. Brooks, a fiery-tempered South Carolina congressman. Brooks confronted Sumner at his Senate desk on May 22. He accused him of slander and began beating him about the head with a cane while stunned senators, including Douglas, looked on. Sumner, struggling to rise, wrenched the desk from the floor and collapsed.

Brooks had satisfied his rage, but in the process he had created a martyr for the antislavery cause. For two and a half years Sumner's empty seat was a solemn reminder of the violence done to him. Some thought the senator was feigning injury, others that he really was physically disabled. In fact, although his injuries were bad enough, including two gashes to the skull, he seems to have suffered psychosomatic shock that left him incapable of functioning. When the House censured Brooks, he resigned, but he was triumphantly reelected. His southern admirers presented him with new canes.

Sectional Politics

Within the span of five days in May of 1856, "Bleeding Kansas," "Bleeding Sumner," and "Bully Brooks" had set the tone for another presidential year. The major parties could no longer evade the slavery issue. Already it had split the American party wide open. Southern delegates, with help from New York, killed a resolution to restore the Missouri Compromise, and they nominated Millard Fillmore for president. Later, what was left of the Whig party endorsed him as well.

At its first national convention, the new Republican party followed the Whig tradition by seeking out a military hero, John C. Frémont, the "Pathfinder" and leader in the conquest of California. The Republican platform owed much to the Whigs too. It favored a transcontinental railroad and, in general, more internal improvements. It condemned the repeal of the Missouri Compromise and the Democratic policy of expansion. The campaign slogan echoed that of the Free Soilers: "Free soil, free speech, and Frémont." It was the first time a major party platform had taken a stand against slavery.

The Democrats rejected Pierce, the hapless victim of so much turmoil. They also spurned Douglas because of the damage done by his Kansas-Nebraska Act. The party therefore turned to James Buchanan of Pennsylvania, who had long sought the nomination. The Democratic platform endorsed the Kansas-Nebraska Act and urged Congress not to interfere with slavery in either states or territories. The party reached out to its newly acquired Irish and German Catholic voters by condemning nativism and endorsing religious liberty.

The campaign of 1856 resolved itself into two sectional campaigns. The "Black Republicans," as the new party was called by proslavery forces, had few southern supporters and only a handful in the border states, where fears of disunion held many Whigs in line. Buchanan thus went into the campaign as the candidate of the only remaining national party. Frémont swept the northernmost states with 114 electoral votes, but Buchanan added five free states to his southern majority for a total of 174.

Few presidents before Buchanan had a broader experience in politics and diplomacy. He had been in Congress, had served as minister to Russia and Britain, and had been Polk's secretary of state in between. His long quest for the presidency had been built on a southern alliance, and his political debts reinforced his belief that saving the Union depended on concessions to the South. Republicans charged that he lacked the backbone to stand up to the southerners who dominated the Democratic majorities in Congress. To them his choice of four slave-state and only three free-state men for his cabinet seemed a bad omen.

The Deepening Sectional Crisis

During Buchanan's first six months in office, he encountered three crises in succession: the Supreme Court's Dred Scott decision, new troubles in Kansas, and a widespread business panic.

The Dred Scott Case

On March 6, 1857, two days after the inauguration, the Supreme Court rendered a decision in the long-pending case of *Dred Scott* v. *Sandford.* Dred Scott, born a slave

in Virginia about 1800, had been taken to St. Louis in 1830 and sold to an army surgeon, who took him as a body servant to Illinois, then to the Wisconsin Territory (later Minnesota), where slavery was prohibited, and finally returned him to St. Louis in 1842. While in the Wisconsin Territory, Scott met and married Harriet Robinson, and they eventually had two daughters.

After his master's death in 1843, Scott tried unsuccessfully to buy his freedom. In 1846, Harriet Scott convinced her husband to file suit in Missouri courts claiming that residence in Illinois and Wisconsin Territory had made them free. A jury decided in their favor, reaffirming the widespread notion that "once free, forever free." But the state supreme court ruled against the Scotts, arguing that a slave state did not have to honor freedom granted to slaves by free states. When the case rose on appeal to the Supreme Court, the country anxiously awaited its opinion on the issue of whether freedom once granted could be lost by returning to a slave state.

Each of the eight justices filed a separate opinion, except one who concurred with Chief Justice Roger B. Taney. By different lines of reasoning, seven justices ruled that Scott reverted to slave status upon his return to Missouri. The aging Taney ruled that Scott lacked standing in court because he lacked citizenship. At the time the Constitution was adopted, Taney added, blacks "had for more than a century been regarded as . . . so far inferior, that they had no rights which the white man was bound to respect."

To clarify the definition of Scott's status, Taney moved to a second major question. He argued that the Missouri Compromise, by ruling that certain new territories were to exclude slaves, had deprived citizens of property in slaves, an action "not warranted by the Constitution." The Supreme Court had declared an act of Congress unconstitutional for the first time since *Marbury* v. *Madison* (1803). Congress had repealed the Missouri Compromise in the Kansas-

Nebraska Act three years earlier, but the Dred Scott decision now challenged the concept of popular sovereignty. If Congress itself could not exclude slavery from a territory, as Taney argued, then presumably neither could a territorial government created by act of Congress.

Proslavery elements, of course, greeted the court's opinion with glee. Many northerners denounced Taney's ruling. Little wonder that Republicans protested: the Court had declared their free-soil program unconstitutional. It had also reinforced the suspicion that the slavocracy was hatching a conspiracy. Were not all but one of the justices who joined Taney southerners? And had not Buchanan chatted with the chief justice at the inauguration and then urged the people to accept the early decision as a final settlement, "Whatever this may be?"

And what of Dred Scott himself? Ironically, his owner, now a widow, married a prominent Massachusetts abolitionist, who saw to it that the slave and his family were freed in 1857. A year later Scott died of tuberculosis.

The Lecompton Constitution

Out in Kansas, meanwhile, the struggle continued through 1857. The contested politics in the territory now resulted in an antislavery legislature and a proslavery constitutional convention. The convention, meeting at Lecompton, drew up a constitution under which Kansas would become a slave state. A referendum on the document was set for December 21, 1857, with rules and officials chosen by the convention.

Although Kansas had only about 200 slaves at the time, free-state men boycotted the election, claiming that it was rigged. At this point President Buchanan took a fateful step. Influenced by southern advisers and politically dependent upon southern congressmen, he decided to support the action of the proslavery Lecompton Convention.

The election went according to form: 6,226 votes for the constitution with slavery, 569 for the constitution without slavery. Meanwhile, the acting governor had convened the antislavery legislature, which called for another election to vote the Lecompton Constitution up or down. Most of the proslavery settlers boycotted this election, and the result on January 4, 1858, was overwhelming: 10,226 against the constitution, 138 for the constitution with slavery, 24 for the constitution without slavery.

The combined results suggested a clear majority against slavery, but Buchanan stuck to his support of the Lecompton Constitution, driving another wedge into the Democratic party. Senator Douglas, up for reelection in Illinois, broke dramatically with the president in a tense confrontation, but Buchanan persisted in trying to drive Lecompton "naked" through the Congress. In the Senate, administration forces held firm, and in 1858 Lecompton was passed. In the House, enough anti-Lecompton Democrats combined to put through an amendment for a new and carefully supervised popular vote in Kansas. Enough senators went along to pass the House bill. Southerners were confident that a new vote in Kansas would favor slavery, because to reject slavery the voters would have to reject the constitution, which would postpone statehood until the population reached 90,000. On August 2, 1858, Kansas voters nevertheless rejected Lecompton by 11,300 to 1,788. With that vote, Kansas, now firmly in the hands of its antislavery legislature, largely ended its role in the sectional controversy.

The Panic of 1857

The third crisis of Buchanan's first half year in office, a financial panic, broke in August 1857. It was brought on by a reduction in Europe's demand for American grain, a surge in manufacturing production that outran the growth of markets, and the continued weakness and confusion of the state bank-note system. Failure of the Ohio Life Insurance and Trust Company precipitated the panic, which brought on a depression from which the country did not emerge until 1859.

The panic further highlighted sectional differences. Northern businessmen tended to blame the depression on the Democratic Tariff of 1857, which had put rates at their lowest level since 1816. The agricultural South weathered the crisis better than the North. Cotton prices fell, but slowly, and world markets for cotton quickly recovered. The result was an exalted notion of King Cotton's importance to the world, and apparent confirmation of the growing argument that the southern system was superior to the free-labor system of the North.

Douglas versus Lincoln

Amid the recriminations over Dred Scott, Kansas, and the depression, the center could not hold. The Lecompton battle put severe strains on the most substantial cord of Union that was left, the Democratic party. To many, Douglas seemed the best hope, one of the few remaining Democratic leaders with support in both sections. But now Douglas was being whipsawed between the extremes. Kansas-Nebraska had cast him in the role of "doughface," a southern sympathizer. His opposition to Lecompton, the fraudulent fruit of popular sovereignty, however, had alienated him from Buchanan's southern junta. But for all his flexibility and opportunism, Douglas had convinced himself that popular sovereignty was a point of principle, a bulwark of democracy and local self-government. In 1858 he faced reelection to the Senate against the opposition of both "Buchanan Democrats" and Republicans. The year 1860 would give him a chance for the presidency, but first he had to secure his home base in Illinois.

To oppose him, Illinois Republicans named Abraham Lincoln of Springfield, the former Whig state legislator and one-term congressman. Born in a Kentucky log cabin in 1809, raised on frontier farms in Indiana and Illinois, the young Lincoln had the wit and will to rise above his coarse beginnings. Striking out on his own, he managed a general store in New Salem, Illinois, learned surveying, served in the Black Hawk War (1832), won election to the legislature in 1834 at the age of twenty-five, read law, and was admitted to the bar in 1836.

As a Whig regular, Lincoln stayed in the state legislature until 1842, and in 1846 he won a term in Congress. After a single term he retired from active politics to cultivate his law practice in Springfield.

In 1854 the Kansas-Nebraska debate drew Lincoln back into the political arena. In 1856 he joined the Republicans, getting over 100 votes for their vice-presidential nomination. By 1858 he was the obvious Republican choice to oppose Douglas himself for the Senate, and Douglas knew he was up against a formidable foe. Lincoln resorted to the classic ploy of the underdog: he challenged the favorite to a debate. The legendary Lincoln-Douglas debates took place that summer and fall.

The two men presented a striking contrast. Lincoln was well over six feet tall, sinewy, and craggy-featured, with a long neck and deep-set, brooding eyes. Unassuming in manner, he conveyed an air of simplicity, sincerity, and common sense. Douglas was short, rotund, bulb-nosed, stern, and cocky, attired in the finest custom-tailored suits and possessed of supreme self-confidence. A man of considerable abilities and even greater ambition, he strutted to the platform with the pugnacious air of a predestined champion.

At the time and since, much attention focused on the second debate, at Freeport, where Lincoln asked Douglas how he could reconcile popular sovereignty with the Dred Scott ruling that citizens had the right to

Abraham Lincoln.

carry slaves into any territory. Douglas's answer, thenceforth known as the Freeport Doctrine, was to state the obvious. Whatever the Supreme Court might say about slavery, it could not exist anywhere unless supported by local police regulations. Thus, if settlers did not want slavery, they simply should refuse to adopt a local code protecting it.

Douglas then tried to set some traps of his own. He accused Lincoln of advocating racial equality. Lincoln countered with a statement affirming white supremacy. There was, he asserted, a "physical difference between the white and black races," and it would "forever forbid the two races living together on terms of social and political equality." But Lincoln insisted that blacks did have an "equal" right to their freedom and the fruits of their labor. He favored the containment of slavery where it existed so that "the public mind shall rest in the belief that it is in the course of ultimate extinction." But the basic difference between the two men, Lincoln insisted, lay in Douglas's professed indifference to the moral question of slavery.

If Lincoln had the better of the argument, at least in the long view, Douglas had the better of the election, which he won on a vote by the Illinois legislature. Across the nation, the elections recorded one loss after another for Buchanan Democrats. The administration had lost control of the House.

John Brown's Raid

The gradual return of prosperity in 1859 offered hope that the political storms of the 1850s might yet pass. But the sectional issue still haunted the public mind, and like lightning on the horizon, it warned that a storm was still brewing. In 1859 John Brown once again surfaced, this time in the East. Since the Pottawatomie Massacre in 1856, he had led a furtive existence, engaging in fund-raising, recruiting, and occasional bushwhacking. His commitment to abolish the "wicked curse of slavery," meanwhile, had intensified to a fever pitch.

On October 16, 1859, Brown launched his supreme gesture. From a Maryland farm he crossed the Potomac with about twenty men, including five blacks, and occupied the federal arsenal in Harper's Ferry, Virginia (now West Virginia). He apparently intended to arm the Maryland slaves he assumed would flock to his cause, set up a black stronghold in the mountains of western Virginia, and provide a nucleus of support for slave insurrections across the South.

What Brown actually did was to take the arsenal by surprise, seize a few hostages, and hole up in the fire-engine house. There he and his band were quickly surrounded by militiamen and town residents. The next morning Brown sent his son Watson and another supporter out under a white flag, but the enraged crowd shot them both. Intermittent shooting then broke out, and another Brown son was mortally wounded.

That night Lieutenant-Colonel Robert E. Lee, U.S. Cavalry, arrived with his aide, Lieutenant J. E. B. Stuart, and a force of marines. The following morning, on October 18, Stuart and his troops broke down the barricaded doors and captured Brown and his men. Brown was quickly tried for treason, convicted, and sentenced to be hanged. When Brown, still unflinching, met his end, northern sympathizers held solemn observances. "That new saint," Ralph Waldo Emerson predicted, ". . . will make the gallows glorious as the Cross." William Lloyd Garrison, the lifelong pacifist, now wished "success to every slave insurrection at the South and in every slave country." By far the gravest effect of Brown's raid was to leave proslavery southerners in no mood to distinguish between John Brown and the Republican party. All through the fall and winter of 1859–1860, rumors of conspiracy and insurrection swept the region. Every northern visitor, commercial traveler, or schoolteacher came under suspicion, and many were driven out.

John Brown.

The Center Comes Apart

The Democrats Divide

Amid emotional hysteria, the nation approached a presidential election destined to be the most fateful in its history. The Democrats met in Charleston, South Carolina, for their 1860 convention. Douglas's supporters reaffirmed the platform of 1856, which simply promised congressional non-interference with slavery. Southern firebrands, however, now demanded a federal code protecting slavery in the territories. Buchanan supporters, hoping to stop Douglas, encouraged the strategy. The platform debate reached a heady climax when the Alabama extremist William L. Yancey informed the northern Democrats that they had erred by failing to defend slavery as a positive good. An Ohio senator offered a blunt reply: "Gentlemen of the South," he declared, "you mistake us—you mistake us. We will not do it."

When the southern planks lost, Alabama's delegation walked out of the convention, followed by delegates from Georgia, South Carolina, Arkansas, and Delaware. The convention then decided to leave the overwrought atmosphere of Charleston and reassemble in Baltimore on June 18. The Baltimore convention finally nominated Douglas on the 1856 platform. The Charleston seceders met first in Richmond, then in Baltimore, where they adopted the slave-code platform defeated in Charleston and named Vice-President John C. Breckinridge of Kentucky for president. Another cord of union had snapped: the last remaining national party.

Lincoln's Election

The Republicans meanwhile gathered in Chicago. There everything suddenly came together for "Honest Abe" Lincoln, "the Railsplitter," the uncommon common man.

Lincoln had suddenly emerged in the national view during his senatorial campaign two years before and had since taken a stance designed to make him available for the nomination. He was strong enough on the containment of slavery to satisfy the abolitionists, yet moderate enough to seem less threatening than they were.

Lincoln won the Republican nomination on the third ballot. The party platform foreshadowed future policy better than most. It denounced John Brown's raid as "among the gravest of crimes" and affirmed that each state should "order and control its own domestic institutions." The party repeated its resistance to the extension of slavery and, in an effort to gain broader support, endorsed a higher protective tariff for manufacturers, free homesteads for farmers, a more liberal naturalization law, and internal improvements, including a transcontinental railroad. With this platform, Republicans made a strong appeal to eastern businessmen, western farmers, and the large immigrant population.

Both major conventions revealed that opinion tended to become more radical in the upper North and Deep South. Attitude seemed to follow latitude. In the border states a sense of moderation aroused the die-hard Whigs there to make one more try at reconciliation. Meeting in Baltimore a week before the Republicans met in Chicago, they reorganized into the Constitutional Union party and named John Bell of Tennessee for president. Their platform simply called for the preservation of the Constitution and the Union.

Of the four candidates, not one was able to command a national following, and the campaign resolved into a choice between Lincoln and Douglas in the North, Breckinridge and Bell in the South. One consequence of these separate campaigns was that each section gained a false impression of the other. The South never learned to distinguish Lincoln from the radicals; the North failed to gauge the force of southern intransigence—and in this Lincoln was among the worst. He stubbornly refused to offer the South assurances or to explain his position on slavery, which he insisted was a matter of public record.

The one man who tried to break through the veil that was falling between the sections was Douglas, who tried to mount a national campaign. Only forty-seven, but already weakened by excessive drink, ill health, and disappointments, he wore himself out in one final glorious campaign. Throughout the South, he carried appeals on behalf of the Union. "I do not believe that every Breckinridge man is a disunionist," he said, "but I do believe that every disunionist is a Breckinridge man."

By midnight of November 6, however, Lincoln's victory was clear. In the final count he had about 39 percent of the total popular vote, but a clear majority with 180 votes in the electoral college. He carried all eighteen free states by a wide margin. Among all the candidates, only Douglas had electoral votes from both slave and free states, but his total of 12 was but a pitiful remnant of Democratic Unionism. He ran last. Bell took Virginia, Kentucky, and Tennessee, and Breckinridge swept the other slave states to come in second with 72 electoral votes.

Secession of the Deep South

Soon after the election, the South Carolina legislature, which had assembled to choose the state's electors, set a special election for December 6 to choose delegates to a convention. In Charleston on December 20, 1860, the convention unanimously voted an Ordinance of Secession, declaring the state's ratification of the Constitution repealed and the union with other states dissolved. By February 1, 1861, Mississippi, Florida, Alabama, Georgia, Louisiana, and Texas had also seceded from the Union. On February 4, a convention of those seven states met in Montgomery, Alabama, and on February 7 it adopted a provisional constitution for the Confederate States of America. Two days later, the delegates elected Jefferson Davis as its president. He was inaugurated February 18, with Alexander Stephens of Georgia as vice-president.

In all seven states of the southernmost tier, a solid majority had voted for secessionist convention delegates, but their combined vote would not have been a

ELECTION OF 1860	Electoral vote	Popular vote
Abraham Lincoln (Republican)	**180**	**1,866,000**
Stephen A. Douglas (Democrat, Northern)	12	1,383,000
John C. Breckinridge (Democrat, Southern)	72	848,000
John Bell (Constitutional Union)	39	593,000

majority of the presidential vote in November. What happened, it seemed, was what often happens in revolutionary situations: a determined minority acted quickly in an emotionally charged climate and carried its program against a confused and indecisive opposition. Trying to decide if a majority of southern whites actually favored secession probably is beside the point—a majority was vulnerable to the decisive action of the secessionists.

Southern Unionists lamented this situation, noting that the "fire-eaters" rather than true statesmen were in control. "Webster and Clay are gone," mourned one Louisianan, "and God has given us over to fools and mad men." Others predicted that secession, instead of conserving traditional southern society, would in fact accelerate its demise.

Buchanan's Waiting Game

History is full of might-have-beens. A bold stroke, even a bold statement, by the lame-duck president at this point might have defused the crisis, but there was no Jacksonian will in Buchanan. Besides, a bold stroke might simply have hastened the conflict. No bold stroke came from Lincoln either, nor would he consult with the administration during the long months before his inauguration on March 4, 1861. He inclined all too strongly to the belief that secession was just another bluff.

Seeking compromise, in his annual message on December 3, 1860, Buchanan argued that secession was illegal, but that he lacked authority to coerce a state. "Seldom have we known so strong an argument come to so lame and impotent a conclusion," the *Cincinnati Enquirer* editorialized. There was, however, a hidden weapon in the president's reaffirmation of a duty to "take care that the laws be faithfully executed" insofar as he was able. If the president could enforce the law upon all citizens, he would

have no need to "coerce" a state. Indeed, Buchanan's position became the policy of the Lincoln administration, which fought a war on the theory that individuals but not states as such were in rebellion.

Buchanan held firmly to his resolve. On the day after Christmas, the small federal garrison at Charleston's Fort Moultrie had been moved into the nearly completed Fort Sumter by Major Robert Anderson, a Kentucky Unionist. Anderson's move struck South Carolina authorities as provocative. Commissioners of the newly "independent" state demanded withdrawal of all federal forces, but they had overplayed their hand. Buchanan's cabinet, with only one southerner left, insisted it would be a gross violation of duty, perhaps grounds for impeachment, for the president to yield. His backbone thus stiffened, he sharply rejected the South Carolina ultimatum to withdraw. He decided instead to hunker down and ride out the remaining weeks of his term, hoping against hope that one of several compromise efforts would yet prove fruitful.

Last Efforts at Compromise

Forlorn efforts at compromise continued in Congress until the dawn of Lincoln's inauguration day. On December 18, Senator John J. Crittenden of Kentucky had proposed a series of resolutions that recognized slavery in the territories south of 36° 30' and guaranteed to maintain it where it already existed. The fight for a compromise was carried to the floor of each house, and Crittenden's resolutions were subjected to intensive but inconclusive debate during January and February.

Meanwhile, a peace conference met in a Washington hotel in February 1861. Twenty-one states sent delegates and former president John Tyler presided, but the convention's proposal, substantially the same as the Crittenden Compromise, failed to win the support of either house of Congress. The only compromise proposal that met with any success was an amendment guaranteeing slavery where it existed. Many Republicans, including Lincoln, were prepared to go that far to save the Union, but they were unwilling to repudiate their stand against slavery in the territories. As it happened, after passing the House, the amendment passed the Senate without a vote to spare, by 24 to 12, on the dawn of inauguration day. It would have become the Thirteenth Amendment, with the first use of the word "slavery" in the Constitution, but the states never ratified it. When a Thirteenth Amendment was ratified in 1865, it did not guarantee slavery—it abolished slavery.

The War of the Union

This chapter focuses on

- The main course and major strategies of the Civil War.

- How the war affected the home front, North and South.

- The reasons for, and results of, Lincoln's Emancipation Proclamation.

THE *ESSENTIAL AMERICA* ON-LINE TUTOR

www.wwnorton.com/eamerica/ch16

- **Topic: The Battle of Gettysburg**
  www.wwnorton.com/eamerica/ch16/topic.htm

  In July of 1863 Union troops confronted Confederate soldiers at Gettysburg in an attempt to prevent Southern forces from advancing further into Union territory. Using maps, personal accounts, photographs, and historical analyses, explore the Battle of Gettysburg. Who won at Gettysburg, and how did that victory affect the course of the war?

- **Chapter review: On-line quiz and chapter summary**
  www.wwnorton.com/eamerica/ch16/review.htm

- **Chapter resources: Multimedia index**
  www.wwnorton.com/eamerica/ch16/media.htm

The Civil War has become shrouded in an ever-thickening mist of gallant images and larger-than-life mythology. As a result, the Union triumph has acquired the mantle of inevitability. Was not the North destined to win? The Confederacy's fight for independence, on the other hand, has taken on the aura of a romantic lost cause, doomed from the start by the region's sparse industrial development, smaller pool of able-bodied men, paucity of capital resources and warships, and spotty transportation network.

But in 1861 the military situation was by no means so clear-cut. For all of the South's obvious disadvantages, it initially enjoyed a captive labor force, superior officers, the prospects of foreign assistance, and the benefits of fighting a defensive campaign on familiar territory. Jefferson Davis and other Confederate leaders were genuinely confident that their cause would prevail on the battlefields. It is important to remember that this epochal event was endowed from the start not with inevitability but with uncertainty, and its outcome was decided as much by human decisions and human willpower as by physical resources.

End of the Waiting Game

In early 1861, as Abraham Lincoln prepared to take office and the possibility of civil war captured the attention of a divided nation, no one imagined that a conflict of horrendous scope and intensity awaited them. On both sides, people believed that the fighting would be over quickly and that their daily lives would go on as usual.

Lincoln and Secession

In his inaugural address on March 4, 1861, Lincoln reassured southerners that he had no intention of interfering with "slavery in the States where it exists." But secession was another matter. He insisted that the "Union of these States is perpetual," and he promised to "hold, occupy, and possess" areas belonging to the federal government.

But the momentum of secession took control of events. The day after Lincoln's inauguration, word arrived from Charleston that time was running out for the federal garrison at Fort Sumter. The fort had enough supplies for only a month. On April 4, 1861, Lincoln decided to resupply Ft. Sumter. The Confederate government demanded that Ft. Sumter surrender. The federal commander refused, and just before dawn on April 12, Confederate batteries began shelling the fort. After thirty-three hours, the federal troops surrendered.

The guns of Charleston signaled the end of the tense waiting game. On April 15, Lincoln issued a proclamation calling upon the loyal states to supply 75,000 militiamen to put down the rebellion. Volunteers in both the North and the South soon crowded recruiting stations for both sides, and huge new armies began to form. On April 19, Lincoln proclaimed a blockade of southern ports, which, as the Supreme Court later ruled, confirmed the existence of a state of war.

Taking Sides

Lincoln's call to arms led four upper South states to join the Confederacy—Virginia, Arkansas, Tennessee, and North Carolina. Each had areas (mainly in the mountains) where both slaves and secessionists were scarce and where Union sentiment ran strong. In fact, Unionists in western Virginia, bolstered by a Union army from Ohio under General George B. McClellan, formed a new state. In 1863 Congress admitted West Virginia with a state constitution that provided for emancipation of the few slaves there.

Of the other slave states, Delaware remained firmly in the Union, but Maryland, Kentucky, and Missouri went through bitter struggles for control. The secession of Maryland would have encircled Washington,

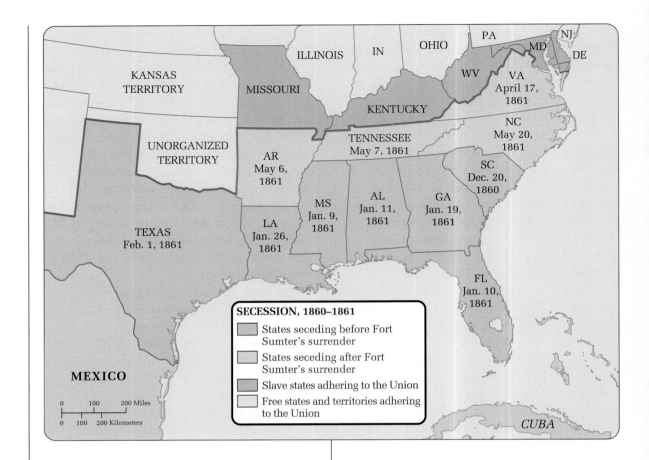

SECESSION, 1860–1861

- States seceding before Fort Sumter's surrender
- States seceding after Fort Sumter's surrender
- Slave states adhering to the Union
- Free states and territories adhering to the Union

D.C., with Confederate states. To hold the state, Lincoln took drastic measures: he suspended the writ of habeas corpus (under which judges could require arresting officers to produce their prisoners and justify their arrest) and jailed pro-Confederate leaders. The fall elections ended the threat of Maryland's secession by returning a solidly Unionist majority in the state.

The Kentucky legislature proclaimed its "neutrality" in the conflict, but that only lasted until September 3, 1861, when a Confederate force captured several towns. General Ulysses S. Grant then moved troops into Paducah. Thereafter, Kentucky for the most part remained with the Union. It joined the Confederacy, some have said, only after the war.

In Missouri, Unionists had a numerical advantage, but secessionist sympathies were strong, and a Confederate militia began to gather near St. Louis. Unionist forces

broke the back of Confederate resistance in Missouri at the battle of Pea Ridge (March 6–8, 1862), just over the state line in Arkansas. Nevertheless, border warfare continued in Missouri, pitting against each other rival bands of gunslingers who kept up their feuding and banditry for years after the war ended.

Robert E. Lee epitomized the agonizing choice facing many border-state residents. Son of "Lighthorse Harry" Lee, a Revolutionary War hero, and married to a descendant of Martha Washington, Lee had graduated second in his class from West Point, had fought with distinction during the Mexican War, and had served in the United States Army for thirty years. Now a colonel and master of Arlington, an elegant estate facing Washington across the Potomac, he was summoned by Lincoln's seventy-five-year-old general-in-chief, Winfield Scott, another Virginian, and offered command of the new Federal forces. After a sleepless night pacing the floor, he told Scott he could not go against his "country," meaning Virginia. Lee resigned his commission, retired to his estate, and soon answered a call to command the Virginia—later the Confederate—military forces.

In contrast, many southerners made great sacrifices to remain loyal to the Union. Some left their native region once the fighting began. Others who remained in the South found ways to support the Union. In every Confederate state except South Carolina, whole regiments were organized to fight for the Union, and at least 100,000 men from the southern states fought against the Confederacy. Of course, some of these southern "Tories" changed sides out of expediency rather than loyalty. Confederate soldiers who had been captured occasionally chose to switch sides and serve on the Indian frontier rather than remain in prison. Others, however, never embraced the Confederate cause. Many of the southern Unionists were Irish or German immigrants who had no love for slavery or the planter elite.

Northern and Southern Advantages

A balance sheet of the sections in 1860 shows that the Union held twenty-three states, including four border slave states, while the Confederacy had eleven, claiming also Missouri and Kentucky. Ignoring conflicts of allegiance within various states, which might roughly cancel each other out, the population count was about 22 million in the Union to 9 million in the Confederacy, and about 3.5 million of the latter were slaves. To help redress the imbalance, the Confederacy mobilized 80 percent or more of its military-age white males, and a third of them would die during the prolonged war.

An even greater advantage for the North was its industry. The states that joined the Confederacy produced just 7.4 percent of the nation's manufactures on the eve of the war, and little of this was in heavy industry. The Union states, in addition to making most of the country's shoes, textiles, and iron products, turned out 97 percent of the firearms and 96 percent of the railroad equipment. They had most of the trained mechanics, most of the shipping and mercantile firms, and the bulk of the banking and financial resources.

Even in farm production the northern states overshadowed the rural South, for most of the North's population was still rooted in the soil. As the progress of the war upset southern agricultural output, northern farms managed to increase theirs, despite the loss of workers to the army. The Confederacy produced enough food to meet minimal needs, but the disruption of transport caused shortages that led to inflation.

The North's advantage in transport weighed heavily as the war went on. The Union had more wagons, horses, and ships than the Confederacy, and an impressive edge in railroads: about 20,000 miles to the South's 10,000. The actual discrepancy was even greater, for southern railroads were mainly short lines built to different gauges (widths), and they had few replacements for train cars that broke down or wore out.

However, the South did have the advantage of geography: the Confederates could fight a defensive war on their own territory. In addition, the South initially had more experienced military leaders.

Bull Run

Caught up in the frothy excitement of military preparation, both sides predicted an easy and quick victory.

Nowhere was this naive optimism more clearly displayed than at the first battle at Bull Run (Manassas).* An impatient public

* The Federals most often named battles for natural features; the Confederates, for nearby towns, thus Bull Run (Manassas), Antietam (Sharpsburg), Stone's River (Murfreesboro), and the like.

pressured both armies to strike quickly and decisively. The battle-hungry Confederate general P. G. T. Beauregard hurried his forces in Virginia to Manassas Junction, about twenty-five miles west of Washington. Lincoln decided that General Irvin McDowell's hastily assembled army of some 30,000 might overrun the outnumbered Confederates and quickly march on to Richmond, the Confederate capital.

It was a dry summer day on July 21, 1861, when McDowell's raw recruits encountered Beauregard's army dug in behind a little stream called Bull Run. The two generals, who had been classmates at West Point, adopted similar plans—each would try to turn the other's left flank. The Federals almost achieved their purpose early in the afternoon, but Confederate reinforcements poured in to check the Union offensive. Amid the fury, a South Carolina general rallied his men by pointing to Thomas Jackson's brigade of Virginians: "Look at Jackson standing there like a damned stone wall." It was true, and Jackson was called "Stonewall" thereafter.

Their attack blunted, the exhausted Union troops eventually broke, and their confused and frantic retreat turned into a panic as fleeing soldiers and civilian spectators clogged the Washington road. Lincoln read a gloomy dispatch from the front: "The day is lost. Save Washington and the remnants of this army. The routed troops will not re-form." But the Confederates were almost as disorganized and exhausted by the battle as the Yankees were, and they failed to give chase.

The Battle of Bull Run was a sobering experience for both sides. Much of the new war's romance—the splendid uniforms, bright flags, fervent songs—gave way to the agonizing realization that this would be a long, mean, and costly struggle. *Harper's Weekly* bluntly warned: "From the fearful day at Bull Run dates war. Not polite war . . . but war that breaks hearts and blights homes."

The War's Early Course

The Battle of Bull Run demonstrated that the war would not be decided with one sudden stroke. Union general Winfield Scott had predicted as much, and now Lincoln fell back upon the three-pronged "Anaconda strategy" that Scott had long before proposed. It called first for the Army of the Potomac to defend Washington and exert constant pressure on the Confederate capital at Richmond. At the same time, the navy would blockade the southern coast and dry up the Confederacy's access to foreign goods and weapons. The final component of the plan would divide the Confederacy by sending navy gunboats and transports to invade the South along the main water routes: the Mississippi, Tennessee, and Cumberland Rivers.

The Confederate strategy was simpler. If the Union forces could be stalemated, Davis and others hoped, then the British or French might be convinced to join their cause, or perhaps public sentiment in the North would force Lincoln to seek a negotiated settlement. So at the same time that armies were forming in the South, Confederate diplomats were seeking assistance in London and Paris, and Confederate sympathizers in the North were urging an end to the Union's war effort.

Naval Actions

After the Battle of Bull Run and for the rest of 1861 and early 1862, the most important military actions involved naval warfare and a blockade of southern ports. The Union navy grew from 90 ships at the start of the war to 650 vessels of all types. It never completely sealed off the South, but it raised to desperate levels the hazards of blockade running.

The one great threat to the Union navy proved to be short-lived. The Confederates in Norfolk had fashioned an ironclad ship from an abandoned Union steam frigate, the *Merrimack.* Rechristened the *Virginia,* it ventured out on March 8, 1862, and wrought havoc among the Union ships at the en-trance to Chesapeake Bay. But as luck would have it, a new Union ironclad, the *Monitor,* arrived from New York in time to engage the *Virginia* the next day. They fought to a draw, and the *Virginia* returned to port, where the

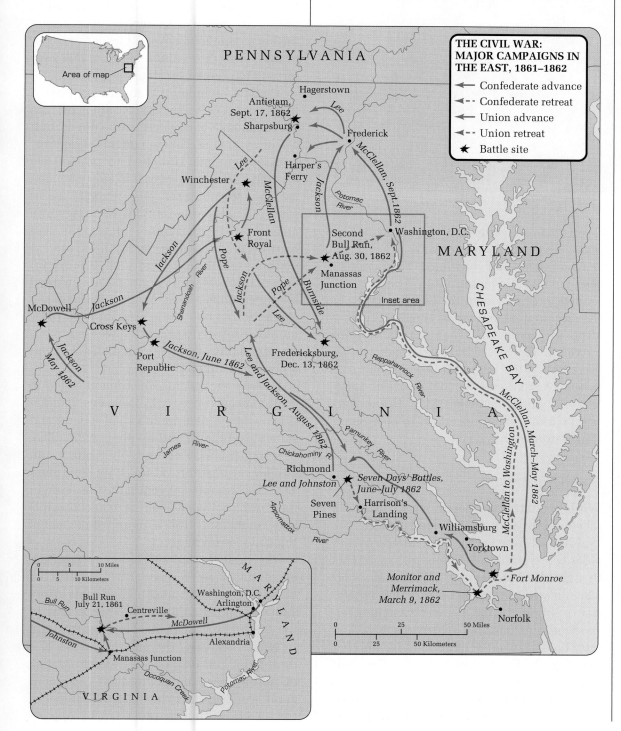

THE CIVIL WAR:
MAJOR CAMPAIGNS IN
THE EAST, 1861–1862

- ← Confederate advance
- ◄--- Confederate retreat
- ← Union advance
- ◄--- Union retreat
- ★ Battle site

Enlisting Union soldiers. Neither side was prepared for the magnitude of the nation's first "modern" war.

Confederates destroyed it when they had to give up Norfolk soon afterward.

Gradually, the northern "Anaconda" tightened its grip on the South. The navy extended its bases down the Carolina coast in the late summer and fall of 1862, first laying siege to Charleston. Then in the Gulf of Mexico, Flag Officer David Farragut's ships forced open the lower Mississippi and surprised New Orleans in the spring of 1862. The city surrendered on May 1, and Farragut's forces then moved on to take Baton Rouge in the same way.

Forming Armies

While the navy was beginning its blockade of southern ports and commissioning the building of new ships, the armies on both sides were recruiting men to form regiments to fight the land battles of the war. After Lincoln's initial request for 75,000 ninety-day militiamen, the Federal Congress authorized a call for 500,000 more men, and after the Battle of Bull Run it added another 500,000. By the end of 1861, the first half million had enlisted in the Union Army.

In the Confederacy, the first mass enlistment put a great strain on limited means. After first trying to recruit volunteers, the

Confederates turned to conscription. On April 16, 1862, all white male citizens, eighteen to thirty-five, were declared members of the army for three years, and those already in service were required to serve out three years. In 1862 the upper age was raised to forty-five, and in 1864 the age limits were further extended to cover all from seventeen to fifty, with those under eighteen and over forty-five reserved for state defense.

The law included two loopholes. First, a draftee might escape service either by providing an able-bodied substitute not of draft age or by paying $500 in commutation. Second, exemptions, designed to protect key civilian work, were subject to abuse by men seeking "bombproof" jobs. Exemption of state officials, for example, was flagrantly abused by the governors of Georgia and North Carolina, who were in charge of defining which jobs were vital. The exclusion of teachers with twenty pupils inspired a sudden educational renaissance, and the exemption of one white man for each plantation with twenty or more slaves led to bitter complaints about "a rich man's war and a poor man's fight."

In 1863 the federal government began to draft men aged twenty to forty-five. Exemptions were granted to specified federal and state officeholders and to others on medical or compassionate grounds, but one could still buy a substitute or, for $300, have one's service commuted. Eventually the draft in the North produced about 46,000 conscripts and 118,000 substitutes, or only 6 percent of the Union armies.

The draft flouted an American tradition of voluntary service and was widely held to be arbitrary and unconstitutional. Widespread opposition limited enforcement of the draft acts both in the North and South. In New York City, the announcement of a draft lottery on July 11, 1863, led to a week of rioting in which roving bands of immigrant working-class toughs took control of the streets. Although provoked by opposition to the draft, the riots exposed emerging racial and ethnic tensions. The mobs assaulted conscription offices, factories, docks, and the homes of prominent Republicans. But they directed their wrath most furiously at blacks. In their tortured reasoning, they blamed blacks for causing the war and for threatening to take their own unskilled jobs. The violence ran completely out of control; 120 people died, and an estimated $2 million in property was destroyed before soldiers brought from Gettysburg restored order.

The West and the Civil War

During the Civil War, western settlement continued. New discoveries of gold and silver along the eastern slopes of the Sierra Nevadas and in Montana and Colorado lured thousands of prospectors and their suppliers. Dakota, Colorado, and Nevada gained territorial status in 1861, Idaho and Arizona in 1863, and Montana in 1864. Silver-rich Nevada gained its statehood in 1864.

With the firing on Fort Sumter, many of the regular army units assigned to frontier outposts in the West moved east to meet the Confederate threat. In Texas, the Indian Territory (Oklahoma), and southern New Mexico, Union soldiers left altogether. Elsewhere they left behind skeleton units to man the forts. Despite the lessened federal presence, Texas was the only western state to join the Confederacy. For the most part, the federal government maintained its control of the other western territories during the war.

Many Indian tribes found themselves caught up in the Civil War. Indian regiments fought on both sides, and in the Indian Country they fought against each other. Many Oklahoma Indians owned African-American slaves and felt a natural bond with southern whites. Oklahoma's proximity to Texas also influenced the Choctaws and Chickasaws to support the Confederacy. The Cherokees, Creeks, and Seminoles were more divided in their loyalties.

Actions in the Western Theater

After the Battle of Bull Run, little happened in the Eastern Theater (east of the Appalachians) before May 1862. The Western Theater (from the mountains to the Mississippi), on the other hand, flared up with several clashes and an important penetration of the Confederate states. In western Kentucky, Confederate general Albert Sidney Johnston had perhaps 40,000 men stretched over some 150 miles. Early in 1862 Union general Ulysses S. Grant attacked the weak center of Johnston's overextended lines. Moving out of Paducah, Kentucky, with a gunboat flotilla, Grant's army swung southward up the Tennessee River toward Fort Henry. After a pounding from the Union gunboats, the fort fell on February 6. Grant then moved overland to attack Fort Donelson, and on February 16 his army captured its 12,000 men. Grant's blunt demand of "immediate and unconditional surrender" and his quick success sent a thrill through the dispirited North.

Ulysses S. "Unconditional Surrender" Grant had not only opened a water route to Nashville but had thrust his forces between the two strongholds of the western Confederates. Johnston therefore had to give up his foothold in Kentucky and abandon Nashville to General Don Carlos Buell's Army of the Ohio. The disheveled Grant, who had graduated from West Point in the lower half of his class and had resigned from the army in disgrace for drunkenness in 1854, was now a national hero. But not for long.

Shiloh

After defeats in Kentucky and Tennessee, General Johnston regrouped the Confederate forces in Corinth, Mississippi, in hopes of retaking control of the Mississippi Valley. As Grant prepared to assault Corinth, he made a costly mistake. He clumsily placed his troops on a rolling plateau between two creeks flowing into the Tennessee River and

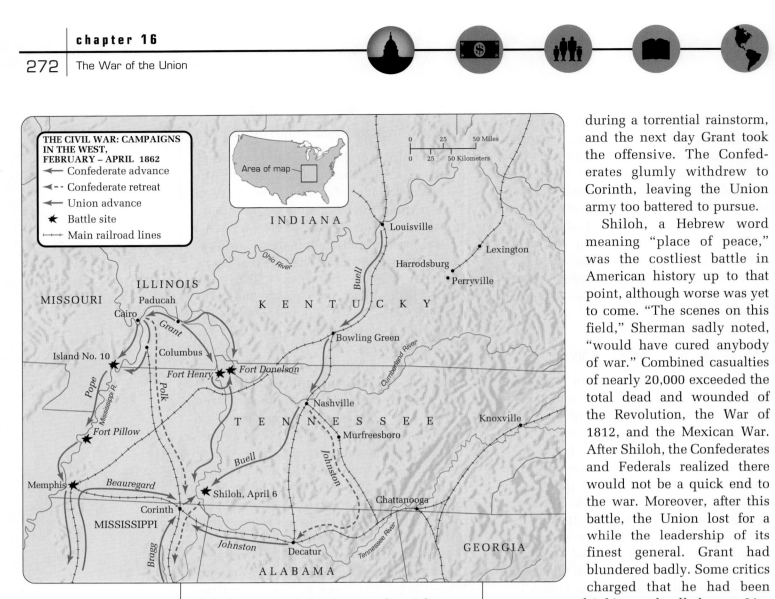

THE CIVIL WAR: CAMPAIGNS IN THE WEST, FEBRUARY – APRIL 1862
→ Confederate advance
◄--- Confederate retreat
→ Union advance
★ Battle site
╫── Main railroad lines

during a torrential rainstorm, and the next day Grant took the offensive. The Confederates glumly withdrew to Corinth, leaving the Union army too battered to pursue.

Shiloh, a Hebrew word meaning "place of peace," was the costliest battle in American history up to that point, although worse was yet to come. "The scenes on this field," Sherman sadly noted, "would have cured anybody of war." Combined casualties of nearly 20,000 exceeded the total dead and wounded of the Revolution, the War of 1812, and the Mexican War. After Shiloh, the Confederates and Federals realized there would not be a quick end to the war. Moreover, after this battle, the Union lost for a while the leadership of its finest general. Grant had blundered badly. Some critics charged that he had been drinking and called upon Lincoln to replace him. But the president, faced with the dithering of his other generals (especially George McClellan in the Eastern Theater), declined: "I can't spare this man; he fights." Grant's superior, General Henry Halleck, however, was not as forgiving. He relieved Grant of his command for several months, and as a result the Union thrust southward ground to a halt. For the remainder of 1862 the chief action in the Western Theater was a series of inconclusive maneuvers and a few sharp engagements.

McClellan's Peninsular Campaign

The Eastern Theater remained fairly quiet for nine months after Bull Run. After the Union defeat, Lincoln had replaced McDowell with the brilliant, if theatrical and

failed to set up defensive trenches. Johnston shrewdly recognized Grant's oversight, and on the morning of April 6, his forces attacked the vulnerable Federals.

The Confederates struck suddenly at Shiloh, a log church in the center of the Union camp. There they found most of Grant's troops still sleeping or eating breakfast. Some died in their bedrolls. After a day of bloody carnage and confusion, Grant's men were pinned against the river. They may well have been annihilated had the Confederate commander, General Johnston, not been mortally wounded at the peak of the battle. His second in command called off the attack. Under the cover of gunboats and artillery at nearby Pittsburg Landing, Grant and the brilliant general from Ohio, William Tecumseh Sherman, rallied their troops. Reinforcements arrived that night hesitant, General George B. McClellan. As head of the Army of the Potomac, he instituted a rigid training regimen, determined that his men would be ready for their next battle. On the surface, McClellan exuded confidence. Yet for all of his organizational ability and dramatic flair, his innate caution would prove crippling. His foremost concern was to avoid defeat rather than inflict it on the enemy.

Time passed, and McClellan kept building his forces to meet the superior numbers he always claimed were facing him. Lincoln initially gave McClellan his complete support, yet after nine months of such prolonged preparation, the president and much of the public had grown understandably impatient. An exasperated Lincoln, convinced that his general "has got the slows," ordered McClellan to begin forward movement by February 22, 1862. McClellan brashly predicted: "I will be in Richmond in ten days."

In mid-March 1862, McClellan's army finally embarked, and before the end of May his advance units sighted the church steeples in Richmond. Thousands of Richmond residents fled the city in panic. President Davis sent his own family to a safe haven west of the city. But McClellan failed to capitalize on his situation. On May 31 Confederate general Joseph E. Johnston struck at Union forces isolated by floodwaters on the south bank of the Chickahominy River. In the battle of Seven Pines (Fair Oaks), only the arrival of reinforcements prevented a disastrous Union defeat. Both sides took heavy casualties, and Johnston was severely wounded.

At this point, the fifty-five-year-old Robert E. Lee assumed command of the Army of Northern Virginia, changing the course of the war. Lee was a reticent Christian gentleman in private, but a slashing, daring leader in uniform. Unlike Johnston, he enjoyed Davis's trust and assembled a galaxy of superb field commanders led by Stonewall Jackson, the fearless, pious math-ematics professor from the Virginia Military Institute.

Once in command, Lee quickly decided to hit the Union forces north of the Chickahominy River on June 26, 1862, leaving only a token force in Richmond. But heavy losses prevented the Confederates from sustaining their momentum. Lee launched a final desperate attack at Malvern Hill (July 1), where the Confederates were riddled by artillery. This week of intense fighting, lumped together as the Seven Days' Battles, failed to dislodge the Union forces.

Second Bull Run

McClellan evacuated the peninsula and joined forces with the bombastic John Pope for a new assault against Richmond from the north. As McClellan's Army of the Potomac pulled out, Lee moved northward to strike Pope before the Union forces could be joined. Dividing his forces, he sent Stonewall Jackson's famous "foot cavalry" on a sweep around Pope's right flank to attack his supply lines and the federal depot at Manassas Junction.

At Second Bull Run (or Second Manassas), fought on almost the same site as the earlier battle, the Confederates thoroughly confused Pope. On August 30, 1862, General James Longstreet's corps of 30,000 Confederates, screaming the Rebel yell "like demons emerging from the earth," drove the Union forces from the field. One New York regiment lost 124 of its 490 men, the highest percentage of deaths in any battle of the war. In the next few days, the whipped Union forces pulled back into fortifications around Washington, where McClellan once again took command and reorganized. The disgraced Pope was dispatched to Minnesota to fight in the Indian wars.

Antietam

Still on the offensive, Lee determined to move the battlefield out of the South and perhaps thereby gain foreign recognition of the Confederacy. In September 1862 he led his troops into western Maryland and headed for Pennsylvania. As luck would have it, however, his bold strategy was uncovered when a Union soldier picked up a bundle of cigars and discovered a secret order from Lee wrapped around them. The paper revealed that Lee had again divided his army, sending Jackson off to take Harper's Ferry.

McClellan, instead of leaping at his unexpected opportunity, delayed for sixteen crucial hours, still worried—as always—about enemy strength. Lee was thereby able to reassemble most of his tired army behind Antietam Creek.

On September 17, 1862, McClellan's forces attacked, and the furious Battle of Antietam (Sharpsburg) began. Still outnumbered more than two to one, the Confederates forced a standoff in the bloodiest single day of the Civil War, a day participants thought would never end.

In the late afternoon McClellan backed off, letting Lee slip away across the Potomac. Lincoln fumed at McClellan's failure to follow up and gain a truly decisive victory. He fired off the following tart message to the general: "I have just read your dispatch about sore-tongued and fatigued horses. Will you pardon me for asking what the horses of your army have done . . . that fatigues anything?" Later the president sent his commander a one-sentence letter: "If you don't want to use the army, I should like to borrow it for a while." Failing to receive a satisfactory answer, Lincoln then removed McClellan and assigned him to recruiting duty in New Jersey. Never again would he command troops.

Fredericksburg

Lee's failed invasion had dashed the Confederacy's hopes of foreign recognition. A Rebel victory might have convinced England and France to assist the Confederacy.

But however disappointing the Confederates were after Lee's failed offensive, the war was far from over. In his search for a fighting general, Lincoln now turned to Ambrose E. Burnside, a modest figure whose main achievement to that time had been to grow his famous whiskers ("sideburns").

On December 13, 1862, Burnside sent his men across the icy Rappahannock River to face Lee's forces, well entrenched behind a stone wall and on high ground just west of Fredericksburg, Virginia. Blessed with a clear field of fire, Confederate artillery and muskets chewed up the valorous Union ranks as they crossed a mile of open land west of the town.

Six times the courageous but suicidal Union assaults melted under the murderous fire coming from protected Confederate positions above and below them. The scene was both awful and awe-inspiring, prompting Lee to remark: "It is well that war is so terrible—we should grow too fond of it."

After seeing his men suffer more than 12,000 casualties, twice as many as the Confederates, Burnside wept as he gave the order to withdraw, and his battered forces limped back across the river. A northern reporter aptly summarized the battle: "It can hardly be in human nature for men to show more valor, or generals to manifest less judgment."

Thus the year 1862 ended with forces in the East deadlocked and the Federal advance in the West stalled since midyear. Union morale reached a low ebb. Northern Democrats were calling for a negotiated peace, while the so-called Radical Republicans were pushing Lincoln to prosecute the war even more forcefully. Several questioned the president's competence.

In the midst of such second-guessing and carping, the deeper currents of the war were in fact turning in favor of the Union: in a lengthening war, its superior resources began to tell on the morale of the Confederacy. In both the Eastern and Western Theaters, the Confederate counterattack had been

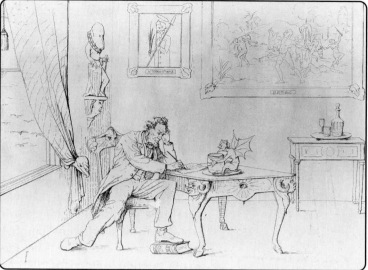

repulsed. And while the armies clashed, Lincoln by a stroke of a pen changed the conflict from a war for the Union into a revolutionary struggle for abolition. On January 1, 1863, he signed the Emancipation Proclamation.

Emancipation

The Emancipation Proclamation was the product of long and painful deliberation, as opinion was divided even in the North as to whether the slaves should all be freed. While most abolitionists favored both complete emancipation and social integration of the races, many antislavery activists only wanted to prohibit slavery from new territories and states, and they were willing to allow slavery to continue in the South.

Lincoln had always insisted that the purpose of the conflict was to restore the Union, and that he did not have the authority to free the slaves. Yet the prolonged war forced the issue. Slaves began to turn up in Union army camps, and generals did not know whether to declare them free or not. Some put these "contrabands" to work building fortifications; others liberated those who belonged to Confederate owners,

thus risking upsetting border-state slaveholders. Lincoln himself edged toward emancipation.

As the war ground on, Lincoln eventually decided that complete emancipation was required for several reasons: slave labor bolstered the Confederate cause; sagging morale in the North needed the lift of a transcendent moral ideal; and public opinion was swinging that way as the war continued. Proclaiming a war on slavery, moreover, would end forever any chance that France or Britain would support the Confederacy.

The time to act came after Antietam. It was a dubious victory, but it did force Lee's withdrawal from the North. On September 22, 1862, Lincoln issued a preliminary Emancipation Proclamation to warn that on January 1, 1863, all slaves in Confederate states or areas still under active rebellion would be "thenceforward and forever free."

The proclamation, with few exceptions, freed only those slaves still under Confederate control, as cynics noted then and later. But critics missed a point that slaves readily grasped. "In a document proclaiming liberty," wrote a black historian, "the unfree never bother to read the fine print."

Lincoln's Emancipation Proclamation

Two views of the Emancipation Proclamation. The Union view (*left*) shows a thoughtful Lincoln composing the proclamation with the Constitution and the Holy Bible in his lap. The Confederate view (*right*) shows a demented Lincoln with his foot on the Constitution using an inkwell held by the devil.

reaffirmed the policy that blacks could enroll in the Union armed services and sparked efforts to organize new all-black units. The War Department authorized general recruitment of blacks all over the country, which transformed a war to preserve the Union into a revolution to overthrow the social, economic, and racial status quo in the South. The first challenge for black troops, however, was to overcome embedded racial fears of northern whites and to get an opportunity to prove themselves in battle. Finally, by mid-1863, black soldiers were involved in significant combat both in the Eastern and Western Theaters. Lincoln reported that several of his commanders believed that "the use of colored troops constitutes the heaviest blow yet dealt to the rebels."

Altogether, between 180,000 and 200,000 black men served in the Union army, providing around 10 percent of its total. Some 38,000 gave their lives. Blacks accounted for about a fourth of all enlistments in the navy, and of these, almost 3,000 died.

As the war entered its final months, freedom emerged more fully as a legal reality. The Thirteenth Amendment, which abolished slavery everywhere, was ratified by three-fourths of the states and became part of the Constitution on December 18, 1865, thus removing any lingering doubts about the legality of emancipation. By then, in fact, slavery remained only in the border states of Kentucky and Delaware.

Women and the War

While breaking the bonds of slavery, the Civil War also loosened traditional restraints on female activity. Women on both sides played prominent roles in the conflict, and in the process many saw their outlook and status transformed. Initially the call to arms revived heroic images of female self-sacrifice and domestic skills. Women in the North and South sewed uniforms, composed uplifting poetry and songs, and raised money and supplies. Thousands of northern women worked with the United States Sanitary Commission, which organized medical relief and other services for soldiers. Others supported the freedmen's-aid movement to help ex-slaves.

In the North alone, some 20,000 women served as nurses or other health-related volunteers. The two most famous nurses were Dorothea Dix and Clara Barton, both untiring volunteers in service to the wounded and dying. Dix, the veteran reformer of the nation's insane asylums, became the Union Army's first Superintendent of Women Nurses. Barton was a former schoolteacher who worked as a nurse in the Civil War. Instead of accepting an assignment to a general hospital, she followed the troops on her own, working in makeshift field hospitals. At Antietam, she came so close to the fighting that, as she worked on a wounded soldier, a Confederate bullet ripped through the sleeve of her dress and killed the man. Barton challenged both male doctors' control of battlefield medicine and male bureaucrats' efforts to restrict the nurses' sphere of operations.

The war experience of women helped generate greater confidence in their abilities. The departure of hundreds of thousands of men for the battlefields forced women to assume the public and private roles the men left behind. A resident of Lexington, Virginia, reported in 1862 that there were "no men left" in town by mid-1862. Women in both the North and South suddenly found themselves in charge of households, farms, and businesses. They became farmers or plantation managers, clerks, munitions plant workers, and schoolteachers. In North Carolina in 1860, for example, only 7 percent of teachers were women. By the end of the Civil War, a majority of the state's teachers were women. Some 400 women disguised themselves as men and fought in the war; dozens worked as spies; others traveled with the armies, cooking meals,

Clara Barton was one of 200,000 women serving the Union Army as nurses or other health-related volunteers.

writing letters, and assisting with amputations.

Government during the War

Striking the shackles from 4 million slaves and loosening the restraints on female activity constituted a monumental social and economic revolution. But an even broader revolution developed as political power shifted from South to North after secession. Before the war, southern congressmen had been able to frustrate the legislative initiatives of both Free Soilers and Whigs. But once the secessionists abandoned Congress to the Republicans, a dramatic change occurred. A new protective tariff, a transcontinental railroad to run through Omaha to Sacramento, a homestead act that granted free farms of 160 acres to settlers who occupied the land for five years—all acts that had been stalled by sectional controversy—were adopted before the end of 1862. That year also saw the passage of the Morrill Land Grant Act, which provided federal aid to state colleges of "agricultural and mechanic arts." The National Banking Act, which created a uniform system of banking and bank-note currency, followed in 1863 and helped the Union address a critical problem: how to finance the war.

Union Finances

Congress had three options for solving the problem of financing the war: raising taxes, printing paper money, and borrowing. The higher taxes came chiefly in the form of the Morrill Tariff and excise taxes, which fell on manufacturers and nearly every profession. An income tax rounded out the revenue measures.

But tax revenues trickled in so slowly that Congress in 1862 ordered the printing of paper money. Eventually $450 million in "greenbacks" were printed, enough to pay the bills but not unleash the kind of run-

Women workers filling cartridges with gunpowder at the Federal arsenal in Watertown, Massachusetts.

away inflation that burdened the Confederacy after Jefferson Davis allowed the unlimited issue of paper money.

Still, paper money and taxes provided only about two-thirds of the money to finance the war. The rest came chiefly from the sale of bonds. A Philadelphia banker named Jay Cooke mobilized a network of agents and propaganda for the sale of government war bonds. It worked well, and over $2 billion was raised in the process.

All wars provide opportunities for quick profits, and the Civil War was no different. Many American entrepreneurs reaped quick riches from war contracts. Several cut corners in the process, providing shoddy goods, paying bribes and kickbacks, or in some cases, not delivering supplies at all. Not all wartime fortunes, however, were made dishonestly. Their long-run importance was in promoting the capital accumulation that fueled the phenomenal postwar expansion of the national economy.

Confederate Finances

Confederate finances were a disaster from the start. Tariffs were tried, but imports were low and therefore raised little revenue. In 1863 the Confederate Congress passed a measure that taxed nearly everything. A 10 percent tax on all agricultural products, however, did more to outrage farmers and planters than to supply the army. Enforcement was so lax and evasion so easy that the taxes produced only negligible income.

The last resort, printing paper money, was in fact resorted to early. Beginning in 1861, the new Confederate government began an extended inflationary binge. Altogether the Confederacy turned out more than $1 billion in paper money, forcing prices up geometrically. By 1864, a turkey sold in a Richmond market for $100, flour went for $425 a barrel, and bacon for $10 a pound. Those living on fixed incomes were caught in a merciless inflationary squeeze.

Confederate Diplomacy

No sooner had the war begun than the Confederate government focused on gaining help from foreign governments in the form of supplies, formal recognition, or perhaps even armed intervention. The first Confederate emissaries to England and France took hope when the British foreign minister received them informally after their arrival in London in 1861. In Paris, French leader Napoleon III even promised them that he would recognize the Confederacy if England would lead the way. But when the agents returned to London, the government refused to see them, partly because of Union pressures and partly out of British self-interest.

Confederate negotiators were far more successful at getting supplies than gaining formal recognition. The most spectacular feat was the procurement of raiding ships. Although British law prohibited the sale of warships to belligerents, a southern agent was able to have the ships built and then, on trial runs, to escape and be outfitted with guns. In all, eighteen such ships were activated and saw action in the Atlantic, Pacific, and Indian Oceans, where they sank hundreds of Yankee ships and sparked terror in the rest.

Union Politics and Civil Liberties

On the home fronts during the Civil War, there was no moratorium on partisan politics, North or South. Within his own party, Lincoln faced a Radical wing composed mainly of prewar abolitionists. Led by House members such as Thaddeus Stevens and George Julian, and senators such as Charles Sumner, Benjamin Wade, and Zachariah Chandler, the so-called Radical Republicans formed a Joint Committee on the Conduct of the War, which increasingly pressured Lincoln to emancipate the slaves, confiscate southern plantations, and prosecute the war more vigorously. The majority of Republicans, however, supported the president, and the party was virtually united on economic matters.

The Democratic party suffered the loss of its southern wing as well as the death of its leader, Stephen A. Douglas, in June 1861. By and large, northern Democrats supported a war for the "Union as it was" before 1860, giving reluctant support to war policies but opposing wartime constraints on civil liberties and the new economic legislation. "War Democrats" such as Senator Andrew Johnson from Tennessee and Secretary of War Edwin Stanton fully supported Lincoln's policies, however, while a Peace Wing of the Democratic party preferred a negotiated end to the fighting, even at the risk of the Union. An extreme fringe among the Peace Democrats even flirted with outright disloyalty. The "Copperheads," as they were called, were strongest in Ohio, Indiana, and Illinois, states with many transplanted southerners, some of whom were pro-Confederate.

Such open sympathy for the enemy provoked Lincoln to crack down hard. Early in the war, he assumed certain emergency powers such as the suspension of the writ of habeas corpus (which entitled people who had been jailed to demand that a court hear their case). Lincoln also asserted his right to invoke martial law. When critics charged that such measures violated the Constitution, Lincoln's congressional supporters pushed through the Habeas Corpus Act of 1863, which authorized the suspension of the writ. Some 14,000 arrests of Confederate sympathizers resulted.

At their 1864 national convention, the Democrats called for an immediate armistice to stop the war and named General McClellan as their candidate, but he distanced himself from the peace platform by declaring that the two sides must agree on reunion before the fighting should stop. Radical Republicans, who still regarded Lincoln as being too soft on the traitorous southerners, tried to thwart his renomination, but Lincoln outmaneuvered them at every turn. In a shrewd move, he named as his vice-presidential running mate Andrew Johnson, a War Democrat from Tennessee, and called their ticket the "National Union" so as to minimize partisanship. As the war ground on through 1864, with General Grant's forces taking heavy losses in Virginia, Lincoln fully expected to lose the election, but key military victories in August and September turned the tide. McClellan carried only New Jersey, Delaware, and Kentucky.

Confederate Politics

Unlike Lincoln, Jefferson Davis never had to contest a presidential election. Both he and his vice-president, Alexander Stephens, were elected for a six-year term. But discontent flourished in the South as events went from bad to worse. Food was in short supply, and prices had skyrocketed by the spring of 1863. A bread riot in Richmond in 1863 ended only when Davis himself persuaded the mob (mostly women) to disperse.

Davis, like Lincoln, also had to contend with dissenters. Especially troublesome were those committed to states' rights who had supported secession but steadfastly opposed the centralizing tendencies of the government in Richmond. Georgia and North Carolina were strongholds of such sentiment. They challenged, among other things, the legality of conscription, taxes on farm produce, and above all, the suspension of habeas corpus. Vice-President Stephens himself carried on a running battle with Davis, accusing the president of trying to establish a "military despotism."

Such internal bickering did not alone cause the Confederacy's defeat, but it certainly contributed to it. Whereas Lincoln was the consummate pragmatist, Davis was a brittle dogmatist with a waspish temper. His fundamental insecurity made him indecisive, but once he made a decision, nothing could change his mind. Such a personality was ill suited to the chief executive of an infant nation.

The Faltering Confederacy

In 1863 the hinges of fate began to close the door on the brief career of the Confederacy. After the Union disaster at Fredericksburg, Lincoln's frustrating search for a capable general turned to one of Burnside's disgruntled lieutenants, Joseph E. Hooker, a hard-drinking character whose pugnacity had earned him the nickname "Fighting Joe." But he was no more able to deliver the goods than Burnside. Hooker failed his test at Chancellorsville in May 1863.

Chancellorsville

With a force of perhaps 130,000 men, the largest Union army yet gathered, and a brilliant plan, Hooker suffered a loss of control at the critical juncture during the Battle of Chancellorsville. Lee, with perhaps half that number of troops, staged what became a textbook classic of daring and maneuver. Hooker's plan was to leave his base, opposite Fredericksburg, on a sweeping movement upstream across the Rappahannock

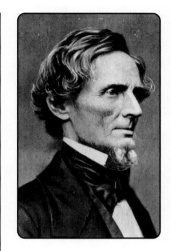

Jefferson Davis.

and Rapidan Rivers, and flank Lee's position. A large diversionary force was to cross the Rappahannock below the town. Initially all went well, but Lee sniffed out the ruse. He moved his main force to meet Hooker and dispatched Stuart's cavalry to disrupt the Union lines of communications. Hooker suddenly lost sight of his opponents and was caught by surprise when rebel skirmishers fired on his advance columns. He then ordered his troops to pull back to the Chancellorsville crossroads. "I just lost faith in Joe Hooker," Hooker himself later admitted, and Lee quickly took advantage of his opponent's failure of nerve. He divided his army again, sending Jackson with more than half the men on a long march to hit the enemy's exposed right flank.

On May 2, Jackson surprised Hooker's right flank at the edge of a densely wooded area called the Wilderness. The Confederates slammed into the Union lines with such furor that the defenders panicked and ran. The thick undergrowth made troop movements more chaotic than usual, and the fighting died out in confusion as darkness fell. The next day was Lee's, however, as his troops forced Hooker's army to recross the Rappahannock. It was the peak of Lee's career, but Chancellorsville was his last significant victory, and his costliest: the South suffered more than 12,000 casualties, including 1,600 killed, among them Stonewall Jackson, mistakenly shot by his own men in the confused fighting. "I have lost my right arm," lamented Lee.

Vicksburg

While Lee held the Federals at bay in the East, Grant, his command now restored, had been groping his way down the Mississippi River toward Vicksburg in western Mississippi. Grant knew that if he could capture Vicksburg, the Union forces could gain control of the Mississippi River and thereby split the Confederacy in two. Located on a bluff 200 feet above the river, Vicksburg had

withstood repeated naval attacks. For months Grant tried to discover a way to penetrate the city's heavily fortified defenses. His army crossed to Louisiana, took a roundabout route to Jackson, Mississippi, where it routed the Confederates, and headed back to Vicksburg. The Federals pinned down 30,000 Confederates in Vicksburg, and Grant resolved to starve them out.

Gettysburg

The plight of besieged Vicksburg put the Confederate high command in a quandary. Lee proposed a diversion. If he could win a great victory on northern soil, he reasoned, he might do more than just relieve the pressure on Vicksburg; he might bring an end to the war. In June 1863 he moved his forces into the Shenandoah Valley and headed north across Maryland. Neither side chose Gettysburg, Pennsylvania, as the site for the climactic battle, but a Confederate foraging party entered the town in search of shoes and encountered units of Union cavalry. The main forces then quickly converged there.

On July 1, a hot, steamy day, the Confederates pushed the Federals out of the town, but into stronger positions on high ground to the south. The new Union commander, George G. Meade, hastened reinforcements to the new lines along the heights. On July 2, Lee, hampered by a lack of information, ordered assaults at both the extreme left and the extreme right flanks of Meade's army. The Confederates fought fiercely, but the Federals, who outnumbered their attackers almost two to one, fought just as bravely—and the assaults were repulsed.

The next day Lee staked everything on one final attack on the Union center at Cemetery Ridge. His plan, however, suffered from a fatal problem: his generals were not unified in their support of it. As a result, General James Longstreet, who remained skeptical of a frontal assault, did not position his forces to assist General George Pick-

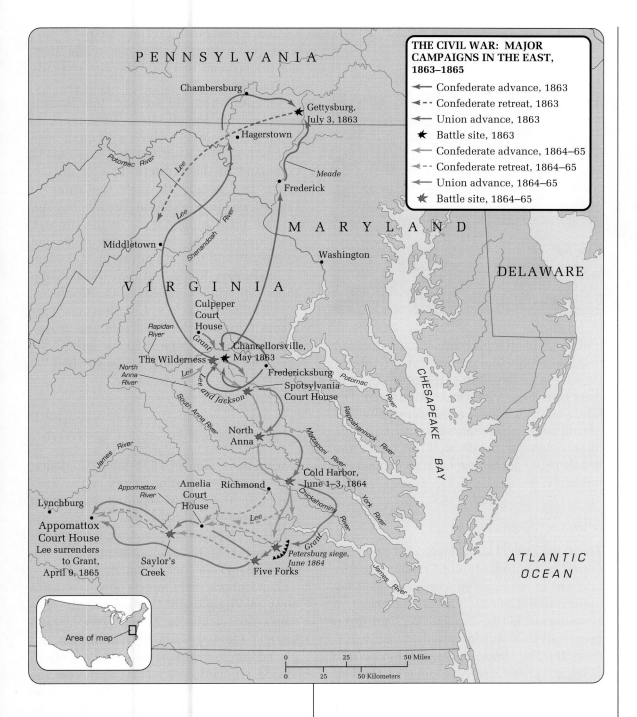

THE CIVIL WAR: MAJOR CAMPAIGNS IN THE EAST, 1863–1865

⟵ Confederate advance, 1863
⟵-- Confederate retreat, 1863
⟵ Union advance, 1863
★ Battle site, 1863
⟵ Confederate advance, 1864–65
⟵-- Confederate retreat, 1864–65
⟵ Union advance, 1864–65
✦ Battle site, 1864–65

ett's division, which Lee had ordered to take Cemetery Ridge.

About 2 P.M. Pickett's 15,000 troops emerged from the woods west of Cemetery Ridge and began their advance across rising open ground commanded by Union artillery. It was as hopeless as Burnside's assault at Fredericksburg. Those who avoided the shelling by Federal cannons were devastated by a wall of musket fire. Of the 14,000 attackers, barely half returned, leading Lee to mutter: "All this has been my fault."

With nothing left to do but retreat, Lee's mangled army began to slog south in a driving rain. They left about a third of their number behind on the ground. They also

Harvest of Death.
T. H. O'Sullivan's grim photograph of the dead at Gettysburg.

had failed in all their purposes, not the least being to relieve the pressure on Vicksburg. On that same day, July 4, the entire Confederate garrison at Vicksburg surrendered. The Confederacy was now irrevocably split. Had Meade aggressively pursued Lee he might have delivered the final blow before the Rebels could get back across the flooded Potomac.

Chattanooga

The third great Union victory of 1863 occurred in fighting around Chattanooga, the railhead of eastern Tennessee and gateway to northern Georgia. On September 9, a Union army led by General William Rosecrans took Chattanooga and then rashly pursued General Braxton Bragg's forces into Georgia, where the two sides clashed at Chickamauga (an old Cherokee word meaning "river of death"). The battle (September 19–20) had the makings of a Union disaster, because it was one of the few times when the Confederates had a numerical advantage (about 70,000 to 56,000). On the second day, Bragg smashed the Federal right, and only the stubborn stand on the left under Virginia Unionist George H. Thomas (thenceforth known as the "Rock of Chickamauga") pre-

vented a general rout. The battered Union forces fell back to Chattanooga, while Bragg cut the railroad and held the city virtually under siege.

Lincoln then dispatched Joe Hooker with reinforcements from Virginia, and Grant and Sherman arrived with more fresh troops from the west. Grant, given overall command of the Western Theater on October 16, pushed through the rings of Confederate troops around Chattanooga and opened up a supply route in the process. On November 24, the Federals broke out of the city and took up positions at the foot of Missionary Ridge. But they did not stop there. Still fuming because the Confederates had jeered them at Chickamauga, they charged toward the crest without orders. Despite Bragg's "cursing like a sailor," his men fled as the Federal troops reached the summit.

The Confederacy's Defeat

During the winter of 1863–1864, Confederates began to despair of victory. Mary Chesnut of South Carolina reported that "gloom and despondency hang like a pall everywhere." Union leaders, sensing the momentum swinging their way, stepped up the pressure on Confederate forces.

The Union's main targets now were Lee's army in Virginia and General Joseph Johnston's in Georgia. In March 1864 Lincoln brought General Grant to Washington and placed him in charge of the entire war effort. Meade retained direct command over the Army of the Potomac; operations in the West were entrusted to Grant's longtime lieutenant, William T. Sherman. As Sherman later wrote, Grant "was to go for Lee, and I was to go for Joe Johnston." Grant brought with him a new strategy against Lee. Whereas his predecessors had all hoped for the climactic single battle, he adopted a war of attrition. He would keep the pressure on the Confederates, grinding down their numbers and sapping their will to fight. Victory, he had decided, would come to the side "which never counted its dead." Grant ordered his commanders to wage total war, confiscating or destroying any and all civilian property of military use. It was a brutal, costly, but ultimately effective plan.

Grant's Pursuit of Lee

In May 1864 the Army of the Potomac, numbering about 115,000 to Lee's 64,000, moved south across the Rappahannock into the Wilderness, where Hooker had earlier come to grief in the Battle of Chancellorsville. In the Battle of the Wilderness (May 5–6), the armies fought blindly through the tangled brush and vines. Grant's men suffered heavier casualties than Lee's, but the Confederates were running out of replacements. Always before, Lee's adversaries had retreated to lick their wounds, but Grant slid off to the left and continued his relentless advance southward, now toward Spotsylvania Court House.

There the armies settled down for five days of carnage, May 8–12. Along the Chickahominy River, the two sides clashed again at Cold Harbor (June 1–3). In twenty minutes, 7,000 attacking Federals were killed or wounded. Battered and again repulsed, Grant soon had his men moving again, headed for Petersburg, the junction of railroads into Richmond from the south. "I shall take no backward steps," he declared.

Lee's army dug in around the town while Grant laid siege. For nine months the two forces faced each other down while Grant kept trying to break the railroad arteries that were Lee's lifeline. Grant's men were generously supplied by vessels moving up the James River, while Lee's forces, beset by hunger, cold, and desertion, wasted away in their muddy trenches. Petersburg had become Lee's prison, while disasters piled up for the Confederacy elsewhere.

Sherman's March

While Grant was chasing Lee in Virginia, the battle-hardened Sherman was doggedly pursuing Joe Johnston's army through north Georgia toward Atlanta. Tightly strung, profane, and plagued by fits of depression, Sherman was one of the few generals to appreciate the concept of total war. Whereas Sherman loved a toe-to-toe fight, Johnston preferred retreat and evasion, determined not to risk a single life until the perfect conditions for fighting were obtained.

An impatient President Davis finally exploded at Johnston's retreat and replaced him with the towering, blond-bearded Texan John B. Hood, who did not know the meaning of retreat or evasion. As Lee once noted, he was "all lion, none of the fox." During late July 1864, Hood's army struck three times from his base at Atlanta, each time fighting desperately but meeting a bloody rebuff. Sherman then circled the city and cut off the rail lines, forcing Hood to evacuate on September 1.

Sherman now resolved to make all of "Georgia howl," as his army embarked on its devastating march southeast through central Georgia. His intention was to "whip the rebels, to humble their pride . . . and

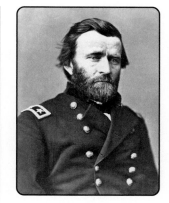

General Ulysses S. Grant.

The tattered colors of the 56th and 36th Massachusetts regiments, marching through Virginia, 1864.

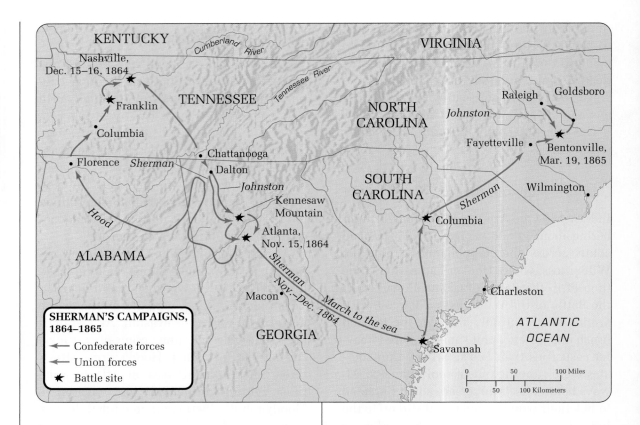

SHERMAN'S CAMPAIGNS, 1864–1865
⟵ Confederate forces
⟵ Union forces
★ Battle site

William T. Sherman.

make them fear and dread us." Hood went in the other direction, cutting through northern Alabama and into Tennessee in the hope of luring Sherman away from the undefended Deep South. But Sherman refused to take the bait, although he did dispatch 30,000 men to keep watch on Hood and his troops.

They did more than observe, however. In the Battle of Franklin (November 30), Hood sent his army across two miles of open Tennessee ground. Six waves of Confederate soldiers crashed against the Union lines but never broke through. "It is impossible to exaggerate the fierce energy with which the Confederate soldiers . . . threw themselves against the

works," recalled a Union colonel. They fought "with what seemed the very madness of despair." One dead general had been hit by forty-nine bullets. A month later, on December 27, Hood suffered another devastating defeat at Nashville that effectively ended Confederate activity in Tennessee.

During all this, Sherman and the main Union force were marching triumphantly through Georgia, pioneering the modern practice of total war against the enemy's resources and will to resist. "War is war," Sherman bluntly declared, "not a popularity contest." On November 15, 1864, his men burned much of Atlanta. When, after a month, Sherman's army approached Savannah, it had cut a swath of desolation 250 miles long.

On December 21 Sherman rode into Savannah, and three days later he offered the city as a Christmas gift to Lincoln. Sherman paused only long enough to resupply his forces, who then moved on across the river into that "hell-hole of secession," South Carolina. There his men wrought even greater destruction. More than a dozen towns were torched, including the state capital of Columbia, captured on February 17, 1865. That same day, the Confederates defending Charleston abandoned the city and headed north to join an army Joe Johnston was desperately trying to form.

Appomattox

During this final season of the Confederacy, Grant kept pushing, probing, and battering the Petersburg defenses. News of Sherman's devastating sweep through Dixie only added to the Confederacy's gloom. Under siege for almost ten months, Lee decided to sneak away and try to join Johnston's forces in North Carolina. In Richmond President Davis, exhausted but still defiant, gathered what papers and treasure he could carry and escaped by train. Torching everything of military and industrial value in Richmond, the Confederate army left the city, and the Union army entered, accompanied by Abraham Lincoln himself. Jefferson Davis would be captured in Georgia on May 10 by Union cavalry, but by then the Confederacy was already dead.

As Richmond lay burning, Lee pulled his shrunken army out of the trenches around Petersburg with Grant's men in hot pursuit. Lee soon found his escape route cut by Philip Sheridan's cavalry. While the Confederates fought desperately to hold their lines, their hunger, weariness, and the loss of so many men by death or desertion enabled the Union soldiers to break through and cut the rail lines that would have carried Lee and his men to the Carolinas. Lee decided it was senseless to waste any more lives.

On April 9 (Palm Sunday), 1865, Lee donned a crisp dress uniform and met the mud-spattered Grant in the parlor of the McLean home at Appomattox to tender his surrender. Grant, at Lee's request, let the Confederate officers keep their sidearms and permitted soldiers to keep their own horses and mules. Three days later, the Confederate troops formed ranks for the last time as they prepared for the formal surrender. As the ceremony unfolded, there was not a sound—no trumpets or drums, no cheers or jeers, simply "an awed stillness . . . as if it were the passing of the dead." On April 18, Johnston surrendered his forces to Sherman near Durham, North Carolina.

A Modern War

The Civil War was in many respects the first modern war. Its scope was unprecedented. One out of every twelve adult American males served in the war, and few families were unaffected by the event. Over 630,000 combatants died in the conflict, 50 percent more than in World War II. Because battlefield surgeons were constantly overworked and frequently lacked equipment, supplies, and knowledge, almost any stomach or head wound proved fatal, and gangrene was rampant. Fifty thousand of the survivors returned home with one or more limbs amputated. Disease, however, was the greatest threat to soldiers, killing twice as many as were lost in battle.

The Civil War was a total war, fought not solely by professional armies but by and against whole societies. Farms became battlefields, cities were transformed into armed encampments, and homes were commandeered for field hospitals.

The Civil War was also modern in that much of the killing was distant, impersonal, and mechanical. The opposing forces used an array of new weapons and instruments of war: artillery with "rifled" or grooved barrels for greater accuracy, repeating rifles, ironclad ships, and observation balloons.

Robert E. Lee. Mathew Brady took this photograph in Richmond eleven days after Lee's surrender at Appomattox.

Men were killed without even knowing who had fired the shot that felled them.

The debate over why the North won and the South lost the Civil War will probably never end, but as in other modern wars, firepower and manpower were essential factors. Lee's own explanation of the Confederate defeat retains an enduring legitimacy: "After four years of arduous service marked by unsurpassed courage and fortitude, the Army of Northern Virginia has been compelled to yield to overwhelming numbers and resources."

Reconstruction: North and South

This chapter focuses on

- The different approaches to Reconstruction.

- Congressional efforts to reshape southern society.

- The role of African Americans in the early postwar years.

- National politics in the 1870s.

THE *ESSENTIAL AMERICA* ON-LINE TUTOR

www.wwnorton.com/eamerica/ch17

- **Topic: The Radical Reconstruction plan**
  www.wwnorton.com/eamerica/ch17/topic.htm

  Following the conclusion of the Civil War in April 1865, the nation underwent twelve tumultuous years of Reconstruction. Relying on historical analyses, government documents, hand bills, photographs, and maps, study the significance of Reconstruction. How did Radical Republicans believe Reconstruction ought to proceed?

- **Chapter review: On-line quiz and chapter summary**
  www.wwnorton.com/eamerica/ch17/review.htm

- **Chapter resources: Multimedia index**
  www.wwnorton.com/eamerica/ch17/media.htm

In the spring of 1865 the wearying war was over. At the frightful cost of 630,000 lives and the destruction of the southern economy and much of its landscape, American nationalism emerged triumphant, and some 4 million slaves emerged free. But peace had come only on the battlefields. Now the North faced the imposing task of "reconstructing" a ravaged and resentful South.

The War's Aftermath

In the war's aftermath, important questions faced the victors in the North: Should the Confederate leaders be tried for treason? How should new governments be formed? How and at whose expense was the South's economy to be rebuilt? What was to be done with the freed slaves? Were they to be given land? social equality? education? voting rights? Such complex questions required sober reflection and careful planning, but policy makers did not have the luxury of time or the benefits of consensus.

Economic Development in the North

To some Americans the Civil War had been more truly a social revolution than the War of Independence, for it reduced the once-dominant power of the planter elite in national politics and elevated that of the northern "captains of industry." Government became more friendly to businessmen and unfriendly to those who would probe into their activities. The wartime Republican Congress had delivered on the major platform promises of 1860, which had cemented the allegiance of northeastern businessmen and western farmers.

In the absence of southern members, Congress during the war had seized the opportunity to expand national power. In this regard, it passed the Morrill Tariff, which doubled the average level of import duties.

The National Banking Act created a uniform system of banking and bank-note currency and helped to finance the war. Congress also passed legislation to construct the first transcontinental railroad along a north-central route from Omaha to Sacramento. In the Homestead Act of 1862, moreover, Congress voted free farms of 160 acres to settlers who occupied the land for five years before gaining title. The Morrill Land Grant Act of the same year conveyed to each state 30,000 acres of public land per member of Congress from the state, the proceeds from the sale of which went to create colleges of "agriculture and mechanic arts." Such measures helped stimulate the North's economy in the years after the Civil War.

Devastation in the South

The postwar South, where most of the fighting had occurred, offered a sharp contrast to the victorious North. Along the path of General William T. Sherman's army, one observer reported in 1866, the countryside "looked for many miles like a broad black streak of ruin and desolation." The border states of Missouri and Kentucky had experienced a guerrilla war that lapsed into postwar anarchy. Marauding bands of bushwhackers such as the notorious James boys, Frank and Jesse, turned into outlaws.

Throughout the South, property values had collapsed. Confederate war bonds and money were worthless; railroads were damaged or destroyed. Cotton that had escaped destruction was seized as Confederate property or in forfeit of federal taxes. Emancipation of the slaves wiped out perhaps $4 billion of human capital and left the labor system in disarray. The great age of expansion in the cotton market was over. Not until 1879 would the cotton crop again equal the record harvest of 1860; tobacco production did not regain its prewar level until 1880, the sugar crop of Louisiana not until 1893.

According to a former Confederate general, recently freed blacks had "nothing but freedom."

A Transformed South

The defeat of the Confederacy transformed much of southern society. The freeing of slaves, the destruction of property, and the free-fall in land values left many among the former planter elite destitute and homeless. Genteel southerners accustomed to relying on slaves for their every need were unprepared for the tasks at hand. Those who still had some money often recruited former slaves to work as domestic servants. Now, however, they had to pay for the services. "It seems humiliating to be compelled to bargain and haggle with our servants about wages," wrote one exasperated woman.

After the Civil War, many former Confederates were so embittered by defeat and so resistant to the idea of living under northern rule that they abandoned their native region rather than submit to "Yankee rule." Some migrated to Canada, Europe, Mexico, South America, and Asia. Others preferred the western territories and states. Still others moved north, settling in northern and midwestern cities on the assumption that their educational and economic opportunities would be better among the victors.

Legally Free, Socially Bound

In the former Confederate states, the newly freed slaves suffered as well. According to Frederick Douglass, the black abolitionist, the former slave remained dependent: "He had neither money, property, nor friends. He was free from the old plantation, but he had nothing but the dusty road under his feet. . . . He was turned loose, naked, hungry, and destitute to the open sky."

A few northerners argued that what the ex-slaves needed most was their own land. There was talk of giving each freed slave "forty acres and a mule" to provide them with an economic foundation. But even dedicated abolitionists shrank from endorsing measures of land reform that might have given the freed slaves self-support and independence. Citizenship and legal rights were one thing, wholesale confiscation of property owned by whites andland redistribution quite another. Instead of land or material help, the freed slaves more often got advice and moral platitudes.

The Freedmen's Bureau

On March 3, 1865, Congress set up within the War Department the Bureau of Refugees, Freedmen, and Abandoned Lands, to provide "such issues of provisions, clothing, and fuel" as might be needed to relieve "destitute and suffering refugees and freedmen and their wives and children." The Freedmen's Bureau would also take over abandoned or confiscated land, but the amount of such land was limited. Agents of the Freedmen's Bureau were entrusted with negotiating labor contracts (something new for both blacks and planters), providing medical care, and setting up schools.

White intransigence and racial prejudice, however, thwarted the efforts of Freedmen's Bureau agents to protect and assist the former slaves. Congress was not willing to strengthen the powers of the Freedmen's Bureau to deal with such problems. Beyond temporary relief measures, no program of Reconstruction ever incorporated much more than constitutional and legal rights for freedmen. These rights were important in themselves, of course, but the extent to which even these should go was very uncertain, to be settled more by the course of events than by any clear-cut commitment to equality.

The Battle over Reconstruction

The problem of reconstructing the South involved creating new governments in the defeated states. As Federal forces advanced into the Confederacy, Lincoln in 1862 named military governors for Tennessee, Arkansas, and Louisiana. By the end of the following year, he had formulated a plan for regular civilian governments in those states and any others that might be liberated from Confederate rule.

Lincoln's Plan and Congress's Response

Acting under his pardon power, President Lincoln issued late in 1863 a Proclamation of Amnesty and Reconstruction, under which any Rebel state could form a Union government whenever a number of citizens equal to 10 percent of those who had voted in 1860 took an oath of allegiance to the Constitution and to the Union and received a presidential pardon. Participants also had to swear support for laws and proclamations dealing with emancipation. Excluded from the pardon, however, were certain groups: civil, diplomatic, and high military officers of the Confederacy; judges, congressmen, and military officers of the United States who had left their federal posts to aid the rebellion; and those accused of failure to treat captured black soldiers and their officers as prisoners of war.

Under Lincoln's plan, loyal governments appeared in Tennessee, Arkansas, and Louisiana, but Congress refused to recognize them. In the absence of any specific provisions for Reconstruction in the Constitution, politicians disagreed as to where authority properly rested. Lincoln claimed the right to direct Reconstruction under the presidential pardon power, and also under the Constitutional obligation to guarantee each state a republican form of government.

A few conservative and most moderate

Republicans supported Lincoln's program of immediate restoration. A small but influential group known as Radical Republicans, however, demanded a sweeping transformation of southern society that would include making the freed slaves full-fledged citizens. The Radicals hoped to reconstruct southern society so as to mirror the North's emphasis on small-scale capitalism. This meant thwarting the efforts of the old planter class to reestablish a caste system and keep the freed blacks in a state of peonage.

The Radicals maintained that Congress, not the president, should supervise the Reconstruction program. To this end, they helped pass in 1864 the Wade-Davis Bill, sponsored by Senator Benjamin Wade of Ohio and Representative Winter Davis of Maryland. In contrast to Lincoln's 10 percent plan, the Wade-Davis Bill required that a *majority* of white male citizens declare their allegiance. Only those who swore an "ironclad" oath that they had always remained loyal to the Union could vote or serve in the state constitutional conventions. The conventions, moreover, would have to abolish slavery, deny political rights to high-ranking civil and military officers of the Confederacy, and repudiate Confederate war debts. Passed during the closing days of the 1864 session, the Wade-Davis Bill went unsigned by Lincoln, and this "pocket veto" provoked the bill's sponsors to issue the

Glimpses at the Freedmen. The Freedmen's Union Industrial School in Richmond, Virginia, was set up by the War Department in 1865.

Wade-Davis Manifesto, a blistering statement that accused the president of usurping power and attempting to use readmitted states to ensure his reelection.

Lincoln issued his final statement on Reconstruction in his last public address, on April 11, 1865. Speaking from the White House balcony, he dismissed the theoretical question of whether the Confederate states had technically remained in the Union as "good for nothing at all—a mere pernicious abstraction." These states were simply "out of their proper practical relation with the Union," and the object was to get them "into their proper practical relation" as quickly as possible. Lincoln wanted "no persecution, no bloody work," no dramatic restructuring of southern social and economic life.

That evening Lincoln went to Ford's Theater and his rendezvous with death. Shot in the head by John Wilkes Booth, a crazed actor and Confederate zealot, the president died the next morning. Pursued into Virginia, Booth was trapped and shot in a burning barn. Three collaborators were tried and hanged.

Johnson's Plan

Lincoln's death elevated to the White House Vice-President Andrew Johnson of Tennessee, a man whose state remained in legal limbo and whose party affiliation was unclear. He was a War Democrat who had been put on the Union ticket with the Republican Lincoln in 1864 as a gesture of bipartisan unity.

Of humble origins like Lincoln, Johnson had moved as a youth from his birthplace in Raleigh, North Carolina, to Greenville, Tennessee, where he became proprietor of a tailor shop. Over the years he grew prosperous, acquiring several slaves in the process. A bitter critic of the "swaggering" planter aristocracy "who are too lazy and proud to work," Johnson was a fervent populist who promoted free land for the poor, defended slavery, and promoted white supremacy. A notoriously stubborn man, he became a self-righteous, hot-tempered orator who enjoyed

Andrew Johnson (detail).

strong drink and employed abusive language to belittle his opponents. His fiery speeches and firm principles helped him win election as mayor, congressman, governor, and senator.

Like many other whites in mountainous eastern Tennessee, Johnson ardently believed in the Union. In 1861 he was the only southern senator from a Confederate state to vote against secession, leading critics to denounce him as a "traitor" to the region. Yet his devotion to the Union did not include opposition to slavery. He hated the Confederacy because he hated the planter elite. "Damn the Negroes," Johnson bellowed to a friend during the war, "I am fighting those traitorous aristocrats, their masters."

Some of the Radicals at first thought Johnson, unlike Lincoln, was one of them, but his loyalty to the Union sprang from a strict adherence to the Constitution. The Confederate states, Johnson believed, should be brought back into their proper relation to the Union because the states and the Union were indestructible. In 1865 Johnson declared that "there is no such thing as Reconstruction. Those states have not gone out of the Union. Therefore Reconstruction is unnecessary."

Johnson's plan to restore the Union thus closely resembled Lincoln's. A new Proclamation of Amnesty (May 29, 1865) added to the list of those Lincoln had excluded from pardon everybody with taxable property worth more than $20,000. These wealthy planters and merchants were the people Johnson believed had led the South into secession. But those in the excluded groups might make special applications for presidential pardon, and before the year was out Johnson had issued some 13,000 pardons.

In each of the Rebel states not already organized by Lincoln, Johnson named a Unionist provisional governor with authority to call a convention of men elected by loyal voters. Lincoln's 10 percent requirement was omitted. Johnson called upon the conventions to invalidate the secession ordinances, repudiate all debts incurred to aid the Confederacy, and ratify the Thirteenth Amendment, which ended slavery. Like Lincoln, Johnson endorsed limited voting rights for blacks. He reminded the provisional governor of Mississippi, for example, that the state conventions might "with perfect safety" extend suffrage to those blacks with education or with military service so as to "disarm the adversary"—the adversary being "radicals who are wild upon Negro franchise [voting]."

Southern Intransigence

When Congress met in December 1865, for the first time since the end of the war, it faced the fact that new state governments were functioning in the South, according to Johnson's requirements, and they were remarkably like the old. Among the new members presenting themselves to Congress were Georgia's Alexander H. Stephens, late vice-president of the Confederacy, four Confederate generals, eight colonels, six cabinet members, and a host of lesser Rebel officials. The Congress forthwith defied Johnson by denying seats to all members from the eleven former Confederate states. It was too much to expect, after four bloody years, that Unionists would welcome ex-Confederates back like prodigal sons.

Furthermore, the new southern legislatures, in passing repressive "Black Codes" restricting the freedom of blacks, baldly revealed that they intended to preserve the trappings of slavery as nearly as possible. As one southerner stressed, the "ex-slave was not a free man; he was a free Negro."

The details of the Black Codes varied from state to state, but some provisions were common. On the one hand, existing black marriages were recognized (although interracial marriages were prohibited), and testimony by blacks was accepted in legal cases involving them—in six states in all cases. Blacks could own property. They could sue and be sued in the courts. On the other hand, blacks in Mississippi could not own farm lands, and in South Carolina they could not own city lots. Unlike whites, blacks were required to enter into annual labor contracts, with provision for punishment in case of violation. Dependent children were subject to compulsory apprenticeship and corporal punishment by masters. Vagrant blacks were punished with severe fines, and, if unable to pay, they were forced to work in the fields for whites who paid the courts for such cheap labor. To many people, it seemed that slavery was being revived in another guise.

The Radicals

Faced with such evidence of southern intransigence, moderate Republicans drifted more and more toward the Radical camp. The new Congress set up a Joint Committee on Reconstruction, with nine members from the House and six from the Senate, to gather evidence and submit proposals. As a parade of witnesses testified to the Rebels' impenitence, initiative on the committee fell to determined Radicals: Benjamin Wade of Ohio, George W. Julian of Indiana, Henry Wilson of Massachusetts—and most conspicuously of all, Thaddeus Stevens of Pennsylvania and Charles Sumner of Massachusetts.

Stevens, a crusty bachelor with a chiseled face and brooding eyes, was the domineering floor leader in the House. Driven by a genuine, if at times fanatical, idealism, he insisted that the "whole fabric of southern society *must* be changed." Sumner, Stevens's counterpart in the Senate, agreed. He strove to see the South *reconstructed* rather than simply restored. This put him at odds with Johnson. After visiting the White House, Sumner found the president "harsh, petulant, and unreasonable." He was especially disheartened by Johnson's "prejudice, ignorance, and perversity" regarding the treatment of blacks. Sumner and other Radicals resolved to take matters into their own hands. The southern plantations, seedbeds of aristocratic pretension and secession, he declared, "must be broken up, and the freedmen must have the pieces."

Most of these Radical Republicans had long been connected with the antislavery cause, and they approached the question of black rights with a sincere humanitarian impulse. Few, however, could escape the bitterness bred by the long and bloody war or remain unaware of the partisan advantage that would come to the Republican party from "Negro suffrage." But they reasoned that their party, after all, could best guarantee the fruits of victory and that granting suffrage could best secure black rights.

The growing conflict of opinion over Reconstruction policy brought about an inversion in constitutional reasoning. Secessionists—and Johnson—were now arguing that their states had in fact remained in the Union, and some Radicals were contriving arguments that they had left the Union after all. Most congressmen embraced the "forfeited rights theory," which held that the southern states continued to exist, but by the acts of secession and war had forfeited "all civil and political rights under the Constitution." And Congress was the proper authority to determine conditions under which such rights might be restored.

Johnson's Battle with Congress

A long year of political battling remained, however, before this idea triumphed. By the end of 1865, Radical views had gained only a slight majority in Congress, insufficient to override presidential vetoes. But the critical year 1866 saw the gradual waning of Johnson's power and influence, much of this self-induced. Johnson first challenged Congress in February, when he vetoed a bill to extend the life of the Freedmen's Bureau. Since it was no longer valid as a war measure, Johnson believed it violated the Constitution. For the moment, Johnson's prestige remained sufficiently intact that the Senate upheld his veto.

Three days after the veto, however, Johnson undermined his already weakening prestige by launching an intemperate assault on Radical leaders during an impromptu speech on George Washington's Birthday. From that point forward, moderate Republicans backed away from the president, and Radical Republicans went on the offensive.

In mid-March 1866, Congress passed the Civil Rights Act. A direct response to the Black Codes, this bill declared that "all persons born in the United States . . . excluding Indians not taxed," were citizens entitled to "full and equal benefit of all laws." The grant of citizenship to native-born blacks, Johnson claimed, went beyond anything formerly held to be within the scope of federal power. It would, moreover, "foment discord among the races." He vetoed the measure, but this time, in April 1866, Congress overrode the presidential veto. Then in July it enacted a revised Freedmen's Bureau Bill, again overturning a veto. From that point on, Johnson's public and political support steadily eroded.

The Fourteenth Amendment

To remove all doubt about the validity of the new Civil Rights Act, the Joint Committee recommended a new constitutional amendment, which passed Congress in 1866 and was ratified by the states in 1868. The Fourteenth Amendment, however, went far beyond the Civil Rights Act, and it would have significant effects long thereafter. The first section asserted four principles: it reaffirmed state and federal citizenship for all persons—regardless of race—born or naturalized in the United States, and it forbade any *state* to abridge the "privileges and immunities" of citizens; to deprive any *person* of life, liberty, or property without "due process of law"; or to deny any person "the equal protection of the laws."

The last three of these clauses have been the subject of lawsuits resulting in applications not foreseen at the time. The "due-process clause" has come to mean that state as well as federal power is subject to the Bill of Rights, and it has been used to protect corporations, as legal "persons," from "un-reasonable" regulation by the states. Other provisions of the amendment had less far-reaching effects. One section specified that the debt of the United States "shall not be questioned," but it declared "illegal and void" all debts contracted in aid of the re-bellion.

Johnson's home state was among the first to ratify the Fourteenth Amendment. In Tennessee, which had harbored proba-bly more Unionists than any other Confed-erate state, the government had fallen under Radical control. But the rest of the South steadfastly resisted the Radical challenge to Johnson's program. In 1866 bloody race riots in Memphis and New Orleans added fuel to the flames. Both incidents sparked massacres of blacks by local police and white mobs. The rioting, Radicals argued, was the natural fruit of Johnson's foolish policy.

Reconstructing the South

The Triumph of Congressional Reconstruction

As 1866 drew to an end, the upcoming con-gressional elections promised to be a refer-endum on the growing split between John-son and the Radicals. Johnson embarked on a speaking tour of the Midwest, a "swing around the circle," which provoked undig-nified shouting contests between the presi-dent and his audiences. Johnson's tour backfired; when the election returns came in, the Republicans had well over a two-thirds majority in each house, a comfortable margin with which to override any presi-dential vetoes.

The Congress actually enacted a new pro-gram even before new members took office. On March 2, 1867, two days before the old Congress expired, it passed three basic laws of congressional Reconstruction over John-son's vetoes: the Military Reconstruction Act, the Command of the Army Act, and the Tenure of Office Act.

The first of the three acts prescribed con-ditions under which new southern state governments should be formed. The other two sought to block obstruction by the pres-ident. The Command of the Army Act re-quired that all orders from the president as commander-in-chief go through the general of the army, Ulysses S. Grant. The Radicals trusted Grant, who was already leaning their way. The Tenure of Office Act re-quired the consent of the Senate for the president to remove any officeholder whose appointment the Senate had to confirm in the first place. In large measure, it was in-tended to retain Secretary of War Edwin M. Stanton, the one Radical sympathizer in Johnson's cabinet. But an ambiguity crept into the wording of the act. Cabinet offi-cers, it said, should serve during the term of the president who appointed them—and Lincoln had appointed Stanton, although, to be sure, Johnson was serving out Lincoln's term.

The Military Reconstruction Act, often hailed or denounced as the triumphant vic-tory of "Radical" Reconstruction, actually fell short of a thoroughgoing transformation. Originally intended by the Radical Republi-cans to give military commanders in the South ultimate control over law enforce-ment and to leave open indefinitely the terms of future restoration, it was diluted by moderate Republicans, until it boiled down to little more than a requirement that south-ern states accept black suffrage and ratify the Fourteenth Amendment.

Tennessee, which had already ratified the Fourteenth Amendment, was exempted from the act. The other ten southern states were divided into five military districts, and the commanding officer of each was authorized to keep order and protect the "rights of persons and property." The Johnson governments remained intact for the time being, but new constitutions were to be framed "in conformity with the Constitution of the United States," in conventions elected by male citizens twenty-one and older "of whatever race, color, or previous condition." Each state constitution had to provide the same universal male suffrage. Then, once the constitution was ratified by a majority of voters and accepted by Congress, and once the state legislature had ratified the Fourteenth Amendment, and once the amendment became part of the Constitution, any given state would be entitled to representation in Congress. Persons excluded from officeholding by the proposed amendment were also excluded from participation in the process. Before the end of 1867, new elections had been held in all the states but Texas.

Having clipped the president's wings, the Republican Congress moved a year later to safeguard its program from possible interference by the Supreme Court. On March 27, 1868, Congress simply removed the power of the Supreme Court to review cases arising under the Military Reconstruction Act, which Congress clearly had the constitutional right to do under its power to define the Court's appellate jurisdiction. The Court accepted this curtailment of its authority on the same day it affirmed the notion of an "indestructible Union" in *Texas* v. *White* (1868). In that case, it also acknowledged the right of Congress to reframe state governments, thus endorsing the Radical point of view.

The Impeachment and Trial of Johnson (1868)

By 1868, Radical Republicans were convinced that Johnson had to be removed from office. Johnson had continued to pardon

former Confederates and transferred several of the district military commanders who had displayed Radical sympathies. Johnson was revealing himself to be a man of limited ability and narrow vision. He lacked Lincoln's resilience and pragmatism.

The Republicans unsuccessfully tried to impeach Johnson early in 1867, alleging a variety of flimsy charges, none of which represented an indictable crime. But Johnson himself provided the occasion for impeachment when he deliberately violated the Tenure of Office Act in order to test its constitutionality. Secretary of War Edwin Stanton had become a thorn in the president's side, refusing to resign despite his disagreements with Johnson's Reconstruction policy. On August 12, 1867, during a congressional recess, Johnson suspended Stanton and named General Grant in his place. When the Senate refused to confirm Johnson's action, however, Grant returned the office to Stanton.

The Radicals now saw their chance to remove the president, and they were quite explicit about their political purposes. As Charles Sumner declared, "Impeachment is a political proceeding before a political body with a political purpose." The debate in the House was clamorous and vicious. One congressman denounced the president as "an ungrateful, despicable, besotted traitorous man—an incubus." On February 24, 1868, the House passed eleven articles of impeachment by a party-line vote of 126 to 47.

Of the eleven articles of impeachment, eight focused on the charge that Johnson had unlawfully removed Stanton and had failed to give the Senate the name of a successor. Article 9 accused the president of issuing orders in violation of the Command of the Army Act. The last two articles in effect charged him with criticizing Congress by "inflammatory and scandalous harangues." Article 11 also accused Johnson of "unlawfully devising and contriving" to violate the

Reconstruction Acts, contrary to his obligation to execute the laws. At the very least, it stated, Johnson had tried to obstruct Congress's will while observing the letter of the law.

The Senate trial began on March 5, 1868, and continued until May 26, with Chief Justice Salmon P. Chase presiding. It was a great spectacle before a packed gallery. However, as the weeks passed, the trial grew tedious. Senators slept during the proceedings, spectators passed out in the unventilated room, and poor acoustics prompted repeated cries of "We can't hear." Debate eventually focused on Stanton's removal, the most substantive impeachment charge. Johnson's lawyers argued that Lincoln, not Johnson, had appointed Stanton, so the Tenure of Office Act did not apply to him. At the same time, they claimed (correctly, as it turned out) that the law was unconstitutional.

When the five-week trial ended and the voting began in May 1868, seven moderate Republicans and all twelve Democrats voted to acquit. The final tally was 35 to 19 for conviction, one vote short of the two-thirds needed for removal from office. The renegade Republicans offered two primary reasons for their controversial votes: they feared damage to the separation of powers among the branches of government if Johnson were removed, and they were assured by Johnson's attorneys that he would stop obstructing congressional policy in the South.

Although the Senate failed to remove Johnson, the trial crippled his already weak presidency. During the remaining ten months of his term, he initiated no other clashes with Congress. In 1868 Johnson sought the Democratic presidential nomination but lost to New York governor Horatio Seymour, who then lost to Republican Ulysses Grant in the general election. A bitter Johnson refused to attend Grant's inauguration. His final act as president was to

The Senate transformed into a court of impeachment for the trial of Andrew Johnson.

issue a pardon to former Confederate president Jefferson Davis.

Impeachment of Johnson was in the end a great political mistake, for the failure to remove the president damaged Radical morale and support. Nevertheless, the Radical cause did gain something. To blunt the opposition, Johnson agreed not to obstruct the process of Reconstruction, and thereafter Radical Reconstruction began in earnest.

Radical Republican Rule in the South

In June 1868 Congress agreed that seven states had met its conditions for readmission, all but Virginia, Mississippi, and Texas. Congress rescinded Georgia's admission, however, when the state legislature expelled twenty-eight black members and seated some former Confederate leaders. The military commander of Georgia then forced the legislature to reseat the black members and remove the Confederates, and the state was compelled to ratify the Fifteenth Amendment before being readmitted in July 1870. Virginia, Mississippi, and Texas had returned earlier in 1870, under the added requirement that they too ratify the Fifteenth Amendment. This amendment, ratified in 1870, forbade the states to deny any citizen the right to vote on grounds of race, color, or previous condition of servitude.

Long before the new governments were established, partisan Republican groups began to spring up in the South, promoted by the Union League, an organization founded in 1862 to rally support for the federal government. Its representatives enrolled blacks and loyal whites as members, initiated them into the secrets and rituals of the order, and instructed them "in their rights and duties." These Union Leagues became a powerful source of Republican political strength in the South and as a result drew the ire of unreconstructed whites.

The Reconstructed South

The Freed Slaves

To focus solely on what white Republicans did to reconstruct the defeated South creates the false impression that the freed slaves were simply pawns in the hands of others. In fact, however, southern blacks were active agents in affecting the course of Reconstruction activities. Although many of them found themselves liberated but destitute after the fighting ended, and often widely separated from family members, the mere promise of freedom raised their hopes about achieving a biracial democracy, equal justice, and economic opportunity.

Participation in the Union army or navy gave many freedmen a training ground in leadership. Black military veterans would form the core of the first generation of African-American political leaders in the postwar South. Military service provided many former slaves with the first opportunities to learn to read and write. Army

life also alerted them to alternative social choices and to new opportunities for advancement and respectability.

Former slaves established independent black churches after the war, churches that would serve as the foundation of African-American community life. Blacks preferred Baptist churches over other denominations, in part because of their decentralized structure that allowed each congregation to worship in its own way. By 1890, there were over 1.3 million black Baptists in the South, nearly three times as many as any other black denomination.

As for making a living, the freed slaves had little money or technical training and were thus faced with the prospect of becoming wage laborers to support themselves. To avoid this and to retain as much autonomy as possible over their productive energies and those of their children on both a daily and seasonal basis, many former slaves chose to become sharecroppers. This meant that they were tenant farmers who gained access to separate plots of land owned by whites in exchange for a share of their crop. In payment for the use of the land and cabin, and sometimes even for use of the tools, seed, and fertilizer needed to farm the land, they gave between one-half and two-thirds of the harvested crops to the white landowners. This gave them higher status than they would have had as wage laborers; it gave them the freedom to set their own hours and work as much or as little as they pleased; and it enabled mothers and wives to devote more of their time to domestic needs while still contributing to family income.

Blacks in Southern Politics

The new role of blacks in politics caused the most controversy, then and afterward. Several hundred black delegates participated in the statewide political conventions. Most had been selected by local political meetings or by churches, fraternal societies,

Union Leagues, and black federal army units, although a few simply appointed themselves.

By 1867, former slaves began to gain political influence and to vote in large numbers, and this revealed emerging tensions within the black community. Some southern blacks resented the presence of northern brethren who moved south after the war, while others complained that few ex-slaves were represented in leadership positions. Northern blacks and the southern free black elite, most of whom were urban dwellers, tended to oppose efforts to confiscate and redistribute land to the rural freedmen, and many insisted that political equality did not mean social equality. In general, however, unity rather than dissension prevailed, and blacks focused on common concerns such as full equality under the law.

Brought suddenly into politics in times that tried the most skilled of statesmen, many blacks served with distinction during so-called Radical Reconstruction. Nonetheless, the derisive label "black Reconstruction" used by later critics exaggerates black political influence, which was limited mainly to voting, and overlooks the large numbers of white Republicans, especially in the mountain areas of the upper South. Only one of the new state conventions, South Carolina's, had a black majority, 76 to 41. Louisiana's was evenly divided racially, and in only two other conventions were more than 20 percent of the members black: Florida's, with 40 percent, and Virginia's, with 24 percent.

In the new state governments, any black participation was a novelty. Although some 600 blacks served as state legislators, no black was elected governor and few served as judges. In Louisiana, however, Pinckney B. S. Pinchback, a northern black and former Union soldier, won the office of lieutenant-governor and served as acting governor when the white governor was indicted for corruption. Several blacks were elected lieutenant-governors, state treasurers, or secretaries of state. There were two black senators in Congress, Hiram Revels and Blanche K. Bruce, both from Mississippi, and fourteen black members of the House during Reconstruction. Among these were some of the ablest congressmen of the time.

Carpetbaggers and Scalawags

The top positions in southern state governments went for the most part to white Republicans, whom the opposition soon labeled "carpetbaggers" and "scalawags," depending on their place of birth. Northern opportunists who allegedly came south with all their belongings in carpetbags to reap political spoils were more often than not Union veterans who had arrived as early as 1865 or 1866, drawn south by the hope of economic opportunity. Others were lawyers, businessmen, editors, teachers, social workers, or preachers who came on missionary endeavors.

The "scalawags," or southern white Republicans, were even more reviled and misrepresented. Most "scalawags" had opposed secession, forming a Unionist majority in many mountain counties as far south as Georgia and Alabama, and especially in the hills of eastern Tennessee. Though many were indeed crass opportunists who indulged in corruption at the public's expense, several were quite distinguished figures. They included former Confederate general James A. Longstreet, who decided after Appomattox that the Old South must change its ways. To that end, he became a successful cotton broker in New Orleans, joined the Republican party, and supported the Radical Reconstruction program.

A freedman casts his vote in 1867. Although the Fifteenth Amendment was not passed until 1870, former slaves had been registering and voting in state elections since 1867.

The Radical Republican Record

Former Confederates resented carpetbaggers and scalawags, and they also objected to the new state constitutions, primarily because of their provisions for black suffrage and civil rights. Nonetheless, most of the state constitutions remained in effect for some years after the end of Radical control, and later constitutions incorporated many of their features. Conspicuous among Radical innovations were steps toward greater democracy such as requiring universal manhood suffrage, reapportioning legislatures more nearly according to population, and making more state offices elective.

Given the hostile circumstances in which the Radical governments arose and operated, their achievements were remarkable. In most of the South, they established the first state school systems. Some 600,000 black pupils were in schools by 1877. State governments under the Radicals also gave more attention to orphanages, asylums, and institutions for the disabled of both races. Public roads, bridges, and buildings were repaired or rebuilt. Blacks achieved new rights and opportunities that would never again be taken away, at least in principle: equality before the law, and the right to own property, carry on business, enter professions, attend schools, and learn to read and write.

Yet several of these Republican regimes also practiced systematic corruption. Public money and public credit were often voted to privately owned corporations, notably railroads, under conditions that invited influence peddling. Bids for contracts were accepted at absurd prices, and some public officials took their cut. Taxes and public debt rose in every state. Still, corruption was not invented by the Radical regimes, nor did it die with them. In Mississippi, the Republican governments of Reconstruction were quite honest compared to their Democratic successors.

White Terror

The case of Mississippi suggests that whites were hostile to Republican regimes less because of their corruption than because of their inclusion of blacks. Most white southerners remained unreconstructed, so conditioned by slavery that they were unable to conceive of blacks as citizens or even free agents. In some places, hostility to the new regimes took the form of white terror. Efforts to oust Republican rule focused largely on violence.

The prototype of terrorist groups was the Ku Klux Klan (KKK), first organized in 1866 by some young men of Pulaski, Tennessee, as a social club with the costumes, secret ritual, and mumbo-jumbo common to fraternal groups. At first a group of pranksters, they soon began to intimidate blacks and white Republicans, and the KKK spread rapidly across the South in answer to the Republican party's Union League. Klansmen rode about the countryside hiding under masks

(*Left*) This Thomas Nast cartoon accuses the Ku Klux Klan and the White League of promoting conditions "worse than slavery" for southern blacks after the Civil War. (*Right*) Alabama Klansmen, 1868.

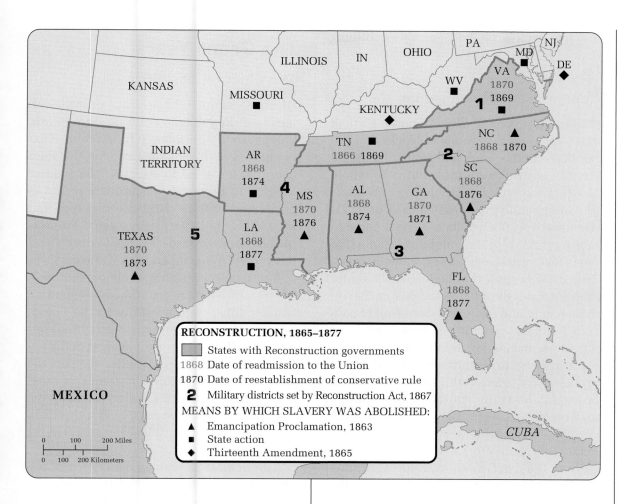

RECONSTRUCTION, 1865–1877

      States with Reconstruction governments
1868 Date of readmission to the Union
1870 Date of reestablishment of conservative rule
2 Military districts set by Reconstruction Act, 1867
MEANS BY WHICH SLAVERY WAS ABOLISHED:
▲ Emancipation Proclamation, 1863
■ State action
♦ Thirteenth Amendment, 1865

and robes, spreading horrendous rumors, harassing blacks, and wreaking violence and destruction.

In Mississippi, Klansmen mutilated a black Republican leader in front of his family. Three white "scalawag" Republicans were murdered in Georgia in 1870. That same year, an armed mob of whites disrupted a Republican political rally in Alabama, killing four blacks and wounding fifty-four. In South Carolina the Klan was especially active. Virtually the entire white male population of York County joined the Klan, and they were responsible for eleven murders and hundreds of whippings. In 1871 some 500 masked men laid siege to the Union County jail and eventually lynched eight black prisoners. Although most Klansmen were poor farmers and tradesmen, middle-class whites—planters, merchants, bankers, lawyers, doctors, even ministers—also joined the group and participated in its brutalities.

Congress responded to such racial terrorism with three Enforcement Acts (1870–1871) to protect black voters. The first of these measures levied penalties on persons who interfered with any citizen's right to vote. A second placed the election of congressmen under surveillance by federal election supervisors and marshals. The third (the Ku Klux Klan Act) outlawed the characteristic activities of the Klan—forming conspiracies, wearing disguises, resisting officers, and intimidating officials. The program of federal enforcement broke the back of the Klan, whose activities declined steadily as recalcitrant southerners resorted to more subtle methods of racial intimidation.

Conservative Resurgence

Perhaps the Klan's most important effect was to weaken the morale of blacks and Republicans in the South and strengthen in the North a growing weariness with the whole "southern question." Republican control in the South gradually loosened as "Conservative" parties—Democrats used that name to mollify former Whigs—mobilized the white vote. Scalawags, and many carpetbaggers, drifted away from the Radical ranks under pressure from their white neighbors. Few of them had joined the Republicans out of concern for black rights in the first place. And where persuasion failed to work, Democrats were willing to manipulate the electoral process. As one enthusiastic Democrat boasted, "the white and black Republicans may outvote us, but we can outcount them."

Such factors led to the collapse of Republican control in Virginia and Tennessee as early as 1869, in Georgia and North Carolina in 1870. Reconstruction lasted longest in the Deep South states with the heaviest black population, where whites abandoned Klan hoods for barefaced intimidation in paramilitary groups like the Mississippi Rifle Club and the South Carolina Red Shirts. By 1876, Radical regimes survived only in Louisiana, South Carolina, and Florida, but these all collapsed after the elections of that year.

The erosion of northern interest in promoting civil rights in the postwar South reflected both weariness with Reconstruction as well as interest in other activities. Western expansion, Indian wars, economic development, and political debates over the tariff and currency distracted attention from southern outrages. In addition, a business panic that occurred in 1873 led to a sharp depression and created both social problems and new racial tensions in the North and the South.

The Grant Years

The Election of 1868

Ulysses S. Grant, who presided over the collapse of Republican rule in the South, brought to the presidency little political experience. But in 1868 the rank-and-file voter could be expected to support "the Lion of Vicksburg" because of his brilliant record as a war leader. Both parties wooed him, but his falling-out with President Johnson pushed him toward the Republicans and built trust in him among the Radicals.

The Republican platform endorsed Radical Reconstruction, cautiously defending black suffrage as a necessity in the South, but a matter each northern state should settle for itself. It also urged payment of the nation's war debt in gold rather than in the new "greenback" paper currency printed during the war. More important than the platform were the great expectations of a soldier-president and his slogan: "Let us have peace."

The Democrats took an opposite position on both Reconstruction and the debt. The Republican Congress, the platform charged, had "subjected ten states, in the time of profound peace, to military despotism and Negro supremacy." As to the public debt, the party endorsed Representative George H. Pendleton's "Ohio idea" that, since most bonds had been bought with depreciated greenbacks, they should be paid off in greenbacks unless they specified payment in gold. With no conspicuously available candidate in sight, the convention turned to Horatio Seymour, war governor of New York and chairman of the convention. The Democrats made a closer race than expected, attesting to the strength of traditional party loyalties. While Grant swept the electoral college by 214 to 80, his popular majority was only 307,000 out of a total of over 5.7 million votes. More than 500,000 black voters accounted for Grant's margin of victory.

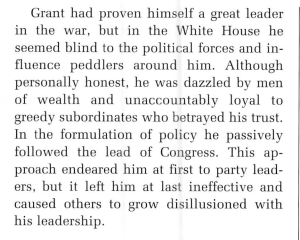

Grant had proven himself a great leader in the war, but in the White House he seemed blind to the political forces and influence peddlers around him. Although personally honest, he was dazzled by men of wealth and unaccountably loyal to greedy subordinates who betrayed his trust. In the formulation of policy he passively followed the lead of Congress. This approach endeared him at first to party leaders, but it left him at last ineffective and caused others to grow disillusioned with his leadership.

The Government Debt

Financial issues dominated the political agenda during Grant's presidency. After the war, the Treasury had assumed that the $432 million worth of greenbacks issued during the conflict would be retired from circulation and that the nation would revert to a "hard-money" currency—gold coins. Congress in 1866 granted the Treasury discretion to redeem the paper money gradually. Many agrarian and debtor groups resisted this contraction of the money supply, believing that it would mean lower crop prices and harder-to-pay debts. In 1868 "soft money" supporters in Congress halted the retirement of greenbacks, leaving $356 million outstanding. There matters stood when Grant took office.

The "sound" or "hard" money advocates, mostly bankers, merchants, and other creditors, claimed that Grant's election was a mandate to save the country from the Democrats' "Ohio idea" of using greenbacks to repay government bonds. Quite influential in Republican circles, the "sound-money" advocates also had the benefit of a deeply ingrained popular assumption that hard money was morally preferable to paper currency. Grant agreed, and in his inaugural address he endorsed payment of the national debt in gold as a point of national honor.

Scandals

Within less than a year of his election, Grant fell into a cesspool of scandal. In the summer of 1869 two young railroad entrepreneurs, Jay Gould and Jim Fisk, connived with the president's brother-in-law to corner the gold market. Gould concocted an argument that the government should refrain from selling gold on the market because the resulting rise in gold prices would raise temporarily depressed farm prices. Grant apparently smelled a rat from the start, but he was seen in public with the speculators. As the rumor spread on Wall Street, gold prices rose sharply. Finally, on "Black Friday," September 24, 1869, Grant ordered the Treasury to sell a large quantity of gold, and the bubble burst. Fisk got out by repudiating his agreements and hiring thugs to intimidate his creditors.

The plot to corner the gold market was only the first of several scandals that rocked the Grant administration. In 1872 the public first learned about the financial buccaneering of the Crédit Mobilier, a construction company that had milked the Union Pacific Railroad for exorbitant fees to line the pockets of insiders who controlled both firms. Rank-and-file Union Pacific shareholders were left holding the bag. This chicanery

The People's Handwriting on the Wall. An 1872 engraving comments on the corruption engulfing Grant.

had transpired before Grant's election in 1868, but it now touched a number of prominent Republican congressmen who had been given shares of Crédit Mobilier stock in exchange for favorable votes. Of thirteen congressmen involved, only two were censured.

Even more odious disclosures followed, and some involved the president's cabinet. Grant's secretary of war, it turned out, had accepted bribes from merchants who traded with Indians at army posts in the West. He was impeached, but he resigned in time to elude trial. Postoffice contracts, it was revealed, went to carriers who offered the highest kickbacks to government officials. In St. Louis a "Whiskey Ring" bribed tax collectors to bilk the government of millions in revenue. Grant's private secretary was enmeshed in that scheme, taking large sums of money and other valuables in return for inside information. There is no evidence that Grant himself participated in any of the fraud, but his poor choice of associates earned him widespread censure.

Reform and the Election of 1872

Long before Grant's first term ended, Republicans broke ranks with the president. Their alienation was a reaction against the Radical Reconstruction measures and the incompetence and corruption in the administration. The so-called Liberal Republicans favored free trade, gold to redeem greenbacks, a stable currency, the restoration of the rights of former Confederates, and civil service reform. Open revolt broke out first in Missouri, where Carl Schurz, a German immigrant and war hero, led a group of Liberal Republicans that, with Democratic help, elected a governor in 1870 and sent Schurz to the Senate.

In 1872 the Liberal Republicans held a clamorous national convention that produced a compromise platform condemning the Republican party's "vindictive" southern policy and favoring civil service reform, but which remained silent on the protective tariff.

The delegates stampeded toward an anomalous presidential candidate: Horace Greeley, editor of the *New York Tribune*, traditionally a strong protectionist and enthusiastic reformer. During his long journalistic career, Greeley had promoted vegetarianism, brown bread, free-thinking, socialism, and spiritualism. His image as a visionary eccentric was complemented by his open hostility to Democrats, whose support the Liberals needed. The Democrats swallowed their reservations and gave their nomination to Greeley as the only hope of beating Grant and the Radical Republicans. Greeley's promise to end Radical Reconstruction and restore "self government" to the South won over Democrats who otherwise despised the man and his beliefs.

The 1872 election result surprised no one. Republican regulars duly endorsed Radical Reconstruction and the protective tariff. Grant still had seven carpetbag states in his pocket, generous support from business and banking interests, and the stalwart support of the Radicals. Above all he still evoked the glory of Vicksburg and Appomattox. Greeley, despite an exhausting tour of the country—still unusual for a presidential candidate—carried only six southern and border states and none in the North. Devastated by his crushing defeat and the simultaneous death of his wife, Greeley entered a mental sanitarium and died three weeks later.

Panic and Redemption

A paralyzing economic panic followed closely upon the public scandals besetting the Grant administration. Contraction of the money supply brought about by the Treasury's postwar withdrawal of greenbacks and the reckless overexpansion of the railroads helped precipitate a financial crisis.

During 1873 some twenty-five strapped railroads defaulted on their interest payments. Caught short, the prominent investment firm of Jay Cooke and Company went bankrupt on September 18, 1873. A financial panic in Vienna forced many financiers to unload American stocks and bonds. The ensuing stampede of selling forced the stock market to close for ten days. The Panic of 1873 set off a depression that lasted for six years. It was the longest and most severe that Americans had yet suffered, marked by widespread bankruptcies, chronic unemployment, and a drastic slowdown in railroad building.

The hard times and corruption hurt Republicans in the midterm elections of 1874, allowing the Democrats to win control of the House of Representatives and gain seats in the Senate. The new Democratic House immediately launched inquiries into the Grant scandals and unearthed further evidence of corruption in high places. The panic meanwhile focused attention once more on greenback currency. Since greenbacks were valued less than gold, most people spent greenbacks first and held their gold or used it to settle foreign accounts, which drained much gold out of the country. To relieve this deflationary spiral and stimulate business, therefore, the Treasury reissued $26 million in greenbacks previously withdrawn.

For a time, the advocates of paper money were riding high. But Grant vetoed an attempt to issue more greenbacks in 1874, and in his annual message he called for their gradual withdrawal and the resumption of payments of gold for greenbacks. Congress obliged the president by passing the Resumption Act of 1875. The resumption of paying gold to customers who turned in their greenbacks began on January 1, 1879, after the Treasury had built a gold reserve for that purpose and reduced the value of greenbacks in circulation. This act infuriated those promoting an inflationary monetary policy and provoked the formation of the National Greenback party. The much debated "money question" would remain one of the most divisive issues in American politics until the end of the century.

The Compromise of 1877

Grant yearned to run for president again in 1876, but the recent scandals precluded any challenge to the tradition of presidents serving no more than two terms. James G. Blaine of Maine, former Speaker of the House, emerged as the Republican front-runner, but he too bore the taint of scandal. Letters in the possession of James Mulligan of Boston linked Blaine to some dubious railroad dealings. Newspapers soon published these "Mulligan Letters," and Blaine's candidacy was dealt a body blow.

The Republican convention therefore eliminated Blaine and several other hopefuls in favor of Ohio's favorite son, Rutherford B. Hayes. Three times governor of Ohio and an advocate of hard money, Hayes had a sterling character and had been a civil service reformer. But his chief virtue, as Henry Adams put it, was "that he is obnoxious to no one."

The Democratic convention was abnormally harmonious from the start. The nomination went on the second ballot to Samuel J. Tilden, corporation lawyer and reform governor of New York, who had directed a campaign to overthrow first the corrupt Tweed Ring that controlled New York City politics and then the Canal Ring in Albany that had bilked New York State of millions.

The campaign generated no burning issues, and early election returns pointed to a Tilden victory. Tilden had a 300,000 edge in the popular vote and had 184 electoral votes, just one short of a majority. Hayes had 165 electoral votes, but Republicans also claimed 19 disputed electoral votes from Florida, Louisiana, and South Carolina. The Democrats laid a counterclaim to 1 of Oregon's 3 votes. The Republicans had clearly carried Oregon, but the outcome in the South was less certain, and given the fraud and intimidation perpetrated on both sides, nobody will ever know the truth of the matter. In all three of the disputed southern states, rival canvassing boards sent in different returns. The Constitution offered no guidance in this unprecedented situation.

The impasse dragged on for months, and there was even talk of public violence. Finally, on January 29, 1877, Congress set up a special Electoral Commission. It had fifteen members, five each from the House, the Senate, and the Supreme Court. The decision on each disputed state went by a vote of 8 to 7 along party lines, in favor of Hayes. After much bluster and threat of filibuster by Democrats, the House voted on March 2 to declare Hayes elected by an electoral vote of 185 to 184.

Critical to this outcome was the defection of southern Democrats who had made several informal agreements with the Republicans. On February 26, 1877, a secret bargain was struck at the Wormley House, a Washington hotel, between prominent Ohio Republicans (including James A. Garfield) and powerful southern Democrats. The Republicans promised that, if elected, Hayes would withdraw federal troops from Louisiana and South Carolina, letting the Republican governments there collapse. In return, the Democrats pledged to withdraw their opposition to Hayes, and to accept in good faith the Thirteenth, Fourteenth, and Fifteenth Amendments.

Southern Democrats could now justify deserting Tilden. This so-called Compromise of 1877 brought a final "redemption" from the "Radicals" and a return to "home rule" in the South, which actually meant rule by native white Democrats. Other, more informal promises bolstered the secret agreement. Hayes's friends pledged more

support for Mississippi River levees and other internal improvements, including a federal subsidy for a transcontinental railroad along a southern route. Southerners extracted a further promise that Hayes would name a white southerner as postmaster-general, the cabinet position with the most patronage jobs at hand. In return, southerners would let Republicans make James Garfield Speaker of the new House. Such a deal illustrates the relative weakness of the presidency compared to Congress during the period.

The End of Reconstruction

In 1877 Hayes withdrew federal troops from the state houses in Louisiana and South Carolina, and the Republican governments there soon collapsed—along with much of Hayes's claim to legitimacy. Hayes chose a Tennessean as postmaster-general. But after southern Democrats failed to permit the choice of Garfield as Speaker, Hayes expressed doubt about any further subsidy for southern railroad building, and none was voted. Most of the other Wormley House promises were either renounced or forgotten.

As to southern promises regarding the civil rights of blacks, only a few Democratic leaders remembered them for long. Over the next three decades, those rights crumbled under the pressure of white rule in the South and the force of Supreme Court decisions narrowing the application of the Fourteenth and Fifteenth Amendments. Radical Reconstruction never offered more than an uncertain commitment to racial equality before the law. Yet it left an enduring legacy, the Thirteenth, Fourteenth, and Fifteenth Amendments—not dead but dormant, waiting to be revived. If Reconstruction did not provide social equality or substantial economic opportunities for blacks, it did create the opportunity for future transformation.

Further Reading

Chapter 1

A fascinating study of Pre-Columbian migration is Brian M. Fagan's *The Great Journey: The Peopling of Ancient America* (1987). Alice B. Kehoe's *North American Indians: A Comprehensive Account* (1992) provides an encyclopedic treatment of Native Americans. An evocative portrait of the Aztecs can be found in Michael E. Smith's *The Aztecs* (1997). An excellent introduction to the prehistory of the American Southwest, its people, and archaeology is Stephen Plog's *Ancient Peoples of the American Southwest* (1997).

The most comprehensive overviews of European exploration are two volumes by Samuel E. Morison, *The European Discovery of America: The Northern Voyages, A.D. 500–1600* (1971), and *The Southern Voyages, 1492–1616* (1974). David B. Quinn's *North America from Earliest Discovery to First Settlements* (1977) is also useful. A good outline of the forces of exploration is John H. Parry's *The Age of Renaissance* (1963).

The voyages of Columbus are surveyed in William D. Phillips, Jr., and Carla Rahn Phillips's *The Worlds of Christopher Columbus* (1992). David J. Weber examines Spanish colonization in *The Spanish Frontier in North America* (1993). For the French experience, see William J. Eccles's *France in America* (1972).

Bernard Bailyn's multivolume work *The Peopling of British North America,* the first two volumes of which have appeared (*The Peopling of British North America: An Introduction,* 1986, and *Voyagers to the West: A Passage in the Peopling of America on the Eve of the Revolution,* 1986), provides a comprehensive view of European migration. Carl Bridenbaugh's *Vexed and Troubled Englishmen, 1590–1642* (1968) helps explain why so many sought a new home in a strange land. English constitutional traditions and their effect on the colonists are examined in Edmund S. Morgan's *Inventing the People: The Rise of Popular Sovereignty in England and America* (1988). Jack P. Greene provides a brilliant synthesis of British colonization in *Pursuits of Happiness: The Social Development of Early Modern British Colonies and the Formation of American Culture* (1988). Carl Bridenbaugh's *Jamestown, 1544–1699* (1980) traces the English experience on the Chesapeake. Alfred W. Crosby's *Ecological Imperialism: The Biological Expansion of Europe, 900–1900* (1986) explores the ecological effects of European settlement.

Daniel K. Richter's *The Ordeal of the Longhouse: The Peoples of the Iroquois League in The Era of European Colonization* (1992) provides a history of the northeastern Iroquois Nation. The conflict between Native Americans and Europeans is treated well in James Axtell's *The Invasion Within: The Contest of Cultures in Colonial North America* (1986) and *Beyond 1492: Encounters in Colonial North America* (1992). Karen O. Kupperman's *Settling with the Indians: The Meeting of English and Indian Cultures in America, 1580–1640* (1980) stresses the racist nature of the conflict. Alfred A. Cave's *The Pequot War* (1996) and Jill Lepore's *The Name of War: King Philip's War and the Origins of American Identity* describe the conditions leading to war between settlers and Indians. An excellent description of the go-betweens who for a time helped to maintain peace between settlers and Indians along the Pennsylvania frontier is provided by James Merrell's *Into the American Woods: Negotiators on the Pennsylvania Frontier* (1999).

A succinct overview on Puritanism can be found in Alan Simpson's *Puritanism in Old and New England* (1955). Andrew Delbanco's *The Puritan Ordeal* (1989) is a powerful study of the tensions inherent in the Puritan outlook. Useful works on the problem of dissent in a theocracy include Edmund S. Morgan's *Roger Williams, the Church, and the State* (1967) and Emery Battis's *Saints and Sectaries: Anne Hutchinson and the Antinomian Controversy in Massachusetts Bay Colony* (1962).

The pattern of settlement in the middle colonies is illuminated in Barry Levy's *Quakers and the American Family: British Settlement in the Delaware Valley* (1988). Randall Balmer's *A Perfect Babel of Confusion: Dutch Religion and English Culture in the Middle Colonies* (1989) describes how the English conquest of New Netherlands intensified the cultural complexity of the middle colonies. The influence of Quakers can be studied through Gary B. Nash's *Quakers and Politics: Pennsylvania, 1681–1726* (1968).

Settlement of the areas along the South Atlantic is traced in Wesley F. Craven's *The Southern Colonies in the Seventeenth Century, 1607–1689* (1949) and Clarence L. Ver Steeg's *Origins of a Southern Mosaic* (1975). Robert M. Weir's *Colonial South Carolina* (1983) covers the activities of the Lords Proprietors. For a study of race and the settlement of South Carolina, see Peter Wood's *Black Majority: Negroes in Colonial South Carolina from 1670 through the Stono Rebellion* (1975). Those interested in the colonization of Georgia should consult *Oglethorpe in Perspective: Georgia's Founder after Two Hundred Years* (1989), edited by Phinizy Spalding and Harvey H. Jackson. A brilliant book on relations between the Catawba Indians and their black and white neighbors is James H. Merrell's *The Indians' New World: Catawbas and Their Neighbors from European Contact through the Era of Removal* (1989).

Chapter 2

The diversity of colonial societies may be seen in David Hackett Fischer's *Albion's Seed: Four British Folkways in America* (1989). Timothy H. Breen's *Puritans and Adventurers: Change and Persistence in Early America* (1980) describes early settlement patterns, especially in Virginia and Massachusetts. Gary B. Nash examines early race relations in *Red, White, and Black* (2nd ed., 1982) and the growth of seaports in *The Urban Crucible* (1979). David Hall's *Worlds of Wonder, Days of Judgment* (1979) describes New Englanders' religious experiences and beliefs. Other useful works include Richard F. Hofstadter's *America at 1750: A Social Portrait* (1971), and James A. Henretta's *The Evolution of American Society, 1700–1815* (1973). Also see Jack P. Greene's *Imperatives, Behaviors, and Identities: Essays in Early American Cultural History* (1992).

Until recently, Puritan communities received the bulk of scholarly attention. Studies of the New England town include Darrett B. Rutman's *Winthrop's Boston: Portrait of a Puritan Town, 1630–1649* (1965) and Kenneth A. Lockridge's *A New England Town: The First One Hundred Years* (2nd ed., 1985). John Frederick Martin's *Profits in the Wilderness: Entrepreneurship and the Founding of New England Towns in the Seventeenth Century* (1991) indicates that economic concerns rather than spiritual motives were driving forces in many New England towns.

Paul S. Boyer and Stephen Nissenbaum's *Salem Possessed* (1974) connects the notorious witch trials to changes in community structure. For an interdisciplinary approach, see John Demos's *Entertaining Satan: Witchcraft and the Culture of Early New England* (1982). Bernard Rosenthal challenges many myths concerning the Salem witch trials in *Salem Story: Reading the Witch Trials of 1692* (1993).

Of the more recent works dealing with New England society, see Janice Knight's *Orthodoxies in Massachusetts: Rereading American Puritanism* (1994), and Stephen Innes's *Creating the Commonwealth: The Economic Culture of Puritan New England* (1995).

Discussions of women in the New England colonies can be found in Laurel Ulrich's *Good Wives: Image and Reality in the Lives of Women in Northern New England, 1650–1750* (1982), Joy Buel and Richard Buel, Jr.'s *The Way of Duty* (1984), and Carol Karlsen's *The Devil in the Shape of a Woman: Witchcraft in Colonial New England* (1987). John Demos describes family life in *A Little Commonwealth: Family Life in Plymouth Colony* (1970).

For the social history of the southern colonies, see Allan Kulikoff's *Tobacco and Slaves: The Development of Southern Cultures in the Chesapeake, 1680–1800* (1986) and *Colonial Chesapeake Society* (1988), edited by Lois Green Carr. Family life along the Chesapeake is described in Gloria L. Main's *Tobacco Colony* (1982) and Daniel B. Smith's *Inside the Great House: Planter Family Life in Eighteenth-Century Chesapeake Society* (1980).

Edmund S. Morgan's *American Slavery, American Freedom: The Ordeal of Colonial Virginia* (1975) examines Virginia's social structure, environment, and labor patterns in a biracial context. More specific on the racial nature of the origins of slavery are Winthrop D. Jordan's *White over Black: American Attitudes toward the Negro* (1968) and David B. Davis's *The Problem of Slavery in Western Culture* (1986). Philip D. Curtin's *The Atlantic Slave Trade* (1969) is a valuable quantitative study. On the interaction of the cultures of blacks and whites, see Mechal Sobel's *The World They Made Together: Black and White Values in Eighteenth Century Virginia* (1987). Black viewpoints are presented in Timothy H. Breen and Stephen Innes's *"Myne Owne Ground": Race and Freedom on Virginia's Eastern Shore, 1640–1676* (1980). David W. Galenson's *White Servitude in Colonial America* (1981) looks at the indentured labor force.

Henry F. May's *The Enlightenment in America* (1976) examines intellectual trends in eighteenth-century America. Lawrence A. Cremin's *American Education: The Colonial Experience, 1607–1783* (1970) surveys educational developments.

On the Great Awakening, see Edwin S. Gaustad's *The Great Awakening in New England* (1957), Patricia U. Bonomi's *Under the Cope of Heaven: Religion, Society, and Politics in Colonial America* (1986), and Timothy D. Hall's *Contested Boundaries: Itinerancy and the Reshaping of the Colonial Religious World* (1994). The political impact of the new religious enthusiasm is shown in Rhys Issac's *The Transformation of Virginia, 1740–1790* (1982). Patricia J. Tracy's *Jonathan Edwards, Pastor* (1980) stresses the Northampton minister's relations to his community.

Chapter 3

The economics motivating colonial policies are covered in John J. McCusker and Russell R. Menard's *The Economy of British America, 1607–1789* (rev. ed., 1991). The problems of colonial customs administration are explored in Micheal Kammen's *Empire and Interest: The American Colonies and the Politics of Mercantilism* (1970).

Jack P. Greene's *The Quest for Power: The Lower Houses of Assembly in the Southern Royal Colonies, 1689–1776* (1963) describes the politics of the southern colonies, and Richard P. Johnson's *Adjustment to Empire* (1981) examines New England. The Andros crisis and related topics are treated in Jack M. Sosin's *English America and the Revolution of 1688* (1982). Stephen S. Webb's *The Governors-General: The English Army and the Definition of Empire, 1569–1681* (1979) argues that the crown was more concerned with military administration than with commercial regulation, and Webb's *1676: The End of American Independence* (1984) shows how the Indian wars undermined the autonomy of colonial governments.

The early Indian wars are treated in Jill Lepore's *The Name of War: King Philip's War and the Origins of American Identity* (1998) and Francis Jennings's *The Invasion of America* (1975). See also Jennings's *The Ambiguous Iroquois Empire* (1984) and *Empire of Fortune: Crowns, Colonies, and Tribes in the Seven Years War in America* (1988) and Richard Aquila's *The Iroquois Restoration: Iroquois Diplomacy on the Colonial Frontier, 1701–1754* (1983).

A good introduction to the imperial phase of the colonial conflicts is Howard H. Peckham's *The Colonial Wars, 1689–1762* (1964). More analytical is Douglas Leach's *Arms for Empire: A Military History of the British Colonies in North America* (1973). Fred Anderson's *A People's Army* (1984) is a social history of the Seven Years' War.

Chapter 4

For a narrative survey of the events leading to the Revolution, see Edward Countryman's *The American Revolution* (1985). For the perspective of Great Britain on the imperial conflict, see Sir Lewis Namier's *England in the Age of the American Revolution* (2nd ed., 1961) and Ian Christie, *Crisis of Empire* (1966).

The intellectual foundations of revolt are traced in Bernard Bailyn's *The Ideological Origins of the American*

Revolution (1967) and in John Phillip Reid's *Constitutional History of the American Revolution: The Authority of Rights* (1987). To understand how these views were connected to organized protest, see Pauline Maier's *From Resistance to Revolution: Colonial Radicals and the Development of American Opposition to Britain, 1765–1776* (1972). The transfer of allegiance from king to Congress is examined in Jerrilyn Marston's *King and Congress: The Transfer of Political Legitimacy, 1774–1776* (1987).

Profiles of the Revolutionary generation of leaders can be found in Bernard Bailyn's *Faces of Revolution: Personalities and Themes in the Struggle for American Independence* (1990), in Pauline Maier's *The Old Revolutionaries: Political Lives in the Age of Samuel Adams* (1980), and in A.J. Langguth's *Patriots: The Men Who Started the American Revolution* (1988).

A number of books deal with specific events in the chain of crisis. Oliver M. Dickerson's *The Navigation Acts and the American Revolution* (1951) stresses the change from trade regulation to taxation in 1764. Edmund S. Morgan and Helen M. Morgan's *The Stamp Act Crisis* (rev. ed., 1962) gives the colonial perspective on that crucial event. Also valuable are Hiller B. Zobel's *The Boston Massacre* (1970), Benjamin W. Labaree's *The Boston Tea Party* (1964), and David Ammerman's *In the Common Cause: American Response to the Coercive Acts of 1774* (1974). Thomas Doerflinger's *A Vigorous Spirit of Enterprise: Merchants and Economic Development in Revolutionary Philadelphia* (1986) describes the role of that influential group in the imperial crisis.

Pauline Maier's *American Scripture: Making the Declaration of Independence* (1997) is the best analysis of the framing of that document. For accounts of the imperial controversy at the colony level, see Edward Countryman's *A People in Revolution* (1981), on New York; Richard L. Bushman's *King and People in Provincial Massachusetts* (1985); James H. Hutson's *Pennsylvania Politics, 1746–1770* (1972); Rhys Isaac's *The Transformation of Virginia, 1740–1790* (1982), and A. Roger Ekirch's *"Poor Carolina": Politics and Society in Colonial North Carolina, 1729–1776* (1981).

Events west of the Appalachians are chronicled concisely by Jack M. Sosin in *The Revolutionary Frontier, 1763–1783* (1967). Military affairs in the early phases of the war are handled in John W. Shy's *Toward Lexington: The Role of the British Army in the Coming of the American Revolution* (1965) and in other works listed in Chapter 5.

Chapter 5

The Revolutionary War is the subject of Colin Bonwick's *The American Revolution* (1991), Theodore Draper's *A Struggle for Power: The American Revolution* (1996), Gordon S. Wood's *The Radicalism of the American Revolution* (1991), and Benson Bobrick's *Angel in the Whirlwind: The Triumph of the American Revolution* (1997). David Hackett Fischer's *Paul Revere's Ride* (1994) details the events surrounding the immediate outbreak of fighting, while Jeremy Black's *War for America: The Fight for Independence, 1775–1783* (1991) focuses on the war itself.

On the social history of the Revolutionary War, see John W. Shy's *A People Numerous and Armed* (1976), Charles Royster's *A Revolutionary People at War* (1979), Lawrence D. Cress's *Citizens in Arms* (1982), and E. Wayne Carp's *To Starve the Army at Pleasure: Continental Army Administration and American Political Culture, 1775–1783* (1984). Colin G. Calloway tells the neglected story of the Indian experiences in the Revolution in *The American Revolution in Indian Country: Crisis and Diversity in Native American Communities* (1995).

Why some Americans remained loyal to the crown is the subject of Bernard Bailyn's *The Ordeal of Thomas Hutchinson* (1974), Robert M. Calhoon's *The Loyalists in Revolutionary America, 1760–1781* (1973), and Mary Beth Norton's *The British-Americans* (1972).

A superb community-level study of Revolutionary change is Robert A. Gross's *The Minutemen and Their World* (1976). The definitive study of African Americans during the Revolutionary era remains Benjamin Quarles's *The Negro in the American Revolution* (1961). Mary Beth Norton's *Liberty's Daughters* (1980) and Linda K. Kerber's *Women of the Republic* (1980) document the role women played in securing independence. Joy D. Buel and Richard Buel, Jr.'s *The Way of Duty* (1984) shows the impact of the Revoluton on one New England family.

The standard introduction to the diplomacy of the Revolutionary era is Jonathan R. Dull's *A Diplomatic History of the American Revolution* (1985). Richard B. Morris's *The Peacemakers* (1965) examines more closely the negotiations for the Peace of Paris.

Chapter 6

A good overview of the Confederation period is Richard B. Morris's *The Forging of the Union, 1781–1789* (1987).

Another useful analysis of this period is Richard Buel, Jr.'s *Securing the Revolution: Ideology in American Politics, 1789–1814* (1974). Relevant chapters of Gordon S. Wood's *The Creation of the American Republic, 1776–1787* (1969) trace the changing contours of political philosophy during these years.

David P. Szatmary's *Shays' Rebellion: The Making of an Agrarian Insurrection* (1980) covers that fateful incident. For a fine account of cultural change during the period, see Joseph J. Ellis's *After the Revolution: Profiles of American Culture* (1979) and Oscar Handlin and Lillian Handlin's *A Restless People: America in Rebellion, 1770–1787* (1982).

Excellent treatments of the post-Revolutionary era include Edmund S. Morgan's *Inventing the People* (1988), Michael Kammen's *Sovereignty and Liberty* (1988), and Forrest McDonald's *Novus Ordo Seclorum: The Intellectual Origins of the Constitution* (1985). Among the better collections of essays on the Constitution are *Toward a More Perfect Union* (1988), edited by Neil L. York, and *The Framing and Ratification of the Constitution* (1987), edited by Leonard W. Levy and Dennis J. Mahoney.

Bruce Ackerman's *We the People: Foundations* (1990) examines Federalist political principles. For the Bill of Rights that emerged from the ratification struggles, see Robert A. Rutland's *The Birth of the Bill of Rights, 1776–1791* (1955).

Michael Kammen's *A Machine That Would Go of Itself: The Constitution in American Culture* (1986) is a comprehensive cultural history of the Constitution that shows how it has become revered by the American public.

Chapter 7

The best introduction to the early Federalists remains John C. Miller's *The Federalist Era, 1789–1800* (1960). Other works analyze the ideological debates among the nation's first leaders. Richard Buel, Jr.'s *Securing the Revolution: Ideology in American Politics, 1789–1815* (1974), Joyce Appleby's *Capitalism and a New Social Order* (1984), Drew McCoy's *The Elusive Republic: Political Economy in Jeffersonian America* (1982) and *The Last of the Fathers: James Madison and the Republican Legacy* (1989), and Stanley Elkins and Eric McKitrick's *The Age of Federalism* (1993) trace the persistence and transformation of ideas first fostered during the Revolutionary crisis. John F. Hoadley's *Origins of American Political Parties, 1789–1803* (1986) is superb.

The 1790s may also be understood through the views and behavior of national leaders. See the following biographies: Forrest McDonald's *Alexander Hamilton: A Biography* (1979), Richard Brookhiser's *Founding Father: Rediscovering George Washington* (1996), E. Harrison Clark's *All Cloudless Glory: The Life of George Washington* (1996), Joseph J. Ellis's *Passionate Sage: The Character and Legacy of John Adams* (1993), and John Ferling's *John Adams: A Life* (1996). For a female perspective, see Phyllis Lee Levin's *Abigail Adams* (1991) and Edith B. Gelles's *Portia: The World of Abigail Adams* (1992). The opposition viewpoint is the subject of Lance Banning's *The Jeffersonian Persuasion: Evolution of a Party Ideology* (1978).

Federalist foreign policy is explored in Jerald A. Comb's *The Jay Treaty* (1970), William C. Stinchcombe's *The XYZ Affair* (1980), and Felix Gilbert's *To the Farewell Address: Ideas of Early American Foreign Policy* (1961).

For specific domestic issues, see Thomas Slaughter's *The Whiskey Rebellion: Frontier Epilogue to the American Revolution* (1986) and Harry Ammon's *The Genêt Mission* (1973). Patricia Watlington's *The Partisan Spirit: Kentucky Politics, 1779–1792* (1972) examines the Kentucky Resolutions. The treatment of Indians in the Old Northwest is explored in Richard H. Kohn's *Eagle and Sword: The Federalists and the Creation of the Military Establishment in America, 1783–1802* (1975). For the Alien and Sedition Acts, consult James Morton Smith's *Freedom's Fetters: The Alien and Sedition Laws and American Civil Liberties* (1956). Daniel Sisson's *The American Revolution of 1800* (1974) is useful for its treatment of that important election.

Several books focus on social issues of the post-Revolutionary period, including *Keepers of the Revolution: New Yorkers at Work in the Early Republic* (1992), edited by Paul A. Gilje and Howard B. Rock, Ronald Schultz's *The Republic of Labor: Philadelphia Artisans and the Politics of Class, 1720–1830* (1993), and Peter Way's *Common Labour: Workers and the Digging of North American Canals, 1780–1860* (1993).

The African-American experience in the Revolutionary era is detailed in Mechal Sobel's *The World They Made Together: Black and White Values in Eighteenth-Century Virginia* (1988) and Gary B. Nash's *Forging Freedom: The Formation of Philadelphia's Black Community, 1720–1840* (1988).

Chapter 8

Marshall Smelser's *The Democratic Republic, 1801–1815* (1968) presents an overview of the Republican administrations. The standard biography of Jefferson is Joseph J. Ellis's *American Sphinx: The Character of Thomas Jefferson* (1997). On the life of Jefferson's friend and successor, see Drew R. McCoy's *The Last of the Fathers: James Madison and the Republican Legacy* (1989). McCoy's *The Elusive Republic* (1982) discusses the political economy of these years in the context of republicanism; Joyce Appleby's *Capitalism and a New Social Order* (1984) minimizes the impact of republican ideology.

Linda K. Kerber's *Federalists in Dissent: Imagery and Ideology in Jeffersonian America* (1970) explores the Federalists while out of power. The concept of judicial review and the courts can be studied in Richard E. Ellis's *The Jeffersonian Crisis* (1971). On John Marshall, see G. Edward White's *The Marshall Court and Cultural Change, 1815–1835* (1991). Milton Lomask's two-volume *Aaron Burr: The Years from Princeton to Vice President, 1756–1805* (1979) and *The Conspiracy and the Years of Exile, 1805–1836* (1982) trace the career of that remarkable American.

For the Louisiana Purchase, consult Alexander De Conde's *This Affair of Louisiana* (1976). For a captivating account of the Lewis and Clark expedition, see Stephen Ambrose's *Undaunted Courage: Meriwether Lewis, Thomas Jefferson and the Opening of the American West* (1996). Bernard W. Sheehan's *Seeds of Extinction* (1973) is more analytical about the Jeffersonians' Indian policy and opening of the West.

Burton Spivak's *Jefferson's English Crisis: Commerce, the Embargo, and the Republican Revolution* (1979) discusses Anglo-American relations during Jefferson's administration; Clifford L. Egan's *Neither Peace nor War* (1983) covers Franco-American relations. An excellent revisionist treatment of the events that brought on war in 1812 is J. C. A. Stagg's *Mr. Madison's War* (1983). The war itself is the focus of Donald R. Hickey's *The War of 1812: A Forgotten Conflict* (1989). See also David Curtis Skaggs and Gerard T. Altoff's *A Signal Victory: The Lake Erie Campaign, 1812–1813* (1997).

Chapter 9

The standard overview of the Era of Good Feelings remains George Dangerfield's *The Awakening of American Nationalism, 1815–1828* (1965). The gathering sense of a national spirit, hindered by an equally growing sectionalism, can be traced in Daniel J. Boorstin's *The Americans: The Nationalist Experience* (1965).

For discussions of the American System, see Bray Hammond's *Banks and Politics in America from the Revolution to the Civil War* (1957) and George R. Taylor's *The Transportation Revolution, 1815–1860* (1951). A classic overview of the economic trends of the period is Douglas C. North's *The Economic Growth of the United States, 1790–1860* (1961).

The political temper of the times is treated in biographical studies of principal figures: Irving Bartlett's *Daniel Webster* (1981) and *John C. Calhoun: A Biography* (1993), Noble Cunningham's *The Presidency of James Monroe* (1996), Clement Eaton's *Henry Clay and the Art of American Politics* (1957), Paul C. Nagel's *John Quincy Adams: A Public Life, A Private Life* (1997), and Jean Edward Smith's *John Marshall: Definer of a Nation* (1997).

A stimulating synthesis of economic, social, and political developments is Sean Wilentz's *Chants Democratic: New York City and the Rise of the American Working Class, 1788–1850* (1983). The emergence of slavery as the most divisive sectional issue is treated in Donald L. Robinson's *Slavery in the Structure of American Politics, 1765–1820* (1971).

On diplomatic relations during James Monroe's presidency, see William Earl Weeks's *John Quincy Adams and American Global Empire* (1992). For relations after 1812, see Ernest R. May's *The Making of the Monroe Doctrine* (1975) and Dexter Perkin's *A History of the Monroe Doctrine* (1955).

Background on Andrew Jackson can be obtained from works cited in Chapter 11. The campaign that brought Jackson to the White House is analyzed in Robert V. Remini's *The Election of Andrew Jackson* (1963).

Chapter 10

A survey of events covered in the chapter is Daniel Feller's *The Jacksonian Promise: America, 1815–1840* (1995). A more political focus can be found in Harry L. Watson's *Liberty and Power: The Politics of Jacksonian America* (1990). Lee Benson's *The Concept of Jacksonian Democracy* (1961) remains an important revisionist interpretation. Edward Pessen's *Jacksonian America: Society,*

Personality, and Politics (rev. ed., 1979) stresses the lack of genuine democracy in society and politics.

A still valuable standard introduction to the development of political parties of the 1830s is Richard P. McCormick's *The Second Party System* (1966). For an outstanding analysis of women in New York City during the Jacksonian period, see Christine Stansell's *City of Women: Sex and Class in New York, 1789–1860* (1986). In *Chants Democratic: New York City and the Rise of the American Working Class, 1788–1850* (1984), Sean Wilentz analyzes the social basis of working-class politics. John Marszalek's *The Petticoat Affair: Manners, Mutiny, and Sex in Andrew Jackson's White House* (1997) assesses the Peggy Eaton controversy.

The best biography of Jackson remains Robert V. Remini's three volume work: *Andrew Jackson: The Course of American Empire, 1767–1821* (1977), *Andrew Jackson: The Course of American Freedom, 1822–1832* (1981), and *Andrew Jackson: The Course of American Democracy, 1833–1845* (1984). On Jackson's successor, consult John Niven's *Martin Van Buren: The Romantic Age of American Politics* (1983). Studies of other major figures of the period include John Niven's *John C. Calhoun and the Price of Union* (1988), Merrill Peterson's *The Great Triumvirate: Webster, Clay, and Calhoun* (1987), and Robert Remini's *Henry Clay: Statesman for the Union* (1992) and *Daniel Webster: The Man and His Time* (1997).

The political philosophies of Jackson's opponents are treated in Daniel W. Howe's *The Political Culture of the American Whigs* (1979) and William P. Vaughn's *The Antimasonic Party in the United States, 1826–1843* (1983).

Two studies of the impact of the Bank controversy are William G. Shade's *Banks or No Banks: The Money Question in the Western States, 1832–1865* (1972) and James R. Sharp's *The Jacksonians versus the Banks: Politics in the States after the Panic of 1837* (1970). Daniel Feller's *The Public Lands in Jacksonian Politics* (1984) is a good introduction to that important topic.

The outstanding book on the nullification issue remains William W. Freehling's *Prelude to Civil War: The Nullification Controversy in South Carolina, 1816–1836* (1966). John M. Belohlavek's *"Let the Eagle Soar!": The Foreign Policy of Andrew Jackson* (1985) is a thorough study of Jacksonian diplomacy. Ronald N. Satz's *American Indian Policy in the Jacksonian Era* (1974) surveys that tragedy; Michael P. Rogin's *Fathers and Children: Andrew Jackson and the Subjugation of the American Indian* (1975) is a psychological interpretation of Jackson's Indian policy.

Chapter 11

On economic development in the nation's early decades, see Stuart W. Bruchey's *Enterprise: The Dynamic Economy of a Free People* (1990). The classic study of transportation and economic growth is George R. Taylor's *The Transportation Revolution, 1815–1860* (1951). A fresh view is provided in Sarah H. Gordon's *Passage to Union: How the Railroads Transformed American Life, 1829–1929* (1997).

The impact of technology is traced in David J. Jeremy's *Transatlantic Industrial Revolution: The Diffusion of Textile Technologies between Britain and America, 1790–1830s* (1981) and Merritt R. Smith's *Harper's Ferry Armory and the New Technology: The Challenge of Change* (1977). The evolution of the nation's postal system is ably recounted in Richard R. John's *Spreading the News: The American Postal System from Franklin to Morse* (1996).

Paul Johnson's *A Shopkeeper's Millennium: Society and Revivals in Rochester, New York, 1815–1837* (1978) studies the role religion played in the emerging industrial order. The attitude of the worker during this time of transition is surveyed in Edward E. Pessen's *Most Uncommon Jacksonians: The Radical Leaders of the Early Labor Movement* (1967). Detailed case studies of working communities include Anthony F. C. Wallace's *Rockdale: The Growth of an American Village in the Early Industrial Revolution* (1978); Thomas Dublin's *Women at Work: The Transformation of Work and Community in Lowell, Massachusetts, 1826–1860* (1979); Stephan Thernstrom's *Poverty and Progress: Social Mobility in a Nineteenth-Century City* (1964), on Newburyport, Massachusetts; and Sean Wilentz's *Chants Democratic* (1984), on New York City. Walter Licht's *Working for the Railroad: The Organization of Work in the Nineteenth Century* (1983) is rich in detail.

For a fine treatment of urbanization, see Charles N. Glaab and A. Theodore Brown's *A History of Urban America* (1976). A valuable case study is Edward K. Spann's *The New Metropolis: New York City, 1840–1857* (1981). Another excellent study of New York City is Edwin G. Burrows and Mike Wallace's *Gotham: A History of New York City to 1898* (1998). On immigration, see Michael Coffey and Terry Golway, *The Irish in America* (1997). The rise of an indigenous American musical tradition is detailed in Ken Emerson's *Doo-Dah! Stephen Foster and the Rise of American Popular Culture* (1997).

Chapter 12

Russel B. Nye's *Society and Culture in America, 1830–1860* (1974) provides a wide-ranging survey. On the reform impulse, consult Ronald G. Walter's *American Reformers, 1815–1860* (1978). Revivalist religion is treated in Nathan O. Hatch's *The Democratization of American Christianity* (1989), and Christine Heyrman's *Southern Cross: The Beginnings of the Bible Belt* (1997). On the Mormons, see Leonard J. Arrington's *Brigham Young: American Moses* (1985).

The best introduction to transcendentalist thought is Paul Boller's *American Transcendentalism, 1830–1860* (1974). A more recent treatment is Carlos Baker's *Emerson Among the Eccentrics: A Group Portrait* (1997). Several good works describe various aspects of the antebellum reform movement. For temperance, see W. J. Rorabaugh's *The Alcoholic Republic: An American Tradition* (1979) and Barbara Leslie Epstein's *The Politics of Domesticity: Women, Evangelism, and Temperance in Nineteenth-Century America* (1981). Stephen Nissenbaum's *Sex, Diet, and Debility in Jacksonian America* (1980) looks at health reform. On prison reform and other humanitarian projects, see David J. Rothman's *The Discovery of the Asylum* (1971), Gerald N. Grob's *Mental Institutions in America* (1973), Charles Rosenberg's *The Care of Strangers: The Rise of America's Hospital System* (1987), and Thomas J. Brown's biography, *Dorothea Dix: New England Reformer* (1998).

Lawrence A. Cremin's *American Education: The National Experience, 1783–1876* (1980) traces early school reform. For other views, see Stanley K. Schultz's *The Culture Factory: Boston Public Schools, 1789–1860* (1973) and Carl F. Kaestle and Eric Foner's *Pillars of the Republic* (1983).

On women during the antebellum period, see Nancy F. Cott's *The Bonds of Womanhood: "Woman's Sphere" in New England, 1780–1835* (1977) and Ellen C. DuBois's *Feminism and Suffrage: The Emergence of an Independent Women's Movement in America, 1848–1869* (1978). Also valuable are Shirley Samuels's *The Culture of Sentiment: Race, Gender, and Sentimentality in Nineteenth-Century America* (1992), Jeanne Boydston's *The Limits of Sisterhood: The Beecher Sisters on Women's Rights and Woman's Sphere* (1988), and Mary P. Ryan's *Women in Public: Between Banners and Ballots, 1825–1880* (1990).

A small but growing literature on ideals of masculinity and changing roles of men in the nineteenth century includes David Leverenz's *Manhood and the American Renaissance* (1989), Mark C. Carnes's *Secret Ritual and Manhood in Victorian America* (1989), Mary Ann Clawson's *Constructing Brotherhood: Class, Gender, and Fraternalism* (1989), and E. Anthony Rotundo's *American Manhood: Transformations in Masculinity from the Revolution to the Modern Era* (1993). Changing ideals of the family in the nineteenth century are described in Steven Mintz and Susan Kellogg's *Domestic Revolutions: A Social History of American Family Life* (1988).

Michael Fellman's *The Unbounded Frame: Freedom and Community in Nineteenth-Century American Utopianism* (1973) surveys the utopian movements. Specific experiments are treated in Robert D. Thomas's *The Man Who Would Be Perfect* (1977), on John Humphrey Noyes; J. F. C. Harrison's *Robert Owen and the Owenites in Britain and America: The Quest for the New Moral World* (1969), Maren L. Carden's *Oneida* (1969); and Henri Desroche's *The American Shakers: From Neo-Christianity to Pre-Socialism* (1971). Lawrence Foster's *Religion and Sexuality* (1981) discusses the Oneida, Shaker, and Mormon communities.

Chapter 13

For background on Whig programs and ideas, see Richard P. McCormick's *The Second American Party System: Party Formation in the Jacksonian Era* (1966). Several works help interpret the expansionist impulse. Frederick Merk's *Manifest Destiny and Mission in American History* (1963) remains a classic. Another treatment of expansionist ideology is Thomas R. Hietala's *Manifest Design: Anxious Aggrandizement in Late Jacksonian America* (1985).

The best survey of western expansion is Richard White's *"It's Your Misfortune and None of My Own": A New History of the American West* (1991). Robert M. Utley's *A Life Wild and Perilous: Mountain Men and the Paths to the Pacific* (1997) tells the dramatic story of the rugged pathfinders who found corridors over the Rocky Mountains. The movement of settlers to the West is ably documented in John Mack Faragher's *Women and Men on the Overland Trail* (1979). The best account of the California gold rush is Malcolm J. Rohrbough's *Days of Gold: The California Gold Rush and the American Nation* (1997).

Gene M. Brack's *Mexico Views Manifest Destiny, 1821–1846* (1975) takes Mexico's viewpoint on American designs on the West. On James K. Polk, see John H. Schroeder's *Mr. Polk's War* (1973). The best survey of the military conflict is John S. D. Eisenhower's *So Far from*

God: The U.S. War with Mexico, 1846–1848 (1989). For a textured account of the soldier's life in the war, see Richard Bruce Winders's *Mr. Polk's Army: The American Military Experience in the Mexican War* (1997). John S. D. Eisenhower's *Agent of Destiny: The Life and Times of General Winfield Scott* (1997) illuminates the greatest American soldier between George Washington and Ulysses S. Grant.

An excellent analysis of the diplomatic aspects of Mexican-American relations is David M. Pletcher's *The Diplomacy of Annexation: Texas, Oregon, and the Mexican War* (1973). On California, see Kevin Starr's *Americans and the California Dream, 1850–1915* (1973). On Oregon, see Earl Pomeroy's *The Pacific Slope: A History of California, Oregon, Washington, Idaho, Utah, and Nevada* (1965).

Chapter 14

Those interested in the problem of discerning myth and reality in the southern experience should consult William R. Taylor's *Cavalier and Yankee: The Old South and American National Character* (1961) and W. J. Cash's *The Mind of the South* (1941). Two efforts to understand the mind of the Old South and its defense of slavery are Eugene D. Genovese's *The Slaveholders' Dilemma: Freedom and Progress in Southern Conservative Thought, 1820–1860* (1992) and Eric H. Walther's *The Fire-Eaters* (1992).

Contrasting analyses of the plantation system are Eugene D. Genovese's *The World the Slaveholders Made* (1969) and Gavin Wright's *The Political Economy of the Cotton South* (1978). Stephanie McCurry's *Masters of Small Worlds: Yeoman Households, Gender Relations, and the Political Culture of the Antebellum South Carolina Low Country* (1995) greatly enriches our understanding of households, religion, and political culture.

Other essential works on southern culture and society include Bertram Wyatt-Brown's *Honor and Violence in the Old South* (1986), Elizabeth Fox-Genovese's *Within the Plantation Household: Black and White Women of the Old South* (1988), Suzanne Lebsock's *The Free Women of Petersburg* (1984), Catherine Clinton's *The Plantation Mistress: Woman's World in the Old South* (1982), Joan Cashin's *A Family Venture: Men and Women on the Southern Frontier* (1991), and Theodore Rosengarten's *Tombee: Portrait of a Cotton Planter* (1987).

William J. Cooper, Jr.'s *Liberty and Slavery: Southern Politics to 1860* (1983) and Robert F. Durden's *The Self-*

Inflicted Wound (1985) cover southern politics of the era. For a look at the role of religion in southern political life, see Mitchell Snay's *Gospel of Disunion: Religion and Separatism in the Antebellum South* (1993).

A provocative discussion of the psychology of black slavery can be found in Stanley M. Elkins's *Slavery: A Problem in American Institutional and Intellectual Life* (3rd ed., 1976). John W. Blassingame's *The Slave Community: Plantation Life in the Antebellum South* (2nd ed., 1979); Eugene D. Genovese's *Roll, Jordan, Roll: The World the Slaves Made* (1974), and Herbert G. Gutman's *The Black Family in Slavery and Freedom, 1750–1925* (1976) all stress the theme of a persisting and identifiable slave culture. Discussions of the diversity of the experience of slavery in particular places can be found in John C. Inscoe's *Mountain Masters: Slavery and the Sectional Crisis in Western North Carolina* (1989) and Randolph B. Campbell's *An Empire for Slavery: The Peculiar Institution in Texas, 1821–1865* (1989).

On the question of slavery's profitability, see Robert W. Fogel and Stanley L. Engerman's *Time on the Cross: The Economics of Negro Slavery* (2 vols., 1974), which argues that not only did planters benefit financially from bondage, but the slaves themselves incorporated a Victorian work ethic based on incentives. Herbert G. Gutman reviewed this controversy in *Slavery and the Numbers Game* (1975). See also Robert Fogel's reflections on the subject in *Without Consent or Contract* (1992).

Other works on slavery include Lawrence W. Levine's *Black Culture and Black Consciousness: Afro-American Folk Thought from Slavery to Freedom* (1977), Albert J. Raboteau's *Slave Religion: The "Invisible Institution" in the Antebellum South* (1978), Dorothy Sterling's *We Are Your Sisters* (1984), Deborah Gray White's *Ar'n't I a Woman? Female Slaves in the Plantation South* (1985), and Joel Williamson's *The Crucible of Race* (1985). Charles Joyner's *Down by the Riverside* (1984) offers a vivid reconstruction of one slave community. Editors Alonzo Johnson and Paul Jersild have compiled insightful essays dealing with slave culture in *"Ain't Gonna Lay My 'Ligion Down": African American Religion in the South* (1996).

Useful surveys of abolitionism include Ronald G. Walters's *The Antislavery Appeal: American Abolitionism after 1830* (1976) and James B. Stewart's *Holy Warriors: The Abolitionists and American Slavery* (1976). William S. McFeely's *Frederick Douglass* (1990) portrays the most eminent black male abolitionist while Nell Painter's *Sojourner Truth: A Life, A Symbol* (1996) profiles the leading female activist. For the proslavery argument as it developed in the South, see Larry Tise's *Proslavery: A History of the Defense of Slavery in America, 1701–1840* (1988), and James Oakes's *The Ruling Race: A History of American Slaveholders* (1982). The problems southerners had in justifying slavery are explored in Drew G. Faust's *A Sacred Circle: The Dilemma of the Intellectual in the Old South, 1840–1860* (1977), Kenneth S. Greenberg's *Masters and Statesmen: The Political Culture of American Slavery* (1985), and Carl N. Degler's *The Other South: Southern Dissenters in the Nineteenth Century* (1974)

Chapter 15

The best surveys of the forces and events leading to the Civil War include James M. McPherson's *Battle Cry of Freedom: The Civil War Era* (1988), Stephen B. Oates and Buz Wyeth's *The Approaching Fury: Voices of the Storm, 1820–1861* (1997), and Bruce Levine's *Half Slave and Half Free: The Roots of the Civil War* (1992). The most recent narrative of the political debate leading to secession is Michael A. Morrison's *Slavery and the American West: The Eclipse of Manifest Destiny and the Coming of the Civil War* (1997). Interpretive analyses can be found in Eric Foner's *Politics and Ideology in the Age of the Civil War* (1980) and Joel H. Silbey's *The Partisan Imperative: The Dynamics of American Politics before the Civil War* (1985).

Mark Stegmaier's *Texas, New Mexico, and the Compromise of 1850: Boundary Dispute and Sectional Crisis* (1996) probes that crucial dispute while Michael F. Holt's *The Political Crisis of the 1850s* (1978) traces the demise of the Whigs. Eric Foner shows how events and ideas combined in the formation of a new political party in *Free Soil, Free Labor, Free Men: The Ideology of the Republican Party before the Civil War* (1970). A more straightforward study of the rise of the Republicans is William E. Gienapp's *The Origins of the Republican Party, 1852–1856* (1987). The economic, social, and political crises of 1857 are examined in Kenneth Stampp's *America in 1857: A Nation on the Brink* (1990).

Robert W. Johannsen's *Stephen A. Douglas* (1973) analyzes the issue of popular sovereignty. A more national perspective is provided in James A. Rawley's *Race and Politics: "Bleeding Kansas" and the Coming of the Civil War* (1969). On the role of John Brown in the sectional crisis, see Stephen B. Oates's *To Purge This Land with Blood: A Biography of John Brown* (2nd ed., 1984). Two other is-

sues that divided the nation can be studied in Stanley W. Campbell's *The Slave Catchers* (1970), on attempts to enforce the Fugitive Slave Act, and in Don E. Fehrenbacher's *Slavery, Law, and Politics* (1981), on the Dred Scott case.

An excellent study on the South's journey to secession is William Freehling's *The Road to Disunion* (1990). Studies of southern states include J. Mills Thornton's *Politics and Power in a Slave Society: Alabama, 1800–1860* (1978), Michael P. Johnson's *Toward a Patriarchal Republic: The Secession of Georgia* (1977), and Steven A. Channing's *Crisis of Fear: Secession in South Carolina* (1970). For developments in the border states, see Daniel W. Croft's *Reluctant Confederates: Upper South Unionists in the Secession Crisis* (1989).

On Lincoln's role in the coming crisis of war, see Don E. Fehrenbacher's *Prelude to Greatness* (1962). Harry V. Jaffa's *Crisis of the House Divided* (1959) details the Lincoln-Douglas debates, and Maury Klein's *Days of Defiance: Sumter, Secession, and the Coming of the Civil War* (1997) treats the Fort Sumter controversy.

Chapter 16

The best one-volume overview of the Civil War period is James M. McPherson's *Battle Cry of Freedom: The Civil War Era* (1988). A good introduction to the military events is Herman Hattaway's *Shades of Blue and Gray: An Introductory Military History of the Civil War* (1997). The outlook and experiences of the common soldier are explored in James M. McPherson's *For Cause and Comrades: Why Men Fought in the Civil War* (1997) and Earl J. Hess's *The Union Soldier in Battle: Enduring the Ordeal of Combat* (1997).

For emphasis on the South, turn first to Gary W. Gallagher's *The Confederate War* (1997). For a sparkling account of the birth of the Rebel nation, see William C. Davis's *"A Government of Our Own": The Making of the Confederacy* (1994). The same author provides a fine biography of the Confederate president in *Jefferson Davis: The Man and His Hour* (1992). The best study of Confederate political culture is George C. Rable's *The Confederate Republic: A Revolution Against Politics* (1994).

Insightful biographies of southern military leaders are Emory Thomas's *Robert E. Lee* (1995), Jeffrey D. West's *General James Longstreet: the Confederacy's Most Controversial Soldier* (1992), and James I. Robertson, Jr.'s *Stonewall Jackson: The Man, the Soldier, the Legend* (1997).

Analytical scholarship on the military conflict includes Joseph L. Harsh's *Confederate Tide Rising: Robert E. Lee and the Making of Southern Strategy, 1861–1862* (1998), Steven E. Wordworth's *Jefferson Davis and His Generals: The Failure of Confederate Command in the West* (1990), and Paul D. Casdorph's *Lee and Jackson: Confederate Chieftains* (1992). A cultural interpretation of Confederate military behavior is Grady McWhiney and Perry D. Jamieson's *Attack and Die: Civil War Military Tactics and the Southern Heritage* (1982). Lonnie R. Speer's *Portals to Hell: The Military Prisons of the Civil War* (1997) details the ghastly experience of prisoners of war.

The history of the North during the war is surveyed in Philip S. Paludan's *"A People's Contest": The Union and Civil War, 1861–1865* (1988) and J. Matthew Gallman, *The North Fights the Civil War: The Home Front* (1994). Treatments of northern politics during the war include Harold M. Hyman's *A More Perfect Union: The Impact of the Civil War and Reconstruction on the Constitution* (1973), and Allan G. Bogue's *The Earnest Men: Republicans of the Civil War Senate* (1981).

The central northern political figure, Abraham Lincoln, is the subject of many books. Two good biographies are David H. Donald's *Lincoln* (1995) and Stephen B. Oates's *With Malice toward None* (1977). The election of 1864 is treated in John C. Waugh's *Reelecting Lincoln: The Battle for the 1864 Presidency* (1998). On Lincoln's assassination, see William Hanchett's *The Lincoln Murder Conspiracies* (1983). For a fine biography of Lincoln's wife, see Jean H. Baker's *Mary Todd Lincoln: A Biography* (1987).

Concerning specific military campaigns, see Larry J. Daniel's *Shiloh: The Battle That Changed the Civil War* (1997), Thomas Goodrich's *Black Flag: Guerrilla Warfare on the Western Border, 1861–1865* (1995), Stephen W. Sears's *Landscape Turned Red: The Battle of Antietam* (1983) and *To the Gates of Richmond: The Peninsula Campaign* (1993), James Lee McDonough and James Pickett Jones's *War So Terrible: Sherman and Atlanta* (1992), Robert Garth Scott's *Into the Wilderness with the Army of the Potomac* (1985), and Albert Castel and Laura K. Poracsky's *Decision in the West: The Atlanta Campaign of 1864* (1992).

Biographical studies of the northern military leaders include Michael Fellman's *Citizen Sherman: A Life of William Tecumseh Sherman* (1995), Brooks D. Simpson's *Let Us Have Peace: Ulysses S. Grant and the Politics of War and Reconstruction, 1861–1868* (1991), John F. Marszalek's *Sherman: A Soldier's Passion for Order* (1992), Charles

Royster's *The Destructive War: William Tecumseh Sherman, Stonewall Jackson, and the Americans* (1991), and William S. McFeely's *Grant: A Biography* (1981).

The experience of the black soldier is surveyed in Joseph T. Glatthaar's *Forged in Battle: The Civil War Alliance of Black Soldiers and White Officers* (1989); Ira Berlin, Joseph P. Reidy, and Leslie S. Rowland's *Freedom's Soldiers: The Black Military Experience in the Civil War* (1998); and *On the Altar of Freedom: A Black Soldier's Civil War Letters from the Front* (1991), edited by James H. Gooding, James M. McPherson, and Virginia M. Adams. Louis S. Gerteis's *From Contraband to Freedman: Federal Policy toward Southern Blacks, 1861–1865* (1973) traces the federal government's policies dealing with freed slaves during the war. For the black woman's experience, see Susie King Taylor and Patricia W. Romero's *A Black Woman's Civil War Memoirs: Reminiscences of My Life in Camp with the 33rd U.S. Colored Troops* (1988) and Jacqueline Jones's *Labor of Love, Labor of Sorrow: Black Women, Work and the Family from Slavery to the Present* (1985).

Recent gender and ethnic studies include *Divided Houses: Gender and the Civil War*, edited by Catherine Clinton and Nina Silber (1992), Drew Gilpin Faust's *Mothers of Invention: Women of the Slaveholding South in the American Civil War* (1997), Shirley Samuels's *The Culture of Sentiment: Race, Gender, and Sentimentality in Nineteenth-Century America* (1992), George C. Rable's *Civil Wars: Women and the Crisis of Southern Nationalism* (1989), and William L. Burton's *Melting Pot Soldiers: The Union's Ethnic Regiments* (2nd ed., 1998). For a fine biography of the North's most famous nurse, see Stephen B. Oates's *A Woman of Valor: Clara Barton and the Civil War* (1994).

Chapter 17

Reconstruction has long been "a dark and bloody ground" of conflicting interpretations. The most comprehensive treatment is Eric Foner's *Reconstruction: America's Unfinished Revolution, 1863–1877* (1988). More specialized works give closer scrutiny to the aims of the principal political figures. For a study of Andrew Johnson, see Hans L. Trefousse's *Andrew Johnson: A Biography* (1989).

Scholars have been fairly sympathetic to the aims and motives of the Radical Republicans. See, for instance,

Herman Belz's *Reconstructing the Union* (1969) and Richard Nelson Current's *Those Terrible Carpet-baggers: A Reinterpretation* (1988). The ideology of these Radicals is explored in Michael Les Benedict's *A Compromise of Principle: Congressional Republicans and Reconstruction, 1863–1869* (1974).

The intransigence of southern white attitudes is examined in Michael Perman's *Reunion without Compromise* (1973), Dan T. Carter's *When the War Was Over: The Failure of Self-Reconstruction in the South, 1865–1867* (1985), and Richard Zuczek's *State of Rebellion: Reconstruction in South Carolina* (1996). Allen W. Trelease's *White Terror* (1971) covers the various organizations that practiced vigilante tactics, chiefly the Ku Klux Klan. The difficulties former laborers had in adjusting to the new labor system are documented in James L. Roark's *Masters without Slaves* (1977). Books on southern politics during Reconstruction include Michael Perman's *The Road to Redemption* (1984), Terry L. Seip's *The South Returns to Congress* (1983), and Mark W. Summer's *Railroads, Reconstruction, and the Gospel of Prosperity* (1984).

Numerous works have appeared on the freed blacks' experience in the South. Start with Leon F. Litwack's *Been in the Storm So Long* (1979), which covers the transition from slavery to freedom. Willie Lee Rose's *Rehearsal for Reconstruction* (1964) examines Union efforts to define the social role of former slaves during wartime emancipation. Joel Williamson's *After Slavery* (1965) argues that South Carolina blacks took an active role in pursuing their polit-ical and economic rights. For discussions of the political activity of freed slaves in other areas of the South, see Howard N. Rabinowitz's *Southern Black Leaders of the Reconstruction Era* (1982) and Edmund L. Drago's *Black Politicians and Reconstruction in Georgia: A Splendid Failure* (1982). Peter Kolchin's *First Freedom* (1972), a study of freed slaves in Alabama, is also useful. The role of the Freedmen's Bureau is explored in William S. McFeely's *Yankee Stepfather: General O.O. Howard and the Freedmen* (1968). The situation of freed slave women, which was often quite different from that of freed slave men, is discussed in Jacqueline Jones's *Labor of Love, Labor of Sorrow: Black Women, Work, and the Family from Slavery to Present* (1985).

The land confiscation issue is discussed in Eric Foner's *Politics and Ideology in the Age of the Civil War* (1980); Beth Bethel's *Promiseland* (1981), on a South Carolina black community; and Janet S. Hermann's *The Pursuit of a Dream* (1981), on the Davis Bend experiment in Mississippi.

The politics of corruption outside the South is depicted in William S. McFeely's *Grant: A Biography* (1981). The political maneuvers of the election of 1876 and the resultant crisis and compromise are explained in C. Vann Woodward's *Reunion and Reaction* (1951) and William Gillette's *Retreat from Reconstruction, 1869–1879* (1979).

For an examination of the lives of southern men and women who moved North between 1865 and 1880, see Daniel E. Sutherland's *The Confederate Carpetbaggers* (1992).

The Declaration of Independence

WHEN IN THE COURSE OF HUMAN EVENTS, it becomes necessary for one people to dissolve the political bands which have connected them with another, and to assume among the Powers of the earth, the separate and equal station to which the Laws of Nature and of Nature's God entitle them, a decent respect to the opinions of mankind requires that they should declare the causes which impel them to the separation.

We hold these truths to be self-evident, that all men are created equal, that they are endowed by their Creator with certain unalienable rights, that among these are Life, Liberty, and the pursuit of Happiness. That to secure these rights, Governments are instituted among Men, deriving their just powers from the consent of the governed. That whenever any Form of Government becomes destructive of these ends, it is the Right of the People to alter or to abolish it, and to institute new Government, laying its foundation on such principles and organizing its powers in such form, as to them shall seem most likely to effect their Safety and Happiness. Prudence, indeed, will dictate that Governments long established should not be changed for light and transient causes; and accordingly all experience hath shown, that mankind are more disposed to suffer, while evils are sufferable, than to right themselves by abolishing the forms to which they are accustomed. But when a long train of abuses and usurpations, pursuing invariably the same Object evinces a design to reduce them under absolute Despotism, it is their right, it is their duty, to throw off such Government, and to provide new Guards for their future security.—Such has been the patient sufferance of these Colonies; and such is now the necessity which constrains them to alter their former Systems of Government. The history of the present King of Great Britain is a history of repeated injuries and usurpations, all having in direct object the establishment of an absolute Tyranny over these States. To prove this, let Facts be submitted to a candid world.

He has refused his Assent to Laws, the most wholesome and necessary for the public good.

He has forbidden his Governors to pass Laws of immediate and pressing importance, unless sus-pended in their operation till his Assent should be obtained; and when so suspended, he has utterly neglected to attend to them.

He has refused to pass other Laws for the accommodation of large districts of people, unless those people would relinquish the right of Representation in the Legislature, a right inestimable to them and formidable to tyrants only.

He has called together legislative bodies at places unusual, uncomfortable, and distant from the depository of their public Records, for the sole purpose of fatiguing them into compliance with his measures.

He has dissolved Representative Houses repeatedly, for opposing with manly firmness his invasions on the rights of the people.

He has refused for a long time, after such dissolutions, to cause others to be elected; whereby the Legislative powers, incapable of Annihilation, have returned to the People at large for their exercise; the State remaining in the mean time exposed to all dangers of invasion from without, and convulsions within.

He has endeavoured to prevent the population of these States; for that purpose obstructing the Laws of Naturalization of Foreigners; refusing to pass others to encourage their migrations hither, and raising the conditions of new Appropriations of Lands.

He has obstructed the Administration of Justice, by refusing his Assent to Laws for establishing Judiciary powers.

He has made Judges dependent on his Will alone, for the tenure of their offices, and the amount and payment of their salaries.

He has erected a multitude of New Offices, and sent hither swarms of Officers to harass our People, and eat out their substance.

He has kept among us, in times of peace, Standing Armies without the Consent of our legislature.

He has affected to render the Military independent of and superior to the Civil Power.

He has combined with others to subject us to a jurisdiction foreign to our constitution, and unacknowledged by our laws; giving his Assent to their Acts of pretended Legislation:

For quartering large bodies of armed troops among us:

For protecting them, by a mock Trial, from Punishment for any Murders which they should commit on the Inhabitants of these States:

For cutting off our Trade with all parts of the world:

For imposing taxes on us without our Consent:

For depriving us of many cases, of the benefits of Trial by jury:

For transporting us beyond Seas to be tried for pretended offences:

For abolishing the free System of English Laws in a neighbouring Province, establishing therein an Arbitrary government, and enlarging its Boundaries so as to render it at once an example and fit instrument for introducing the same absolute rule into these Colonies:

For taking away our Charters, abolishing our most valuable Laws, and altering fundamentally the Forms of our Governments:

For suspending our own Legislatures, and declaring themselves in vested with Power to legislate for us in all cases whatsoever.

He has abdicated Government here, by declaring us out of his Protection and waging War against us.

He has plundered our seas, ravaged our Coasts, burnt our towns, and destroyed the lives of our people.

He is at this time transporting large armies of foreign mercenaries to compleat the works of death, desolation, and tyranny, already begun with circumstances of Cruelty & perfidy scarcely paralleled in the most barbarous ages, and totally unworthy the Head of a civilized nation.

He has constrained our fellow Citizens taken Captive on the high Seas to bear Arms against their Country, to become the executioners of their friends and Brethren, or to fall themselves by their Hands.

He has excited domestic insurrections amongst us, and has endeavoured to bring on the inhabitants of our frontiers, the merciless Indian Savages, whose known rule of warfare, is an undistinguished destruction of all ages, sexes, and conditions.

In every stage of these Oppressions We have Petitioned for Redress in the most humble terms: Our repeated Petitions have been answered only by repeated injury. A Prince, whose character is thus marked by every act which may define a Tyrant, is unfit to be the ruler of a free people.

Nor have We been wanting in attention to our British brethren. We have warned them from time to time of attempts by their legislature to extend an unwarrantable jurisdiction over us. We have re-minded them of the circumstances of our emigration and settlement here. We have appealed to their native justice and magnanimity, and we have conjured them by the ties of our common kindred to disavow these usurpations, which, would inevitably interrupt our connections and correspondence. They too must have been deaf to the voice of justice and of consanguinity. We must, therefore, acquiesce in the necessity, which denounces our Separation, and hold them, as we hold the rest of mankind, Enemies in War, in Peace Friends.

WE, THEREFORE, the Representatives of the UNITED STATES OF AMERICA, in General Congress, Assembled, appealing to the Supreme Judge of the world for the rectitude of our intentions, do, in the Name, and by Authority of the good People of these Colonies, solemnly publish and declare, That these United Colonies are, and of Right ought to be FREE AND INDEPENDENT STATES; that they are Absolved from all Allegiance to the British Crown, and that all political connection between them and the State of Great Britain, is and ought to be totally dissolved; and that as Free and Independent States, they have full Power to levy War, conclude Peace, contract Alliances, establish Commerce, and to do all other Acts and Things which Independent States may of right do. And for the support of this Declaration, with a firm reliance on the Protection of Divine Providence, we mutually pledge to each other our Lives, our Fortunes, and our sacred Honor.

The foregoing Declaration was, by order of Congress, engrossed, and signed by the following members:

John Hancock

NEW HAMPSHIRE
Josiah Bartlett
William Whipple
Matthew Thornton

MASSACHUSETTS BAY
Samuel Adams
John Adams
Robert Treat Paine
Elbridge Gerry

RHODE ISLAND
Stephen Hopkins
William Ellery

CONNECTICUT
Roger Sherman
Samuel Huntington
William Williams
Oliver Wolcott

NEW YORK
William Floyd
Philip Livingston
Francis Lewis
Lewis Morris

NEW JERSEY
Richard Stockton
John Witherspoon
Francis Hopkinson
John Hart
Abraham Clark

PENNSYLVANIA
Robert Morris
Benjamin Rush
Benjamin Franklin
John Morton
George Clymer
James Smith
George Taylor
James Wilson
George Ross

DELAWARE
Caesar Rodney
George Read
Thomas M'Kean

MARYLAND
Samuel Chase
William Paca
Thomas Stone
Charles Carroll, of Carrollton

VIRGINIA
George Wythe
Richard Henry Lee
Thomas Jefferson
Benjamin Harrison
Thomas Nelson, Jr.
Francis Lightfoot Lee
Carter Braxton

NORTH CAROLINA
William Hooper
Joseph Hewes
John Penn

SOUTH CAROLINA
Edward Rutledge
Thomas Heyward, Jr.
Thomas Lynch, Jr.
Arthur Middleton

GEORGIA
Button Gwinnett
Lyman Hall
George Walton

Resolved, That copies of the Declaration be sent to the several assemblies, conventions, and committees, or councils of safety, and to the several commanding officers of the continental troops; that it be proclaimed in each of the United States, at the head of the army.

Articles of Confederation

TO ALL TO WHOM these Presents shall come, we the undersigned Delegates of the States affixed to our Names send greeting.

Whereas the Delegates of the United States of America in Congress assembled did on the fifteenth day of November in the Year of our Lord One Thousand Seven Hundred and Seventy-seven, and in the Second Year of the Independence of America agree to certain articles of Confederation and perpetual Union between the States of Newhampshire, Massachusetts-bay, Rhodeisland and Providence Plantations, Connecticut, New York, New Jersey, Pennsylvania, Delaware, Maryland, Virginia, North-Carolina, South-Carolina and Georgia in the Words following, viz.

Articles of Confederation and perpetual Union between the States of Newhampshire, Massachusetts-bay, Rhodeisland and Providence Plantations, Connecticut, New-York, New-Jersey, Pennsylvania, Delaware, Maryland, Virginia, North-Carolina, South-Carolina and Georgia.

ARTICLE I. The stile of this confederacy shall be "The United States of America."

ARTICLE II. Each State retains its sovereignty, freedom and independence, and every power, jurisdiction and right, which is not by this confederation expressly delegated to the United States, in Congress assembled.

ARTICLE III. The said States hereby severally enter into a firm league of friendship with each other, for their common defence, the security of their liberties, and their mutual and general welfare, binding themselves to assist each other, against all force offered to, or attacks made upon them, or any of them, on account of religion, sovereignty, trade or any other pretence whatever.

ARTICLE IV. The better to secure and perpetuate mutual friendship and intercourse among the people of the different States in this Union, the free inhabitants of each of these States, paupers, vagabonds and fugitives from justice excepted, shall be entitled to all privileges and immunities of free citizens in the several States; and the people of each State shall have free ingress and regress to and from any other State, and shall enjoy therein all the privileges of trade and commerce, subject to the same duties, impositions and restrictions as the inhabitants there of respectively, provided that such restrictions shall not extend so far as to prevent the removal of property imported into any State, to any other State of which the owner is an inhabitant; provided also that no imposition, duties or restriction shall be laid by any State, on the property of the United States, or either of them.

If any person guilty of, or charged with treason, felony, or other high misdemeanor in any State, shall flee from justice, and be found in any of the United States, he shall upon demand of the Governor or Executive power, of the State from which he fled, be delivered up and removed to the State having jurisdiction of his offence.

Full faith and credit shall be given in each of these States to the records, acts and judicial proceedings of the courts and magistrates of every other State.

ARTICLE V. For the more convenient management of the general interests of the United States, delegates shall be annually appointed in such manner as the legislature of each State shall direct, to meet in Congress on the first Monday in November, in every year, with a power reserved to each State, to recall its delegates, or any of them, at any time within the year, and to send others in their stead, for the remainder of the year.

No State shall be represented in Congress by less than two, nor by more than seven members; and no person shall be capable of being a delegate for more than three years in any term of six years; nor shall any person, being a delegate, be capable of holding any office under the United States, for which he, or another for his benefit receives any salary, fees or emolument of any kind.

Each State shall maintain its own delegates in a meeting of the States, and while they act as members of the committee of the States.

In determining questions in the United States, in Congress assembled, each State shall have one vote.

Freedom of speech and debate in Congress shall not be impeached or questioned in any court, or place out of Congress, and the members of Congress shall be protected in their persons from arrests and imprisonments, during the time of their going to and from, and attendance on Congress, except for treason, felony, or breach of the peace.

ARTICLE VI. No State without the consent of the United States in Congress assembled, shall send any embassy to, or receive any embassy from, or enter into any conference, agreement, alliance or treaty with any king, prince or state; nor shall any person holding any office of profit or trust under the United States, or any of them, accept of any present, emolument, office or title of any kind whatever from any king, prince or foreign state; nor shall the United States in Congress assembled, or any of them, grant any title of nobility.

No two or more States shall enter into any treaty, confederation or alliance whatever between them, without the consent of the United States in Congress assembled, specifying accurately the purposes for which the same is to be entered into, and how long it shall continue.

No State shall lay any imposts or duties, which may interfere with any stipulations in treaties, entered into by the United States in Congress assembled, with any king, prince or state, in pursuance of any treaties already proposed by Congress, to the courts of France and Spain.

No vessels of war shall be kept up in time of peace by any State, except such number only, as shall be deemed necessary by the United States in Congress assembled, for the defence of such State, or its trade; nor shall any body of forces be kept up by any State, in time of peace, except such number only, as in the judgment of the United States, in Congress assembled, shall be deemed requisite to garrison the forts necessary for the defence of such State; but every State shall always keep up a well regulated and disciplined militia, sufficiently armed and accoutred, and shall provide and constantly have ready for use, in public stores, a due number of field pieces and tents, and a proper quantity of arms, ammunition and camp equipage.

No State shall engage in any war without the consent of the United States in Congress assembled, unless such State be actually invaded by enemies, or shall have received certain advice of a resolution being formed by some nation of Indians to invade such State, and the danger is so imminent as not to admit of a delay, till the United States in Congress assembled can be consulted: nor shall any State grant commissions to any ships or vessels of war, nor letters of marque or reprisal, except it be after a declaration of war by the United States in Congress assembled, and then only against the kingdom or state and the subjects thereof, against which war has been so declared, and under such regulations as shall be established by the United States in Congress assembled, unless such State be infested by pirates, in which case vessels of war may be fitted out for that occasion, and kept so long as the danger shall continue, or until the United States in Congress assembled shall determine otherwise.

ARTICLE VII. When land-forces are raised by any State of the common defence, all officers of or under the rank of colonel, shall be appointed by the Legislature of each State respectively by whom such forces shall be raised, or in such manner as such State shall direct, and all vacancies shall be filled up by the State which first made the appointment.

ARTICLE VIII. All charges of war, and all other expenses that shall be incurred for the common defence or general welfare, and allowed by the United States in Congress assembled, shall be defrayed out of a common treasury, which shall be supplied by the several States, in proportion to the value of all land within each State, granted to or surveyed for any person, as such land and the buildings and improvements thereon shall be estimated according to such mode as the United States in Congress assembled, shall from time to time direct and appoint.

The taxes for paying that proportion shall be laid and levied by the authority and direction of the Legislatures of the several States within the time agreed upon by the United States in Congress assembled.

ARTICLE IX. The United States in Congress assembled, shall have the sole and exclusive right and power of determining on peace and war, except in the cases mentioned in the sixth article—of sending and receiving ambassadors—entering into treaties and alliances, provided that no treaty of commerce shall be made whereby the legislative power of the respective States shall be restrained from imposing such imposts and duties on foreigners, as their own people are subjected to, or from prohibiting the exportation or importation of and species of goods or commodities whatsoever—of establishing rules for deciding in all cases, what captures on land or water shall be legal, and in what manner prizes taken by land or naval forces in the service of the United States shall be divided or appropriated—of granting letters of marque and reprisal in times of peace—appointing courts for the trial of piracies and felonies committed on the high seas and establishing courts for receiving and determining finally appeals in all cases of captures, provided that no member of Congress shall be appointed a judge of any of the said courts.

The United States in Congress assembled shall also be the last resort on appeal in all disputes and differences now subsisting or that hereafter may arise between two or more States concerning boundary, jurisdiction or any other cause whatever; which authority shall always be exercised in the manner following. Whenever the legislative or executive authority or lawful agent of any State in controversy with another shall present a petition to Congress, stating the matter in question and praying for a hearing, notice thereof shall be given by order of Congress to the legislative or executive authority of the other State in controversy, and a day assigned for the appearance of the parties by their lawful agents, who shall then be directed to appoint by joint consent, commissioners or judges to constitute a court for hearing and determining the matter in question: but if they cannot agree, Congress shall name three persons out of each of the United States, and from the list of such persons each party shall alternately strike out one, the petitioners beginning, until the number shall be reduced to thirteen; and from that number not less than seven, nor more than nine names as Congress shall direct, shall in the presence of Congress be drawn out by lot, and the persons whose names shall be so drawn or any five of them, shall be commissioners or judges, to hear and finally determine the controversy, so always as a major part of the judges who shall hear the cause shall agree in the determination: and if either party shall neglect to attend at the day appointed, without reasons, which Congress shall judge sufficient, or being present shall refuse to strike, the Congress shall proceed to nominate three persons out of each State, and the Secretary of Congress shall strike in behalf of such party absent or refusing; and the judgment and sentence of the court to be appointed, in the manner before prescribed, shall be final and conclusive; and if any of the parties shall refuse to submit to the authority of such court, or to appear or defend their claim or cause, the court shall nevertheless proceed to pronounce sentence, or judgment, which shall in like manner be final and decisive, the judgment or sentence and other proceedings being in either case transmitted to Congress, and lodged among the acts of Congress for the security of the parties concerned: provided that every commissioner, before he sits in judgment, shall take an oath to be administered by one of the judges of the supreme or superior court of the State where the case shall be tried, "well and truly to hear and determine the matter in question, according to the best of his judgment, without favour, affection or hope of reward:" provided also that no State shall be deprived of territory for the benefit of the United States.

All controversies concerning the private right of soil claimed under different grants of two or more States, whose jurisdiction as they may respect such lands, and the states which passed such grants are adjusted, the said grants or either of them being at the same time claimed to have originated antecedent to such settlement of jurisdiction, shall on the petition of either party to the Congress of the United States, be finally determined as near as may be in the same manner as is before prescribed for deciding disputes respecting territorial jurisdiction between different States.

The United States in Congress assembled shall also have the sole and exclusive right and power of regulating the alloy and value of coin struck by their own authority, or by that of the respective States—fixing the standard of weights and measures throughout the United States—regulating the trade and managing all affairs with the Indians, not members of any of the States, provided that the legislative right of any State within its own limits be not infringed or violated—establishing and regulating post-offices from one State to another, throughout all of the United States, and exacting such postage on the papers passing thro' the same as may be requisite to defray the expenses of the said office—appointing all officers of the land forces, in the service of the United States, excepting regimental officers—appointing all the officers of the naval forces, and commissioning all officers whatever in the service of the United States—making rules for the government and regulation of the said land and naval forces, and directing their operations.

The United States in Congress assembled shall have authority to appoint a committee, to sit in the recess of Congress, to be denominated "a Committee of the States," and to consist of one delegate from each State; and to appoint such other committees and civil officers as may be necessary for managing the general affairs of the United States under their direction—to appoint one of their number to preside, provided that no person be allowed to serve in the office of president more than one year in any term of three years; to ascertain the necessary sums of money to be raised for the service of the United States, and to appropriate and apply the same for defraying the public expenses—to borrow money, or emit bills on the credit of the United States, transmitting every half year to the respective States an account of the sums of money so borrowed or emitted,—to build and equip a navy—to agree upon the number of land forces, and to make requisitions from each State for its quota, in proportion to the number of white inhabitants in such State; which requisition shall be binding, and thereupon the Legislature of each State shall appoint the regimental officers, raise the men and cloath, arm and equip them in a soldier like manner, at the expense of the United States; and the officers and men so cloathed, armed and equipped shall march to the place appointed, and within the time agreed on by the United States in Congress assembled: but if the United States in Congress assembled shall, on consideration of circumstances judge proper that any State should not raise men, or should raise a smaller number of men than the quota thereof, such extra number shall be raised, officered, cloathed, armed and equipped in the same manner as the quota of such State, unless the legislature of such State shall judge that such extra number cannot be safely spared out of the same, in which case they shall raise officer, cloath, arm and equip as many of such extra number as they judge can be safely spared. And the officers and men so cloathed, armed and equipped, shall march to the place appointed, and within the time agreed on by the United States in Congress assembled.

The United States in Congress assembled shall never engage in a war, nor grant letters of marque and reprisal in time of peace, nor enter into any treaties or alliances, nor coin money, nor regulate the value thereof, nor ascertain the sums and expenses necessary for the defence and welfare of the United States, or any of them, nor emit bills, nor borrow money on the credit of the United States, nor appropriate money, nor agree upon the number of vessels to be built or purchased, or the number of land or sea forces to be raised, nor appoint a commander in chief of the army or navy, unless nine States assent to the same: nor shall a question on any other point, except for adjourning from day to day be determined, unless by the votes of a majority of the United States in Congress assembled.

The Congress of the United States shall have power to adjourn to any time within the year, and to any place within the United States, so that no period of adjournment be for a longer duration than the space of six months, and shall publish the journal of their proceedings monthly, except such parts thereof relating to treaties, alliances or military operations, as in their judgment require secresy; and the yeas and nays of the delegates of each State on any question shall be entered on the Journal, when it is desired by any delegate; and the delegates of a State, or any of them, at his or their request shall be furnished with a transcript of the said journal, except such parts as are above excepted, to lay before the Legislatures of the several States.

ARTICLE X. The committee of the States, or any nine of them, shall be authorized to execute, in the recess of Congress, such of the powers of Congress as the United States in Congress assembled, by the consent of nine States, shall from time to time think expedient to vest them with; provided that no power be delegated to the said committee, for the exercise of which, by the articles of confederation, the voice of nine States in the Congress of the United States assembled is requisite.

ARTICLE XI. Canada acceding to this confederation, and joining in the measures of the United States, shall be admitted into, and entitled to all the advantages of this Union: but no other colony shall be admitted into the same, unless such admission be agreed to by nine States.

ARTICLE XII. All bills of credit emitted, monies borrowed and debts contracted by, or under the authority of Congress, before the assembling of the United States, in pursuance of the present confederation, shall be deemed and considered as a charge against the United States, for payment and satisfaction whereof the said United States, and the public faith are hereby solemnly pledged.

ARTICLE XIII. Every State shall abide by the determinations of the United States in Congress assembled, on all questions which by this confederation are submitted to them. And the articles of this confederation shall be inviolably observed by every State, and the Union shall be perpetual; nor shall any alteration at any time hereafter be made in any of them; unless such alteration be agreed to in a Congress of the United States, and be afterwards confirmed by the Legislatures of every State.

And whereas it has pleased the Great Governor of the world to incline the hearts of the Legislatures we respectively represent in Congress, to approve of, and to authorize us to ratify the said articles of confederation and perpetual union. Know ye that we the undersigned delegates, by virtue of the power and authority to us given for that purpose, do by these presents, in the name and in behalf of our respective constituents, fully and entirely ratify and confirm each and every of the said articles of confederation and perpetual union, and all and singular the matters and things therein contained: and we do further solemnly plight and engage the faith of our respective constituents, that they shall abide by the determinations of the United States in Congress assembled, on all questions, which by the said confederation are submitted to them. And that the articles thereof shall be inviolably observed by the States we respectively represent, and that the Union shall be perpetual.

In witness thereof we have hereunto set our hands in Congress. Done at Philadelphia in the State of Pennsylvania the ninth day of July in the year of our Lord one thousand seven hundred and seventy-eight, and in the third year of the independence of America.

The Constitution of the United States

WE THE PEOPLE OF THE UNITED STATES, in order to form a more perfect Union, establish Justice, insure domestic Tranquility, provide for the common defence, promote the general Welfare, and secure the Blessings of Liberty to ourselves and our Posterity, do ordain and establish this Constitution for the United States of America.

ARTICLE. I.

Section. 1. All legislative Powers herein granted shall be vested in a Congress of the United States, which shall consist of a Senate and House of Representatives.

Section. 2. The House of Representatives shall be composed of Members chosen every second Year by the People of the several States, and the Electors in each State shall have the Qualifications requisite for Electors of the most numerous Branch of the State Legislature.

No Person shall be a Representative who shall not have attained to the Age of twenty five Years, and been seven Years a Citizen of the United States, and who shall not, when elected, be an Inhabitant of that State in which he shall be chosen.

Representatives and direct Taxes shall be apportioned among the several States which may be included within this Union, according to their respective Numbers, which shall be determined by adding to the whole Number of free Persons, including those bound to Service for a Term of Years, and excluding Indians not taxed, three fifths of all other Persons. The actual Enumeration shall be made within three Years after the first Meeting of the Congress of the United States, and within every subsequent Term of ten Years, in such Manner as they shall by Law direct. The Number of Representatives shall not exceed one for every thirty Thousand, but each State shall have at Least one Representative; and until such enumeration shall be made, the

State of New Hampshire shall be entitled to chuse three, Massachusetts eight, Rhode-Island and Providence Plantations one, Connecticut five, New-York six, New Jersey four, Pennsylvania eight, Delaware one, Maryland six, Virginia ten, North Carolina five, South Carolina five, and Georgia three.

When vacancies happen in the Representation from any state, the Executive Authority thereof shall issue Writs of Election to fill such Vacancies.

The House of Representatives shall chuse their Speaker and other Officers; and shall have the sole Power of Impeachment.

Section. 3. The Senate of the United States shall be composed of two Senators from each State, chosen by the legislature thereof, for six Years; and each Senator shall have one Vote.

Immediately after they shall be assembled in Consequence of the first Election, they shall be divided as equally as may be into three Classes. The Seats of the Senators of the first Class shall be vacated at the Expiration of the second Year, of the second Class at the Expiration of the fourth Year, and of the third Class at the Expiration of the sixth Year, so that one third maybe chosen every second Year; and if Vacancies happen by Resignation, or otherwise, during the Recess of the Legislature of any State, the Executive thereof may make temporary Appoint-ments until the next Meeting of the Legislature, which shall then fill such Vacancies.

No Person shall be a Senator who shall not have attained to the Age of thirty Years, and been nine Years a Citizen of the United States, and who shall not, when elected, be an Inhabitant of that State for which he shall be chosen.

The Vice President of the United States shall be President of the Senate, but shall have no Vote, unless they be equally divided.

The Senate shall chuse their other Officers, and also a President pro tempore, in the Absence of the Vice President, or when he shall exercise the Office of President of the United States.

The Senate shall have the sole Power to try all Impeachments. When sitting for that Purpose, they shall be on Oath or Affirmation. When the President of the United States is tried, the Chief Justice shall preside: And no Person shall be convicted without the Concurrence of two thirds of the Members present.

Judgment in Cases of Impeachment shall not extend further than to removal from Office, and disqualification to hold and enjoy any Office of honor, Trust or Profit under the United States: but the Party convicted shall nevertheless be liable and subject to Indictment, Trial, Judgment and Punishment, according to Law.

Section. 4. The Times, Places and Manner of holding Elections for Senators and Representatives, shall be prescribed in each State by the Legislature thereof; but the Congress may at any time by Law make or alter such Regulations, except as to the Places of chusing Senators.

The Congress shall assemble at least once in every Year, and such Meeting shall be on the first Monday in December, unless they shall by Law appoint a different Day.

Section. 5. Each House shall be the Judge of the Elections, Returns and Qualifications of its own Members, and a Majority of each shall constitute a Quorum to do Business; but a smaller Number may adjourn from day to day, and may be authorized to compel the Attendance of absent Members, in such Manner, and under such Penalties as each House may provide.

Each House may determine the Rules of its Proceedings, punish its Members for disorderly Behaviour, and, with the Concurrence of two thirds, expel a Member.

Each House shall keep a Journal of its Proceedings, and from time to time publish the same, excepting such Parts as may in their Judgment require Secrecy; and the Yeas and Nays of the Members of either House on any question shall, at the Desire of one fifth of those Present, be entered on the Journal.

Neither House, during the Session of Congress, shall, without the Consent of the other, adjourn for more than three days, not to any other Place than that in which the two Houses shall be sitting.

Section. 6. The Senators and Representatives shall receive a Compensation for their Services, to be ascertained by Law, and paid out of the Treasury of the United States. They shall in all Cases, except Treason, Felony and Breach of the Peace, be privileged from Arrest during their Attendance at the Session of their respective Houses, and in going to and returning from the same; and for any Speech or Debate in either House, they shall not be questioned in any other Place.

No Senator or Representative shall, during the Time for which he was elected, be appointed to any civil Office under the Authority of the United States, which shall have been created, or the Emoluments whereof shall have been encreased during such time; and no Person holding any Office under the United States, shall be a Member of either House during his Continuance in Office.

Section. 7. All Bills for raising Revenue shall originate in the House of Representatives; but the Senate may propose or concur with Amendments as on other Bills.

Every Bill which shall have passed the House of Representatives and the Senate shall, before it become a Law, be presented to the President of the United States; If he approve he shall sign it, but if not he shall return it, with his Objections to that House in which it shall have originated, who shall enter the Objections at large on their Journal, and proceed to reconsider it. If after such Reconsideration two thirds of that House shall agree to pass the Bill, it shall be sent, together with the Objections, to the other House, by which it shall likewise be reconsidered, and if approved by two thirds of that House, it shall become a Law. But in all such Cases the Votes of both Houses shall be determined by yeas and Nays, and the Names of the Persons voting for and against the Bill shall be entered on the Journal of each House respectively. If any Bill shall not be returned by the President within ten Days (Sundays excepted) after it shall have been presented to him, the Same shall be a Law, in like Manner as if he had signed it, unless the Congress by their Adjournment prevent its Return, in which Case it shall not be a Law.

Every Order, Resolution, or Vote to which the Concurrence of the Senate and House of Representatives may be necessary (except on a question of Adjournment) shall be presented to the President of the United States; and before the Same shall take Effect, shall be approved by him, or being disapproved by him, shall be repassed by two thirds of the Senate and House of Representatives, according to the Rules and Limitations prescribed in the Case of a Bill.

Section. 8. The Congress shall have Power To lay and collect Taxes, Duties, Imposts and Excises, to pay the Debts and provide for the common Defence and general Welfare of the United States; but all Duties, Imposts and Excises shall be uniform throughout the United States;

To borrow Money on the credit of the United States;

To regulate Commerce with foreign Nations, and among the several States, and with the Indian Tribes;

To establish an uniform Rule of Naturalization, and uniform Laws on the subject of Bankruptcies throughout the United States;

To coin Money, regulate the Value thereof, and of foreign Coin, and fix the Standard of Weights and Measures;

To provide for the Punishment of counterfeiting the Securities and current Coin of the United States;

To establish Post Offices and Post Roads;

To promote the Progress of Science and useful Arts, by securing for limited Times to Authors and Inventors the exclusive Right to their respective Writings and Discoveries;

To constitute Tribunals inferior to the supreme Court;

To define and punish Piracies and Felonies committed on the high Seas, and Offences against the Law of Nations;

To declare War, grant Letters of Marque and Reprisal, and make Rules concerning Captures on land and Water;

To raise and support Armies, but no Appropriation of Money to that Use shall be for a longer Term than two Years;

To provide and maintain a Navy;

To make Rules for the Government and Regulation of the land and naval Forces;

To provide for calling forth the Militia to execute the Laws of the Union, suppress Insurrections and repel Invasions;

To provide for organizing, arming, and disciplining, the Militia, and for governing such Part of them as may be employed in the Service of the United States, reserving to the States respectively, the Appointment of the Officers, and the Authority of training the Militia according to the discipline prescribed by Congress.

To exercise exclusive Legislation in all Cases whatsoever, over such District (not exceeding ten Miles square) as may, by Cession of Particular States, and the Acceptance of Congress, become the Seat of the Government of the United States, and to exercise like Authority over all Places purchased by the Consent of the Legislature of the State in which the Same shall be, for the Erection of Forts, Magazines, Arsenals, dock-Yards, and other needful Buildings;—And

To make all Laws which shall be necessary and proper for carrying into Execution the foregoing Powers, and all other Powers vested by this Constitution in the Government of the United States, or in any Department or Officer thereof.

Section. 9. The Migration or Importation of such Persons as any of the States now existing shall think proper to admit, shall not be prohibited by the Congress prior to the Year one thousand eight hundred and eight, but a Tax or duty may be imposed on such Importation, not exceeding ten dollars for each Person.

The Privilege of the Writ of Habeas Corpus shall not be suspended, unless when in Cases of Rebellion or Invasion the public Safety may require it.

No Bill of Attainder or ex post facto Law shall be passed.

No Capitation, or other direct, Tax shall be laid, unless in Proportion to the Census or Enumeration herein before directed to be taken.

No Tax or Duty shall be laid on Articles exported from any State.

No Preference shall be given by any Regulation of Commerce or Revenue to the Ports of one State over those of another: nor shall Vessels bound to, or from, one State, be obliged to enter, clear, or pay Duties in another.

No Money shall be drawn from the Treasury, but in Consequence of Appropriations made by Law; and a regular Statement and Account of the Receipts and Expenditures of all public Money shall be published from time to time.

No Title of Nobility shall be granted by the United States: And no Person holding any Office of Profit or trust under them, shall, without the Consent of the Congress, accept of any present, Emolument, Office, or Title, of any kind whatever, from any King, Prince, or foreign State.

Section 10. No State shall enter into any Treaty, Alliance, or Confederation; grant Letters of Marque and Reprisal; coin Money; emit Bills of Credit; make any Thing but gold and silver Coin a Tender in Payment of Debts; pass any Bill of Attainder, ex post facto Law, or Law impairing the Obligation of Contracts, or grant any Title of Nobility.

No State shall, without the Consent of the Congress, lay any Imposts or Duties on Imports or Exports, except what may be absolutely necessary for executing its inspection Laws: and the net Produce of all Duties and Imposts, laid by any State on Imports or Exports, shall be for the Use of the Treasury of the United States; and all such Laws shall be subject to the Revision and Controul of the Congress.

No State shall, without the Consent of Congress, lay any Duty of Tonnage, keep Troops, or Ships of War in time of Peace, enter into any Agreement or Compact with another State, or with a foreign Power, or engage in War, unless actually invaded, or in such imminent Danger as will not admit of delay.

ARTICLE. II.

Section. 1. The executive Power shall be vested in a President of the United States of America. He shall hold his Office during the term of four Years, and, together with the Vice President, chosen for the same Term, be elected, as follows:

Each State shall appoint, in such Manner as the Legislature thereof may direct, a Number of Electors, equal to the whole Number of Senators and Representatives to which the State may be entitled in the Congress: but no Senator or Representative, or Person holding an Office of Trust or Profit under the United States, shall be appointed an Elector.

The Electors shall meet in their respective States, and vote by Ballot for two Persons, of whom one at least shall not be an Inhabitant of the same State with themselves. And they shall make a List of all the Persons voted for, and of the Number of Votes for each; which List they shall sign and certify, and transmit sealed to the Seat of the Government of the United States, directed to the President of the Senate. The President of the Senate shall, in the Presence of the Senate and House of Representatives, open all the Certificates, and the Votes shall then be counted. The Person having the greatest Number of Votes shall be the President, if such Number be a Majority of the whole Number of Electors appointed; and if there be more than one who have such Majority, and have an equal Number of Votes, then the House of Representatives shall immediately chuse by Ballot one of them for President; and if no Person have a Majority, then from the five highest on the List the said House shall in like Manner chuse the President. But in chusing the President, the Votes shall be taken by States, the Representation from each State having one Vote; A quorum for this Purpose shall consist of a Member or Members from two thirds of the States, and a Majority of all the States shall be necessary to a Choice. In every Case, after the Choice of the President, the Person having the greatest Number of Votes of the Electors shall be the Vice President. But if there should remain two or more who have equal Votes, the Senate shall chuse from them by Ballot the Vice President.

The Congress may determine the Time of chusing the Electors, and the Day on which they shall give their Votes; which Day shall be the same throughout the United States.

No Person except a natural born Citizen, or a Citizen of the United States, at the time of the Adoption of this Constitution, shall be eligible to the Office of President; neither shall any Person be eligible to that Office who shall not have attained to the Age of thirty five Years, and been fourteen Years a Resident within the United States.

In Case of the Removal of the President from Office, or of his Death, Resignation, or Inability to discharge the Powers and Duties of the said Office, the Same shall devolve on the Vice President, and the Congress may by Law provide for the Case of Removal, Death, Resignation or Inability, both of the President and Vice President, declaring what Officer shall then act as President, and such Officer shall act accordingly, until the Disability be removed, or a President shall be elected.

The President shall, at stated Times, receive for his Services, a Compensation, which shall neither be encreased or diminished during the Period for which he shall have been elected, and he shall not receive within that Period any other Emolument from the United States, or any of them.

Before he enters on the Execution of his Office, he shall take the following Oath or Affirmation:—"I do solemnly swear (or affirm) that I will faithfully execute the Office of President of the United States, and will to the best of my Ability, preserve, protect and defend the Constitution of the United States."

Section. 2. The President shall be Commander in Chief of the Army and Navy of the United States, and of the Militia of the several States, when called into the actual Service of the United States; he may require the Opinion, in writing, of the principal Officer in each of the executive Departments, upon any Subject relating to the Duties of their respective Offices, and he shall have Power to grant Reprieves and Pardons for Offences against the United States, except in Cases of Impeachment.

He shall have Power, by and with the Advice and Consent of the Senate, to make Treaties, provided two thirds of the Senators present concur; and he shall nominate, and by and with the Advice and Consent of the Senate, shall appoint Ambassadors, other public Ministers and Consuls, Judges of the supreme Court, and all other Officers of the United States, whose Appointments are not herein otherwise provided for, and which shall be established by Law; but the Congress may by Law vest the Appointment of such inferior Officers, as they think proper, in the President alone, in the Courts of Law, or in the Heads of Departments.

The President shall have Power to fill up all Vacancies that may happen during the Recess of the Senate, by granting Commissions which shall expire at the End of their next Session.

Section. 3. He shall from time to time give to the Congress Information of the State of the Union, and recommend to their Consideration such Measures as he shall judge necessary and expedient; he may, on extraordinary Occasions, convene both Houses, or either of them, and in Case of Disagreement between them, with Respect to the Time of Adjournment, he may adjourn them to such Time as he shall think proper; he shall receive Ambassadors and other public Ministers; he shall take Care that the Laws be faithfully executed, and shall Commission all the Officers of the United States.

Section. 4. The President, Vice President and all civil Officers of the United States, shall be removed from Office on Impeachment for, and Conviction of, Treason, Bribery, or other high Crimes and Misdemeanors.

ARTICLE. III.

Section. 1. The judicial Power of the United States, shall be vested in one supreme Court, and in such inferior Courts as the Congress may from time to time ordain and establish. The Judges, both of the supreme and inferior Courts, shall hold their Offices during good Behavior, and shall, at stated Times, receive for their Services, a Compensation, which shall not be diminished during their Continuance in Office.

Section. 2. The judicial Power shall extend to all Cases, in Law and Equity, arising under this Constitution, the Laws of the United States, and Treaties made, or which shall be made, under their Authority;—to all Cases affecting Ambassadors, other public Ministers and Consuls;—to all Cases of admiralty and maritime Jurisdiction;—the Controversies to which the United States shall be a Party;—to Controversies between two or more States;—between a State and Citizens of another State;—between Citizens of different States;—between Citizens of the same State claiming Lands under Grants of different States, and between a State, or the Citizens thereof, and foreign States, Citizens or Subjects.

In all cases affecting Ambassadors, other public Ministers and Consuls, and those in which a State shall be Party, the supreme Court shall have original Jurisdiction. In all the other Cases before mentioned, the supreme Court shall have appellate Jurisdiction, both as to Law and Fact, with such Exceptions, and under such Regulations as the Congress shall make.

The Trial of all Crimes, except in Cases of Impeachment, shall be by Jury; and such Trial shall be held in the State where the said Crimes shall have been committed; but when not committed within any State, the Trial shall be at such Place or Places as the Congress may by Law have directed.

Section. 3. Treason against the United States, shall consist only in levying War against them, or in adhering to their Enemies, giving them Aid and Comfort. No Person shall be convicted of Treason unless on the Testimony of two Witnesses to the same overt Act, or on Confession in open Court.

The Congress shall have Power to declare the Punishment of Treason, but no Attainder of Treason shall work Corruption of Blood, or Forfeiture except during the Life of the Person attainted.

ARTICLE. IV.

Section. 1. Full Faith and Credit shall be given in each State to the public Acts, Records, and judicial Proceedings of every other State. And the Congress may by general Laws prescribe the Manner in which such Acts, Records and Proceedings shall be proved, and the Effect thereof.

Section. 2. The Citizens of each State shall be entitled to all Privileges and Immunities of Citizens in the several States.

A Person charged in any State with Treason, Felony, or other Crime, who shall flee from Justice, and be found in another State, shall on Demand of the executive Authority of the State from which he fled, be delivered up, to be removed to the State having Jurisdiction of the Crime.

No Person held to Service or Labour in one State, under the Laws thereof, escaping into another, shall, in Consequence of any Law or Regulation therein, be discharged from such Service or Labour, but shall be delivered up on Claim of the Party to whom such Service or Labour may be due.

Section. 3. New States may be admitted by the Congress into this Union; but no new State shall be formed or erected within the Jurisdiction of any other State; nor any State be formed by the Junction of two or more States, or Parts of States, without the consent of the Legislatures of the States concerned as well as of the Congress.

The Congress shall have Power to dispose of and make all needful Rules and Regulations respecting the Territory or other Property belonging to the United States; and nothing in this Constitution shall be so construed as to Prejudice any Claims of the United States, or of any particular States.

Section. 4. The United States shall guarantee to every State in this Union a Republican Form of Government, and shall protect each of them against Invasion; and on Application of the Legislature, or of the Executive (when the Legislature cannot be convened) against domestic Violence.

ARTICLE. V.

The Congress, whenever two thirds of both Houses shall deem it necessary, shall propose Amendments to this Constitution, or, on the Application of the Legislatures of two thirds of the several States, shall call a Convention for proposing Amendments, which, in either Case, shall be valid to all Intents and Purposes, as Part of this Constitution, when ratified by the Legislatures of three fourths of the several States, or by Conventions in three fourths thereof, as the one or the other Mode of Ratification may be proposed by the Congress; Provided that no Amendment which may be made prior to the Year One thousand eight hundred and eight shall in any Manner affect the first and fourth Clauses in the Ninth Section of the first Article; and that no State, without its Consent, shall be deprived of its equal Suffrage in the Senate.

ARTICLE. VI.

All Debts contracted and Engagements entered into, before the Adoption of this Constitution, shall be as valid against the United States under this Constitution, as under the Confederation.

This Constitution, and the Laws of the United States which shall be made in Pursuance thereof; and all Treaties made, or which shall be made, under the Authority of the United States, shall be the supreme Law of the Land; and the Judges in every State shall be bound thereby, any Thing in the Constitution or Laws of any State to the Contrary notwithstanding.

The Senators and Representatives before mentioned, and the Members of the several State Legislatures, and all executive and judicial Officers, both of the United States and of the several States, shall be bound by Oath or Affirmation, to support this Constitution; but no religious Test shall ever be required as a Qualification to any Office or public Trust under the United States.

ARTICLE. VII.

The Ratification of the Conventions of nine States, shall be sufficient for the Establishment of this Constitution between the States so ratifying the Same.

Done in Convention by the Unanimous Consent of the States present the Seventeenth Day of September in the Year of our Lord one thousand seven hundred and Eighty seven and of the Independence of the United States of America the Twelfth. In witness thereof We have hereunto subscribed our Names,

Gº. WASHINGTON—Presdt.
and deputy from Virginia.

New Hampshire
{ John Langdon
Nicholas Gilman

Massachusetts
{ Nathaniel Gorham
Rufus King

Connecticut
{ Wm Saml Johnson
Roger Sherman

New York: . . . Alexander Hamilton

New Jersey
{ Wil: Livingston
David A. Brearley.
Wm Paterson.
Jona: Dayton

Pennsylvania
{ B Franklin
Thomas Mifflin
Robt Morris
Geo. Clymer
Thos FitzSimons
Jared Ingersoll
James Wilson
Gouv Morris

Delaware
{ Geo: Read
Gunning Bedford jun
John Dickinson
Richard Bassett
Jaco: Broom

Maryland
{ James McHenry
Dan of St Thos Jenifer
Danl Carroll

Virginia
{ John Blair—
James Madison Jr.

North Carolina
{ Wm Blount
Richd Dobbs Spaight.
Hu Williamson

South Carolina
{ J. Rutledge
Charles Cotesworth Pinckney
Charles Pinckney
Pierce Butler.

Georgia
{ William Few
Abr Baldwin

AMENDMENTS TO THE CONSTITUTION

ARTICLES IN ADDITION TO, and Amendment of the Constitution of the United States of America, proposed by Congress, and ratified by the Legislatures of the several States, pursuant to the fifth Article of the original Constitution.

AMENDMENT I.

Congress shall make no law respecting an establishment of religion, or prohibiting the free exercise thereof; or abridging the freedom of speech, or of the press; or the right of the people peaceably to assemble, and to petition the Government for a redress of grievances.

AMENDMENT II.

A well regulated Militia, being necessary to the security of a free State, the right of the people to keep and bear Arms, shall not be infringed.

AMENDMENT III.

No Soldier shall, in time of peace be quartered in any house, without the consent of the Owner, nor in time of war, but in a manner to be prescribed by law.

AMENDMENT IV.

The right of the people to be secure in their persons, houses, papers, and effects, against unreasonable searches and seizures, shall not be violated, and no Warrants shall issue, but upon probable cause, supported by Oath or affirmation, and particularly describing the place to be searched, and the persons or things to be seized.

AMENDMENT V.

No person shall be held to answer for a capital, or otherwise infamous crime, unless on a presentment or indictment of a Grand Jury, except in cases arising in the land or naval forces, or in the Militia, when in actual service in time of War or public danger; nor shall any person be subject for the same offence to be twice put in jeopardy of life or limb; nor shall be compelled in any criminal case to be a witness against himself, nor be deprived of life, liberty, or property, without due process of law; nor shall private property be taken for public use, without just compensation.

AMENDMENT VI.

In all criminal prosecutions, the accused shall enjoy the right to a speedy and public trial, by an impartial jury of the State and district wherein the crime shall have been committed, which district shall have been previously ascertained by law, and to be informed of the nature and cause of the accusation; to be confronted with the witnesses against him; to have compulsory process for obtaining witnesses in his favor, and to have the Assistance of Counsel for his defence.

AMENDMENT VII.

In Suits at common law, where the value in controversy shall exceed twenty dollars, the right of trial by jury shall be preserved, and no fact tried by a jury, shall be otherwise re-examined in any Court of the United States, than according to the rules of the common law.

AMENDMENT VIII.

Excessive bail shall not be required, nor excessive fines imposed, nor cruel and unusual punishments inflicted.

AMENDMENT IX.

The enumeration in the Constitution, of certain rights, shall not be construed to deny or disparage others retained by the people.

AMENDMENT X.

The powers not delegated to the United States by the Constitution, nor prohibited by it to the States, are reserved to the States respectively, or to the people. [The first ten amendments went into effect December 15, 1791.]

AMENDMENT XI.

The Judicial power of the United States shall not be construed to extend to any suit in law or equity, commenced or prosecuted against one of the United States by Citizens of another State, or by Citizens or Subjects of any Foreign State. [January 8, 1798.]

AMENDMENT XII.

The Electors shall meet in their respective states, and vote by ballot for President and Vice-President, one of whom, at least, shall not be an inhabitant of the same state with themselves; they shall name in their ballots the person voted for as President, and in distinct ballots the person voted for as Vice-President, and they shall make distinct lists of all persons voted for as President, and of all persons voted for as Vice President, and of the number of votes for each, which lists they shall sign and certify, and transmit sealed to the seat of the government of the United States, directed to the President of the Senate;—The President of the Senate shall, in the presence of the Senate and House of Representatives, open all the certificates and the votes shall then be counted;—The person having the greatest number of votes for President, shall be the President, if such number be a majority of the whole number of Electors appointed; and if no person have such majority, then from the persons having the highest numbers not exceeding three on the list of those voted for as President, the House of Representatives shall choose immediately, by ballot, the President. But in choosing the President, the votes shall be taken by states, the representation from each state having one vote; a quorum for this purpose shall consist of a member or members from two-thirds of the states, and a majority of all the states shall be necessary to a choice. And if the House of Representatives shall not choose a President whenever the right of choice shall devolve upon them, before the fourth day of March next following, then the Vice-President shall act as President, as in the case of the death or other constitutional disability of the President.—The person having the greatest number of votes as Vice-President, shall be the Vice-President,

if such number be a majority of the whole number of Electors appointed, and if no person have a majority, then from the two highest numbers on the list, the Senate shall choose the Vice-President; a quorum for the purpose shall consist of two-thirds of the whole number of Senators, and a majority of the whole number shall be necessary to a choice. But no person constitutionally ineligible to the office of President shall be eligible to that of Vice-President of the United States. [September 25, 1804.]

AMENDMENT XIII.

Section 1. Neither slavery nor involuntary servitude, except as a punishment for crime whereof the party shall have been duly convicted, shall exist within the United States, or any place subject to their jurisdiction.

Section 2. Congress shall have power to enforce this article by appropriate legislation. [December 18, 1865.]

AMENDMENT XIV.

Section 1. All persons born or naturalized in the United States, and subject to the jurisdiction thereof, are citizens of the United States and of the State wherein they reside. No State shall make or enforce any law which shall abridge the privileges or immunities of citizens of the United States; nor shall any State deprive any person of life, liberty, or property, without due process of law; nor deny to any person within its jurisdiction the equal protection of the laws.

Section 2. Representatives shall be apportioned among the several States according to their respective numbers, counting the whole number of persons in each State, excluding Indians not taxed. But when the right to vote at any election for the choice of electors for President and Vice President of the United States, Representatives in Congress, the Executive and Judicial officers of a State, or the members of the Legislature thereof, is denied to any of the male inhabitants of such State, being twenty-one years of age, and citizens of the United States, or in any way abridged, except for participation in rebellion, or other crime, the basis of representation therein shall be reduced in the proportion which the number of such male citizens shall bear to the whole number of male citizens twenty-one years of age in such State.

Section 3. No person shall be a Senator or Representative in Congress, or elector of President and Vice President, or hold any office, civil or military, under the United States, or under any State, who, having previously taken an oath, as a member of Congress, or as an officer of the United States, or as a member of any State legislature, or as an executive or judicial officer of any State, to support the Constitution of the United States, shall have engaged in insurrection or rebellion against the same, or given aid or comfort to the enemies thereof. But Congress may by a vote of two-thirds of each House, remove such disability.

Section 4. The validity of the public debt of the United States, authorized by law, including debts incurred for payment of pensions and bounties for services in suppressing insurrection or rebellion, shall not be questioned. But neither the United States nor any State shall assume or pay any debt or obligation incurred in aid of insurrection or rebellion against the United States, or any claim for the loss or emancipation of any slave; but all such debts, obligations and claims shall be held illegal and void.

Section 5. The Congress shall have power to enforce, by appropriate legislation, the provisions of this article. [July 28, 1868.]

AMENDMENT XV.

Section 1. The right of citizens of the United States to vote shall not be denied or abridged by the United States or by any State on account of race, color, or previous condition of servitude—

Section 2. The Congress shall have power to enforce this article by appropriate legislation.—[March 30, 1870.]

AMENDMENT XVI.

The Congress shall have power to lay and collect taxes on incomes, from whatever source derived, without appor-

tionment among the several States, and without regard to any census or enumeration. [February 25, 1913.]

AMENDMENT XVII.

The Senate of the United States shall be composed of two senators from each State, elected by the people thereof, for six years; and each Senator shall have one vote. The electors in each State shall have the qualifications requisite for electors of the most numerous branch of the State legislature.

When vacancies happen in the representation of any State in the Senate, the executive authority of such State shall issue writs of election to fill such vacancies: *Provided,* That the legislature of any State may empower the executive thereof to make temporary appointments until the people fill the vacancies by election as the legislature may direct.

This amendment shall not be so construed as to affect the election or term of any senator chosen before it becomes valid as part of the Constitution. [May 31, 1913.]

AMENDMENT XVIII.

After one year from the ratification of this article, the manufacture, sale, or transportation of intoxicating liquors within, the importation thereof into, or the exportation thereof from the United States and all territory subject to the jurisdiction thereof for beverage purposes is hereby prohibited.

The Congress and the several States shall have concurrent power to enforce this article by appropriate legislation.

This article shall be inoperative unless it shall have been ratified as an amendment to the Constitution by the legislatures of the several States, as provided in the Constitution, within seven years from the date of the submission thereof to the States by Congress. [January 29, 1919.]

AMENDMENT XIX.

The right of citizens of the United States to vote shall not be denied or abridged by the United States or by any State on account of sex.

The Congress shall have power by appropriate legislation to enforce the provisions of this article. [August 26, 1920.]

AMENDMENT XX.

Section 1. The terms of the President and Vice-President shall end at noon on the twentieth day of January, and the terms of Senators and Representatives at noon on the third day of January, of the years in which such terms would have ended if this article had not been ratified; and the terms of their successors shall then begin.

Section 2. The Congress shall assemble at least once in every year, and such meeting shall begin at noon on the third day of January, unless they shall by law appoint a different day.

Section 3. If, at the time fixed for the beginning of the term of the President, the President-elect shall have died, the Vice-President-elect shall become President. If a President shall not have been chosen before the time fixed for the beginning of his term, or if the President-elect shall have failed to qualify, then the Vice-President-elect shall act as President until a President shall have qualified; and the Congress may by law provide for the case wherein neither a President-elect nor a Vice-President-elect shall have qualified, declaring who shall then act as President, or the manner in which one who is to act shall be selected, and such person shall act accordingly until a President or Vice-President shall have qualified.

Section 4. The Congress may by law provide for the case of the death of any of the persons from whom the House of Representatives may choose a President whenever the right of choice shall have devolved upon them, and for the case of the death of any of the persons from whom the Senate may choose a Vice-President whenever the right of choice shall have devolved upon them.

Section 5. Sections 1 and 2 shall take effect on the 15th day of October following the ratification of this article.

Section 6. This article shall be inoperative unless it shall have been ratified as an amendment to the Constitution by the legislatures of three-fourths of the several States within seven years from the date of its submission. [February 6, 1933.]

AMENDMENT XXI.

Section 1. The eighteenth article of amendment to the Constitution of the United States is hereby repealed.

Section 2. The transportation or importation into any State, Territory or possession of the United States for delivery or use therein of intoxicating liquors, in violation of the laws thereof, is hereby prohibited.

Section 3. This article shall be inoperative unless it shall have been ratified as an amendment to the Constitution by convention in the several States, as provided in the Constitution, within seven years from the date of the submission thereof to the States by the Congress. [December 5, 1933.]

AMENDMENT XXII.

Section 1. No person shall be elected to the office of the President more than twice, and no person who has held the office of President, or acted as President, for more than two years of a term to which some other person was elected President shall be elected to the office of the President more than once. But this Article shall not apply to any person holding the office of President when this Article was proposed by the Congress, and shall not prevent any person who may be holding the office of President, or acting as President, during the term within which this Article becomes operative from holding the office of President or acting as President during the remainder of such term.

Section 2. This article shall be inoperative unless it shall have been ratified as an amendment to the Constitution by the legislatures of three-fourths of the several states within seven years from the date of its submission to the States by the Congress. [February 27, 1951.]

AMENDMENT XXIII.

Section 1. The District constituting the seat of government of the United States shall appoint in such manner as the Congress may direct:

A number of electors of President and Vice-President equal to the whole number of Senators and Representatives in Congress to which the District would be entitled if it were a State, but in no event more than the least populous State; they shall be in addition to those appointed by the States, but they shall be considered, for the purposes of the election of President and Vice-President, to be electors appointed by a State; and they shall meet in the District and perform such duties as provided by the twelfth article of amendment.

Section 2. The Congress shall have the power to enforce this article by appropriate legislation. [March 29, 1961.]

AMENDMENT XXIV.

Section 1. The right of citizens of the United States to vote in any primary or other election for President or Vice President, for electors for President or Vice President, or for Senator or Representative in Congress, shall not be denied or abridged by the United States or any State by reason of failure to pay any poll tax or other tax.

Section 2. The Congress shall have power to enforce this article by appropriate legislation. [January 23, 1964.]

AMENDMENT XXV.

Section 1. In case of the removal of the President from office or of his death or resignation, the Vice President shall become President.

Section 2. Whenever there is a vacancy in the office of Vice President, the President shall nominate a Vice President who shall take office upon confirmation by a majority vote of both Houses of Congress.

Section 3. Whenever the President transmits to the President pro tempore of the Senate and the Speaker of the House of Representatives his written declaration that he is unable to discharge the powers and duties of his office, and until he transmits to them a written declaration to the contrary, such powers and duties shall be discharged by the Vice President as Acting President.

Section 4. Whenever the Vice President and a majority of either the principal officers of the executive departments or of such other body as Congress may by law provide, transmit to the President pro tempore of the Senate and the Speaker of the House of Representatives their written declaration that the President is unable to discharge the powers and duties of his office, the Vice President shall immediately assume the powers and duties of the office as Acting President.

Thereafter, when the President transmits to the President pro tempore of the Senate and the Speaker of the House of Representatives his written declaration that no inability exists, he shall resume the powers and duties of his office unless the Vice President and a majority of either the principal officers of the executive departments or of such other body as Congress may by law provide, transmit within four days to the President pro tempore of the Senate and the Speaker of the House of Representatives their written declaration that the President is unable to discharge the powers and duties of his office. Thereupon Congress shall decide the issue, assembling within forty-eight hours for that purpose if not in session. If the Congress, within twenty-one days after receipt of the latter written declaration, or, if Congress is not in session, within twenty-one days after Congress is required to assemble, determines by two-thirds vote of both Houses that the President is unable to discharge the powers and duties of his office, the Vice President shall continue to discharge the same as Acting President; otherwise, the President shall resume the powers and duties of his office. [February 10, 1967.]

AMENDMENT XXVI.

Section 1. The right of citizens of the United States, who are eighteen years of age or older, to vote shall not be denied or abridged by the United States or by any State on account of age.

Section 2. The Congress shall have power to enforce this article by appropriate legislation. [June 30, 1971.]

AMENDMENT XXVII.

No law, varying the compensation for the services of the Senators and Representatives shall take effect, until an election of Representatives shall have intervened. [May 8, 1992.]

Presidential Elections

Year	Number of States	Candidates	Parties	Popular Vote	% of Popular Vote	Electoral Vote	% Voter Partici- pation
1789	11	**GEORGE WASHINGTON**	No party designations			69	
		John Adams				34	
		Other candidates				35	
1792	15	**GEORGE WASHINGTON**	No party designations			132	
		John Adams				77	
		George Clinton				50	
		Other candidates				5	
1796	16	**JOHN ADAMS**	Federalist			71	
		Thomas Jefferson	Democratic-Republican			68	
		Thomas Pinckney	Federalist			59	
		Aaron Burr	Democratic-Republican			30	
		Other candidates				48	
1800	16	**THOMAS JEFFERSON**	Democratic-Republican			73	
		Aaron Burr	Democratic-Republican			73	
		John Adams	Federalist			65	
		Charles C. Pinckney	Federalist			64	
		John Jay	Federalist			1	
1804	17	**THOMAS JEFFERSON**	Democratic-Republican			162	
		Charles C. Pinckney	Federalist			14	
1808	17	**JAMES MADISON**	Democratic-Republican			122	
		Charles C. Pinckney	Federalist			47	
		George Clinton	Democratic-Republican			6	
1812	18	**JAMES MADISON**	Democratic-Republican			128	
		DeWitt Clinton	Federalist			89	
1816	19	**JAMES MONROE**	Democratic-Republican			183	
		Rufus King	Federalist			34	
1820	24	**JAMES MONROE**	Democratic-Republican			231	
		John Quincy Adams	Independent			1	
1820	24	**JAMES MONROE**	Democratic-Republican			231	
		John Quincy Adams	Independent			1	
1824	24	**JOHN QUINCY ADAMS**	Democratic-Republican	108,740	30.5	84	26.9
		Andrew Jackson	Democratic-Republican	153,544	43.1	99	
		Henry Clay	Democratic-Republican	47,136	13.2	37	
		William H. Crawford	Democratic-Republican	46,618	13.1	41	
1828	24	**ANDREW JACKSON**	Democratic	647,286	56.0	178	57.6
		John Quincy Adams	National-Republican	508,064	44.0	83	

Year	Number of States	Candidates	Parties	Popular Vote	% of Popular Vote	Electoral Vote	% Voter Partici- pation
1832	24	**ANDREW JACKSON**	Democratic	688,242	54.5	219	55.4
		Henry Clay	National-Republican	473,462	37.5	49	
		William Wirt	Anti-Masonic	101,051	8.0	7	
		John Floyd	Democratic			11	
1836	26	**MARTIN VAN BUREN**	Democratic	765,483	50.9	170	57.8
		William H. Harrison	Whig			73	
		Hugh L. White	Whig	739,795	49.1	26	
		Daniel Webster	Whig			14	
		W. P. Mangum	Whig			11	
1840	26	**WILLIAM H. HARRISON**	Whig	1,274,624	53.1	234	80.2
		Martin Van Buren	Democratic	1,127,781	46.9	60	
1844	26	**JAMES K. POLK**	Democratic	1,338,464	49.6	170	78.9
		Henry Clay	Whig	1,300,097	48.1	105	
		James G. Birney	Liberty	62,300	2.3		
1848	30	**ZACHARY TAYLOR**	Whig	1,360,967	47.4	163	72.7
		Lewis Cass	Democratic	1,222,342	42.5	127	
		Martin Van Buren	Free Soil	291,263	10.1		
1852	31	**FRANKLIN PIERCE**	Democratic	1,601,117	50.9	254	69.6
		Winfield Scott	Whig	1,385,453	44.1	42	
		John P. Hale	Free Soil	155,825	5.0		
1856	31	**JAMES BUCHANAN**	Democratic	1,832,955	45.3	174	78.9
		John C. Frémont	Republican	1,339,932	33.1	114	
		Millard Fillmore	American	871,731	21.6	8	
1860	33	**ABRAHAM LINCOLN**	Republican	1,865,593	39.8	180	81.2
		Stephen A. Douglas	Democratic	1,382,713	29.5	12	
		John C. Breckinridge	Democratic	848,356	18.1	72	
		John Bell	Constitutional Union	592,906	12.6	39	
1864	36	**ABRAHAM LINCOLN**	Republican	2,206,938	55.0	212	73.8
		George B. McClellan	Democratic	1,803,787	45.0	21	
1868	37	**ULYSSES S. GRANT**	Republican	3,013,421	52.7	214	78.1
		Horatio Seymour	Democratic	2,706,829	47.3	80	
1872	37	**ULYSSES S. GRANT**	Republican	3,596,745	55.6	286	71.3
		Horace Greeley	Democratic	2,843,446	43.9	66	
1876	38	**RUTHERFORD B. HAYES**	Republican	4,036,572	48.0	185	81.8
		Samuel J. Tilden	Democratic	4,284,020	51.0	184	
1880	38	**JAMES A. GARFIELD**	Republican	4,453,295	48.5	214	79.4
		Winfield S. Hancock	Democratic	4,414,082	48.1	155	
		James B. Weaver	Greenback-Labor	308,578	3.4		
1884	38	**GROVER CLEVELAND**	Democratic	4,879,507	48.5	219	77.5
		James G. Blaine	Republican	4,850,293	48.2	182	
		Benjamin F. Butler	Greenback-Labor	175,370	1.8		
		John P. St. John	Prohibition	150,369	1.5		

Year	Number of States	Candidates	Parties	Popular Vote	% of Popular Vote	Electoral Vote	% Voter Partici- pation
1888	38	**BENJAMIN HARRISON**	Republican	5,477,129	47.9	233	79.3
		Grover Cleveland	Democratic	5,537,857	48.6	168	
		Clinton B. Fisk	Prohibition	249,506	2.2		
		Anson J. Streeter	Union Labor	146,935	1.3		
1892	44	**GROVER CLEVELAND**	Democratic	5,555,426	46.1	277	74.7
		Benjamin Harrison	Republican	5,182,690	43.0	145	
		James B. Weaver	People's	1,029,846	8.5	22	
		John Bidwell	Prohibition	264,133	2.2		
1896	45	**WILLIAM McKINLEY**	Republican	7,102,246	51.1	271	79.3
		William J. Bryan	Democratic	6,492,559	47.7	176	
1900	45	**WILLIAM McKINLEY**	Republican	7,218,491	51.7	292	73.2
		William J. Bryan	Democratic; Populist	6,356,734	45.5	155	
		John C. Wooley	Prohibition	208,914	1.5		
1904	45	**THEODORE ROOSEVELT**	Republican	7,628,461	57.4	336	65.2
		Alton B. Parker	Democratic	5,084,223	37.6	140	
		Eugene V. Debs	Socialist	402,283	3.0		
		Silas C. Swallow	Prohibition	258,536	1.9		
1908	46	**WILLIAM H. TAFT**	Republican	7,675,320	51.6	321	65.4
		William J. Bryan	Democratic	6,412,294	43.1	162	
		Eugene V. Debs	Socialist	420,793	2.8		
		Eugene W. Chafin	Prohibition	253,840	1.7		
1912	48	**WOODROW WILSON**	Democratic	6,296,547	41.9	435	58.8
		Theodore Roosevelt	Progressive	4,118,571	27.4	88	
		William H. Taft	Republican	3,486,720	23.2	8	
		Eugene V. Debs	Socialist	900,672	6.0		
		Eugene W. Chafin	Prohibition	206,275	1.4		
1916	48	**WOODROW WILSON**	Democratic	9,127,695	49.4	277	61.6
		Charles E. Hughes	Republican	8,533,507	46.2	254	
		A. L. Benson	Socialist	585,113	3.2		
		J. Frank Hanly	Prohibition	220,506	1.2		
1920	48	**WARREN G. HARDING**	Republican	16,143,407	60.4	404	49.2
		James M. Cox	Democratic	9,130,328	34.2	127	
		Eugene V. Debs	Socialist	919,799	3.4		
		P. P. Christensen	Farmer-Labor	265,411	1.0		
1924	48	**CALVIN COOLIDGE**	Republican	15,718,211	54.0	382	48.9
		John W. Davis	Democratic	8,385,283	28.8	136	
		Robert M. La Follette	Progressive	4,831,289	16.6	13	
1928	48	**HERBERT C. HOOVER**	Republican	21,391,993	58.2	444	56.9
		Alfred E. Smith	Democratic	15,016,169	40.9	87	
1932	48	**FRANKLIN D. ROOSEVELT**	Democratic	22,809,638	57.4	472	56.9
		Herbert C. Hoover	Republican	15,758,901	39.7	59	
		Norman Thomas	Socialist	881,951	2.2		
1936	48	**FRANKLIN D. ROOSEVELT**	Democratic	27,752,869	60.8	523	61.0
		Alfred M. Landon	Republican	16,674,665	36.5	8	
		William Lemke	Union	882,479	1.9		

Year	Number of States	Candidates	Parties	Popular Vote	% of Popular Vote	Electoral Vote	% Voter Participation
1940	48	**FRANKLIN D. ROOSEVELT**	Democratic	27,307,819	54.8	449	62.5
		Wendell L. Willkie	Republican	22,321,018	44.8	82	
1944	48	**FRANKLIN D. ROOSEVELT**	Democratic	25,606,585	53.5	432	55.9
		Thomas E. Dewey	Republican	22,014,745	46.0	99	
1948	48	**HARRY S. TRUMAN**	Democratic	24,179,345	49.6	303	53.0
		Thomas E. Dewey	Republican	21,991,291	45.1	189	
		J. Strom Thurmond	States' Rights	1,176,125	2.4	39	
		Henry A. Wallace	Progressive	1,157,326	2.4		
1952	48	**DWIGHT D. EISENHOWER**	Republican	33,936,234	55.1	442	63.3
		Adlai E. Stevenson	Democratic	27,314,992	44.4	89	
1956	48	**DWIGHT D. EISENHOWER**	Republican	35,590,472	57.6	457	60.6
		Adlai E. Stevenson	Democratic	26,022,752	42.1	73	
1960	50	**JOHN F. KENNEDY**	Democratic	34,226,731	49.7	303	62.8
		Richard M. Nixon	Republican	34,108,157	49.5	219	
1964	50	**LYNDON B. JOHNSON**	Democratic	43,129,566	61.1	486	61.9
		Barry M. Goldwater	Republican	27,178,188	38.5	52	
1968	50	**RICHARD M. NIXON**	Republican	31,785,480	43.4	301	60.9
		Hubert H. Humphrey	Democratic	31,275,166	42.7	191	
		George C. Wallace	American Independent	9,906,473	13.5	46	
1972	50	**RICHARD M. NIXON**	Republican	47,169,911	60.7	520	55.2
		George S. McGovern	Democratic	29,170,383	37.5	17	
		John G. Schmitz	American	1,099,482	1.4		
1976	50	**JIMMY CARTER**	Democratic	40,830,763	50.1	297	53.5
		Gerald R. Ford	Republican	39,147,793	48.0	240	
1980	50	**RONALD REAGAN**	Republican	43,901,812	50.7	489	52.6
		Jimmy Carter	Democratic	35,483,820	41.0	49	
		John B. Anderson	Independent	5,719,437	6.6		
		Ed Clark	Libertarian	921,188	1.1		
1984	50	**RONALD REAGAN**	Republican	54,451,521	58.8	525	53.1
		Walter F. Mondale	Democratic	37,565,334	40.6	13	
1988	50	**GEORGE H. BUSH**	Republican	47,917,341	53.4	426	50.1
		Michael Dukakis	Democratic	41,013,030	45.6	111	
1992	50	**BILL CLINTON**	Democratic	44,908,254	43.0	370	55.0
		George H. Bush	Republican	39,102,343	37.4	168	
		H. Ross Perot	Independent	19,741,065	18.9	0	
1996	50	**BILL CLINTON**	Democratic	47,401,185	49.0	379	49.0
		Bob Dole	Republican	39,197,469	41.0	159	
		H. Ross Perot	Independent	8,085,295	8.0	0	

Candidates receiving less than 1 percent of the popular vote have been omitted. Thus the percentage of popular vote given for any election year may not total 100 percent.
Before the passage of the Twelfth Amendment in 1804, the Electoral College voted for two presidential candidates; the runner-up became vice-president.

Admission Of States

Order of Admission	State	Date of Admission	Order of Admission	State	Date of Admission
1	Delaware	December 7, 1787	26	Michigan	January 26, 1837
2	Pennsylvania	December 12, 1787	27	Florida	March 3, 1845
3	New Jersey	December 18, 1787	28	Texas	December 29, 1845
4	Georgia	January 2, 1788	29	Iowa	December 28, 1846
5	Connecticut	January 9, 1788	30	Wisconsin	May 29, 1848
6	Massachusetts	February 7, 1788	31	California	September 9, 1850
7	Maryland	April 28, 1788	32	Minnesota	May 11, 1858
8	South Carolina	May 23, 1788	33	Oregon	February 14, 1859
9	New Hampshire	June 21, 1788	34	Kansas	January 29, 1861
10	Virginia	June 25, 1788	35	West Virginia	June 30, 1863
11	New York	July 26, 1788	36	Nevada	October 31, 1864
12	North Carolina	November 21, 1789	37	Nebraska	March 1, 1867
13	Rhode Island	May 29, 1790	38	Colorado	August 1, 1876
14	Vermont	March 4, 1791	39	North Dakota	November 2, 1889
15	Kentucky	June 1, 1792	40	South Dakota	November 2, 1889
16	Tennessee	June 1, 1796	41	Montana	November 8, 1889
17	Ohio	March 1, 1803	42	Washington	November 11, 1889
18	Louisiana	April 30, 1812	43	Idaho	July 3, 1890
19	Indiana	December 11, 1816	44	Wyoming	July 10, 1890
20	Mississippi	December 10, 1817	45	Utah	January 4, 1896
21	Illinois	December 3, 1818	46	Oklahoma	November 16, 1907
22	Alabama	December 14, 1819	47	New Mexico	January 6, 1912
23	Maine	March 15, 1820	48	Arizona	February 14, 1912
24	Missouri	August 10, 1821	49	Alaska	January 3, 1959
25	Arkansas	June 15, 1836	50	Hawaii	August 21, 1959

Population of the United States

Year	Number of States	Population	% Increase	Population per Square Mile
1790	13	3,929,214		4.5
1800	16	5,308,483	35.1	6.1
1810	17	7,239,881	36.4	4.3
1820	23	9,638,453	33.1	5.5
1830	24	12,866,020	33.5	7.4
1840	26	17,069,453	32.7	9.8
1850	31	23,191,876	35.9	7.9
1860	33	31,443,321	35.6	10.6
1870	37	39,818,449	26.6	13.4
1880	38	50,155,783	26.0	16.9
1890	44	62,947,714	25.5	21.1
1900	45	75,994,575	20.7	25.6
1910	46	91,972,266	21.0	31.0
1920	48	105,710,620	14.9	35.6
1930	48	122,775,046	16.1	41.2
1940	48	131,669,275	7.2	44.2
1950	48	150,697,361	14.5	50.7
1960	50	179,323,175	19.0	50.6
1970	50	203,235,298	13.3	57.5
1980	50	226,504,825	11.4	64.0
1985	50	237,839,000	5.0	67.2
1990	50	250,122,000	5.2	70.6
1995	50	263,411,707	5.3	74.4

Source: U.S. Census Bureau.

Immigration to the United States, fiscal years 1820–1998

Year	Number	Year	Number	Year	Number	Year	Number
1820–1989	**55,457,531**	**1871–80**	**2,812,191**	**1921–30**	**4,107,209**	**1971–80**	**4,493,314**
		1871	321,350	1921	805,228	1971	370,478
1820	8,385	1872	404,806	1922	309,556	1972	384,685
		1873	459,803	1923	522,919	1973	400,063
1821–30	**143,439**	1874	313,339	1924	706,896	1974	394,861
1821	9,127	1875	227,498	1925	294,314	1975	386,914
1822	6,911	1876	169,986	1926	304,488	1976	398,613
1823	6,354	1877	141,857	1927	335,175	1976	103,676
1824	7,912	1878	138,469	1928	307,255	1977	462,315
1825	10,199	1879	177,826	1929	279,678	1978	601,442
1826	10,837	1880	457,257	1930	241,700	1979	460,348
1827	18,875					1980	530,639
1828	27,382	**1881–90**	**5,246,613**	**1931–40**	**528,431**		
1829	22,520	1881	669,431	1931	97,139	**1981–90**	**7,338,062**
1830	23,322	1882	788,992	1932	35,576	1981	596,600
		1883	603,322	1933	23,068	1982	594,131
1831–40	**599,125**	1884	518,592	1934	29,470	1983	559,763
1831	22,633	1885	395,346	1935	34,956	1984	543,903
1832	60,482	1886	334,203	1936	36,329	1985	570,009
1833	58,640	1887	490,109	1937	50,244	1986	601,708
1834	65,365	1888	546,889	1938	67,895	1987	601,516
1835	45,374	1889	444,427	1939	82,998	1988	643,025
1836	76,242	1890	455,302	1940	70,756	1989	1,090,924
1837	79,340					1990	1,536,483
1838	38,914	**1891–1900**	**3,687,564**	**1941–50**	**1,035,039**		
1839	68,069	1891	560,319	1941	51,776	**1991–98**	**7,605,068**
1840	84,066	1892	579,663	1942	28,781	1991	1,827,167
		1893	439,730	1943	23,725	1992	973,977
1841–50	**1,713,251**	1894	285,631	1944	28,551	1993	904,292
1841	80,289	1895	258,536	1945	38,119	1994	804,416
1842	104,565	1896	343,267	1946	108,721	1995	720,461
1843	52,496	1897	230,832	1947	147,292	1996	915,900
1844	78,615	1898	229,299	1948	170,570	1997	798,378
1845	114,371	1899	311,715	1949	188,317	1998	660,477
1846	154,416	1900	448,572	1950	249,187		
1847	234,968						
1848	226,527	**1901–10**	**8,795,386**	**1951–60**	**2,515,479**		
1849	297,024	1901	487,918	1951	205,717		
1850	369,980	1902	648,743	1952	265,520		
		1903	857,046	1953	170,434		
1851–60	**2,598,214**	1904	812,870	1954	208,177		
1851	379,466	1905	1,026,499	1955	237,790		
1852	371,603	1906	1,100,735	1956	321,625		
1853	368,645	1907	1,285,349	1957	326,867		
1854	427,833	1908	782,870	1958	253,265		
1855	200,877	1909	751,786	1959	260,686		
1856	200,436	1910	1,041,570	1960	265,398		
1857	251,306						
1858	123,126	**1911–20**	**5,735,811**	**1961–70**	**3,321,677**		
1859	121,282	1911	878,587	1961	271,344		
1860	153,640	1912	838,172	1962	283,763		
		1913	1,197,892	1963	306,260		
1861–70	**2,314,824**	1914	1,218,480	1964	292,248		
1861	91,918	1915	326,700	1965	296,697		
1862	91,985	1916	298,826	1966	323,040		
1863	176,282	1917	295,403	1967	361,972		
1864	193,418	1918	110,618	1968	454,448		
1865	248,120	1919	141,132	1969	358,579		
1866	318,568	1920	430,001	1970	373,326		
1867	315,722						
1868	138,840						
1869	352,768						
1870	387,203						

Source: U.S. Immigration and Naturalization Service, 1999.

Immigration By Region And Selected Country Of Last Residence, Fiscal Years 1820-1998

Region and Country of Last Residence[1]	1820	1821–30	1831–40	1841–50	1851–60	1861–70	1871–80	1881–90
All countries	8,385	143,439	599,125	1,713,251	2,598,214	2,314,824	2,812,191	5,246,613
Europe	7,690	98,797	495,681	1,597,442	2,452,577	2,065,141	2,271,925	4,735,484
Austria-Hungary	—[2]	—[2]	—[2]	—[2]	—[2]	7,800	72,969	353,719
Austria	—[2]	—[2]	—[2]	—[2]	—[2]	484[3]	63,009	226,038
Hungary	—[2]	—[2]	—[2]	—[2]	—[2]	7,124[3]	9,960	127,681
Belgium	1	27	22	5,074	4,738	6,734	7,221	20,177
Czechoslovakia	—[4]	—[4]	—[4]	—[4]	—[4]	—[4]	—[4]	—[4]
Denmark	20	169	1,063	539	3,749	17,094	31,771	88,132
France	371	8,497	45,575	77,262	76,358	35,986	72,206	50,464
Germany	968	6,761	152,454	434,626	951,667	787,468	718,182	1,452,970
Greece	—	20	49	16	31	72	210	2,308
Ireland[5]	3,614	50,724	207,381	780,719	914,119	435,778	436,871	655,482
Italy	30	409	2,253	1,870	9,231	11,725	55,759	307,309
Netherlands	49	1,078	1,412	8,251	10,789	9,102	16,541	53,701
Norway-Sweden	3	91	1,201	13,903	20,931	109,298	211,245	568,362
Norway	—[6]	—[6]	—[6]	—[6]	—[6]	—[6]	95,323	176,586
Sweden	—[6]	—[6]	—[6]	—[6]	—[6]	—[6]	115,922	391,776
Poland	5	16	369	105	1,164	2,027	12,970	51,806
Portugal	35	145	829	550	1,055	2,658	14,082	16,978
Romania	—[7]	—[7]	—[7]	—[7]	—[7]	—[7]	11	6,348
Soviet Union	14	75	277	551	457	2,512	39,284	213,282
Spain	139	2,477	2,125	2,209	9,298	6,697	5,266	4,419
Switzerland	31	3,226	4,821	4,644	25,011	23,286	28,293	81,988
United Kingdom[5,8]	2,410	25,079	75,810	267,044	423,974	606,896	548,043	807,357
Yugoslavia	—[9]	—[9]	—[9]	—[9]	—[9]	—[9]	—[9]	—[9]
Other Europe	—	3	40	79	5	8	1,001	682
Asia	6	30	55	141	41,538	64,759	124,160	69,942
China[10]	1	2	8	35	41,397	64,301	123,201	61,711
Hong Kong	—[11]	—[11]	—[11]	—[11]	—[11]	—[11]	—[11]	—[11]
India	1	8	39	36	43	69	163	269
Iran	—[12]	—[12]	—[12]	—[12]	—[12]	—[12]	—[12]	—[12]
Israel	—[13]	—[13]	—[13]	—[13]	—[13]	—[13]	—[13]	—[13]
Japan	—[14]	—[14]	—[14]	—[14]	—[14]	186	149	2,270
Korea	—[15]	—[15]	—[15]	—[15]	—[15]	—[15]	—[15]	—[15]
Philippines	—[16]	—[16]	—[16]	—[16]	—[16]	—[16]	—[16]	—[16]
Turkey	1	20	7	59	83	131	404	3,782
Vietnam	—[11]	—[11]	—[11]	—[11]	—[11]	—[11]	—[11]	—[11]
Other Asia	3	—	1	11	15	72	243	1,910
America	387	11,564	33,424	62,469	74,720	166,607	404,044	426,967
Canada & Newfoundland [17,18]	209	2,277	13,624	41,723	59,309	153,878	383,640	393,304
Mexico[18]	1	4,817	6,599	3,271	3,078	2,191	5,162	191,319
Caribbean	164	3,834	12,301	13,528	10,660	9,046	13,957	29,042
Cuba	—[12]	—[12]	—[12]	—[12]	—[12]	—[12]	—[12]	—[12]
Dominican Republic	—[20]	—[20]	—[20]	—[20]	—[20]	—[20]	—[20]	—[20]
Haiti	—[20]	—[20]	—[20]	—[20]	—[20]	—[20]	—[20]	—[20]
Jamaica	—[21]	—[21]	—[21]	—[21]	—[21]	—[21]	—[21]	—[21]
Other Caribbean	164	3,834	12,301	13,528	10,660	9,046	13,957	29,042
Central America	2	105	44	368	449	95	157	404
El Salvador	—[20]	—[20]	—[20]	—[20]	—[20]	—[20]	—[20]	—[20]
Other Central America	2	105	44	368	449	95	157	404
South America	11	531	856	3,579	1,224	1,397	1,128	2,304
Argentina	—[20]	—[20]	—[20]	—[20]	—[20]	—[20]	—[20]	—[20]
Colombia	—[20]	—[20]	—[20]	—[20]	—[20]	—[20]	—[20]	—[20]
Ecuador	—[20]	—[20]	—[20]	—[20]	—[20]	—[20]	—[20]	—[20]
Other South America	11	531	856	3,579	1,224	1,397	1,128	2,304
Other America	—[22]	—[22]	—[22]	—[22]	—[22]	—[22]	—[22]	—[22]
Africa	1	16	54	55	210	312	358	857
Oceania	1	2	9	29	158	214	10,914	12,574
Not specified [22]	300	33,030	69,902	53,115	29,011	17,791	790	789

See footnotes at end of table.

— represents zero.

Region and Country of Last Residence[1]	1891–1900	1901–10	1911–20	1921–30	1931–40	1941–50	1951–60	1961–70
All countries	3,687,564	8,795,386	5,735,811	4,107,209	528,431	1,035,039	2,515,479	3,321,677
Europe	3,555,352	8,056,040	4,321,887	2,463,194	347,566	621,147	1,325,727	1,123,492
Austria-Hungary	592,707[23]	2,145,266[23]	896,342[23]	63,548	11,424	28,329	103,743	26,022
Austria	234,081[3]	668,209[3]	453,649	32,868	3,563[24]	24,860[24]	67,106	20,621
Hungary	181,288[3]	808,511[3]	442,693	30,680	7,861	3,469	36,637	5,401
Belgium	18,167	41,635	33,746	15,846	4,817	12,189	18,575	9,192
Czechoslovakia	—[4]	—[4]	3,426[4]	102,194	14,393	8,347	918	3,273
Denmark	50,231	65,285	41,983	32,430	2,559	5,393	10,984	9,201
France	30,770	73,379	61,897	49,610	12,623	38,809	51,121	45,237
Germany	505,152[23]	341,498[23]	143,945[23]	412,202	114,058[24]	226,578[24]	477,765	190,796
Greece	15,979	167,519	184,201	51,084	9,119	8,973	47,608	85,969
Ireland[5]	388,416	339,065	146,181	211,234	10,973	19,789	48,362	32,966
Italy	651,893	2,045,877	1,109,524	455,315	68,028	57,661	185,491	214,111
Netherlands	26,758	48,262	43,718	26,948	7,150	14,860	52,277	30,606
Norway-Sweden	321,281	440,039	161,469	165,780	8,700	20,765	44,632	32,600
Norway	95,015	190,505	66,395	68,531	4,740	10,100	22,935	15,484
Sweden	226,266	249,534	95,074	97,249	3,960	10,665	21,697	17,116
Poland	96,720[23]	—[23]	4,813[23]	227,734	17,026	7,571	9,985	53,539
Portugal	27,508	69,149	89,732	29,994	3,329	7,423	19,588	76,065
Romania	12,750	53,008	13,311	67,646	3,871	1,076	1,039	2,531
Soviet Union	505,290[23]	1,597,306[23]	921,201[23]	61,742	1,370	571	671	2,465
Spain	8,731	27,935	68,611	28,958	3,258	2,898	7,894	44,659
Switzerland	31,179	34,922	23,091	29,676	5,512	10,547	17,675	18,453
United Kingdom[5,8]	271,538	525,950	341,408	339,570	31,572	139,306	202,824	213,822
Yugoslavia	—[9]	—[9]	1,888[9]	49,064	5,835	1,576	8,225	20,381
Other Europe	282	39,945	31,400	42,619	11,949	8,486	16,350	11,604
Asia	74,862	323,543	247,236	112,059	16,595	37,028	153,249	427,642
China[10]	14,799	20,605	21,278	29,907	4,928	16,709	9,657	34,764
Hong Kong	—[11]	—[11]	—[11]	—[11]	—[11]	—[11]	15,541[11]	75,007
India	68	4,713	2,082	1,886	496	1,761	1,973	27,189
Iran	—[12]	—[12]	—[12]	241[12]	195	1,380	3,388	10,339
Israel	—[13]	—[13]	—[13]	—[13]	—[13]	476[13]	25,476	29,602
Japan	25,942	129,797	83,837	33,462	1,948	1,555	46,250	39,988
Korea	—[15]	—[15]	—[15]	—[15]	—[15]	107[15]	6,231	34,526
Philippines	—[16]	—[16]	—[16]	—[16]	528[16]	4,691	19,307	98,376
Turkey	30,425	157,369	134,066	33,824	1,065	798	3,519	10,142
Vietnam	—[11]	—[11]	—[11]	—[11]	—[11]	—[11]	335[11]	4,340
Other Asia	3,628	11,059	5,973	12,739	7,435	9,551	21,572	63,369
America	38,972	361,888	1,143,671	1,516,716	160,037	354,804	996,944	1,716,374
Canada & Newfoundland[17,18]	3,311	179,226	742,185	924,515	108,527	171,718	377,952	413,310
Mexico[18]	971[19]	49,642	219,004	459,287	22,319	60,589	299,811	453,937
Caribbean	33,066	107,548	123,424	74,899	15,502	49,725	123,091	470,213
Cuba	—[12]	—[12]	—[12]	15,901[12]	9,571	26,313	78,948	208,536
Dominican Republic	—[20]	—[20]	—[20]	—[20]	1,150[20]	5,627	9,897	93,292
Haiti	—[20]	—[20]	—[20]	—[20]	191[20]	911	4,442	34,499
Jamaica	—[21]	—[21]	—[21]	—[21]	—[21]	—[21]	8,869[21]	74,906
Other Caribbean	33,066	107,548	123,424	58,998	4,590	16,874	20,935[21]	58,980
Central America	549	8,192	17,159	15,769	5,861	21,665	44,751	101,330
El Salvador	—[20]	—[20]	—[20]	—[20]	673[20]	5,132	5,895	14,992
Other Central America	549	8,192	17,159	15,769	5,188	16,533	38,856	86,338
South America	1,075	17,280	41,899	42,215	7,803	21,831	91,628	257,954
Argentina	—[20]	—[20]	—[20]	—[20]	1,349[20]	3,338	19,486	49,721
Colombia	—[20]	—[20]	—[20]	—[20]	1,223[20]	3,858	18,048	72,028
Ecuador	—[20]	—[20]	—[20]	—[20]	337[20]	2,417	9,841	36,780
Other South America	1,075	17,280	41,899	42,215	4,894	12,218	44,253	99,425
Other America	—[22]	—[22]	—[22]	31[22]	25	29,276	59,711	19,630
Africa	350	7,368	8,443	6,286	1,750	7,367	14,092	28,954
Oceania	3,965	13,024	13,427	8,726	2,483	14,551	12,976	25,122
Not specified[22]	14,063	33,523[25]	1,147	228	—	142	12,491	93

See footnotes at end of table.

— represents zero.

Region and Country of Last Residence[1]	1971–80	1981–90	1991-94	1995	1996	1997	1998	Total 179 Years 1820–1998
All countries	4,493,314	7,338,062	4,509,852	720,461	915,900	798,378	660,477	64,599,082
Europe	800,368	761,550	631,921	132,914	151,898	122,358	92,911	38,233,062
Austria-Hungary	16,028	24,885	13,426	2,190	2,325	1,964	1,435	4,364,122
Austria	9,478	18,340	9,600	1,340	1,182	1,044	610	1,842,722[3]
Hungary	6,550	6,545	3,826	850	1,143	920	825	1,675,324[3]
Belgium	5,329	7,066	3,055	694	802	633	557	216,297
Czechoslovakia	6,023	7,227	3,050	1,057	1,299	1,169	931	153,307
Denmark	4,439	5,370	2,799	588	795	507	447	375,548
France	25,069	32,353	16,021	3,178	3,896	3,007	2,961	816,650
Germany	74,414	91,961	42,667	7,896	8,365	6,941	6,923	7,156,257
Greece	92,369	38,377	10,096	2,404	2,394	1,483	1,183	721,464
Ireland[5]	11,490	31,969	46,564	4,851	1,611	932	907	4,779,998
Italy	129,368	67,254	48,841	2,594	2,755	2,190	1,966	5,431,454
Netherlands	10,492	12,238	5,891	1,284	1,553	1,197	1,036	385,193
Norway-Sweden	10,472	15,182	8,149	1,607	2,015	1,517	1,344	2,160,586
Norway	3,941	4,164	2,572	465	552	391	327	758,026[6]
Sweden	6,531	11,018	5,577	1,142	1,463	1,126	1,017	1,257,133[6]
Poland	37,234	83,252	96,482	13,570	15,504	11,729	8,202	751,823
Portugal	101,710	40,431	11,588	2,611	3,024	1,690	1,523	521,697
Romania	12,393	30,857	19,142	4,565	5,449	5,276	4,833	244,106
Soviet Union	38,961	57,677	193,077	54,133	61,895	48,238	28,984	3,830,033
Spain	39,141	20,433	8,251	1,664	1,970	1,607	1,185	299,825
Switzerland	8,235	8,849	4,752	1,119	1,344	1,302	1,090	369,046
United Kingdom[5,8]	137,374	159,173	76,780	14,207	15,564	11,950	10,170	5,247,821
Yugoslavia	30,540	18,762	11,507	7,828	10,755	9,913	7,264	183,538
Other Europe	9,287	8,234	9,783	4,874	8,583	9,113	9,970	224,297
Asia	1,588,178	2,738,157	1,314,833	259,984	300,574	258,561	212,799	8,365,931
China[10]	124,326	346,747	170,191	41,112	50,981	44,356	41,034	1,262,050
Hong Kong	113,467	98,215	58,676	10,699	11,319	7,974	7,379	398,277[11]
India	164,134	250,786	149,374	33,060	42,819	36,092	34,288	751,349
Iran	45,136	116,172	32,828	5,646	7,299	6,291	4,945	233,860[12]
Israel	37,713	44,273	20,252	3,188	4,029	2,951	2,546	170,506[13]
Japan	49,775	47,085	31,982	5,556	6,617	5,640	5,647	517,686[14]
Korea	267,638	333,746	76,901	15,053	17,380	13,626	13,691	778,899[15]
Philippines	354,987	548,764	248,466	49,696	54,588	47,842	33,176	1,460,421[16]
Turkey	13,399	23,233	14,036	4,806	5,573	4,596	4,016	445,354
Vietnam	172,820	280,782	110,300	37,764	39,922	37,121	16,534	699,918[11]
Other Asia	244,783	648,354	401,827	53,404	60,047	52,072	49,543	1,647,611
America	1,982,735	3,615,225	2,429,423	282,270	407,813	359,619	298,156	16,844,829
Canada & Newfoundland[17,18]	169,939	156,938	87,613	18,117	21,751	15,788	14,295	4,453,149
Mexico[18]	640,294	1,655,843	1,400,108	90,045	163,743	146,680	130,661	5,819,966
Caribbean	741,126	872,051	436,471	96,021	115,991	101,095	72,948	3,525,703
Cuba	264,863	144,578	47,565	17,661	26,166	29,913	15,415	885,421[12]
Dominican Republic	148,135	252,035	180,055	38,493	36,284	24,966	20,267	810,201[20]
Haiti	56,335	138,379	80,867	13,872	18,185	14,941	13,316	375,938[20]
Jamaica	137,577	208,148	71,927	16,061	18,732	17,585	14,819	568,624[21]
Other Caribbean	134,216	128,911	56,066	9,934	16,624	13,690	9,131	885,519
Central America	134,640	468,088	267,591	32,020	44,336	43,451	35,368	1,242,394
El Salvador	34,436	213,539	117,463	11,670	17,847	17,741	14,329	453,717[20]
Other Central America	100,204	254,549	150,128	20,350	26,489	25,710	21,039	788,677
South America	295,741	461,847	237,615	46,063	61,990	52,600	44,884	1,693,441
Argentina	29,897	27,327	13,760	2,239	2,878	2,055	1,649	153,699[20]
Colombia	77,347	122,849	55,407	10,641	14,078	12,795	11,618	399,892[20]
Ecuador	50,077	56,315	30,627	6,453	8,348	7,763	6,840	215,798[20]
Other South America	138,420	255,356	137,821	26,730	36,686	29,987	24,777	924,052
Other America	995	458	25	4	2	5	–	110,176
Africa	80,779	176,893	108,645	39,818	49,605	44,668	37,494	614,375
Oceania	41,242	45,205	24,846	5,472	6,008	4,855	4,403	250,206
Not specified[22]	12	1,032	184	3	2	8,317	14,714	290,679

Source: U.S. Immigration and Naturalization Service, 1999.
See footnotes next page.

[1] Data for years prior to 1906 relate to country whence alien came; data from 1906–79 and 1984–1998 are for country of last permanent residence; and data for 1980–83 refer to country of birth. Because of changes in boundaries, changes in lists of countries, and lack of data for specified countries for various periods, data for certain countries, especially for the total period 1820–1998, are not comparable throughout. Data for specified countries are included with countries to which they belonged prior to World War I.
[2] Data for Austria and Hungary not reported until 1861.
[3] Data for Austria and Hungary not reported separately for all years during the period.
[4] No data available for Czechoslovakia until 1920.
[5] Prior to 1926, data for Northern Ireland included in Ireland.
[6] Data for Norway and Sweden not reported separately until 1871.
[7] No data available for Romania until 1880.
[8] Since 1925, data for United Kingdom refer to England, Scotland, Wales, and Northern Ireland.
[9] In 1920, a separate enumeration was made for the Kingdom of Serbs, Croats, and Slovenes. Since 1922, the Serb, Croat, and Slovene Kingdom recorded as Yugoslavia.
[10] Beginning in 1957, China includes Taiwan.
[11] Data not reported separately until 1952.
[12] Data not reported separately until 1925.
[13] Data not reported separately until 1949.
[14] No data available for Japan until 1861.
[15] Data not reported separately until 1948.
[16] Prior to 1934, Philippines recorded as insular travel.
[17] Prior to 1920, Canada and Newfoundland recorded as British North America. From 1820 to 1898, figures include all British North America possessions.
[18] Land arrivals not completely enumerated until 1908.
[19] No data available for Mexico from 1886 to 1893.
[20] Data not reported separately until 1932.
[21] Data for Jamaica not collected until 1953. In prior years, consolidated under British West Indies, which is included in "Other Caribbean."
[22] Included in countries "Not specified" until 1925.
[23] From 1899 to 1919, data for Poland included in Austria-Hungary, Germany, and the Soviet Union.
[24] From 1938 to 1945, data for Austria included in Germany.
[25] Includes 32,897 persons returning in 1906 to their homes in the United States.
—represents zero.

NOTE: From 1820 to 1867, figures represent alien passengers arrived at seaports; from 1868 to 1891 and 1895 to 1897, immigrant aliens arrived; from 1892 to 1894 and 1898 to 1998, immigrant aliens admitted for permanent residence. From 1892 to 1903, aliens entering by cabin class were not counted as immigrants. Land arrivals were not completely enumerated until 1908. For this table, fiscal year 1843 covers 9 months ending September 1843; fiscal years 1832 and 1850 cover 15 months ending December 31 of the respective years; and fiscal year 1868 covers 6 months ending June 30, 1868.

Presidents, Vice-Presidents, and Secretaries of State

	President	Vice-President	Secretary of State
1.	George Washington, Federalist 1789	John Adams, Federalist 1789	Thomas Jefferson 1789 Edmund Randolph 1794 Timothy Pickering 1795
2.	John Adams, Federalist 1797	Thomas Jefferson, Dem.-Rep. 1797	Timothy Pickering 1797 John Marshall 1800
3.	Thomas Jefferson, Dem.-Rep. 1801	Aaron Burr, Dem.-Rep. 1801 George Clinton, Dem.-Rep. 1805	James Madison 1801
4.	James Madison, Dem.-Rep. 1809	George Clinton, Dem.-Rep. 1809 Elbridge Gerry, Dem.-Rep. 1813	Robert Smith 1809 James Monroe 1811
5.	James Monroe, Dem.-Rep. 1817	Daniel D. Tompkins, Dem.-Rep. 1817	John Q. Adams 1817
6.	John Quincy Adams, Dem.-Rep. 1825	John C. Calhoun, Dem.-Rep. 1825	Henry Clay 1825
7.	Andrew Jackson, Democratic 1829	John C. Calhoun, Democratic 1829 Martin Van Buren, Democratic 1833	Martin Van Buren 1829 Edward Livingston 1831 Louis McLane 1833 John Forsyth 1834
8.	Martin Van Buren, Democratic 1837	Richard M. Johnson, Democratic 1837	John Forsyth 1837
9.	William H. Harrison, Whig 1841	John Tyler, Whig 1841	Daniel Webster 1841

	President	Vice-President	Secretary of State
10.	John Tyler, Whig and Democratic 1841	None	Daniel Webster 1841 Hugh S. Legaré 1843 Abel P. Upshur 1843 John C. Calhoun 1844
11.	James K. Polk, Democratic 1845	George M. Dallas, Democratic 1845	James Buchanan 1845
12.	Zachary Taylor, Whig 1849	Millard Fillmore, Whig 1849	John M. Clayton 1849
13.	Millard Fillmore, Whig 1850	None	Daniel Webster 1850 Edward Everett 1852
14.	Franklin Pierce, Democratic 1853	William R. King, Democratic 1853	William L. Marcy 1853
15.	James Buchanan, Democratic 1857	John C. Breckinridge, Democratic 1857	Lewis Cass 1857 Jeremiah S. Black 1860
16.	Abraham Lincoln, Republican 1861	Hannibal Hamlin, Republican 1861 Andrew Johnson, Unionist 1865	William H. Seward 1861
17.	Andrew Johnson, Unionist 1865	None	William H. Seward 1865
18.	Ulysses S. Grant, Republican 1869	Schuyler Colfax, Republican 1869 Henry Wilson, Republican 1873	Elihu B. Washburne 1869 Hamilton Fish 1869
19.	Rutherford B. Hayes, Republican 1877	William A. Wheeler, Republican 1877	William M. Evarts 1877

	President	Vice-President	Secretary of State
20.	James A. Garfield, Republican 1881	Chester A. Arthur, Republican 1881	James G. Blaine 1881
21.	Chester A. Arthur, Republican 1881	None	Frederick T. Frelinghuysen 1881
22.	Grover Cleveland, Democratic 1885	Thomas A. Hendricks, Democratic 1885	Thomas F. Bayard 1885
23.	Benjamin Harrison, Republican 1889	Levi P. Morton, Republican 1889	James G. Blaine 1889 John W. Foster 1892
24.	Grover Cleveland, Democratic 1893	Adlai E. Stevenson, Democratic 1893	Walter Q. Gresham 1893 Richard Olney 1895
25.	William McKinley, Republican 1897	Garret A. Hobart, Republican 1897 Theodore Roosevelt, Republican 1901	John Sherman 1897 William R. Day 1898 John Hay 1898
26.	Theodore Roosevelt, Republican 1901	Charles Fairbanks, Republican 1905	John Hay 1901 Elihu Root 1905 Robert Bacon 1909
27.	William H. Taft, Republican 1909	James S. Sherman, Republican 1909	Philander C. Knox 1909
28.	Woodrow Wilson, Democratic 1913	Thomas R. Marshall, Democratic 1913	William J. Bryan 1913 Robert Lansing 1915 Bainbridge Colby 1920
29.	Warren G. Harding, Republican 1921	Calvin Coolidge, Republican 1921	Charles E. Hughes 1921
30.	Calvin Coolidge, Republican 1923	Charles G. Dawes, Republican 1925	Charles E. Hughes 1923 Frank B. Kellogg 1925

President	Vice-President	Secretary of State
31. Herbert Hoover, Republican 1929	Charles Curtis, Republican 1929	Henry L. Stimson 1929
32. Franklin D. Roosevelt, Democratic 1933	John Nance Garner, Democratic 1933 Henry A. Wallace, Democratic 1941 Harry S. Truman, Democratic 1945	Cordell Hull 1933 Edward R. Stettinius, Jr. 1944
33. Harry S. Truman, Democratic 1945	Alben W. Barkley, Democratic 1949	Edward R. Stettinius, Jr. 1945 James F. Byrnes 1945 George C. Marshall 1947 Dean G. Acheson 1949
34. Dwight D. Eisenhower, Republican 1953	Richard M. Nixon, Republican 1953	John F. Dulles 1953 Christian A. Herter 1959
35. John F. Kennedy, Democratic 1961	Lyndon B. Johnson, Democratic 1961	Dean Rusk 1961
36. Lyndon B. Johnson, Democratic 1963	Hubert H. Humphrey, Democratic 1965	Dean Rusk 1963
37. Richard M. Nixon, Republican 1969	Spiro T. Agnew, Republican 1969 Gerald R. Ford, Republican 1973	William P. Rogers 1969 Henry Kissinger 1973
38. Gerald R. Ford, Republican 1974	Nelson Rockefeller, Republican 1974	Henry Kissinger 1974
39. Jimmy Carter, Democratic 1977	Walter Mondale, Democratic 1977	Cyrus Vance 1977 Edmund Muskie 1980

	President	Vice-President	Secretary of State
40.	Ronald Reagan, Republican 1981	George Bush, Republican 1981	Alexander Haig 1981 George Schultz 1982
41.	George Bush, Republican 1989	J. Danforth Quayle, Republican 1989	James A. Baker 1989 Lawrence Eagleburger 1992
42.	William J. Clinton, Democratic 1993	Albert Gore, Jr., Democratic 1993	Warren Christopher 1993 Madeleine Albright 1997

Credits